The Southern Pacific, 1901–1985

An eastbound, TOFC train is being readied at the Los Angeles Transportation Center.

The Southern Pacific,
1901–1985

by

Don L. Hofsommer

Foreword by
Richard C. Overton

TEXAS A&M UNIVERSITY PRESS

COLLEGE STATION

Library of Congress Cataloging-in-Publication Data
Hofsommer, Donovan L.
    The Southern Pacific, 1901–1985.

    Bibliography: p.
    Includes index.
    1. Southern Pacific Railroad—History.   I. Title.
HE2791.S794H63   1986   385'.065'78   85-40745
ISBN 0-89096-246-4

Manufactured in the United States of America
FIRST EDITION

To the men and women of the Southern Pacific

Contents

List of Maps

Foreword

WOULD anyone in his or her right mind set out to write a single-volume history covering the twentieth-century story of the massive transport complex known casually as "Espee," the Southern Pacific—especially if that history had to be researched, written, revised, and published within an outside limit of five years?

The offhand answer would have to be "No." Why? In 1935, to pick a representative date, Espee's steam and electric lines, truck and bus operations, plus its maritime system sprawled across a wide domain from Portland, San Francisco, and Los Angeles on the west, to New Orleans on the south, to Saint Louis in the Heartlands, and, by sea, on to Norfolk, Baltimore, and New York.

The mere thought of fitting the history of such a vast complex into a single volume is staggering. Yet the "bargain" was struck. Espee's Chairman Benjamin F. Biaggini promised Professor Donovan L. Hofsommer that the company's records would be made available and that the requisite research, writing, and publication of "a fair assessment" would have financial support from SP. The author was given freedom to tell the story as he saw it, the company retaining only the right to state its own views in a clearly labeled footnote if it wished to do so. Both parties to the agreement recognized that academic freedom, as well as academic responsibility, constituted the essence of the arrangement between scholar and corporation.

Reassured by these mutual commitments, Hofsommer has completed a text notable for both its substance and its style. His product does not pretend to be the final word on the subject; he closes his introduction by saying: "My fond hope is that this book will point the way for further investigation into particularized areas of SP's remarkable past." This modest statement represents an honest approach to an honest undertaking.

Hofsommer's study is a treasure house of information about the Southern Pacific Company. Based firmly on original sources, many of them not previously available, it covers the story of the parent company as well as the evolution and growing pains of its many subsidiaries. His account follows a generally chronological pattern, but every relevant topic has received careful attention. Beyond the text, but hardly less important, illustrations and maps are, as one would expect, well chosen and superbly presented.

In passing, it is worth remembering that existing SP source records revealing top-level decision making are measured in tons. Small wonder that heavy reliance has had to be placed on judicious summary and sampling. Technical terms have had to be carefully explained. Yet the story breathes and moves; monotony is avoided by changes of pace and a generous (but restrained) use of analogy and anecdote. Indeed, this book is a joy to read. It will surely charm the general reader and enlighten even the most sophisticated specialist in railway history.

An organization as large, as venerable, and as essential to the nation as SP inevitably attracts its share of adverse criticism. In respect to such matters, Hofsommer assumes the role of investigative reporter. For example, he reminds us that in the early 1960s, Espee, as well as Santa Fe and Great Northern, sought to control Western Pacific, which had a longer but more efficient main stem than SP between Salt Lake City and San Francisco. Ultimately the ICC decreed that WP should remain independent. "Strangely, however," Hofsommer observes, "the SP was lethargic and ineffective in advancing opportunities on its eastern front." The Chicago & Eastern Illinois, he says, might have been a valuable partner for SP's Cotton Belt, but in San Francisco conventional wisdom prevailed *not* to press the matter. "In retrospect," Hofsommer concludes, that "decision was a monumental blunder." This blunt observation is typical, not exceptional. Although the author frankly expresses his view that overall SP has done a creditable job down through the years, he does not hesitate to note clearly the less happy occurrences.

The author's central and pervasive theme is that the SP, over the years, has been able to adapt to and surmount the rapidly changing challenges of the transportation industry. Since 1900 successive leaders have coped with booms and busts, radical advances in technology, basic new developments in labor and public relations, shifting political trends, and any number of emergency situations. The company, for example, made heroic efforts to make passenger service both distinguished and remunerative, only to find that financial salvation lay, if anywhere, in further diversification.

Hofsommer does not try to make instant history out of the events of the last fifteen years or so. He fully appreciates the importance of perspective and is guided accordingly. He is perfectly willing to take a stand, but insists on labeling it as tentative if that's what it is. Throughout the book, he has compiled and digested the record; it is now up to those who read it to evaluate its significance.

Richard C. Overton
Manchester Center, Vermont
September 4, 1985

Preface

EARLY in 1981 senior officers of the Southern Pacific contemplated the merits of having a history of the company prepared and then made available to the public. In the end, they decided to support two studies. The first would cover the earlier period, up to 1930, and would be a developmental history detailing the impact of the SP on its service area. There would be some topical as well as chronological overlap, they agreed, with the second, which would be essentially a history of the company itself during the twentieth century. Richard J. Orsi, professor of history at California State University-Hayward, was chosen for volume one; I, for volume two.

The entire undertaking reflects a particularly enlightened corporate policy. "What we want from you," Chairman Benjamin F. Biaggini told me on May 28, 1981, "is a fair assessment." I took him at his word and over the next many months never found reason to doubt his sincerity or that of his subordinates. Indeed, all company archives were opened to me, and personnel from one end of the property to the other were uniformly cordial and candid. Moreover, I retained editorial control; the company had the right to review the manuscript with the corollary right to enter a contrary explanatory footnote in the case of conflicting interpretations. None was requested.

This is, then, a twentieth-century history of the Southern Pacific Company and its subsidiaries, and to a lesser extent, their service areas. The focus is on SP's senior managers and on the decisions they made—how they were made, why they were made, and their results. I have

felt an obligation to describe, to the best of my ability, the context in which these men worked and to seek an understanding of their motives, aspirations, and policies. I have also implicitly compared successive management teams against standards set by E. H. Harriman (1901–1909), implicitly compared SP's railroads with their premier competitors, and probed SP's record as a corporate citizen. Not surprisingly, I have found a company with strengths and weaknesses, one that has tasted the sweetness of triumph and the bitterness of failure. Yet on the whole, the SP has enjoyed a significant, exciting, and profitable existence that does credit to its owners, managers, and employees.

Given the restrictions of time, the need to compress the lengthy twentieth-century story into a single volume, and given the company's multifaceted activities, ranging from steamships and pipelines, trunk railroads and communication satellites to leasing, real estate, and insurance companies, I have not been able to cover all aspects in the detail preferred. Moreover, the body of available source materials proved rich to the point of frustration and forced me to exercise a degree of subjective judgment in the selecting and sampling process. As a consequence, this study is, in a sense, a "snapshot" view of the Southern Pacific experience in this century, but my fond hope is that it will motivate others to report on particular elements of SP's remarkable past.

This volume would not have been possible without the sincere interest and assistance of scores of persons within and without the company. Although most of the support material has come from internal records and oral history, important archival materials have also been used. In this regard, I wish to thank W. Thomas White, James J. Hill Reference Library, Saint Paul; Helen M. Rowland, Association of American Railroads, Washington, D.C.; and Hilary Cummings, University of Oregon Library, Eugene. The staff at Harvard's Baker Library also showed me every courtesy during the time I spent there.

Among others outside the SP family who provided materials or otherwise helped me were Arthur L. Lloyd, G. B. Aydelott, Harry E. Hammer, Martin M. Pomphrey, Robert E. Gehrt, Fred A. Stindt, Prime F. Osborn, W. Averell Harriman, James R. Sullivan, David P. Morgan, John W. Barriger, John B. McCall, Russ E. Frame, and Ken Longe. Photographs were provided or processed by Richard E. Wilkinson, Bill Robertson, Harry M. Williamson, Bart C. Nadeau, James E. Sanders, and Peter H. Whitney, among others. The fine maps were prepared by John L. Hodson and John R. Signor.

From trainmen at Strang, Texas, to engine crews at Klamath Falls, Oregon, I was warmly received by all hands in every department and at every subsidiary. These included L. M. Phelps, Andrew Anderson, Stan August, Gloria G. Pacis, Anne E. Xanders, James A. Loveland, Robert A. Sederholm, Gerald D. Pera, Natalia W. Allen, Robert B. Hoppe, George Kraus, A. A. Adams, Joe L. Bart, Antonio Aleman, Henry M. Ortiz, B. B. Arro, R. E. Dipprey, George H. Durbala, Earl L. Eckhoff, Merle Kelly, J. W. Lynch, Michael E. McGinley, O. R. Thurston, Robert G. Thruston, W. Theo Eskew, J. G. Montfort, Thor H. Sjostrand, Thomas D. Ellen, Dale D. Holder, Conrad Weil, Kris K. Perez, Henry M. Chidgey, Ed N. Brown, Diane L. Young, Don H. Skelton, Dorane Humphrey, B. B. Garrett, W. H. Hudson, Jackye Vandenberg, Jimmy L. Bates, Ed P. Ahearn, Judy A. Holm, Randolph Karr, Marshall Hamil, Duane M. Autrey, John Mac-

Donald Smith, Don E. Enright, Al G. Richards, and C. E. Lamb.

The operating departments of SPTCo and St. Louis Southwestern saw to it that I got a firsthand look at their railroads. Those who assisted in this way included Lon P. Marsh, Mel J. Eshler, Dan L. Andreason, H. Declan Brown, Douglas F. Dupre, W. Brendt Eckardt, Jim R. Efaw, H. David Fischer, Jack L. Fuller, Art M. Henson, Robert G. Huff, Michael L. Irvine, David K. Medley, Ken A. Moore, Tom P. Russell, Ed J. Seil, C. R. Urbick, LeRoy Williams, Gary A. Greblo, John J. Tierney, W. J. Lacy, Roy G. McWhirter, Larry L. Phipps, Michael D. Ongerth, Charles T. Babers, W. C. Hoenig, Michael L. Burke, and Peter K. Baumhefner.

Several persons within the company and others in the railroad industry were joined by several academics who read all or parts of the manuscript and offered their own special insights and constructive criticisms. In this, special thanks go to Lynn D. Farrar, Rollin D. Bredenberg, Lloyd G. Simpson, Allen D. DeMoss, Richard D. Spence, Harry M. Williamson, W. Theo Eskew, Thomas C. Buckley, Lewis M. Phelps, Andrew Anderson, David F. Myrick, Robert I. Melbo, Michael D. Ongerth, John MacDonald Smith, Donald J. Russell, Benjamin F. Biaggini, Robert D. Krebs, Ed P. Ahearn, Guerdon S. Sines, Richard L. Tower, Arthur L. Lloyd, Thomas J. Lamphier, David P. Morgan, Keith L. Bryant, Richard C. Overton, Albro Martin, H. Roger Grant, and Leland L. Sage.

During the course of research and writing I was favored with materials, encouragement, wise counsel, and in a host of other ways by several who went far beyond the call of duty. Donald J. Russell inevitably responded with enthusiasm and candor to my every question during more than a dozen interviews; it was the same with Harold J. McKenzie; the door to the office of Robert D. Krebs was always open; Rollin D. Bredenberg, J. Earl Hare, L. Jack Jenkins, Robert R. McClanahan, Robert I. Melbo, and James T. McNamara provided generous travel opportunities and otherwise gave their cheery assistance; Lynn D. Farrar, Thomas C. Buckley, Allen D. DeMoss, Jim Johnson, Gary A. Laakso, Robert D. McIntyre, David F. Myrick, and Kenneth W. Jones graciously responded to endless requests and even more questions. Throughout all, Jana McClendon turned in her usual stellar performance by transcribing my illegible handwriting into clean manuscript.

Most of all, I am indebted to Ben Biaggini, who authorized the project.

Finally, I am grateful to my wife and family whose tolerance seems inexhaustible. To all of the above, and to any others whom I might have regretably overlooked, I am indebted. For errors of fact and for infelicities of style that remain, I alone am responsible.

Don L. Hofsommer

List of Acronyms and Shortened Names

A&P	Atlantic & Pacific Railroad	EP&SW	El Paso & Southwestern Railway
A&S	Alton & Southern Railroad	Frisco	St. Louis & San Francisco Railroad; St. Louis–San Francisco Railway
ALCO	American Locomotive Company		
ALCOA	Aluminum Company of America		
AT&SF	Atchison, Topeka & Santa Fe Railway	GE	General Electric Company
		GH&SA	Galveston, Harrisburg & San Antonio Railway
AT&T	American Telephone & Telegraph Company		
		GM	General Motors Corporation
B&MR	Burlington & Missouri River	GN	Great Northern Railway
BBB&C	Buffalo Bayou, Brazos & Colorado Railway	GTE	General Telephone & Electronic Corporation
BN	Burlington Northern Railroad	GWT&P	Gulf, Western Texas & Pacific Railway
BTR	Bureau of Transportation Research, SP	H&TC	Houston & Texas Central Railroad
Burlington	Chicago, Burlington & Quincy Railroad	HE&WT	Houston, East & West Texas Railway
C&EI	Chicago & Eastern Illinois Railroad	IBM	International Business Machines
C&NW	Chicago & North Western System	IC	Illinois Central Railroad
		ICC	Interstate Commerce Commission
CB&Q	Chicago, Burlington & Quincy Railroad		
CM&StP	Chicago, Milwaukee & St. Paul Railroad	Katy	Missouri-Kansas-Texas Railroad
		KCS	Kansas City Southern
		L&N	Louisiana & Nashville
COFC	Container On Flat Car	LCL	Less-than-Carload
Cotton Belt	St. Louis Southwestern Railway	M&StL	Minneapolis & St. Louis Railroad
CP	Central Pacific Railroad		
CRI&P	Chicago, Rock Island & Pacific Railroad	MCI	Microwave Communications Incorporated
CTC	Centralized Traffic Control	Milwaukee	Chicago, Milwaukee & St. Paul Railroad; Chicago, Milwaukee, St. Paul & Pacific Railroad
D&RGW	Denver & Rio Grande Western Railroad		
EMD	Electro Motive Division of General Motors	M-K-T	Missouri-Kansas-Texas Railroad

ML&T	Morgan's Louisiana & Texas Railroad & Steamship Co.	SD&AE	San Diego & Arizona Eastern Railway
MoPac	Missouri Pacific Railroad. For consistency, the term MoPac, coined in 1972, is used throughout.	Seaboard	Seaboard Coast Line
		SFSP	Santa Fe Southern Pacific Corporation
		SP	Southern Pacific Company
Morgan Lines	Southern Pacific Steamship Lines	SP&S	Spokane, Portland & Seattle Railway
NCO	Nevada-California-Oregon Railway	SPCC	Southern Pacific Communication Company
NP	Northern Pacific Railroad	SPID	Southern Pacific Industrial Development Company
NS	Norfolk Southern		
NWP	Northwestern Pacific Railroad	SPdeMex	Southern Pacific Railroad Company of Mexico
NYC	New York Central System		
OR&N	Oregon Railroad & Navigation Company	SPPL	Southern Pacific Pipe Line Company
O&W	Oregon & Washington	SPTCo	Southern Pacific Transportation Company
P&E	Phoenix & Eastern Railroad		
PE	Pacific Electric Railways	SSW	St. Louis Southwestern Railway
PFE	Pacific Fruit Express Company	T&L	Texas & Louisiana Lines
PMT	Pacific Motor Trucking Company	T&NO	Texas & New Orleans Railroad
PRR	Pennsylvania Railroad	T&P	Texas & Pacific Railway
Rio Grande	Denver & Rio Grande Railroad; Denver & Rio Grande Western Railroad	TOFC	Trailer on Flat Car
		TOPS	Total Operations Processing System
Rock Island	Chicago, Rock Island & Pacific Railroad	TRRA	Terminal Railroad Association of St. Louis
RPO	Rail Post Office	UP	Union Pacific Railroad
Santa Fe	Atchison, Topeka & Santa Fe Railway	V&T	Virginia & Truckee Railroad
		VP&GM Files	Vice President and General Manager's Files
SAP	San Antonio & Aransas Pass Railway		
SCL	Seaboard Coast Line	WP	Western Pacific Railroad
SD&A	San Diego & Arizona Railway		

The Southern Pacific, 1901–1985

CHAPTER I

Promontory Prelude

"... the celebration at Promontory was for
them [the Big Four] the beginning rather
than the end of a great task."—Robert Glass
Cleland, *A History of California*

THE simple message was dispatched at 12:47
P.M.: "Done." That unusually brief telegraphic
notice on May 10, 1869, set off what may have
been the most widespread celebration the
United States had witnessed to that time. Fifty
tugboats whistled salutes as they paraded
along the lakefront in Chicago; New Yorkers
shouted with glee at the conclusion of a 100-
gun salute; the national capital staged ban-
quets, parades, and a spectacular fireworks
display; and, prayers and toasts were inter-
mingled throughout the thirty-seven states
and territories. Asa Whitney the aging vision-
ary must have smiled; Bret Harte pondered
what the locomotives said as they faced each
other head to head. The locomotives, of course,
were Central Pacific's *Jupiter* and Union Pacific's 119, and the event that gave such pleasure to Whitney and his fellow citizens was
the completion of the country's first transcontinental railroad. The rails joined at Promontory, a desolate, windswept, and heretofore
unremarked spot in what became the state of
Utah—some 690 miles east of Sacramento
and 1,086 miles west of the Missouri River.[1]

Whitney had been arguing for such a railroad since the mid-1840s. The matter was inextricably linked with sectional tensions related to slavery or the extension of it, however,
and little, other than military surveys and
a lot of talk, was accomplished during the
1850s. Yet public support for such an enterprise became evident. The 1860 platforms of

the Republican party and the Democratic candidates—Douglas as well as Breckinridge—
included planks urging the construction of "a
Pacific Railroad." The Civil War intensified
interest, at least in the North and on the part
of the federal government, and resulted in the
passage of important legislation designed to
promote such a line. The Pacific Railroad Act
of 1862 and a similar act in 1864 spelled out a
policy of cooperative enterprise that authorized governmental support for two private
companies, the Union Pacific Railroad (UP),
building from the east, and the Central Pacific
Railroad (CP), from the west. Even with such
support, it was an awesome physical, not to
mention financial, undertaking. Few thought
it would be readily accomplished; Gen. W. T.
Sherman had not expected the project to be
completed in his lifetime although he thought
it likely his grandchildren would one day ride
the cars between America's heartland and the
Pacific Ocean. But now it was done. Out of
the ashes of the house divided came this great
national triumph; the country was united by
thin but effective bands of iron.[2]

Promoters of the Union Pacific had anticipated that a single company, theirs, would
build the entire line. They were surprised and
not a little displeased that four audacious Californians upstaged them by forming the Central Pacific Rail Road Company on June 28,
1861, and then convincing the Congress and
President Lincoln to authorize two companies,

not one, to build the line and share in government support. The four, Charles Crocker, Mark Hopkins, Collis Potter Huntington, and Leland Stanford, initially had neither the technical knowledge nor the massive capital support required to construct such a railway. Yet they were determined men who, as they gained success, took on the label "Big Four." Their greatest early asset proved to be Theodore D. Judah, who conceived the idea of conquering the Sierra Nevada and who surveyed and championed the famous Donner Pass route, which eventually was selected. Judah, sad to say, did not live to see the undertaking completed.[3]

The Big Four could ill afford to waste time celebrating the driving of the Golden Spike at Promontory. They and the CP were deeply in debt, and there was little reason to expect that circumstances soon would change. Completion of the Suez Canal in 1869 drained traffic to the Orient that the railroaders had counted on, and Nevada business declined as the silver mining industry lapsed into a long depression. Moreover, California itself was largely underpopulated and capital poor. The Big Four quickly learned that it was a dangerous business to build a railroad ahead of the frontier. On the other hand, they understood that rail lines could and would expand business and agricultural opportunities, so they plunged ahead.

The Central Pacific was recast twice in 1870 to absorb other lines. By then it had forged an agreement with the Union Pacific to purchase 47.5 miles of its track from Promontory east to the established community of Ogden. This made good sense, as Promontory was a poor junction for the two roads. The CP also acquired and completed the 151-mile Western Pacific Railroad (not to be confused with a later independent company of the same name), which had a line from Oakland to Brighton (near Sacramento) via Niles with a branch from Niles to San Jose. Additional mileage was acquired near Lathrop, between Roseville and Chico, from the California & Oregon Railroad and in and around Oakland, where a ferry operation was included. In this fashion CP forged a through line from Oakland over the Coast Range (Altamont Pass) to Sacramento and Ogden.[4]

San Francisco—queen city of the Bay Area, gateway to the Far East, and a logical target for the Big Four—had been reached, if indirectly, when the associates acquired the Southern Pacific Railroad in mid-1868. That company had acceded to the San Francisco & San Jose Rail Road, whose lines linked the two important peninsula cities of its corporate namesake. Another important addition followed. The California Pacific Railroad, which owned a water-level route in competition with the Central Pacific's Altamont line between Oakland and Sacramento, came into the fold of the Big Four during 1876.[5]

Not all mileage was acquired by purchase; much was constructed on behalf of both the CP and SP. By the end of the 1870s, lines pointed northward toward Oregon and southward along the coast. Additionally, during that decade the Big Four pushed a major artery down the San Joaquin Valley through Merced, Fresno, Bakersfield, and Mojave and then over the Tehachapis and through the San Fernando tunnel to Los Angeles. All of this was impressive enough, but orders were passed to company engineers for even more construction. To capture new territory and to forestall competition, Huntington and his associates drove rails east from Los Angeles to Yuma, reaching that point on the Colorado River in 1877. Construction resumed after only a brief pause. Crews labored through the hot, dry country of Arizona and New Mexico territories to reach the Rio Grande at El Paso, Texas, on May 19, 1881.[6]

Meanwhile, Huntington had emerged as the major figure among the Big Four (now down to three—Mark Hopkins had died in 1878) and had involved himself personally and on behalf of his associates in the railroad affairs of Texas. There he persuaded the owners of the Galveston, Harrisburg & San Antonio Railway

(GH&SA), which had recently opened a route from Houston to San Antonio, to push west for a connection with the Southern Pacific at El Paso. During the summer of 1881, crews from El Paso and from San Antonio began to close the gap; they met at the west bank of the Pecos River on January 12, 1883. The degree of financial involvement in the GH&SA by the SP or Huntington himself at this early date is not clear. However, the Southern Development Company was responsible for the actual construction of the San Antonio–El Paso line, and it was paid in bonds and capital stock of the GH&SA.[7]

Texans are quick to point out that Southern Pacific's earliest antecedent derived not from California but from the Lone Star State. The Buffalo Bayou, Brazos & Colorado Railway (BBB&C), chartered in 1850, placed in service a 20-mile route from Harrisburg to Stafford during 1853. This mileage, west of Houston, eventually passed to the GH&SA, which itself would become an integral part of the SP. As such, the BBB&C represented the first construction of any trackage that became the Southern Pacific.[8]

There was even more to be done, and Huntington was equal to the task. Between 1852 and 1881 several companies in Texas and Louisiana, including the Sabine, Galveston Bay Railroad & Lumber Company (later styled the Texas & New Orleans Railroad); the Louisiana Western Railroad; Morgan's Louisiana & Texas Railroad & Steamship Company; and the New Orleans, Opelousas & Great Western Railroad built end-to-end lines that, taken together, formed a through route linking Houston and New Orleans. Each one passed, in time, to the hands of the Southern Pacific. The first through passenger trains to operate between Los Angeles and New Orleans left their respective terminals on February 5, 1883. This important new artery was properly christened the Sunset Route.[9]

Huntington's hand moved broadly across Texas, and soon he and his associates owned, leased, or otherwise controlled not only the GH&SA—which itself would acquire numerous additional companies—but also the New York, Texas & Mexican Railroad, the Gulf, Western Texas & Pacific Railway, the Sabine & East Texas Railway, and the Houston & Texas Central Railway. More followed. The Houston & Shreveport Railroad and the Houston, East & West Texas Railway, forming a completed route from Houston to Shreveport, came into the Huntington camp on May 8, 1893. The reward was sweet. By 1900 the SP was the premier carrier in Texas in terms of miles operated.[10]

It was much the same in Oregon and California. Between 1872 and 1887 the Central Pacific finished a route from Red Bluff to the California-Oregon border; additional construction in 1887 saw the line reach Ashland, Oregon. Two companies, the Oregon & California Railroad and the Oregon Central Railroad, both originally independent but soon a part of the Southern Pacific, provided an extension through Eugene and Salem to Portland. Other important additions included a Tracy-Fresno line, completed during the summer of 1892, and Soledad to Saugus, built between 1886 and 1901, which provided a "Coast Line" route between the Bay Area and Los Angeles. Finally, the SP fleshed out its operations in the Los Angeles Basin with a spaghetti-like system of branches and feeders.[11]

Although the Central Pacific, its leased lines, and, later, the Southern Pacific Railroad were from the beginning under unified control, Huntington and his associates felt the need to simplify the corporate structure and met to discuss the matter in New York during 1884. A suggestion that all lines theretofore acquired be consolidated into one company was inexplicably rejected. However, they did agree to formation of the Southern Pacific Company, incorporated under the laws of Kentucky on March 17 of that year. Securities of the Southern Pacific Railroad Company and its subsidiaries (including properties in Texas and Louisiana then controlled) were exchanged for those of the new firm, and in the following

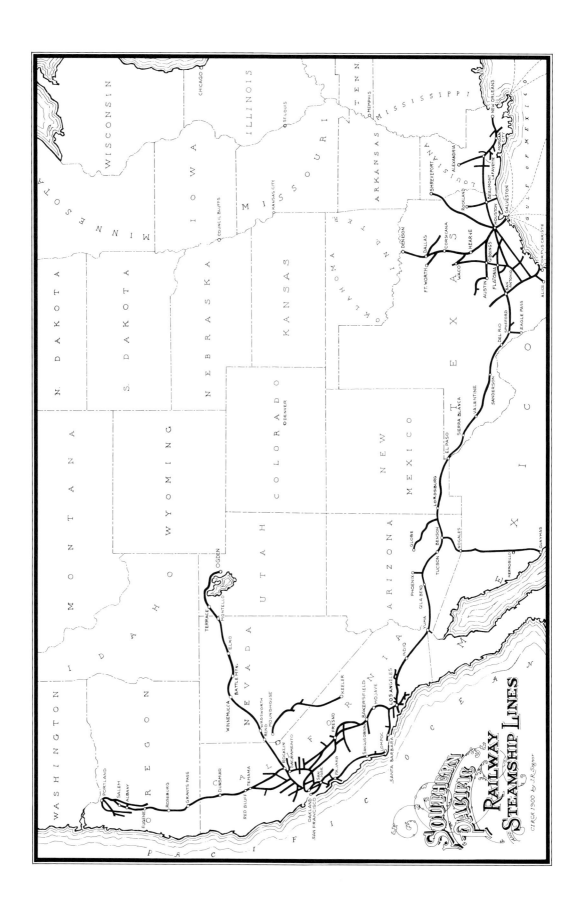

season the properties of the Central Pacific were leased for operation to the newly organized company. Then, in 1899, the Central Pacific Railroad itself was reorganized as the Central Pacific Railway. In that process virtually all holders of CP stock chose to receive stock and bonds of the Southern Pacific Company. The "new" CP then issued all of its stock to the Southern Pacific Company, which continued to operate the properties as lessee. An important ramification of these proceedings was that the federal government, which had loaned its bonds to CP in the amount of $58 million for construction of the original transcontinental line between Sacramento and Ogden, received payment in full with interest.[12]

C. P. Huntington could not rest; he was an early advocate of a true, single-company transcontinental railroad. In addition to his well-known activities on behalf of the CP and SP, Huntington was also associated with the Chesapeake & Ohio Railroad, becoming its president in 1869. His transcontinental dreams matured during the 1870s, and in 1882 he told a reporter in Louisville, Kentucky, that "our plans have grown as we advanced and now we will connect ocean with ocean." He did not spell out the precise route; he may have been thinking of an eastern connection for the Sunset Route from Los Angeles to New Orleans, or he may have been referring to his dream of a new line from Memphis through Albuquerque and on to a connection with an existing SP line in California—utilizing assets of the Atlantic & Pacific (A&P). The Atchison, Topeka & Santa Fe and the St. Louis & San Francisco, of course, and not Huntington, ultimately acceded to the Atlantic & Pacific. Huntington and his associates had discussed in 1884 the possibility of forming a through line from San Francisco to Newport News, Virginia, but as Huntington recalled, his associates "did not think well of it." One can only speculate as to the history of American railroading if they had.[13]

Nevertheless, the Big Four had created a truly prodigious enterprise. They transformed

Collis Potter Huntington shortly before his death on August 13, 1900.

California and much of the West and did so in an excitingly brief time. Their railroad operations opened many opportunities for the general public and provided direct employment for thousands. Indeed, they became wealthy themselves. The citizenry, however, was not uniformly appreciative. Many persons, for reasons of fantasy as much as fact, came to dislike the Big Four and, consequently, the Southern Pacific. The writer Frank Norris gave the railroad a particularly onerous label: The Octopus. It is unlikely that the company ever had the power that many ascribed to it. Still, as the nineteenth century passed into the twentieth, the SP was a railroad to be reckoned with: it controlled 8,206 route miles stretching from Portland to New Orleans, linking with the Union Pacific to form the Overland Route via Ogden, owned impressive operations throughout California, and boasted its own steamship company linking

New York and other points with the railroad at New Orleans.[14]

Impressive as the Southern Pacific was at the turn of the century, it needed a constant and growing source of cash to develop the property fully. That would not come from the Big Four. Mark Hopkins had died in 1878 and was followed in death by Crocker in 1888 and Stanford in 1893. On August 13, 1900, the most talented railroader of the four, Collis P. Huntington, joined them.[15]

CHAPTER 2

Enter Edward Henry Harriman

"We have bought not only a railroad, but an
empire."—Edward Henry Harriman

BECAUSE the inherent and strategic value of
the Southern Pacific was well recognized by
the investment and transportation communities, there was keen interest in the properties even before Huntington died. Edward
Henry Harriman was one of many who were
captivated by the opportunities presented by
the SP. Harriman had implored Huntington to
sell him his interest, but the old man stead-
fastly refused. Death finally released Huntington's grip. However, Speyer & Company,
SP's financial agents, continued to resist Harriman's overtures. Fully determined, Harriman
ordered the Union Pacific Railroad, which
he controlled, to buy SP stock. Yet, unless
he could secure that which Huntington had
willed his wife and nephew, there was no hope
that he could gain similar control of the Southern Pacific.[1]

The opportunity Harriman yearned for developed in 1901 when Edwin Hawley, an in-
timate business associate of Huntington's,
pledged his own holdings and openly advocated the sale of the estate's stock to the Union
Pacific. In the end, Hawley and not Speyer &
Company prevailed. By March 31, 1901, the
UP owned 38 percent of SP stock—20 percent
acquired from the Huntington estate and the
remainder purchased by Kuhn, Loeb & Company, bankers for the Union Pacific, on the
open market or by private sale. Harriman
later increased UP's holdings in SP to 46 percent. With 38 percent, Harriman claimed control; with just under half, the matter was beyond question. "We have finally landed the

Southern Pacific bird," exulted Jacob Schiff, a
friend and associate of Harriman.[2]

Western control of the Southern Pacific and
its heritage of freedom from "eastern entangle-
ments" evaporated with the sale of the Huntington shares to Harriman interests. Yet the
railroad was in good hands, yea, excellent
hands. Of Harriman, contemporaries and later
historians have said that he was "the foremost
railroad economist of the day"; "the most
powerful figure in the railroad situation in the
United States"; "the most competent railroad
man in the world"; "the greatest railroad man
since railroads began"; "the greatest of all
American railroad leaders."[3]

There was nothing to predict that E. H.
Harriman would ultimately emerge at the center of railroad affairs in this country. He
was born on February 25, 1848, the son of
the Reverend Mr. Orlando and Mrs. Cornelia
Harriman. School did not yield the reward
young Harriman was seeking, and he left it at
the tender age of fourteen to become an office
boy for the Wall Street house of D. C. Hays.
He quickly became familiar with the brokerage business and, when he was twenty-
two, purchased a seat on the New York Stock
Exchange. Fortune was kind to him. Prominent customers sought his talents, and the
firm of E. H. Harriman & Company grew accordingly. Good fortune also followed him in
marriage. During the late 1870s Harriman
was attracted to Mary Williamson Averell, a
pleasant young lady from a prominent Ogdensburg, New York, family. Mary's father

was a leading banker of the community and also president of the Ogdensburg & Lake Champlain Railroad. His marriage to her in 1879 not only provided Harriman with a charming and talented mate but also introduced him to the opportunities provided by the railroad industry.[4]

During the next two decades Harriman moved from relative obscurity to national prominence. In 1881 he acquired an interest in a tiny railroad in upstate New York; two years later he was elected to the directory of the prestigious Illinois Central Railroad; and in 1887 he became vice-president of that company. He jousted successfully with J. P. Morgan for control of the Dubuque & Sioux City Railroad and bested him again over plans for reorganization of the Erie. All of this, it seems, was preparatory for his forthcoming campaigns in the West.[5]

The fabled Union Pacific, with which the Central Pacific had been joined in 1869 to effect the nation's first transcontinental artery, had been victimized by the Credit Mobilier scandal, increased regional competition, periodically inadequate management, and the humiliation of a bankruptcy that stripped the road of important outlets and productive branches. Most observers had come to see it as a broken-down property—"two dirt ballasted streaks of rust," according to one source, and "a melancholy imitation of a railroad," according to another. Sidney Dillon was slightly more charitable; he called it an "apple tree without a limb." J. P. Morgan, a member of an early reorganization committee, declared the case hopeless. His was the prevailing view.[6]

A few saw it otherwise. New reorganization efforts implied hope through a new and powerful transcontinental alliance that would link the UP with the Chicago & North Western and the New York Central. The respected Gen. Grenville M. Dodge asserted that the road's organization was good and that its physical condition was as good as any carrier west of the Missouri River. Another respected railroader, Charles E. Perkins of the Chicago, Bur-

lington & Quincy Railroad, likewise thought the UP a worthy plum. He and others purchased "some hundreds of shares" of it and in 1893 suggested to James J. Hill that it might be wise to make "up a party now to buy a good block of it with the view of making the property a paying one on a *neutral basis*." (The emphasis is Perkins's.) Hill and Perkins failed to act, however, and so did C. P. Huntington, who also studied the possibility during the early 1890s.[7]

Harriman, too, had seen promise in the UP. He told Otto H. Kahn that the Union Pacific was "intrinsically worth as much as St. Paul [the CM&StP], and with good management it will get there." Initially, Harriman wanted to unite the Illinois Central with the UP, but eventually, for whatever reason, he gave up on that prospect. In any event, Harriman invested in the UP, became a director of the reorganized company on December 6, 1897, a member of its executive committee shortly thereafter, and chairman of that powerful body in May, 1898. The decisiveness that characterized his style for the remainder of his life was soon manifest. In 1898 he requested and received authorization from the UP board to spend no less than $25 million to rehabilitate the road. One season later he saw to the acquisition of the Oregon Railroad & Navigation Company and the reacquisition of the Oregon Short Line; in this way UP increased its mileage from 2,848 to 5,391 and recovered its West Coast outlet at Portland. The metamorphosis was as astonishing for its swiftness as for its completeness. Harriman, according to one writer, had "given to the West an entirely new Union Pacific." John W. Gates said in 1901 that the UP was "the most magnificent railroad property in the world."[8]

Relations between the Southern Pacific and the Union Pacific in the nineteenth century had always been unpredictable and not always cordial. An official of the neighboring Denver & Rio Grande Railroad (D&RG) in 1883 commented that "one day the Union Pacific and the Central Pacific are like two chums in bed, the next day they are like two cats hanging over a clothes line." Goodwill was clearly absent in 1885 when a rate dispute between the two companies resulted in the loss of the Pacific mail subsidy. Angry at this, UP officials diverted westbound traffic away from the Central Pacific to their own Oregon Short Line; Huntington retaliated by exacting local rates on traffic that the Central Pacific interchanged with the UP at Ogden. Peace returned in 1890 when the quarreling carriers signed a complicated agreement essentially pledging that they would, insofar as the law allowed, favor each other. Both, of course, were further bound by federal statutes that designated the Overland Route (Council Bluffs–Oakland via Ogden) as one continuous line available for all time to "the business and necessities of" the American people. A Supreme Court decision likewise affirmed that the UP was forever guaranteed "a connection with the Central Pacific upon terms as favorable as might be given any other connection."[9]

Each company nevertheless looked out for its own best interests. That included studies, plans, and even strategies designated to tap the territory of the other. Collis P. Huntington, in 1870, could have purchased the strategically located Utah Central, which if extended eastward to a connection with the Kansas Pacific—as was then rumored—would have structured a through line from Pacific tidewater to the Missouri River and would have challenged the very existence of the UP. Huntington, for reasons that are unknown, failed to act on the matter. For its part, the Union Pacific considered extension westward from Ogden to San Francisco, and its management ultimately authorized construction of the Oregon Short Line from Ogden to the Northwest because, in part, it feared Huntington would, as Sidney Dillon said, "shut down the gate at Ogden" and divert SP traffic to the Sunset Route. To fail in expansion toward Oregon would have, Dillon allowed, dead-ended the UP in Utah. The Union Pacific was also concerned that the newly completed

Northern Pacific would drain traffic through incursions into UP country and that the fledgling Denver & Rio Grande would similarly divert business by building its own line westward from Utah. Accordingly, the UP acted to thwart what it thought to be D&RG plans by purchasing an obscure and otherwise irrelevant short line in Nevada that, Dillon had heard, would be used to connect the Rio Grande with the Central Pacific.[10]

The tiny Denver & Rio Grande clearly could not be ignored, for it constantly kept the caldrons brewing. A decision was made, perhaps as early as 1880, by Rio Grande management to push that company from Colorado into Utah with the idea that it would, in fact, become a mighty link in a new Pacific rail chain. With that in mind, the Rio Grande and the much larger Chicago, Burlington & Quincy Railroad (CB&Q) during the summer of 1881 entered into an agreement whereby the Burlington & Missouri River (B&MR), a CB&Q satellite, was to complete a line into Denver from the east and the D&RG was to push its line to Salt Lake City and then Ogden for a connection with the Central Pacific. Ironically, the Rio Grande in 1880 had anticipated the construction of its own line through central Utah to Los Angeles. Its agreement with Chicago, Burlington & Quincy thus served to redefine the Rio Grande's goals away from Southern California toward Salt Lake City and Ogden. Connecting service began in May, 1883, when the Rio Grande Western Railway, a friendly associate of the Denver & Rio Grande, completed its road into Ogden. Earlier memoranda guaranteed through shipments from the Atchison, Topeka & Santa Fe at Pueblo and the B&MR at Denver over the Denver & Rio Grande–Rio Grande Western to Central Pacific rails at Ogden. The Union Pacific, not surprisingly, fought to undermine the new operation but failed.[11]

The redoubtable William Jackson Palmer, president of the Rio Grande Western, personally solicited and authorized reconnaissance of various routes to the Pacific between 1891 and 1901. The *San Francisco Chronicle* of November 5, 1891, boldly proclaimed that "the Rio Grande Western is sure to build to San Francisco" over a route that, the paper had to admit, had not yet been defined. The line, of course, was not built, but public speculation in the matter persisted.[12]

The Denver & Rio Grande itself continued to look westward. It scoured the area but did not find a suitable route across the badlands of southern Utah from Durango, Colorado. Nevertheless, it did eventually construct a standard-gauge line from Durango to Farmington, New Mexico—possibly with the idea that it would be used as part of a new through route to Los Angeles via Gallup. The Rio Grande's dream of reaching California or at least another connection with the Southern Pacific ultimately failed to materialize.[13]

The plans and dreams of still other aspirants further shaped or modified the strategies of the Union Pacific and SP. The Chicago, Burlington & Quincy in 1876 inquired of the CP as to its impartiality in the event the Burlington built west to Ogden. The same company in 1883 made line locations west of Denver and accelerated its plans with property acquisitions in 1885–86. During the latter part of the same decade the CB&Q also conducted surveys west of the Rockies with the idea of extending its operation to Salt Lake City and even into the Pacific Northwest. The Burlington was not alone in hopes of tapping California trade directly or through a friendly connection with the SP. Jay Gould, for instance, once threatened to build his Kansas Pacific Railroad to a junction with the Central Pacific. Moreover, the Colorado Midland Railway aspired to build an independent line from Colorado Springs to Salt Lake City, and in 1887 it had surveyors looking for such a route in Utah. (The plan, strange to say, surfaced again in the second decade of the twentieth century.) Finally, the *Railway Review* for March 31, 1888, reported that the Chicago & North Western System planned to extend its recently opened Casper, Wyoming, line to a connection with the Central Pacific at Ogden and possibly on to Los Angeles.[14]

Construction of competing rail routes into California was not a prospect warmly received by SP's management, but it obviously perceived no similar threat in additional eastern connections at Ogden. The Union Pacific viewed such competition otherwise. Harriman understood the implications. The UP was flanked on one side by the growing power of the Hill Lines, and on the other by SP's Sunset Route, the Gould empire, and the increasingly important Santa Fe. Moreover, UP's crucial connection at Ogden was always subject to competitive attack as well as potentially unfriendly action by the SP. Most importantly, there was the possibility after Huntington's death that the SP would fall into hands unalterably hostile to the interests of the Union Pacific. Harriman was properly concerned. He had succeeded in making the Union Pacific an admirable property, and he had regained its Oregon Short Line outlet to the Pacific. Yet it was inadequate. Harriman had one overarching need: the SP. Nothing less would suffice.

While he lived, of course, C. P. Huntington held Harriman at bay. He resisted the efforts of Harriman to secure common management of the two properties, just as he had resisted Jay Gould in an earlier day; he declined to sell just the Central Pacific to Harriman; and he even refused to sign an agreement guaranteeing the Harriman road perpetual access to the Pacific. Like Harriman, Huntington had boldness and vision. If either road would take over the other, Huntington must have thought, it would be the Southern Pacific that would accede to the Union Pacific.[15]

But Collis Potter Huntington died suddenly on August 13, 1900. Four days later, at 11:00 A.M., employees of the Southern Pacific stood at silence for a full seven minutes in honor of the man. All trains, boats, and ships paused, company offices were hushed, and even the telegraph instruments fell silent. His fellow directors on the SP called him "one of the greatest men of his generation." It was hardly an overstatement. Huntington was a man of awe-inspiring talent and tenacity. His labors—joined by and supported by his associates—resulted in accomplishments so rapid and dramatic as to tax comprehension.[16]

Early in 1901, at Harriman's recommendation, the board of directors of the Union Pacific moved to take advantage of the opportunity now presented. It authorized the issuance of convertible bonds secured by several hundred miles of improved road as well as bonds of the Oregon Short Line and stock of both the Oregon Short Line and the Oregon Railroad & Navigation Company. In this way the Union Pacific—Harriman—raised money to acquire stock control of the SP and unified the two great companies under a single management.[17]

Harriman offered several arguments to justify the massive new association. He told Union Pacific stockholders that control of the Southern Pacific was strategically necessary "to maintain and protect the position of the system and to safeguard its future against combinations of other lines, which might divert much business by changes in existing channels of transportation." On another occasion Harriman contended that the UP purchased control of the SP "not because it needed the additional mileage, but rather that it might indirectly acquire the Central Pacific and a direct outlet to the Pacific Coast." Neither the report to shareholders nor Harriman's assertion—even the two in combination—represented the whole truth. Clearly, Harriman was scrambling to protect heavy investments in and massive expenditures made for improvements of the Union Pacific. Furthermore, acquisition of the SP neutralized Central Pacific's advantages over the UP, curtailed competition from the Denver & Rio Grande, and rendered impotent plans or hopes of the Burlington, the Chicago & North Western, or the Colorado Midland to connect without prejudice at Ogden or any other location with the SP. There was some short-term disagreement on Wall Street, but as one ob-

server put it, "the majority opinion seems to be that it will be a good thing for the Union Pacific."[18]

There were other, equally understandable reasons why Harriman wanted the SP. The Southern Pacific was an astonishingly large operation by comparison with other carriers at the time. Indeed, it was, as Harriman's biographer observed, "the greatest transportation system in the world." Unlike the Union Pacific, which was forced to rely primarily on transcontinental traffic for its livelihood, SP boasted a desirable and diversified traffic mix, long average hauls, and high average earnings. "Lacking the Southern Pacific," said transportation observer Frank H. Spearman, "the Union Pacific never had been and never could be a great railway." When Harriman gained control of the UP he "really got hold of the transcontinental traffic dog; in the Southern Pacific he got the traffic dog itself." Harriman understood as much. "We have bought not only a railroad, but an empire," he declared.[19]

After Harriman rehabilitated the Union Pacific, the SP, in terms of its physical condition, was not at par. However, the property was, to quote William Hood, SP's respected chief engineer, in "suitable condition for its traffic." Other assessments corroborated Hood's. After Chauncey M. Depew and Cornelius Vanderbilt had toured the SP in 1896, they told Huntington they were "much impressed by the evidences of system and completeness in all the appointments, and by the perfection of your roadbed." Huntington was no doubt pleased to receive such compliments, but he was not one to rest on his laurels. Considerable line improvement and plans for more of the same typified the SP in his last years. To be sure, many of the improvements that occurred during the Harriman years originated in the Huntington era and could be completed expeditiously.[20]

Harriman's control of both the SP and the Union Pacific represented, in truth, a radical change in the railroad situation of the West. He would work to knit the two giants into a fine—perhaps the finest—U.S. rail system. He would seek to reduce curvature, to lower grades, and to improve rolling stock. Harriman had not only access to necessary financial resources but, in addition, all skills necessary to oversee and manage a giant enterprise. The writer Burton K. Kendrick said that in comparison to Harriman, "the Vanderbilts, the Goulds, the Garrets, the Huntingtons, represent the parochial period of our railroad history." The earlier leaders had, Hendrick argued, "consolidated small railroad principalities into kingdoms." Harriman, on the other hand, federalized "their kingdoms into an empire." William Hood, who worked under both Huntington and Harriman and who admired both, thought Harriman's power a positive good. "It is exceedingly fortunate for the territory served by the Southern Pacific Lines that E. H. Harriman acquired control and gave of his abilities for the benefit of this railroad and its patrons," said Hood. If Harriman had not followed Huntington in the leadership of SP, Hood believed, "there would have been a delay of many years in the development of the resources of the Great West." [21]

Internal changes at SP came quickly. Charles M. Hayes, who had succeeded C. P. Huntington as president, survived only briefly under Harriman, who on September 26, 1901, assumed that office himself. The chairman of the board of directors after Huntington's death, Charles H. Tweed, held that position into 1902, at which time the office was abolished; Tweed remained on the board, however. Another personality from the Huntington days, Edwin Hawley—the man who had arranged sale of the Huntington estate shares to Harriman interests—was given a seat on the SP board and served on its executive committee. Nevertheless, his term was brief since Harriman, who was also chairman of the executive committee, would not take Hawley fully into his confidence. The composition of the board itself changed radically. Only Henry E. Huntington, Collis's nephew, saw continuous service through the Harriman years. If Harriman substantially altered the composition of

Edward Henry Harriman loved nothing if not a challenge.

the SP board, he chose another course with its top officers. Most of them retained their positions, and several were moved to the highest positions in the combined system. [22]

Harriman immediately made good a pledge to spend money in the amount necessary to realize Southern Pacific's potential. Early plans focused on the Central Pacific line from Roseville, California, to Ogden, Utah. The board authorized expenditures of $18 million, and when Julius Kruttschnitt, under whose supervision the money would be spent, asked Harriman what speed should be made in the prosecution of the task, Harriman replied, "Spend it in a week if you can." Not all of the money was allocated to improvement of the Overland Route, but Harriman promised that the most impressive changes would occur there. [23]

Harriman's immediate purpose was to make the Central Pacific capable of carrying as much freight between Ogden and San Francisco

The Lucin Cut-off, which was placed in service on March 8, 1904, cost over $8 million. Side-dump cars, known as "battleships," carried eighty-ton payloads.

as the Union Pacific could handle between Ogden and Council Bluffs. Of particular concern was the portion between Reno and Ogden, where the road was burdened by excessive curvature and intolerable grades—the heaviest of which were located east of Lucin, north of the Great Salt Lake. In Nevada alone, 221 of Central Pacific's 433 miles of main track were relocated to reduce grades and curvature. For the entire route, 321 miles of new main track were built. When completed, it was 50.89 miles shorter, had 12,736 degrees less curvature, and maximum grades for the reconstructed portions were reduced to about twenty-one feet to the mile (0.4 percent).[24]

The most impressive aspect of the Central Pacific project was the construction of the Lucin Cut-off. Like virtually all of the major betterment programs executed during the Harriman years, it had been on the drawing boards before Huntington died. In 1898, after he had considered and rejected a new Wells, Nevada–to–Salt Lake City route, Huntington ordered William Hood to make studies

and surveys for a cut-off to Ogden. The issue was in limbo pending a suitable settlement with the federal government over Central Pacific's construction debts, but when that issue was resolved in 1899, Hood went forward with plans for right-of-way acquisition and the procurement of massive steam shovels.[25]

In November, 1899, the company announced further and even more spectacular plans—for a mammoth pile trestle across Great Salt Lake. Engineers were already taking soundings. Huntington believed that the cross-lake trestle was feasible because, in his view, the level of the lake would continue to drop because streams feeding it were increasingly tapped for irrigation purposes. Harriman, though, was initially unconvinced that the lake's level would drop, and plans for the trestle were shelved until he changed his mind in mid-1902. The first piles were driven on August 21, 1902.[26]

Meanwhile, work had already commenced on the new grades leading to the lake from Lucin, on the west, and Ogden, on the east.

Special trains brought E. H. Harriman (*second from left*) and other dignitaries to a Thanksgiving Day celebration at Midlake. The Lucin Cut-off involved building 102.9 miles of new railroad.

Three hundred huge side-dump cars known as
"battleships" were purchased for the enterprise; they were commonly loaded with eighty
tons of payload. A constant problem resulted
from the need to supply water—in the amount
of 500,000 gallons daily—for the locomotives,
pile drivers, steam shovels, and boats employed
on the project. Much of it was hauled from
Deeth, Nevada, to Lakeside, 145 miles.[27]

The cross-lake venture comprised over 15
miles of filled embankments and 23 miles of
temporary and permanent trestles. The lake
bottom was at once unstable and treacherous;

there were times when it appeared that fills
and trestles alike would be swallowed up in
mud. Perseverance was required. At one time
3,000 men and nineteen pile drivers were
at work. On October 26, 1903, after 535
miles of piling (if placed end to end) had been
driven, the bridgemen finished their work.
Three trains brought dignitaries, including
E. H. Harriman and William Hood (who had
designed the Lucin Cut-off and executed its
construction) to a Thanksgiving Day celebration at Midlake, or Camp No. 23, as it was
then known.[28]

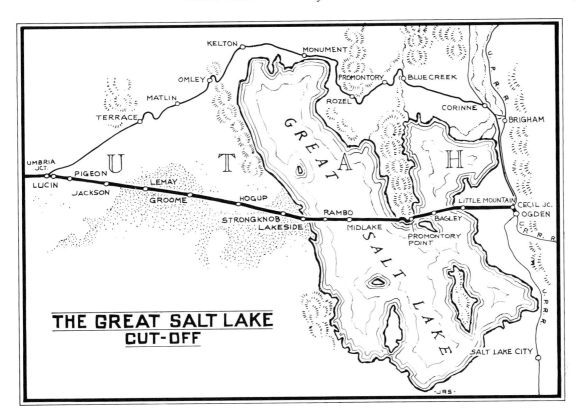

THE GREAT SALT LAKE CUT-OFF

Here was something worth celebrating. The Lucin project had involved building 102.9 miles of new railroad and had cost $8.359 million. It was clearly the most striking of Harriman's achievements in modernizing the Central Pacific line and was also one of the most remarkable and courageous engineering accomplishments of the time. The trestle, in particular, caught the public's attention. "The Salt Lake [*sic*] cut-off is certainly a bold piece of engineering and well worth seeing," Thomas A. Edison wrote enthusiastically in a letter to the company. The Lucin Cut-off was officially placed in service on March 8, 1904.[29]

A similar project was known as the Bay Shore Cut-off. This one, built at the astonishing cost of nearly $1 million per mile, replaced the old line built in 1863 between San Francisco and San Bruno. Feasibility studies had been made as early as 1873 and again in 1878. Subsequently, land was purchased for right-of-way, but SP management eventually concluded that traffic volume would not justify such a massive expenditure. Then, in 1899, while the construction of the Coast Line via Santa Barbara was going forward, the Bay Shore Cut-off project was resuscitated. Huntington's death postponed it again, but Harriman was easily convinced of the merits. Construction began in October, 1904. It proved a difficult bit of work involving extensive grading, the construction of heavy bridging, and the boring of five tunnels aggregating nearly 10,000 feet. In the end, however, the Bay Shore Cut-off provided the SP with an entirely new, handsome, double-track main-line into the heart of San Francisco. It was opened for traffic on December 8, 1907.[30]

Still another project undertaken by Huntington and completed by Harriman was the Montalvo Cut-off. When in the 1880s SP management had determined to build its railroad into Santa Barbara from Los Angeles (the southern end of the Coast Line), two routes were considered, and both were deemed desirable in terms of local traffic. The one selected for immediate construction, Saugus–Montalvo–Santa Barbara, could be built faster and more inexpensively than the other, Burbank–Montalvo–Santa Barbara. Later on, when the Coast Line (San Jose–San Luis Obispo–Santa Barbara) was nearing completion, C. P. Huntington directed his engineering department to proceed with the Montalvo Cut-off. When placed in service on March 20, 1904, it featured an impressive alignment—facilitated in part by the Chatsworth, Santa Susana, and Simi tunnels—and was the short route between Santa Barbara and Los Angeles.[31]

The Lucin, Bay Shore, and Montalvo projects represented monuments to the philosophies and foresightedness of both Huntington and Harriman. Each understood the need to reduce distances, grades, and curvatures. Each man also understood the savings in operating expenses facilitated by these improvements—8 to 10 percent on the money invested in them.[32]

One seemingly prosaic element of Harriman's progressive program of improvements merits special consideration. In 1901 the SP had a bare 50 miles of block signal protection along its massive plant. A plan to increase such was soon instituted; by mid-1907, a total

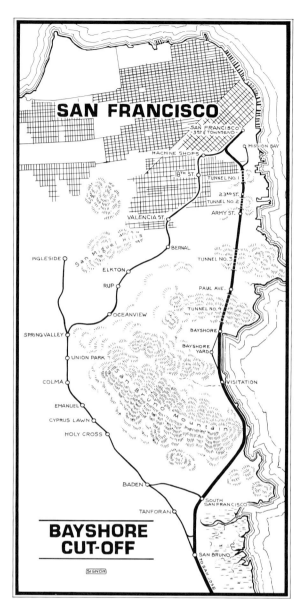

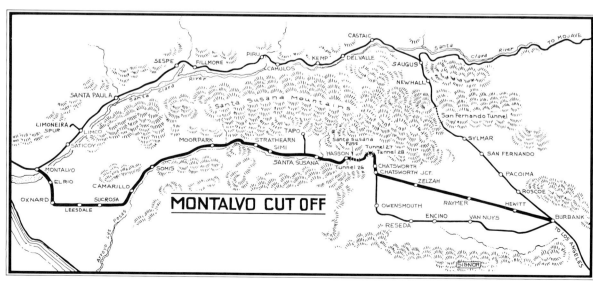

The Bay Shore Cut-off was another massive construction project undertaken by Huntington and completed by Harriman. It required five tunnels, aggregating nearly ten thousand feet in length.

of 1,263 miles of road were thus protected, and plans called for an additional 360 miles. Signaling of this type, Harriman matter-of-factly observed, would "give additional safety and despatch to the movement of trains." The Southern Pacific under Harriman became the industry leader in terms of miles of line protected by automatic block signals.[33]

On the great trunk routes and, indeed, across the breadth and width of the SP, Harriman spent money to make the road all it was ca-pable of. New sidings were built and old ones were lengthened; new ties (27 million of them during the Harriman years) were inserted; millions of tons of ballast were dumped; heavier rail was installed; stronger bridges replaced weaker ones; real estate was acquired for new terminals; portions of the Overland Route in California and Nevada were double-tracked; and facilities of all types were acquired. Harriman was—could there be any doubt?—a planner and a builder.[34]

CHAPTER 3

The Napoleon of Railroading

"The way to save money is to spend it wisely and productively."—Edward Henry Harriman

THE impact of Edward Henry Harriman on the Southern Pacific was both immediate and long term. What motivated this extraordinary man? What were his principles, his beliefs? What was his business philosophy? What was his style?

Religion and the institutional church were important to Harriman. He was born the son of an Episcopalian rector, was reared in an ecclesiastical environment, and was, as his son W. Averell Harriman recalled, "very quietly religious, not ostentatious about it." He had no time for those whom he labeled "fair-weather Christians." Rather, he urged that responsibility did not end with oneself but extended to those over whom one had influence. This belief led Harriman to an activist role. His best-known efforts were on behalf of New York's Tompkins Square Boy's Club, an unusually successful venture that served thousands. He also participated in campaigns against saloons and in various charitable enterprises.[1]

Harriman firmly believed that a man is duty-bound to leave a property in better condition than he found it. For him it was a matter of moral principle as well as a cardinal rule of business practice. He saw railroads as public service properties that required constant infusions of capital if they were to handle traffic efficiently and thus contribute properly to the development of the continent. At the same time, Harriman understood that if his lines were in superior condition, they would attract additional traffic at the expense of less well-equipped competitors. A hallmark of his philosophy was to build up and not tear down; railroads under his control were uniformly better off as a result of his stewardship.[2]

Few railroaders of the time better understood the fact that additional net income could be derived by reducing the cost of transportation, and that costs could be reduced by acquiring higher capacity cars and larger and more efficient locomotives. Implementing this policy on the Harriman Lines increased the carrying capacity of trains without damaging operating ratios and reflected a basic tenet of Harriman's philosophy. "The way to save money is to spend it wisely and productively," he once observed. This did not mean squandering resources; it did mean spending freely when doing so would promote earning power and increase revenue. Harriman particularly favored spending during periods when money was cheap but counseled against borrowing "from the substance of a road."[3]

Harriman was not averse to investing large sums of his personal fortune in projects he felt were worthy, and he had an amazing ability to persuade others to join him. Jacob A. Schiff, James Stillman, Henry H. Rogers, William Rockefeller, William K. Vanderbilt, and Henry C. Frick were among those who at one time or another associated themselves with Harriman's ventures. Several banking and insurance firms provided additional monies;

Harriman relied in particular on Kuhn, Loeb & Company and National City Bank. With his fiduciary standing well established, he moved with increased boldness and vigor. His policy was to use the credit of his stronger properties to advance the capacity of newly acquired or weaker ones. This tactic, as it developed, was especially beneficial to the Southern Pacific. The SP, of course, was hardly weak, but on its own it could not have generated the $242 million that Harriman spent on the property during his brief tenure.[4]

Some thought Harriman's spending policies were extravagant—especially when compared with his seemingly parsimonious dividend policy. Harriman believed that the railroad's main business was to serve the public and shippers and that this responsibility had to be put ahead of the payment of dividends to shareholders. Thus, SP's earnings were typically put into improvements rather than dividends. Not surprisingly, there were those who disapproved of that policy. Indeed, it excited the active opposition of James R. Keene and others, who formed a pool of SP stock with the idea of forcing Harriman to declare dividends. Litigation followed, but Keene was defeated. Harriman relented somewhat, however. A 2.5 percent dividend on common stock was paid in 1906; 5.25 percent in 1907; 6 percent in 1908 and 1909.[5]

Harriman believed that American society would best be served by private enterprise railroads created to provide inexpensive, efficient, and dependable transportation. The public generally agreed. However, to facilitate such service, all carriers, Harriman argued, had to insist on rates that were compensatory and, in conformity with long-established patterns, based on what traffic would bear; such rate making, of course, rested on studied assumptions by railroad management regarding the ability of shippers to pay and yet stay in business. Such an approach, however, took on an unfortunate and onerous meaning; many if not most Americans interpreted "all the traffic

will bear" as a policy to squeeze the last dollar from a forlorn and helpless public. Nevertheless, "costs-plus-profit" rates would have had a deleterious effect on most small shippers and infant industries. For that reason, Harriman and other railroad leaders often chose to formulate artificially low rates to create new traffic and new markets—rates that were ultimately beneficial to shippers and carriers alike.

On balance, Harriman's policy of rate making was fair. He knew that it was not possible for a railroad to separate its own interests from those of its patrons. If a railroad failed to build up its service territory, it would, in effect, make that same territory less competitive and thus threaten the prosperity of the transportation company itself. Harriman faced the issue squarely:

It would be suicidal for a railroad company to throttle or paralyze the industries along its lines by charging exorbitant rates. Even if there is no direct competition by parallel roads, every industrial plant located along a line of railroad is competing with plants located on other lines, and every railroad is forced to make sure low and reasonable rates as will permit the industries in the territory tributary to it to make sales in competitive markets, and thus furnish the traffic from which the railroad company derives its earnings.

Harriman, in effect, laid a tremendous wager on the future of "his" territory—the West. He doubtless would have lost that wager had the Harriman Lines charged its customers ruinous rates.[6]

For E. H. Harriman, the essence of life was planning, creating, and building. He possessed an active imagination and saw vividly into a future whose needs he anticipated. In 1904 he bluntly told President Theodore Roosevelt that the massive improvement program of the nation's railroads in the preceding several years would in fact prove to be woefully inadequate to meet their future needs. He predicted that every single-track operation in the country would eventually have to be double tracked. He might be faulted for having failed to foresee the rise of the auto and the competition it would represent, but this example nevertheless illustrates Harriman's ability to think in large terms and his willingness to plan in advance.[7]

Harriman's abilities and strategies brought him handsome financial rewards; as a consequence of his wealth, there were those who despised him. Yet Harriman had achieved financial independence early; at the apex of his life money meant little to him except for the power that it gave him for constructive works. Money, he said, was simply the reflection of a successful undertaking; satisfaction should not come merely from the accumulation of money but rather from the warm feeling of a job well done. He told a San Antonio newspaperman that he and his railroad associates were "in the attitude of the deeply interested professional man or scientist who prosecutes his work, not alone for the money they can make out of it, but for the beautiful service they can render." Although his statement sounded trite and self-serving, Harriman was sincere.[8]

Like most successful men, Harriman was devoted to specific values. He despised waste, worshiped efficiency, and was impatient with stupidity in all forms. His word was good to friend and foe alike. This slight, walrus-mustached man, frail during his later years, was not one to seek conflict, but neither did he avoid it. In all cases he was considered a "fair fighter."[9]

Other qualities further characterized Harriman. He was bold, sagacious, and self-assured. Julius Kruttschnitt thought Harriman had "the most wonderful intellect" he had ever known; SP's W. F. Herrin likewise marveled at his quick and nimble mind. He had an insatiable thirst for information, asked blunt questions that were difficult to evade, and could quickly reduce a multitude of facts to the nub. He did not believe it necessary to have all details of a plan perfected before proceeding. Harriman gave the naturalist John Muir a full dose of his philosophy when he felt his friend was overplanning and brooding too much over a book project. "The trouble with you," Harriman told Muir, "is that you are too slow in your beginnings. . . . Begin, begin, begin!" The advice was vintage Harriman. The great railroader always began boldly, and he could balance his realism with the fruits of his remarkable imagination. Complementing all this was his ability to successfully conduct affairs on a large scale.[10]

Investment banker Otto Kahn and railroad builder Grenville Dodge were among many who marveled at Harriman's ability to bring others around to his way of thinking. Dodge referred to it as Harriman's "great power in argument." Kahn recalled the lucidity of his arguments, his indomitable persistence, and his good judgment. Harriman himself saw it as an ability to harmonize varying opinions. Others thought of it, rather, as his capacity to "Harrimanize."[11]

Harriman loved a challenge. He was at his best when confronted with a seemingly impossible problem. It was, in a sense, a matter of sport; he pitted his mental powers and personality against physical tasks or talented rivals. The rewards were intrinsic; a sense of accomplishment, mastery, and the successful exercise of power.[12]

Harriman firmly believed in the voluntary consolidation of railroads, in the need to form railway territories or baronial districts, and in the necessity of the overlords to cooperate in a community of interests. He despised unstable rate structures and destructive competition—both of which, he considered, were antithetical to the best interests of the public and the railroads themselves. This led Harriman to push for regional domination and to promote use of the most efficient and expeditious routes under his command. Some saw in his work only the threat of monopoly, and they came to fear both Harriman and the philosophies he advocated.[13]

Harriman's difficulties with the public were ofttimes self-inflicted. Indeed, this nervous, rapid-fire, little man seemingly had little sense of good public relations. His friend Otto Kahn thought Harriman took unnecessary chances with his reputation. He was brutally frank, brusque to the point of being rude, and had little regard for appearances. Consequently, although he did not set out to offend others, he did so with reckless abandon. He made needless enemies by simply rubbing people the wrong way. Such behavior paid negative dividends at a time when the average citizen was increasingly concerned about the growing size and power of basic industries and those who controlled them. Harriman would have profited from Kahn's advice: "A man, especially a man at the head of a great corporation, must not only *do* right, but he must be very careful to avoid even appearances tending to arouse the suspicion of his not doing right." Like it or not, Kahn observed, a man holding power and a conspicuous place in society is a legitimate object for public scrutiny. Harriman was unmoved. After playing into the hands of his detractors, he remained characteristically aloof. The railroader regarded public controversy as a waste of time. "Let them kick," he said of his opponents. "They have the advantage because they tell lies about me, and I won't about them. . . . The people always find out what's what in the end, and I can wait . . . I need my time to *do* things." His was a noble and honorable position, but naive. Some thought his silence represented indifference to public opinion; others felt his lack of response proved any accusation, however utterly foolish.[14]

Harriman was not silent, however, in the matter of safety. Indeed, safety and its increase was a hallmark of Harriman's philosophy. His approach was to spend money—"like water," according to one contemporary—on advanced signal systems and other devices designed to enhance safe passage. Material changes, however, were inadequate in and of themselves; human error also had to be reckoned with. Harriman's operating personnel eventually discerned that threatening a violator of safety

rules with his job did little good, since labor was relatively scarce and all the man had to do, if dismissed, was locate another job. "Surprise testing" of operating personnel was more effective in reducing violations but, ironically, did little to diminish accidents. Management naturally was puzzled but remained no less interested in isolating responsibility for each accident, particularly serious ones. Boards of inquiry, consisting of the division superintendent, master mechanic, and resident engineer, were always empaneled for such. Yet each of these officers had investments in both turf and ego and thus could rarely be relied on to render impartial assessment. A serious and independent voice was added to the traditional committee when the Harriman Lines did the unthinkable—it tapped the public for outsiders, in no way connected with the railroad. "Cause unknown" reports were no longer accepted, nor were split decisions. If a committee could not reach a unanimous verdict, a new committee made up of general officers, was formed. If this group also rendered an unacceptable report, an outside and unbiased expert was employed. Internal objections to the new procedures were great at first but gradually were overcome. The number of accidents as well as the loss of life and property per incident was materially reduced on the combined Southern Pacific–Union Pacific system as a consequence of these policies and Harriman's vigorous interest in safety.[15]

The term "Harriman Lines" defined no corporation or combination of firms but was merely a familiar designation of those properties over which Harriman held control. All such companies maintained legal independence but, as a practical matter, each was operated rather like an autonomous division of a larger system, and each retained its own vice-president and general manager who was in charge of that particular line. Harriman's new organizational structure employed the mechanics of creative tension: He wanted to bring the various entities into close relationship but, at the same time, grant to them maximum independence. It would require a delicate balancing act. Yet, if successful, it would bring maximum efficiency, and Harriman admired that above all.

Why did Harriman not simply fold all of these railroad properties into one? There were several reasons. First, Harriman was not convinced that one man could manage or even perform responsibly in the management of even a single major department in a transportation company as large as his would be if fully merged. Second, because of a variety of circumstances he thought numerous of his properties could be managed more efficiently on a local basis. Third, neither Harriman singly nor he and his financial associates together could command monetary resources adequate to acquire equity fully in every property. Fourth, any attempt to thus merge the properties during the early part of the twentieth century would have been, at best, a public relations disaster since the national mood generally feared such "bigness." Finally, given the political climate of the time, and the growing gulf between Harriman and Theodore Roosevelt, merger would have invited an antitrust action by the "Trust Buster."[16]

Otto Kahn once recalled that Collis Huntington's admonition on the business of managing a great property was simple and direct: "Watch the details. Then the whole organization will watch the details." Kahn also recalled the advice of another eminently successful person on the same subject: "Don't waste your strength on non-essentials. Never do yourself what you can hire someone else to do equally well for you." Harriman's style was somewhere between these two, depending on the time and issue. He could divide labor and fix responsibility in a most effective way. On the other hand, he clearly kept close watch on all important matters and, as those who recalled his inspection trips said, the smaller ones, too.[17]

Opinions regarding Harriman's style and his very persona varied greatly. That he was a born leader is beyond dispute. Neither is there question that he was imperious—although he mellowed in later years. "He was rather small in stature," son Averell remembered, but "he dominated a room whenever he was in it, in a quiet way." Otto Kahn admired his "generalship." So did C. C. Goodwin, a westerner, who considered Harriman "a general in marshaling both his forces and his finances." George Kennan thought "his genius was the genius of a Bismarck, of a Roman Caesar." Goodwin thought him "a statesman in foreseeing the effects that would follow certain causes." Others offered less charitable interpretations of Harriman's imperiousness. His good friend Otto Kahn admitted that some of Harriman's associates chafed under "his undisguised autocracy." A contemporary writer called him "a tyrant, harsh and overbearing, absolutely without tact . . . the sovereign, the dictator." A similar assessment labeled him "Napoleonic—small, forceful, enduring, victorious, believing himself appointed by Providence." Even the writer of a sterile government report noted that Harriman exercised powers that were "well-nigh absolute." Those who were put off or those who were genuinely offended by his style likely embraced the view of the writer C. M. Keys: "His idea of cooperation is that all men shall assist him in carrying out his plans. His conception of harmony . . . is that no man shall lift up his voice and object to the dictum. . . ."[18]

Nevertheless, one of Harriman's most striking talents as a successful executive was his ability to attract strong and able men to his employ. Moreover, once in the Harriman fold, subordinates were not likely to leave. They were loyal to Harriman because he was loyal to them. The way to reward faithfulness and loyalty, he knew, was not by discharging old hands. He had a kind word for those who were trying to succeed and encouraged those in whom he saw strength and potential. On the other hand, he was intolerant of incompetence and weeded out those in whom he saw no prospects. He hired college graduates, of course, but was not impressed by a person simply because he attended a fashionable school or possessed prestigious degrees. Rather, he was impressed by the person who, irrespective of educational background, could reason, plan, execute—he was impressed by those who could be trusted to handle assigned duties. He chose executives from among those thoroughly tested and seasoned officers who had learned their business "from the ground up." Harriman always desired officers who looked to the future, who contributed new and practical ideas that would make the Harriman Lines even more efficient. His subordinates, he observed on one occasion, must be provided with adequate and accurate information but must never be covered up with paper work. Once, when he saw an officer at a desk littered with paper, he said: "I want to find him leaning back in his chair with his feet on the desk—thinking! thinking!"[19]

Perhaps the most remarkable of Harriman's traits as a businessman was his facility to organize his vast holdings into a workable and efficient system. In the case of the Southern Pacific and Union Pacific, he planned for a generally common directorate, with the two companies operated by a combined management. Solicitation for traffic was to be accomplished by common agents. There was no precedent in the nation's railroad history for such a massive undertaking. The Harriman organization would preside over 18,000 miles of track; many thought it an impossible task. But it worked. Harriman's combined Southern Pacific–Union Pacific system functioned wonderfully, in no small part because of its excellent organization. It was by 1909, according to one observer, the peer "of the standard railways of the East." Harriman considered the issue matter-of-factly: "If an obstruction should come in the path of a well-organized railroad company there would be no noise made about it; the company would just go to work and overcome it."[20]

Central to success for such an undertaking was Harriman himself. He had to be self-

If Harriman was the "Napoleon of railroading," Julius Kruttschnitt was the "Von Moltke of transportation."

confident enough to allow individual freedom and initiative at lower levels, to give full authority to subordinates, to leave detail to others, to stand behind all of them, and not be afraid to take responsibility for their decisions. Most of all, he had to pick his highest executives with the greatest care. Harriman was up to all of it. The truest mark of this man is found in his selection of top officers for the combined system. Interestingly, he chose not from properties that he had known longer—the Illinois Central and the Union Pacific, for instance—but, rather, from the Southern Pacific. He picked for the combined system Julius Kruttschnitt, John C. Stubbs, Robert S. Lovett, and William Mahl, among others.[21]

If some thought Harriman the Napoleon of railroading, others considered Kruttschnitt the Von Moltke of transportation. Born on July 30, 1854, at New Orleans, Kruttschnitt graduated from Washington and Lee University with a degree in civil engineering. He taught for five years, then realized his boyhood ambition of becoming a railroader when in 1878 he entered the employ of Morgan's Louisiana & Texas Railroad & Steamship Company. In 1887 he became general manager of SP's Texas & Louisiana Lines. At the time Harriman tapped him, he was vice-president and general manager for the entire Southern Pacific Company.[22]

John C. Stubbs was born at Ashland, Ohio, in 1847 and began his railroad career twenty-two years later as chief clerk in Central Pacific's general freight office at Sacramento. He was promoted several times by the Central Pacific before being transferred to the Southern Pacific in 1885. Stubbs was third vice-president and in charge of the traffic department for SP in 1901.[23]

Another outstanding talent Harriman found at the SP was Robert S. Lovett. A Texan, born at San Jacinto in 1860, Lovett became local attorney for the Houston, East & West Texas Railway in 1884. He represented the Southern Pacific in Texas and served as president of the Houston & Texas Central Railroad before Harriman appointed him vice-president and general counsel for the combined roads.[24]

Of all those selected from the SP ranks for service in the top management of the new system, William Mahl had the broadest experience in the industry. Born in Germany in 1843, Mahl worked in the mechanical department of the Louisville & Nashville and then held various positions in the operating, accounting, and purchasing departments of the Louisville, Cincinnati & Lexington Railway. Huntington hired him in 1882; in 1901 he was vice-president and comptroller for the SP. Ability, industry, and integrity were attributes generally ascribed to Mahl; many considered him the country's finest railway comptroller. Harriman placed him in charge of expenditures for the Southern Pacific–Union Pacific as well as several other of his enterprises.[25]

Yet another prominent member of Harri-

Robert S. Lovett began his career with the Southern Pacific on the T&L Lines. Eventually he went on to head the Union Pacific.

man's management team was William Hood. Although Harriman did not establish a central engineering department for the combined system, his esteem for SP's chief engineer was clear: Hood retained his position throughout Harriman's tenure and was in charge of SP's massive upgrading program during those same years. Hood was born in 1846 at Concord, New Hampshire, graduated from Dartmouth College, entered the service of the Central Pacific's engineering department in 1867, and rose rapidly through the ranks.[26]

In general, Harriman felt the need to place officers of the combined companies where they would be closest to their duties. His office and those of Lovett and Mahl were in New York—the financial center of the country. Hood remained in San Francisco. Kruttschnitt and Stubbs, however, were moved to

William Hood was in charge of the SP's massive upgrading program.

Chicago in 1904, when Harriman established a unique management system by authorizing two new positions: director of maintenance and operations, to which Kruttschnitt was appointed, and traffic director, the position for Stubbs. By creating these new positions, Harriman in effect delegated administrative control and supervision of the combined companies to these trusted lieutenants. They shared adjoining offices in Chicago—midpoint between the railroads themselves and the New York headquarters—and answered directly to the president.

Traditionally, the operating department of a railroad was responsible for providing transportation facilities and running the trains while the traffic department was charged with selling the service. Not surprisingly, in those days before any meaningful modal competi-

tion, the operating department was the apple of any railroad's eye and its operating chief, its major domo. That person on the combined Southern Pacific–Union Pacific was, of course, Julius Kruttschnitt. His responsibilities included bringing the operation of the separate lines under central authority, overseeing the general managers, otherwise defining authority, and authorizing new construction. Recommendations for physical changes ordinarily originated with division superintendents or general managers, but neither of these could authorize construction. All such suggestions were forwarded to the Chicago office, where Kruttschnitt reviewed them, turned them down, or approved them and sent them on to Harriman for his assessment. The system was not without fault. Delays and local frustration were inevitable, but in this process both Harriman and Kruttschnitt gained an important overview of construction and repair activity across the length of the combined roads. Once plans were approved, an Authority for Expenditure (AFE) was issued and purchase could be made or work commence. AFEs expired yearly; their annual sum gave Harriman and Kruttschnitt still another means by which to proctor their projects.[27]

Kruttschnitt received additional data in several ways. One took the form of a monthly "information letter" from each of his five general managers. A small statistical bureau likewise provided important materials. This bureau also supervised and checked accounting procedures and prescribed methods and forms for accounts.[28]

Harriman agreed that adequate and accurate information was essential for management to make proper judgments, but he was concerned that Kruttschnitt, "being so far from the direct operations of the properties," would unintentionally "establish a corresponding bureau." Harriman reminded Kruttschnitt that "every letter you require one of the subordinate officers to write to you incurs some effort on his part." Consequently, said

Harriman and his subordinates made frequent inspections of the sprawling Southern Pacific. This inspection train is headed west from Ogden toward the new Lucin Cut-off.

Harriman, "the necessity for such correspondence should be reduced to a minimum." Harriman saw another potential problem for Kruttschnitt. He feared that his director of maintenance and operations would lose touch with the realities of his operation, and so he issued an oblique order: "I presume you . . . will spend some time in going out over the various lines and keep things smooth. . . ."[29]

Harriman's devotion to efficiency led him to insist on common standards, central purchasing, and pooling of equipment for the properties under his control. Although these policies offended the "this-is-the-way-we-have-always-done-it" mentality, firmly entrenched on the various lines, the efficiencies resulting from implementation of the new standards were remarkable. Common standards for structures, equipment, stationery, and even operating rules were eventually drawn up and adopted. Before standardization, fifty different patterns

of switch frogs were used on the Harriman Lines; after standardization, only four were used. Changes were not formulated lightly. Common standards were adopted only after thorough investigation and discussion by the department heads and general managers. Kruttschnitt had final authority. Specifications were drawn following his approval, and the new standards became common to all lines— subject to revision and review, of course, as they were implemented and after the test of time. Temptations to overdo were great, especially for Harriman. A case in point involved his desire for uniform classes of locomotives on both the Southern Pacific and Union Pacific. This was impractical because of dissimilar operating conditions, said Kruttschnitt, and would impair rather than increase efficiency. Harriman fortunately yielded to Kruttschnitt's better judgment in this matter.[30]

So that the lines could make the most of

common standards, a director of purchases was appointed and his office established in New York City. W. V. S. Thorn, who held this position, pointed out the advantages of common standards and centralized purchasing as he saw them:

(1) The number of items for inventory was substantially reduced.

(2) Standardized equipment was interchangeable and thus inventory stocks were further reduced.

(3) Larger volume orders resulted in lower unit costs.

(4) Downtime on equipment was reduced because of interchangeable parts for equipment.

(5) Standardized equipment could be expeditiously moved from division to division according to need.[31]

Pooling of equipment, particularly freight equipment, was likewise a requisite for the efficient operation of the combined properties. It was utterly foolish for the Southern Pacific, for instance, to haul empty or bad-order freight cars hundreds of miles simply to return them to the Union Pacific. To remedy that glaring inefficiency, general managers received detailed daily reports on the location of equipment in their regions; this information was then condensed and forwarded to Kruttschnitt's office three times monthly. All hands were ordered to use commonly owned cars in the most advantageous way. As a consequence of these pooling arrangements, the number of empty car miles on the combined system was reduced by 54 million miles in just two years.[32]

Kruttschnitt's counterpart, and the man in charge of the traffic department and sales for the combined properties, was John C. Stubbs. Harriman involved himself in matters of traffic very little, leaving Stubbs with practically a free hand. Stubbs viewed his responsibilities as being threefold: to build volume through sales; to make rates and divisions; and to arrange with Kruttschnitt for the most expeditious and economical routing of traffic among

the various options provided by the Southern Pacific–Union Pacific system. As a practical matter, transcontinental traffic moving to or from locations south of a line from Buffalo–Pittsburgh–Cincinnati–Cairo was routed via SP's Sunset Route; traffic to or from points above that line was dispatched via the Ogden Gateway. Stubbs's subordinates thus solicited and routed business accordingly. It was simply a matter of efficiency. The combined system provided new sales opportunities for both the Southern Pacific and Union Pacific and, just as importantly, for shippers located along their lines. An example was the establishment of rates on dried fruits, fresh vegetables, and citrus from points in California to the Canadian provinces of Alberta, Saskatchewan, and Manitoba via Harriman's SP and Oregon Railroad & Navigation companies, then to the Spokane International, and on for delivery by the Canadian Pacific. Over 700 carloads of new business moved annually as a result of these arrangements, benefiting carriers and producers alike.[33]

Two other important officers, the chief engineer and the superintendent of motive power, were really Kruttschnitt's assistants. Both reported directly to him but their jurisdiction was mixed—"concurrent," Kruttschnitt said, with division superintendents. The chief engineer was responsible for all new construction, contracts for construction, inspections and maintenance of bridges, signal systems, and interlocking plants; the operation of tie-preserving plants, and recommendations for the appointment of division engineers. It was much the same for the superintendent of motive power. He was in charge of the general shops and all things pertaining to equipment, power plants, and tools. He was also responsible for recommendations to the posts of division master mechanic, division foremen, and traveling engineer.[34]

Responsibilities for division superintendents were many, but their powers were defined simply by Kruttschnitt: "They shall exercise upon their respective divisions the same authority as is exercised by the Vice President and General Manager over the entire property. . . . The control over all matters under their jurisdiction shall be complete." The divisions, as a consequence, became small fiefs ruled by a feudal lord—the superintendent. These men reported to a general manager who then reported to Kruttschnitt.[35]

The general auditor for the combined system was located at Omaha. However, even here, too, the division superintendent held sway since division accounting departments were his responsibility and its personnel were on his payroll.[36]

All of this was a reflection of the "unit" system, introduced by Major C. D. Hine. Central to it was the idea of "home rule," which encouraged individuality and initiative. Kruttschnitt nevertheless expected the divisions to cooperate and he demanded that superintendents visit other units and exchange information. He also expected his superintendents to spend fifteen days per month on the road. That, however, presented problems, for the superintendent's chief clerk, who traditionally handled the office in his absence, had no executive authority. Thus, the unit idea was broadened to include assistant superintendents who, like the superintendent, had division-wide authority. Each of these served four- to six-month terms as senior assistant to the superintendent; they handled correspondence, served as the superintendent's administrative assistant, and acted for him when he was away from the office. The rotation of assistant superintendents gave them excellent experience as well as an overview of the entire operation of the division. It similarly provided the company with a pool of experienced talent and at the same time provided junior officers with better chances for advancement. Not all components of the unit plan were new, but the Harriman Lines were early in their break with traditional practices and departmental procedures and early in their embrace of advanced systems.[37]

Harriman prized education. He encouraged his companies to hire college graduates, but he also conducted a constant internal campaign to locate nonlettered talent. He perceived that the college man brought to his job not only the knowledge acquired through formal education but, more importantly, an ongoing ability to learn. On the other hand, Harriman no doubt subscribed to a general complaint regarding college graduates of the period—that they lacked backbone and that they were disinclined to involve themselves in the dirt and grime of the railroad business. Of particular note was his policy of placing "employee students" on each of the Harriman Lines operating divisions. These men, usually degree-holders, underwent a rigorous, forty-two-month program of work, instruction, and reading designed to prepare them for advanced positions. Each man spent time in station service and in the maintenance of way, stores, mechanical, accounting, and signal departments; each served a lengthy on-the-job stint with a trainmaster. All were graded and subject to minimum requirements. Students were paid from $80 to $100 per month during the training period. Others, if Harriman's managers detected aptitude in them, were recruited from the ranks and "drilled." Arithmetic skills were a minimum requirement for selection.[38]

Education was promoted on the Harriman Lines in other ways. If a man on one division developed a new policy or program that top management ultimately adopted, he was detailed as a special representative to all divisions where he introduced it. Always alert to the danger of provincialism and territorial despotism that threatened both logic and system procedures, Harriman and his managerial lieutenants insisted that division officers be dispatched on periodic fifteen-day tours of other portions of the property. Additionally, general officers met semiannually at various cities along the line so that they could be exposed to regional differences and problems. Harriman was particularly desirous that his subordinates be well informed in all matters pertaining to the company and that they concern themselves in corporate matters well beyond the confines of their immediate responsibilities.[39]

The value of history and the constant need for communication were corollaries to Harriman's views on education. He had no intention of being captive to the past, nor did he have time for nostalgia. And he worried not at all about his own place in history. His was a practical view. He would be instructed by the past, but he insisted on "looking forward as well as backward." It was the same with contemporary information. A sophisticated system was necessary to facilitate the constant and essential flow of information to and from all points along the vast expanse of the Harriman Lines. Information on crop conditions and commercial forecasts were gathered by local agents and funneled to division offices and then to the general headquarters, where weekly dispatches were assembled for the executive officers and board of directors. Press reports were gathered and passed along in similar fashion. This upward flow of information kept all levels of management apprised regarding traffic developments and the public's view of various issues, including those related to the Harriman Lines. Downward communications ordinarily involved suggestions and advice along with occasional instructions.[40]

Harriman's concerns were not restricted to his managerial subordinates but extended to contract employees as well. For a man of considerable means, he had an impressive ability to empathize with the ordinary workmen on his properties. He paid good wages, studied

Harriman hoped that clubs established by the company would counteract the influence of saloons and at the same time increase morale, efficiency, and safe working habits.

their needs, and urged programs for pensions, hospitals, educational plans, and employees' clubs. He was especially concerned about the need of operating personnel at division points in remote western regions for recreation. He established clubs, maintained by the company, where employees at "away from home terminals" could dine, bathe, sleep, or engage in billiards or cards. Such an environment, Harriman hoped, would counteract the influence of the ubiquitous saloons and at the same time increase morale, efficiency, and safe working habits.[41]

The Napoleon of railroading? The label seems fitting. Like Napoleon, Edward H. Harriman was imperfect, but like Napoleon, the great railroader had qualities of leadership adequate to earn an impressive niche in history.

Trump Cards

"He has made travel safer, swifter and more comfortable from the Rivers to the Pacific Ocean. By his methods he has contributed largely to the growth of the whole South Pacific Coast in wealth and commercial life."—C. M. Keys, "Harriman IV"

EDWARD H. Harriman loved nothing if not a contest. That was fortunate since he was confronted by several during his last years. These included challenges to the Harriman Lines from other railroads, natural disasters, and a changing national mood styled the Progressive Era.

The first problem occurred in lower California when the Colorado River threatened productivity of the newly opened Imperial Valley and trackage of SP's vital Sunset Route. Until a plan for irrigation had been implemented, the Imperial Valley was a soul-repelling desert, imprisoned by mountains, and essentially devoid of human life. Water, diverted from the Colorado, changed that. Earlier efforts had not matured, but in 1901 the California Development Company opened a seam in the bank of the river near Yuma and a small amount of water was delivered by canal to irrigable land in Mexico. During the following season it was also made available in the Imperial Valley.[1]

All went well at first. Then, in the fall of 1904, another intake was opened southwest of Yuma in Mexico, but heavy rains and resultant floods prevented its planned closure; in short order the entire flow of the river passed through the cut. A crisis was at hand. Itinerant waters rushed into and across the Salton Sink through canals and normally dry stream-

beds instead of emptying southward into the Gulf of California by way of its usual course. The investments made by those who had pioneered the valley were obviously threatened, but the California Development Company itself had not adequate resources to meet the emergency. Its officers anxiously sought assistance from the Southern Pacific's Julius Kruttschnitt, but he declined to provide financial support.[2]

Harriman himself interceded, however, and agreed to loan the development company $200,000 on condition that its capital stock be placed in the hands of a trustee named by the SP and that its management be assumed by the railroad. Consequently, on June 20, 1905, the SP took control; Epes Randolph, a man familiar with the country, was named president. Randolph had reservations. Frankly, he was not convinced that Harriman understood the implications of the deal. Randolph bluntly told Harriman that he was "not merely making a loan of $200,000, but was getting behind a most difficult undertaking of indefinite magnitude." If it was simply a matter of money, Randolph said, "it would be very much cheaper to raise the grade of the Southern Pacific track to an elevation above sea level and let the Valley become a sea." Harriman asked how many persons lived in the affected area and wondered if they would lose their homes. Randolph estimated that 15,000 were vulnerable and said their domiciles "certainly" would be lost. Harriman considered the matter briefly and then, with characteristic directness, asked Randolph if he was convinced that he could "stop that river." Randolph replied, "I am," but added, "I cannot say how much it will cost." Harriman did not hesitate: "Go ahead," he ordered.[3]

Harriman was, of course, looking after SP's interests, but he was also attentive to the needs of those who had settled the Imperial Valley. In his view, railroads were public service properties that had distinct social obligations. The response of the SP to this crisis, a response dictated by Harriman himself, reflected these beliefs.

During the seasons of 1905 and 1906 the SP engaged in repeated if heartbreaking attempts to return the Colorado to its banks and keep it there and at the same time to provide adequate water for irrigation. The major crevasse was closed on November 6, 1906, but several days later heavy rains resulted in new flooding and another break, through which the destructive waters roared. The Salton Sea rose at the rate of seven inches per day and gradually covered 400 square miles. SP engineers made new grades for the Sunset Route at higher ground on five occasions during 1906 alone.[4]

It was enough to frustrate even the most indomitable soul. Harriman, Randolph later recalled, reluctantly determined that "he had done about his share toward saving the valley from destruction." Harriman believed the U.S. Reclamation Service should now turn its hand to the new break; residents of the area urgently wired President Theodore Roosevelt asking for relief. Roosevelt responded by saying that the Reclamation Service could not act without congressional authority, that Congress had just adjourned for the holidays, and that, in any event, the federal government could not act without the concurrence of the Mexican government. Haste was necessary. Roosevelt asked Harriman to act indepen-

dently, "to close the break at once," and promised that he would request compensation from Congress.[5]

Harriman agreed and ordered a veritable army to attack the problem. Earlier efforts and arrangements finally paid off. A labor force composed of Indians, Mexicans, and itinerant Americans was already on hand. So were commissary facilities, dredges, and pile drivers. Mexican authorities agreed to place the entire region under martial law and to ban liquor from all camps. A branch railroad, already in place, brought additional forces and material. Five quarries—one as far away as Colton, some two hundred miles distant—began to load riprap and gravel. Battleship cars, used earlier at Lucin, were ladened with heavy payloads and dispatched on trains that had precedence over all others on the Sunset Route. Other high-speed trains brought piling from the farthest corners of SP's domain. Company engineers prepared plans to bolster existing levees and to build a double trestlework from which the battleships could drop their cargo.[6]

Work went forward around the clock. The first trestle was completed on January 27, 1907. Over the next fifteen days, 600 men dumped 2,626 carloads of rock, gravel, and clay into the swirling waters. On February 10, at 11:00 P.M., the break was closed and water again returned to the old channel.[7]

In all, the SP built 17 miles of railway, 15.6 miles of levee, and 2,250 feet of dam; it had placed or handled 1,545,000 cubic yards of material. The cost was staggering. The SP had already advanced $1.490 million to the California Development Company and, at the request of Theodore Roosevelt, spent another $1.663 million in finally conquering the wayward Colorado.[8]

In 1905 Harriman had been able to tell SP shareholders that the company's properties had been "free from serious losses or damages by floods and fires." Because of the severe flooding of the Colorado he was unable to say as much in 1906. Neither could he report that

The heartbreaking efforts to stem the Colorado River flow were finally rewarded on February 10, 1907.

the property or its service area had been spared by fire. At 5:13 a.m. on April 18, 1906, the San Francisco Bay area was subjected to a severe 48-second tremor, part of a general earthquake that shook the coast from Oregon to Mexico. The temblor itself would not have ruined the city, but unfortunately small, separate fires combined in less than five hours to form a conflagration that remained essentially unchecked for seventy-two hours. By then, the homes of at least 200,000 were gone, as was much of the city's business and commercial district.[9]

Harriman was immediately advised of the tragedy by SP officials in San Francisco who, under trying conditions, did their best to keep him informed during the day. General officers met at the Merchants Exchange Building for a conference at 9:00 A.M. to ascertain damage to the company's property and to prepare contingency plans. Like virtually all San Franciscans, they believed that the fires "would not prove serious," although as a precaution they did order freight and passenger equipment moved to safer locations. But the fires *were* serious and eventually destroyed the office building at Fourth and Townsend as well as the offices in the Merchants Building. Lost were most of the company's books, vouchers, accounts, records, undelivered paychecks, and the like.[10]

The SP hospital at Fourteenth and Mission streets received little damage from the earthquake and thus became a haven for 250 victims who had sustained injury elsewhere. By early evening of the eighteenth the hospital, however, was threatened by fire; consequently, its patients were evacuated by way of "dead" streetcars pulled by horses to the car barns of the United Railroads of San Francisco. These facilities, too, were threatened the following day and another evacuation was necessary— this time by special SP passenger train to San Mateo, where authorities had readied a large athletic hall. Patients who were SP employees were moved again a few days later to the company hospital at Sacramento.[11]

Harriman himself left New York for San Francisco on the morning of the nineteenth. Before that, he telegraphed officers of the combined systems "directing them to act quickly and to co-operate with officers in charge at San Francisco in doing all that could be done to relieve the distress." Before the first awful day had ended, all forces of the Southern Pacific and Union Pacific were actively engaged in that relief work.[12]

Such efforts took many forms. SP's chief counsel, W. F. Herrin, became the company's liaison with military, state, and city authorities, who met daily at Fort Mason. Telegraph operators from the SP were loaned to the hard-pressed Western Union Company; its lines were restored collaterally with those of the SP. Throughout the downtown area, company track gangs worked furiously to build temporary facilities on street surfaces in order for trains to haul out debris and then bring in building materials.[13]

SP's passenger department was called on for a variety of special duties. Its representatives handled hundreds of inquiries, particularly from railway offices in the East, regarding missing persons. The department also established information bureaus at several locations in the most heavily damaged areas of the city and kept them posted with the latest news by means of horseback riders and auto couriers dispatched from the SP's temporary headquarters at the Ferry Building. Putting down rumors and restoring confidence were concomitant duties. An active rumor that Harriman planned the permanent removal of SP's headquarters from San Francisco as a result of the fire was quickly quelled. "San Francisco, the Imperishable" and "Progress" were two publications utilized by SP's passenger department in an effort to restore confidence in the city and to promote its rebuilding. On April 20 the department began furnishing the Associated Press and local newspapers with information regarding the resumption of regular train service.[14]

All other departments contributed similarly. Operating officers limited all inbound freight trains to from ten to fifteen cars so that they could "make passenger train time," and for thirty-five days following the quake the SP handled without charge over 1,600 carloads of relief supplies and 224,000 passengers. On April 19, the day of heaviest travel, 1,073 carloads of refugees were transported. Gasoline from the stores department was furnished to emergency vehicles; the same department issued free explosives at the request of the San Francisco Fire Department. Furthermore, all of SP's freight sheds in San Francisco were tendered for the immediate relief of the homeless.[15]

The company's transbay ferries remarkably maintained regular twenty-minute schedules throughout—except for a brief period when fresh boiler water could not be supplied to them. SP's river steamers and extra ferry boats were also used to take passengers from outlying wharves and landings to the Oakland side of the bay, and three of its steamers were placed at the disposal of the Army Quartermaster Department.[16]

Finally, the worst was over. Harriman took particular and rightful pride in the performance of SP's personnel. Given the fact that there was no warning and thus no way to prepare for the disaster, Harriman thought it nearly miraculous "that such a large traffic could be handled under these trying conditions without serious injury to any person." He was uncharacteristically effusive. "The perfect discipline maintained by the working staff of the Company," he told its shareholders, "reflects most highly on its organization, and the prompt and efficient service rendered contributed largely to the feeling of courage and confidence with which the people of San Francisco faced this calamity."[17]

He cautioned, however, that much remained "to be done before the city could be rehabilitated" but pledged that it would "be not only the duty but the pleasure of the Company to continue in all legitimate ways its assistance in restoring and rebuilding the city." This new San Francisco would be, he freely predicted, "larger, more beautiful, stronger and more inviting in every way than the one whose ashes now cover nearly twelve square miles."[18]

This was not lost on observers near and far. *Railway World* said editorially, "When San Francisco was laid in ashes, it was Mr. Harriman who took personal charge of the situation. . . . It was primarily due to his organizing genius and energy that San Francisco so quickly rallied from its great disaster." The far-off *New York Times* noted that a "large fraction of the city's populace were for a considerable period dependent for their very lives on the course persued by the Southern Pacific

SP's fleet of ferry boats maintained their schedules throughout the frantic period following the temblor and fire. The *Berkeley*, shown here, entered service in 1898.

. . ." and considered the course chosen by the company "to have been the best of business." Even as late as 1954 the company and its president were honored in remembrance. "The tireless zeal with which E. H. Harriman served old San Francisco was equalled only by the inspiration he supplied to the rebuilding of the new," said the 1906 Club in honoring Harriman with a posthumous award.[19]

Harriman faced many other challenges on the SP during the 1900s, although none were as dramatic or immediately newsworthy as the Colorado River break and the San Francisco earthquake. For instance, the matter of expanding or strengthening Harriman's railroad barony was important, in both short- and long-range prospects. Harriman understood that there were few remaining areas to pioneer, but he was determined to expand into those that were open to him or that he considered a rightful part of his service area.

In one case, however, he failed to secure important gateway opportunities, gain local traffic from an area already known for its agricultural productivity, and at the same time, tweak the ego of his major rival, James J. Hill.

Harriman, of course, long had been associated with the Illinois Central Railroad (IC) and remained a powerful member of its directorate until his death. At essentially the same time that he undertook the reorganization of the Union Pacific, the Illinois Central had authorized the construction of a new line from near Fort Dodge, Iowa, to Council Bluffs and Omaha—thus forging an important connection between the two roads controlled by Harriman. Rumors in the industry simultaneously suggested that the IC would purchase the Minneapolis & St. Louis Railroad (M&StL). Much of M&StL's stock was held by Collis P. Huntington, and one of his trusted associates, Edwin Hawley, was its president. Appearances if not hard historical data urge that Huntington and Hawley were attempting to make the M&StL attractive to Harriman and that he was responding favorably. In 1900 the IC also extended a principal branch reaching from Waterloo to the northern boundary of Iowa on to Albert Lea, Minnesota, and a connection there with the Minneapolis & St. Louis. In the same season Hawley was driving a new M&StL line through western Iowa

Harriman was rightfully proud of the part the SP played in rebuilding San Francisco following the earthquake and fire. Indeed, the company threw its full resources into the campaign.

that, if completed to Council Bluffs, as he promised, would be the short route between the Twin Cities and the easternmost point of the Union Pacific.[20]

After Huntington died in 1900, Hawley was the intermediary who facilitated the sale of the Huntington interests in the Southern Pacific to Harriman, and he likewise attempted to sell the Minneapolis & St. Louis to Harriman, who agreed to study the matter. Others were watching. In 1903 J. P. Morgan reminded James J. Hill of the "importance of this road and its terminals." Morgan said he could gain control of the M&StL and the Iowa Central (another Hawley road to which the M&StL was connected at Albert Lea) because Hawley was "short and must have relief." Morgan was willing to do this on behalf of the "CB&Q or Northern Pacific or jointly" and warned Hill that Harriman and Stuyvesant Fish (president of the Illinois Central) were aware of this prospect. Hill hedged; he was not interested in the Iowa Central. Morgan argued that the Hill Lines could "throw upon the Iowa Central the traffic needed to

make it pay" and considered the M&StL's terminal facilities in the Twin Cities worth the entire price if only to keep it away from others. "What would be the result if the Illinois Central or Union Pacific should get them?" he wondered. Hill decided he would go halfway. The Iowa Central, he reaffirmed, was "too great a burden," but he agreed to place the Minneapolis & St. Louis with the Northern Pacific if Morgan could acquire it independently.[21]

In the end, neither Harriman nor Hill moved to acquire the Hawley roads. Hill missed an opportunity to acquire valuable trackage in the Twin Cities and to block potential invasion. Harriman, who ordinarily favored acquisition of existing properties to gain new territory, failed to exercise such a policy in this case. His reasons, unfortunately, are lost to history.

If Harriman and Hill avoided territorial conflict in the Twin Cities area, they failed miserably to do so in Oregon, where each felt vested. Hill claimed rights by way of Northern Pacific's line between Seattle, Tacoma, and

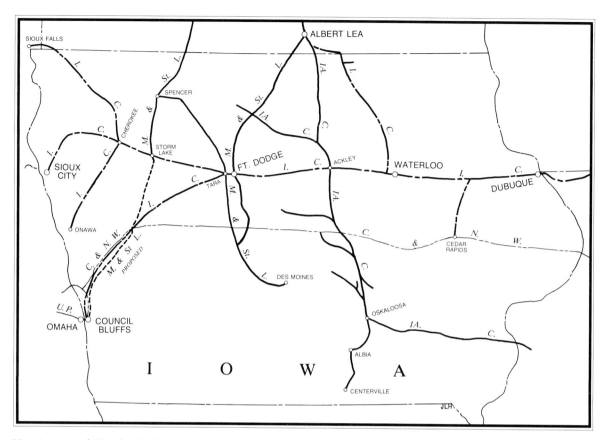

Harriman and Hawley in Iowa

Portland and later by virtue of the Spokane, Portland & Seattle Railway, which followed the north bank of the Columbia River. Harriman, on the other hand, felt Oregon was his province because of SP's extensive network in the western portion of the state and by way of the Oregon Railroad & Navigation Company (OR&N), which reached Portland by hugging the south bank of the Columbia.

A brainchild of the redoubtable Henry Villard, the OR&N had been organized on June 13, 1879, with, Villard thought, the firm and friendly backing of the Union Pacific, which saw in the new company a means to avoid Central Pacific's domination at Ogden. However, C. P. Huntington had threatened retaliation against the Union Pacific if it or one of its subsidiaries built to the planned junction with the Oregon Railroad & Navigation Company on the Oregon-Idaho boundary. As

a consequence, the OR&N was forced to go it alone, but to good advantage, since Henry Villard soon expanded his power, at least temporarily, to include the Northern Pacific, a transcontinental line, which utilized Oregon Railroad & Navigation to gain Pacific shores. Moreover, the UP soon ignored Huntington's warning and authorized one of its subsidiaries, the Oregon Short Line, to complete a route to a connection with the OR&N. Although it completed its own road over the Cascades to the Pacific at Tacoma in 1887, the Northern Pacific, to forestall wasteful duplication of construction, agreed with the Union Pacific, through its Oregon Short Line, to a joint lease of the OR&N.[22]

Railroad matters in the Pacific Northwest became rather more confused over the next decade. In 1893 the Union Pacific suffered severe financial reverses and, partly in consequence, lost control of both the Oregon Short Line and the Oregon Railroad & Navigation Company. Adrift and in financial difficulties themselves, they were appointed separate receivers two years later; both railroads were, as a result, independent of Union Pacific and of each other. That situation changed shortly when in March, 1897, the Oregon Short Line took over Oregon Railroad & Navigation and then itself reverted to the Union Pacific camp as a consequence of Harriman's skillful maneuvering. Meanwhile, the Great Northern Railway, under the aegis of James J. Hill, completed its own independent line from the Upper Midwest to Puget Sound in 1893— adding greatly to the woes of neighboring Northern Pacific. Indeed, Hill soon gathered that important company into his own camp; Great Northern and Northern Pacific henceforth were known as the Hill Lines. All of this set the stage for more than a decade of tilting between Harriman and Hill.

Hill understandably wished to keep options open in regard to Northern Pacific's joint lease of the Oregon Railroad & Navigation Company and, for that matter, the entire service area. He urged Harriman and his associates not to "inaugurate policies that would end in unnecessary construction of additional railroad" for, as Hill maintained, "the country is now supplied with all the railway facilities necessary for years to come." He was particularly fretful regarding the OR&N's joint lease, now subject to Harriman's considerations. "I do not think we should be compelled to either abandon our share of that [Portland] business or be forced to build a line of our own," worried Hill. A face-to-face discussion was necessary. Harriman, Hill, Charles S. Mellen, Jacob H. Schiff, and others thus met at Northern Pacific's New York headquarters on October 3, 1898, for the purpose of considering the Oregon Railroad & Navigation's lease and the broader issues of traffic and territorial dominion in the Pacific Northwest. Each man professed to admire harmony, but each clearly sought to protect or expand his own interests.

Since the Great Northern had no independent line from Spokane to Portland, Hill sought parity between the Spokane, Washington, and Huntington, Oregon, gateways. The NP representative, C. H. Coster, argued that the Oregon Railroad & Navigation Company ought to be "an independent company," but, under Harriman's guidance, he charged, it had become a Union Pacific satellite. Harriman, however, contended that the OR&N "should be used in the interest of all three companies," i.e., the Union Pacific, Great Northern, and Northern Pacific. On the other hand, he pointedly asserted that he did "not want to divide territory," an indirect warning that he did not expect others to divide territory, either. NP's Coster suggested that, to "avoid quarrels and trouble," the parties should establish territorial boundaries and then agree "that we not go into certain territory." Coster and Charles Mellen quickly added, however, that within this context the Northern Pacific should be allowed to build a Missoula, Montana–Pasco, Washington, cut-off through the Bitterroot Mountains over Lolo Pass. Hill defended the plan as one that would reduce both miles and grades. Harriman suspected, though, that the NP wanted to gain local traffic west of Lewiston, Idaho, as much as it wanted a more efficient route. And he remained obdurate in the matter of "territorial division." The meeting settled little.[23]

Matters shifted by degree. Hill pressed Harriman for joint ownership instead of joint lease of the Oregon Railroad & Navigation Company, but Harriman presently insisted on the desirability of the UP having "its own line to Portland." Hill sweetened the pot. The Northern Pacific, he said, "would be willing to arrange for the business of the Union Pacific to go over its lines between Portland and Puget Sound" if Harriman would agree to give the Northern Pacific and Great Northern "the same rights and benefits" on the OR&N "as would accrue under separate lines owned by each." In other words, Hill was willing to give Harriman access to Seattle over the Northern

Pacific from Portland in exchange for joint ownership of Oregon Railroad & Navigation and use of it by the Northern Pacific and the Great Northern as well as the Union Pacific. Failing in that, Hill threatened to act independently. "I think that with five million dollars I could build a much better line from our road [the Great Northern at Spokane] into Portland and with say two million more reach the most productive sections of the Navigation Company." Harriman was unmoved. Hill was forced to bide his time. Eventually, when Harriman acted to acquire control of the Southern Pacific, a business associate of Hill's suggested that "it was just the right time . . . to go ahead and build the line on the north side of the Columbia." Hill instead persisted in efforts with Harriman to obtain traffic arrangements satisfactory to both the Union Pacific, on the one hand, and the Great Northern and the Northern Pacific, on the other. By the summer of 1904 Hill thought he had a deal with Harriman by which his roads would send their business over the OR&N, that the Hill companies would have their own respective terminals in Portland—so that, as he said, the Navigation line "had only to hitch its engines to the cars and pull the trains." Harriman backed out. It infuriated Hill. In a very real way, then, it was Harriman as much as Hill who was responsible for the creation of the Spokane, Portland & Seattle Railway (SP&S).[24]

Originally chartered as the Portland & Seattle Railway in 1905, Hill's new railroad was rechristened three years later as the Spokane, Portland & Seattle. Neither precisely defined the company's purpose: to link Spokane with Portland. Hill never intended that the line reach Seattle. Rather, he had the Northern Pacific double track its route between Seattle and Portland to handle expanded business. Earthwork on the SP&S began in 1906, but it proved to be more difficult and significantly more expensive than Hill had estimated back in 1899 when he said it could be built for $5 million. By 1906 he was

estimating its cost at $40 to $45 million, and four years later Hill considered that at least $10 million had been misspent on the project. "On the whole it is the most unsatisfactory thing that has ever occurred in my experience," he lamented. The SP&S was opened in sections between 1907 and 1909 and was owned in equal portions by the Great Northern and the Northern Pacific. Hill finally had independent access to Portland from the east on a direct route.[25]

Unfortunately for Harriman, the Spokane, Portland & Seattle was not the only Hill project to annoy him in Oregon. Both men understood the traffic potential of central Oregon and the strategic value of the Deschutes River Canyon, and both moved to advance their own claims to each. Harriman's effort took the form of the Deschutes Railroad, a subsidiary of the Oregon Railroad & Navigation Company, and Hill's the Oregon Trunk Railway, a satellite of the SP&S. Each focused on the route south from the Columbia River to Bend via the Deschutes River Canyon, and each sparred for advantage. Activity ceased temporarily in the aftermath of the Panic of 1907, but two years later Hill pressed on. There simply was no room in certain sections of the canyon for two railroads, and eventually, an accommodation was reached under which the two companies used a single track through these. The Oregon Trunk was opened for service from Fallbridge, Washington (later renamed Wishram), to Bend on November 1, 1911. Southern Pacific officials in San Francisco were not amused. They knew that Hill projected the Oregon Trunk on to Klamath Falls and even west to Medford. They wondered: Was his goal really San Francisco?[26]

There were other contentious issues between the two giants of the industry. One of these involved Harriman's growing desire to reach Seattle from Portland and, following his usual policy, his wish to reach Puget Sound without building a new line. During the mid-1900s Northern Pacific's Howard Elliott tentatively agreed to grant the Union

Pacific trackage rights between South Tacoma and Vancouver, Washington, but withdrew the offer before Harriman could ratify it. In 1908 Harriman approached Hill himself who, of course, had, a few years earlier in the Oregon Railroad & Navigation matter, offered Harriman trackage rights over the NP's line the entire distance from Portland to Puget Sound. (Interestingly, Hill, as early as 1890, had proposed joint ownership of a Portland-Seattle line to Union Pacific's William H. Holcomb.) Hill initially suggested to Harriman that the Northern Pacific, Union Pacific, and Great Northern be equally interested by lease or purchase of NP's Portland-Seattle line and that it then be operated by an independent company for the benefit of all. Harriman countered by offering $7 million for joint ownership of only the Tacoma-Vancouver (Washington) section. Northern Pacific attorneys then advised that none of this was possible because of congressional land-grant and mortgage restrictions. In any event, NP's board eventually turned down Harriman's proposition.[27]

Harriman persisted, and he was not without ammunition. Hill's forces were well aware of the problems between the two powers in the Deschutes River area: that Harriman was pushing an SP road northward from California toward Klamath Falls, Oregon; that Harriman was contemplating a cross-state route in Oregon; and that Harriman engineers had already surveyed a line between Portland and Seattle. Harriman thought the time ripe for action. In 1909 he told Julius Kruttschnitt to solicit bids on a first-class, low-grade line between Vancouver and Tacoma. Matters moved quickly. On May 21, 1909, at Harriman's home, a memo of agreement was forged by which the Oregon & Washington Railroad (O&W, a Union Pacific subsidiary) and the Great Northern were to be given "joint and equal use of the Northern Pacific" between Vancouver and South Tacoma. A contract to this end took effect on July 1, 1909, and joint use began on January 1, 1910. Additional

construction and joint ownership with the Chicago, Milwaukee & Puget Sound Railway of another segment took the Harriman Lines on to Seattle. All parties professed to be pleased. Even the Northern Pacific asserted in 1911 that the "arrangements . . . have worked advantageously to all parties and to the public."[28]

The SP's involvement in this matter, on the one hand, and the lack of it, on the other, were curious. When arrangements nearly had been completed with the Northern Pacific on the joint track agreement, its management demanded that the Union Pacific *and* the Southern Pacific "jointly and severally guarantee the performance" of the contract with the Oregon & Washington Railroad because, the Northern Pacific said, the O&W was, in fact, a wholly owned subsidiary of the Union Pacific and could at its pleasure be reduced to a condition of financial irresponsibility. Harriman agreed to this on behalf of the Union Pacific and the Southern Pacific because, as he and Robert S. Lovett contended, the Puget Sound extension was considered beneficial to both companies. The arrangement was certainly beneficial to the Union Pacific, but the contract, insofar as the SP was concerned, involved it in an obligation without consideration. The Southern Pacific was not even given the option of trackage rights over the Northern Pacific to Tacoma and, in fact, all that was immediately obvious by way of benefit to it was a friendly connection to and from Puget Sound in the form of UP's Oregon & Washington Railroad. Nobody knew it at the time, but the contract held unpleasant ramifications for the SP.[29]

Elsewhere, Harriman and Hill tilted for control of the territory south of Astoria, Oregon, to Tillamook Bay. At stake was not only valuable traffic if Tillamook developed as a port but also the absolute guarantee of heavy timber and lumber business from the impressive stand of fir that typified the region. To secure the area on behalf of the SP, the impressive-sounding Pacific Railway & Navigation Company was formed on October 16, 1905. Construction began immediately at Hillsboro, west of Portland on SP's West Side Branch, and from Tillamook the following year. Hill was slow to respond, but eventually he sent his trusted engineer, John F. Stevens, to investigate the region. Stevens was enthusiastic and so was Hill. A Great Northern line from Astoria to Tillamook would take two years to build and would require one 6,000-foot tunnel and two or three shorter ones, but the promise of traffic in lumber products was so great that the investment would, Hill enthused, "pay from two to three times as much as the extension of branch lines east of the main range of the Rocky Mountains." Nevertheless, Hill, for reasons not recorded, failed to prosecute construction. Meanwhile, the SP, which had the jump on him from the beginning in this venture, slowed its activity, finally placing the completed Tillamook Branch in operation on January 1, 1912.[30]

Other Southern Pacific activity in Oregon during the Harriman era was undertaken with an eye toward frustrating Hill's options, fleshing out the system, and reducing grades and curvature. The entire issue of stock and bonds of the Corvallis & Eastern Railway—142 miles, reaching eastward from the coast at Yaquina to Corvallis, Albany, and Idanha—was acquired during fiscal 1907. The Corvallis & Eastern, which ran at right angles to SP's general north-south orientation in Oregon, once considered eastward expansion all the way to the Oregon Railroad & Navigation line. The new property furnished valuable feeder traffic to the SP. More important than the Corvallis & Eastern in terms of ultimate utility was the beginning of what eventually would be the Natron Cut-off, or SP's Cascade line; the California Northeastern Railway was organized in 1905 for the purpose of prosecuting this venture. It then acquired the 22-mile railroad of the Weed Lumber Company extending from Weed, California, 27 miles north of Dunsmuir, to Grass Lake. Subsequently, between 1906 and 1909, the California Northeast-

ern completed construction from Grass Lake, California, to Klamath Falls, Oregon. In a collateral development, the Oregon Eastern Railway was formed on August 22, 1905, in order to foster construction of the Natron Cut-off from the Oregon end. Work went slowly. Only 34 miles were completed by mid-1912, and the longed-for line over the Cascades—one that would seal off competition, yield lucrative traffic, and avoid the difficult operation over SP's older Siskiyou Line—was to remain on hold for several years.[31]

Harriman's attention also focused on other areas of SP's sprawling domain. During the mid-1900s Harriman approved construction designed to solidify SP's competitive position in eastern California and western Nevada. He had attempted to acquire the fabled Virginia & Truckee Railroad (V&T) but, rebuffed in this and not wanting to share Tonopah business with the V&T, determined to drive a new north-south line through the region. To this end, the Nevada & California Railway was chartered on April 7, 1905; it was authorized to construct and operate a line from Hazen, Nevada, a station on the Central Pacific's Overland Line east of Reno, to Mojave, located on Southern Pacific's Sacramento–Los Angeles route in southeastern California. On May 11, 1905, the Nevada & California purchased from parent Southern Pacific the assets of the narrow-gauge Carson & Colorado Railroad, which had been acquired by the SP in 1900. A "third-rail" operation on the northern portion of the Carson & Colorado allowed it to serve as the required link between Nevada & California's Hazen-Churchill and Mojave-Owenyo lines. The completed route was turned over to operation on October 22, 1910.[32]

Harriman faced another adversary—the Atchison, Topeka & Santa Fe Railway (AT&SF)—in the Southwest. If skirmishing with the Santa Fe was new for Harriman, it certainly was not for the SP. Much earlier, in 1881, the Santa Fe had driven its main line to a junction with SP's Sunset Route at Deming, in New Mexico Territory. The Santa Fe hoped to gather significant overhead traffic via Deming, but C. P. Huntington initially refused to make rates of any type and then modified his position only enough to, as Santa Fe saw it, establish charges that were exorbitant. In an attempt to outflank the SP, the Santa Fe then built to deep water at Guaymas, Mexico, but the venture was not financially satisfactory. As a consequence, Santa Fe management determined to attack the Southern Pacific in its heartland—California.[33]

The Atlantic & Pacific Railroad, then controlled jointly by the AT&SF and the St. Louis & San Francisco Railway, had rights to the thirty-fifth-parallel route, but its congressional charter pledged a connection with the SP at the eastern California border for any new line to San Francisco. Managements of both the Santa Fe and the Frisco agreed that this charter provision could be challenged and raised money for penetration into California. However, Huntington—whose Golden State empire was thereby threatened by the Santa Fe—and Jay Gould—whose Texas & Pacific venture was similarly menaced—joined forces to buy a controlling interest in the Frisco and thus share in Atlantic & Pacific's rights. In that way Santa Fe found itself checkmated. A compromise of sorts was arranged. The SP, at that time building southeastward from Mojave, would not go, Huntington agreed, beyond Needles, California—242.5 miles— and the Santa Fe, through the Atlantic & Pacific, would forge a junction there with the SP and not penetrate California with its own line. Service via Needles was begun in August, 1883, but the arrangement quickly proved unsatisfactory from Santa Fe's point of view since the SP, for its part, vowed not to shorthaul itself and continued to favor the Overland and Sunset routes.[34]

The stalemate was short-lived. Santa Fe's management threatened construction of a line parallel to SP's; Huntington was forced to capitulate. He agreed to a "lease and contract of sale" arrangement under which the At-

lantic & Pacific (AT&SF) gained immediate possession and later acquired as payment in kind the Mojave-Needles route. The SP agreed to handle Atlantic & Pacific business above Mojave into San Francisco on a coordinated basis, and the Atlantic & Pacific promised not to purchase terminal facilities in the Bay Area. On the other hand, Santa Fe management had other arrows in its California quiver. It reached San Diego by way of acquisition and new construction in 1885 and two years later drove its own line into Los Angeles. That was not the end of it. The Santa Fe acquired the locally owned San Francisco & San Joaquin Valley Railroad between Stockton and Bakersfield in 1898, gained trackage rights from the SP over the Tehachapis between Mojave and Bakersfield, and in 1900 finished its own new line from Stockton to Point Richmond on San Francisco Bay. The Southern Pacific's monopoly in California, if ever it existed, was surely shattered by the time E. H. Harriman came to lead its affairs.[35]

The circumstance of the two powerful carriers in Arizona Territory was roughly analogous. The SP had enjoyed a monopoly there very briefly before the Atlantic & Pacific (Santa Fe) built its distant if parallel line across the northern portion of the area. Peace between the two was threatened in 1895 when an independent road was completed between Ashfork, on Atlantic & Pacific's main line west of Flagstaff, and Phoenix, in the south central portion of the territory, above the Sunset Route. SP's management was even more concerned when this property passed to the AT&SF in 1901 and became thoroughly alarmed when the Santa Fe announced an extension of it, as the Phoenix & Eastern Railroad, toward the southeast into what SP assumed was its preserve. The matter was not unimportant. If Santa Fe's Phoenix & Eastern were to reach Benson, it would, of course, have an opportunity to exchange traffic with the SP, but it would more likely forge agreements with a competitor—the El Paso & Southwestern Railroad, which was itself com-

pleting a line roughly parallel with the SP between the Rio Grande River and Tucson and
which offered alternate routing opportunities
via El Paso.[36]

Harriman in early 1902 asked the Santa Fe
to stop building into what he considered SP's
service area. His request was ignored. The
Phoenix & Eastern built nearly 100 miles of
road toward Benson in 1903 and 1904, initi-
ating service to Winkelman on September 28,
1904. Another Santa Fe affiliate pledged construction of a cut-off linking Phoenix with the
AT&SF main line near Cadiz, in southeastern
California. The independent El Paso & Southwestern, as might be expected, urged swift
completion of this cut-off as well as extension
of the Phoenix & Eastern to Benson. With
those lines in place, the El Paso & Southwestern stood to share in lucrative overhead traffic.
Harriman was not amused by the prospect.[37]

These matters soon became related to others
in Northern California, where the SP and the
Santa Fe were also squabbling over territorial
rights. Each had acquired formerly independent but disjointed rail operations northwest
of the Bay Area between San Francisco and
Eureka, but the northern segment, owned by
the Santa Fe, and the southern, owned by SP,
were of little value to either of the giants unless connected by new construction—which
would be expensive because of the character
of the country involved. Harriman counseled
cooperation in the spirit of community interest. It was slow to come. The Santa Fe apparently was willing to sell the Phoenix & Eastern to the SP but insisted on resolution of the
Northern California issue at the same time.
Harriman would not hear of it.

The entire matter reached a boiling point
when the Santa Fe announced plans to extend
the Phoenix & Eastern from its end-of-tracks
to a junction with the AT&SF line at Deming,
New Mexico Territory. If completed, the route
would give the Santa Fe a low-grade through
route from El Paso to Phoenix and, if the
Phoenix cut-off was similarly finished, on into
California. Construction in Arizona would

take the Phoenix & Eastern through the narrow canyon of the Gila River, one that Huntington and his engineers had known of and
the very one they had expected to use eventually in a line relocation designed to reduce
operating costs on the Sunset Route. To
counter the AT&SF, Harriman ordered creation of an SP satellite, the Arizona Eastern
Railroad, designed, not surprisingly, to build a
low-grade line across Arizona through, of
course, the valley of the Gila.[38]

Epes Randolph was placed in charge. He
quickly but quietly located two engineer corps
in "that portion of the canyon where construction would be the most difficult" and
then, on March 14, 1904, filed requisite maps
with the Tucson Land Office. Representatives
of the Santa Fe's Phoenix & Eastern arrived
a little over two hours later with their own
maps covering the "same territory." The issue
quickly went before the territorial courts;
Randolph anticipated "no possible chance of
defeat" because the SP's Arizona Eastern controlled the "most strategic ground" by "prior
location" and because the Arizona Eastern
had filed its papers in advance of those presented by the Phoenix & Eastern. The Arizona Eastern's case, as Randolph predicted,
was eventually sustained by the local courts,
but the Santa Fe determined to make an appeal before the U.S. Supreme Court. Meanwhile, Harriman elected to play trump cards.[39]

Early in the fall of 1904, Harriman advised
Santa Fe's E. P. Ripley that he and several
others had purchased $30 million of Atchison,
Topeka & Santa Fe stock, or 14 percent of the
total. Under Santa Fe's cumulative system of
voting, Harriman could place four representatives on its board but chose to seat only two,
Henry C. Frick and Henry H. Rogers. Resolution of the Arizona and California problems
came quickly. In the next year the Santa Fe
agreed to sell, and the SP agreed to buy, the
Phoenix & Eastern at cost plus 4.5 percent interest. Both companies also agreed to reciprocal trackage rights—between Phoenix and
Deming over the new line for the Santa Fe and

between Phoenix and Mojave over the cut-off for the SP. (These agreements were never executed.) Harriman and Ripley likewise covenanted that in the future the SP would not build into the territory north of Phoenix and the Santa Fe would not engage in construction south of that location.[40]

Disposition of the operations northwest of San Francisco followed a similar pattern. On January 8, 1907, the Southern Pacific and the Santa Fe formed a new company, the Northwestern Pacific Railroad, of which the parent companies each owned half. The two then vested the Northwestern Pacific with several smaller lines and, with new construction linking them, formed a through route serving the northern coastal and redwood-bearing areas of California. It was an example of Harriman's belief that relationships between railroads would be bettered by dealing "more frankly with each other" and by operating them "not for the purpose of destroying one another but to help one another."[41]

Harriman was impressed with the Santa Fe itself and apparently would have pursued its acquisition had it not been for the threat of antitrust action by the Roosevelt administration. As it developed, the Harriman interests sold their holdings in 1906, although Frick and Rogers remained on the Santa Fe board until their respective deaths. Interestingly, the Union Pacific, also in 1906, through its Oregon Short Line acquired over $10 million in Santa Fe's preferred issue, but this, too, was sold after three years.[42]

The development of the Southern Pacific Railroad Company of Mexico (SPdeMex) was likewise intertwined in the histories of the Southern Pacific and Santa Fe companies. When it found SP an unenthusiastic connection for its recently completed line to Deming, New Mexico Territory, back in 1881, the Santa Fe had gambled on an extension to tidewater in Mexico. This took the form of the Sonora Railway from the Arizona-Sonora boundary to Guaymas, on the Gulf of California, and the New Mexico & Arizona Railroad

between Benson and Nogales in Arizona Territory (SP granted Santa Fe trackage rights from Deming to Benson). The venture was not successful for Santa Fe and, in 1898, as a part of the Mojave-Needles agreement, the SP leased the Sonora and the New Mexico & Arizona operations.[43]

The Southern Pacific gradually expanded this Mexican adventure during the Harriman years. In 1902 it acquired from the Green Consolidated Copper Company the Cananea, Yaqui River & Pacific Railroad, which possessed several concessions from the Mexican government to construct mileage in that country. The SP itself gained a concession to construct a line of road from an undesignated point convenient on the Cananea line to a junction with the National Railways of Mexico between San Marcos and Guadalajara. Work began near Guaymas at Empalme in 1905, and crews reached Navojoa, 117 miles south, two years later. All concessions, rights, and properties in Mexico were consolidated and transferred to the SPdeMex upon its incorporation on June 24, 1909.[44]

The SP during the Harriman era engaged in still other construction projects or property acquisitions. Its Texas and Louisiana subsidiaries engaged themselves in extensive fleshing out between 1902 and 1907. And, in 1903, the SP purchased 50 percent of the capital stock of the Pacific Electric Railway, which was expanding a vast network of electric traction throughout the Los Angeles Basin.[45]

Yet another major Harriman venture in Southern California, but one in which the SP was not directly involved, was the acquisition of lines and rights that brought the Union Pacific into Los Angeles. That company had early contemplated a line from Ogden and Salt Lake City to Los Angeles, and certain rights-of-way were purchased to that end, but the deadly panic of 1893 prevented its full development. In 1900 Montana's Senator William A. Clark and others who had interest in a local line, the Los Angeles Terminal Railway, announced their intention to tie that concern

with a new one of interregional importance—
the San Pedro, Los Angeles & Salt Lake Railroad, established, as its corporate title urged,
to link Los Angeles and its port with Salt Lake
City and connections there with the Union
Pacific as well as the Denver & Rio Grande.
The implications of the Clark road were not
lost on Harriman, who met the interloper
with competitive construction and litigation. Parallel lines clearly were not justified,
and Clark's company simply could not prevail
against Harriman's power. Compromise followed. The partly completed lines of each
were consolidated, retaining the Clark name—
San Pedro, Los Angeles & Salt Lake—but
managed by Harriman's men. It was opened
for through traffic in 1905. The threat to the
Harriman Lines from Clark's road was obviated. The San Pedro Road adopted SP's rates
as its own on local traffic that was subject to
competition with the Southern Pacific.[46]

Harriman was not always victorious in
warding off intruders. Hill had challenged him
with varying success in Oregon, and the Santa
Fe had not been without accomplishment in
the Southwest. Harriman failed completely,
however, to prevent invasion by George Jay
Gould's Western Pacific.

When he died in 1892, Jay Gould had controlled several railroads that passed to the
management of his son, George, who apparently embraced his father's dream of a true
transcontinental system under one flag. Central to such a plan, as the Goulds saw it, was
the Denver & Rio Grande Railroad. As a result, George Gould saw to it that additional
Rio Grande stock was acquired by his Missouri Pacific, with which the D&RG connected at Pueblo, Colorado. More acquisitions followed. By folding the Rio Grande
Western into the D&RG George Gould, by
the summer of 1901, had a friendly line of
railroad from Saint Louis to Ogden. Rio
Grande's historic link to the Bay Area via
the Central Pacific seemed assured, Gould
thought, although its control had by now
passed to Harriman. Relations between Har-

riman and Gould at the turn of the century
and shortly thereafter were, after all, friendly
and, according to one source, "rather inti-
mate." Both were directors of the Chicago,
Burlington & Quincy; Harriman served on
the boards of Gould's Rio Grande Western
and his Denver & Rio Grande; and Gould
was a member of the executive committee for
SP's directorate and also a member of Union
Pacific's board.[47]

Trouble, nevertheless, was not slow in bud-
ding. The Union Pacific had long since resented the presence of the Rio Grande at
Ogden because, during the Huntington era,
the Central Pacific had allowed and even encouraged through rate agreements with UP's
competition. Harriman, who after 1901 controlled the historic Overland Route, understandably determined not to allow short-
hauling of his own lines and thus demanded
local instead of through rates for business interchanged with the Rio Grande at Ogden.
This had the immediate consequence of diverting a larger tonnage to the Union Pacific
and away from the Gould System. Prosperity
for the Rio Grande was further subverted
when Harriman succeeded in capturing Senator Clark's San Pedro line—one that, had it remained independent, surely would have benefited the Gould system against Harriman's
Union Pacific.[48]

Whether Gould felt penned-in by Harriman
at Ogden (and El Paso, too, on SP's Sunset
Route), or whether he hoped to make real his
father's dream of a true transcontinental railroad, Gould ultimately concluded to strike
out on his own for the Pacific. To this end, the
Western Pacific (WP) Railway was incorporated on March 6, 1903, for the purpose of
building a new line of road from the Bay Area
to Salt Lake City. Its financial sponsorship was
publicly shrouded but, although he denied his
involvement, Gould's name was usually attached to it. The charade was all the more bizarre because Gould and Harriman served on
each other's boards. Finally, in 1905 each resigned from the other's directorate after Gould

publicly admitted that he was fully behind the Western Pacific venture; Harriman pledged to do all he could to prevent the reality of a Gould line between Utah and San Francisco Bay. Part of Harriman's response was pique— he was jealous of his domain; part of it was Harriman's feeling that Gould had betrayed him. Yet there was another aspect. Harriman recognized what the American public generally did not: that destructive competition made the rate structure unstable and resulted in practices that were not in the interests of the railroads themselves or the public at large. For him the Western Pacific was an archetypical example of wasteful duplication of facilities.[49]

Although the Southern Pacific made every effort to prevent the interloper from obtaining a waterfront terminal at Oakland, and Harriman missed no tricks in a heavy-handed campaign to forestall its construction, work on the Western Pacific went forward. The financial burden for the effort was thrown to Gould's Rio Grande, although its own capacity was suspect. California aspirations were not new, of course, to that company. William J. Palmer, president of the Rio Grande Western, had authorized reconnaissance of various routes to the Pacific between 1891 and 1901, and the D&RG itself had studied a potential westward route from Durango, Colorado. Now it would have its wish, if only indirectly. In the Western Pacific endeavor the Rio Grande and presumably the entire Gould System would profit from valuable transcontinental traffic secured at the expense of the Harriman Lines. It was a promise adequate to spur the efforts of all of Gould's forces. Western Pacific engineers staked out a low-level route through the Sierra at an elevation of 5,000 feet—one that Grenville M. Dodge had examined much earlier and, as he recalled, "the Union Pacific would have built [in the late 1860s] if it had not been for the progress of the Central Pacific East." Regular freight operations on the Western Pacific began on December 1, 1909; passenger service, the following August.[50]

The Western Pacific was derided at the SP and elsewhere as the "Wobbly Pacific," and in a sense it deserved the epithet. Costs of constructing and equipping the WP proved to be double the estimates and revenues were slack. In short order the Gould empire collapsed; both the Western Pacific and the Rio Grande slid into receivership. Contemporary observers were not gentle with Gould. One said, "His preeminent characteristic is indecision of character. . . . He is a good deal of a dreamer but he lacks the physical force, the 'nerve,' to see his operations through." He was known as the "sick man of Wall Street." Neither have historians been kind: Gould had a "weakness for aggression" and displayed "faulty field-generalship" that "forced him to build west of Salt Lake City," according to an historian of the Rio Grande. Yet the Western Pacific remained in place. Nobody then could have foreseen the ironic circumstance and strangely strategic importance that the "Wobbly" would assume in the era of the mega-merger, several decades later.[51]

Throughout this period the very character of the United States was changing. The number of people in the country, their average age, average per capita income, and gross national product all increased. So did capital investment. Henry Morgenthau proclaimed that the decade from 1896 to 1906 "was the period of the most gigantic expansion of business in all . . . history. . . . The cry everywhere was for money—more money—and yet more money." An astonishing array of huge industries sprouted abroad the land, but corporate prosperity was uneven during the first decade of the twentieth century. There were three economic downturns, the worst being the short-lived panic of 1907, although the overall trend was upward. All was not well, however. Workers' productivity increased markedly, but real wages of labor remained virtually stable. Moreover, the average citizen was increasingly concerned over the size, power, and concentration of the country's great industries as well as those who owned and managed them. This, after all, was the decade that witnessed the formation of United States Steel, the country's first billion-dollar corporation.[52]

This was also the decade of the Northern Securities case, in which Harriman and James J. Hill were the leading participants. To promote longer hauls for his Great Northern and Northern Pacific companies and to eliminate handling by intermediate carriers between the Twin Cities and eastern roads at Chicago, Hill had seen to the acquisition of the Chicago, Burlington & Quincy, a handsomely located and marvelously managed property. In addition to its Chicago-Minneapolis line, however, the Burlington also had a route stretching from Omaha to Denver and served a territory that lay between Harriman's Overland Route and his Kansas Pacific line. The two men talked of a combined purchase but could not agree; the Chicago, Burlington & Quincy thus passed to Hill, its stock held by the Great Northern and the Northern Pacific. Harriman thereupon began the purchase of Northern Pacific stock with the idea of getting at the Burlington by way of the back door. Hill responded with a campaign of his own. Northern Pacific stock rose to $1,000 per share on the market, a small panic developed, and in the end Hill and his banker, J. P. Morgan, agreed to include Harriman in the creation of Northern Securities, a massive holding company formed in 1901. Nevertheless, three years later the Supreme Court ordered the dissolution of Northern Securities; the decision caused consternation in the business world but was widely applauded by the general public.[53]

Attitudes hardened. The idea grew popular that corporations were greedy and without social responsibility, that business leaders were at best selfish and at worst dishonest, that management exploited labor, and that the rich grew richer while the poor grew poorer, and the big got bigger and the small grew smaller.

Much of this focused on the nation's rail-roads, which, for the brief era of the steamcar civilization, suffered virtually no modal competition. Every citizen had an immediate and unavoidable contact with the railroads. The public—rightly or wrongly—gradually came to perceive that the country had a "railroad problem"; the issue was a constant in its political debates. Westerners and others became concerned that those who controlled the carriers lived in the East and were absentee landlords or alien powers. Furthermore, critics noted, the gross incomes of the larger railroads frequently were larger than those of the states they served. It mattered little if these were really problems or not; the public perceived them as problems and responded accordingly. One of the country's overarching values, its citizens believed, was competition. Yet in the railroad industry true competition was virtually impossible except where parallel lines served the same communities, and even this could result in circumstances counterproductive to all. In many parts of the country, particularly the West, there was inadequate business to support side-by-side lines. When they were constructed, they resulted in overcapacity, waste of capital, and ultimately higher rates for customers.[54]

Theodore Roosevelt, who acceded to the presidency after the assassination of William McKinley in 1901, accurately discerned that the relatively sudden emergence of huge corporations ("trusts") ran contrary to the view of ordinary citizens, who felt that such concentration of private power was inconsistent with individualistic free enterprise. Not surprisingly, the public—and Roosevelt, too, after their unfortunate falling out—focused on Harriman as the archvillain. His melding of the SP and Union Pacific had been the most significant combination of railroad properties made to that time; the Harriman Lines were "the best-run and most thoroughly integrated of the railroad combinations" of the time; and Harriman himself was "the unquestioned leader of the American railroad industry."

Roosevelt and much of the public, however, had come to think of Harriman as an "undesirable citizen."[55]

If he did not actually order the Interstate Commerce Commission to investigate Harriman and his railroad interests, Roosevelt certainly approved and applauded such action. Formally styled an inquiry into "The Consolidation and Combination of Carriers," it did not include all carriers, consolidations, and combinations and, in reality, was a thinly veiled attack on Harriman himself. It provided a stage for his detractors—"the Harriman Extermination League," said Otto Kahn.[56]

Unfortunately for himself, for his properties, and for the industry at large, Harriman in his frankness played into the hands of his opponents. The recent 10 percent dividend on Union Pacific stock not only amazed the financial world but for the general public "proved" charges that rail rates were no less than exorbitant. Shortly thereafter, Harriman made what his friend Otto Kahn called "the one serious mistake" of his career. Following the dissolution of the Northern Securities Company ordered by the U.S. Supreme Court in 1904, Harriman decided to sell Northern Pacific stock held by the UP. The impressive profits thus earned, Harriman decided, should be reinvested to the advantage of the Union Pacific. To him, that meant acquiring stock in other railroads. Consequently, by 1909, the UP owned stock in more than ten of the country's best known carriers. Harriman saw it simply as a change of investments. For the public, however, it appeared as bald-faced attempt to establish a gigantic and illegal monopoly. Kahn thought Harriman's decision a public relations disaster. It was that and more.[57]

Harriman was categorically impolitic as a witness before the hearing. On the one hand, he stoutly defended his view that economic reasons required the voluntary consolidation of the railroads, but on the other he was unwilling to defend himself against either straightforward accusations or innuendo; his demeanor was one of impatience, resentment, and defiance. When asked to answer certain questions regarding stock transactions, he properly refused and the Supreme Court sustained his rights—but the damage was enormous. It was not so much what he said or did not say; rather, it was Harriman's bearing that stood him convicted before the public. Times had changed. It was no longer the Gilded Age, it was the Progressive Era. Harriman, usually a shrewd observer, had failed to note the shift. This time he was his own enemy.[58]

Given the political mood of the time, the commission's recommendations, if regrettable, were predictable. Among other things, the ICC urged that surplus funds be "expended in developing the country and building feeder lines instead of in stock acquisition." There was more, much more, that involved the Harriman Lines directly. It was "contrary to public policy," said the ICC, "for one railroad to acquire control of parallel or competing lines." The implications were ominous. Rumors quickly urged that the government would in one way or another seek to dissolve the strong ties that Harriman had forged between the Southern Pacific and the Union Pacific.[59]

Harriman appeared undaunted. "I've been a pack horse all my life," he commented; "I guess I can pack this too." Certainly his work went on. He approved plans for the Dumbarton Point bridge south of Oakland in San Francisco Bay and urged SP engineers to seek governmental permission for yet another and more impressive structure across San Francisco Bay. At the same time he contemplated an underwater tube through which trains could pass between San Francisco and Oakland, an elevated railway in San Francisco between the passenger station at Third and Townsend and the Ferry Building, and a massive tunnel in the Sierra. He likewise encouraged a variety of electrification projects in the Bay Area and in Oregon as well as hydroelectric generating possibilities in the mountains. He pondered a line extension from Arizona to Durango, Colorado, and planned a light-grade route from Kansas City to Denison, Texas, and corollary upgrading of SP's Houston & Texas Central from Denison all the way to Houston. On a more theoretical level, Harriman advocated broadening all standard-gauge railroads to six feet in order to improve efficiency. Unfortunately, much of this remained unfinished business. Edward Henry Harriman died on September 9, 1909.[60]

His measure was taken broadly. On the SP, trains paused briefly as a manner of respect but then, as Harriman would have had it, moved off on their appointed rounds. He was mourned variously as the "last individualist," the "world's greatest railroad man," and "one who played the game of life upon a large scale." Otto Kahn was not blind to his shortcomings but believed Harriman's "faults were largely those of his generation." The editor of the *Illinois Central Magazine* considered Harriman "at once the best loved and the most misunderstood man of his generation." His peers on the Union Pacific board of directors thought him "one of the most remarkable men this country has ever produced and certainly the greatest man of his generation," and the directors of the Southern Pacific pointed with pride to what they considered his crowning achievement: "A record of development and organization in railroad affairs without parallel, which will live as an important part of the industrial history of the country, a lasting monument to his memory."[61]

Raw statistics do not adequately tell the story of Harriman's years at the Southern Pacific, but they imply much.

	1901	1909
Route miles, rail	9,016.9	9,976.5
Route miles, water	5,365.0	5,385.0
Second track (miles)	107.3	228.8
Sidings (miles)	2,104.5	3,199.5
Total receipts	$81,107,672	$120,521,908
Operating ratio	63.56	66.34
Locomotives (average weight, tons)	51.9	71.06
Passenger cars	1,261	1,771
Freight cars	35,709	44,578
Freight cars (average capacity, tons)	26.88	37.58

During Harriman's tenure the SP purchased 918 new locomotives (net gain of 540), 930 new passenger cars (net gain of 510), and 25,447 new freight cars (net gain of 8,859). Much of this reflected the burgeoning economy, particularly in SP's service area, and the increase in the average capacity of freight cars and the average weight in locomotives is explained in part by advanced standards. Yet these acquisitions also mirrored Harriman's devotion to efficiency and his understanding that it was necessary to spend money in order to make it. His mark was clear and Frank Spearman saw it as such: "The Union Pacific Railroad—and the same can be said of the Southern Pacific—is the peer physically of the standard railway lines of the East."[62]

CHAPTER 5

The Wide-Awake West

"The West Needs More People—More People
Need to Come West."—*Salt Lake City and
the State of Utah*

HARRIMAN was dead and, as John Moody observed, "the wizard touch was clearly gone." Grenville M. Dodge concurred but added an optimistic note: "It is fortunate that he built up and organized the properties so completely and efficiently that it will not be difficult to find someone in them to take his place and carry out his plans. . . ." It was true that Harriman's excellent management team of Robert Lovett, Julius Kruttschnitt, John Stubbs, William Hood, and William Mahl—led now by Lovett—remained in place. It was also true that many if not most of Harriman's policies would go forward as if he were still alive. However, the country was becoming more entranced with what it thought was progressive reform. Lovett's job, difficult enough following in the shadow of Harriman, was sure to be exacerbated by a significantly changed political circumstance.[1]

Even before Harriman's death the Roosevelt Administration, on February 1, 1908, had brought suit under the Sherman Antitrust Act, contending that Union Pacific's control of Southern Pacific through majority stock ownership was in violation of the law. At issue was the matter of competition or, as the government asserted, the lack of it between the Southern Pacific and Union Pacific after Harriman combined them in 1901. The government's contention that the two roads had engaged in aggressive competition before that time was beyond debate. However, its view that none existed thereafter was suspect, at

best. Federal lawyers pointed out that transcontinental traffic moving via Ogden earned only a 30 percent division for the SP, whereas such business handled via its steamship line and Sunset Route could earn 100 percent of the tariff. Logic, they implied, favored the single line. It was not as simple as that. A formula, based on rules of efficiency, had long since applied to the movement of transcontinental business on the Harriman Lines: shipments to or from points above Buffalo, Pittsburgh, Cincinnati, and Cairo moved via Ogden, and those below by way of the Sunset Route. In fact, of business moving through Ogden and El Paso gateways—in other words by way of the Overland Route and the Sunset Route—a full 53 percent moved via Ogden during fiscal 1912.[2]

Company attorneys argued, in rebuttal, that combination of the properties was right and proper because it was by way of stock acquisition rather than contract or other agreement. This contention, however meritorious, was unimportant. The issue, pure and simple, was competition. The lower court saw it thus and, although it found little between the Ogden and Sunset routes, dismissed the case on June 11, 1911.[3]

Senior officers of the Harriman Lines wondered nervously if that would end the matter. Eventually they decided to seek a face-to-face meeting with President William Howard Taft. The youthful W. Averell Harriman, who had met Taft in 1905 when they sailed together aboard a specially scheduled Pacific Mail steamship from the Far East, joined Robert Lovett early in 1912 for a visit with the president "about keeping the railroads together." Taft listened courteously but told his visitors that he would not interfere with the considerations of his attorney general, George W. Wickersham. The implication was ominous: a political decision and not an economic decision would govern the fate of the combined Southern Pacific and Union Pacific.[4]

Shortly thereafter the government appealed to the U.S. Supreme Court, and on December 2, 1912, that body handed down a momentous decision. The court held that, although the amount of business that was competitive between the Overland and Sunset routes was small compared with total transcontinental traffic, the two companies nevertheless were competitors for substantial traffic. Consequently, said the court, combination of the two was in contravention to the Sherman Act. Moreover, the court added an important corollary. Nothing in its decision, it said, should prevent the government or any other party of interest from presenting a plan to the lower court that would effect a continuity of operation from the Missouri River to San Francisco as, suggested the justices, was contemplated under the Pacific Railroad acts. The court's decision brought immediate trauma to the Southern Pacific, but its implications were even worse.[5]

Although disposition of Southern Pacific shares held by Union Pacific (in its own name or through its Oregon Short Line) was a problem not resolved for several months, internal divorcement proceedings began immediately. Joint traffic offices and solicitation agreements were terminated at the end of January, 1913, less than two months after the court's decision. New office facilities were easily located, but a more pressing problem involved personnel. Who would go to the Union Pacific and who would remain with the SP? Another among a plethora of nagging questions that required immediate response involved pooled equipment. Julius Kruttschnitt observed that if the historic pool was dissolved, each of the roads would have to provide more equipment to perform the same amount of carriage and, of course, new equipment could not be acquired instantaneously. On the other hand, it would not be that much of a problem, E. E. Calvin contended, since pooling of equipment had "been of greater advantage to the Union Pacific" than to the SP. In any event, the arrangement ended on April 1, 1913. Yet another crucial decision involved the appointment of executive officers. Robert S. Lovett, whose railroad origins were with the SP, elected to retain his position as chairman of the Union Pacific's executive committee, but in the main those who had been with the SP before 1901 returned. Chairman of the new executive committee was Julius Kruttschnitt; William Sproule, named president in 1911, retained that position.[6]

Earlier in 1913 a fire had destroyed the Equitable Life Assurance Society building at 120 Broadway in New York and with it Harriman's papers as well as executive office files, minutes of the Union Pacific and Southern Pacific board of directors, and the minutes of the executive committees. Records held by Julius Kruttschnitt and moved from Chicago to new offices at 165 Broadway in New York only days before the Equitable Fire immediately became invaluable. As the managements of the two companies went through divorcement proceedings as a result of the court's decree, these files were painstakingly evaluated, and those "which seemed to relate purely to UP matters were turned over to that company."[7]

A consummately peculiar chapter in SP's history then unfolded. An agreement was made between the two companies for the cancellation of Southern Pacific's lease of the Central Pacific, sale of that historic entity to the Union Pacific, and the granting to Union Pacific of important trackage rights and other concessions. There was nothing in this that was advantageous to the Southern Pacific. Rather, as SP's top officers said, darkly, it was

Julius Kruttschnitt (*right*) was assisted during the hard days of divorcement and unmerger proceedings by Paul Shoup (*left*) and William Sproule (*center*).

a condition demanded by the attorney general in settlement of the Supreme Court's decision separating the Southern Pacific from the Union Pacific. Indeed, the SP was told privately by the attorney general that unless it voluntarily terminated its control of the Central Pacific, the government would institute legal proceedings to accomplish such. The merits or lack of merits in the government's position aside, there were other reasons why the SP agreed to mutilation. The company was still controlled by Union Pacific and it remained, after all, under combined management until February 1, 1913; independence of thought was not yet an option. Moreover, SP management worried over the prospect of Union Pacific's dumping its huge block of SP stock on the market at one time. It also considered that SP's credit would be severely clouded by any suit from the attorney general's office. SP's management viewed its situation much as would a man who has a gun at his head. "Southern Pacific . . . would not consent to the severance of the Central Pacific from its lines . . . if left to its own will," said William Sproule. Yet that was not an alternative early in 1913. Thus SP yielded, quietly if reluctantly, as Sproule said, "simply as an expedient."[8]

Many essential features of the plan to divest the Central Pacific in favor of the Union Pacific required approval of the California Railroad Commission, a body recently strengthened in its regulatory power and composed of men appointed by Governor Hiram Johnson, hardly known as a friend of the Southern Pacific. Ironically, however, that body, the pesky Western Pacific Railway, the ornery *San Francisco Chronicle*, and the rebellious California public all combined to provide the SP with lifesaving support.

The Western Pacific insisted on a variety of concessions should the Union Pacific be successful in its quest of Central Pacific, and the Railroad Commission concurred. More importantly, the commissioners called attention to the fact that the U.S. attorney general had interjected a new and crucial requirement not specifically cited by the Supreme Court—that the Southern Pacific sell the stock of the Central Pacific to the UP. Coupled with Union Pacific's own powerful arteries to both Portland and Los Angeles, the Central Pacific in UP hands would, the commissioners worried, reduce the Southern Pacific to the status of "an inferior road" and leave California with "one dominant line [the UP] and one much impaired line" [the SP]. Privately, the commissioners went further: they would, insofar as their power extended, oppose any severance of the Central Pacific from the SP.[9]

In a succession of hotly worded editorials the *San Francisco Chronicle* charged the U.S. attorney general with "bullheaded obstinacy" for pursuing a plan for "the certain, direct and serious injury to the people of California." Under the pretense "of serving the public the government has injured the public," roared the editorialist. "By compelling the divorce of the Union and Southern Pacific pigheaded officials have done mischief enough," but now, continued the exasperated writer, the government wished to take the SP "by the throat and tear from it one of its largest assets, the Central Pacific Railroad." It amounted to "robbing the stockholders of the Southern Pacific, whether they like it or not." The government's efforts "could not be too heartily or emphatically condemned" for, if successful, "it would weaken the Southern Pacific, whose greatest interests lie in the development of California."[10]

It was an unusual if pleasant position for the Southern Pacific, which had not so long before been labeled as an octopus by a relatively well-known novelist. Yet the public opinion in California clearly was that Southern Pacific was being victimized by the government, and prevailing sentiment was against Central Pacific's divorcement. This was just as certainly not a matter of stockholder power. In early 1913, only 196 Californians held equity in the SP, and none had more than 1,000 shares. Collectively, they controlled a mere one-half of 1 percent of the total issue.[11]

All of the major western carriers watched the contest with interest. The Union Pacific itself worried about SP's plans for the routing of traffic once it gained independence, but its fears were groundless; the SP pledged to solicit traffic above Santa Barbara on the Coast Line and Mojave on the Valley Line preferentially via Ogden. The AT&SF was similarly concerned. It dispatched W. B. Storey to San Francisco as a firsthand observer. The Western Pacific was also anxious to protect its interests against the giant rivals. And even the Kansas City, Mexico & Orient Railway, which was about to forge a potentially important connection with the Sunset Route at Alpine, Texas, wondered if new circumstances might work to its advantage. Most optimistic was the Chicago, Rock Island & Pacific, which saw a grand opportunity to expand transcontinental volume by way of El Paso and the Golden State Route.[12]

Meanwhile, Union Pacific's management agonized over two critical and related questions. Should it press energetically for acquisition of the Central Pacific, which it desperately wanted? What method should be employed in the disposal of its SP stock?

The Union Pacific was deeply troubled by the continuing opposition of the California Railroad Commission to separation of Central Pacific from SP. After thorough consideration it announced on March 15, 1913, that a new program for the divorcement, one that would look at the CP matter differently, would have to be designed. There was a nearly audible sigh of relief in San Francisco.[13]

Meanwhile, the government decided not to allow the Union Pacific to implement a pro rata program for distribution of its SP shares to UP stockholders. Alternative plans were considered and, finally, approval was won for a complicated proposal that took effect early in July. As a consequence, those shares of SP held by UP's Oregon Short Line were exchanged for shares in the Baltimore & Ohio Railroad held by the Pennsylvania Railroad; those held directly by the Union Pacific were transferred to the Central Trust Company of New York as trustee. Undramatically, the Harriman era at Southern Pacific ended.[14]

Internally, opposition among company officers to the government's attempt to dispossess SP of the Central Pacific grew after the SP gained independence of management in February, 1913. Initially they had been shocked by the idea, then stoically accepted it, then became mutually discontent and, finally, outright assertive. Early correspondence among the principals at SP bears no emotion but merely reflects their going about what they perceived as necessary routine under the circumstances. In May, Sproule cautiously admitted that he hoped "we will be able to retain the Central Pacific," but one month later SP's William F. Herrin could contain himself no longer: the government's action was, he said, "unconscionable . . . in view of the history of the Central Pacific and its unified ownership at all times with the Southern Pacific." Simply stated, Herrin thought the government's "vexing us" was "absolute in its inequity and injustice." Herrin reflected a growing sentiment among company executives—a sentiment that was much more vigorously enunciated after the Union Pacific disposed of its SP stock in July. Two months later Sproule told an Oregon journalist that the divorcement process had been completed, but that the SP would resist any further attempt "to dispossess it of the Central Pacific," and that the CP was "not for sale at any price." Sproule admitted that the SP had "prospered under" Harriman's stewardship but added, correctly if defensively, "we would have done so anyway." He chastised the several attorneys general who had made mischief for the Harriman Lines and hoped that the incumbent, James C. McReynolds, would "be so busy that he will forget about the Central Pacific." This statement brought an immediate rebuke from Julius Kruttschnitt, who disapproved of any "public criticism" of the attorney general and urged Sproule to "let sleeping dogs lie." A few days later, however, Kruttschnitt himself pledged a "fight to retain the Central Pacific if the government" brought suit.[15]

A fight was the last thing the SP needed at the moment. There was skepticism in many quarters as to the SP's ability to compete outside of the Harriman Lines' umbrella-like protection and, at least briefly, with the quality of SP's management. There were other concerns. SP's indebtedness to the Union Pacific was well known, as was its need for equipment following cancellation of its longstanding pooling agreement with Union Pacific. The mood was grim. Sproule was moved to exhort "all hands to steady down and row the boat." He urgently demanded that the traffic department get to work "everywhere drumming the trade vigorously." The entire SP family, he urged, should "work most actively to improve our earnings and keep down our expenditures." The situation was critical; a dispute with the government or the UP in regard to the Central Pacific would be most untimely. Kruttschnitt was convinced, nevertheless, that a fight was coming. He was right. On February 11, 1914, the government renewed its attack by filing suit to force the SP to sell its stock in Central Pacific.[16]

The unmerger issue had already consumed a half-dozen years and, amazingly, was to last

another nine. It hung over the Southern Pacific like a pall; it unnecessarily sapped the company's resources and diverted the talents of its management; it resulted in the unhappy delay, postponement, and in some cases eventual cancellation of improvements that would have made the Southern Pacific a more effective and efficient carrier in the face of challenges from other railroads as well as new modal competition. The government's proceedings were no doubt well-intentioned, but they were also wrongheaded. In the end they were equally counterproductive for SP's current and future shareholders, employees, and patrons. Meanwhile, the railroad continued to function during the difficult years 1910 to 1920. It grew, if slowly, and continued, if unevenly, to mature.

Some, but not all, of SP's expansion and improvement program after Harriman's death in 1909 represented his legacy. This was the case on the historic Overland Route, where a program of installing a second main track between Oakland and Ogden was under way. At the end of 1912, 167 miles had been finished and another 112 miles were in varying states of completion. No authorization had been made for the remaining 505 miles, and, sad to say, none would be forthcoming until the unmerger matter was resolved.[17]

SP's program of construction and acquisition in Arizona likewise moved haltingly. Plans to link the Phoenix-Christmas line with the Bowie-Globe Branch (the Gila Valley, Globe & Northern Railway, an affiliate) as part of a new low-grade relocation of the Sunset Route was shelved permanently when the federal Reclamation Service built a dam in Gila Canyon between San Carlos and Christmas. Plans for the western portion of this, between Phoenix and Yuma, proceeded, at least between Phoenix and Hassayampa, about 40 miles, which was placed in service by the Arizona Eastern during fiscal 1911. The program for the remaining segment toward Yuma was postponed, though. South of Tucson, a subsidiary of the SP acquired a tiny independent road, completed a short construction project, and by utilizing trackage of the former New Mexico & Arizona Railroad (leased from the Santa Fe since 1898 and soon to be acquired outright), began service to Nogales on the Mexican border effective June 19, 1910. In the same season, a half-dozen subsidiaries in Arizona were consolidated under the flag of the Arizona Eastern Railroad.[18]

During the years 1902–11, the SP also completed an interesting U-shaped route from Niland, California, south through the Imperial Valley to the international boundary at Calexico, then looping into Mexico for over 50 miles before rejoining the Sunset Route just west of Yuma. A portion of this route had been used earlier during the Colorado River crisis, and all of it was operated by the Inter-California Railway under lease from the SP.[19]

The situation in the northwestern part of SP's service area was analogous to that in its southwestern section. Some plans matured, others did not. Construction of the Tillamook Branch, begun in 1905, was finally concluded in 1911, and regular operations commenced on January 1, 1912. A heavy volume of fine forest products moved to market over this new feeder, and for several years summer passenger specials handled eager patrons to popular vacation spots at or near Tillamook. Elsewhere, however, work on the important Natron Cut-off remained on hold pending the outcome of unmerger proceedings.[20]

Another major undertaking in Oregon, one that not only garnered remunerative traffic but also sealed off rail competition, was the Coos Bay Branch. SP's interest dated from 1906, when it purchased the tiny but strategically located Coos Bay, Roseburg & Eastern Railroad & Navigation Company, which owned a 28-mile pike in the Coos Bay area. The new property was not connected to other rail carriers, and none were close at hand, but the SP offered connecting service to San Francisco and Portland by way of its S.S. *Breakwater*. SP then projected a new road between Drain, on the Siskiyou Line south of Eugene and above

Roseburg, and the newly acquired property near Coos Bay. Work on the 82-mile Oregon Western Railway, as it was called, continued from 1907 through 1910, but it was later abandoned and the material salvaged. For whatever reason—strategic, most likely—SP's interests were redirected in favor of a dog-legged line running westward from Eugene and then southward to Coos Bay, 120 miles. To prosecute this venture, SP established the Willamette Pacific Railroad on June 14, 1911. Grading was commenced in a few months, but it was not until five years later that the line was opened to traffic over its entire route. A celebration to honor the Southern Pacific for introducing "Coos Bay to the World" began on August 24, 1916 and ran for three days. There was good reason to salute this achievement. The area was one of the richest undeveloped sections in the country, and Coos Bay itself was a wonderful natural harbor, possibly the finest between San Francisco and Puget Sound. Railroad transportation was sure to foster enhancement of the entire region.[21]

Harassment by the Hill Lines in Oregon continued, however, and, under SP's constricted circumstance, it seems strange that James J. Hill did not seek further advantage there. He did acquire the Oregon Electric Railway in 1910. That company had a line parallel with the SP from Portland to Albany and, under Hill's leadership, was extended to Eugene in 1912. SP's traffic department had wanted the company to buy the Oregon Electric before it passed to Hill, but because Oregon Electric competed side-by-side with the SP, company attorneys considered that its acquisition was likely illegal under the Sherman Antitrust Act. Kruttschnitt chafed under what he considered an invasion of the "territory served by us in the Willamette Valley" and hoped one day to "have an opportunity to balance the account." More troubling psychologically than otherwise was Hill's Pacific & Eastern Railway, a 32-mile pest located in southwestern Oregon, not connected to the rest of his empire nor anywhere near it. An-

The Southern Pacific Railway Introduces Coos Bay to the World

The Coos Bay Branch in Oregon garnered remunerative traffic and also sealed off rail competition. *From the Coos Bay Times, April 8, 1916.*

other relatively unimportant Hill operation involved the United Railways Company, a tiny interurban route serving metropolitan Portland.[22]

Relations with the Santa Fe during this period were, if not cordial, at least stable. On December 27, 1911, the SP sold to the Santa Fe the Mojave-Needles line, which had been under lease to it since 1898. At the same time the AT&SF, in exchange for this trackage, conveyed to the SP the New Mexico & Arizona Railroad, which owned the line from Benson to Nogales, and the Sonora Railway, which held the line from Nogales to Guaymas, Mexico. These former Santa Fe properties had been leased by the SP since 1898. (The Sonora Railway passed to the Southern Pacific of Mexico on June 30, 1912.) To the

north, the heavy construction required to link the disconnected entities of the jointly owned Northwestern Pacific Railroad was completed on October 23, 1914, and through passenger service between San Francisco and Eureka began a few days later.[23]

Fortune did not smile on the Southern Pacific of Mexico. The revolutionary movement in Mexico affected its construction plans and even its operations. Bridges, trestles, and other properties were destroyed during the years 1910 to 1916. The situation so deteriorated during that period that the SPdeMex was only "open for traffic from time to time." Losses were compounded by that country's "generally demoralized business conditions" and a resulting loss of revenue as well as slowness on the part of the government in satisfy-

In 1916, under a series of compromise agreements, the SP advanced the monies necessary to complete the San Diego & Arizona. An inspection train is shown here at the second crossing of the Tijuana River.

ing reparations and payments by the military for its transportation charges. Conditions improved late in the decade but not sufficiently to warrant completion of planned construction.[24]

Yet another colorful element of Southern Pacific's history involved the San Diego & Arizona Railway (later the San Diego & Arizona Eastern Railway). Early railroad planners predicted that San Diego would be the western terminus of a transcontinental line, but the surprising growth of Los Angeles, due in large measure to its successful campaign to lure the SP, changed all that. San Diego did receive rail services of the Atchison, Topeka & Santa Fe but, much to its chagrin, by way of a spur, and the Santa Fe increasingly concerned itself with Los Angeles. SP's interest in reaching San Diego dated from 1902 when Julius Kruttschnitt ordered William Hood to make a thorough study for an outlet to the east, striking the Inter-California Railway near El Centro.[25]

An arrangement was made at E. H. Harriman's behest between the SP and John D. and A. B. Spreckels, under which the Spreckels in-

terests were to organize the company. This was done on December 15, 1906; SP's participation and backing were not immediately divulged to the public. Grading began in September, 1907, and continued until Harriman's death in 1909. SP's management then had a change of heart and suspended support. The Spreckels interests determined to carry out the venture on their own and in September, 1910, agreed to purchase SP's investment. Later, however, the Spreckels forces came to feel betrayed, and, in fact, the SP had acted badly in the matter. Lengthy litigation resulted. Finally, in 1916 a series of compromise agreements resulted in SP's advancing monies necessary to complete the road, which was to be owned equally by the Spreckels interests and SP. The reasons for SP's decision to compromise were complex and involved moral, financial, and policy considerations. There was great concern, for instance, in the company's general offices that the territory to be served was ripe for invasion by the Union Pacific, the Santa Fe, or even the Rock Island.[26]

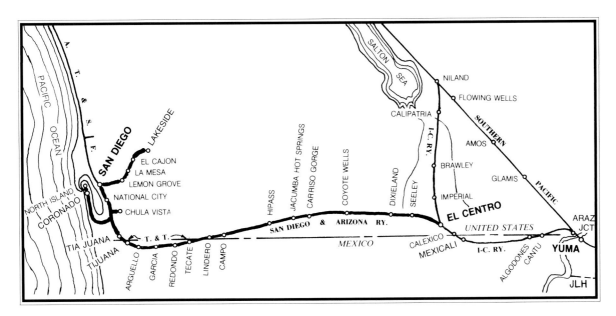

San Diego & Arizona Railway

In any event, through internal merger, line construction from both ends, and lease of a short piece of SP trackage, the route was opened for through service on December 1, 1919. The route led southeastward from San Diego to Tijuana, where it crossed into Mexico, continued in a generally easterly direction, crossed back into the United States 44 miles later, passed over the summit of the Coast Range, and then dropped into the Imperial Valley. Much of it was characterized by rugged, mountainous country requiring a profile of stiff grades and difficult curvature. Of particular note was the construction through Carrizo Gorge—which a New York writer labeled "one of the seven wonders of America"—where much tunneling was required to defeat the narrow canyon and steep cliffs. The line in Mexico was technically the property of the Tijuana & Tecate Railway, a wholly owned subsidiary. San Diego & Arizona trains reached El Centro and Calexico from Seeley by way of the SP line; through business to and from Yuma was carried over the Inter-California. In any event, the San Diego & Arizona provided what its incorporators dreamed—a shorter rail route from San Diego to the east that at the same time served the burgeoning Imperial Valley.[27]

Another construction project involved a branch from the Overland Route at Fernley, Nevada, northwestwardly to Susanville and Westwood, California. Its ultimate strategic value was obscured because it began and ended in a remote region. Begun as a project of the Fernley & Lassen Railway to tap remunerative business from the Red River Lumber Company but actually accomplished by the Central Pacific, the line was opened to Susanville in 1913 and to Westwood the next year.[28]

During the first two decades of the twentieth century the Southern Pacific moved vigorously into the field of electric traction. For instance, in 1903 it acquired 50 percent interest in the Pacific Electric Railway (PE), and on November 1, 1910, it purchased the remainder. The Pacific Electric itself owned several subsidiaries, and these in addition to other lines in the Los Angeles Basin owned by the SP were consolidated under PE's charter. Three years later Pacific Electric advertised itself as "the largest electric railway system in the world," running "2300 scheduled interurban trains daily to points of interest in Southern California." In 1912, it operated just under 600 route miles and, as the "Wonderland Trolley Trail," it offered an "economical, quick, and satisfactory way to see the Southland." Several tours were available, among them the "Orange Empire Trolley Trip," a 175-mile tour through "Orange Land," at only $3.50 per ticket. Pacific Electric promised "competent guides, comfortable service, and reserved seats" for this and other excursions.[29]

Other formerly independent electric traction operations in California were acquired during the same period. These included the Stockton Electric Railroad, the Peninsular Railway in Palo Alto and San Jose, the Visalia Electric Railroad in and around Visalia, the Fresno Traction Company, and the San Jose Railroads serving San Jose and Santa Clara. These provided passenger and also effective pick-up and distribution services that were beneficial to the public and the corporate parent as well.[30]

Farther north in the Golden State, the SP, at Harriman's direction in 1908, made plans for the electrification of its suburban network connecting Oakland, Alameda, and Berkeley with its cross-bay ferry operations at Oakland Mole and Alameda Mole. When completed in 1912, SP's system was the first in the nation to embrace a high-voltage DC overhead system; power was generated at the company's Fruitvale plant and distributed to substations at West Oakland and Berkeley. The initial rolling stock of 60 steel multiple-unit cars was eventually increased to 140 as business increased.[31]

Active consideration was given in 1912 for a dramatic program to expand SP's electrified operations in the Bay Area. Early in that year Thomas Ahearn, an operating officer, pointed out that the "main line down the Peninsula" from San Francisco to San Jose was "taxed to handle present business" and suggested, by way of relief, electrification of "the old line" plus use of the already electrified Peninsular Railway and additional construction if neces-

The Pacific Electric building in Los Angeles.

sary to "handle the commutation business down the Peninsula" and "relieve the present steam line." Ahearn also urged extension of East Bay electrified suburban operation by way of new construction to Hayward and San Jose in order to similarly relieve pressure on the existing steam line between Oakland and San Jose. Ahearn, in reality, was advocating electrification of a horseshoe-shaped system reaching all the way from Berkeley, in the East Bay, to San Jose and back up the west side to San Francisco.[32]

Ahearn won the support of his superior, E. E. Calvin, at least for the San Francisco–San Jose segment. Calvin observed that electrification would facilitate more flexible service, lower employee numbers, release fifty coaches and ten locomotives, and reduce the steam-powered commuter trains to only the heaviest San Francisco–San Jose "expresses." Paul Shoup, president of Pacific Electric, likewise supported the proposal and urged haste in implementation lest a situation develop like that in Oregon where Hill's Oregon Electric had invaded the Willamette Valley. The esti-

SP's East Bay electric operation connected Oakland, Alameda, and Berkeley with its cross-bay ferry operations. Business was brisk. This view shows the approach to the Oakland Mole in 1912.

Ticket clerks at the Ferry Building in 1907 were a busy lot, indeed.

mated cost for electrification of the Peninsula line was $4 million; William Sproule signed the "authority for expenditure" on December 11, 1912. No monies were spent, however. The project died, the result of uncertainties occasioned by the government's unmerger proceedings.[33]

At the same time, SP's management gave thoughtful consideration to the creation of a separate corporation vested with all of SP's electric operations as well as its ferry boat business. William Sproule likely belied the prejudice of a steam railroader as he assessed the matter. "The operation of electric lines is," he told W. F. Herrin, "very much of a streetcar business." On the other hand, Sproule acknowledged that "the methods and organization of steam railroads are too cumbersome and not flexible enough to fit electric traction." However, Paul Shoup, whose devotion to electrification was clear, doubted the value of combining the various and disjointed segments. His concerns were various and complex, but he was particularly bothered by the possibility that combination might invite additional government regulation and by the even more likely possibility of union grievances and demand for increased wages among those employed by what might be styled "Southern Pacific Electric Company." Shoup carried the argument. Thoughts of combination died accordingly.[34]

In Oregon an enterprising electrical engineer by the name of Alvadore Welch had long dreamed of forging an electrified railroad from Portland to California. To this end he acquired several streetcar lines and labeled his collection the Portland, Eugene & Eastern Railway. Unfortunately for him, he had not adequate financial resources. E. H. Harriman soon purchased his heavily mortgaged lines; he and his successors used the Portland, Eugene & Eastern as a vehicle to combat Hill's growing influence in the greater Portland area and to capture for itself a larger dominion. In 1914, on January 17, electric service began on the West Side loop from Portland to Oswego,

Newburg, Saint Joseph, and back by way of Forest Grove and Hillsboro. The equipment used in the new service was composed of forty-eight passenger and combination cars outfitted at the nearby Beaverton Shops and were copies of those used at Oakland. Painted in a smart red color, they were, not surprisingly, called the "big Red Electrics."[35]

Portland, Eugene & Eastern's president, Robert E. Strahorn, promised an eager public that his company had "outlined extensive plans for further work in Oregon." Strahorn was true to his word. He urged further electrification—from Whiteson, south of Saint Joseph and McMinnville and where the electrification currently ended, to Corvallis and Eugene as well as between Salem and Dallas. All of this, he told William Sproule, could be accomplished inexpensively and would "vastly increase local business." Sproule was impressed with the net income of 33¢ per train mile from electric operations in Oregon during the summer of 1914, but because of SP's impaired ability resulting from the unmerger confusion, Sproule concluded that it was impossible "to extend the PE&E to Corvallis or any where else at this time." Sproule did modify his position later, however, to facilitate electrification to Corvallis, but catenary never reached Eugene on the Portland, Eugene & Eastern.[36]

Southern Pacific's management also interested itself in electrification of a very different character. Beginning in 1903 and lasting for ten years, SP officers studied the feasibility of electrifying the company's mountain lines over the Siskiyous in Oregon and the Sierra and Tehachapis in California. The initial assessments were made by both General Electric and Westinghouse, and their reports were favorable. SP thereupon began its own review, principally under the direction of Allen H. Babcock. After detailed analysis, Babcock concluded that there was not "a reasonable chance for profitable electrification" on either the Siskiyou or Sierra line. Study of electrification for the Tehachapi route began in 1912 when

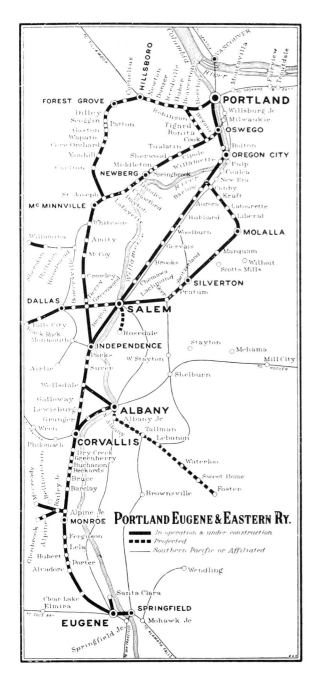

PORTLAND EUGENE & EASTERN RY.

━━━ *In operation & under construction*
▪▪▪▪ *Projected*
──── *Southern Pacific or Affiliated*

possible economies were so much reduced" by them that, in regard to the Sierra and Siskiyous, "consideration of the matter was dropped." There was another problem. The railroad would be obliged by the power supplier to stand the expense of a high peak load because the movement of trains tended to bunch and could not be spread evenly over a twenty-four-hour period. For these reasons the SP had opted for additional Mallets and double track instead of electrification. Nevertheless, Kruttschnitt was willing to consider the issue as it applied to the Tehachapis. Negotiations were conducted with Pacific Power & Light, which agreed to provide the necessary electricity on a long-term basis and offered a rather attractive rate. Paul Shoup, however, was at best lukewarm to the proposal, although he did point out that the cost of oil for fueling steam locomotives was likely to rise over twenty years whereas the power company's proposal would make that factor a constant if the electrification proposal became a reality. Babcock's appraisal was more direct: "On the basis of present traffic . . . electrification of this division would not be justified from a financial viewpoint, whether the power" was generated by a plant owned by the railroad or purchased from a supplier. Kruttschnitt duly reported this to Ripley, who was both "quite surprised" and "disappointed." He wondered if the investigation had "been undertaken by somebody who was prejudiced against the change." It was not likely; Babcock was SP's electrical engineer. Moreover, it is worth noting that Ripley's Santa Fe chose not to electrify its own route over Raton Pass.[38]

Santa Fe's E. P. Ripley, who was then considering a similar possibility for his road between Trinidad, Colorado, and Raton, New Mexico, asked Julius Kruttschnitt to look into the matter.[37]

Kruttschnitt told Ripley in reply that "before the development of the Mallet locomotive the question offered some attractions but the

The dramatic surge in population throughout SP's service area, but particularly in California, resulted in a concomitant increase in the company's passenger offerings. These were as diverse as the territory's requirements. Eighteen weekday trains plied in each direction between San Francisco and San Jose; additional commuter service was provided between Los

In terms of continuous service, the oldest of the SP's name trains was the *Sunset Limited*.

Angeles and Pasadena, San Bernardino, Colton, and Riverside. Locals and mixed trains served other constituencies, but the pride of the company was in its growing fleet of named trains. The oldest of these in terms of continuous service, beginning its life in November, 1884, was a delightful train initially labeled *Sunset Express* and later *Sunset Limited*. It served, as its name implied, the Sunset Route, which, as SP advertised during cold seasons in the North, was "the summer way on a winter day." Additionally, the SP and its leased lines in Texas for several years joined with the Southern Railway, West Point Route, and Louisville & Nashville to advertise what they called the "Washington-Sunset Route" for direct connections through the cooperating carriers at New Orleans from Washington, Atlanta, and Montgomery for all points on the Sunset Route as well as California's Valley and Coast lines. Additional premier passenger service over the western portion of SP's Sunset

Route was provided by the "sleeping cars only" *Golden State Limited*, a gem of a train begun in 1902 and sponsored jointly by the SP, Rock Island, and El Paso & Southwestern between Los Angeles and Chicago via El Paso.[39]

The Overland Route, however, traditionally claimed the company's greatest attention, and this was reflected in its passenger service there. Three daily trains in each direction during 1906 were expanded to four "over the Main Highway . . . via the famous Lucin Cut-Off" a year later. The flagship train among them was appropriately named the *Overland Limited*—a superb all-Pullman "De Luxe—Extra Fare Train—Electric Lighted." It featured a buffet club car with barbershop, shower bath, and valet services in addition to a drawing room compartment car with library, stenographer, ladies' maid, newspapers, and the latest stock market reports. As a name train, the *Overland* dated from 1887 on the

Union Pacific but only 1899 on the SP. Interestingly, SP kept its options open, even during the years of Union Pacific control, by handling scheduled cars over the Overland Route from several carriers out of Chicago, Omaha, Denver, and Saint Louis.[40]

On other of the company's routes there was a heavy volume of business to and from San Jose, Monterey, Tracy, and Sacramento. Oregon traffic was not as impressive, but the SP nevertheless provided impeccable service on the *Shasta Express*, later the *Shasta Limited*—a "de luxe daily extra fare train" with surprisingly fine amenities.[41]

The requirements of passenger carriage put a special strain on SP's terminal facilities, at San Francisco and Los Angeles in particular. A new facility for San Francisco, near the Ferry Building on Market Street, was under consideration before the 1906 earthquake and fire, but construction of it was thereafter postponed and eventually canceled. William Sproule correctly perceived the growing rivalry between the two California cities and warned Julius Kruttschnitt that it would not be politic for the SP "to erect a depot in one city and not the other." Finally, by the summer of 1912 the company was able to announce that new stations were authorized for both. There was great pleasure in Los Angeles when on June 12, 1915, gates were opened at the impressive Central Station, but the mood was mixed a few weeks later when SP's Third & Townsend Street terminal entered service. Peninsula commuters were indignant that the company had chosen to make a heavy investment at that location instead of closer to the business district. As one journalist said, "This peninsula controversy will never be settled until it is settled on the basis of a Market Street terminal."[42]

Improvements in rolling stock also typified SP's operations. In 1906 the SP placed in service its first all-steel passenger car and four years later commenced a policy of acquiring only steel equipment for passenger operations. At the end of fiscal 1913, SP owned 2,292 pas-

The *Shasta Express*, later called the *Shasta Limited*, offered fine amenities.

senger cars; of these, 738, or fully 32 percent, were of steel construction.[43]

The acquisition of all-steel equipment, construction of new stations, and the location of downtown ticket offices handy for busy patrons were necessary ingredients if the SP was to deal effectively in the business of passenger carriage and to ward off increasing competitive attacks. These took the form of the Western Pacific interloper and other steam rail competitors, interurban electric lines, and, more importantly, motor vehicles. The continued growth of population in SP country notwithstanding, a decline in the volume of through and local passengers on the SP began in 1914 and continued through 1916, but rebounded during World War I to a peak in 1919. As it developed, the 1914–16 experience and not that of the war years and 1919 was a harbinger.[44]

Revenues derived from passenger operations were extremely important to SP's income statement in those years. That aspect of the business was also implicitly understood to be

SP's 3rd & Townsend Street station in San Francisco opened during the summer of 1915.

the company's advertising, public relations, and promotional arm. A classic example of this interconnection involved San Francisco's Panama-Pacific Exposition in 1915. Located near Fort Mason, the 635-acre extravaganza attracted more than 13 million sightseers. Southern Pacific, a California-oriented company, predictably felt obliged to eclipse all other rail competitors, and it did so. SP subsidized the Exposition, offered incentive rates to attract visiting crowds, and constructed an award-winning Renaissance-style building to showcase itself. The Southern Pacific Building, as it was known, was opened with gala festivities on March 10; a general holiday was declared by the company, and over 8,500 active and retired employees attended. Inside was the "Sunset Theatre," which hosted illustrated lectures and pipe organ recitals; a diorama called "The Road of a Thousand Wonders" made up of scenes from along SP's famous Sunset, Overland, and Shasta routes; a reading room where "newspapers from

principal cities were on file"; and women's and men's restrooms. There were "no charges of any kind," boasted SP. Nearby, in the Transportation Building, the company proudly displayed its tiny and elderly 4-2-4T, *C. P. Huntington*, next to a modern 2-8-8-2 Mallet. For the SP, and the other carriers, too, the Exposition provided an opportunity to stage a popular industrial exhibit in home territory. It was successful in that and also in stimulating extraordinary passenger revenues.[45]

SP's advertisement of California was hardly restricted to the Exposition. Indeed, that was a year-round project. "In the good old summer time," said the SP, California was "where the flowers are sweetest, the waters are clearest, the skies are bluest, and the joys are keenest." On the other hand, "winter travel to and from California" was also a pleasure if, of course, one traveled on the Southern Pacific with its "automatic block signals, smokeless comfort with oil-burning locomotives, direct service, and perfect roadbed." California, the

SP pledged to prospective tourists, had anything a person could want: ocean beaches, missions, mountain and seaside resorts, big trees, and beautiful agricultural valleys. "Descriptive California literature free on request," the SP always promised.[46]

An important adjunct to SP's double-edged policy of promoting its service area while promoting itself was its sponsorship of *Sunset Magazine*. Begun in May, 1898, the aim of *Sunset* was to present "information concerning the great states of California, Oregon, Nevada, Texas, Louisiana, and the territories of Arizona and New Mexico—a rich and inexhaustible field over which the dawn of future commercial and industrial importance is just breaking." Named for SP's well-known *Sunset Limited*, the magazine was initially edited by a small staff in the passenger department. Editorially it was concerned with the challenges and opportunities of the West; its contents reflected the spirit of the time. The first issue contained, not surprisingly, an article on Yosemite Valley. Its writers were also intrigued with auto transportation and later reported on the dawn of the air age. Among its contributors were Bret Harte, Jack London, John Muir, Sinclair Lewis, and even SP's own Paul Shoup. Advertisers eager to find placement in *Sunset* included, for instance, Cadillac, Ford, the Palace and Del Monte hotels, Victor Talking Machines, Bon Ton Corsets, and Jell-O. Neither did *Sunset* hesitate to advertise itself. It was, it said, the magazine that told "by story and picture all about the Pacific Coast and the Wide-Awake West," available for only 15¢ per copy at newsstands or $1.50 yearly by mail. SP sold *Sunset* in 1914. Today it is the property of the Lane Publishing Company and remains the West's oldest popular magazine.[47]

The Southern Pacific throughout the first three decades of the twentieth century energetically lured colonists to its service area. This was not new but rather the continuation of a program begun early in the company's history by the Big Four, who clearly understood that the development of local freight and passenger traffic—so important to SP's financial health—depended on a productive population located along its lines. As early as 1875 a company broadside asserted California's advantages: "The Laborer's Paradise!! Salubrious Climate, Fertile Soil, Large Labor Returns, No Severe Winters, No Lost Time, No Blight or Insect Pests." Migrants were offered tickets at "low rates." Furthermore, during the late 1880s and early 1890s, the SP sent five-car "California on Wheels" trains throughout the Middle West with exhibits of California products and agricultural displays from various California regions. It was a pioneer method of advertising and an important factor in attracting home-seekers.[48]

Sunset Magazine during the years 1909 through 1913 conducted its own large-scale campaign in cooperation with on-line counties and municipalities, which joined its Homeseekers Bureau in issuing thousands of beautiful booklets ballyhooing their respective territories. These were distributed by the railroad, chambers of commerce, boards of trade, county supervisors, and other agencies.[49]

The railroad itself engineered still other campaigns. A series of booklets, as diverse as *California Fishing* and *The New Arizona*, were published by the SP and placed on trains, in depots, and otherwise made available to the general public by mail. Particular stress was laid on the Sacramento, San Joaquin, Imperial, Coachella, and Indian Wells valleys, western and southern Oregon, and southern and central Arizona. Amazingly, over 80 million pieces of literature promoting the Pacific coast states were distributed between 1912 and 1922.[50]

Additional efforts to colonize Southern Pacific country were expended in western Europe. These included, for example, participation and advertising at the Paris Fair of 1900 and the Royal Galleries of London in 1910. The reception was enthusiastic. Those enticed to migrate were urged to seek the assistance of SP's European representative, who could, the company promised, arrange "through ticket-

The SP engaged in a strong campaign of colonization, and it developed an enthusiastic symbiotic relationship with its agricultural shippers.

ing" with any steamship company that had service to Atlantic or Gulf Coast ports. "To meet their personal needs for a reasonable length of time," SP urged, immigrants should have at least twenty-five dollars in cash when they arrive in the New World.[51]

Other campaigns were conducted closer to home. Twice each year, in the spring and in the fall, SP agents sold one-way colonist tickets to aspiring candidates who sought new opportunity along the Sunset Route west of El Paso and the Overland Route west of Ogden. Rates in 1901 were reasonable: $30.00 from Chicago, $25.50 from Mississippi River points, and $25.00 from Council Bluffs or Sioux City. A decade later the tariffs were only slightly higher. Ten-day stopovers were allowed at any station in California, Utah, Nevada, Arizona, and at Deming and Lordsburg in New Mexico. Before the inexpensive promotional rates were suspended in 1916, an amazing total of 798,824 persons availed themselves of them.[52]

The Southern Pacific understandably en-

couraged a strong symbiotic relationship with its agricultural shippers. To this end, it worked actively with existing agricultural agencies such as the Farm Bureau, the Grange, the Farmers Union, various schools, and civic organizations to promote the welfare of husbandry. The company also hired its own agricultural agents to conduct soil surveys, set standards for production, develop irrigation districts, and instruct growers in the best methods of cultivation. It likewise sponsored food demonstration and promotion trains and supported local projects such as Fresno's Raisin Festival and California's Orange Day.[53]

The development of fresh fruit and vegetable production and SP's involvement in support, particularly in the states of Oregon, California, and later Arizona, was impressive. Indeed, the prosperity of this important new industry was dependent on the efficient and economical transportation offered by the Southern Pacific, and, in turn, the SP's income statement reflected the importance of such traffic tendered by the growers. By 1914 California's fruit industry was responsible for more of SP's gross revenue from that state than any other commodity group.[54]

Indeed, California held the focus. Interstate shipments of produce from that state began in 1869 but amounted to a mere thirty-three tons. Nine years later SP convinced the Union Pacific and its eastern connections to handle "not more than two cars per day of California fruit" on passenger trains to New York City. Then, on June 24, 1886, the SP dispatched the first special fruit train from Sacramento; in the same year Boston received its first carload of California fruit. As volume grew, so did the need for sophisticated equipment. Boxcars were replaced by ventilator cars, which themselves were replaced by refrigerator cars in this carriage. Cooperation flourished. To promote sales of California citrus, the SP joined the California Fruit Growers Exchange in an advertising campaign in which each party paid an equal share. The two found other ways to assist each other. An experimental marketing campaign focused on the state of Iowa. "Oranges for Health—California for Wealth" was the wisdom spread throughout that state before specially bannered trains arrived there with Sunkist lemons and oranges. Each train was accompanied by a messenger who, upon arrival at scheduled locations, had the news telegraphed ahead. A 50 percent increase in sales was the result for the growers, and a fine increase in traffic was the reward for SP. The promise of continuing demand was reward for both.[55]

Production and consumption of western produce leaped. By 1916 over one billion oranges were shipped annually from California. Citrus, however, was not the only commodity rolling east to hungry markets. Strawberries, peaches, watermelons, apples, potatoes, pears, apricots, grapes, figs, cherries, onions, asparagus, and cantaloupe joined the parade—often in special trains. The rates were reasonable: $1 to $1.15 per hundredweight (phw) to Chicago, slightly more to the East Coast.[56]

The SP found still other ways to promote the welfare of growers while promoting its own well-being. The infant table grape industry provides an example. SP allowed one stop in transit for grapes, packed in barrels and billed in carload lots, for growers who might discover that the market had fallen after the car had been loaded. In that way the grower could stall sale and delivery in the hope that the market would rise. The SP also allowed part unloading at stop-in-transit points east of Colorado. None of this was immediately rewarding for the SP but represented the company's gamble that the grape industry would make market inroads and thus generate regular traffic for years to come.[57]

To more expeditiously handle the mushrooming growth of perishables business, the Southern Pacific joined the Union Pacific on an equal basis in forming the Pacific Fruit Express Company. PFE commenced operations on October 1, 1907, with a fleet of 6,600 new refrigerator cars. It was charged with the responsibility of operating and maintaining cars and services for perishable shippers on both lines. Although owned in equal shares by the SP and the UP, PFE loadings were made mostly on the SP and moved eastbound to Ogden for forwarding by the Union Pacific. Business was good. PFE handled 70,000 carloads of Pacific Coast perishables in 1913 alone. Four years later it was, during some weeks, billing 300 cars daily.[58]

The very nature of perishables traffic demanded the most expeditious handling, which only the railroads at that time could provide. On the other hand, much business that was not time-sensitive was susceptible to the competition of water carriers, a problem exacerbated for the SP and other railroads by the opening of the Panama Canal in 1914. Julius Kruttschnitt anticipated the need to reduce operating costs on SP's Sunset Route in order for the company to more adequately meet the threat. He contemplated "a reciprocal trackage agreement" with the Atchison, Topeka & Santa Fe using the most efficient lines of the

The SP joined the Union Pacific on an equal basis to form the Pacific Fruit Express Company. Business was good; PFE handled seventy thousand carloads of Pacific Coast perishables in 1913 alone. Here a fruit block is just east of Roseville, California.

two roads between Galveston and San Francisco via Mojave. He also planned extensive grade reductions in Texas on the 122-mile route between San Antonio and Glidden. Sad to say, nothing came of the joint venture, the Texas project was postponed, and other proposals for upgrading the SP to meet steamship competition were put off or canceled because of the uncertainties presented by the un-merger matter. The negative impact of the Panama Canal on the SP was consequently greater than it should have been.[59]

One issue that would not long be postponed involved the location of general offices in San Francisco. Space in the Flood Building, rebuilt after the 1906 earthquake and fire, was both inadequate and expensive. Moreover, SP's lease was subject to expiration in 1917. Relocation studies began in 1913; three years later SP announced the construction of a new ten-story, E-shaped general office building on the south side of Market Street near the Ferry Building. Of Class A construction, the new structure rested on 60 lineal miles of piling driven to a depth of 130 feet and was

ready for occupancy in September, 1917. Each office in the building faced daylight. The company boasted that the 280,000-square-foot structure was "one of the largest office buildings west of Chicago." It cost $1,878,881.[60]

The matter of safety, so forcefully advanced by E. H. Harriman, continued to be of great interest to his successors at SP. The company's management actively promoted a campaign of "Safety First" among its employees, made "generous expenditures for safety devices," and enthusiastically reported as much to the shareholders. When the derailment of a mixed train in June, 1914, cost a passenger his life, it was the first fatality among patrons in nearly six years. Indeed, SP's record in accident prevention earned for it the American Museum of Safety's first annual E. H. Harriman Gold Medal in 1913. Safety campaigns, of course, were not directed solely toward the secure passage of patrons; they also focused on safe habits among workers. Small wonder. Railroading was a dangerous business. From 1908 through 1914 SP employees who lost their lives in service numbered 123.[61]

Safety was only one of many themes stressed by the *Bulletin*, SP's company publication, which issued its first number on November 20, 1913. Other topics were predictable and reflected the business and management ethos of the times: loyalty to the company, means by which a person could improve himself within the company, and opportunities for employees to solicit business on behalf of the company. The *Bulletin* also contained stories dealing with events and circumstances that involved the railroad, stories related to vacation and tourist travel to locations on the SP, as well as notices regarding SP passenger trains and those operated by principal connections. The new magazine also provided a vehicle for management to disseminate information and for it to communicate the company's side of stories (such as unmerger) to employees.[62]

Like railroad managers elsewhere during those years, SP's general officers were forced to spend an increased portion of their time on issues that were inextricably linked—rates, regulation, demands of labor, and dividends. The public, whether its complaints against railroads were based on fact or not, demanded and succeeded in gaining additional federal regulation of the carriers. The Elkins Act of 1903 and the Hepburn Act of 1906 greatly increased the powers of the Interstate Commerce Commission. The carriers, as a consequence, lost the ability to set rates and thus regulate their own income. Julius Kruttschnitt blasted "the demagogues and the well intentioned though unenlightened reformers," who together were responsible for the passage of "many unreasonable laws . . . which serve no public good and which add unnecessarily to the cost of operation." William Sproule tried to put a better face on it: "The era of regulation had definitely arrived. The principle of regulation is accepted. The question of what is good in regulation and what is bad in regulation remains debatable," however.[63]

Unfortunately, difficulties with SP's contract employees and with labor's demands accelerated during the teens. In 1911 the company experienced a general strike but broke it by hiring replacements for those who left. Strikes elsewhere were no more successful. Organized labor then adopted a new tack: it sought federal legislation to attain its goals. Premier among them was the demand for an eight-hour day, in reality a demand for time-and-a-half rates for work over eight hours. The Adamson Act in 1916 guaranteed it.[64]

Earlier legislation had curbed the railroads' ability to control its income; the Adamson Act, in essence, eliminated the carriers' ability to control outgo. Parity might have been achieved if the ICC had allowed rates to rise in relation to costs. Alas, it was not to be. In 1918 alone on the SP, revenues gained from paltry rate increases failed to cover increased operating expenses by a whopping $14 million. SP's operating ratio jumped from 62.2 in 1917 to a disappointing 85.8 in 1920. The entire matter resulted in the flow of investment capital away from the railroad industry. This, in turn, resulted in what Albro Martin has called the demise of the spirit of enterprise in the industry—a loss that sapped the energy of that crucial sector, diminished its capacity to offer cost-effective service in a transportation world that was increasingly subject to modal alternatives. Under the circumstance, SP's ability to present its shareholders with a regular annual dividend of 6 percent was remarkable.[65]

Events growing out of the assassination of Archduke Franz Ferdinand on June 28, 1914, quickly had impact not just in Europe but the entire world. At home, and on the SP, the initial result was a most unpleasant war depression. This economic downturn—linked directly to the outbreak of World War I—coupled with the loss of traffic resulting from the opening of the Panama Canal combined to sharply reduce SP revenue in 1914 and 1915.[66]

The situation then changed dramatically. Europe at war soon craved American produc-

Events growing out of the assassination of Archduke Franz Ferdinand finally drew the United States into World War I.

tion; as a consequence, domestic depression turned to prosperity. Industrial activity stimulated by the war in 1916 and 1917 plus increased traffic resulting from diversion of ships from the Panama route to transatlantic service caused a leap in revenues. The heavy flow of traffic was increased further when the United States declared itself to war early in April, 1917. The industry moved immediately to deal with new challenges by creating what it called the Railroads' War Board. This agency pledged to support the war effort by running the country's several and independent carriers as a "continental railway system," by organizing carpools, and by eliminating duplication of services. But problems were great. War traffic generally moved in one direction—east— and when Atlantic seaboard port facilities and ocean transport proved inadequate, rail cars simply became warehouses. A severe car

shortage was the consequence. The war enflamed an already difficult imbalance—one reflected by the example of Central Pacific's car 83622, which was absent from home rails for over seven years.[67]

With William Sproule as chairman of the Western Department of the Railroads' War Board, the SP took a special interest in the success of this voluntary association. Sproule promised that public convenience would be subordinate to national need, that government interests would have first call on all transportation facilities, and that the company would diligently seek to render efficient service. The movement of troops, especially, presented problems. Thousands of trains were required to move the "new national army" and National Guard troops to cantonments around the country. A case in point involved the movement of 18,500 men to Camp Lewis,

Washington, during the fall of 1917. This required several trains of mixed equipment, including baggage and stock cars; it confronted the commissary department with the problem of serving 40,000 meals en route. The undertaking required the cooperation of the Red Cross and civic organizations at twenty-two on-line points where the men were detrained and partook of open-air barbecues and other home-cooked meals. SP's dining car fleet was simply inadequate to the swell of such traffic.[68]

SP's San Francisco Committee of the Commission on Car Service meanwhile tackled the matter of efficient use of freight equipment. This committee forcefully urged shippers to use car space fully. "You need it. Your neighbor needs it. Uncle Sam must have it," was the resolute message of that group. "Transportation Will Win the War," it reminded. Company agents also urged consignees to unload cars promptly, to notify the company when this was accomplished, to pool shipments, to load cars promptly, and to load them to capacity or even "ten per cent above." The response was gratifying. Company auditors discovered that SP equipment was doing thrice the service of only three years earlier.[69]

Yet even this was inadequate. On December 1, 1917, the Interstate Commerce Commission recommended to President Woodrow Wilson that the federal government take possession of the railroads. Wilson agreed; on December 28 control passed to the U.S. Railroad Administration and to William G. McAdoo, director general. McAdoo promised stringent control and centralized management of routing and distribution of freight traffic as well as joint use of terminals, shops, and equipment. Kruttschnitt was understandably nervous about the new arrangement. There was nothing in the history of American railroading parallel to the new federal control; for that matter, however, there was nothing in American experience like its involvement in "the Great War." Kruttschnitt would keep a stiff upper lip. He reminded all employees that they should "continue to perform their cus-

tomary duties and to obey orders" of the regulatory bodies, and he "earnestly requested" that all hands "maintain the character of service on the Southern Pacific Lines so as to keep them in the highest rank of American railroads."[70]

McAdoo was firm. He expected "every possible effort to increase efficiency" as well as the "hearty cooperation" of SP officers and directors. Indeed, in McAdoo's view, it was "obligatory upon every officer and employee . . . to apply himself with unreserved energy and unquestioned loyalty to his work." It was a matter of patriotism. Railroaders, he said, were "just as important . . . in winning the war as the men in uniform who are fighting in the trenches." Only through "united effort, unselfish service, and effective work" could this war be won and "America's future be secured." The USRA's rallying cry was direct: "First of All, Win the War." William R. Sproule and W. R. Scott, among others at SP, were appointed by the USRA to positions of responsibility in the administration of the company's affairs.[71]

There was, to be sure, discomfort among virtually all railroad managers regarding government control. Critics of the industry interpreted this feeling as disloyalty, but when the *San Francisco Examiner* suggested that railroad officials hampered efforts of the USRA, William Sproule saw red. "Every officer of this company," he exploded in a letter to Julius Kruttschnitt, "believes it to be his duty as a citizen, besides being his duty as a railroad man, to do at this time everything that can be done to make the operations of this railroad a success." Sproule was still upset when he addressed the San Francisco Transportation Club a few weeks later. Such accusations were false, deceitful, and traitorous, he said.[72]

Common control by the USRA brought notable changes. Ticket offices in several cities were consolidated; traffic solicitation offices were closed; SP's Oakland Pier became a joint operation with Western Pacific and Santa Fe; the SP ferry operation now served WP and

AT&SF patrons in addition to its own; congestion on the Sunset Route between Yuma and El Paso was relieved in part by using the parallel El Paso & Southwestern as a double-track line; and SP's *Bulletin* became the Southern Pacific–Western Pacific *Bulletin*. Under pressure from the USRA, the SP and the Western Pacific, which for some years before federal control had been discussing the matter, also agreed to forge a 182-mile paired-track operation between Weso, two miles east of Winnemucca, and Alazon, four miles west of Wells, in Nevada.[73]

"Waste and extravagance are Germany's silent allies," said the editor of the *Bulletin* during the summer of 1918. His views reflected the wisdom of the day. The country, in prosecution of its war effort, after all, was devoted to both conservation and efficiency. Stenographers were urged to get the fullest use of carbon sheets; station agents were counseled to exercise the greatest care in saving and storing scrap wood; firemen were called upon to save fuel; engineers were warned against wasting boiler water; and section laborers were encouraged to cultivate "war gardens" along company rights-of-way. All employees were asked to "Hooverize" on stationery supplies. The ongoing campaign against lost and damaged freight now became a patriotic duty. Consequently, the director general caused to be established a bureau to check all cases of pilferage, false claims, or embezzlement; stealing from the railroad during World War I was viewed as stealing from the government. The National Council of Defense also asked station agents in California to assist in locating idle land capable of growing wheat. At the same time, SP's commissary department announced that, in accordance with a request from food administrator Herbert Hoover, the company would suspend the use of baked goods made from wheat flour on all diners. Director General McAdoo reflected the conservation movement as well as the country's move toward prohibition when he banned the sale of "liquor and intoxicants of every char-

W.S.S.
WAR SAVINGS STAMPS
ISSUED BY THE
UNITED STATES
GOVERNMENT

Waste and Extravagance

Are Germany's Silent Allies

They will help the Kaiser. They will kill American soldiers.

Every bit of waste, every extravagance takes force from the power America must put into the war to win. Every penny spent for luxuries and unnecessary things is a penny lost to the production and purchase of food, clothing, supplies, ships, and munitions for our soldiers.

As long as we spend wastefully, Germany will receive silent but powerful help from America; just so much farther away is the Day of Peace.

Don't spend thoughtlessly or unnecessarily. *Save!* With high wages and plenty of work for everyone there never was such an *opportunity* to *help yourself* and *help your country.*

Save to help the Government. Lend your savings to your Country—

Buy War Savings Stamps

—and drive out the enemy's silent allies. Put your dimes and quarters, as well as your dollars, at work.

Every man, woman, and child can buy War Savings Stamps—and keep buying them. Put all you can save into War Savings Stamps and watch your savings grow. *They are a profitable, simple, and secure investment.* You'll never find a better road to Prosperity.

Become a War Saver *and*

Help Yourself to Prosperity
Help Your Country to Victory

The editor of the *Bulletin* was gripped with patriotic fervor.

acter in dining cars, restaurants, and railroad stations." The country even determined to conserve sunlight; federal daylight savings legislation went into effect on March 31, 1918.[74]

SP employees found an amazing variety of ways to serve the national effort. Most remained on the job as part of what one officer called "the great industrial army." In San Francisco they packed the Columbia Theatre on "Southern Pacific Night" to see *Pershing's Crusaders*, and across the system they saved khaki and gray knitted articles "for the boys in the field" and otherwise supported the Red Cross and the Red Cross Auxiliary. Others volunteered or were drafted. Nearly 3,000 from SP's Pacific Lines family served in the armed forces; forty-six died in action. A standard service flag with numerals indicating the number of SP employees then in the service was proudly placed in prominent display at the company's general office building.[75]

All could participate and contribute in at least one way—through the Liberty Bond and War Savings Stamp programs. The SP advanced up to 25 percent of annual salaries to

The Fourth Liberty Loan Bond Drive was greeted with typical enthusiasm. *Collection of Harry M. Williamson.*

those employees who wished to use that money for the purchase of Liberty Bonds; the company was reimbursed through monthly deductions. There were several drives. Over 50,000 SP employees joined to purchase $5,218,500 in bonds during one campaign alone. The USRA encouraged competition in this regard and among specified western roads—the Santa Fe, the Union Pacific, the Rock Island, and the Milwaukee—SP's employees almost always subscribed more on a percentage basis and in net dollars. The company itself subscribed to at least $19 million. It also found more prosaic ways to encourage the campaigns. "Save Your Child from Autocracy and Poverty. Buy War Savings Stamps" and "Halt the Hun. Buy War Savings Stamps" were the injunctions of campaign posters plastered on the walls of depot waiting rooms across the

system. Such stamps, in denominations of 25¢ and $5.00, were sold in the general office building by the company librarian, who reported sales of $2,000 weekly.[76]

The editor of the *Bulletin* was especially energetic in boosting the Liberty Bond campaigns. "He who is not actively for America in these days is against her," he bellowed. "Idle money is enemy money," and, he continued, "idle men and women are giving comfort to the enemy." The editor mirrored the patriotic fervor of the time. Not surprisingly, his views darkened as the war progressed. In 1917 he joked that the Kaiser was "facing red signals all around him and is headed for the derail," but later he approvingly reported the story from an off-line city where a deputy sheriff took it upon himself to post his personal message: "This is an American town. Don't criti-

cize our President or our Government. If you
don't like our country, go back to your own
country. If you have no country, go to hell."
The editor urgently exhorted his readers to
know Germany for what it was—"the mighti-
est outlaw nation in history," one that heartily embraced "incredible barbarous doctrines
and vicious teachings." At home each citizen
should, he said, "weigh each question on the
scales of Americanism, and if it doesn't measure up discard it at once." The editor was
not alone in his growing hysteria. Americans
increasingly shed their idealism in favor of
xenophobia and other fashionable irresponsi-
bilities. On the SP a formal program of "Ameri-
canization" fortunately embraced a positive
policy of education instead of hateful discrimination. On the Los Angeles and Tucson division "school cars" and portable schoolhouses
provided educational opportunities for the
children of SP track laborers who, in the main,
were foreign born. "The children are taught
respect for the American flag, American history, and our constitution," reported the editor of the *Bulletin*. "This is a mighty good
movement," he concluded.[77]

The war, of course, brought a boom economy for the United States. Traffic on the SP reflected it. Material of war represented an impressive portion, since it took four tons to
maintain a single soldier in France. On the SP
military shipments were as diverse as Oregon's
Tillamook County cheese, northern California's timber products (for "the construction
of war plants and aeroplanes"), and steel for
the Pacific Coast's shipbuilding industry. The
railroad itself was at the highest state of
mobilization.[78]

Then, suddenly, the war ended; an armistice
was declared on November 11, 1918. Servicemen who had left their jobs at the SP, who fortunately survived the conflict and who remained "in competent physical and mental
condition," reclaimed their jobs with full se-
niority and pension rights. On Labor Day,
1919, for an hour and twenty minutes SP's
ferryboats "stood at attention" in their slips as

the U.S. fleet passed through San Francisco
Bay. It seemed a fitting salute to the "war to
end all wars" and to all who had served in it.[79]

Meanwhile, the railroad industry's nervousness with the USRA turned to fear as elements
of the country's citizenry clamored loudly for
outright ownership of the railroads by the federal government. Director General McAdoo
himself suggested five years of government
control following the end of hostilities, and
the Hearst and other newspapers began to
beat the same drum. SP's management was
caught flatfooted by this turn of events. It had
assumed that railroads under federal control
would be returned to their owners within
twenty-one months after the end of the war, as
the law provided. Now it seemed that events
might turn out otherwise.

Indecision among SP's top officers was the
immediate result. Epes Randolph urged that a
campaign be started on behalf of the railroads
to retain their properties but thought it really
"a fight between the substantial citizenship on
the one hand and the laborites and the irre-
sponsible politicians on the other." He hoped
that railroad officers would be able to stay in
the background. Frank Karr, Pacific Electric's
chief counsel, suggested that railroad managers quickly formulate and "advocate a concrete form of proposed legislation" that would
"protect the owners, employees, and the public." A program of public awareness and education was advocated by Paul Shoup. Kruttschnitt encouraged open discussion among
senior officers, for, as he told them, the matter
was "of the most vital importance." Gradually
a consensus took shape: Railroads should not
seek to escape regulation in matters reason-
ably demanded by the public but should, instead, attempt to bring about a more scientific, orderly, and just system.[80]

It is questionable if the Esch-Cummins or
Transportation Act of 1920 resulted in the
kind of system idealized by SP's senior officers.
However, under its provisions the carriers at
least were returned to private management
effective March 1, 1920.[81]

That did not end the matter. Government management had been essentially satisfactory from the standpoint of moving traffic but it had been otherwise from the point of maintenance. Rolling stock, which had been pooled for efficiency by the USRA, had not been adequately maintained by "foreign" roads, and locomotives had been pushed to the limit during the war years. Kruttschnitt was particularly vexed by the condition of SP's lines in Texas and Louisiana. Tie renewals there had been grossly neglected, and damage and inefficiencies were the result. There was an additional problem. The SP wanted Washington authorities to prosecute a claim against the German government for "war risk insurance"—in the amount of $42,347.22.[82]

The problems of World War I and the USRA became bittersweet memories as time passed. However, other events afforded SP managers no relief from problems—chief among them was "unmerger."

CHAPTER 6

Unmerger

> "If the impending hardship of having one's life work ruthlessly destroyed for no public benefit does not enlist your sympathy in *our* behalf, may I hope that it will at least deter you from helping those who seek, and have long sought, to destroy the Southern Pacific body and to dismember and feast upon it before even its corpse is cold."—Julius Kruttschnitt, 1922, to Gen. Charles G. Dawes

NEITHER the Wilson administration nor the Union Pacific Railroad had been happy with the agreement made in 1913 whereby the Southern Pacific was divorced from the UP. At issue was the Central Pacific Railway, which represented not just SP's part of the Overland Route but also other important arteries, feeders, and terminal facilities. The government ostensibly was concerned with the matter of competition; the Union Pacific, clearly, with reacquiring at least a part of Harriman's former SP empire and expanding its dominion as a result.

As 1913 passed to 1914, Julius Kruttschnitt and other senior officials at the SP were increasingly certain that the government would involve itself again in the company's fortunes. Early in January, 1914, Kruttschnitt suggested to William Sproule that "the present is a peculiarly propitious time" to mobilize public opinion and governmental leaders in California on behalf of the SP. In this way, Kruttschnitt thought, the Wilson administration might be dissuaded from its apparent untoward intentions. There would be no problem generating enthusiasm among most Californians, who continued in their love-hate relationship with the SP; they saw the company

both as an octopus, and as their own local road. In the main, Californians agreed with Kruttschnitt's argument that the SP and the Central Pacific were, in fact, "interdependent, having been conceived, constructed and operated as one connected whole." Neither company, promised Kruttschnitt, was self-sufficient. The prospect of a weakened Southern Pacific thoroughly alarmed the directors of the San Francisco Chamber of Commerce, who unanimously resolved that any proposed suit by the government to dispossess the SP of Central Pacific was not in the public interest. Across the continent, New York's *Financial America* approvingly reported on the "determined opposition by Californians to unmerging."[1]

The Wilson administration was unmoved. On February 11, 1914, Attorney General J. C. McReynolds brought suit in the U.S. district court to separate the Central Pacific from the Southern Pacific because, he argued, their union was in violation of the Sherman Antitrust Act of 1890 as well as the Pacific Railroad Acts of the 1860s.[2] The suit created an extremely murky environment in which SP's management had to operate. One day before the government announced its intentions, the SP had begun the sale of convertible bonds among company stockholders; the suit had an understandably chilling effect. Said one blunt Louisville shareholder, "I have no desire to increase my holdings in the Southern Pacific Company, either in stock or bonds, if a suit is to be brought by the Attorney General to divorce the Southern Pacific and the Central Pacific." Programs for improvements and expansion, confused since the government's decision in 1908 to separate SP from Union Pacific, were now in disarray. Among primary projects thus affected were the Natron Cut-off in Oregon and the program to double-track the Overland Route all the way from Sacramento to Ogden. Competitive conditions in central California posed another problem. Independent carriers there, particularly the electric lines, were cutting into revenues of the Central Pacific, but since they frequently paralleled the CP, they could not be acquired without violating antitrust laws. Should the government be successful in divesting Central Pacific, the SP could legally acquire these. However, by the time a decision on the case could be reached, they might be lost to competition. It was, at best, a dilemma for Kruttschnitt and his associates.[3]

The government's suit was of regional but also national interest and received much attention in the press. Support for the SP was impressive. William Randolph Hearst, whose jousting with the Southern Pacific was legendary, vowed to lend his inestimable support and to "preserve" SP's "views as convincingly as possible." Hearst considered that the public did not at all times receive its "proper share of advantages" and, in his view, when those advantages were not appropriately shared, it was "the duty of government" to help. However, that did not mean, in Hearst's view, the destruction of "combination and cooperation which makes such advantage possible."[4]

His and other newspapers soon thundered opposition to the government's suit. "The Sherman Anti-Trust law was intended to improve conditions, not make life more expen-

sive," said the *New York American*. In Chicago the *Examiner* quoted Talleyrand as it condemned the attorney general for action "worse than a crime—it is a blunder." Editorial writers for the *San Francisco Chronicle* considered that McReynolds was "bent on doing a great mischief to California and the whole Pacific Coast." The "persecution of the Southern Pacific Company," they said, was "morally ex-post facto" since the government was attempting to punish current management and owners "for wicked acts committed in the last generation by persons who got rich and," they added with consummate irony, "incidentally conferred a public benefit." The *New York American* thought there was "something awful about a government using its immense weight to destroy its citizens, its institutions, and their values." Other writers focused on the financial and legal ramifications of the matter. Theodore H. Price, in the *Outlook*, wondered if "the agencies of government shall become agencies of economic destruction?" An editorialist for *Leslie's Weekly* pursued the same theme. He urged "every security holder of the Southern Pacific, and of every other corporation whose interests are being jeopardized by the trust-busting program of the Attorney General, take up the cudgel in behalf of fair treatment for corporations that are obeying the law." Elsewhere, Kenneth C. Kerr, editor of *Railway and Marine News*, worried that the government's success in this case would "establish the most disastrous precedent tending toward the dissolution of various other railroads."[5]

The view of California journalists was remarkably consistent. Among some seventy-five members of the California Press Association, there was universal support for the SP in its contest with the federal government.[6]

Not surprisingly, men of business were positively alarmed by implications of the suit. "If the lines [SP and CP] are separated each of them will be obliged to expend millions of dollars to build necessary connecting lines and secure terminals," complained William H.

Crocker of the Crocker National Bank. This would, he concluded, "result in increased rates and impaired service." Santa Fe's E. P. Ripley expected "a howl . . . from the people" that would "surprise the government." However, he regarded the loss of the Central Pacific "improbable."[7]

The SP filed answers to the attorney general's allegations on April 30, 1914. The Central Pacific was, said company attorneys, a fully integrated entity of the Southern Pacific: the lines of the two companies were managed commonly, and they had been developed as one property. All alleged violations of antitrust were denied.[8]

The trial was held in San Francisco and New York during March, 1915; it lasted twenty-nine days. The UP did not publicly admit that it wanted the Central Pacific for itself but at this stage urged only that an independent CP would offer Southern Pacific some much-needed competition. UP's Robert S. Lovett reiterated his company's historic fear that the SP would divert traffic away from Ogden to the Sunset Route. Lovett had to admit, however, that UP's circumstances in 1915 were very much different from those in 1901, when Harriman had taken SP into his fold. Union Pacific now had strong arteries reaching Pacific tidewater at both Portland and Los Angeles. Moreover, it had an alternative independent connection to the Bay Area in the form of the Western Pacific from Salt Lake City. Lovett also admitted that the Southern Pacific was "working the Central Pacific very efficiently" and at no disadvantage to his road. Lovett likewise conceded that he was not certain the Union Pacific would garner more business if Central Pacific were independent or even if it became UP's own line into central California.[9]

William Sproule confirmed that, all factors being equal, SP preferred to solicit business for the Sunset Route as its longest haul. Important variables had to be considered, however. SP did not encourage the waste of ton miles and, depending on origin or destination

points, much traffic moved automatically via Ogden. Time-sensitive traffic to or from Central Pacific points likewise moved by way of the Overland Route. Sproule insisted that no change of policy in this regard had occurred since SP's separation from Union Pacific.[10]

Crusty Julius Kruttschnitt went further. He said that relations with the Union Pacific, particularly from the point of operations, remained as they had been during his entire tenure—"harmonious . . . cordial . . . cooperative." Kruttschnitt thought transcontinental service, passenger as well as freight, via Ogden was "the best . . . of any . . . in the United States." In fact, said SP's chairman, the Union Pacific connection at Ogden was likely treated with greater care than those made at El Paso, where tariff divisions were more favorable to the SP.[11]

Much that the court heard in 1915 was a rehash of testimony offered earlier in the government's successful attempt to separate the Southern Pacific from the Union Pacific. Several witnesses hostile to the SP recalled that it had been willing to sell the Central Pacific to the Union Pacific early in 1913 and wondered why the SP took such a dramatically different position now. It was a good point, and Kruttschnitt welcomed a chance to address it. He and other senior officers of both firms knew the answer, if the public did not. The attorney general in 1913, George W. Wickersham, had simply "used compulsion," testified Kruttschnitt. Only the energetic activities of the press and the California Public Utilities Commission had then convinced the government and, incidentally, the Union Pacific to back off. Kruttschnitt could not forswear an opportunity to add an editorial postscript. The current fiasco was nothing less than an attempt to "rob the Southern Pacific of its rightful property," he contended.[12]

Newspapers continued to watch the affair with great interest; all seemed to take an editorial position. The "continuous and spectacular 'kicking' of the poor old political corpse of the Southern Pacific Company is grotesque"—a fact, said the *San Francisco Chronicle*, as strange as it was barbarous, since "in a political sense the Southern Pacific Company has long been dead as a door nail." The same newspaper asserted that "never was anything more unjust or injurious attempted by the most despotic government on earth than the unmerging of the Union and Southern Pacific, and the attempted unmerging of the Southern and Central." The support of the California press must have bemused and pleased SP's management, since it had until recently been the state's chief whipping boy.[13]

There was good news for the SP on March 10, 1917, when the district court denied the government's petition. J. P. Blair, SP's general counsel, said the decision was a good one not just for his company but for all of the larger railroads, which, had the government's case been upheld, presumably would have been subject to their own dismemberment proceedings. For the SP the victory was all the more gratifying because in its fight it had been "backed by the sympathy and support of the communities it served."[14]

The euphoria at SP and among its supporters was short-lived, for the government immediately appealed the case to the Supreme Court. Before that body could study the case, however, the country's railroads became subject to USRA regulations during World War I—regulations that among other things demanded discontinuance of competition among routes and, instead, demanded coordination and combination. The irony was incredible. The SP and the Union Pacific *had been* coordinated and combined before 1913—only to be separated by zealous proponents of "trust busting." In any event, arguments before the Supreme Court on this case were deferred until the end of federal control.[15]

The Transportation Act of 1920, of course, resulted in the release of the railroads to their owners but it also strengthened the hand of the Interstate Commerce Commission in several ways. For instance, mergers or consolidation of railroads now became subject to ICC approval. Additionally, Congress ordered the regulatory agency to study and in fact to promote the consolidation of the nation's railroads into a limited number of systems. To this end, the ICC hired Professor William Z. Ripley, who eventually suggested nineteen large railroads. All of this, as it developed, proved timely for the Southern Pacific.[16]

Officers of the company, however, were concerned when Ripley wondered if SP's lines in Oregon might not be better held by the Union Pacific. Kruttschnitt told Ripley that the "loss of its Oregon lines would be a staggering blow" and UP's Robert S. Lovett advised the respected professor that "even if they were for sale . . . the Union Pacific could use the money elsewhere very much more to the advantage of the public and its own stockholders." Ripley dropped that idea but then floated another. Kruttschnitt was thoroughly alarmed, but Lovett was greatly pleased when Ripley proposed to place the main line of the Central Pacific with the Union Pacific.[17]

Lovett reflected on the idea and then dispatched a most remarkable letter to Kruttschnitt. Frankly, he said, "the Union Pacific would much prefer to be let alone" and, for that matter, he assumed the entire industry would prefer to seek its own ends. However, Lovett was pleased that the government seemed to be taking a softer line toward mergers. The very best of these, in his judgment, would be a combination of the Union Pacific and the Southern Pacific that would also take in "the Chicago & North Western and portions of the Wabash and perhaps some other minor lines." He felt strongly that this was "the most natural relationship of any and would accord with the natural lines of traffic"; it would be "the wise and logical combination." Such a merger would have another important benefit, as it would simultaneously "settle the Central Pacific question." Lovett acknowledged that rejoining the SP and Union Pacific "would be contrary to the decision of the Supreme Court in our merger case [1912], but" he observed, "so are all the other combinations as proposed" by Ripley as a consequence of the Transportation Act. Kruttschnitt was reserved in response. He had "not given much consideration to possible combinations between the Southern Pacific System and other railway systems." However, Kruttschnitt used the opportunity to remind his former boss that the SP would "fight to the bitter end against any plan of consolidation that involves the separation of the Central Pacific lines from the other Southern Pacific lines."[18]

Meanwhile, the government's case against the Southern Pacific, deferred since 1917, was taken before the Supreme Court early in 1921. The issue was the same as it had been at the federal district court level: should the Central Pacific be stripped from its historic owner, the Southern Pacific? The stake for the SP was also the same: could it long survive with the heart of its operations removed?

On May 29, 1922, the highest court in the land handed down a decision that presented the Southern Pacific with the greatest crisis in its history. The court ruled that SP's acquisition of the Central Pacific's stock in 1899 constituted an unlawful combination in restraint of trade and ordered the severance of control by stock ownership or by lease. Among other losses that were obvious, the decision, if carried into effect, would have the impact of isolating some 1,300 miles of SP trackage in Oregon from the rest of the system. Kruttschnitt and the others at SP were dumbfounded by the ruling and, for the moment, nearly immobilized. Two days later William Sproule canceled "capital expenditures on the CP unless essential to the proper upkeep of property."[19]

Fortunately, composure replaced hysteria, and before a week had passed SP's executive committee ordered the official family to go on the offensive, to gain both time and friends. "Raise as much 'cain' as possible in California," read a directive from the company's executive offices in New York. It was not hard to energize the California press, which was already alert to the issues. In a statement dated

June 10, William Sproule reminded journalists that the Central Pacific had been leased by the SP in 1885, five years before the passage of the Sherman Act—the law by which the SP had been prosecuted. Indeed, the two companies had been under common management for nearly five decades and had grown and matured as a single system under two corporate names. Many in SP's service area, but especially in California, doubted that they stood to gain anything by the court's action. Chambers of commerce and other groups quickly took up SP's cause—to preserve its great trunk-line system—a cause, incidentally, they perceived as their own. Soon there were three hundred such groups made up of shippers located principally in California, Arizona, Oregon, and Nevada.[20]

A new variable, one that had immediate as well as long-term implications, now presented itself in public. On the surface, at least, SP's sole opponent in the Central Pacific matter since 1914 had been the federal government. SP's management knew, of course, that the Union Pacific, its assertions to the contrary notwithstanding, coveted the Central Pacific not only for its main route from Ogden to the Bay Area but also for its impressive gathering and distribution system in central California. To date, however, the UP had remained as a shadow, maintaining a gentlemanly aloofness. Its pretense disappeared early in June, 1922, following the Supreme Court's decision, when Union Pacific representatives began to call on chambers of commerce from Portland to San Diego in what SP officials viewed as an unseemly effort to dissuade them from support of "the home road." After all, fumed William Sproule, the Central Pacific was not yet "actually on the market for sale."[21]

The Union Pacific quickly warmed to its task. President C. R. Gray pledged that the UP was solely interested in an "independent" Central Pacific "performing its duties" as "the westerly half of the Federal railway system from the Missouri River to the Pacific Ocean." Gray strained credulity when he said the

Union Pacific "was not seeking to acquire the Central Pacific," but his veracity returned when he admitted that his company was willing to purchase the Central Pacific from the SP "if fair and reasonable terms can be agreed on." Should the UP be favored with the Central Pacific, Gray promised to complete the long-delayed Natron Cut-off. "An independent Central Pacific cannot operate in Oregon" without it, he said.[22]

Those were only the opening volleys. As one SP officer later recalled, the Union Pacific launched a most vigorous and bitter war of publicity against the SP and certain of its officers. The campaign was led by Fred G. Athearn, UP's western counsel, and formerly an attorney for the SP. Athearn's position and that of his employer appeared benign: "A Plain Statement of the Facts" was the title of a pamphlet written by him and distributed by the UP. Athearn hired newspapermen, attorneys, and others; Stuart Daggett, respected professor of railway economics at the University of California, also lent his support. Together these forces advertised Union Pacific's contentions:

(1) The Union Pacific would free the West Coast from the clutches of a corporation that had never built up the territory.

(2) Central Pacific, as the western arm of the Union Pacific, would bring stern competition to central and northern California and much of Oregon.

(3) The Southern Pacific was a rapacious villain whose coffers overflowed only because of the government's munificent grant of land.

(4) The SP was attempting to evade the wishes of the Supreme Court in its Central Pacific decision.[23]

The Union Pacific's campaign, well funded and initially better managed than SP's, tended, however, to be heavy-handed and ultimately counterproductive. Athearn's style was abusive, and he did not wear well. By mid-August, Sproule could legitimately tell Kruttschnitt

that the "Union Pacific organizations" were "falling into discredit" and were "known as empty shells." Elsewhere, the *Wall Street Journal* frowned on UP's handling of the situation. Even Samuel Rea, stately head of the Pennsylvania Railroad, considered comments made by UP's Gray "ill-advised and inappropriate."[24]

By mid-summer of 1922 Kruttschnitt was willing to establish SP's own press bureau in Washington. However, he placed several caveats on its operation. As a matter of review, he told Paul Shoup that the Union Pacific's campaign had been conducted without regard for "any consideration of friendship or fair dealing and in utter disregard of the truth." In an oblique reference to the way he wanted the SP's promotion conducted, Kruttschnitt said, "I am willing to admit at the outset both our unwillingness and our inability to equal or excel them in their campaign of vilification and misrepresentation." At the same time, he did not want the SP to "follow up on every misrepresentation made by the Union Pacific and to rush into print about it. It would be undignified," argued the plainspoken Kruttschnitt.[25]

SP's campaign to garner public support and to gain time gathered speed: The *Bulletin* was mobilized to carry the company's case to employees, who were told of their losses should the Central Pacific fall to the Union Pacific. Rail patrons attended meetings at various locations and pledged to fight against dismemberment. And *Barron's* chided the government for failing to note what the American public already knew—"the trust-buster as a popular hero is dead!" Instead "of being an unnatural and vicious combination in restraint of trade the lease of the Central Pacific by the Southern Pacific in 1885 merely consolidated in the legal sense properties which had from the very beginning been constructed and operated as an integral whole," observed *Barron's*.[26]

Railroaders thus became politicians, in a sense, campaigning before large audiences and for high stakes. They understood this only in part, and as an unfortunate result took quite personally and were deeply hurt by the verbal arrows hurled by the other side. Kruttschnitt, for instance, thought C. R. Gray's "attack" on the SP immediately after the Supreme Court had rendered its decision both "unwarranted and uncalled-for." Feelings ran high. Personal friendships and business associations, rooted deeply in the Harriman era, snapped under the pressure. Even the internal reputation of Harriman was somewhat diminished during the late years of the unmerger process, as SP veterans, particularly Kruttschnitt, understated his contributions. Feelings of betrayal, distrust, and hostility permeated SP's official family and, rightly or wrongly, were institutionalized—to be passed from one generation of managers to the next.

On October 9, 1922, the Supreme Court refused SP's petition to rehear the case. This, on its face, meant that the matter would be mandated back to the district court, which would "give effect to the decision." The Union Pacific immediately took upon itself to spread this good news. Advertisements were placed in newspapers along Central Pacific's main line; they included "an announcement" of the court's decision, promises of what the Union Pacific now would do to maximize development of the region, and praised the fact that "Competition—The Public's Right" had been restored. Yet it was not a fait accompli. The SP had one more card to play.[27]

The Sherman Antitrust Act, signed into law by President Benjamin Harrison in 1890, mirrored a strong contemporary value of the time—unrestricted competition as the life of trade. During the ensuing thirty years a gradual reassessment of that value took place, at least as it applied to the railroad industry, and the Transportation Act of 1920 reflected the change. Indeed, during the brief period of USRA control, competition had been forbidden; and this was perceived as consistent with the public's interest. During that same period of federal control the SP properly considered itself in an ironic position—prosecuted by the

attorney general who insisted on competition and told by the director general that there could be none. In fact, the unmerger case represented a test of strong values, old and new, the Sherman Act and the Transportation Act. The SP had lost in the courts under the former; it now staked its life as a first-class railroad before the Interstate Commerce Commission on the latter.

The idea of seeking refuge under the new legislation had originated as early as June 1 when SP's executive committee, in review of the Supreme Court's May 29 ruling, noted that the case had turned on law current with the institution of the proceedings in 1914 and did not take account of the new powers vested in the ICC as a result of the Transportation Act. Ripley had allocated Central Pacific's main line to the Union Pacific in his suggested plan of combination, but the ICC's own proposal of 1921 called for retention of the entire Central Pacific as a part of the Southern Pacific. The SP waited until the Supreme Court ruled against rehearing and then, on October 17, 1922, before any action could be taken by the lower court pursuant to the mandate, made application before the regulatory body to acquire control of the Central Pacific by stock ownership and lease under authority of the Interstate Commerce Act as amended by the Transportation Act. This strategy did not seek a review by the commission of the court's decision but sought instead a new status, "lawful" control of the Central Pacific. The Union Pacific quickly filed a petition in opposition. The stage was set for a new round of jousting; the stakes were the same as always.[28]

The hearing began on November 21 in Washington, D.C. Nearly every western state acted as intervenor; this was not an unimportant intramural contest but one of substantial import for the entire region.

The Union Pacific trotted out its traditional complaint that Southern Pacific was diverting or in the future would divert traffic via El Paso and away from the Overland Route. The argu-

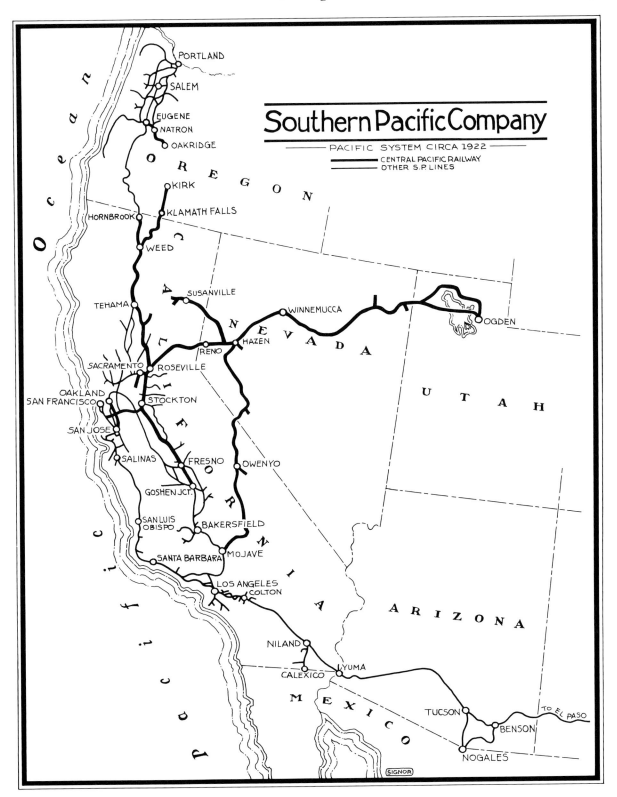

Southern Pacific Company

PACIFIC SYSTEM CIRCA 1922

CENTRAL PACIFIC RAILWAY
OTHER S.P. LINES

Competi-tion--

The Public's Right

Restored!

UP's jubilant if self-serving ad, which appeared in the *San Francisco Chronicle* for October 12, 1922.

ment was, for that era, conceptually sound. Soliciting for the long haul was fine as long as labor and capital were relatively inexpensive. Nevertheless, in practical terms, the issue of sending transcontinental freight via the Sunset Route to Gulf Coast connections, or even via SP's own ship line between New Orleans and New York, was essentially moot—made so by the opening of the Panama Canal in 1914. By 1922, only 4 percent of traffic on the Sunset-Gulf Route (i.e., moving via El Paso on SP's Texas & Louisiana Lines) could be classified as transcontinental. Moreover, in 1921 the SP moved nearly three times the tonnage via Ogden as it did via El Paso.

OGDEN GATEWAY
To Union Pacific: 1,332,000
From Union Pacific: 580,000
EL PASO GATEWAY
To SP (T&L Lines): 348,000 tons
From SP (T&L Lines): 412,000.[29]

The Union Pacific in 1922, let there be no mistake, was a formidable opponent. It was a well-maintained, well-managed, and well-financed property that owned blocks of stock in the Illinois Central, New York Central, Baltimore & Ohio, Chicago & North Western, and Chicago, Milwaukee & St. Paul and held bonds, notes, or equipment trust certificates of no fewer than thirty-one carriers. Its management understandably wished to protect the company's admirable position and worried that, if the Supreme Court's decision was negated and the ICC ruled that the SP could retain the Central Pacific, the SP would, or at least could—with impunity—divert traffic away from Ogden. "If they succeed, what is to become of this important line of railroad," wondered Union Pacific's R. S. Lovett.[30]

Much of the ICC's energy focused, not surprisingly, on the venerable Julius Kruttschnitt, SP's chairman and a man who had the advantage of having served the SP as well as the

SP's losses due to unmerger proceedings cannot be calculated. Not the least was the loss from its management team's being distracted for over a decade. Kruttschnitt had his team in Los Angeles during 1922; *left to right*: F. S. McGinnis, J. T. Saunders, J. H. Dyer, T. M. Schumacher, W. Sproule, J. Kruttschnitt, A. D. McDonald, Paul Shoup, G. W. Boschke, D. W. Pontius, T. H. Williams, and F. Karr.

combined systems during the Harriman era. Kruttschnitt himself had become very active in SP's campaign for support and was not without emotion. It was "a vital question" to him, he told future vice-president Charles G. Dawes, "as all of my life has been spent building up Southern Pacific properties." He hoped that Dawes and others whom he could influence would at least refrain from "helping those who seek, and have long sought, to destroy the Southern Pacific's body and to dismember and feast upon it before even its corpse is cold." Dawes assured Kruttschnitt that he would support SP's position since they were "unquestionably based upon justice,

public convenience and common sense." Kruttschnitt received similar letters of support from a variety of persons, including officials of friendly connecting railroads like the Virginia & Truckee and determined competitors such as the Santa Fe.[31]

Kruttschnitt, though, could be heavy-handed. In his zeal to protect and advance SP's cause before the ICC, he provoked a nasty and unproductive campaign designed to prove, in essence, that his plant was more tightly and effectively managed than that of the Union Pacific. What resulted was the distribution of materials that showed each to be a fine company but with such dramatic differences in

operating conditions as to make comparative analyses meaningless.[32]

Paul Shoup, by now an SP vice-president and assistant to the president, was responsible for monitoring the day-to-day proceedings in Washington. After a month of testimony Shoup perceived that momentum was moving in favor of the Southern Pacific. He thereupon sought a private meeting with C. B. Seger, a member of Union Pacific's executive committee and a former company official whom Shoup knew from the period of combined systems. The two, with the blessings of their respective companies, subsequently drew up a proposal that was mutually agreeable. On January 3, 1923, copies were distributed to the Interstate Commerce Commission, which forwarded them to all intervenors. After study and discussion, the regulatory body and most of the participants were willing to abide by tenets of the proposal. On February 6 the ICC then handed down a decision authorizing control and lease of the Central Pacific by the SP.[33]

The ICC, however, imposed numerous conditions, most of which already had been agreed to by the SP and Union Pacific, among them:

(1) The two carriers would, "as part of one continuous line, maintain through train service between San Francisco and Chicago equal in quality afforded by either party between Los Angeles or Portland and Chicago.

(2) The two carriers would afford parity of schedules and service for perishable traffic via Ogden, as opposed to their respective services from southern California.

(3) The two would cooperate in the matter of freight train scheduling and would not discriminate in favor of the Denver & Rio Grande Western or Western Pacific at Ogden or Salt Lake.

(4) The two would cooperate in the matter of joint rate making to protect movement via Ogden.[34]

Most importantly, the SP was obliged to solicit preferentially for the Union Pacific via Ogden on traffic originating or terminating

north of Caliente and Santa Margarita in California, south of Kirk on the Cascade line in Oregon, and north of the Oklahoma-Texas boundaries to the Ohio River and on to Buffalo. This, incidentally, was not appreciably different from the internal agreement instituted during the Harriman era to determine whether traffic would move via Ogden or El Paso.[35]

The ICC did not impose conditions regarding the Western Pacific but, to obviate any, the SP signed an agreement with that company which, among other things, guaranteed rates, routes, and gateways; provided for interchange or common operation of Pacific Fruit Express and Western Pacific refrigerator cars; and, reflecting previous arrangements that had lapsed following federal control, arranged to utilize the properties of each as a 183-mile double-track operation in Nevada.[36]

In the course of his testimony Julius Kruttschnitt had promised to complete the Natron Cut-off and construct new passenger stations at Sacramento and Reno if SP's petition to control the Central Pacific was approved. These were not included among the ICC conditions but became moral obligations for the SP.[37]

There was general approval in the financial world and in the California press. The ICC's decision, said the *Wall Street Journal*, "prevents disruption of the Southern Pacific and at the same time assures the Union Pacific of every service and facility . . . which it could expect if it owned the Central Pacific." The *San Francisco Chronicle* was pleased that California had gotten what it fought for and pointed out broader implications. The decision had national importance: The Transportation Act repealed the "Sherman Act as far as it relates to railroads," said the *Chronicle*.[38]

Yet there remained one very large hurdle. The district court, of course, had by this time received the mandate from the Supreme Court ordering it to enter a final decree against the Southern Pacific that would have the effect of severing the CP from it. Parties of the case quickly appeared before the court to argue that control of the Central Pacific by the SP had been made lawful by the ICC's order. On June 18, 1923, the district court affirmed that position. Politicians from throughout SP's service area immediately urged Attorney General Harry M. Daugherty to, as Nevada governor J. G. Scrugham said, "refrain from further litigating the issue." Daugherty accepted that wisdom and on May 5, 1924, the Southern Pacific and the Union Pacific signed a contract that bound them to the tenets of the ICC order.[39]

Not to be forgotten in all of this were the ICC's efforts under the Transportation Act of 1920 to suggest the structuring of the nation's railways into giant systems. Its early energies were expended simultaneously with the unmerger case before the Supreme Court and then the ICC commissioners themselves. For his part, William Ripley was intrigued with the possibilities offered by a combination of the SP and the Chicago, Rock Island & Pacific, which, as he correctly observed, might create a system "stronger than the Atchison [AT&SF] in terminals" such as San Francisco and Chicago and would at the same time offer the SP Mississippi River gateways other than New Orleans at Memphis and Saint Louis. The ICC's own recommendation in 1921 was also to combine the SP and Rock Island. Union Pacific's R. S. Lovett took early and energetic exception to that proposition: "The proposal to merge the Rock Island while leaving the Southern Pacific in control of the Central Pacific would obviously be disastrous to the Union Pacific." Lovett, early in 1922, was likewise concerned that merging of the SP and Rock Island would "mean legal sanction and requirement for forcing traffic between Chicago and San Francisco and even Portland down via El Paso."[40]

The whole matter was perplexing for SP's executive officers who, on the one hand, cov-

eted all that the Rock Island offered but, on the other hand, dared not enflame the unmerger issue. They chose the safe course. They did not advocate the inclusion of the Rock Island in the SP system but instead urged the ICC to make "the Rock Island the nucleus of a third Southwestern System" which, added the SP ironically, could be much strengthened by the addition of the St. Louis Southwestern Railway (Cotton Belt).[41]

Following resolution of the unmerger case in which it gained impressive protective conditions, Union Pacific softened its position toward the SP remarkably. Indeed, it no longer objected to combining the Rock Island with the SP, although it felt keenly that in such event the Rock Island's Omaha–Colorado Springs/Denver line should be severed from the much-enlarged SP. It mattered not at all. The idealistic movement to arrange and combine the nation's railways into larger and equally blessed systems died aborning.[42]

The gigantic cloud occasioned by the unmerger efforts finally passed. The Southern Pacific had survived and it was intact. The entire episode had been filled with ironies. Not the least of these were the strange bedfellows who assisted the SP in one way or another during the hour of its greatest need—California politicians and shippers, the California Public Utilities Commission, the Western Pacific Railroad, the Hearst newspapers, and, through the changes brought about by the Transportation Act of 1920, the same federal government that had harassed it. Other ironies, ones that would not become apparent until the passage of nearly sixty years, were similarly rooted in the events and decisions of "unmerger." None at the SP in 1924, however, were concerned by such implications now that this overriding concern had been safely set aside.

CHAPTER 7

The Roaring Twenties

"The United States is bounded on the east,
west and south by the S.P. and on the north
by Canada."—Arizona schoolboy, quoted by
the *Saturday Evening Post*

SOUTHERN Pacific's victory in the unmerger campaign was likely savored more by Julius Kruttschnitt than by any other person. His service had begun in 1878; by 1924 he was not only the tireless chairman of SP's executive committee but also the respected elder statesman of the industry.

Quiet and dignified, Kruttschnitt was without bombast. Patience and courtesy characterized his relationship with others; his "orders" to subordinates were couched as requests. He valued hard work and loyal attention to the company's interests, but he also understood the need for detachment. Kruttschnitt's hobbies included chemistry, astronomy, gardening, and golf. He was an omnivorous reader whose interests ranged from science to fiction.[1]

Making decisions was not a problem for Kruttschnitt. Written requests for expenditures presented to him on the road were evaluated and decided without comment; those he approved were stuffed into the right pocket of his greatcoat; those rejected, into the left pocket. In his massive office at 165 Broadway in New York City, Kruttschnitt pondered weightier matters in a more unhurried fashion, considering the details before making a conclusion.[2]

Kruttschnitt considered the most important duty of a company's chief executive to be the selection of his "official staff," as he called it. That required, he believed, "a fair knowledge of the functions of each department." Krutt-

schnitt also believed it important to, as much as possible, promote from within, and during his tenure the company fielded a remarkable array of "home grown" talent.[3]

Kruttschnitt looked for particular traits in candidates for managerial positions. He insisted that they have a fundamental understanding of science, the ability "to think logically and quantitatively" and "to write and speak clearly and correctly," an adequate understanding of economic theories, and "an unlimited capacity to learn." Other requirements, equally important, included "the habit of looking forward" and a "pronounced firmness combined with a high sense of fairness and charity"—essential qualities, said Kruttschnitt, "needed to control men."[4]

Kruttschnitt's definition of a railroad was disarmingly simple: "A railroad is a huge manufacturing plant designed to convert the energy locked up in fuel into work for transporting persons and property on specially designed roadways." Yet the business of managing railroads was not simple; it had become complex in the twentieth century because of rising wages and inadequate increases in rates that put a tight squeeze on the percentage of net that "could be turned in to the treasury." The problem of lower net returns required, said Kruttschnitt, "the closest kind of management and the services of very much more highly trained executives to meet all the money requirements." Small wonder that he counseled the sparing of no expense "in establishing an Accounting Department to keep track of earnings and expenses, to record the history of operations, to act as general inspectors to expose poor results . . . and to . . . work up cost data."[5]

Kruttschnitt declared often the importance of besting the competition and seeing to the needs of shippers. "I believe that in meeting competition . . . nothing but cold business conditions should govern, and we should seek by all legitimate means to retain traffic that we have enjoyed, and if we have not enjoyed enough we should endeavor strenuously to get more," he told William Sproule in 1922. Kruttschnitt entreated SP's sales force to encourage a shipper "to come to us and to tie him to us with bands of steel." He was not content simply to attract new shippers; once they were "captured," it was necessary, he admonished, to keep them satisfied. Kruttschnitt mixed with customers at every opportunity and encouraged them to bare their complaints. Only in that way, he understood, could problems be alleviated.[6]

Kruttschnitt similarly understood the need for positive public relations. His attitude toward disclosure of information about accidents is illustrative. Under the chairman's direction, SP provided the press with detailed information "developed by thoroughgoing investigation." This policy of directness and honesty resulted in a curtailment of what Kruttschnitt called "sensational stories."[7]

SP's chairman wrote much and appeared frequently in public as an exponent of the industry's interests. He was not simply an apologist. "If the railway is guilty of acts of omission or commission which are inconsistent with its public duty" the government "should adequately restrain and punish it." On the other hand, "when the railway is doing its best to perform its duty it is obviously contrary to the interests of the public for it to be subjected to unnecessary restraints and penalties." Kruttschnitt firmly supported the Transportation Act of 1920, which he saw as a means to strengthen the credit of the carriers and thereby restore attractiveness of railroad securities sufficiently to induce investors to buy them. He was dismayed by those who attacked the new legislation or urged its repeal. He was even more distressed by the ICC; in his view, it nullified the clear purposes of the act through maladministration. The 6 percent return on investment (later reduced to 5.75 percent) permitted under the law, in fact, had been negated by the regulatory commission's unwillingness to grant adequate rate increases, growled Kruttschnitt. The ICC, among its other failings, he thought, simply refused to acknowledge that federal laws regarding the Panama Canal restricted railroads' ability to compete for transcontinental business and that several of the states had succeeded in establishing "make work" legislation while forcing a reduction in intrastate rates. Moreover, concluded Kruttschnitt, the ICC was blind to new modal competition in the form of "freight and passenger motors."[8]

Kruttschnitt viewed SP's victory in the unmerger case as vindication of his support for the Transportation Act of 1920 and vowed to do all he could to make certain that the agreements made with the Union Pacific as a consequence would be carried out in good faith. Sales forces were told immediately and emphatically "to cooperate with the Union Pacific R.R. to secure by active solicitation the routing of the maximum of freight traffic via the lines of the UPRR and the CPR through the Missouri River and Ogden, Utah, as part of one connected, continuous line." Kruttschnitt felt the election of C. B. Seger, a former associate, as chairman of Union Pacific's executive committee to be especially fortuitous—"a pleasure that is enhanced by the conviction that much of the bad feelings engendered in the Central Pacific controversy will now disappear." If cordiality did not return, at least the two companies maintained proper and formal relationships. In 1927 executive officers and board members from the two companies even casually discussed the reestablishment of "the old association of Union Pacific and Southern Pacific in common ownership." Paul Warburg, a member of UP's board, suggested inclusion of both the Chicago & North Western and the Chicago, Rock Island & Pacific. Warburg skillfully argued that the four railroads and their subsidiaries, could be operated independently pending consolidation under a holding company. The idea died, however.[9]

With the unmerger problems behind him, Kruttschnitt authorized a plethora of capital expenditures. Among those long delayed by unmerger was the plan, dating from 1906, to double-track the Overland Route from Oakland to Ogden. Most of the congested sections had been completed by the end of 1914, when plans were canceled because of the government's suit. However, following the favorable decision in the Central Pacific case, 112 miles of second track were built and, with the new Western Pacific arrangement for paired track, the SP by the end of the 1920s had nearly 600 miles of double track on its 782-mile route from Oakland to Ogden. These splendid improvements facilitated a new speed record over the Sierra—when the government's mine rescue car was rushed to a disaster—and a new monthly record for traffic in September, 1927, when 54,107 cars were handled over the mountains.[10]

Consideration was also given in 1926 to the possibility of extending the paired-track agreement with the Western Pacific all the way to Sacramento. One of SP's directors, Walter Douglas, pointed out that Western Pacific's eastbound grades through the Feather River Canyon were much less than those of the Central Pacific over the Sierra, although, as he noted, the WP line was appreciably longer. Douglas considered that the Western Pacific could be used as the eastbound main and the Central Pacific could provide the other. WP's Arthur Curtiss James had not previously considered the idea but said his road would "cooperate in every possible way with the Southern Pacific." SP's A. D. McDonald

took exception to the notion: "Now that we have a double track over the Mountain, I take it that we have sufficient track capacity for many years to come." McDonald's argument prevailed.[11]

Another major uncompleted project dating from the Harriman era and long delayed by the unmerger matter was the Natron Cut-off in Oregon. When the government's suit had been instituted in 1914, the SP had acquired or placed in operation 160 miles of disconnected railroad from Natron, southeast of Eugene, to Oakridge, Oregon, and from Weed, California, above Dunsmuir, to Kirk, Oregon. The Natron project captivated the interests of Oregonians, who were sensitive because it was incomplete. Consequently, on June 15, 1922, SP's executive committee authorized Kruttschnitt "to make a definite promise to the people of Oregon that the Southern Pacific Company would complete the line of railroad between Weed and Oakridge, forming a part of the so-called Natron Cut-off plan, as soon as its right to hold the Central Pacific shall have been definitely and finally established." As quickly as the unmerger decision was known, the SP filed with the ICC for permission to close the 118-mile gap. Approval was given on August 15, 1923.[12]

Renewed construction on the cut-off began at Kirk on September 1, 1923. A month later Klamath Falls, whose citizens long had agitated for completion of the line, staged a celebration styled "Passing of the Covered Wagon." As a part of the event, local leaders and visiting dignitaries were taken by special trains to Kirk where, as William Sproule had promised, they were given a "show to beat the movies—a drama with live people in action." Some six months later SP announced that 32.5 miles of the new line had been built.[13]

The situation then became cloudy. The Public Service Commission of Oregon filed suit and also petitioned the ICC to, among other things, force joint and common use of SP's Natron Cut-off by other aspirants. William Sproule suggested that, in the event Oregon's

End-of-track at Kirk, Oregon, in 1923.

petition was granted, SP stop all work on the project. Kruttschnitt disagreed. He thought joint use would be objectionable, unnecessary, and unfair, but, he reminded Sproule, "our promise to construct the Natron Cut-off was unconditional." Both were appalled, though, when the hearing examiner went well beyond the scope of Oregon's petition; he suggested that SP's lines in Oregon be stripped from their owner and transferred to the Union Pacific.[14]

Another variable, introduced by the Hill Lines, made the situation even more awkward. As early as 1912 the Great Northern (GN) and the Northern Pacific had advertised a projected line of their Oregon Trunk Railway southwestward from Bend to Butte Falls and a connection there with Hill's isolated Pacific & Eastern stub. Rumors of this extension, which many including SP officers saw as the Hill Lines' plan to invade California, circulated from time to time. They were resurrected in earnest during the late summer of 1924 when senior officers of both the Great Northern and the Northern Pacific were reported to be "on a scouting trip in Southern Pacific's domain in Southern Oregon." This time the rumors were based on fact. The Oregon Trunk soon applied for a certificate of public convenience and necessity to extend its line southward from Bend to Klamath Falls. NP's Charles Donnelly told William Sproule that the appli-

cation had been made simply to "protect our position." Donnelly, whose railroad had become SP's favored connection at Portland and likely stood to lose more than it gained by the Trunk's extension, hoped, however, that compromise might yet "avoid a conflict of interests."[15]

Sproule did not favor accommodation. "It would give the Hill system a new entrance into our field of activity" and, he fumed, "it is one stride toward California." Sproule's fears appeared confirmed a few days later when the press reported that Hill interests had purchased right-of-way from Klamath Falls to the Pacific Coast. This was denied by Great Northern's Louis W. Hill, who insisted, however, that there was "an immense amount of timber to be reached" by Oregon Trunk's extension to Klamath Falls. SP's executive officers looked for options. They wished to protect the company's heavy investments in the Natron Cut-off from "direct competition," to "retain markets tributary to the new line," but at the same time wished to "avoid having the Northern Lines find it convenient or necessary to extend southward . . . into California" and a possible "connection there with the Western Pacific and Santa Fe." Accommodation was required, but what form should it take? Meetings were scheduled among executive officers of the various companies. Northern Pacific's Donnelly sat in on these but had already withdrawn his company's support for the Bend–Klamath Falls extension by Oregon Trunk; the Trunk, he reminded, was owned by the Spokane, Portland & Seattle, itself owned in halves by the NP and GN. The application before the ICC continued in the name of Oregon Trunk although only the Great Northern, of the owning parties, remained interested in it. Ralph Budd of the GN insisted that his road reach "Klamath Falls with its own trains" but offered the SP trackage rights over the Oregon Trunk extension to Bend. Sproule could "see no practical advantage in that." In the end, Sproule and Budd "agreed to disagree." The hearing officers' recommendation,

Great Northern's request, the Oregon utility commission's complaint, and various related issues passed to the ICC for judgment.[16]

One of the related issues was SP's application to acquire the Oregon, California & Eastern Railway, a short line reaching into rich timber-bearing regions east of Klamath Falls and to extend those operations by way of branches. Acquisition of the line was certain, thought SP's managers, to bring welcome revenues and at the same time serve as a block to the aspirations of the Hill interests.[17]

The ICC's decision was announced on May 3, 1926. The earlier recommendation of the hearing officer to strip SP of its Oregon lines was thrown out, the petition of the Oregon commission was denied, the SP was given the right to acquire the Oregon, California & Eastern, and the Oregon Trunk was authorized to tap Klamath Falls. But the regulatory body added significant conditions. The SP was obligated to grant the Oregon Trunk trackage rights over the Natron Cut-off or over the Oregon, California & Eastern by way of entry to Klamath Falls. The two companies subsequently entered into negotiations but were unable to formulate mutually agreeable contracts. Part of this reflected Northern Pacific's disenchantment with the Hill Lines' plan, and in time the ICC allowed the Great Northern to formally replace the Oregon Trunk in the negotiations and as applicant.[18]

While this was going on, work progressed, if slowly, on the Natron project as well as another smaller one. The original line in California, from Weed to Grass Lake, purchased from the Weed Lumber Company, had been constructed to logging-road standards, with heavy grades and tight curves, and was inadequate to handle traffic efficiently in the volume certain to result when the Cascade line was placed in operation. New construction, labeled the Black Butte Cut-off, 23.7 miles, was added to the Natron project. The costs for the Natron and Black Butte undertakings were enormous, 15 percent beyond estimates and authorization. The executive committee of the board took an exceedingly dim view of the matter. Sproule told chief engineer George W. Boschke early in 1926 "that no dollar may be spent except where it will be of telling value beyond debate." Boschke was hard pressed. He told Sproule that the country between Oakridge and the summit of the Cascades was so difficult as to "make closer estimates impossible." Slides, he noted, were a constant problem.[19]

Finally, it was over. The Cascade Line was officially completed on August 7, 1926, although, to allow for proper settling of the roadbed, through passenger service would not be instituted until the following spring. The cost was a staggering $39.4 million, but Cascade's advantages over the older Siskiyou Line were great—shorter by 25 miles between San Francisco and Portland and easier by far in grades and curvature. Eugene staged an appropriate "Trail to Rail" celebration to commemorate the event.[20]

For the SP there was no time to celebrate. Problems with the Oregon Trunk remained, and presently to these was added a threat from the Oregon Public Utility Commission to reopen the Central Pacific case for the purpose of demanding construction by the SP of what it called a "cross-state line" (east-west line across the center of Oregon).

Arduous negotiations among executives of the SP and Great Northern failed to resolve the matter of the Hill Lines' entry into Klamath Falls. Political conditions did not favor the SP. Furthermore, Ralph Budd proved a stern negotiator for the opposition. The situation dragged on. Public relations campaigns and even ICC intervention failed to resolve the issue. Ultimately, public opinion and political pressure forced a decision that favored the Great Northern against the SP. As a consequence, the Great Northern built a new line from Bend to Chemult and reached Klamath Falls by "equal joint use" of 72 miles of SP's new Cascade Line. The Great Northern gained another important concession when SP sold one-half interest in its recently acquired Ore-

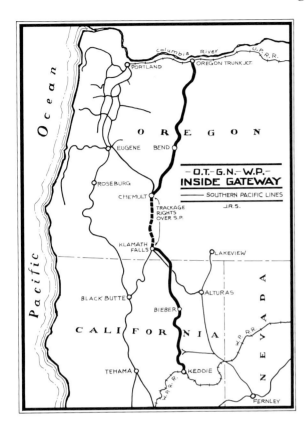

gon, California & Eastern Railway. Formal contracts were signed on November 18, 1927; the first GN train rolled into Klamath Falls on May 6, 1928.[21]

Oregonians were similarly interested in a related construction project undertaken by the SP. In 1911 the company had quietly sent a reconnaissance party to study the country between Fernley, Nevada, and Klamath Falls because the SP was interested in the potential movement of forest products traffic from the Susanville, California, area and also in sealing off that region from possible incursions by the Western Pacific and the Great Northern. The Western Pacific, after all, was nearby at Keddie, and the Great Northern, through the Oregon Trunk, was then building southward to Bend. SP's management fully believed the Oregon Trunk would continue into the Susanville area because the Weyerhaeuser Company, with which the Hill Lines had strong ties, had purchased holdings there.[22]

The SP had already reached into the Susan-

ville region during 1912 when it completed a line from the southeast but thereafter had deferred additional construction because of the government's unmerger suits. However, the company retained a commercial and strategic interest in the country above Susanville to Klamath Falls and in its survey between these two points. Agitation for rail service among those living in Klamath Falls and to the southeast grew during the early 1920s when these citizens became increasingly discontent with SP's promises and demanded action. There were other considerations. Since 1913, when the SP and the Union Pacific had been separated, the UP had energetically solicited Oregon traffic via its lines to Portland against SP's right-angle route via Roseville. A Klamath Falls–Susanville–Fernley line would, SP officers understood, simultaneously serve to attract transcontinental traffic, save ton miles, and frustrate potential competition. In 1922 Julius Kruttschnitt pledged the SP to build such a route.[23]

Kruttschnitt had second thoughts a year later when construction costs on the Cascade Line proved "much higher than had been imagined." However, by the summer of 1925, SP's executive officers felt compelled to go forward, albeit nervously, with the proposal as a part of the Natron, the Oregon, California & Eastern, the Oregon Trunk, and other proceedings before the ICC at that time. The regulatory agency quickly gave its blessing.[24]

The Modoc Line, as the Klamath Falls–Fernley line was called, involved a curious combination of old and new. On October 8, 1926, the SP acquired control of the narrow-gauge Nevada-California-Oregon Railway (NCO), which owned a rickety road from Reno to Wendel, California, on SP's Fernley-Susanville line, and on to Lakeview, Oregon, via Alturas. The SP, of course, faced the requirement of standard gauging the railway as well as providing new construction from Klamath Falls to Alturas. Internal indecision coupled with regulatory confusion in the Oregon Trunk–Great Northern matters delayed plans and even threatened their completion. SP's management carefully studied potential traffic volumes and patterns. Frankly, there would be little local traffic on the Modoc, especially from Fernley to Alturas; the new line would be dependent on overhead traffic heavily oriented to the timber industry. Much of the internal speculation centered on a double-edged question: What would happen to competitive traffic if the Modoc Line were *not* built and if the Oregon Trunk–Great Northern finally reached southward to Klamath Falls—or beyond? Sproule had cold feet. "I am frank to say that where so much money is involved I am less and less disposed to be pressed into conclusions in apprehension of what a competitor might do," he confided to A. D. McDonald. Ultimately the fate of the Modoc Line rested with the Union Pacific and the divisions it would permit on traffic moving to it via the new route. "Whatever we hold as against the Great Northern or gain through development of business that otherwise would not be created inures substantially as much to your benefit as ours and possibly more," William Sproule told Union Pacific's C. R. Gray.[25]

The Union Pacific saw it likewise and agreed to the same rate divisions the two roads shared on Oregon traffic moving via the historic if long-mile route through Roseville. Paul Shoup recommended going ahead with the project although its immediate and even ultimate benefits were unclear. "I dislike very much to recommend the expenditure of this large sum of money under existing conditions for a line that is almost altogether dependent" on a single industry for its traffic base. Nevertheless, on May 18, 1928, SP's executive committee authorized the company's chief engineer to make final surveys. Work commenced on the new construction between Klamath Falls and Alturas in January, 1929, and in the following summer the gauge of the NCO was changed from narrow to standard. The Modoc Line was "turned over for operation" on September 15 following appropriate ceremonies. There was limited rejoicing among

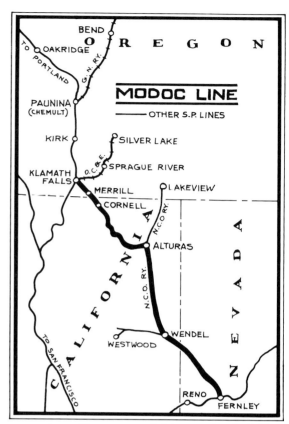

executive officers; acquisition and rehabilitation of the Nevada-California-Oregon plus new construction necessary to form the Modoc had cost nearly $16 million, well above estimates.[26]

The saga of railroad expansion in southern Oregon and Northern California was extended in 1929 when SP's chief rivals in that territory, the Western Pacific and the Great Northern, applied to the ICC for permission to expand their respective lines to form a joint operation, an "inside gateway" between the Pacific Northwest and the Bay Area via Bieber, California. The Southern Pacific understandably saw this as "unnecessary duplication" of rail operations, but the GN and WP countered by promising to run Great Northern's famous *Empire Builder* as well as through passenger trains from Vancouver and Seattle into San Francisco if the request was granted. The Santa Fe was not disinterested in this; it agreed to establish joint rates and divisions on through freight traffic via Stockton, California. In the end, the ICC favored the concept of a new competitive route, its positive impact on a "new territory," and opportunities for additional passenger travel. The joint request was granted to SP's competitors. Paul Shoup was philosophical. "We have to face the fact that the public everywhere wants expenditures of money that does not directly involve it in taxation, and for this and other reasons wants more railroads, which at least give the impression of additional life to the communities served." As it developed, the Great Northern–Western Pacific's Inside Gateway never saw regular passenger service, and its long-mile route proved to be little more than an irritant.[27]

SP's management in the late 1920s also had to consider the Hill Lines in a larger context. During 1927 stockholders of the Northern Pacific and the Great Northern approved a plan of merger for those two companies, which was then sent to the ICC for decision. Sproule did not see much threat to the SP if the merger was concluded but asked Shoup for his views. "Unquestionably the new company with a stronger unified policy and one financial and operating program will be stronger than the two apart," said Shoup, who saw "no evidence upon which" the SP "could properly oppose the consolidation." Furthermore, "if it be one of improving service and developing their own territory by bringing more people to the West, the Southern Pacific as a north and south line on the Pacific Coast will be benefited rather than injured." It mattered little. The ICC granted the request of the Hill Lines but with an overriding caveat—that they be divorced from control of the lucrative Chicago, Burlington & Quincy, a condition they could not accept.[28]

During the same period SP quietly analyzed its own strategic options north of the Columbia River. In July, 1925, a management team was assigned to study the feasibility of constructing a line "from Portland via Longview to a connection with the Milwaukee Road" and with additional trackage rights over the rails of that company "establishing our own

line between Portland and Puget Sound points." In that way, as Shoup told A. D. McDonald, the SP "would serve the entire coast territory from Guadalajara to the Canadian boundary as one company." A new SP route above Portland would certainly yield impressive long hauls for the system but would place the company in severe competition with the Union Pacific, Great Northern, and Northern Pacific. Other problems became apparent after thorough evaluation. The costs for construction of a new line would be great, the Milwaukee's terminal facilities—which SP would likely use—were inadequate, the Milwaukee Road itself was frankly not financially robust, and overall prospective freight earnings did not look good. Accordingly, studies were terminated by Shoup during the summer of 1929.[29]

All of SP's experiences in Oregon and its strategic planning in the Pacific Northwest were of special interest to the Union Pacific. Relations between the former bedmates warmed slightly. Shoup told McDonald that senior UP officers had promised that they "would do nothing to invade our territory," and Shoup, in turn, told the management team studying SP's possible expansion above Portland "to confer with the Union Pacific . . . to determine how their interests might be protected." After all, said Shoup, the UP had "been friendly in [SP's] southern Oregon operations." The thaw continued. A few years later, for instance, the Union Pacific fashioned a new alliance with the Chicago, Burlington & Quincy for transcontinental traffic moving via Sidney, Nebraska, that favored the UP and SP against the Denver & Rio Grande Western and the Western Pacific.[30]

Elsewhere, the capacity of SP's route over the Tehachapis was brought into question during the second decade of the twentieth century. The Santa Fe complained hotly in 1912 that it was "suffering a good many delays" to its trains "because of a lack of facilities." E. P. Ripley, president of the Atchison, Topeka & Santa Fe, suggested in the next season that there was "getting to be a little too much traffic for a single-track line" and urged the SP to double-track a portion of the Tehachapi route, say, between Caliente and Bakersfield and between Tehachapi and Mojave. The Southern Pacific had already begun to acquire right-of-way for the second track, but William Hood remained unconvinced that it was required. The subject surfaced again during World War I, but when traffic dropped off thereafter, discussions ceased. The Santa Fe, however, pressed the matter once more in 1921 when it complained of congestion resulting in undue labor costs and delay to lading. The "very rapid development in the San Joaquin Valley within the next two years," said W. B. Storey of the Santa Fe, would necessitate "additional facilities." Freight tonnage handled over the Tehachapis was then essentially equal between the two roads, although SP's passenger volume (measured in gross ton miles) was one-third greater than Santa Fe's.[31]

In 1919 the SP began a bit-by-bit project of double-tracking the line eastward toward the mountains from Bakersfield. Business did increase for both companies, although disproportionately in favor of the SP except during the brief perishables season, and so did the congestion. In 1927 during the peak season—September and October—an average of sixty-five trains used the line daily, seventy-four on October 13 alone. Helper engines were woefully delayed, and many crews had to be relieved because they had been on duty for sixteen hours. The Santa Fe again urged the SP "to provide double track over that entire hill," but the SP, to Santa Fe's great disgust, moved slowly. By the end of the decade several passing tracks were lengthened, but only 24.5 miles were double tracked. Santa Fe then, on its own, sought to find a location better than one closely paralleling the existing line and even explored for a new route totally divorced from SP's.[32]

During the same years and stretching into the next decade the SP pondered again the benefits of electrifying certain of its strategic lines. In 1927 Paul Shoup considered as a prime candidate the Sunset Route from Los Angeles to El Paso, but the master study of that year contemplated only Bakersfield to Los Angeles (over the Tehachapis) and Los Angeles to Yuma. Based on statistics from 1926, SP's assessment favored electrification, especially if savings in transportation of fuel oil for steam locomotives, overtime, and rail wear were considered. By late 1929, though, there was no need for the increase in track capacity that electric operations would facilitate, and potential net return on investment was minuscule. That did not end the discussion, however. Paul Shoup suggested that gas from SP landholdings could be traded to utility companies for electricity, and Hale Holden wanted the possibility of electrifying the Sierra and Tehachapi reexamined. Shoup added for consideration the Peninsula line from San Francisco to San Jose, at least for the commuter business. The Sierra study was the most optimistic—promising an increase in track capacity, gross ton miles per train, and speed as well as a reduction in rail wear and general operating expenses. A decade earlier John M. Scott had urged Sproule to authorize a new alignment between Blue Canyon and Truckee, a seven-mile tunnel, and electrification between Roseville and Sparks. The most recent study built on Scott's logic, but unfortunately the timing was poor. Traffic fell off badly in 1930 and deteriorated thereafter. The General Electric Company attempted to rekindle interest during 1934, but, as Paul Shoup told its representatives, there was "no early prospect of our tackling such a job."[33]

Expansion of the Southern Pacific in the Southwest during these years took two forms—construction and acquisition. Of particular importance was purchase of the El Paso & Southwestern System (EP&SW) in 1924.

The El Paso & Southwestern owed its inception to the presence of an abundant and rich supply of copper ore in the area of Bisbee, Arizona Territory, and the decision of the

Santa Fe to locate its New Mexico & Arizona/Sonora line some distance away. Phelps, Dodge & Company had purchased many mining claims around Bisbee, developed impressive mines, and had constructed a smelter. To provide itself with adequate transportation, Phelps Dodge then saw to the incorporation of the Arizona & South Eastern Rail Road, which constructed a 36-mile line from Bisbee northwestward to a connection with Santa Fe's New Mexico & Arizona at Fairbank. A conflict with the Santa Fe over freight rates later caused Phelps Dodge to extend its Arizona & South Eastern another 19 miles from Fairbank to SP's Sunset Route at Benson in 1894.[34]

The country was increasingly turning to electricity as the twentieth century dawned, and demand for copper supplies expanded accordingly. To meet these requirements, Phelps Dodge replaced the smelters at Bisbee with larger ones at the newly formed town of Douglas, on the flats southeast of Bisbee along the Mexican boundary. Collaterally, the El Paso & Southwestern Railroad was formed on June 25, 1901, to take over the properties of the Arizona & South Eastern and to continue the railroad construction projects and operations of Phelps Dodge. The immediate need was to drive a new road from Bisbee to Douglas, but that was only part of a more dramatic project. There had been concern among Phelps Dodge officers that their Arizona operations were captive of the SP after it leased the New Mexico & Arizona/Sonora lines from the Santa Fe in 1898. To obviate this monopoly the EP&SW continued construction northeastward from Douglas to a new junction with the Santa Fe at Deming. That was not all. The El Paso & Southwestern continued on to additional outlets at El Paso, reaching that important location late in 1902.[35]

E. H. Harriman, who by this time had acceded to control of the Southern Pacific, watched these events without amusement. Then, when the El Paso & Southwestern threatened to seek an independent outlet to the Pacific coast, either on its own or through a cooperative venture, Harriman retaliated with various forms of harassment, including litigation. Harriman viewed the transportation enterprise of Phelps Dodge as wasteful duplication, but Phelps Dodge perceived Harriman's covetousness as the bullying tactics of a monopolist. Several years later Paul Shoup admitted that SP's "policy at the time had been a bad one . . . which resulted in competitive building."[36]

With its finances assured by parental support and lucrative traffic, the El Paso & Southwestern confidently expanded by way of branches and acquisitions. It built short spurs during 1902 and 1903; more importantly, it took over the various properties of Charles R. Eddy on July 1, 1905.[37]

The "Eddy empire" included several lines that, when taken together, reached from El Paso, Texas, northeastward to Tucumcari, New Mexico, with branches from Alamogordo to Cloudcroft and Russia; Carrizozo to Capitan; and Tucumcari to Dawson. These could be enumerated as follows:

Company	Miles	Dates of Operation
El Paso & North Eastern Railroad (El Paso to Texas-N. Mex. boundary)	19.2	Jan. 1, 1899
El Paso & North Eastern Railway (Texas-N. Mex. boundary to Capitan)	144.8	Oct. 31, 1899
Alamogordo & Sacramento Northern Railway (Alamogordo to Toboggan)	19.3	Nov. 30, 1898
(Toboggan to Cox Canyon)	7.3	Jan. 31, 1900
(Cox Canyon to Russia)	4.5	July 31, 1905
El Paso & Rock Island Railway		

(Carrizozo to Santa Rosa)	127.5	Feb. 1, 1902
Dawson Railway (Tumcumcari to Dawson)	132.0	Jan. 31, 1903

Most importantly, Eddy had enticed the Chicago, Rock Island & Pacific Railroad to extend its line from Liberal, Kansas, to a junction with his El Paso & Rock Island at the Pecos River, and when the two met there on February 1, 1902, a new transcontinental option—styled the Golden State Route—was forged.[38]

The El Paso & Southwestern rounded out its operations with additional branches, a short incursion into Mexico with the Nacozari Railroad from Douglas to serve an affiliated mining and smelting operation, acquisition of the Mexico & Colorado Railroad to form its Courtland Branch, and on July 1, 1907, lease of Rock Island's track between Santa Rosa and Tucumcari. It also built from Fairbank to Tucson, in 1911–12, and acquired the Arizona & New Mexico Railway from Lordsburg and Hachita, New Mexico, to Clifton, Arizona, in 1922.[39]

The former Eddy lines gave Phelps Dodge an outstanding eastern outlet as well as long-haul potential. Coal from the Dawson region was hauled to Tucumcari for use in fueling locomotives of the Rock Island and to the Phelps Dodge copper smelters for coking. Yet there were problems on the eastern portion of the El Paso & Southwestern. Water was scarce and what was available was bad for steaming. Indeed, during the Eddy years new locomotives failed to make a single round trip without severe damage to flues and boilers because available water had "more than 100 grains of encrusting solids per gallon" and "could not be made suitable by treatment." In 1905 it was "common for trains to be laid out in numbers along the entire route and extra engines" died "for lack of steam before they reached the crippled trains." The company finally solved the problem by building long pipe lines to bring spring water from distant mountains. Only in that way could the railroad be operated during the era of the steam locomotive.[40]

Julius Kruttschnitt, following the death of Harriman in 1909, felt the need to seek "satisfactory traffic arrangements" and maintain "harmonious and cordial" relations with the El Paso & Southwestern. This was all the more the case as SP's unmerger plague deepened. Small wonder that Kruttschnitt was concerned when Phelps Dodge took a financial interest in the Rock Island and when that road in turn looked covetously toward California.[41]

Matters remained relatively stable until the spring of 1923. By then the unmerger crisis had passed, traffic congestion on the Sunset Route's single track demanded resolution, and the El Paso & Southwestern's vaunted profitability was in doubt because of the glut of primary metals following World War I. There was another important local matter: the strong and growing desire of Phoenix to be located on a "main line."

The desire of Phoenix for a main-line railroad was played to by James S. Douglas, son of Dr. James Douglas, the well-known metallurgist and principal in both Phelps Dodge and its railroad. The younger Douglas, against the wishes of his father, Kruttschnitt believed, had fostered the development of the high-sounding Tucson, Phoenix & Tidewater Railroad and gained impressive franchises in Phoenix. Epes Randolph looked into the matter in 1914 and learned that the El Paso & Southwestern had "studied very carefully for several years past the question of building a line to Phoenix" but had always "decided that the building of such a line was not desirable." The EP&SW denied then and later that it was behind the younger Douglas's project.[42]

When it surfaced again in the early 1920s, SP officers worried that the Tucson, Phoenix

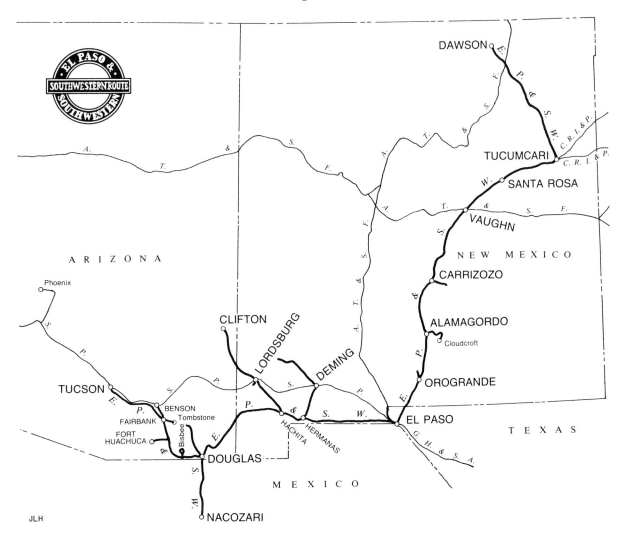

& Tidewater might be the "missing link" in a powerful new competitive line connecting El Paso and Los Angeles by way of the EP&SW from El Paso to Tucson and the Santa Fe from Phoenix westward. Harriman and E. P. Ripley had reached an agreement in 1904 to the effect that, as Ripley said, "the Southern Pacific should not construct anything north of an east and west line drawn through Phoenix and that the Santa Fe would preserve a like attitude as to anything south of this line." The Santa Fe presently assured William Sproule that it stood by the Harriman-Ripley agreement and had no involvement in the Douglas venture. Sproule was not convinced. He con-

sidered that an allied El Paso & Southwestern and Santa Fe—after constructing a Tucson-Phoenix line—would demand favorable connections and divisions with SP's Texas & Louisiana Lines that would "complicate our relations with both the Southwest and Southeast." Adding to Sproule's alarm was a story in the *Los Angeles Times* that correctly reported that the EP&SW had purchased terminal properties in that city.[43]

Sproule also had reason to be concerned by the public attitude in and about Phoenix where, said the *Arizona Gazette*, "the Southern Pacific has done and is doing all in its power to keep this valley from having a main line railroad." That organ likely represented local thinking. Its "platform for Phoenix" was unashamedly attuned to boosterism:

(1) Fight for Main Line railways
(2) Abate the unsightly weeds
(3) Iron and shackle the speed devil
(4) Sixty thousand population in 1928.

Items one and four were clearly linked. SP's management could ignore these feelings and local favoritism for the Douglas road only at peril to the company's best interests. "A real problem confronts us," admitted Sproule. It was time to go on the offensive.[44]

Sproule considered that there was only one way to defuse the situation—to appease the local constituency and prevent unacceptable competitive challenges—and that was to put Phoenix on a main line, SP's. To that end he suggested new construction to complete the Phoenix-Hassayampa line to Yuma, a direct Tucson-Phoenix link, and upgrading trackage in and around Phoenix to higher standards. Then came the big surprise for the public. An SP press release on June 11, 1924, announced "that negotiations between the Southern Pacific Company and the El Paso & Southwestern Railroad looking toward the" merger of the EP&SW into SP had "been practically completed." Petitions for construction of the new SP lines and acquisition of the Southwestern properties would go forward together.[45]

"Public information" meetings were staged throughout the affected area. Kruttschnitt, experienced campaigner that he was, insisted that benefits of the merger be fully explained and defended. The public relations departments of both companies went into high gear. Opposition, and there was little of it except at El Paso where civic leaders worried over the possible loss of jobs among El Paso & Southwestern employees, was effectively obliterated. *Traffic World* enthusiastically applauded the SP for an effective program of taking "its plans to all concerned" and of laying its "groundwork so carefully" that only two protestants appeared before the ICC. The SP also skill-

fully allayed fears among EP&SW personnel by praising them and the company's modern equipment, its substantial structures, and its high standards of efficiency in maintenance and operation.[46]

The effort paid off. On September 24, 1924, the ICC granted the SP permission to acquire "control of the carriers comprising the El Paso & Southwestern System by lease and stock ownership" and at the same time authorized SP's construction plans. The *New York Herald-Tribune* thought the ICC's prompt approval represented a "new railroad era" and approvingly remarked on the passage of the old, which had been typified by "railroad baiters" who considered railroad combinations an anathema. In the present case the chambers of commerce in every town along the EP&SW had supported the consolidation. This was explained, said the *Herald-Tribune*, by their faith in the SP: "The Southern Pacific has become a great and prosperous system through cultivating the esteem of the people in its territory and continually raising transportation standards." The SP took control of the El Paso & Southwestern on November 1, 1924, after agreeing to pay $28 million in capital stock and $29.4 million in twenty-year trust bonds to the shareholders of the Southwestern (stockholders of the Phelps Dodge Corporation).[47]

Construction in Arizona moved briskly as crews labored concurrently between Welton (37 miles east of Yuma) and Hassayampa and between Picacho (47 miles west of Tucson) and a point on the Chandler Branch southeast of Phoenix. When completed, the Phoenix line would, with the acquisition of the EP&SW, give the SP a much-needed second primary route from near Yuma to El Paso and, at the same time, grant the capital city of Arizona its historic desire to be located on a main-line railroad. Phoenix already boasted an impressive new station used jointly by the Arizona Eastern (SP) and the Santa Fe; it offered the proper setting when Phoenix staged "one of the largest and most enthusiastic celebrations ever held in Arizona" to cheer the formal

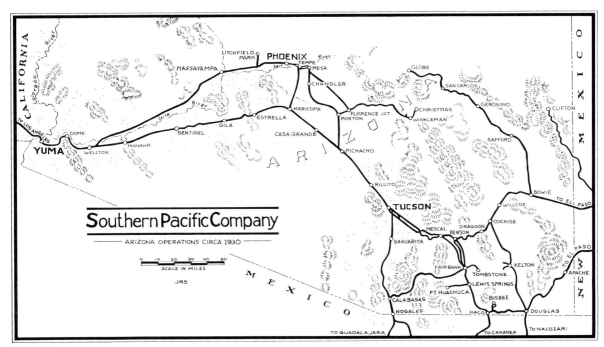

opening of the new line. Two special trains, one bearing delegations from California and another carrying visitors from Texas, arrived simultaneously at the Phoenix station on October 5, 1926. General manager J. H. Dyer announced that regular passenger operations would be initiated by the *Californian* on November 14.[48]

SP's recent activity in Arizona made the Santa Fe rather uneasy. In 1927 Paul Shoup and W. K. Etter from AT&SF reaffirmed the earlier Harriman-Ripley agreement, and a year later Shoup pledged "that the Southern Pacific would not invade the Grand Canyon either by rail or directly or indirectly through the agency of motor vehicles." For its part, the Santa Fe agreed not to "invade the Apache Trail" (SP's rail-highway tourist attraction between Phoenix and Globe). Looking to the future, both companies agreed that the term "motor vehicles" as used in this understanding covered "airplane service."[49]

If the Santa Fe was concerned with SP's intentions in Arizona, the SP was worried about those of the Santa Fe and the Western Pacific in California. With that in mind, Paul Shoup late in 1925 ordered the company's local offi-

cers to "determine what protective measures" might be taken within the next five years to "prevent encroachment" on SP's territories. Concern centered on Sacramento, Stockton, Modesto, Fresno, San Jose, and San Francisco. Most of these cities were already well served, and additional investment, whether to forestall incursions by competition or not, would be redundant. A less expensive way to deal with the issue was to wait until applications were made before the ICC and then fight them. This was the case when WP hoped to build trackage parallel to the SP in the San Joaquin Valley. In this instance, however, the Santa Fe joined with the SP to defeat the Western Pacific.[50]

The SP and the Santa Fe found themselves uneasy partners on other matters, too. Cooperation required soul-searching on both sides to find equity or, as Henry de Forest said, to keep Santa Fe from increasing "its takings and reduce ours." On the other hand, SP management felt itself forced to work with the AT&SF, especially when both could keep down costs. There was precedent for this. Under agreement dated October 1, 1900, the SP and the Santa Fe pledged to own the Sunset

Two trains, one bearing delegations from California and another carrying visitors from Texas, arrived simultaneously at the Phoenix station on October 5, 1926.

The SP gained full control of the picturesque NWP in 1929.

Railway in equal shares and to operate independently on alternating five-year periods the properties reaching from Bakersfield into the oil fields. The two had also agreed to jointly acquire and prosper the Northwestern Pacific (NWP) and on June 27, 1928, they jointly acquired the Petaluma & Santa Rosa Railroad through the NWP. Although the SP and the Santa Fe often combined against the Western Pacific, the three joined in 1927 to acquire the 54-mile Central California Traction Company, a third-rail operation between Sacramento and Stockton with a branch to Lodi. Cooperation between the SP and AT&SF took an ironic turn on January 17, 1929, when the SP agreed to acquire Santa Fe's portion of the Northwestern Pacific. Finally, in that same year the SP and its Pacific Electric joined with the Santa Fe and the Union Pacific in forming the Harbor Belt Line Railroad to serve the needs of the Port of Los Angeles.[51]

The SP also acted on its own to solidify positions or to keep smaller roads from falling into the hands of competitors. This was the case in 1925–26 when it purchased the capital stock of the Holton Inter-Urban Railway, a 10-mile pike with which it connected at El Centro. In another but very different part of California, the SP leased the scenic Lake Tahoe Railway & Transportation Company on

The cartoonist for the *San Francisco Chronicle* (Sept. 7, 1928) urged support for SP's drive to acquire full control of the NWP.

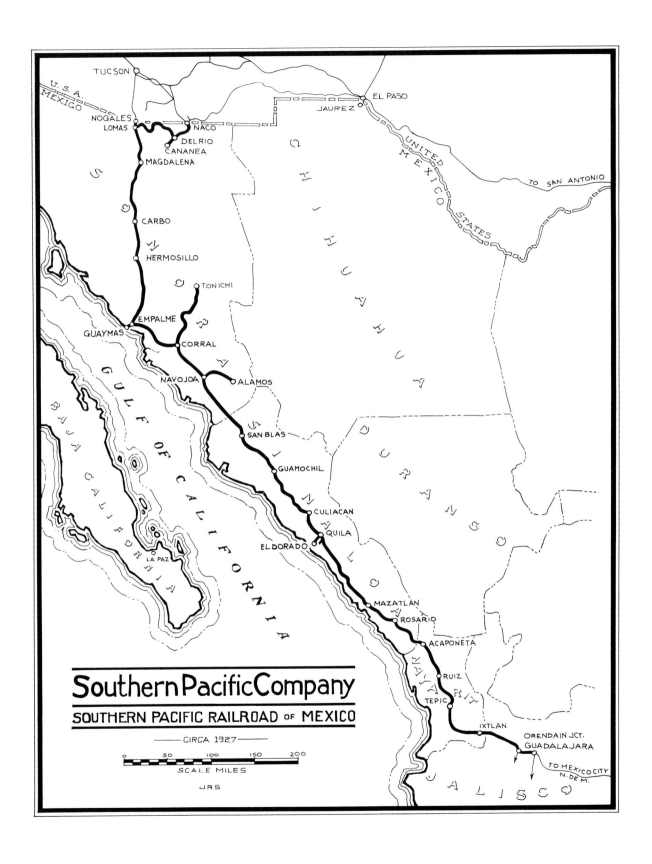

TUCSON

U.S.A
MEXICO

EL PASO
JAUREZ

NOGALES
LOMAS

NACO

DEL RIO
CANANEA

MAGDALENA

TO SAN ANTONIO

CARBO

C H I H U A H U A

HERMOSILLO

TONICHI

UNITED   MEXICO   STATES

EMPALME

GUAYMAS

CORRAL

NAVOJOA

ALAMOS

SAN BLAS

GUAMOCHIL

D U R A N G O

CULIACAN

AQUILA

EL DORADO

MAZATLÁN

ROSARIO

ACAPONETA

RUIZ

TEPIC

IXTLAN

ORENDAIN JCT.
GUADALAJARA

TO MEXICO CITY
N. DE M.

GULF OF CALIFORNIA

BAJA CALIFORNIA

LA PAZ

N A Y A R I T

J A L I S C O

Southern Pacific Company

SOUTHERN PACIFIC RAILROAD of MEXICO

—— CIRCA 1927 ——

0   50   100   150   200

SCALE MILES

JRS

Arrival of first through train from Nogales over the new line of the SPdeMex, Guadalajara, April 17, 1927.

October 16, 1925, and had its gauge changed from narrow to standard during the next year.[52]

During the 1920s the SP made dramatic expenditures for the construction of new yards at Eugene and Los Angeles and additions to those at Fresno, Roseville, and Santa Clara. PFE facilities at Fresno and Roseville were similarly upgraded, and passenger facilities also received attention. New stations were built at Glendale, Ogden (with the Union Pacific), Phoenix, Sacramento, Reno, Yuma, and Stockton.

One project that, for good or for ill, was not carried to fruition involved constructing new facilities, upgrading trackage, and modifying the general office building at 65 Market Street to become additionally SP's passenger terminal in San Francisco. Harriman had toyed with the notion of a new office building and terminal, and the issue had again received serious attention in 1911. Paul Shoup brought up the matter again in 1927, but for whatever reason nothing was done.[53]

Not to be forgotten during the so-called Roaring Twenties were affairs of the Southern Pacific of Mexico. As the decade opened, the SPdeMex continued to reflect the domestic difficulties of that country; only skimpy maintenance was authorized by the parent to keep portions of the line open. Work to restore and rehabilitate lines damaged during the revolution began in 1923 after various agreements were made with the Mexican government to pay claims presented to the railroad. Construction was advanced on the main line but went very slowly because of heavy volcanic formations requiring extensive tunneling. Finally, on April 19, 1927, the 1,095-mile line from Nogales to Guadalajara was opened to through service, with connections to Mexico City. All was not well, however. Raids by Yaqui Indians and bandits combined with acts of nature to disrupt service. Furthermore, affairs in Mexico generally deteriorated, and in 1929 revolutionary disturbances "which continued for several months resulted in heavy damage to the property" as well as lost revenue.[54]

CHAPTER 8

Signal Masts and 2-10-2s

"My blessings on the Prosperity Special: May her speed be steadily maintained and may God grant a safe arrival."—President Warren G. Harding

THE history of the Southern Pacific was not solely that of dealing in the rarefied atmosphere of strategy and intrigue, building impressive new lines and acquiring others, jousting with the government, or outwitting or being outwitted by the competition. Much of it involved the more prosaic but crucial business of running the railroad on a day-to-day basis.

Its communications system was of early and continuing interest to the Southern Pacific. Environmental difficulties—from desert heat to mountain blizzards, from isolation to congestion—had to be met and overcome by those who strung the lines and those who maintained them. Because of the impressive volume of perishables indigenous to its operations, adequate and reliable communication was more important to the SP than to other carriers. The company's telegraph system not only provided an efficient means of dispatching trains but, since it was shared by Western Union, facilitated a marketing system by which growers could ship produce when ready and sell it en route according to diversion procedures.[1]

Telephone dispatching began on the SP between Bakersfield and Fresno and Los Angeles and Indio before World War I and gradually replaced Morse systemwide. In a similar vein, the SP pioneered the use of "simultaneous telegraphy and telephony" between Sparks and

Imlay, Nevada on September 4, 1912. Printer circuits were added on line and before the end of the 1920s linked New York and Chicago passenger offices with those in San Francisco, Los Angeles, Houston, and El Paso. In 1923 the SP's Pacific System (west of El Paso and Ogden) boasted 7,328 miles of pole line and 68,991 miles of wire, and it handled an amazing 21,297,000 telegrams at 688 telegraph offices.[2]

In 1894 the SP general offices had but fourteen telephones, which required the service of only one operator. The operator was assisted by two messenger boys employed to notify those officers who had no "phone" that they had a call on the line. Twenty-five years later much had changed; the general offices then employed thirteen operators, who handled 10,000 calls daily through a $150,000 telephone installation. More improvements followed. On August 5, 1928, the "automatic telephone," or "dial system," was placed in operation there. The new exchange, as the *Bulletin* reported, was "the largest semi-mechanical private branch on the West Coast."[3]

At the same time the growing use of machines, for reasons of efficiency and economy, greatly altered office work. They also saved labor. In 1927 the SP owned an inventory of 5,462 office machines having an aggregate value of $1 million. These included typewriters, which made up the greatest number, but also machines for adding, calculating, dictating, recording, and duplicating. Most of these were used commonly among the several departments, although some required specialized equipment. For instance, the freight accounts office employed "key-punching, tabulating and card-sorting machines" to perform its monumental duties. *Railway Age* complimented SP on its use of such office tools, especially the addressograph, in preparation of time rolls, ICC statements, and paychecks.[4]

Southern Pacific's advertising department, already mature, reached full flower during the 1920s. In 1921 alone, it saw to the distribution of 6.2 million "folders, maps, pamphlets, and other pieces of literature advertising the scenic, industrial and agricultural resources of the states" served by SP. As part of a 1923 campaign to overcome inroads into passenger volume by "auto-stages, private automobiles, and steamer lines," the SP stressed the dedication of its employees to "courtesy and efficiency." This theme was repeated nationwide late in the decade. Special events received particular attention. On the eve of the sixtieth anniversary of the Golden Spike ceremony at Promontory, the SP, in a striking advertisement, pledged that "the 'Last Spike' Will Never Be Driven" because it was "Still Building With the West." Executive-level support for vigorous advertising was manifest in the department's budget—over $1 million in each of the last three years of the decade.[5]

Much, but hardly all, of SP's advertising energies were directed to its fine passenger service. "Four Great Routes to California Offered Only By The Southern Pacific" and "Go One Way—Return Another and See the Whole Pacific Coast" were themes that stressed SP's Overland, Sunset, Golden State, and, after completion of the Natron Cut-off, Cascade routes. Adjunct promotions stressed scenic opportunities afforded by national parks—Sequoia, Yosemite, Lassen Volcanic—and California's famous missions. "California for the Tourist" was an extremely popular and

comprehensive folder distributed without cost for over a decade. SP also advertised the Golden State's excellent hotels, among them the fashionable Del Monte on Monterey Peninsula.[6]

The Southern Pacific did not approach archrival Santa Fe in expenditures to directly or indirectly support art and artists. However, it did grant free transportation to several in the hope that their work showing scenes along SP lines would be shown prominently or published in popular magazines such as *Ladies' Home Journal*, *Saturday Evening Post*, *Country Gentleman*, and *World's Work*. SP also commissioned Maynard Dixon to do "a set of four lunettes on Arizona themes" for the Tucson station; Dixon additionally turned out several travel posters and folders for the SP.[7]

Advertising and promotional efforts on behalf of agriculture continued apace throughout the 1920s. In 1928, for instance, the SP joined with the Agricultural Extension Service of the state university to sponsor a fifteen-car agricultural train that visited twenty-four California locations. The cars were equipped for stock display and demonstration purposes. Professors discussed the advantages of diversified farming and of expanding current markets and developing new ones; SP representatives spoke to the close relationship between marketing and transportation.[8]

The marketing of California's burgeoning harvest of fruits and vegetables was of early interest to both the SP and its wholly owned Pacific Electric. In this regard, Pacific Electric, during 1915, purchased the Los Angeles Public Market and in the following year acquired the Los Angeles Union Terminal Company. Four years later these properties passed directly to the SP. By 1928 the Los Angeles Union Terminal owned nineteen acres of land, seven multistory warehouses and public market buildings, and adjoining shipping sheds.[9]

Sometimes the business of promotion could take a strange twist. Although it did not set out to do so, the SP in 1922 attracted nationwide attention through an order from the Baldwin

The "Last Spike" will never be driven

—Southern Pacific still building with the West

The 60th anniversary of the driving of the Golden Spike, May 10, Southern Pacific's Golden Jubilee, finds this western railroad still building. Weaponed with crude tools, courage and vision, the early pioneer had hand-carved a way to the new West. With the vision of the pioneer, the West has carried on, and with it, step by step, Southern Pacific has builded.

In the last five years Southern Pacific has built more new line than any other railroad in the United States.

In fifteen years Southern Pacific has built 1481 miles of new line at a cost of 88 million dollars. Of this, 40 million dollars has been spent in Northern California and Oregon.

Through the barrier of the mighty Cascades it has created a new north and south railway. It has double-tracked its OVERLAND ROUTE line over the Sierra. A new main line has been built through Arizona. From Wendel, California, to Lakeview, Oregon, has been broad-gauged.

Now Southern Pacific is completing a short line transcontinental railway through Southern Oregon and Northern California. The Cascade line of the SHASTA ROUTE

Thru the mighty Cascades

and the OVERLAND ROUTE will be connected.

From less than 700 miles in 1869 to 16,520 miles today is but one way of recording Southern Pacific's 60 years of work.

Behind this cold fact of miles built is the epic story of the development of the West. A story of progress indelibly written in the traditions of the West.

Across the desert—direct to Phoenix

Southern Pacific

Locomotive Works for fifty 2-10-2 locomotives. The story is surrounded by both curiosity and irony. The decision to purchase these locomotives was made, said Kruttschnitt in his usual straightforward style, "to avoid expected increases in steel entering into construction of locomotives." Intramural struggles followed, however. Company accountants urged accepting the locomotives later in a block to save interest payments, while mechanical staffers urged receipt in small lots as quickly as they could be shipped. The traffic department counseled delivery to the nearest point on the SP to save transportation costs and to receive the first twenty in a "solid train for advertising purposes"; the operating department fussed that moving a solid train of locomotives was "inadvisable and unsafe." William Sproule worried that "if anything happened to the solid engine train we would be exposed to criticism not only for the accident but for having promoted it." Sproule sided with the mechanical and operating staffs.[10]

Nevertheless, Sproule soon experienced pressure from the outside. Samuel M. Vauclain, president of Baldwin, and Samuel Rea, president of the Pennsylvania Railroad—which served the Baldwin works at Eddystone, Pennsylvania—both "attached the greatest importance to the benefits of the publicity that would be given to the movement of these twenty locomotives in a solid train." Sproule then backed off, agreeing that the first twenty machines could move en bloc over the Pennsylvania to East Saint Louis and thence to the SP's Texas & Louisiana Lines at Corsicana via the St. Louis Southwestern, but he continued to demand that the train be broken up upon reaching Corsicana. Meanwhile, the Pennsylvania Railroad arranged to distribute along its lines "over 10,000 copies" of an impressive broadside calling attention to the schedule of what Pennsy and Baldwin styled "the Prosperity Special." As the train headed west from Eddystone on May 26, 1922, Baldwin's Grafton Greenough considered that the

SP was foolishly "overlooking a wonderful opportunity . . . to reap the benefit awakened by the unique features of this shipment."[11]

Attention generated by the Prosperity Special as it moved toward the Pacific astonished SP's management. Indeed, it was adequate to convince Sproule to leave it intact as far as El Paso and to permit stopovers en route. In addition, he grudgingly authorized minimal advertising, including reprints of the broadsides supplied by Pennsylvania/Baldwin—modified, however, to omit the offensive term "Santa Fe type" in favor of 2-10-2.[12]

Excitement within the entire SP organization mounted as the novel train moved toward California. Fox Film's "News Weekly" included the story, as did most of the nation's newspapers. Sproule capitulated. The train passed to the Pacific Lines as a unit and was greeted at all locations by large crowds. It was the heaviest train handled to date over the Los Angeles Division, where three Mikados and three Consolidations were joined by one Mallet locomotive to lift the Prosperity Special over Beaumont Hill. When the new locomotives arrived in Los Angeles, they were put on display for two days at Exposition Park, where the SP invited the public to inspect them. Thousands took advantage of the offer. Sproule was amazed to receive numerous congratulatory telegrams, including one from President Warren G. Harding. Several industrial leaders and fellow railroaders similarly praised the Southern Pacific for, as Samuel Vauclain put it, "earnestly and enthusiastically backing and supporting the President of the United States in his efforts to restore permanent prosperity to all our people." If Sproule was embarrassed by this misinterpretation of SP's timing and intent in purchasing the locomotives or his own obstinate efforts to subvert the public relations potential of the Prosperity Special, he shrewdly camouflaged it. The remaining thirty locomotives trickled in over the next two months, dispatched westward over several roads that SP's traffic department wished to favor; the last four 2-10-2s

SP's management was astonished at the public response to the "Prosperity Special," shown here in Ontario, California, June 30, 1922.

left Baldwin's erecting plant on July 25, 1922. SP paid $78,215.29 per copy, f.o.b., or $3,660,765 for the lot.[13]

The Prosperity Special was only one of innumerable trains safely expedited along SP lines by way of its expanding network of block signals. In 1914 the ICC reported that the SP had more miles of such protection than any other domestic carrier. SP's inventory of them was almost 7,000 three years later, representing an investment of $4.5 million. The program of installation was slowed, unfortunately, by the unmerger difficulties and other problems but was renewed in 1928. Over 95 percent of the Pacific Lines' main routes were thus protected when the decade ended.[14]

As the company matured, so did its work force. Its retirees—alternately referred to as pensioners, veterans, or the "Old Guard"—

began to hold reunions in 1910 and continued them annually on the anniversary date of the Golden Spike ceremony. These were gala affairs staged at the famous Palace Hotel in San Francisco; over a thousand attended the 1923 event. SP's executive officers participated in them and otherwise exhibited a sincere interest in the welfare of former employees. For example, a club room was provided for the veterans in the general office building. Other space there was made available to the board of pensions, which itself dated from 1903 and handled a variety of benefits for those who had at least twenty-five years of continuous service and had reached the mandatory retirement age of seventy or had become disabled. Disbursements reached one-half million dollars annually by 1922.[15]

The Southern Pacific similarly found ways

to express its interest in the welfare of current employees. These included the establishment of clubs and clubhouses at outlying points, begun in the Harriman era, as well as support for the SP Traffic Club in the general offices, and the SP Picnic Association in Los Angeles. Sacramento's SP Band and Glee Club was prominent in the life of that important community, often appearing before charities and public bodies, and the Portland Division Employee Band frequently serenaded employees of the Brooklyn Shops during their noon break. The company also sponsored employee athletic teams for those interested in bowling, baseball, and football, and supported intramural track meets, golf tournaments, and even a women's General Office Indoor Baseball League.[16]

Harriman and his immediate successors considered the further education of company employees to be paramount. External opportunities took the form of courses from the International Correspondence Schools and the Extension Division of the University of California. Internal options included schools to train future station agents and courses to teach apprentices in eleven mechanical trades. SP's "Student Course in Railroading," introduced in 1914, was an impressive three-and-one-half-year laboratory experience designed to introduce prospective managers to "all of the principal departments of the railroad." Still another program, one that mixed education and financial opportunity, was introduced in 1922 when the SP approved an employee stock subscription arrangement that provided for monthly installment payments by those who chose to take advantage of it.[17]

As competitive pressures increased, Julius Kruttschnitt insisted that rank-and-file employees be instructed in the need for good service, good housekeeping, and fuel savings. Good service, he thought, could be promoted if members of the "SP family" were drawn closer and if each member better understood the nature of competitive forces. Good housekeeping was a natural corollary. Competition

was encouraged among stations, shops, and terminals to claim honors for cleanliness and orderliness. Competition was likewise promoted among engine crews and operating divisions in regard to the efficient use of fuel. Winning divisions were allowed to fly the company's "fuel banner," and winning crews had their names printed in the *Bulletin* and were awarded paid trips to represent the SP at annual meetings of the International Railway Fuel Association.[18]

Similar campaigns stressed safety. Contests sought to promote new slogans and pitted operating divisions against one another in pursuit of the highest rankings. A department of safety was established, and the editor of the *Bulletin* constantly stressed the issue. The rewards were gratifying; 1927 proved to be the safest year to date "in the prevention of accidents to passengers and employees of the Southern Pacific." An alarming new variable had entered the scene, however. Engine crews especially were confronted by the danger of grade-crossing accidents. In 1920, 57 persons perished and another 293 were injured in accidents involving SP trains and motor vehicles.[19]

Those employees who were injured in an accident could take solace in the knowledge that Southern Pacific often placed such unfortunate persons on jobs they could still handle. Several became crossing flagmen. Shortly before America's entry into World War I, the SP had 308 employees in what it called the "crippled class"; the average length of employment after injury was 8.7 years.[20]

All who were injured or otherwise in need of health care could avail themselves of the service provided them by the Southern Pacific hospitals. Such care had begun in 1868. During the following season a company hospital was erected at Sacramento; it was the first in the country established for the exclusive care of rail employees. In 1898 another facility was opened in San Francisco, but it burned in the earthquake and fire of 1906 and was replaced by a second structure three years later. Former station properties of the El Paso & Southwestern in Tucson were later utilized in the development of a tubercular sanitorium which, along with a new wing for the San Francisco hospital, were financed in large part through the beneficence of Edward S. Harkness, a member of SP's board of directors.[21]

SP's Hospital Department performed as a nonprofit institution in behalf of the company's employees and was maintained with funds contributed by them in the form of dues. Prior to March, 1920, these were 50¢ monthly, rising to 75¢ in 1922 and $1.00 in 1927. The SP contributed a small monthly supplement, and the department likewise received gifts from several sources, including Mrs. E. H. Harriman. These monies were adequate to provide payment for doctors, nurses, drugs, and all food and other supplies necessary for the operation of the central hospitals as well as fifteen emergency facilities at outlying points.[22]

In spite of its progressive if paternalistic labor policy, the SP, like sister systems across the country, was confronted with unrest and periodic strikes. Before the beginning of the twentieth century the SP came to embrace the "Brown System" of regulating employees' efficiency. Named for George R. Brown of the Fall Brook Railway, the system ostensibly represented a change from the punitive to the corrective system of discipline. However, even under the Brown System an employee was subject to summary dismissal for "disloyalty, dishonesty, intemperance, insubordination, wilful neglect, gross carelessness, immorality, violation of rules resulting in the destruction of company property, making false statements concerning matters under investigation," and the like. When engine and train crews threatened strikes in 1916, William Sproule appealed to all other crafts to bring pressure on their brethren to forestall a disruption. He also issued an implied threat: he hoped the men would "seriously consider their positions, their pensions, their transportation privileges and the welfare of their families."

Striking, in his view, was both disloyal and insubordinate—adequate reasons for dismissal. Not surprisingly, Sproule and most others in railroad management at the time saw the unauthorized strike by switchmen in 1920 as a "war on the American people."[23]

A more ominous situation presented itself in 1922 when shop workers threatened a nationwide walkout. J. H. Dyer's view was that the SP and its employees owed "a duty to the public to render uninterrupted transportation" and suggested that wage increases mandated by the Railroad Labor Board and the USRA since 1917 had been at least adequate and probably generous. At the same time, he noted, SP's operating ratio of 62.17 in 1917 had risen alarmingly to 85.27 in 1920 and stood at 78.88 the next year. SP's situation was mirrored collectively; the carriers therefore argued for reduction in wages because of slack revenues that reflected the postwar recession. Emotions heightened. On July 1, 1922, the shop unions struck over the decision of the United States Railroad Labor Board to lower wages to 1920 scales. Most of SP's shopmen stayed on the job although the strike itself lasted several weeks. It had a great impact on the competition, but the SP was shut down only sixty-seven hours; no passenger trains were annulled and embargoes affected perishable and livestock shipments only briefly. Employees who stayed on received "recognition payments," but deep scars remained. Paternalism gradually passed—to be replaced by a more antagonistic and confrontational style of labor-management relations.[24]

The Southern Pacific Company, virtually from the beginning, was more than a railway. Its vast landholdings—gained in large measure as a grant from a people and government intent on opening the vast resources of the West by way of railroad transportation built at the earliest possible date—provided numerous nontransportation opportunities for SP managers. To locate significant mineral deposits on land owned by the SP and to maximize development of coal and oil resources for the company's fleet of locomotives, a geological department was established in 1898. Its earliest work was done in Mexico and in Texas, but during 1902 the department turned its attention to Kern County, California, where, strangely, the company was disposing land of oil-bearing potential at only grazing land prices. In 1909 Harriman ordered that a complete geological survey of all company lands in California, Nevada, and Utah be made for classification as to oil, mineral, or other valuable rock deposits. Additional work conducted by the department included investigations for water supply and ballast material. In 1926 these tasks were performed by a team of company geologists and mining engineers.[25]

Nevertheless, SP's interest in maturing its nonrailroad properties, particularly those in the western San Joaquin Basin, was inexplicably slow. As early as 1893 C. P. Huntington had been told that company oil lands were likely worth more than the entire railroad. Apparently, he was unmoved because the SP—even as it converted its locomotives from coal-fired to oil—continued to sell these valuable lands. Company geologists easily confirmed the mineral value of the properties, and finally, in 1903, SP established the Kern Trading & Oil Company, a subsidiary. Kern was responsible for developing the oil lands but did not take title to them. Ultimately, its assets and responsibilities passed to another subsidiary, the Southern Pacific Land Company, established on February 12, 1912. For that matter, all of SP's oil properties and its significant holding in an outside company, Associated Oil, were divorced from the railroad properties late in 1920 and placed in the hands of still another subsidiary, Pacific Oil Company.[26]

These changes did not reflect unproductive and foolish bureaucratic shuffling. Rather, they represented management's best effort to preserve shareholder equity. For nearly the entire decade until 1920 the SP had been under legal attack by the federal government, which sought to divest SP of nearly 175,000 acres of

land in California given to it as part of construction grants because, said the government, the SP had known they were mineral and not agricultural when patents had been perfected. The courts ultimately took SP's side—only 6,100 acres were ordered back to the government—but the cases were as long as they were inflammatory. Furthermore, in 1919–20 there was no certainty that the country's railroads would be returned to private control, and the Supreme Court's decision in the U.S. v. Reading Company case suggested that similar future litigation might result in the forced disassociation of SP's oil properties from its transportation holdings. SP's board of directors was understandably worried about protecting the value of all company assets; to that end it ultimately determined to give stockholders an opportunity to purchase, at $15 each, on a one-to-one basis, shares of Pacific Oil. This, reasoned the board, would preserve the value of the properties to the stockholder. In the end, Pacific Oil issued 3.5 million shares, and all but 85,396 (which remained in SP's coffers) were purchased by SP shareholders. By 1926 Standard Oil Company (California) purchased a sufficiency of Pacific Oil's shares to gain control, and on January 1 of that year the assets of the two companies were combined, with Standard Oil as the survivor. Much internal criticism later attached to SP's spinoff of these properties, but given the political circumstances of the time it was likely a wise decision.[27]

Company attorneys were busy during the same period with other sticky litigation concerning SP's administration of the federal government's grant of land in Oregon. These holdings, which the SP had acceded to through the acquisition of predecessor companies, were to be distributed only to actual settlers in quantities not greater than quarter-sections (160 acres) and at a price not to exceed $2.50 per acre. In fact, much of the land was nonarable and unfit for settlement, a view seemingly embraced by the Congress when it passed the Timber and Stone Act (1878). With this understanding, and to gain funds it considered legitimate in satisfaction for completing the legally mandated rail link between Roseville, California, and Portland, Oregon, the SP decided to sell parcels of its land grant in larger blocks, at rates higher than $2.50, and not to actual settlers. Even then sales were hardly brisk; the SP still held more than two-thirds of its grant when the government sought a decree of forfeiture in 1910. The proceedings were complex. Suffice it to say that, in the end, SP lost the unsold portion of its Oregon grant and paid $1.72 million, which the federal government believed to be the difference between what the SP should have received at $2.50 per acre and what it had actually charged. However financially important other government grants proved to the SP over time, the one in Oregon was a bust.[28]

If the "heavy" in the Oregon fracas was the SP, it was the government in the matter of the Colorado River break claim. This issue dated from Theodore Roosevelt's request in 1906 to E. H. Harriman to do whatever was necessary to stop the vagrant flow of water from the Colorado's usual course. Harriman and the SP had responded promptly and vigorously, closing the break, but the government was shamefully obdurate in satisfying the claim. Not even a personal appeal to President Calvin Coolidge moved it to honorable action. The SP finally resorted to litigation through the Court of Claims, and more than twenty-three years after the incident the SP, on April 1, 1930, received a government check of $1.013 million in settlement.[29]

Several of SP's senior officers had been with the company since even before Colorado River break. Not surprisingly, then, significant changes in SP's executive-level personnel and organization took place during the 1920s. The remarkable Julius Kruttschnitt, a man whose roots tapped both the Huntington and Harriman eras, retired on May 31, 1925, after forty-seven years of continuous service. Kruttschnitt was successful in working with the executive team handed to him by Harriman

(Stubbs, Mahl, Hood, et al.) and in building his own (Sproule, Shoup, McDonald, et al.). Kruttschnitt was not the entrepreneur that Huntington had been, nor was he the financial wizard that Harriman was. Rather, he represented the trend to professional management that typified the industry in the twentieth century. And he was an outstanding example of it. Small wonder that upon Kruttschnitt's retirement the editor of the *Bulletin* referred to Kruttschnitt as "our friend," and small wonder that all of SP's trains, ferries, and ships paused in tribute when he died unexpectedly only days after his retirement.[30]

Upon Kruttschnitt's departure, Henry W. de Forest became chairman of the executive committee. Born in New York City on October 29, 1855, de Forest earned a bachelor's degree at Yale and a law degree at Columbia; he remained a member of the de Forest Brothers law firm throughout his tenure at SP. De Forest became an SP vice-president in 1913; serving in that capacity and also as a member of the board of directors, he was responsible for the company's financial affairs. In addition, de Forest served on the boards of Wells Fargo, Western Union, and several other companies.[31]

At the same time, Angus Daniel McDonald was appointed vice-chairman and in 1928 would, as additional duties, assume the presidency of SP's Texas & Louisiana operations. A native Californian, McDonald was born in Oakland on April 14, 1878; he received his higher education at the University of Notre Dame and entered SP's service at Houston in 1901. McDonald had been named to the auditor's position in 1910, to a vice-presidency in 1913, and to the board of directors in 1925.[32]

William R. Sproule retained the presidency of SP's Pacific Lines. Born in Ireland and moving to New York as a boy, Sproule had entered the employ of the SP in 1882 and worked his way up the ranks to become general traffic manager in 1898. He then left the SP, serving as traffic manager for American Smelting &

William R. Sproule retained the presidency of the Pacific Lines following Kruttschnitt's departure.

SP's board of directors broke tradition by reaching outside its organization to tap Hale Holden (*left*) as chairman of the executive committee. Paul Shoup is shown with Holden in this idyllic scene.

Refining and later as president of Wells Fargo before returning in 1911 as president of the SP and a member of its board.[33]

Paul Shoup was another Californian, born at San Bernardino, and another who rose through the ranks. He became president of Pacific Electric in 1912 and, retaining that title and those responsibilities, was also an SP vice-president from 1918 to 1925. As a young telegrapher, Shoup wrote short stories, verses, and essays that he sold to various newspapers and magazines in the West. Friends later gathered them into a privately published book called *Side Tracks from the Main Line*. He was named executive vice-president in 1925.[34]

Additional shuffling was required later in the decade when Sproule retired at the end of 1928. Shoup replaced him as president of the Pacific Lines, and de Forest was elected chairman of the board, a new position. SP then broke tradition by reaching outside of its or-

ganization to tap Hale Holden as chairman of the executive committee. A native of Kansas City, Missouri, where he was born in 1869, a graduate of Williams College and the law school at Harvard, Holden had risen quickly through the legal department of the Chicago, Burlington & Quincy Railroad to become that company's president in 1914.[35]

The trade press, financial analysts, and others found ample reason to praise the Southern Pacific during the last half of the 1920s. In 1926 there were ten billion-dollar companies in the United States; SP ranked number two. Among the elite ten, five were railroads, and among these the SP had the largest total assets and the greatest value in terms of physical properties. One year later it had 58,000 stockholders, 96,000 employees, and served a huge empire with 13,532 route miles of railway and 3,825 miles of water service. The balance sheet showed total assets of $2,206,621,000.

Moreover, the company had paid standard 6 percent dividends since 1907; *Barron's* recommended that investors could "hold this stock with confidence." Others chimed in similarly. Strassburger & Company saw the SP as "an admirably rounded out transportation system" whose strength was "in large measure the result of the reinvestment of surplus earnings in its properties." At "no time in its history has the outlook been brighter," said Strassburg in August, 1929.[36]

Yet there were clouds, serious clouds, on SP's horizon. The board of directors was especially displeased with management for being overly optimistic regarding the estimated rate of return for SP's recent construction projects. These rates varied greatly on expenditures for short branches or extension of branches, but in 1928, for example, major projects such as the Cascade and Phoenix lines yielded only 2.6 percent and 3.8 percent, respectively. For that matter, the return on investment for the entire system was low, only 3.98 percent in 1926, a fact that was all the more regrettable because in that year the company experienced the highest operating revenues yet. "New territory required some time to develop," said Paul Shoup, who noted further that vehicular and Panamanian competition were draining "earnings from investments made" earlier. Shoup, however, was not able to explain away another bothering statistic, the operating ratio, which in 1926 was 72.2, bad enough in and of itself but more disappointing when compared to those for the same season of SP's archrivals—Union Pacific's 68.5, Santa Fe's 65.2. Moreover, SP had made an issue of bonds in nearly every year during the 1920s and felt the need in 1929 to add both equity and debt in the form of a new issue of common stock, trust certificates, and bonds. The timing was awful. A massive wave of sell orders hit Wall Street on October 24, 1929; the crash was at hand and the Great Depression was not far behind.[37]

CHAPTER 9

The Dark Decade

"We face the first necessity of producing a service we can sell successfully in an increasingly competitive market. This means a service constantly revised and improved to meet more exactly the requirements of shippers and travelers, a service our customers will find easy and pleasant to use."—President A. D. McDonald

THE United States slid inexorably into the world depression following the stock market crash of 1929. Except for the worst periods of the Civil War, the nation had never witnessed days as dark as these. In 1930 alone, over 1,500 banks closed, losing $1 billion in deposits. At least one-quarter and possibly as much as one-third of the work force found itself unemployed. However, the nation did endure, survive, and eventually prosper, an experience mirrored by the Southern Pacific. Its profit-and-loss statement did not show a constant downward trend but rather reflected the saw-tooth fortunes of the country itself. SP was not forced into bankruptcy, yet the prospect was very real during the bleak depression decade.

Southern Pacific's financial condition was admittedly grim throughout the 1930s. These unpleasant circumstances, however, were not solely the result of the Great Depression. The company's leaders had matured in an environment of constant expansion; they were, in a sense, captives of SP's past and ill-equipped by psychological orientation or tradition to deal adequately with the new circumstance. They responded sluggishly and, like many others, underestimated the length and depth of the depression. They clung forlornly to the hope

that it was an aberration—that the status quo ante was, as President Herbert C. Hoover affirmed, "just around the corner." He was wrong and so were they. Not only did hard times persist, they energized competition, particularly in the form of over-the-road truck companies, intercity bus operators and, to a lesser extent, air lines. At the same time, and in spite of the depression, the family automobile continued to gain popularity at the expense of the railroads.

The exigencies of the depressed economy coupled with changed and changing competitive forces finally resulted in a significant reorientation of managerial thinking. Before business rebounded in 1940, the SP would be forced to reduce train service, abandon certain lines, discontinue entire operations, and embrace a wide variety of innovations. Meanwhile, the company suffered with its constituents; the agony of one was mirrored by the other. It was, as one of SP's directors said, "the dark decade."[1]

The decline in the number of through and local riders, which had begun before World War I, continued dramatically throughout the 1920s. The average distance traveled did go up sharply during that decade, but the percentage of contribution to total operating

This busy scene at Dunsmuir belied reality. The decline in the number of through and local riders, which had begun before World War I, continued in dramatic fashion throughout the 1920s.

revenues by passengers slid from 25.4 in 1920 to 16.0 in 1929. The depression simply accelerated the process. Ridership in 1933 was nearly as low as it had been in 1898; receipts declined in equal portion.[2]

Freight volume, unlike passenger, had grown impressively during the 1920s but, like passenger, plummeted during the depression. Total revenue tonnage in 1933 approximated that of 1906. Volume in all major categories dropped, but declines in mines, forests, manufactures, and merchandise were precipitous. In the case of forest products, traffic in 1933 was only 36 percent of what it had been in 1930.[3]

Total revenues in 1930 proved to be the lowest in ten years. The balance sheet for that year looked healthy, however, by comparison with the devastated reports of the three seasons following. SP's return on equity for the entire decade of the 1920s had been an unim-pressive 3.84 percent; even that looked good by comparison with the company's performance in 1930. During the following year dividends were reduced and in 1932 were suspended for the duration. For that matter, the company's earnings did not cover fixed charges in 1932 or 1933. These problems understandably disturbed shareholders, whose numbers fell from 54,858 in 1930 to 41,627 in 1941.[4]

The financial picture was so bleak in 1933 that the company applied for and received loans from the Reconstruction Finance Corporation (RFC) and another federal agency. As the situation worsened, the SP also borrowed frequently from banks and even sold some of its lands to reduce the debt. In 1934 a paltry 0.3 percent of SP's budget was available for improvements. Fortunately, after the depression eased somewhat in 1935, the company was able to pay off several bank obligations, and in 1936 it satisfied the RFC debt.[5]

SP's management found few pleasant options during those difficult years. On the one hand, it was confronted with inordinately high fixed costs accompanied by regulatory constraints and innumerable labor agreements that hindered flexible responses and, on the other hand, by faltering traffic and stiffer competition. The operating ratio reflected the dilemma; it rose from 75.52 in 1930 to 80.79 two years later. Cuts were required. These took various forms, including, for instance, line abandonments. The process of reducing a plant had begun in the 1920s when 158 miles had been abandoned, but it was not sufficient. A. D. McDonald in 1932 ordered a vigorous study of potential line reductions, and by the end of the decade another 768.6 miles were pared from the system.[6]

Other nostrums were equally painful. Publication of the *Bulletin* was terminated during the summer of 1931, and employee numbers dropped dramatically, from 89,304 in 1929 to 41,863 in 1933. Those who remained were forced to accept reductions in wages or salaries. All took 10 percent cuts in 1932, and those in the official family who earned in excess of $10,000 annually experienced a further 10 percent reduction later the same year. Yet another 10 percent cut followed for the salaried group in 1933. Among SP's several shops, only those at Bayshore (San Francisco), Sacramento, Los Angeles, and El Paso worked full five-day shifts by early 1934.[7]

Literally thousands of former SP employees suffered from the vicissitudes of the depression. Other than restoring them to their former jobs, an impossibility for several years, there was little the company could do. However, it did join with its officers and contract forces in 1931 to establish an employees' relief loan fund. Those who chose to do so could subscribe 1 percent of their monthly earnings, which the SP promised to match. These funds were then used in making no-interest loans to persons laid off and were to be repaid by them when "circumstances permitted." Such loans, aggregating $349,000,

were made to nearly 3,000 persons before the company was forced to terminate the program in 1932. (About half of the monies were ultimately refunded to the contributors.)[8]

SP's traffic reverses were discouraging, and not all were the result of the depression; modal competition was increasingly a factor in the company's fortunes. The use of automobiles and the introduction of motor buses cut deeply into local business. More important to overall revenues were the significant inroads made by motor trucks, which sliced deeply into less-than-carload (LCL) traffic and then into historically important commodity classes, including agricultural, petroleum, and merchandise. SP's response, like that of the industry generally, was defensive. The "good roads movement" was mere propaganda, the editor of the *Bulletin* had wailed in 1922. "There is not a highway in the United States today that will stand up under truck traffic," he dolefully predicted. The SP fought for regulation and taxation of truckers at the state level and lobbied successfully for the passage of the federal Motor Carrier Act of 1935. Nevertheless, the company had to admit to its shareholders in 1937 that "the severity of competition from this form of transportation has not materially lessened." Furthermore, other modes of transportation levied significant competitive attacks. Intercoastal and unregulated coastal carriers constantly sniped at lucrative bulk traffic, as did a growing network of pipelines.[9]

SP's management had not been slow to recognize threats presented by other modes of transportation, but it was disappointingly lethargic in addressing them. There was irony in this since it had traditionally responded skillfully to threats from other railroads. Apparently, SP's managers thought the company invincible against meaningful attack by anything less than steel rails and iron horses. This reflected, sad to say, a creeping if unfortunate "this-is-the-way-we've-always-done-it" mentality that more and more characterized the entire industry and earned for it a reputation of "reacting" rather than "acting."

SP's operations at Oakland—a complex mixture of rail and water, passenger and freight, steam and electric—served to illustrate changed patterns. As the 1920s had begun, SP's Oakland Mole was unquestionably one of the country's busiest terminals, serving at least 90 steam and over 600 electric trains daily. As late as 1928, SP's Eastbay electric trains offered pleasant and efficient service, with trains operating on twenty-minute headways during daylight hours (forty- to sixty-minute headways until midnight) with modest 21¢ fares (or $6.50 monthly). Nevertheless, traffic peaked in 1920 and then declined. Losses mounted to nearly one-half million dollars annually even before the depression. Not surprisingly, certain line reductions were made in 1933. In a related matter, the SP during the same year entered into agreements with both the AT&SF and Western Pacific that allowed them joint use of the Oakland Pier to originate and terminate their passenger trains.[10]

Employees, who had as great a stake as any in the new environment, sometimes took matters into their own hands. On the San Diego & Arizona (SD&A) they skillfully formed their own solicitation committee and quickly produced improved ticket sales and freight receipts. The SD&A program of "business-getting" eventually spread across the SP system. Interested employees who perceived the company's welfare as their own filled out "prospective business cards" that were forwarded to the sales department for follow-up. This elementary style of employee involvement eventually took the form of a contest among the various operating divisions plus the general office force. Cash prizes were given during the early 1930s for those who made the best suggestions as to how the SP could increase its revenues. During the last part of the depression, meetings were held throughout the system during which officers frankly told employees of the company's difficult position and heartily urged everyone to "ask friends and merchants with whom you trade to patronize the Southern Pacific." Enthusiasm was great even if the total impact on revenues was not. These campaigns also produced important side benefits: the SP "team" tended to pull more in harness and morale was improved.[11]

Adversity clearly strengthened the family bond between the company and its employees. The SP quickly found radio broadcasting and later the new medium of television to be especially useful tools in fostering pride and loyalty while at the same time increasing morale and getting positive publicity. SP broadcasts began in 1923; they originated from KGO, General Electric's station at Oakland, and featured instrumental and vocal selections and readings by talented SP personnel living in the Bay Area. GE received "applause cards" from California and surrounding states complimenting the program and individual performers. To commemorate the sixtieth anniversary of the Golden Spike ceremony on May 10, 1929, the company presented an hour-long "Golden Jubilee Program" featuring the noted baritone Reginald Werrenrath; it boasted broad regional coverage and was well received. Even more impressive was SP's half-hour "All Aboard" program, which aired weekly in 1940 and 1941 from NBC's Hollywood studios. Equally pleasant was the publicity the company gained when its supervising chef was featured for culinary demonstrations on the Mutual–Don Lee television network in 1939.[12]

It was much the same with the Hollywood film industry that grew up in the shadow of SP's operations in Southern California. The railroad discovered early that it could make money and simultaneously receive free publicity by working with the cinematographers. In 1915 such revenues had been only $8,000, but two years later they were over $100,000. The SP provided hundreds of special trains for the industry and even established a "locations bureau" in the Los Angeles city ticket office as an aid to the studios in selecting sites for special pictures and for filming natural scenes. "When you see Mary Pickford enjoying a meal on a train, or Bill Hart waving farewell from the observation platform," said SP's local passenger agent, "the chances are that it is an SP diner or train that is being used." Truckee was a favorite location for mountain scenes and Palm Springs for desert sets.[13]

As much as its financial officers might have wished it, the company could not rely entirely on the incidental publicity that resulted from radio and movie exposure. The SP also had to spend its own money, scarce as it was during the depression. Like virtually all other budgets, that of advertising was slashed and would not regain its 1929 level until 1946. Available money generally was spent to stimulate travel on SP's fleet of passenger trains. Advertising focused on the company's low-fare Sunday excursions such as the *Suntan Special* between San Francisco and Santa Cruz, the *Snowball Specials* to the Sierra, and on "Dollar Day" campaigns, which offered patrons "One Hundred Miles of Travel for $1."[14]

Although the SP traditionally bragged about its "Four Great Routes West," it enjoyed single line–haul advantage only via the relatively short Shasta Route and its longer transcontinental Sunset Route. On the Overland and Golden State routes SP had to rely on the cooperation of midwestern connections not only for goodwill but also for the actual movement of trains. Historically, the SP kept its Overland passenger options open to facilitate joint car routes via Saint Louis, Kansas City, Omaha, Denver, and Ogden, although its premier connections were always by way of the Union Pacific and Chicago & North Western. That relationship had been strained during the late unmerger proceedings when the C&NW sided with the Union Pacific against the Southern Pacific. Julius Kruttschnitt understood that C&NW's "interests were nearly identical" to those of the UP, but like other SP officers, he felt North Western's decision a betrayal—a perception that permanently colored SP's view of the company. The incident also provided the SP an opportunity to favor the Chicago, Milwaukee & St. Paul Railway (CM&StP)—

Examples of roundtrips between OAKLAND and:-

Los Angeles...	$10.15	Reno......	$ 5.20
Fresno	4.10	Portland....	16.10
Sacramento...	1.85	Santa Cruz..	1.70
Salt Lake.....	16.85	Stockton....	1.75

LEAVE FRIDAY, SATURDAY OR SUNDAY ★

OCTOBER 9, 10, 11

BE BACK BY MIDNIGHT, OCTOBER 19

★ *This is the first time "Dollar Day" tickets have been good on Sunday trains. A rare opportunity for a family outing.*

MINIMUM "DOLLAR DAY" ROUNDTRIP FARE, $1.00

Southern Pacific

which had taken no similarly unpleasant position in the unmerger matter—with additional Overland business. Yet there were problems. William Sproule wished to do nothing that might strike the Union Pacific as unfriendly since that "would open the way for it to work passenger business with the Western Pacific" to SP's disadvantage. Additionally, Sproule believed the Chicago & North Western to be "the strongest of the passenger lines" in the Chicago-Omaha corridor, "with the Burlington a close second." The Milwaukee, he feared, did not have "the soliciting force" and was "lacking in organization to deliver

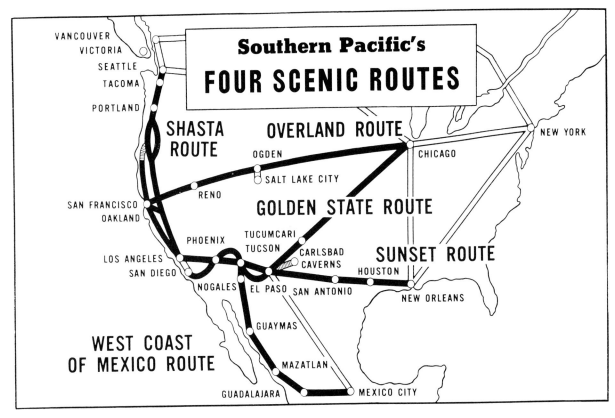

any considerable volume of passenger business" to the SP. Ironically, the Union Pacific had its own complaint with the C&NW, which in 1912 had joined with the Northern Pacific in establishing through passenger service from Chicago to Puget Sound and Portland—"to which the Union Pacific management took vigorous exception," recalled Sproule. Nevertheless, little change in policy developed until the depression when the Milwaukee felt compelled to, as its president H. H. Scandrett said, "accomplish a substantial reduction in passenger train mileage." The Milwaukee withdrew from joint San Francisco–Chicago service; the *Pacific Limited* made its last trip between Chicago and Omaha over the CMStP&P on May 3, 1931. Scandrett took the opportunity, though, to remind Paul Shoup that his company would continue to favor the Union Pacific and Southern Pacific with all California business, and he hoped for a continuation of "cordial relations" and "close cooperation." [15]

More interline passengers moved via Ogden than any other of SP's gateways, and of course the Union Pacific was by agreement and by practice the favored connection. The UP was also the favored connection at Portland—followed there, in order, by the Northern Pacific, Great Northern, and the Spokane, Portland & Seattle. Elsewhere, the SP, after it acquired the El Paso & Southwestern, built stronger alliances with the Rock Island via Tucumcari, New Mexico. Indeed, during the winter months freight and passenger volume moving on the Golden State Route exceeded that via Ogden—much to the consternation of the Union Pacific and of the Santa Fe, which competed with the Southern Pacific–Rock Island for Chicago–Los Angeles business. [16]

Although ridership slipped, and the contribution of passenger earnings to operating revenue mirrored it, passenger business remained an important element in Southern Pacific's thinking. Various physical and operational improvements were made. As a quality-

The Golden State Route represented a cooperative effort by SP with the EP&SW and the Rock Island in order to compete with the Santa Fe for the important Los Angeles–Chicago business. Three sections of the *Golden State Limited* are ready to leave Los Angeles during the great years of the long-haul passenger business.

control measure, train inspectors had been authorized in 1904; to simplify the work of agents and auditors, it adopted multiform coupon tickets a few years later. On-board amenities included expensive nickel-plated typewriters for the *Overland Limited*, radios on the lounge cars of several trains, small Christmas trees on observation cars at the holiday season, and intercar telephones aboard the *Cascade*. *Railway Age* in 1928 celebrated SP's decision to provide convenient free parking lots for patrons at thirty-seven California locations, as well as its experimental "automobile and passenger carrying service" between San Francisco and Monterey (autos moved in baggage cars aboard the same train their owners rode for $24, round trip). The SP's passenger personnel also drew plaudits. For example, the steward on the *Argonaut* arranged to have that train stopped briefly on a hot summer day in 1927 to have a bottle of goat's milk delivered aboard to a sick baby.[17]

Southern Pacific passenger trains served the great as well as the unknown. The popular French "hero of the Marne," Marshal Joffre, was joined in 1922 by other celebrities such as former President William Howard Taft, famous child actor Jackie Coogan, and the winners of the Pacific Coast bathing beauty contest as notables aboard the company's trains. However, most patrons were not well known, and some had no names at all: thirty babies were born on SP passenger trains between 1917 and 1926. The company once had an expectant mother rushed to a hospital, and so great was her gratitude that she christened the newly born child with names giving her the initials "S.P."[18]

Throughout the period before World War II the SP campaigned vigorously for tourist travel. Between 1913 and 1922 it distributed 80 million pieces of promotional literature throughout the world, and in the same years it attracted 4.5 million tourist passengers to its lines. With the end of World War I and with renewed attendance at national conventions

Local trains and branch operations were especially susceptible to attack by rubber tire competition. The Tahoe Branch, however, shown here in 1928, drew heavy tourist traffic.

held in California, SP handled more passengers in 1920 than in any year before the great crush brought on by the second war.[19]

Many travelers rode on one of an incredible array of special passenger trains chartered by organizations as diverse as the National Education Association, Sierra Club, Shriners, and Rexall Drug, to mention a few. Local groups sponsored Tucson's Santa Claus special, Fresno's Hello Neighbor Excursion, and Santa Barbara's Cycle Train. Others were more exotic: the Creole Special carrying revelers by special train to New Orleans, Pullman's Land Cruise Liners, and the Boat Trains that connected at San Francisco with Matson Navigation's SS *Malolo* for Hawaii. A less exotic train paid for by the American Legion carried French Marshal Ferdinand Foch from Portland to Oakland. Hardly dignified, but very popular, were the multiple sections required to handle enthusiastic fans from Berkeley

to football games at Stanford. Easily as uproarious were overnight Snowball Specials from Oakland to Truckee and return, and picnic specials to Santa Cruz. Senior employees later recalled that "after a day at the various resorts the celebrants were well organized by the time the trains reached home."[20]

Special trains likewise transported the nation's presidents on periodic visits to the West. William McKinley was the first of these. His train traversed the Coast Line, the picturesque branch to Monterey, and the Overland Route to Ogden in May, 1901. Woodrow Wilson followed in 1919 as a part of his unsuccessful campaign to win support for America's membership in the League of Nations. Warren G. Harding was celebrated when his train arrived in San Francisco from Portland on July 29, 1923, but mourned five days later when it carried the president's body eastward. Herbert Hoover took his campaign to the West over SP

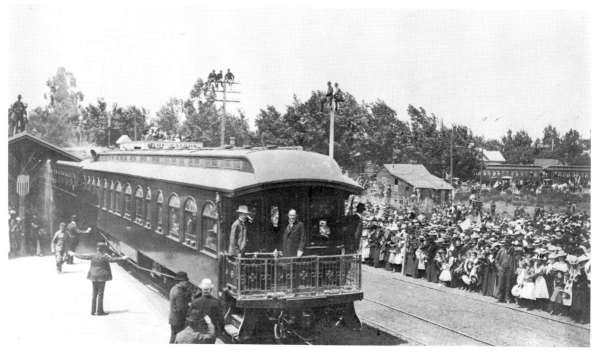

William McKinley was a visitor in SP's service area shortly before his death.

rails following his nomination in 1928, and ten years later his successor in the White House, Franklin Roosevelt, toured the Overland Route and Coast Line.[21]

Not as romantic but much more important to the company's income statement was its freight service. Throughout the 1920s and 1930s freight contributed an increased portion of total operating revenues, rising from 66.9 percent in 1921 to 81.2 percent in 1940. Peak movements in all group commodities for the same period were reached between 1925 and 1929; total tonnage in 1929 was 76,016,073, a record, and one that would stand until World War II. Most commodity classes remained relatively stable throughout, although tonnage in manufactured items jumped dramatically while LCL tonnage declined in the same fashion.[22]

The greatest density in freight traffic remained between Roseville, California, and Ogden, Utah, on the Overland Route, where typically more business moved eastward than toward the West. The Union Pacific was the recipient of roughly 90 percent of the volume in-

terchanged there, the Denver & Rio Grande Western gaining the paltry remaining 10 percent. Divisions on Bay Area–Missouri River revenues interestingly favored the Union Pacific over the SP 54 percent to 46 percent.[23]

The next most important corridor of freight density was between Los Angeles and Tucson—one that also featured an imbalance of eastbound tonnage. Before the opening of the Panama Canal and SP's acquisition of the El Paso & Southwestern, most traffic on the Sunset Route moved to or from the Texas & Louisiana Lines. By 1925, however, the Rock Island became the favored connection (via Tucumcari, New Mexico) for the Sunset Route. Indeed, throughout the late 1920s and all of the 1930s, more tonnage moved to and from the Golden State Route than was interchanged with SP's lines east of El Paso.[24]

The Southern Pacific was called upon to handle a predictably wide variety of carload as well as trainload commodities. Oddities included Easter lilies, pipe organs, Old Forester whisky (dispatched for medicinal purposes to Pacific Coast druggists during prohibition),

Top: The SP reinstated the *Noon Daylight* on April 14, 1946. Each day it marched by the Mission Bay engine facility and Potrero Tower enroute from San Francisco to Los Angeles. *Bottom:* Cuesta Grade and the Horseshoe Curve above San Luis Obispo on the Coast Line have always posed difficult operating conditions. 1957.

Top: SP's Claude E. Peterson urged early improvement of passenger service on the Shasta Route following World War II. Peterson's victory included the resplendent *Shasta Daylight*, which posed for publicity photographs in the upper Sacramento River Valley. *Bottom:* During the early and mid-1950s, the SP frequently assigned its handsome Alco power to the famous *San Francisco Overland*, shown here at Troy, California, in the Sierra Nevadas.

Top: The spectacular beauty of SP's routes to the West not only attracted important passenger trade but posed difficult and expensive operating conditions. To meet the challenge, SP traditionally employed burly locomotives such as SD-45 8898, which delivered massive motive power muscle. *Bottom:* Donald J. Russell marveled that the commander of a Japanese submarine that harassed the area early in World War II failed to shell SP's vital trestles between Surf and Santa Barbara. Here an expedited freight traverses one of those bridges on the Coast Line during the late 1970s.

Top: March 24, 1980, was a red-letter day for residents of Hooker, Oklahoma. The first SSW train over Rock Island trackage meant continued service for local patrons and resurrection of the Golden State Route as a vital transportation artery. *Bottom:* Later the same day, the first train—with an impressive consist of covered hopper cars designed to reassure area wheat shippers that the Cotton Belt intended to meet their needs—crossed over the Cimarron River west of Kismet, Kansas, en route to Armourdale Yard in Kansas City.

candy, mineral water, and even the Liberty Bell. Sugar beets, garbanzo beans, and Christmas trees moved on a seasonal basis. Entire trains of silk and eggs moved eastward, and those of corn and machinery westward.[25]

The transportation of livestock typified SP operations from the beginning. Stocker cattle and lambs moved seasonally to new pasturage, ard mature animals moved regularly to market. A triweekly train known as the Nevada Stock Extra gathered cattle west of Lovelock, Nevada, for Bay Area packers, and twice weekly "lamb specials" moved sheep eastward out of the San Joaquin Valley. During periods of drought the SP instituted special rates to handle livestock from parched areas to mountain valleys such as those near Truckee. Wild horses were rounded up and sent east on SP trains for service in World War II, and in every season the company handled pure-blood animals to livestock shows around the country. Frankly, however, there was little or no profit in it. As early as the Harriman era, SP's managers complained of inadequate rates and frequent claims. One officer groused that livestock producers seemed to know more about filing damage suits than about the care and nourishment of their animals.[26]

Nothing, however, distinguished SP's freight operations more than the impressive movement of perishables to satisfy the needs of roughly half the nation. Every month saw some type of produce moving eastward from Oregon, California, or Arizona. Citrus was joined by a bewildering array of fresh fruits and vegetables, as new growing areas were added or older ones expanded. The Imperial Valley contributed melons and lettuce, the Salinas Valley lettuce, celery, and carrots, while other areas added richly to the cornucopia. The growth of this traffic was prodigious. In the Imperial Valley, for example, only 297 cars of perishables were loaded in 1905, but in 1928 the total reached 36,870. Some produce was consumed nearby and other was transported to regional canners, but the majority was shipped to eastern markets. The SP

The transportation of livestock typified SP operations from the beginning.

handled a total of 176,000 carloads in 1923 alone; several hundred special trains were required annually for this traffic. The busiest day at Roseville in 1928 was September 28, when no fewer than 6,282 carloads of perishables passed in and out of the yard on such trains.[27]

To expedite the movement of perishable commodities, close coordination was required among packers, Pacific Fruit Express, the Southern Pacific, and its connections. Cars had to be marshaled, precooled, spotted, loaded, iced, and switched into trains. The race to waiting connections was slowed only by the need to ice the cars again at long PFE docks located at Roseville and Ogden on the Overland Route and at Yuma, Tucson, and El Paso on the Sunset. PFE required thousands of tons of ice daily, made available mechanically in later years, but earlier cut from mountain lakes and ponds, stored, and then transported to the various PFE docks. Over-the-road speeds for perishables trains increased following World War I. The elapsed times for such trains in 1918 between Roseville and Chicago was 180 hours, but only 146 hours in 1932. The same was true for the Sunset–Golden State Route. Colton-to-Chicago perishables traffic in 1918 required 189 hours, but only 146 hours in 1932. De-

pendability was good. SP perishables trains to
Ogden for a two-year test period built an enviable 92 percent on-time record.[28]

In 1929 the SP convinced the Western Association of Railway Executives to accept a plan
for the equitable scheduling of eastbound perishables and westbound manifest freight—a
concept dear to the hearts of company planners and one steadily promoted throughout
the 1930s. The new scheduling called for uniform seventh-day delivery of perishables from
the Pacific Coast to Chicago, with sixth-day
service to Saint Louis; the agreement additionally promised the same delivery times
via all routes on merchandise traffic from the
Chicago and Saint Louis gateways to the Pacific Coast.[29]

Competition among the railroads and between railroads and other forms of transportation, coupled with demands from shippers,
combined to force ever faster schedules. The
premier timetable for the Portland–San Francisco run, for instance, was reduced to make
third-morning deliveries. Elsewhere, on October 22, 1935, the SP introduced its impressive
"merchandise-only" *Overnight* trains between
San Francisco and Los Angeles. These speedsters stopped only at a few break bulk points
and offered coordinated first morning, store-
door delivery by company-owned trucks. Way-
bills were teletyped ahead. Before the service
was temporarily suspended in World War II,
the SP operated eighteen of these swift nightly
trains over several western routes.[30]

The demand for expedited freight service
was a serious factor in SP's decision in 1929 to
install "signal dispatching" or Centralized
Traffic Control (CTC) on a 40-mile stretch between Sacramento and Stockton that handled
12,000 trains annually. The CTC operation
obviated the need for double track and promised a 30 percent improvement in freight train
performance. Although much impressed with
the efficiencies of CTC, the company's management reluctantly postponed further installations until economic recovery facilitated
such expenditures in 1940 and 1941 on the
Shasta Route and the Coast Line.[31]

A more dramatic program to expedite movements of trains involved the construction of a
spectacular bridge over Suisun Bay near Martinez, California. For years, SP's busy high-
speed main line between the Bay Area and
Sacramento suffered from one severe bottleneck—the need to ferry every locomotive and
car across the Carquinez Straits from Port
Costa to Benicia. This time-consuming and expensive operation was handled by the *Solano*,
built in 1879, and the *Contra Costa*, in service since 1914. By 1927 it was plain that
these veterans would require replacement and
that the increase in traffic over SP's busy artery
would necessitate the service of yet a third vessel. Even then the problem of fog, the possibility of collision, and severe delay to all trains
would not be relieved. Furthermore, the Carquinez ferry operation caused SP to divert
heavy freight traffic over the longer Niles Canyon route, with its heavy grades on Altamont
Pass. Earlier managers were not ignorant of
the advantages offered by replacing the ferries
with a bridge; it was simply a matter of generating adequate funding for such a stupendous
undertaking. Finally, after exhaustive studies
in 1927, the board of directors on May 31,
1928, gave its blessing for a $12 million
double-track bridge. When opened to regular
service on October 15, 1930, the 5,603-foot
Suisun Bridge was heralded as the longest and
heaviest two-track structure west of the Mississippi River and greatest in the country in
terms of load-carrying capacity. Passenger
train schedules were shortened, that of the
Cascade Limited by forty-five minutes. The
quaint ferry steamers, which had served so
long and so well, became scrap.[32]

The devastating impact of the Great Depression severely curtailed, but did not halt,
SP's program of acquisition. In 1930 it purchased the 13-mile Clackamas Eastern Railroad in Oregon; unfortunately, though, this
ill-fated line suffered abandonment before the
decade passed. A more beneficial acquisition
involved the South San Francisco Belt Railway, which SP operated under contract before
its purchase in 1940. Greatly overshadowing

Construction of the spectacular bridge over Suisun Bay near Martinez rendered SP's Carquinez Straight car ferry redundant. *Collection of Harry M. Williamson.*

these, however, was SP's decision in 1931 to gain control of the strategically located St. Louis Southwestern Railway (Cotton Belt), which linked Saint Louis with SP's Texas & Louisiana Lines at Corsicana, Texas, and Shreveport, Louisiana. (See chapter 12.)[33]

During these same years SP's managers came to grips with another issue. On December 5, 1925, *Railway Age* ran a lengthy and sobering study dealing with motor bus and truck transportation; a week later it followed with another that discussed how some railroads were seeking to cope by establishing their own motor systems. The Boston & Maine, New Haven, Pennsylvania, and Great Northern companies were already active in this regard. The Southern Pacific had long recognized the problem presented by vehicular competition but was inexplicably slow to see the wisdom of actually substituting buses for unprofitable local and branch passenger trains. Finally, in April, 1927, it formed the Southern Pacific Motor Transport Company to engage in the motorized transportation of passengers, mail, baggage, and express. The first route was in California, between Santa Cruz and Boulder Creek, established on April 19, 1927.

Expansion thereafter was rapid. SP acquired several local bus companies, added its own routes, and by the end of 1928 featured an interstate system that linked Portland and San Francisco, Los Angeles and El Paso, Grants Pass and Eureka, Truckee and Reno, and Phoenix and Lordsburg over the Apache Trail.[34]

SP's philosophy was, as Paul Shoup told Great Northern's Ralph Budd, to maintain motor stage routes parallel to its own rail lines as "auxiliary thereto in substitution of service." It was not the intent of the SP, promised Shoup, to invade territories of its railway competitors with buses.[35]

Early in 1929 the SP, at the urging of Chauncey McCormick, a director and one well known for his association with the International Harvester Company, agreed to merge the Southern Pacific Motor Transport Company and all of its subsidiaries with the Pickwick Corporation and the Motor Transit Corporation to form a new company which, after a name change, emerged as the Pacific Greyhound Corporation. SP owned a one-third interest in the new firm. A predictably close relationship developed between Pacific Greyhound and the Greyhound Corporation, another of McCormick's interests. There was nothing untoward in this. The Greyhound Corporation was actively expanding to create a national system; in the process it joined with nearly a dozen rail carriers in joint stock ownership of local and regional bus companies. For its part, the SP pledged not to start new bus lines in competition with Pacific Greyhound—although it retained the bus operations of Pacific Electric and other of its electric lines—and agreed to guarantee the revenues of Pacific Greyhound routes substituted for rail service.[36]

The development of SP's trucking operations was roughly analogous. In this case, however, the inception came not from the parent company, but from Pacific Electric, which on October 13, 1928, established the Pacific Electric Motor Transport Company for the purpose of providing store-door pickup-and-delivery service by truck at twenty-three com-

The Southern Pacific Motor Transport Company was formed in April, 1927, to substitute buses for unprofitable local and branch passenger trains. This view was made at Felton, California.

munities it served. The line haul between stations was provided by rail. Since this was experimental, PE hired local draymen for the work; no trucks or other equipment were purchased. However, matters changed quickly. One year later service was expanded to several SP points, and on February 4, 1930, the company was rechristened Pacific Motor Transport Company. Its network spread and its scope was broadened shortly into line-haul truck service with company employees. New incorporation followed in 1933 to form the Pacific Motor Trucking Company (PMT).[37]

PMT initially functioned solely to provide a substitute for rail service where economies could be expected. In all cases its operations sought to benefit the railroad, although its purpose eventually was expanded from simply protecting rail revenues to attracting new business on its own. Traffic surged from 8,525 tons in 1929 to 340,293 tons in 1935. Part of this reflected the company's participation in SP's coordinated *Overnight* train service, which began in 1935, and part of it reflected

Pacific Motor Trucking's own solicitation. Moreover, cooperation between SP and the trucking firm was not restricted to LCL shipments; the two companies also worked to provide carload shippers with a total transportation package. Such was the case between 1934 and 1939 when SP and PMT jointly moved 2,847,660 barrels of bulk cement for Southern California's Metropolitan Water District Aqueduct. All of this proved most satisfactory. The trucking firm's operating ratio was a startling 42 percent, a fact that clearly caught the eye of A. D. McDonald during the trying days of the depression.[38]

Significant changes in the executive suite occurred in 1932. Henry W. de Forest resigned as chairman of the board but retained his position as a member of that body. Hale Holden was elected chairman. Paul Shoup became vice-chairman and A. D. McDonald, president. Responsibility for the day-to-day operations of steamships and the Atlantic Lines passed to H. M. Lull.[39]

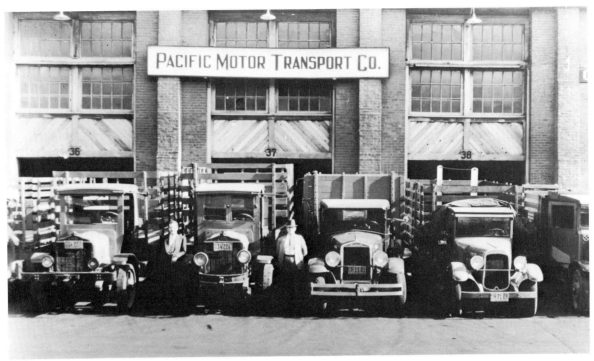

Pacific Motor Trucking, successor to Pacific Electric Motor Transport, was a successful attempt to blend rail and motor modes.

Significant changes in SP's management team occurred in 1932. *From left*: Paul Shoup, Joe Saunders, J. H. Dyer, A. D. McDonald, unidentified, H. M. Lull, W. H. Kirkbride.

Other changes followed. The resurrection of the *Bulletin* early in 1935 was more than symbolic. It reflected, in part, better economic circumstances. The nadir for the company had been reached in 1932; modest increases in freight tonnage and passenger volume raised revenues thereafter. The reemergence of the *Bulletin* also reflected A. D. McDonald's concern for improved internal communications and his belief that it could mobilize "teamwork among us all." McDonald did not minimize the company's continuing problems. The first requirement, he told employees, was to "produce a service we can sell successfully in an increasingly competitive market." This would require hard work and a dedication on the part of all to "some phase of the selling job." It also meant that the company, strapped though it was, would have to come up with monies necessary to fund physical improvements. All of this was pleasant and instructive, but the most promising and poignant portion of McDonald's message was as simple as its validity was obvious. Adequate service, observed McDonald, was one that evolved continuously—in other words, "a service constantly revised and improved to meet more exactly the requirements of shippers and travelers."[40]

CHAPTER 10

The Dark Decade Ended

"With this bottle of California champagne I christen you the *Daylight*. Good luck and Godspeed."—Olivia de Havilland

BY 1935 there was no longer any naive notion at 65 Market Street that "prosperity was just around the corner." Instead, among SP's managers there was a grim determination to proceed and to hope for the best. Their mood was reflected by the entire "SP family," which had drawn closer in the face of common challenges offered by the Great Depression.

Hard times affected Southern Pacific's subsidiaries no less than the parent itself. Revenues of the Southern Pacific of Mexico, for example, slipped modestly in 1930 but deteriorated badly throughout the rest of the decade because of the world depression, storms, floods, the loss of markets in the United States for perishables produced in Mexico, increases in wages, and strikes. Nevertheless, during the decade the SP authorized two significant expenditures. On October 20, 1931, the Inter-California Southern Railway—owned by the SP—placed in service a 43-mile line from Pascualitos, a station on the Inter-California below Mexicali, southeastward toward the Gulf of California. SP hoped the new service area would produce handsome traffic in cotton, alfalfa, and other agricultural commodities. Five years later the West Coast Hotel Company, another subsidiary, opened the Hotel Plaza de Cortes overlooking the Gulf of California near Guaymas in Sonora. Shareholders were told that the excellent winter climate coupled with opportunities for deep-sea fishing and bathing promised significant business for the SPdeMex from American tourists. The

hotel opened in March, 1935. Meanwhile, however, SPdeMex abandoned its 38-mile branch from Navajoa to the picturesque city of Alamos because of inadequate traffic.[1]

Matters came to a head in 1939 after several SP directors toured the lines in Mexico. The SPdeMex was clearly expensive to maintain and had never yielded the traffic expected—only 5,800 cars were interchanged with the SP in 1935—yet the parent had made several internal loans, which unfortunately remained unpaid. Consequently, the board announced that beginning in 1940, "no further cash advances would be made for the relief of" the SPdeMex. The future of the road looked bleak. It was the same for the Inter-California Southern, which had turned in "substantial net losses" every year since its inception; the assets of that company would be conveyed to the government of Mexico in 1941. The case of the Inter-California Railway, which also operated in Mexico, was appreciably better since it handled overhead business to and from the San Diego & Arizona Eastern as well as perishables from the Imperial Valley.[2]

The story of Pacific Fruit Express was much happier than that of the SPdeMex. Traffic in perishables slipped during the first half of the depression, and the fortunes of PFE were reduced accordingly. Nevertheless, that company had modernized its facilities at Roseville and Fresno and had established new ones at Tucson before the full onslaught of the depression hit and, as a result, was able to weather the storm in relatively good order. When business improved in 1936 and 1937, PFE was able to purchase 4,700 new cars without devastating its budget. It was also able to test new technology. With the advent of frozen-food processing in commercial volume, PFE joined with packers in experimenting with "water ice refrigeration" by providing 30 percent salt to the ice supply. That was satisfactory for prefrozen commodities, but the era of the mechanical refrigerator car remained in the future. Until that time, PFE continued to purchase millions of tons of ice annually to cool entire trainloads of perishables.[3]

The fortunes of the Northwestern Pacific Railroad were not as pleasant. It lost money throughout the depression years, $4.2 million in 1938–39 alone. Passengers still flocked to the scenic line during summer months, but otherwise profitable numbers were absent. Freight traffic was no better; it was only a trickle by comparison to that of the 1920s. Consequently, service was reduced or even terminated and branches were pared. Such resources proved inadequate. Losses continued in 1940 and 1941.[4]

On the lines of the parent itself, the reduction in the number of total passengers, a pattern that had been continuous since 1919, understandably caused soul-searching among company officers. Early in 1933 SP sought the counsel of Lord & Thomas, a well-known advertising agency, which bluntly told the railroad that it was going to have to adopt a new mentality regarding passenger service if it was going to stay in that business. The old approach—"Here is the train; Here is the fare; Here is the schedule; Take it or leave it"—had to go. Frankly, said Lord & Thomas, SP was "in the position of a large manufacturer with a product that has become somewhat obsolete." Simply spending more for advertising would not do since "no amount of advertising will sell a thing that won't sell itself."[5]

Lord & Thomas consequently urged a bold plan to "fit services" to passenger desires: mod-

A familiar scene at PFE docks, this one at Watsonville, California, 1937.

ern equipment, faster trains, competitive fares. Experimentation was required. The agency suggested the San Francisco–Sacramento corridor for market testing—using "modern, streamlined gasoline Rocket Cars" operated on two-hour schedules. The design of the train, said Lord & Thomas, should be left to "a real artist who understands the value of modernistic lines"; the Rocket train definitely should not resemble "busses or standard railway coaches." Finally, following the establishment of Rocket service between San Francisco and Sacramento, the SP should, said the advertising firm, turn its attention to the important Coast Line route between San Francisco and Los Angeles.[6]

"Motor train" service on the Southern Pacific was not new. It dated from the era of joint control when, to reduce costs on branches and secondary runs, motor cars had replaced a few steam trains. In 1914, for instance, such trains worked the Davis-Hamilton and Chico–

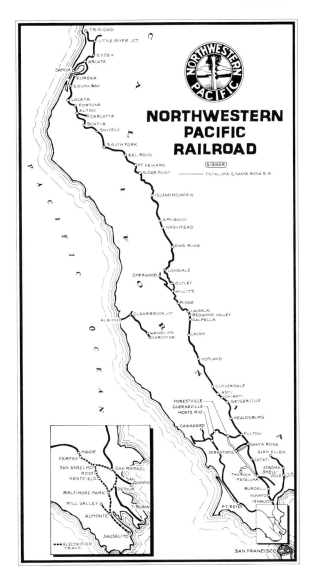

The Great Depression was particularly harsh for the NWP, which lost $4.2 million in 1938–39 alone.

Red Bluff runs in California. More followed. Twenty-one new cars were ordered in 1929 for use in commute service between San Francisco and San Jose, on the Northwestern Pacific, on the Texas & Louisiana Lines, and elsewhere. In Arizona, gas-electric trains between Tucson and Nogales were known as the *Burro*, but between Phoenix and Tucson they took the more usual term—*Doodlebug*. Both terms reflected the status accorded the cars by local patrons as well as by SP's management. Nevertheless, the gas-electric cars afforded SP's mechanical department valuable experience that pointed toward the era of the diesel

and convinced company accountants that internal combustion had much to commend it.[7]

Thus, there was at least some receptivity at the Southern Pacific when the Lord & Thomas report was received. However, executive officers decided to focus primary attention on the Coast Line rather than the San Francisco–Sacramento corridor. Ten years earlier Paul Shoup had suggested that something special be done to establish the Coast Line's *Daylight Limited* as the company's premier train. Perhaps, he suggested, equipment for that train could be painted distinctively— white or cream—to set it apart from the rest of the passenger fleet. The operating department objected, but Shoup persisted. The train's speed was increased, new equipment added to it, and in July, 1929, Shoup finally prevailed: the train would appear in striking pearl gray paint for the 1930 season. The depression caught the *Daylight* in its web, however; its schedule soon was lengthened and its distinctive decor discontinued.[8]

Nevertheless, following the advice of Lord & Thomas in part, SP's mechanical department and the Winton Engine Corporation cooperated in plans for a three-car articulated train that could make the Coast run in eight hours at the cost of a mere 50¢ per train mile. The proposal was vetoed, though, by J. H. Dyer, vice-president of operations, who felt the train was underpowered and inflexible because of its articulated nature. The matter was in limbo until December 12, 1935, when Hale Holden advised A. D. McDonald that archrival Santa Fe was purchasing a diesel-powered steamlined train that, no doubt, would be placed in service against the *Golden State* on the Chicago–Los Angeles route. A few days later the Budd Company, which had provided stainless steel cars for Burlington's famous *Zephyr* in 1934, submitted plans and prints to SP for a fine new streamlined train of its own. Dyer was not impressed. Let other railroads bear the expense of experimentation, he urged; the SP should look at the proposal again a year hence, after operating reports would be available from the others.[9]

For reasons that are not apparent, Dyer had a nearly immediate change of heart. Forty-eight hours later he recommended the acquisition of new equipment to protect the San Francisco–Los Angeles trade and thus "progress the Southern Pacific with the trend of time." It was, in a sense, a sad commentary. Dyer was admitting that the SP was not the trend-setter, that it was reacting and not acting. After all, the Burlington's *Zephyr* had made its famous dawn-to-dusk run from Denver to Chicago on May 27, 1934; UP's *City of Salina* and Milwaukee Road's *Hiawatha* had entered service in 1935; and Santa Fe's spectacular *Super Chief* soon would be a reality.[10]

Happy to say, however, events now moved rapidly. In March, 1936, the executive committee gave approval for a diesel-powered, lightweight train for the Coast Line but strangely specified Pullman instead of Budd for the car order. Equally surprising was the subsequent decision to substitute streamlined and cross-counterbalanced GS 4-8-4 steam locomotives for diesel power; general manager A. T. Mercier explained that operating officials wanted "time to study diesels from afar."

At the same time, the matter of the train's paint scheme occasioned hearty internal debate; F. S. McGinnis, who was in charge of passenger service, urged "flame orange." In the end, a striking combination of red, orange, black, and aluminum was employed.[11]

Champagne bathed the pilots of the new locomotives and network radio carried the story nationwide as the handsome twelve-car *Daylight* trains made their initial nine-hour-and-45-minute runs on Sunday, May 21, 1937. They were instant and profitable stars; by their fourth birthday 1.3 million passengers had ridden them. Luxury service on the Coast Line was doubled in 1940 with the installation of the *Noon Daylight*, and on July 4, 1941, the equally handsome *San Joaquin Daylight* began service between Oakland and Los Angeles through the valley of its namesake. Few perceived it then, but the new service had an ominous implication: each trip of the *Daylight* required the services of forty-five employees "from the locomotive to the observation end."[12]

Even before plans for the *Daylight* matured, the SP joined with the Union Pacific and the Chicago & North Western to sponsor another impressive passenger train venture—the elegant diesel-powered *City of San Francisco*, which, following its inaugural run on June 14, 1936, featured "sailings" from Oakland and Chicago every sixth day. Demand for the extra-fare accommodations provided by the eleven-car beauty was great. Another train set, this one of seventeen cars and powered by three diesel units, soon was ordered; it took to the rails on January 2, 1938. The first train was owned solely by the Union Pacific, but its replacement was the property of the participating carriers, each owning approximately a third. Service was doubled on July 26, 1941, when still another set of equipment was added. Speed of passage was a hallmark of the train's reputation. Fine track conditions on the Overland Route had permitted Harriman's special in 1906 to traverse the Oakland-to-Chicago line in only 51 hours and 7 minutes,

Christening the new *Daylight* at Los Angeles on March 21, 1937. Actress Olivia DeHaviland did the honors.

but even better maintenance and diesel power now allowed the *City* a swift 39-hour-and-45-minute schedule. The train was authorized for 95 mph at several locations on SP's Salt Lake and Western divisions.[13]

Competitive pressures and a slightly improved economy convinced SP's management to institute further passenger service improvements. The program of air conditioning older equipment, begun early in the decade, went forward; company diners were among the first to be modernized in this way. There was irony in this since deficits in the dining car department provided a constant irritant. "The loss on dining cars is too great to be borne; it eats too much of net passenger revenue," concluded a gloomy Paul Shoup in 1930. Shoup proposed to revamp SP's operations by forming a separate company that would function in a way similar to the relationship then existing between the Santa Fe and Fred Harvey. Internal evaluation subsequently found no relative economic advantage, however, and the idea perished. Dining revenues were increased, nevertheless, by introducing "tray service" in coaches and tourist cars and by designing low-priced childrens' menus that attracted families to the diners.[14]

Other changes followed. A "feminine touch" was added to passenger service when graduate nurses were assigned as stewardesses to the *City of San Francisco*, then to the *Overland Limited*, and finally to other of SP's name trains. By 1938, thirty-four such persons were

The SP cooperated with the C&NW and the UP in instituting the *City of San Francisco* in 1936. This view shows ceremonies attending the first eastbound trip from Oakland Mole. The *Overland Limited*, historically the premier train on the Overland Route, is in the background.

A second train set for the *City*—shown here coming off the impressive Martinez Bridge—was acquired in 1941.

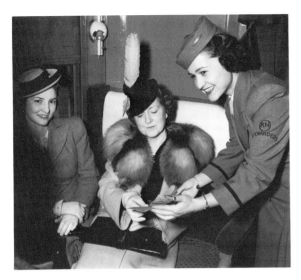

The SP added a feminine touch, stewardesses, to its
passenger service during the 1930s.

employed by the company—a fact much applauded by the traveling public.[15]

More modern trains and new marketing
approaches ensued. A pair of streamlined
Larks for overnight service joined the *Daylights* on the Coast Line; the all-Pullman
Forty-Niner and the economy-oriented *San
Francisco Challenger* complemented the *City
of San Francisco* on the Overland Route; and
the *Californian*—carrying modern coaches,
tourist sleeping cars, and separate cars for
women and children—joined the *Golden
State Limited* in the Chicago–Los Angeles
trade. Average passenger speeds in 1938 were
highest in the history of the company.[16]

Except for expansion of its popular *Overnight* merchandise service, SP's freight operations continued to mirror the industry's traditional form. However, train speeds advanced
slightly, total revenue tons increased after the
low in 1933, the average distance handled
rose impressively, and so did average revenue
tonnage per train.[17]

Longer, heavier, faster trains required more
powerful and sophisticated motive power.
Some of these locomotives were built in SP's
huge shop complex at Sacramento; the first
had entered service in 1872 and sixty-six of
them had been erected there during World

War I, when commercial builders were unable
to handle orders. Sacramento also manufactured boilers, frames, and running gear for locomotives to be assembled in other company
shops at Ogden, Los Angeles, Houston, and
Algiers (New Orleans). As one of the largest,
if not in fact the largest, railroad shop facilities west of Chicago, Sacramento likewise
built, repaired, and maintained thousands of
freight cars.[18]

By the 1930s oil was the primary fuel for
SP's locomotive fleet. The potential advantage
of oil for fueling steam locomotives had been
recognized by SP's mechanical forces as early
as 1879, when experiments began, and for the
next several years these were broadened to include the company's bay steamers and ferries.
The first locomotive converted to oil was a diminutive 4-4-0 in May, 1895, and was an impressive success; some operating divisions
soon had only oil-fired locomotives. The new
fuel offered several advantages to the SP, not
the least of which was its relative cost and extent of supply. It also provided higher heat
value per pound, was less expensive to handle,
and burned cleaner. Advanced design oil-fired
locomotives boasted another impressive asset:
they could make longer runs before being
changed. In 1925 only three locomotive
changes were required for San Francisco–
New Orleans passenger trains; oil-burning
freight locomotives also ran through between
El Paso and Del Rio and between Houston
and Algiers.[19]

Most of SP's modern steam locomotive fleet
came from the country's major commercial locomotive works—Baldwin, American (Alco),
and later Lima. William Sproule in 1922 ex-
claimed that the 2-10-2s recently received from
Baldwin represented "the ultimate achievement in the modern locomotive." Sproule's
temporary euphoria aside, the 2-10-2s proved
to be steady but only pedestrian performers.
Not surprisingly, SP shortly thereafter approached Alco with a design that was, as
the company said, "a step in advance of the
mighty 2-10-2 and 4-8-2 types." The new
4-10-2, or Southern Pacific type, would fea-

SP's complex at Sacramento was impressive by any measure.

ture a third cylinder that would maximize tractive effort, although it would also present additional maintenance problems. Eventually, SP's fleet included 182 2-10-2s, 83 4-8-2s, and 49 4-10-2s.[20]

Although the 4-10-2s bore the label "Southern Pacific type," the company's distinctive cab-forward articulateds were the steam locomotives most readily identifiable with the SP. The advantages of placing the cab ahead included visibility but, more importantly, keeping the cab clear of smoke and gas when operating through tunnels and snowsheds. The new design was made possible only by fueling with oil; the road took delivery of the first models, 2-8-8-2s, from Baldwin in 1909. Although SP experimented with cab-forward 2-6-6-2s and 4-6-6-2s, its most successful versions were class AC 4-8-8-2s, which Baldwin

completed in 1928–30 and 1937–39. Traditional cab-in-the-rear coal-fired articulated 2-8-8-4s arrived from Lima in 1939 for service between El Paso and Tucumcari, where coal could be purchased locally at favorable prices and where tunnels were not a problem.[21]

If the ACs were SP's most distinctive locomotives, its GS 4-8-4s were the handsomest. The first of the series came from Baldwin in 1930 and were split between Atlantic and Pacific lines. SP also turned to the 4-8-4s when it sought power for the *Daylights*, but Lima built these in 1936–37 and 1941. The Lima GSs proved to be the world's largest streamlined locomotives and, according to SP's mechanical department, were "the world's most beautiful locomotives." Few argued otherwise.[22]

Line changes, however desirable to reduce

The 4-10-2, or Southern Pacific type, featured a third cylinder. The SP owned forty-nine of them.

grades and curvature, were rare during the depression. In one case, however, a Bureau of Reclamation project provided a better line at no expense to the company. In 1938 the federal government began construction of the impressive Shasta Dam near Kennet, California, adjacent to SP's main line to Oregon; this required a relocation and, as a consequence, the government provided a new line of railroad between Redding and Delta, 30.1 miles, in exchange for title to the former trackage. The new route would be placed in service in May, 1942.[23]

Southern Pacific's service area was generally spared the tragedy of Dust Bowl conditions that plagued other regions of the country during the 1930s, but it was not spared other vicious acts of nature. Floods in Texas and Oregon during 1935 caused serious damage and delayed traffic. These were minor inconveniences, however, compared with conditions in California during the first weeks of 1938. A continuous storm blanketed most of the central and northern portions from January 27 to February 11, with heavy rains in the lowlands and deep snow in the mountains. Total snowfall at Norden, in the Sierras,

reached a record 805 inches for the season. Farther south, gale winds were followed by severe flooding in the southern portions of the state. The Coast, San Joaquin, and Sunset routes all were out of service for several days.[24]

Snows in the Sierra, of course, are legendary. Huntington and his associates learned that hard lesson even as they were pushing the Central Pacific eastward during the 1860s. Bucking snow in the depths of accumulation natural to the area could not in all cases be accomplished with wedge plows. Miles and miles of expensive snowsheds were required—so many that one writer suggested the line was, in fact, a "railroad in a barn." Rotary snowplows pushed by powerful articulated locomotives obviated the need for some, but not all, of the sheds. In any case, SP found it necessary to maintain a fleet of flangers, spreaders, plows, and locomotives plus a large crew of hearty mountain railroaders to keep the Sierra as well as the Cascade line open for business each winter. The 1938 season was simply more extraordinary than most.[25]

Winter snows in the mountains were expected and, as much as it was possible to do so, the company could and did prepare for

SP's mechanical department boasted that the GS 4-8-4s were "the world's most beautiful locomotives." Few argued otherwise.

The first of SP's handsome GS locomotives came from Baldwin and were split among the Pacific and Atlantic lines. This one was assigned to the famous *Overnighter* freight train.

them. Anticipating economic and financial storms was much more difficult. This was the case not only with the Great Depression but with the unexpected and unfortunate economic downturn of 1937 and 1938. Morale had gone up predictably in the preceding two years, as freight and passenger revenues rose slightly. This plus notable competitive pressures served to explain SP's renewed program of improvements and equipment acquisitions during the mid-1930s. More debt, of course, had been acquired as a consequence. Severe traffic reverses, higher operating expenses in 1937–38, plus a millstone of debt combined to present the SP with an ominous situation in 1938. Moreover, certain major capital projects of the 1920s—the Modoc Line, for example—had yet to provide "economics equal to annual expense incurred by reason

of construction." At the same time, shareholders—who had received nothing on their investment since 1931—were increasingly restive. Grim was the only way to describe 1938; the SP failed even to cover fixed charges in that year. Indeed, it was again forced to institute a policy of reduced wages and salaries and to seek financial assistance from banks and the Reconstruction Finance Corporation. Not surprisingly, executive officers weighed the merits of bankruptcy proceedings. Nor was it surprising that the argument took two sides. It was important to maintain good faith with the banks that had stood by the company over the years, and it was necessary to safeguard the interests of the shareholders. On the other hand, bankruptcy had the obvious value of clearing company books of onerous liabilities. The course of bankruptcy

SP managers learned early that winter operations over the Sierra were tedious and expensive.

was not chosen, but subsequent managers would continue to debate whether or not the company should have gone through the wringer. In any event, recovery eventually turned to prosperity; the RFC loans were repaid in 1941, and the bank notes and serial bank loans shortly thereafter.[26]

Southern Pacific employees were acutely mindful of the struggle their company—and, indeed, their nation—was experiencing during the 1930s, and like Americans everywhere at that time they were susceptible to fear and prone to hysteria. This was evident even at remote locations such as Palomas, New Mexico—along the Golden State Route between El Paso and Tucumcari—when on a memorable evening in 1938 Orson Welles presented his dramatization of H. G. Wells's novel, *The War of the Worlds*. At Palomas the astonishing "news" that the earth was being invaded by Martians was received by a battery-powered radio in the track-side home of section foreman Joshua M. Babers, who dutifully relayed the information by company pony-phone, a

party line arrangement, to other foremen up and down the line. Babers's son, Charles, later a general manager for the company, recalled that the episode "scared the hell out of everybody."[27]

Pressed as they were by hard times, SP employees of all stripes during the 1930s may have looked longingly to the past as a golden era of expansion and prosperity, but they did not mourn the passing of one aspect: train hold-ups. These were, sad to say, not simply the stuff of Hollywood mythology. In fact, several occurred on the SP during the late nineteenth century, and the trend continued into the next. Trains were held up at Copley, California, in 1904; at Goodyear, California, in 1910; at Dryden, Texas, in 1912; and at Jaynes Station near Tucson in 1922. A year later, on October 11, 1923, train 13 was stopped near Siskiyou, Oregon, by the infamous DeAutremont brothers; its Railway Post Office car was dynamited and three railway employees plus an RPO clerk were killed in cold blood. Other if less spectacular rob-

"Railroad in a barn."

When flangers and spreaders proved inadequate, the huge rotaries were called to duty.

The tragic derailment of the *City of San Francisco* at Harney, Nevada, was no accident.

beries occurred near Richmond and Saugus in California during 1929 and 1930, but "get rich quick" schemes of this type nearly disappeared during the hard times of the depression.[28]

One element of railroading that unfortunately did not disappear was accidents. Despite SP's traditional concern for proper maintenance of track and equipment, and despite its constant devotion to compliance with rules and to safety, the road experienced wrecks in the natural course of business that sadly snuffed out lives and fortunes. Nearly 200 persons died in passenger train accidents on SP lines during the first forty years of the century. Most accidents resulted from mechanical, track, or human failure. For example, on

September 20, 1938, a brakeman mistakenly lined a switch that resulted in the head-on collision of the *Argonaut* and the *Californian* at Tortuga, California. Eleven were killed and 139 injured.[29]

There was no human error but certainly human responsibility for the tragic derailment of the westbound *City of San Francisco* at Harney, Nevada, on August 12, 1939, after "a person or persons unknown . . . maliciously tampered with the track." Casualties were great: 24 died and 115 were injured. A large squad of SP special agents and FBI men worked on the case, and SP published reward notices for several days in fifty western newspapers. Nevertheless, the perpetrator or perpetrators were never located.[30]

Many who were on that unfortunate train were bound for the Golden State International Exposition, staged on Treasure Island in San Francisco Bay during 1939 and again in 1940. SP's "Roundhouse" exhibit—which bally-hooed the company's modern freight and passenger service, featured beautiful murals representing the scenic regions of its ser-vice area, and included fitting tributes to its work force—was one of the most popular at-tractions. The SP advertised lower rates for travel to the exposition and, with the UP and C&NW, even instituted a new luxury train, the *Treasure Island Special*.[31]

The Golden State Exposition was essen-tially a statement of optimism and an emanci-pation from the worst days of the depression. The SP saw it that way, and so did its em-ployees, who flocked from all over the system aboard special trains for "Homecoming and Southern Pacific Days" at the fair in May of 1939 and 1940. As the editor of the *Bulletin* said, "They came as railroaders to meet with railroaders in a railroad celebration." The fes-tivities included a parade down Market Street, luncheons, tours of the general office building, a queen contest, various entertainment events, and a grand ball.[32]

The end of the decade was also witness to another statement of optimism—the opening of the elegant Los Angeles Union Passenger Terminal. The SP had completed its own sta-tion in Los Angeles on June 12, 1915, but civic leaders there soon clamored for a facility that would centralize all of the city's rail pas-senger services. Paul Shoup met with the Santa Fe's William B. Storey early in 1929 and offered joint use of SP's station, but Storey be-lieved it "too small to accommodate all the roads for any length of time." Los Angeles officials then took the issue to the California Railroad Commission, but as the depression deepened, and as their financial fortunes soured, all of the roads—the SP, Santa Fe, and Union Pacific—collectively argued against any attempt to force construction of an ex-pensive new terminal. For SP, and likely for

the others, too, the matter was simple: there was little money in the till, and what was available could more advantageously be spent in other ways. Nevertheless, the California regulatory body—backed by a decision of the U.S. Supreme Court in 1933—obligated the railroads to such a venture. The idea, of course, was as good as its timing was bad. Once the matter was determined, however, the carriers worked diligently to conclusion. Three days and four nights of celebration and pageantry heralded the opening of the gorgeous $11 million Mediterranean-style fa-cility on May 7, 1939.[33]

If a spirit of optimism began to permeate 65 Market Street late in the decade, so too did a determination to make hard decisions. Autho-rizations had already been made for massive improvements in track and equipment where continuing operations promised adequate re-turn. In other areas, it was a matter of decid-ing how much to reduce operations or even to vacate them. Such was the case for virtually all of SP's electrified lines. The company had great financial as well as emotional invest-ments in them, but returns ranged from poor to awful. By the late days of the depression SP could take none other than a dry-eyed look at all of them.

Curtailments and abandonments had be-gun earlier. In 1927 buses replaced streetcars at Salem and Eugene; SP's electric operations in and about the Portland area were reduced at the same time; and in 1931 all electric ser-vice from Portland into the Willamette Valley perished. The Peninsular Railway, with almost one hundred miles of lines serving major com-munities in California's Santa Clara Valley, flourished until it fell victim to vehicular com-petition and was abandoned in 1932 and 1933. Similarly, SP's interests in the Fresno Traction Company, Stockton Electric Rail-road, San Jose Railroads, and the San Jose & Santa Clara County Railroad were disposed of on April 1, 1939. Elsewhere, the electric commuter operation of the Northwestern Pa-cific in Marin County, which dated from 1903

"Homecoming and Southern Pacific Days" at the Golden State Exposition in 1939 and 1940 included a parade down Market Street and a tour of the general office building (shown here).

but had been unprofitable for years, became an intolerable loser following the opening of the famous Golden Gate Bridge on May 28, 1937. Lengthy and emotional hearings finally resulted in authority for the line to discontinue all electric service on March 1, 1941. On the Pacific Electric the situation was more complex, but the financial picture was equally bleak. PE had turned to buses as early as 1928, and that policy was accelerated late in the 1930s.[34]

The San Francisco–Oakland Bay Bridge seemed at first to imply longevity but instead quickly extinguished the life of SP's East Bay electric commuter business. This magnificent structure opened to vehicular traffic on No-

vember 12, 1936, although not to electric train service until January 15, 1939. The SP long since had grown weary of the losses incurred by the East Bay operations and as early as 1925 had attempted to unify its electric properties there with those of the Key System, a competitor. These efforts failed, but with the prospect of the Bay Bridge's diverting traffic from both systems, negotiations began anew. Agreement between SP and Key was eventually reached—Key would accede to all of SP's electric lines and on its own would operate service across the new bridge into San Francisco—but labor organizations vetoed the plan. The SP faced a dilemma. Its East Bay commute system, tied to the company's trans-

Pacific Electric had turned to buses as early as 1928, and that policy was accelerated in the 1930s.

The San Francisco–Oakland Bay Bridge seemingly implied longevity for SP's electric commute business, but in reality it extinguished both SP's commute ferry business and its Eastbay electric operation.

bay ferry operation for delivery of passengers to and from San Francisco, faced increased losses with the opening of the bridge, yet regulatory agencies were not likely to authorize abandonment. Nevertheless, something had to be done. SP's executive committee late in 1934 finally determined to form a new company, the Interurban Electric Railway Company, to pass all of SP's East Bay commute properties to it, and to demand a pay-as-you-go basis for its operation. Interurban took over on December 1, 1938, and began transbay runs effective January 15, 1939. (Key System and Sacramento Northern trains likewise used the bridge as well as the Transbay Terminal facility on Mission Street in San Francisco.)[35]

Logic urged that single carrier, direct, rail rapid transit would be both attractive and profitable. Yet Interurban's deficits were nearly $1 million in 1939, and reduced tolls for motor-vehicle traffic passing over the Bay Bridge promised more red ink. The problems simply could not be solved with either increases or reductions in fares. Consequently, applications for abandonment were filed on February 26, 1940. Permission came several months later; the various lines were aban-

doned gradually as substitute service was inaugurated by the Key System. The last to go was the Berkeley line, on July 26, 1941. (Some trackage survived under Key ownership, and SP retained short sections for industries.)[36]

The fortunes of SP's famous and colorful transbay ferry network were made equally precarious by completion of the Bay and Golden Gate bridges. SP's service dated from the late 1860s; passengers arriving from the east by train were delivered from Oakland Pier to San Francisco by ferry beginning in 1869. Inexpensive commute service was initiated in the same season, and car ferry operations began in 1871. Oakland Pier, or Oakland Mole as it was known locally, was modified and expanded several times in its lifetime, as demands required. Daily ferry service for automobiles was inaugurated from that point in April, 1923. Seven years later SP

Oakland Pier, or Oakland Mole as it was known locally, was modified several times as demand required. This early air view dates from 1921.

Streetcars ran down Market Street in front of SP's general office to the busy Ferry Building.

and its affiliates operated no fewer than forty-three boats on San Francisco Bay; as such it represented the world's largest transportation enterprise of that kind. The auto ferries enjoyed their peak year in 1930, handling nearly 6.2 million vehicles and 15 million passengers. All told, over 40.2 million passengers availed themselves of SP's combined ferry service in that season. The operation represented, as Southern Pacific boasted, "a floating bridge on San Francisco Bay."[37]

Change came quickly. To avoid wasteful duplication the SP, Northwestern Pacific, and the independent Golden Gate Ferries Company combined in 1929 to form the Southern Pacific Golden State Ferries, Ltd., for the purpose of handling the auto ferry business. Then, after lengthy negotiations, the Western Pacific and the Santa Fe on April 22, 1933, each began to operate their trains into Oakland Mole and at the same time discontinued their respective transbay ferries, substituting SP's service. The great days were over. Auto ferry service vanished shortly after the opening of the Bay and Golden Gate bridges; so, too, did regular transbay commuter operations on January 14, 1939, the day before Interurban Electric began its ill-fated service over the Bay Bridge. Oakland-Alameda operations ended in 1940, and on February 28,

1941, NWP's San Francisco–Sausalito line perished. Thereafter, SP's sole ferry service was that provided between San Francisco's Ferry Building and the Oakland Mole in conjunction with its intercity rail passenger network.[38]

The situation regarding SP's other marine interests was roughly analogous. The company had a historic and psychological tie to them, but as conditions changed they became redundant. Separation, nevertheless, was painful.

Southern Pacific's interest in oceanic transportation, as with so many other areas, sprang from the farsighted policies of C. P. Huntington. "The railroad cannot traverse the seas," Huntington said shortly before his death in 1900, but "it can own ships which do, and together, the locomotive and the ship can make for all commercial purposes a continuous line across the lands and seas. . . ." In this way, he said, railroads might compete "with the seas and the rivers." Huntington's views, of course, were similar to those of another innovative entrepreneur, James J. Hill, who in 1901 also pointed out the advantages of railroads' owning their "own steamships for carriage across the ocean." Both men did more than philosophize; the railroads they headed each developed steamship extensions.[39]

SP's entry into the steamship business actually resulted from a decision by the Pacific Mail Steamship Company in the early 1870s to cease issuing bills of lading on shipments moving to and from the Orient and points served by rail on the eastern seaboard from San Francisco. Pacific Mail, chartered in 1848, had enjoyed great profits on traffic to the Orient moving via Panama but resented competition from the newly completed transcontinental railroad. Both the Central Pacific and the Union Pacific urged a policy of contracting for specified capacity on San Francisco steamers, but Pacific Mail demurred. The two railroads then sought to bring Pacific Mail to heel by forming their own steamship company, the Occidental & Oriental, chartered in 1874. Accommodations with Pacific Mail were forthcoming, but Huntington wished for more than that. In 1900 SP took control of Pacific Mail when it acquired slightly over half of its stock. (Additional shares were purchased in 1901 and 1912.) Not surprisingly, the Occidental & Oriental was gradually assimilated into Pacific Mail. In 1907 the two operated ten vessels, ranging in size from 9,000 to 27,000 tons, in service to Hawaii, Japan, China, the Philippines, Panama, and Central America.[40]

Pacific Mail's essential value was its excellent reputation in the Orient, its respected fleet of ships, and its ability to funnel business to and from SP's rail lines. For instance, on September 17, 1914, Pacific Mail's *Manchuria* landed the largest cargo of merchandise that had ever reached San Francisco from the Orient. The raw silk and silk pieces it carried were then sped eastward by special train, and the remaining merchandise was similarly dispatched as quickly as transloading could be accomplished.[41]

There were problems, however. By the second decade of the twentieth century the SP earned "only about $800,000 per annum gross" on business interchanged with Pacific Mail—85 percent of it on freight, the rest from passenger traffic. This was alarming enough, but the Panama Canal Act prohibited Pacific Mail from using that waterway or engaging in coastwise business unless SP divested itself of control before the canal opened for business. William Sproule warned that under the circumstance, Pacific Mail could not "continue its operations without serious loss"; but instead of selling out, Sproule urged "that Pacific Mail as such be succeeded by" a new company, "the Southern Pacific Steamship Lines, retaining the name Pacific Mail as a sub-title." Sproule considered that "the Titanic disaster" had "warned the public that big ships are far from insuring safety." He thought "yacht-like ships of about 6,000 tons gross" that could "run at 16 to 18 knots" would protect the Oriental trade and even attract new business. It was not to be. On June 11, 1915, Julius Kruttschnitt announced that Pacific Mail's ships would be sold and the company dissolved because of restrictive conditions imposed by the La Follette Seamen's Law, which was to take effect on November 4, 1915. This legislation required that 75 percent of the crew in each department of the company speak the language of the officers— a requirement particularly objectionable, said Kruttschnitt, since Pacific Mail employed American officers and Asiatic crews for its vessels. Service ended following the departure of the *Mongolia* on November 2, but the company was resurrected in the next year after W. R. Grace & Company purchased SP's holdings.[42]

During the same period the Southern Pacific provided "elegantly equipped steamships with all the latest appliances for comfort and safety" between Portland and San Francisco and between San Francisco and San Pedro (Los Angeles) by way of its San Francisco & Portland Steamship Company. Additional service was offered by the steamer *Breakwater* between San Francisco and Coos Bay, Oregon, and later between Portland and Coos Bay, before full rail service was made available to that location.[43]

More important and longlasting was SP's

nautical involvement in the Gulf of Mexico and along the East Coast. This began on February 1, 1883, when C. P. Huntington gained control of Morgan's Louisiana & Texas Railroad & Steamship Company. These properties were consolidated with others on March 1, 1885, to form SP's Atlantic System, embracing all of its rail lines east of El Paso. Oceanic operations, carried on under the flag name "Morgan Line"—in honor of Charles Morgan, founder—afforded the SP a coordinated through rail-water route between the Pacific and North Atlantic ports. When SP acquired the Morgan Line, its equipment inventory included sixteen ocean-going steamships, transfer ferries, river boats, tugs, and auxiliary barges. Steamship routes at that time were:

New Orleans to New York	1,800 miles
New Orleans to Havana (via Tampa and Key West)	700 miles
Morgan City, La., to Vera Cruz, Mexico (via Galveston)	800 miles
Morgan City, La., to Brazos Santiago (Brownsville)	400 miles
Morgan City, La., to Corpus Christi	300 miles
TOTAL	4,000 miles [44]

In 1902 the SP purchased the Bromwell Steamship Company, a competitor operating three ships between New Orleans and New York, and consolidated its operations with those of the Morgan Line. In the same year regular freight service was established be-

tween Galveston and New York. Also in 1902 navigation responsibilities were divorced from Morgan's Louisiana & Texas Railroad & Steamship Company and thereafter operated as a department of the SP—although the "Morgan Line" flag designation was wisely retained because of its popularity and business value. [45]

Morgan Line passage between New York and New Orleans was promoted by the SP as a wonderful "1800 mile trip—Five Days on the Deep." Weekly sailings were doubled in 1913 as popularity increased. Shippers and travelers alike were told of the many advantages offered by the "100% SP Route." In 1922 and thereafter passengers were urged to take advantage of "One Hundred Golden Hours at Sea" while shippers were surprised to learn that SP's water-rail route schedules were competitive with all-rail options. [46]

As a result of conditions imposed by the Panama Canal Act, Morgan Line routes and service became subject to review by the ICC. In 1917 that agency confirmed Morgan's existing route structure and approved its carriage of Mexican oil in tankers. The ICC eventually also allowed Morgan to expand service to Houston, Baltimore, Boston, New Bedford, and Norfolk. SP's maritime operations, on the other hand, were understandably curtailed by the government when its fleet was "impressed" during World War I. [47]

In 1921 the Morgan fleet was at its apex, with twenty-eight ocean-going steamers (five

For Health Or Pleasure

This is the ideal time to take the Sea Trip of One hundred Golden Hours between

New York and New Orleans
ON
Southern Pacific Steamships
(MORGAN LINE)

It will exhilarate you to breathe the bracing salt air and revel in the warm sunshine. Connections at New Orleans with the SUNSET ROUTE for points in Louisiana, Texas, Mexico, New Mexico, Arizona, and California, including the famous "APACHE TRAIL" auto trip. *Literature on request.*
L. H. NUTTING, General Passenger Agent, 366 Broadway, N. Y.

of which were freight-passenger ships) and sixty-five auxiliary vessels. By the time it celebrated its Golden Jubilee in 1927, however, the Morgan Line had begun an inexorable decline. Service to Havana had ended in 1923 with the sale of the two ships assigned to that route, and six years later its tankers were sold to Richfield Oil in exchange for fuel oil.[48]

Morgan's last hurrah, although unrecognized at the time, came with the launching of the *Dixie* on July 27, 1927. An oil-burning passenger and freight steamer of 12,000-ton displacement, it was clearly the crown jewel of Morgan's fleet; it cost $2.4 million and was placed in service on the New York–New Orleans run during January, 1928. The magnificent vessel was grounded in a fierce hurricane near Miami in 1935, but passengers and crew fortunately escaped serious injury although the vessel itself was damaged. While laid up, it was reconditioned and modified to add several recreational and service facilities. The resplendent *Dixie* resumed service on Decem-

ber 11, 1935, the sole vessel of its type on Morgan's roster, departing from New York and New Orleans every third Wednesday.[49]

Operations of the Morgan Line were under constant scrutiny by SP accountants throughout the depression; it failed to generate net income after 1931, and, as a consequence, older vessels were sold or retired rather than replaced. Lower volumes of traffic were offered the line, but depressed conditions demanded reduced rates to retain even that. Operating costs rose accordingly. Furthermore, the relative value of the Morgan Line to the Southern Pacific had decreased following the acquisition of the St. Louis Southwestern Railway in 1931. Not surprisingly, an internal study in 1937 urged disposal. H. M Lull, who was in charge of steamship operations, took exception. He admitted the urgency of the problem and counseled President A. D. McDonald to curtail operations if necessary but "to continue the Morgan Line without making any heavy investments." In any event, said Lull, "it would be difficult to find a purchaser for an operation which itself has not been profitable for a long time."[50]

McDonald took Lull's advice, but the end was clearly in sight. Services were reduced in 1940, and by the end of that year the fleet was down to twelve freighters and the *Dixie*. Events then took a strange turn. Early in the next season, at the request of the government, the *Dixie* was transferred to the navy; the grande dame of the fleet sailed from New Orleans on February 22, 1941, for the last time under the Morgan flag. With no similar vessel to protect the New York–New Orleans service, it was necessary, said the SP, "to discontinue this service." Two freighters assigned to that run were then sold to other carriers and before midyear the navy directed the SP to hand over the remainder of the fleet, ten vessels, "for national defense purposes." With that passed the famous Morgan Line. It was "with much regret," said SP's press release, that the "company had been forced to quit the business." It was true that there was nostalgia among SP officers for the old line, but in truth

The *Dixie*, outbound from New Orleans.

the war provided the company a convenient and graceful way of terminating business that was a distinct financial liability and offered no future promise.[51]

Another of SP's ventures into water transportation—steamer service on California's Sacramento and San Joaquin rivers—gained much less notice than its transbay ferries or its oceanic subsidiaries. The service dated from March 1, 1854, when it was begun by the California Steam Navigation Company, a firm that was acquired by the California Pacific Railroad and that itself passed to the hands of the Southern Pacific. Wheat shipments in great volume were typical of early billings, but later the steamers carried fruit, wine, hardware, and general lading. Tourists especially appreciated daylight trips through what promoters labeled "the Netherlands of America." To be sure, the wide, flat valley of the Sacramento featured fertile lands behind a system of dykes and levees. Although they owned a proud record of service, the SP's river steamers were doomed by an adequacy of rail lines supplemented by a growing network of roads;

they ceased operations on January 15, 1930.[52]

If SP aggressively sought to curtail or even terminate unremunerative elements of its business during the late 1930s, it also energetically sought to make more money from those it retained. Such was the case for the long-distance passenger train. A massive national advertising campaign in 1939 urged a public long weary of the depression that this was "The Year to See America," especially Northern California, where SP trains served "The Heart of the Snow Region" and, not to be slighted, Southern California, "Where the Winter is Summer." Additional advertising, on billboards strategically located along congested highways, suggested that harried drivers should "take the train next time" for they were, after all, a safe, fast, inexpensive, and relaxing way to travel. And they were air conditioned. Pleasure travel did increase, in part because of gradually improved economic conditions and in part because those who had money to travel chose to do so at home instead of abroad, where conditions were increasingly uncertain. SP's management was

SP's service on the Sacramento River dated, indirectly, from 1854.

also convinced that improved schedules, air conditioning, new equipment, external advertising, and "new economy-type trains" such as the *San Francisco Challenger*, the *Californian*, and the *Beaver* (on the Overland, Golden State, and Shasta routes, respectively) served as attractions.[53]

Executive officers labored on other matters as well. Periodically during the 1930s they sought to simplify SP's inordinately complex corporate structure. Several subsidiaries, as diverse as the Phoenix & Eastern Railroad and the South Pacific Coast Railway, were disincorporated or otherwise merged into the parent corporation. The most impressive of these efforts culminated in 1934 when the numerous entities making up SP's Texas & Louisiana lines were merged into the Texas & New Orleans Railroad. (See chapter 11.)[54]

Another major decision involved the very location of the company's executive offices. Correspondent with the retirement of Hale Holden as chairman in 1939, after lengthy deliberation, and apparently at the strong urging of Jesse H. Jones and the Reconstruction Finance Corporation, the board of direc-

tors announced that executive headquarters would be moved to San Francisco from New York City. Collaterally, responsibilities of the chairman devolved to the president, A. D. McDonald, and an all-California executive committee was appointed. The move, said the company, was designed to put the board in closer contact "with local problems." Most observers thought it long overdue.[55]

The decision to move the executive offices to San Francisco resulted in an increased aggressiveness on the part of SP's board as well as its management team. The economic picture, of course, had brightened for the company as the depression ebbed. Furthermore, difficult but correct decisions by SP's leaders had been made during "the dark decade," especially during the later years. These diverse decisions were centered on such issues as dealing with SP's funded debt, reducing or abandoning marginal or unprofitable elements of its business, focusing on and making greater investments in those elements that promised greater return, advancing its strategic position, and otherwise planning for the future. In the end, SP's senior managers simply gambled on the future. They made impressive capital expenditures for new motive power (including the road's first diesel locomotives—switchers for Oakland, placed in service on April 1, 1939) and equipment, betterments to track structure (SP would have 4,700 track miles of rail that was 110 pound or heavier by 1942), and installation of CTC. All promised lower operating expenses and represented tangible evidence of that gamble.[56]

The SP was not without problems. Nevertheless, its diligent efforts caught the eye of several outside analysts who, like a writer for the *San Francisco News*, applauded "the great changes" that were "the result of definite planning and hard work by men who were given the responsibility to make them." In its financial survey of the SP in 1937, the N. S. Hall Company pointed out that the SP was "the largest transportation system in the country, measured either in terms of mileage or total assets." Hall gave SP a high credit rating, although not as high as that given rivals Santa Fe and Union Pacific. *Fortune* in 1937 observed that SP was "bigger than General Motors, Standard Oil of New Jersey, or U.S. Steel . . . in short, after AT&T and the great Pennsylvania Railroad, [it is] the third-biggest industrial corporation in the land." SP's railroads, it reported, represented 95 percent of the holding company's assets. Others pointed out with admiration that Southern Pacific was going to emerge from the depression without the aid of bankruptcy proceedings. For that matter, they noted, SP had never defaulted on a fixed obligation.[57]

Much of the credit for SP's ultimate success in weathering the depression and preparing the company for the future belonged to A. D. McDonald, "an auditor by training and a Scotsman by birth," as one writer put it. McDonald was an exacting officer who personified a simple creed of dependability, perseverance, courage, and character. Indeed, argued McDonald, "character is the basis of a successful life." To the graduates of Notre Dame in 1931, he said: "Without an ideal of

some kind life has no significance; without a life purpose, opportunities can neither be seen nor grasped." McDonald was clearly a man of exceptional integrity and vision. He advocated what he called "a new era in railroading" and urged every employee to do his utmost to make the Southern Pacific "Your Friendly Railroad" in fact as well as philosophy. The very success or failure of the company, McDonald understood, depended not so much upon physical facilities as upon the individuals who worked for the company in all capacities. Small wonder a family feeling permeated the SP organization during his tenure.[58]

Small wonder, too, that the SP family was shocked when Angus Daniel McDonald died unexpectedly on November 15, 1941. It would fall to Armand T. Mercier to lead the Southern Pacific through the trying but also exhilarating years of World War II.[59]

Angus Daniel McDonald, who had led the SP through the harsh days of the 1930s, died unexpectedly on November 15, 1941.

CHAPTER 11

The Texas & New Orleans Railroad

"This is the oldest, largest and strongest system in Texas."—S. G. Reed, *History of the Texas Railroads*

SP managers in later years complained that an "iron curtain" existed at El Paso. Although the assertion may have been exaggerated, there clearly were difficulties of communication, logistics, and authority at this critical junction, where traffic was channeled to and from the Pacific Lines, Texas & Louisiana Lines, and the Golden State Route. There were several possible explanations for the problem. Before the era of modern communication, division of the sprawling Southern Pacific into two systems—Pacific and Atlantic—for administrative purposes made sense. On the other hand, such division promoted two separate and increasingly disparate corporate cultures. The matter was further confused in Texas by an onerous constitutional requirement that every railroad operating in the state "keep public office in the state" and further that no Texas-chartered railroad could consolidate with a "foreign" company (one chartered in another state). For that reason alone, SP's interests in the Lone Star State for many years could not be integrated with its interests elsewhere. Moreover, as the relative importance of the Texas & Louisiana Lines and its Morgan Line extension decreased—because of the erosion of traffic correspondent with the opening of the Panama Canal and the growing importance of SP's Golden State Route—the cloud of second-class citizenship settled over SP's Sunset Route east of El Paso. Only in later years would SP management seek to break down the "iron curtain" and bring its Texas &

Louisiana Lines fully into the company as an equal partner.[1]

Southern Pacific's early interest in Texas and Louisiana understandably centered on driving the Sunset Route to completion between Los Angeles and New Orleans. Construction of the line west of El Paso was for its own account, but between New Orleans and El Paso the SP forged a through line only by gathering and tying together several separately organized properties. Initial construction by SP's antecedent companies began during the early 1850s in both Louisiana and Texas.

The easternmost portion of the Sunset Route had its origin in April, 1852, when ambitious citizens of Louisiana secured a charter for the romantic-sounding New Orleans, Opelousas & Great Western Railway. Construction of the 5′6″ gauge line began five months later, but progress was slow as crews toiled in the low and poorly drained forest swamps west of Algiers, across the Mississippi River from New Orleans. Five years were required before the line was completed 80 miles to Brashear City, now Morgan City, Louisiana. There the terminus remained until after the Civil War, when Charles Morgan acquired the property and changed its gauge to standard. For some years Morgan had been operating a fleet of small steamers between New Orleans and Mobile and later from New Orleans to Brashear City, Galveston, and Corpus Christi. On June 4, 1873, Morgan also initiated steamer service between New Orleans and Havana. Just before he died in 1878, Morgan disposed of his rail and water interests, which then were recast as Morgan's Louisiana & Texas Railroad & Steamship Company (ML&T).[2]

Under the watchful eye of a young engineer named Julius Kruttschnitt, ML&T construction gangs renewed their activity in 1878, reaching Lafayette with rail in May, 1881, and then turning northward toward Alexandria. Sixty miles of construction and twenty-five miles of trackage rights over the Texas & Pacific allowed the Morgan's Louisiana & Texas to reach that community. Elsewhere, the Louisiana Western Railroad, supported by the SP through Collis P. Huntington, completed its line westward from Lafayette to the Sabine River in 1881.[3]

On the Texas side of the Sabine, land and timber promoters who sought to open up a promising country and at the same time find an outlet through Houston for forest products, broadened the scope of their enterprise to include creation of the Texas & New Orleans Railroad (T&NO)—a company that would satisfy their initial desires and at the same time provide connection for the lines (mentioned above) building from the east across Louisiana. By January, 1861, Texas & New Orleans crews had negotiated the Trinity and Neches rivers and their valleys to provide a line from Houston to Orange. The history of the T&NO during and shortly after the Civil War is unclear, but it was partly dismantled and out of service for a time. New owners rehabilitated the property, and the line to Orange was opened again on October 16, 1876. The short stretch between that place and the Sabine River was closed by the Louisiana Western Extension Railroad before March, 1881, and thus a connecting service between New Orleans and Houston was established.[4]

An important adjunct to the growth and development of Houston and SP's eventual association there involved two unrelated firms, the Texas Transportation Company and the Direct Navigation Company. Incorporated in

Shortly before he died in 1878, Charles Morgan disposed of his water and rail interests, which were then recast as Morgan's Louisiana & Texas Railroad and Steamship Company.

1866, the Texas company ten years later built a strategic line of railroad from Houston along Buffalo Bayou (now called the Houston Ship Channel) to Clinton, 7.4 miles. It was supported by Morgan's Louisiana & Texas Railroad & Steamship Company, which already was laboring to secure federal aid in developing the ship channel and in making Houston a deep-water port. The Direct Navigation Company had been established in 1866 for the purpose of operating steamboats and barges on Buffalo Bayou between Houston and Galveston and also offering lighterage for cotton and other commodities to vessels lying in or about Galveston Bay. After improvements to the channel were made, the relative importance of the navigation company diminished, but that of the Texas Transportation Company was increased. Both, of course, in their own ways served greatly to make Houston an important world port.[5]

The first passenger train west of Morgan City enters Broussard in 1879.

Buffalo Bayou, foot of Main Street in Houston, head of navigation.

On February 11, 1850, by special act, the legislature of Texas chartered the Buffalo Bayou, Brazos & Colorado Railway (BBB&-C), and its construction, begun a year later, was the earliest of any by SP's antecedents. The purpose of the railway was to link the headwaters of Buffalo Bayou, some five miles from Houston, with the twin productive valleys of the Brazos and Colorado rivers to the west. By the fall of 1860 rails had reached Alleyton, 80 miles inland but slightly short of the Colorado River. The gap was closed by the Columbus Tap Railway, which itself became part of the BBB&C in 1866. Four years later the road was sold to promoter Thomas W. Peirce and others, who on July 27, 1870, changed its name to the Galveston, Harrisburg & San Antonio Railway (GH&SA).[6]

Peirce's immediate goal was to extend the line to San Antonio, which was reached on February 5, 1877. A momentous celebration followed, as townsmen applauded the coming of the steamcar civilization. At the same time, C. P. Huntington was contemplating means by which to extend SP's influence eastward from California and simultaneously frustrate the efforts of Thomas Scott, and later Jay Gould, to make reality of the goals implied by the corporate title of the Texas & Pacific Railway (T&P). The SP quickly built eastward through the territories of Arizona and New Mexico. At the same time, the value of the GH&SA was not lost on Huntington, who successfully induced Peirce to link with the SP at El Paso instead of building northwestward from San Antonio to a junction with the Texas & Pacific.[7] Galveston, Harrisburg & San Antonio construction gangs faced no serious problems until they reached a few miles west of Del Rio, where surveyors' stakes led them into the narrow valley of the Rio Grande. Indeed, to maintain standards of grade, tunnels were required near the confluence of the Pecos River and the Rio Grande. The location proved temporary; a viaduct or "high bridge" over the Pecos would be placed in service in March, 1892. As crews from San Antonio worked

westward, others approached from El Paso. On January 27, 1883, they met 227 miles west of San Antonio. The Sunset Route was complete; through trains from New Orleans and San Francisco left their respective terminals on February 5. Furthermore, the joint Southern Pacific–Galveston, Harrisburg & San Antonio enterprise defeated the aspirations of the Texas & Pacific; Jay Gould was reduced to signing an important territorial agreement with Huntington in 1881. Under that compact Huntington agreed to allow the Texas & Pacific trackage rights from Sierra Blanca, Texas, to El Paso, 90 miles, but the T&P laid no rail west of the Rio Grande.[8]

Unfortunately, the record of the early financial involvement of Huntington and the SP in those properties eventually acquired in Texas and Louisiana is incomplete. Certainly this is the case with the Galveston, Harrisburg & San Antonio. Huntington did pledge support for Peirce's extension to El Paso through the Southern Development Company, and he may have exercised authority over the property as a consequence. Control passed to the SP on March 1, 1885, when the GH&SA was leased, and was clearly affirmed on July 1, 1889, when the railroad became one of SP's proprietary lines, operated under its own flag but governed by the parent.[9]

Huntington worked feverishly for further consolidations and acquisitions. Morgan's Louisiana & Texas Railroad & Steamship Company became a proprietary line on March 1, 1885. It was much the same with the Texas & New Orleans Railroad, which with its rights and ancillary holdings also became one of SP's proprietary properties in 1885. New construction in and about Houston then linked several SP properties.[10]

The Houston & Texas Central Railroad (H&TC) offered the SP an opportunity to broaden significantly its service area. Advantageously located on a north-south axis, it had evolved from the Galveston & Red River Railway, chartered as early as 1848. Construction began in January, 1853, from

The Sunset Route was completed early in 1883, when construction crews met at a remote location 227 miles west of San Antonio.

The ML&T became a proprietary line on March 1, 1885. ML&T's handsome locomotive #47 and the business car *Morgan* were visitors at the New Orleans Exposition of 1884–85.

The SP officially reached the important river city of New Orleans when the ML&T became a proprietary line in 1885.

Houston on a 5'6" gauge (altered to standard in 1874–77). Following a change in name to the Houston & Texas Central, its fortunes were inhibited by inadequate financing and then by the Civil War. When that conflict ended, the Houston & Texas Central owned a main line from Houston northward to Millican and a short branch from Hempstead toward Austin. Its rails finally reached Dallas during the summer of 1872, and the Red River at Denison in March of the next year. The branch to Austin had been completed earlier, in December, 1871. The H&TC fleshed out its system by acquiring the Waco & Northwestern Railroad (Bremond to Waco and shortly beyond, 55 miles, in 1873); the 108-mile Austin & Northwestern (built in part to narrow gauge and later converted to standard from Austin to Llano, with branches) in 1901; the Fort Worth & New Orleans Railway (from Fort Worth to Waxahachie, 42 miles) in 1901; and the tiny Central Texas & Northwestern Railway (Garrett to Waxahachie, 13 miles), also in 1901. The Houston & Texas Central itself came under SP's control in 1895 but, pursuant to Texas law, remained in operation by its own offices.[11]

From its earliest entry into the railroad affairs of Texas, the SP favored Houston over Galveston. It did not ignore Galveston; on the contrary, it established service there, by trackage rights, as the result of the Huntington-Gould agreement in 1881. Then, on September 28, 1905, the SP—through its Galveston, Harrisburg & San Antonio—secured an independent entry by acquiring the Galveston, Houston & Northern Railway, which owned a main line from near Houston to Galveston plus a branch from Strang to Sylvan Beach as well as trackage on Galveston Island.[12]

To further strengthen its grip on Houston and to hold much of East Texas for its own development, the SP brought the expansive-sounding Houston East & West Texas Railway into its corporate fold during 1900. The company had been incorporated in 1875; its subsidiary in Louisiana, the Gulf, Shreveport & Kansas City Railroad, was chartered in 1883. Together they had built 232 miles of track between Houston and Shreveport during the period from 1876 to 1885. Originally constructed as a narrow gauge line, the line was changed to standard in 1894.[13]

An especially curious relationship existed between the Southern Pacific and the San Antonio & Aransas Pass Railway. The SAP, as it was known, was incorporated in 1884 as a consequence of the desire of San Antonio's leaders for a connection to the Gulf. Construction in 1885–88 took the line through Kenedy and Beeville to Corpus Christi, with a branch to Aransas Pass and Rockport. Other construction between 1886 and 1888 extended the SAP from Kenedy to Houston and between 1885 and 1887 from San Antonio northwesterly to Kerrville. To secure a connection with the Texas-Mexican Railway, a branch was built south from Skidmore to Alice in 1887–88. Yet another feeder was placed in service during 1891 from Yoakum to Waco. Late in 1903, San Antonio & Aransas Pass's management announced plans to extend its line from Alice into the Rio Grande Valley with a terminus at Brownsville. Con-

On September 28, 1905, the SP—through its GH&SA—secured an independent entry to Galveston.

struction crews reached Falfurrias by mid-1904, but then they were disbanded for lack of money. The SAP had been a part of SP's domain since 1892, but in December, 1903, the Railroad Commission of Texas compelled the SP to divest itself of stock control. This proved, however, to be a temporary setback, as the ICC in 1925 would authorize the lease of the San Antonio & Aransas Pass to SP's Galveston, Harrisburg & San Antonio.[14]

Huntington's insatiable thirst for more rail lines remained unslaked. The high-sounding New York, Texas & Mexican Railway was the pet of Count Joseph Telfener, an Italian nobleman, who dispatched his fellow countrymen to construct a line—from Rosenberg, 37 miles west of Houston on the GH&SA, to Brownsville and then into Mexico. Incorporated

in 1880, the New York, Texas & Mexican began service from Rosenberg to Victoria two years later, but the project failed there. The SP purchased substantially all of its stock in 1885, selling it, in turn, to the GH&SA during 1905.[15]

The New York, Texas & Mexican Railway connected at Victoria with the Gulf, Western Texas & Pacific Railway (GWT&P), which between 1871 and 1873 had built a 28-mile route from Victoria to Cuero. The GWT&P passed to Charles Morgan in 1877, to the SP in 1885, and to the Galveston, Harrisburg & San Antonio in 1905. During 1888–89 the Gulf, Western Texas & Pacific also built a 56-mile connection between Victoria and the San Antonio & Aransas Pass at Beeville.[16]

Rounding out what became SP's network in

The San Antonio & Aransas Pass Railway came into SP's orbit in 1892, left it temporarily, and returned in the 1920s. An SAP train is seen here at San Antonio.

the Victoria area was an undertaking styled the San Antonio & Gulf Shore Railway. Its promoters hoped to link San Antonio with the Gulf, Western Texas & Pacific at Cuero. Only 28 miles were constructed between 1895 and 1898; it fell to the GH&SA in 1905 and was finished to Cuero during the next two years.[17]

Most of the formerly independent companies in Texas and Louisiana that became part of the Southern Pacific had at least one branch or secondary main line. Morgan's Louisiana & Texas and the Louisiana Western had several feeders that tapped much of southern Louisiana. Elsewhere, SP's predecessors so pervaded the landscape in and about Houston that their collective map looked like a plate of wet spaghetti; the Houston & Texas Central owned a second line between Mexia and Navasota; the Galveston, Harrisburg & San Antonio had an important branch from Spofford to Eagle Pass and a connection there for Mex-

ico; and the New York, Texas & Mexican had two short appendages.

Several of these predecessor companies had nicknames that suggested something of their heritage or at least their local reputation. The Houston East & West Texas was known as the "Rabbit" because its profile seemed to hop from hill to hill and its ride was so unpleasant that, as customers said, it was "Hell Either Way You Take It." The Houston & Texas Central took the moniker "Hoboes and Tin Cans," and because it was built by Italian crews, the New York, Texas & Mexican became known as the "Macaroni."[18]

Another of SP's Texas lines with a nickname was the "Dalsa," between Hearne and Flatonia. The word *Dalsa*, as might be expected, stood for Dallas and San Antonio; the line itself represented a shortcut for traffic moving on the SP from San Antonio and the west to Dallas and Fort Worth. Completion of this route by the Houston & Texas Central required acquisition of the tiny Hearne & Brazos Valley Railroad between Hearne and Stone City; new construction between Stone City and Giddings; trackage rights over the San Antonio & Aransas Pass from Giddings to Flatonia; and use of the Sunset Route to San Antonio. It was opened for regular freight service on September 10, 1913, although scheduled passenger service did not begin until October 7, 1920.[19]

SP's interests in the states of Texas and Louisiana were further expanded during the 1920s. The 40-mile Franklin & Abbeville Railway, serving a Louisiana sugar refinery and plantation, was added in November, 1924. So, too, was the Dayton–Goose Creek Railway, a 25-mile pike serving the petroleum industry from Baytown to Dayton in Texas; it became part of the SP empire on May 1, 1926. Longer but not nearly as consequential as the Dayton–Goose Creek was the Texas Midland Railroad, acquired on April 1, 1928. This 125-mile road—made popular by Hetty Green, "The Witch of Wall Street," and her flamboyant son Colonel Ned Green—linked Ennis (on the H&TC) with Paris, in northeast Texas. Also, the San Antonio & Aransas Pass returned to the SP fold on April 8, 1925.[20]

A continuing desire to expand its opportunities in the Lone Star State predictably led SP's management to pursue acquisition of the Texas Mexican Railway, which stretched from the Gulf of Mexico at Corpus Christi westward to the Rio Grande and an important gateway to Mexico at Laredo. Constructed as the Corpus Christi, San Diego & Rio Grande Narrow Gauge Railroad, the line had been completed bit by bit between 1876 and 1881. The corporate designation was changed to Texas Mexican in 1881, and the road was converted to standard gauge in 1902. It connected with the San Antonio & Aransas Pass at Corpus Christi and at Alice. SP's interest in the Texas Mexican dated from early 1920 when W. R. Scott, who was in charge of the T&L Lines, urged Julius Kruttschnitt to au-

thorize its purchase. "Possession of the road," said Scott, "would put us in an ideal position toward future development in Mexico and would give us a preferred location in Laredo, the main gateway to Mexico." Furthermore, Scott warned, "the Gulf Coast Lines [which had trackage rights over the Tex-Mex from Corpus Christi to Robstown] has been making overtures for the control or purchase of this line."[21]

Negotiations followed a serpentine path. It was true that the Gulf Coast Lines proposed to lease the Texas Mexican, but for whatever reason such an agreement was not consummated. Meanwhile, SP officers studied the matter; the executive committee finally authorized lease or purchase of the line in February, 1925. This upset the Missouri Pacific, which had come to control the Gulf Coast Lines as well as the International & Great Northern with which the Tex-Mex connected at Laredo. It also upset the Missouri-Kansas-Texas Railroad (the M-K-T, or Katy), which had no physical connection and, in fact, whose lines were no closer than San Antonio. Consequently, it seemed for a while that the SP, Missouri Pacific (MoPac), and the Katy would collectively purchase the Texas Mexican. The Katy eventually withdrew, but at the outset of the depression the SP and MoPac, through the agency of the Central Hanover Bank and Trust Company, appeared to develop a compatible joint-lease arrangement. Events conspired otherwise. The Missouri Pacific went into bankruptcy in 1933, the SP itself struggled through hard times, and the Texas Mexican remained independent.[22]

Had the Southern Pacific been successful in acquiring the Texas Mexican, it likely would have had those properties leased for operation by the Texas & New Orleans Railroad. SP's managers in Houston long had been faced with the difficulty of administering the affairs of each subsidiary as an operating concern. Fortunately, however, the railroad commissions of Texas and Louisiana and the Interstate Commerce Commission gave their respective blessings to a plan by which all of the entities making up SP's Texas & Louisiana Lines passed under lease to the T&NO which, of all, owned a corporate title that best described the geographic nature of SP's properties in Texas and Louisiana. The new arrangement permitted a desirable concentration of authority, activities, and supervision and facilitated economies in all departments. The unification took effect on March 1, 1927.[23]

Benefits of the new consolidation were immediately evident in the colonization and agricultural promotion efforts of the Texas & New Orleans. Its antecedents had earlier developed their own programs so that the attractions of each area in SP's service area had been properly advertised; the Galveston, Harrisburg & San Antonio, for instance, promoted southwest Texas while the "old" T&NO ballyhooed east and southeast Texas. The GH&SA had early organized an immigration bureau, sent agents abroad to recruit settlers, and authorized a rate of 1.75 cents per mile for all who chose to relocate along its lines. Elsewhere, Morgan's Louisiana & Texas had helped to rejuvenate Louisiana's flagging sugar cane industry shortly after the turn of the century by building high-capacity sugar cane cars and by lowering rates, which allowed producers and processors to concentrate their operations and regain financial stability. Now, under the T&NO's unified leadership, these efforts were more tightly focused. A colonization agent was located in New Orleans for the purpose of promoting the agricultural and industrial potential of Louisiana; a twelve-car farm demonstration train toured Texas in cooperation with that state's A&M College; 160 4-H members from T&NO country in Texas received paid trips to College Station for a short course in 1927; and a flood of new, sophisticated promotional materials emanated from the Houston offices.[24]

All of this was particularly useful given SP's final campaign of expansion in Texas—into the "Magic Valley" or, more precisely, the Lower Rio Grande Valley. The San Antonio &

Aransas Pass had set out for the valley in 1903, but the drive stalled at Falfurrias during the following year. When the SAP returned to SP's orbit in 1925, a thorough assessment of SP's options and opportunities in South Texas was ordered. W. R. Scott told A. D. McDonald that the Missouri Pacific would "always be our chief competitor in Texas" and, noted Scott, the MoPac was—through its Gulf Coast Lines—thoroughly entrenched in the Rio Grande Valley. Much to the consternation of L. W. Baldwin, president of the Missouri Pacific, who considered the "territory already adequately served," the Interstate Commerce Commission nevertheless granted permission to extend the SAP line from Falfurrias to McAllen, with a branch from Edinburg eastward to Harlingen. Construction began on October 5, 1926, and on February 6, 1927, service was initiated to McAllen. Baldwin was even more disturbed when the T&NO asked the ICC for permission to extend its Edinburg branch to Brownsville. He offered the T&NO trackage privileges over the MoPac, "without local rights," between the two places, but Scott saw "nothing of value in this proposition." The ICC went along; service to Brownsville began on November 10, 1927, with a predictable and enthusiastic celebration.[25]

Under the original order the SAP had permission to build "to the international boundary . . . at a practicable crossing of the Rio Grande"; this would have been near McAllen but, although the National Railways of Mexico periodically encouraged it to do so, the T&NO never elected to create another "border port" at that location. Instead, the company sought to develop local business in the "Magic Valley." Small wonder. SP's shareholders were told that it contained "the richest and most productive soil of any agricultural section in the country." T&NO agricultural agents and sales representatives spread this good news far and wide, offering fascinating programs and instructive pamphlets. In a related campaign, agricultural agents promoted

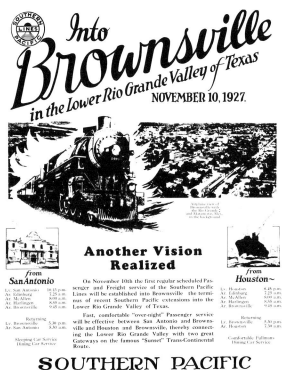

Into Brownsville in the Lower Rio Grande Valley of Texas
NOVEMBER 10, 1927.

Another Vision Realized

from **San Antonio**

Lv. San Antonio 10.15 p.m.
Ar. Edinburg 7.25 a.m.
Ar. McAllen 8.00 a.m.
Ar. Harlingen 8.55 a.m.
Ar. Brownsville 9.45 a.m.

Returning
Lv. Brownsville 5.30 p.m.
Ar. San Antonio 5.30 a.m.

Sleeping Car Service
Dining Car Service

On November 10th the first regular scheduled Passenger and Freight service of the Southern Pacific Lines will be established into Brownsville the terminus of recent Southern Pacific extensions into the Lower Rio Grande Valley of Texas.

Fast, comfortable "over-night" Passenger service will be effective between San Antonio and Brownsville and Houston and Brownsville, thereby connecting the Lower Rio Grande Valley with two great Gateways on the famous "Sunset" Trans-Continental Route.

from **Houston~**

Lv. Houston 8.45 p.m.
Ar. Edinburg 7.25 a.m.
Ar. McAllen 8.00 a.m.
Ar. Harlingen 8.55 a.m.
Ar. Brownsville 9.45 a.m.

Returning
Lv. Brownsville 5.30 p.m.
Ar. Houston 7.30 a.m.

Comfortable Pullmans
Dining Car Service

SOUTHERN PACIFIC

C. K. DUNLAP, Traffic Manager.   W. C. McCORMICK, General Passenger Agent.
HOUSTON, TEXAS

H. H. GRAY, Gen'l Agent Pass. Dept.,
165 Broadway,
New York, N. Y.

the institution of a significant canning industry in the Valley. The rewards were immediate. Much of T&NO's increase in freight volume for 1928 came from billings made along the new 135-mile lines. It was the same for passenger revenues. Vacationers by the thousands detrained each winter at handsome new stations in McAllen, Edinburg, Harlingen, and Brownsville.[26]

A heavy volume of perishable traffic originated on the T&NO or moved overhead. It began in 1884 when two enterprising farmers shipped a carload of watermelons from Prairie View, Texas, to Houston, where they sold them from a stand in front of Grand Central passenger station. Their profits were good; watermelon soon became a principal crop in many parts of the T&NO's service area and, at the same time, an important part of the railroad's traffic mix. Louisiana shippers sent wild dewberries to market, and in 1937 the Rio Grande Valley set a record in the movement of citrus. Bananas moved overhead to

the West, while a full range of California and Arizona produce passed to the East. Pacific Fruit Express iced 43,508 cars at El Paso in 1928 alone. Indeed, PFE represented an imposing enterprise along the T&NO, with icing facilities at El Paso, San Antonio, Del Rio, Hearne, Edinburg, Skidmore, Houston, and Shreveport.[27]

The Texas & New Orleans also handled the usual traffic in merchandise and bulk commodities, and it likewise hosted promotional movements—solid trains of tractors and threshing machines, for example—and early in 1940 it participated in the unit train movement of Plymouth automobiles from Detroit to a consignee in San Antonio. Local loadings included grain, cement, cotton, aggregates, wool, merchandise, and LCL items.[28]

Nothing more characterized local loadings on the T&NO than livestock. Live turkeys moved from Victoria, horses and mules from the San Antonio area, and goats, sheep, and hogs from other localities. Yet, in Texas at least, the term *livestock* was a synonym for cattle. At many locations, particularly on the old Galveston, Harrisburg & San Antonio and on the Llano Branch, cattle billings were extremely important. Huge company-owned stock pens were located at Alpine, Marfa, Ryan, Valentine, Lobo, and Llano; impressive water and feed facilities, necessary to comply with federal water and rest laws, were located at El Paso, Waco, Hearne, and Ennis. In 1916 a total of 5,792 carloads of cattle were shipped from or delivered to stations between San Antonio and El Paso; Marfa and Uvalde had the greatest billings. Handling livestock, however, was a tedious business. Dispatchers watched train sheets carefully to be certain that livestock was delivered within thirty-six hours or otherwise unloaded for feed, water, and rest. Brakemen were responsible for inspecting the animals at every stop and for prodding any "down" animals. And, of course, each car had to be bedded with sand before loading.[29]

Another commodity that characterized Texas & New Orleans country—one that was

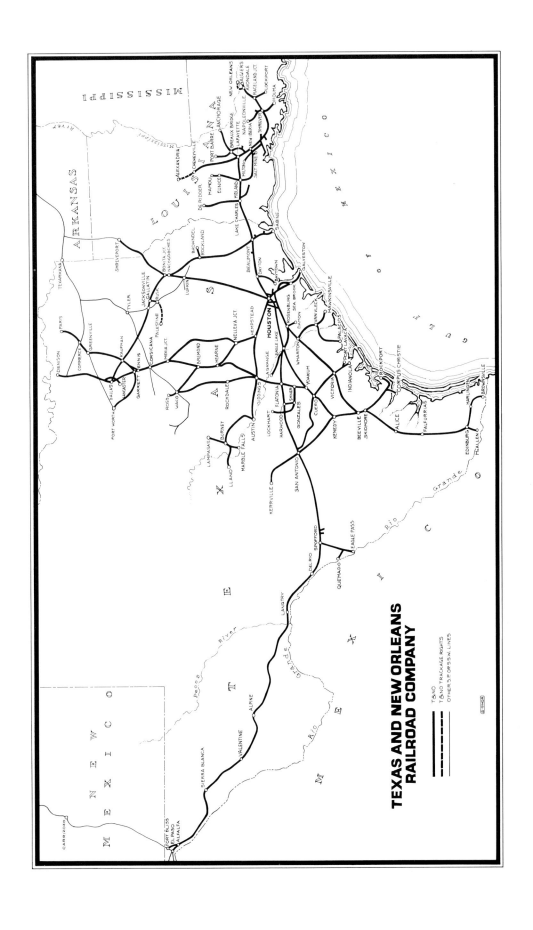

TEXAS AND NEW ORLEANS RAILROAD COMPANY

T&NO	
T&NO TRACKAGE RIGHTS	
OTHER S.P. OR S.S.W. LINES	

A full range of California and Arizona produce moved east over the T&NO. Here a cantaloupe train takes water at Marathon, Texas.

far more important to the ultimate development of the region and to the railroad's fortunes—was oil. Early fields were located near Corsicana, Humble, and Dayton, but the grand-daddy of them all was ushered in on January 10, 1901, at Spindletop dome near Beaumont. Petroleum products promised impressive revenues as well as a constant and inexpensive source of fuel. Three locomotives from the T&L Lines, one each from the GH&SA, H&TC, and T&NO, were soon equipped to burn oil. The experiment was a dramatic success; by July 31, 1901, 500 tank cars and 50 storage tanks were ordered as the first step in converting the entire locomotive fleet of the Texas & Louisiana Lines from coal to oil. Morgan steamers followed in short order. Meanwhile, shipments of crude oil produced generous revenues, but they proved short term. Refiners complained that rail rates were too high compared with those of pipe lines; the carriers had to admit that they could not even meet their operating expenses at pipe line rates. Although they generally lost the haulage of crude oil, Texas railroads continued to handle prodigious volumes of refined products—7.8 million tons from the

Lone Star State in 1940, of which 31 percent was billed on the Texas & New Orleans. Petroleum caused Houston to boom. Shortly before World War II, twenty-five refineries had been located in and about that bustling city.[30]

Reflecting its growing need for a dependable and inexpensive supply of fuel oil for its locomotives and steamships, the SP saw to the creation of the Rio Bravo Oil Company on March 3, 1903. Specifically, this new subsidiary was empowered "to produce, sell and transport oil and other minerals in Texas and Louisiana." It quickly acquired lands and leases in areas that promised production of lignite, coal, and oil. Rio Bravo produced more than 31 million barrels of oil from various fields by 1944. It also produced a precedent-setting case in which the Texas Supreme Court ruled that owners of adjacent lands could claim mineral rights to the center of an easement granted for a railroad right-of-way. That decision in 1932 cost Rio Bravo over $6 million and partly explains SP's need to seek the assistance of the Reconstruction Finance Corporation during the depression.[31]

Many who arrived in the "oil patches" to work for Rio Bravo and other petroleum companies did so aboard Texas & New Orleans passenger trains. Without question, the flagship of T&NO's passenger operation was the *Sunset Limited*, which began life in November, 1894 (as the *Sunset Express*), and served the entire route from San Francisco and Los Angeles to New Orleans. In 1916 the *Sunset Limited* featured a sterling consist of "Pullman drawing room, compartment and observation cars and dining car" and made only nine station stops on the 1,194–mile line between El Paso and New Orleans. The number-two train on the route, later named *The Argonaut*, handled standard equipment plus popular "tourist sleepers."[32]

The rest of T&NO's passenger operations—except for the Houston-Dallas line, which in 1930 boasted four trains daily in each direction including the *Sunbeam*, *Hustler*, *Owl*, and a local—were prosaic. During the same

The T&NO handled a normal traffic in merchandise and bulk commodities. This train of mixed freight has stopped at Taft, Texas, northwest of Corpus Christi.

season gas-electric motor cars held down train assignments on seven runs. Mail and express revenues justified the existence of these and most others, but income from local passengers declined, reflecting the national trend toward automobiles and buses. Sadly but predictably, trains from the Rio Grande Valley handled an increasing number of corpses during the winter months, as more and more elderly refugees fled the North to spend snowy seasons in a warmer climate. On a happier note, passenger business picked up in 1936 when the Texas Centennial Exposition was held in Dallas. The T&NO derived additional income from special trains such as that which carried President Franklin Roosevelt from Houston to San Antonio in 1936. Thousands cheered him in Houston at the SP's fine new passenger station and along the route. Other Texans supported their favorite college football teams each fall by riding special trains that carried them to gridiron clashes at the Cotton Bowl (Dallas), Sugar Bowl (New Orleans), Sun Bowl (El Paso), and even to the Rose Bowl (Pasadena). The annual contest between the Texas A&M College and the University of Texas always guaranteed extra

trains, which required no advertising. That happy situation was not the case generally. However, the T&NO air conditioned its cars, reduced its rates, and advertised these facts. Business on regularly scheduled trains turned up during the 1930s, if only slightly.[33]

Competitive forces likewise had impact on Texas & New Orleans freight operations. Faster and more reliable freight service was required. Perishables received the most expeditious handling; forty-eight hours elapsed time from Edinburg to Memphis, sixty-three hours to East Saint Louis via Shreveport and the St. Louis Southwestern Railway (SSW). The T&NO and SSW, via Corsicana, also cooperated in the operation of the *Motor Special*, which, after automobile manufacturing companies established plants in California, handled parts as an extension of the assembly process. Additional improvements followed in merchandise service. Sixth-day delivery from Los Angeles to New Orleans was improved to fifth day in 1937, and three years later the T&NO instituted the *Corpus Christi Overnight* on the Victoria division to and from Houston.[34]

Signal protection and automatic train control added an important level of sophistication to T&NO's plant. The first automatic block signals had been installed between Houston and Beaumont during 1904, and by the end of 1926 the entire Sunset Route was thus protected. The Houston-Dallas line followed in completion a year later. Additional funding provided for the installation of an electrical control system governing the movement of trains over the Dallas Belt Line. More impressively, 171 miles of track between San Antonio and Rosenberg, west of Houston, were outfitted with automatic train control by the end of 1927.[35]

The Texas & New Orleans's motive power inventory followed a predictable evolution from the American Standard 4-4-0s to the famous Golden State (later called General Service) 4-8-4s. In 1925 there were 665 locomotives assigned to the T&L Lines; they

The *Sunset Limited*, T&NO's flagship train, leaves the Houston station.

averaged twenty years in age and only 71.27 tons weight on the drivers. During the 1930s passenger trains usually drew 4-6-2s; through freights drew workhorse 2-8-2s and 2-10-2s. A host of smaller power handled branch, local, and switching assignments, while the handful of GS engines were true to their "general service" designations, although they usually held passenger runs. Compared to the motive power stable for SP's Pacific Lines, the T&NO's fleet was pedestrian but reliable.[36]

The impact of the Great Depression was

particularly devastating to the service area of the T&NO and thus to the railroad itself. Reduced revenues led to "forced economies." Layoffs were carried out in all departments, resulting in thousands of personal tragedies within the corporate family. H. M. Lull, SP's senior officer in Houston at that time, reminded all employees that recovery had followed every previous depression, and he encouraged his forces to anticipate the future "with renewed faith and courage." Meanwhile, he authorized the establishment of an

T&NO passenger trains proudly called on this impressive station facility at San Antonio.

Employee Relief Loan Fund for unfortunate employees furloughed as a result of hard times. Recovery proved elusive, though. Maintenance programs suffered accordingly. By early 1932 a disappointing 24.3 percent of the T&NO locomotive fleet was "waiting repairs, in shop, or unserviceable." Five years later the company junked nearly one hundred engines.[37]

In November, 1930, the mayor of Houston contacted the Texas & New Orleans, among several of the city's largest employers, asking that the company "give reasonable assurance" to employees that "their jobs are secure" and to "employ force as fast as conditions warrant." Lull promised the mayor that he and all other T&NO officers shared a concern for victims of the depression, especially those former railroad employees now out of work. He took the opportunity to point out, however, that "the situation in which the railroads find themselves at present" was "not due wholly to the present business depression." Lull complained that a variety of laws and governmental policies had circumscribed the inherent efficiencies of railroads. The railroads were tightly regulated by state and federal agencies that granted inadequate rate increases; they were forced to compete with an inland waterway system, an Intercoastal Canal, a growing system of roads and highways, and air carriers—all of which received large governmental subsidies; and they were unfairly taxed. This, said Lull, reduced their profitability, impaired their ability to compete, and restricted their ability to maintain or expand employment. Lull may have been impolitic in speaking so boldly, but he correctly perceived that the railroads were suffering from more than just the current economic trauma.[38]

Lull also correctly understood that successful management and operation of railroads proceeds from an understanding of "cooperative enterprise." Failure was certain unless each department, and indeed each individual, could be counted on to "perform work faithfully and well." Lull was especially pleased with the good work of the T&NO service clubs, which he thought represented "mutual helpfulness." There seems little doubt that the sense of family, strong on the Pacific Lines, was even stronger on the T&NO. This may be explained by the harshness of times in Texas and Louisiana or by the fact that the T&NO itself was restricted to only two states, whereas the Pacific Lines were spread over several. In any event, the tight-knit nature of the T&NO was reflected in the energetic activities of "employee service clubs," which held elaborate annual parties in Houston and lobbied there and elsewhere to increase both passenger and freight business for the railroad. It was similarly manifest in various athletic activities—bowling, golf, basketball tournaments and a remarkably fine system track and field meet staged annually from 1924 until World War II—and in the impressive performances of the railroad's band and glee club. Most of all, it was reflected by the tenor of the *Bulletin* for the T&L Lines.[39]

The editors of the *Bulletin* over the years persistently stressed these themes: safety; the quality of cuisine and service in Texas & New Orleans dining cars; courtesy; the injustice of subsidies given to other forms of transportation; fuel conservation; camaraderie and loyalty; and, most of all, the sense of "one big family." Particularly popular were regular columns devoted to news about the T&L Lines, operations of the Morgan Line, activities of the service clubs, accomplishments of personnel, retirement notices, and especially "Gossip From Along the Line." After resumption of publication in 1936, following a hiatus after 1932, the *Bulletin* featured in-house advertisements boosting T&NO passenger service and exhorting employees to seek every opportunity to sell it. The *Bulletin* likewise mirrored regrettable regional racial attitudes. Activities of the segregated "colored employees service clubs" were reported, as were retirements such as that of one George A. Branford, whom the editor in 1940 identified as one of the company's "most popular colored employees."[40]

The medical welfare of Texas & New Orleans personnel was attended to in company-owned hospitals. The first of these was established by the Galveston, Harrisburg & San Antonio at Columbus, Texas, in 1880; its successor was placed in service at Houston in 1911. Payroll deductions were made in the form of dues as early as 1880, on the GH&SA and later on the other subsidiaries. The standard rate initially was 50¢ per month and guaranteed the employee medical care as well as voting rights in the hospital association.[41]

Therapy of another type was required in an effort to combat the erosion of less-than-carload business on the T&NO. To this end, the Southern Pacific Transport Company was established on August 1, 1930; the Southern Pacific Transport of Louisiana followed on April 16, 1932. Both were organized as trucking arms to coordinate with and supplement T&NO rail lines in "the performance of store-door pick-up and delivery." Initially, contracts were drawn with local drayage operators for pick-up and delivery while the T&NO provided the intercity haul in box cars. Later on, Southern Pacific Transport's operations were expanded to include over-the-road hauls by company-owned trucks driven by its own employees.[42]

Other changes were in the offing. Operating circumstances at New Orleans had been difficult since service began there before the Civil

Historically, T&NO passenger trains reached New Orleans by ferry from Avondale.

War. A bridge across the Mississippi River had not been built because of difficult foundation conditions, low lands in approach to the river, required navigational clearances, plus costly hazards of construction. Consequently, yarding operations for freight were conducted across the river at Algiers; cars were ferried from there to New Orleans. Passenger trains reached New Orleans Union Station (actually the Illinois Central station, which hosted T&NO and Gulf Coast Line trains as tenants) by ferry from Avondale. The SP, through Morgan's Louisiana & Texas, as early as 1892 had proposed a high-level bridge, but the depression of 1893 precluded construction. The matter languished until 1916. In that year the Public Belt Railroad Commission succeeded in gaining passage of a state constitutional amendment that gave the City of New Orleans exclusive right to construct and operate a bridge across the river at that place. The project again fell into obscurity until increased rail business and the development of vehicular transportation made it more popular. Finally, on November 5, 1932, bonds of the Public Belt Railroad Commission were guaranteed by agreement among the SP, the City of New Orleans, and the State of Louisiana; these

The *Hustler* calls at Ennis, Texas.

The first regularly scheduled train to use the $13 million Huey P. Long bridge was the eastbound *Sunset Limited* on December 17, 1935.

were sold to the Reconstruction Finance Corporation shortly thereafter.[43]

Events then moved quickly. Construction began on December 31, 1932, and the 4.35-mile imposing double-track railroad and four-

lane highway structure was placed in service on December 16, 1935—reason enough for a day-long celebration. The first regularly scheduled train to utilize the $13 million Huey P. Long–Mississippi River Bridge was, appropriately, the eastbound *Sunset Limited* on the seventeenth. It was headed by T&NO's GS-1 702, with tires painted white and side-rods and brass polished to a shine. Soon thereafter the venerable ferry ships and transfer vessels were scrapped, and a new freight yard was built at Avondale.[44]

The great bridge at New Orleans understandably served as a valuable "shot in the arm" for the depression-weary railroaders of the T&NO. They received another on September 19, 1937, when their company introduced "the very latest in travel comfort, luxury and convenience"—the new twin streamlined *Sunbeams* on two-stop, 4-hour and 45-minute afternoon runs between Houston and Dallas. The eight-car trains were powered by P-14 4-6-2s, streamlined by the Houston shops especially for *Sunbeam* service; all equipment was painted in *Daylight* colors. So popular were the trains that T&NO's management quickly authorized new streamlined equipment for the morning *Hustler*. On June 5, 1938, the road advertised "double daily air-conditioned service between Houston and Dallas." The *Hustler* performed local work, but the *Sunbeam* now offered a nonstop run of 265 miles in 265 minutes. Even the *Owl* received new bedroom sleeping cars in 1940 to accompany its standard sleepers, chair cars, coaches, and head end equipment.[45]

Opening of the Huey Long Bridge and streamlining of the *Sunbeam* and *Hustler* were not simply of psychological importance; they were also statements of faith. The SP made no more important statement during the grim days of the 1930s, however, than when it wisely and courageously acquired the strategically located St. Louis Southwestern Railway—a property that complemented the SP, as well as the Texas & New Orleans, and secured important gateways at Memphis and East Saint Louis.

CHAPTER 12

The St. Louis Southwestern Railway

"For the future of these lines [SP's Texas &
Louisiana Lines] it is absolutely necessary
that we should own a line extending to the
main distributing point for the Southwest,
St. Louis."—W. R. Scott to A. D. McDonald

As clouds of the Great Depression settled over
the land, the St. Louis Southwestern Railway
(Cotton Belt) operated a modest system of
lines, somewhat under two thousand miles in
all. Lying on a northeast-to-southwest axis
from Saint Louis, it served portions of Missouri, Illinois, Arkansas, Louisiana, and Texas
and met the Southern Pacific's Texas & New
Orleans at several locations, including Shreveport, Dallas, and Waco. It was a logical fit in
SP's network.

The St. Louis Southwestern possessed a
colorful and complex history. Its earliest predecessor, the Tyler Tap Railroad, was formed
when disappointed citizens of Tyler, Texas,
learned that neither the Texas & Pacific Railway nor the International & Great Northern
Railroad had chosen their community for
new lines. Incorporated late in 1871, the Tap
finally began service on October 1, 1877, between Tyler and the T&P at Big Sandy, 21.5
miles to the northeast. Built as a narrow-
gauge road, it quickly fell on hard times and
required reorganization in 1879 as the more
expansive-sounding Texas & St. Louis Railway. Two years later construction crews had
taken the road beyond Big Sandy to Texarkana
as well as southeastward to Waco. In the process, the Texas & St. Louis opened an important new country and provided important
connections for its patrons. For a while at
least, it was also considered an integral part

of a grandiose Great Lakes–to–the–Gulf
narrow-gauge system proposal. That caught
the attention of Jay Gould, who sought to buy
it or kill it. He canceled traffic agreements that
the narrow gauge had with his properties at
Texarkana, but the Texas & St. Louis struck
back by announcing a major incursion into
"Gould country." On August 12, 1883, the
road was opened across Arkansas to Bird's
Point, Missouri, on the west bank of the Mississippi, opposite and slightly above the mouth
of the Ohio River. Traffic alliances then were
forged with the Illinois Central Railroad and
the St. Louis, Alton & Terre Haute Railroad;
transfer boats ferried cars to and from Cairo,
Illinois. Financial difficulties followed, however, and on January 23, 1884, the company
landed in the hands of a receiver.[1]

The properties were sold in 1886 to become
the St. Louis, Arkansas & Texas Railway, but
the new company was not without the problems of the old. Its narrow gauge was a distinct liability, the road lacked feeders, and its
financial circumstance remained precarious.
Nevertheless, it plunged ahead. On the northern portion of its lines the gauge was changed
to standard on October 18, 1886, and on
January 12, 1887, over the remainder; the
cost was nearly $3 million but the alteration was required if the road was to survive.
Construction or acquisition of branches followed. These included: Mount Pleasant to

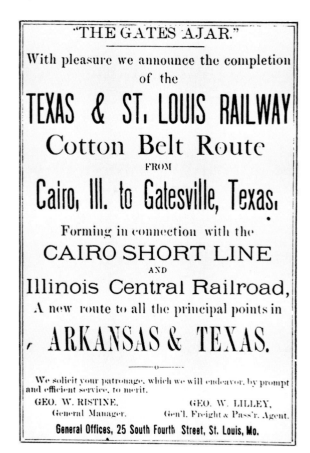

"THE GATES AJAR."

With pleasure we announce the completion
of the

TEXAS & ST. LOUIS RAILWAY

Cotton Belt Route

FROM

Cairo, Ill. to Gatesville, Texas,

Forming in connection with the

CAIRO SHORT LINE

AND

Illinois Central Railroad,

A new route to all the principal points in

ARKANSAS & TEXAS.

———o———

We solicit your patronage, which we will endeavor, by prompt
and efficient service, to merit.

GEO. W. RISTINE,   GEO. W. LILLEY,
General Manager.   Gen'l. Freight & Pass'r. Agent.

General Offices, 25 South Fourth Street, St. Louis, Mo.

The narrow-gauge Texas & St. Louis ended up in
the hands of a receiver.

Sherman, Texas (1887); Commerce, Texas, to
Fort Worth (1888); Corsicana, Texas, to Hillsboro, Texas (1888); Altheimer to Little Rock,
Arkansas (1888); Lewisville, Arkansas, to
Shreveport, Louisiana (1888); and, Malden to
Delta, Missouri (1889). In 1887 it also acquired, but then lost, a narrow-gauge line
southward from Tyler to Lufkin. All of this
was necessary and at the same time too much;
the St. Louis, Arkansas & Texas declared
bankruptcy on May 14, 1889.[2]

Its successor took two titles: the St. Louis
Southwestern Railway, incorporated under the
laws of Missouri on January 16, 1891, and the
St. Louis Southwestern Railway of Texas, necessary to satisfy the constitutional requirements of that state, on January 12, 1891. General offices were located in Saint Louis and in
Tyler, Texas. Pine Bluff, Arkansas, centrally located, became the principal shop location. Although hardly financially robust, the SSW

nevertheless pursued important changes and
made impressive purchases. The Lufkin line
was reacquired in 1899 after it had been standard gauged and then extended through purchase a few miles to Monterey. Two years later
the Cotton Belt also purchased the Stuttgart
& Arkansas River Railroad, a 35-mile artery
that connected Gillett with the SSW main line
at Stuttgart. Even earlier, in 1893, it had taken
control of the Paragould Southeastern Railway, another formerly narrow-gauge road; between 1888 and 1907 the Paragould was extended from near the Arkansas village of its
namesake eastward to Blythesville. It was fully
absorbed into the Cotton Belt in 1914. During 1892 the SSW additionally gained access
to important markets at Memphis when the
St. Louis, Iron Mountain & Southern granted
it traffic concessions via its line from Fair Oaks,
Arkansas (north of Brinkley). The Cotton Belt
secured another major market in 1898 when
it secured trackage rights over the Gulf, Colorado & Santa Fe Railroad from Wylie, Texas,
into Dallas. Elsewhere, the SSW created the
Shreveport Bridge & Terminal Company,
which itself authorized construction of an impressive bridge over the Red River at that location. It opened on December 1, 1907. Of particular importance for the long-range goals of
the company was the incorporation in 1896 of
the Gray's Point Terminal Railway. On De-

cember 1, 1898, that subsidiary completed an extension of line northeastward from Delta, Missouri, to Gray's Point, where a new transfer incline was built to facilitate ferrying operations across the Mississippi to connections at Thebes, Illinois, with the Illinois Central and the Chicago & Eastern Illinois Railroad. Eventually the older transfer facility at Birds Point washed away, although service to Cairo remained by way of Thebes.[3]

If Jay Gould had tried to thwart the aspirations of what became the Cotton Belt, his second son, Edwin, had much to do with its later good fortune. The younger Gould became an officer of the St. Louis Arkansas & Texas in 1888, and after the company's reorganization into the Cotton Belt, became its vice-president. He was elected president during the next year and served in that position until April 22, 1912. Under Edwin Gould cooperation was predictable with the so-called Gould Lines, headed by his brother George. For example, in 1900 the Iron Mountain agreed to handle Cotton Belt passenger trains and freight traffic directly into Saint Louis, and in the same year the Iron Mountain granted the SSW permission for full freight and passenger service into Memphis from Fair Oaks. Also in 1900 the Cotton Belt was joined by the Missouri Pacific and the Iron Mountain (along with two non-Gould lines, the Illinois Central and the Chicago & Eastern Illinois) in forming the Southern Illinois & Missouri Bridge Company to build a new rail line and bridge over the Mississippi between Thebes, Illinois, and Illmo, Missouri. Opened on May 25, 1905, the Thebes Bridge was owned in fifths by the participating carriers, although eventually control would pass to the Missouri Pacific (60 percent) and Cotton Belt (40 percent). The bridge immediately extinguished the need for the nearby transfer incline and ferry. The bridge likewise implied further cooperation with the Iron Mountain. That road was granted trackage rights over the SSW from Illmo to Dexter, Missouri, 47 miles, and, reciprocating in kind, the Iron Mountain in

1903 granted the Cotton Belt trackage rights for passenger trains and in 1904 for freights from Thebes to East Saint Louis, approximately 120 miles. Bridge and passenger station rights were then accorded by the Terminal Railroad Association of Saint Louis, in which the Cotton Belt acquired a proprietary interest during 1910.[4]

Under Edwin Gould's influence the Cotton Belt expanded farther. Twelve miles of new construction in 1903 took the SSW directly into Dallas from Addison, and during the following four years the Lufkin Branch was extended farther, to White City. In Arkansas the SSW absorbed the Central Arkansas & Eastern Railroad in 1911 and then completed that company's construction program—short stubs from Stuttgart to Hazen and from Stuttgart to England. Other acquisitions were not as well advised. The 30-mile Eastern Texas Railroad between Lufkin and Kennard, acquired in 1906, would be abandoned in 1921, and the 106-mile Stephenville, North & South Texas Railway, leased by the Cotton Belt in 1913, would be abandoned between 1934 and 1941. Also, on January 1, 1918, the short Pine Bluff Arkansas River Railway was leased, but it too would be abandoned early, in 1934.[5]

With its system essentially in place, Cotton Belt's management turned to the important business of solidifying previous gains. Early in 1913 the SSW opened a new freight terminal in north Saint Louis, and during the following summer the company purchased a large tract of land in East Saint Louis that eventually became its freight yard there. Elsewhere, on April 1, 1912, the Cotton Belt joined with four other railroads to form the Memphis Union Station Company, and on the same day the Chicago, Rock Island & Pacific Railroad (CRI&P) granted the Cotton Belt the right to use its line for passenger trains only from Brinkley to Memphis. During the next season these two railroads joined with the Iron Mountain in thirds to fund construction of the Harahan Bridge over the Mississippi at Memphis. Cotton Belt's investment in that structure was eventually jeopardized when the Iron Mountain became balky over the contract covering SSW's use of its line to Memphis from Fair Oaks for freight trains. Fortunately, the Rock Island was more flexible and, effective February 28, 1921, the SSW began use of the CRI&P between Brinkley and Memphis for freight and passenger trains alike. Cotton Belt's passenger trains, of course, used Memphis Union Passenger Station; its freights utilized yards of the Illinois Central.[6]

The era of railroad expansion had generally passed except in West Texas, Arizona, and Oregon, but during 1928 Cotton Belt's management foolishly yielded to "construction fever." It took the form of the Saint Francis Basin Project. The company's purpose was to gain fuller access to the rich and productive agricultural territory of southeast Missouri and northeast Arkansas and at the same time shorten its route between Saint Louis and Memphis. To accomplish this, the SSW purchased six tiny railroads and built 30 miles of new line. When operations began on November 10, 1930, the Saint Francis project represented a through line from Saint Louis—by way of McDonald, Arkansas, and then trackage rights over the Missouri Pacific—to Memphis. It was a gigantic bust. Through service ended as early as November 10, 1934, and a portion of the line would be abandoned in 1940.[7]

From 1900 through 1929, SSW's traffic trend in freight was upward; ton miles increased at an annual average rate of 10.8 percent. This was explained by Cotton Belt's expanded system of branches and by the rapid development of the Southwest. The proportion of traffic originated on line hovered at the 50 percent mark, and manufactured goods led among all commodities handled; products of agriculture, mines (mostly crude oil), forests, and LCL followed in order. Competition for local business was brisk, and for overhead traffic, intense. Missouri Pacific's subsidiaries, the St. Louis, Iron Mountain & Southern and the Texas & Pacific, provided

CONSTRUCTION HISTORY
OF THE COTTON BELT ROUTE

immediate and keen rivalries along the entire length and breadth of the Cotton Belt. Vigorous competition for interchange traffic and long-haul business came also from the Missouri-Kansas-Texas Railroad and the St. Louis–San Francisco Railway.[8]

Except for the extremities of the line—Saint Louis and East Saint Louis on the north and Dallas–Fort Worth on the south—the service territory of the St. Louis Southwestern could generally be classified as agricultural. From Illmo to Texarkana the terrain is generally flat to rolling, with river-silt soil in the lowlands and sandy clay elsewhere. Much of the country had been heavily timbered earlier but was gradually cleared and drained for cultivation. Principal crops included corn, rice, potatoes, alfalfa, and—around Tyler—fruits, vegetables, and even roses. Additionally, as the company's popular nickname suggests, cotton was grown at several locations along the SSW. Even the company monogram, if legend be trusted, is the cross-section view of the drive cam from an old cotton gin.[9]

To bolster local business the Cotton Belt in 1908 established an agricultural and in-

dustrial department, which, not surprisingly, tended to emphasize farming projects. During the following year a 300-acre demonstration farm was purchased near the Lufkin Branch south of Tyler. The company's purpose was to prove that crops other than cotton and corn could be profitably produced in that region. Most of the land was initially devoted to the cultivation of peach trees, but experimental acres were also devoted to pears, apples, plums, and figs. The plan to gain greater pro-

duction from the East Texas "poor lands" was demonstrably successful. In 1912 a total of 1,158 carloads of fruits and vegetables were billed from SSW stations in the county where its Brunswick Farm was located. Experiments later centered on tomato production, and, to increase sales potential by expanded marketing, the railroad sponsored a program of picking and wrapping green tomatoes, which ripened enroute. Company horticulturists also experimented with improved cotton-

One of the principal crops grown in the Cotton Belt's service area is rice. Bulk carriage in covered hopper cars was many years in the future.

growing techniques as well as food preservation and preparation; the SSW then spread the news of their work by way of special demonstration trains and in the 1920s by a motor bus fitted with loudspeakers.[10]

The railroad also engaged itself in another innovative service. In 1916 Edwin Gould, who by then was Cotton Belt's chairman, became alarmed by the widespread malarial infection along the company's lines and pledged to see what could be done to relieve the problem. Gould placed certain of his personal securities in a trust fund, specifying that its income was to be used for malaria prevention and control programs. Gould was confident that positive results could be achieved from the programs but felt the company itself should not be burdened with such expense until the value was clearly demonstrated. Malaria, without question, was a serious problem and a special menace to railroad workers and others who labored in the outdoors. It sapped their strength and because of its onerous reputation handicapped the industrial and agricultural development of the entire region. Remedial measures began in 1917 at Tyler, Lufkin, and Texarkana, where "drain-

age and oiling operations" were carried out by a "malaria extra gang" under the supervision of the company's sanitary engineer. During the next two seasons other campaigns to control mosquitoes, and thus malaria, were undertaken at Mount Pleasant, Commerce, and Pine Bluff. At the same time the SSW placed screens on the windows and doors of its cabooses and gang cars. Personnel were simultaneously educated on the matter through exhibits and instructional presentations aboard the Cotton Belt's car *Anopheles*, which toured the company's Arkansas lines and most of those in Texas, with the cooperation of the respective state health departments. The car was equipped with exhibits and models to teach the story of typhoid fever, bubonic plague, and smallpox as well as that of malaria. Results were impressive. The number of malaria patients given treatment by Cotton Belt's Railway Employees' Hospital at Texarkana for the years 1917–20 was but one-third of those for the years 1913–16 (before the program began).[11]

Like most of the country's railways, the St. Louis Southwestern came under control of the federal government's U.S. Railroad Administration on December 28, 1917. The USRA soon cut the railroad's allowances for track maintenance, purchased inadequately treated ties for the company's roadbed, and curtailed services. Meanwhile, the U.S. Labor Board increased pay for employees, but the ICC authorized rate increases that were inadequate to cover these new costs. Capital improvements were few, although the Valley Terminal Yard in East Saint Louis was completed during the USRA years. The Cotton Belt was, sad to say, ill-served by government administration brought on as the result of World War I.[12]

The quality of freight and passenger service on the Cotton Belt, in comparison with that of the major trunk roads, was as pedestrian after the war as it had been before. During the years 1926 through 1928 one daily scheduled time freight in each direction (sometimes a second northbound train) typified all of the principal lines. These were supplemented with

Cotton Belt's secondary routes frequently saw passenger service provided by motorcars.

triweekly local service and extras as needed. Between 1923 and 1929 passenger ridership fell by 76.8 percent, and 1923 was the last year that passenger service generated net earnings. Nevertheless, passenger train miles remained high in comparison with freight. Sleeping cars, diners, and club cars were found on four trains—one in each direction between Saint Louis and Pine Bluff and between Memphis and Dallas—and as late as 1928 the primary lines boasted two passenger trains in each direction. Secondary routes and branches were yet served by steam trains, motorcars, or mixed trains. Pride of the line was the *Lone Star Limited*, which offered daily service between Memphis and Dallas–Fort Worth.[13]

Although it was hardly an impressive money maker, the Cotton Belt was nevertheless attractive to suitors because of its location. This was fully perceived by James E. Gorman, president of the Chicago, Rock Island & Pacific Railroad, who in March, 1925, ordered "the purchase of a dominant interest in the stock of the Cotton Belt." As a consequence of the sale, St. Louis Southwestern for the first time in its history became governed by another railroad company, although the Rock Island determined not to seek a merger or even immediate consolidation of the Cotton Belt into its own system, but rather chose to operate it as an allied and independent company. Rock Island's interest in the Cotton Belt was understandable. It wished to control an increased portion of traffic to and from Texas and southwestern points. However, the Rock Island itself was about to be assaulted by a group holding the St. Louis–San Francisco Railway, a rival of the Cotton Belt. Because of this new development, and because the Interstate Commerce Commission issued an unfavorable decision on the CRI&P's request to acquire an additional interest, the Rock Island disposed of its SSW stock to the Kansas City Southern Railway (KCS) later in 1925.[14]

Thus began a particularly curious chapter in the Cotton Belt's history. On July 24, 1926, the Kansas City Southern asked the ICC for permission to control the Missouri-Kansas-

Texas, which in turn made application to control the Cotton Belt. The enterprise represented the genius of Leonor F. Loree, the intriguing chairman of the KCS, who hoped to forge a large new southwestern rail system. The ICC denied these unusual applications because of what it considered inadequate financial structures, but Loree countered with another proposal: that the M-K-T acquire both the KCS and the Cotton Belt. Meanwhile, the regulatory agency filed proceedings against the KCS, alleging violation of the Clayton Antitrust Act by purchasing capital stock of the Katy and Cotton Belt. Loree threw in the towel; the application was withdrawn and the Kansas City Southern disposed of its Cotton Belt holdings.[15]

Throughout this strange interlude, and even earlier, Cotton Belt's management had prosecuted noteworthy programs of betterments and efficiencies. In 1898 nearly all of the road's track had been 56-pound rail; by 1915 most was 85 pound. Curves and grades, many constructed to narrow-gauge standards, were gradually eased. It was much the same with motive power and rolling stock. By 1915 the road owned 250 locomotives with an average tractive effort of 29,188 pounds, and most of its converted narrow-gauge equipment had been replaced by larger all-steel or steel underframe cars. Additionally, the SSW owned eight gasoline-powered motor cars used in passenger service. The Cotton Belt had early experimented with oil for fueling its locomotives, but it was not until significant fields were developed near or on line that management decided to convert the fleet. This was begun in earnest during 1922–23 and completed shortly thereafter. From 1923 through 1929 significant capital was also invested in heavier rail, ties, ballast, bridge renewal and strengthening, and line revision. All of this was necessary before Cotton Belt could accept its newest power—handsome 4-8-4s built by Baldwin and placed in service between Pine Bluff and Texas points during September, 1930. These programs collectively represented SSW management's belief that expenses could be substantially reduced by building more efficiency into the plant. Cotton Belt's managers likewise faced up to the need to trim unremunerative operations. This was the case, for instance, when service to Cairo, Illinois, over the Chicago & Eastern Illinois and Illinois Central was ended in 1925.[16]

During the years immediately preceding the onset of the Great Depression, Cotton Belt's president, Daniel Upthegrove, demanded that the company recognize and address changing competitive circumstances. Upthegrove understood that modal competition from trucks and buses was not going to disappear, and with that in mind he decided to join the enemy, so to speak, by forming Cotton Belt's own motor vehicle arm, the Southwestern Transportation Company, incorporated on October 1, 1928. Two months later the new company began operation of motor coaches and motor trucks on several routes paralleling the railroad. Even earlier, buses had replaced motor trains on the Lufkin Branch under a contract with an outside company. Indeed, the Cotton Belt was an industry leader in the use of motor vehicles, a matter that was closely monitored by the trade press.[17]

In spite of their persistent efforts, Upthegrove and his sales department watched in dismay as revenues slumped following the Crash of 1929. There was little that could be done to increase volume among Cotton Belt's major freight commodities, but there was clear potential in the movement of LCL freight. Cotton Belt's management recognized that much of this business had been lost to truckers and presently moved to arrest the trend by improving package car service and, through its Southwestern Transportation Company, instituting coordinated rail-truck service with "store-door pick-up and delivery." These innovations not withstanding, SSW's LCL business continued to slump; one final ingredient was required in the design of an integrated transportation package necessary to meet truck competition—speedy overnight trains to provide, as Upthegrove said, "service comparable with trucks." Thus was born Cotton Belt's famous *Blue Streak* merchandise train.[18]

This train, said J. R. Turney, Cotton Belt's vice-president for traffic, would "jettison conventions and taboos of railroading." It would do so by being carded as "first class"; by assigning passenger locomotives to it; by dispatching only carloads of LCL merchandise on it; and, by coordinating its schedules with connecting trains plus pick-up and delivery by Southwestern Transportation Company. In that way, said Turney, merchandise purchased in Saint Louis on one day would be "ready for sale before the next over store counters . . . [at] . . . all points served by the Cotton Belt in Missouri, Arkansas, and Louisiana." The *Blue Streak*, he affirmed, was SSW's answer to "the demand of modern business," and, he predicted, "will prove to be the forerunner of a new breed of freight train." Service began between East Saint Louis and Pine Bluff on October 1, 1931, with much publicity—and much gnashing of teeth by Cotton Belt's rail competition, particularly the Missouri Pacific and the Frisco, both of which considered the service "wasteful and unnecessary." Nevertheless, the *Blue Streak* was an immediate success; it captured new business and gave the company a vital psychological boost. "Again! Cotton Belt Shows the Way!" was the bold assertion made by the company when the *Blue Streak* took to the rails. It was no idle boast.[19]

Southern Pacific officers in New York, San Francisco, and Houston were well aware of the impressive strides that the Cotton Belt had made to improve itself during the last half of the 1920s. They were equally aware of its favorable location and potential for mischief in any merger such as that proposed by the Rock Island and later by Loree. As SP's H. M. Lull said, "sooner or later the Cotton Belt will be merged with some other system." Earlier in the decade William Ripley had wished to place the SSW with the Frisco but later recommended splitting it between the Frisco and

the Rock Island. The ICC itself had similar changes of heart. That body initially thought the SSW should be placed with the Frisco but eventually considered that it would be better as a part of the Illinois Central.[20]

Although it had forged a traffic agreement with the Cotton Belt on business moving via Corsicana as early as 1913, Southern Pacific's interest in the smaller road increased gradually over the next two decades. When J. M. Herbert left the SP to become president of the SSW in 1916, a new general traffic agreement specified that the Cotton Belt "would solicit via Southern Pacific preferentially" but that the SP would only "solicit via Cotton Belt without discrimination." Meanwhile, the historic importance of the Sunset Route east of El Paso for transcontinental business declined because of changed traffic alliances, competition from water carriers using the Panama Canal, and conditions of the Canal Act that hampered the Morgan Line. Additionally, more business, especially perishables, moved via Tucumcari after the SP acquired the El Paso & Southwestern. Perishables and other time-sensitive freight also moved in large volumes by way of El Paso and the Texas & Pacific–Missouri Pacific. In 1928, for instance, the Texas & New Orleans received 18,484 carloads of perishables from the Pacific Lines, but the rival Texas & Pacific was given more, 22,085. On the other hand, most of the cantaloupes from the Imperial Valley and Arizona were handled to Tucumcari for interchange with the Rock Island.[21]

Serious threats to take over the SSW by the Rock Island and Loree during the 1920s thus caused understandable consternation among SP's management personnel. Debate over the matter was continuous and heated. In Houston, W. R. Scott brooded about the future of T&L Lines. He pointed out to A. D. McDonald in 1926 that the SP lines under his direction were, in a sense, captive with "no outlet except to the Gulf Coast and the West." It was absolutely necessary, he maintained, for the SP to "own a line extending to the main dis-

The first run of Cotton Belt's famous *Blue Streak* occurred on October 1, 1931.

tributing point for the Southwest, St. Louis." The Cotton Belt, he thought, was uniquely situated to benefit the SP. It would provide an outlet to the east and northeast for the flood of perishables sure to come, the result of new construction in the Rio Grande Valley; it would yield a long haul for the SP system; and it would facilitate direct connection with the eastern trunk roads and obviate the need for intermediate carriers such as the Missouri-Kansas-Texas and the Frisco, among others. Scott was thinking of Saint Louis but also of Memphis as valued entrepôts reached by the Cotton Belt. For good measure, he shrewdly urged purchase of the important Choctaw, Oklahoma & Gulf Railroad, controlled by the Rock Island but rumored for sale, between Memphis and Tucumcari. Scott waxed enthusiastic about prospects at Memphis, where extremely important connections could be effected with the Louisville & Nashville Railroad; Nashville, Chattanooga & St. Louis Railway; and the Southern Railway. Acquisition of the Choctaw would extend SP's dominion through Oklahoma and Arkansas while providing an excellent short-mile thirty-fifth-

parallel route via El Paso and Tucumcari to Memphis; acquisition of the Cotton Belt would grant the SP access to both Memphis and Saint Louis and give new meaning to its heavy investment in the Texas & Louisiana Lines. In all, it would capture a huge territory for the parent.[22]

Scott's enthusiasm for expansion as well as his growing sense of urgency were not matched by senior executive officers in San Francisco nor initially by those in charge of sales for the entire system. The Cotton Belt, complained T. M. Schumacher, "is the weakest line between North Texas junctions and St. Louis." Schumacher was joined in opposition by Paul Shoup who, at least on the Pacific Lines, historically had been an ardent expansionist. Shoup thought acquisition of the Cotton Belt was undesirable, however, because it would threaten "friendly relationships" with the Rock Island and the Missouri Pacific. Most of all, Shoup was "very much concerned with anything that might result in diversion of traffic from our lines to the Santa Fe." Nevertheless, Scott was not about to be put off. He presided over a part of the SP that was characterized by high costs of "gathering and distributing a large volume of local traffic" and would lose the offsetting advantage of long haul should friendly options to the north and east be lost. Scott's fear was not unfounded. The Missouri Pacific had recently integrated the International & Great Northern and the Gulf Coast Lines into its main system, and controlled the Texas & Pacific; L. F. Loree was still posturing for the amalgamation of the M-K-T, KCS, and SSW; and the Frisco and Rock Island at the time seemed headed for merger. If all else failed, said Scott, the SP should acquire or at least neutralize the Trinity & Brazos Valley Railway (owned jointly by the Rock Island and the Fort Worth & Denver City Railway) from near Dallas to Houston. Nevertheless, his focus was clearly on offensive expansion. "I think it is highly important that the Southern Pacific have system lines to through Mississippi River points, say at Memphis and St. Louis, or should have some line closely allied or in control tapping the St. Louis gateway and later a strong connection with Kansas City."[23]

The internal debate continued. Scott won a convert in the sales department when F. H. Plaisted submitted detailed memoranda demonstrating that "when measured by Southern Pacific revenue," business interchanged with the Cotton Belt was "substantially more than with any other southwestern line." Indeed, he said, "disposition of the Cotton Belt is the crux of our problem." The SSW offered the SP, Plaisted argued, the "strongest southwest connection we have on transcontinental traffic" and, at the same time, afforded the T&NO "an opportunity to participate in transcontinental business [El Paso to Corsicana]" as well as a much-needed outlet to the northeast for traffic originating in Texas and Louisiana. Others in the sales department disagreed. Freight and passenger traffic managers in San Francisco complained that it would be imprudent to acquire the SSW ("it is in our interest to have as many connections as possible friendly and working with us")

and impossible to "compete successfully as a St. Louis line through Corsicana" because routes of the principal competitors were better located and shorter. "Our best interests lie in continuing enthusiastic support for all southwestern lines," concluded J. T. Saunders and F. S. McGinnis. Paul Shoup was willing to make only a marginal concession: If the SSW were purchased at all, the "acquisition should be based wholly upon the needs of the T&NO for additional Mississippi River gateway connections."[24]

The entire scenario was bewildering. The Cotton Belt had gone to the merger altar first with the Rock Island and then with L. F. Loree, but neither marriage had materialized. It had also presented itself to the Santa Fe but was rebuffed. Several observers, including SP's F. H. Plaisted, looked favorably on a combination of the Cotton Belt and the Chicago & Eastern Illinois as natural and unoffensive. Others thought the Chicago & Alton a logical mate for Cotton Belt. In any event, Daniel Upthegrove was in San Francisco during March, 1931, to inquire as to SP's intentions. He found SP officers cordial but coy.[25]

Upthegrove must have understood, though, that senior officials of the larger company were nervously studying maps of the entire trans-Mississippi West. Hale Holden worried privately that the assertive Van Sweringen brothers from Cleveland might, in fact, finally merge former Gould lines—the Missouri Pacific, Denver & Rio Grande Western, and Western Pacific—into a powerful transcontinental operation threatening the Overland Route. A strengthened Missouri Pacific would also, as Holden and other of SP's senior executives slowly came to understand, threaten SP's investments in Texas and Louisiana.[26]

The time for action had arrived, but it took a strange turn. To protect itself, and to expand its options, the SP purchased 44,300 shares of the St. Louis–San Francisco—as an investment in a "friendly connection," according to Holden—and, on October 25, 1929, it also began the purchase of St. Louis Southwestern's stock, both common and preferred. By July 15, 1930, the SP held 35 percent of the total outstanding stock of the SSW but Kuhn, Loeb & Company held another 22 percent for the SP pending approval by the Interstate Commerce Commission of its wish to control the Cotton Belt. Papers were filed with that agency on July 25, 1930.[27]

The results of these steps were mixed. The Frisco entered bankruptcy in 1933 and SP's stock in it, purchased for $5,036,770, was sold eventually at almost a total loss; the investment in a "friendly connection" proved hardly fortuitous. Meanwhile, in spite of a serious challenge by the Missouri Pacific, the ICC on January 12, 1932, gave its blessing to "acquisition by the Southern Pacific Company of control of the St. Louis Southwestern Railway Company by purchase of capital stock." Before that announcement was made, however, minority shareholders in the SSW, led by one Walter E. Meyer, succeeded in persuading the SP to acquire holdings on the basis of one share of SP stock for three shares of Cotton Belt common and three shares of SP for five shares of St. Louis Southwestern preferred. Holdings by the SP were thus increased to 86 percent but, strangely, Meyer and his associates did not subscribe; they remained minority but vocal shareholders.[28]

As all of this transpired, the country slid into the Great Depression. In Cotton Belt country, 134 Arkansas banks failed in 1930 alone, and the value of the state's cotton crop dropped by 68 percent in only one season. This was instantly reflected by the fortunes of the SSW. Net income for the company had fallen annually since 1926, but deficits began in 1930 and would continue through 1940. During those eleven years the company lost a staggering $11.5 million. A crisis was at hand when bank loans and bonds matured in 1932. On January 26 the Cotton Belt asked the ICC to authorize a loan from the Reconstruction Finance Corporation, and the regulatory agency approved the application for $18 mil-

lion, but only on condition that the SP guarantee it. After some grumpy discussions SP's executive committee agreed. However, three years later, when the Cotton Belt asked for an additional loan contingent on SP's guarantee, the larger road balked. The SSW thereupon defaulted in the payment of interest on the RFC loan and on December 12, 1935, filed for reorganization under section 77 of the Bankruptcy Act. A month later Berryman Henwood was appointed trustee.[29]

Fortunately, the news was not all grim. A report by Shields & Company in 1935 remarked favorably on the company, pointing to the quality of its management and Cotton Belt's place in SP's sun. Moreover, Cotton Belt's management had labored diligently to get the property in good order before the onset of the depression, and that policy paid off. So, too, did efforts to develop a strong sales team, which enterprisingly solicited traffic from forty-six offices located as variously as Blytheville, Arkansas, and Mexico City. Additionally, new arrangements called for the SP to solicit preferentially for the Cotton Belt except as governed by the Central Pacific Conditions and other agreements entered into before it secured control of the SSW. The rewards eventually were pleasing. Together, the SP and SSW lured substantial and valuable overhead traffic, especially automobiles, trucks, and parts moving to the Southwest and to California. Perishables received from the SP at Shreveport and Corsicana for handling eastbound during the six-year period from 1936 to 1941 totaled 115,091 carloads. For that matter, the total percentage of freight business that the SP interchanged steadily favored the Cotton Belt.[30]

	1933	1941
Eastbound transcontinental to SSW	19.3%	26%
Westbound transcontinental from SSW	7.8	13
To SSW from T&NO	14.8	19
To T&NO from SSW	24.2%	33%

As the 1930s ended the Cotton Belt's fortunes seemed improved, but the long-term picture remained murky. Nevertheless, like the Pacific Lines and the Texas & New Orleans, the St. Louis Southwestern was about to face the greatest challenge of its history: World War II was at hand.

CHAPTER 13

Its Finest Hour

"Temporarily our entire facilities will have to
be used to handle military business."—A. T.
Mercier, 1942

A lively debate characterized the meeting of Southern Pacific's board of directors on October 15, 1942. At issue was the question of whether the company should energetically discharge its bonded indebtedness or renew the payment of dividends on its stock. During the "dark decade" just past, SP's board had struggled with the company's debt structure, courageously authorized significant expenditures for plant and equipment, and had kept the property out of the bankruptcy courts. Like the nation itself, the SP had survived the Great Depression and, like the nation, was then confronted with the realities of World War II. It was the staggering volume of traffic incident to that conflict that resulted in bittersweet profits adequate to occasion the board's debate over debt and dividends and allowed the company, in the end, to both ease indebtedness and issue dividends.[1]

Events of 1940—Lend-Lease, the first peacetime draft, calling up of reservists, and simultaneous orders for war material—resulted in a huge surge of business. Fortunately, the SP was in relatively good physical condition because of the improvements to property made during the last half of the depression. Moreover, the SP was not without experience in defense matters. National Guard troops had been transported regularly to annual training exercises, and in the summer of 1940 the company participated in a gigantic movement of National Guard and U.S. Army troops aboard forty trains to maneuvers at Fort Lewis,

Washington, and elsewhere. Before the year was out the SP found itself delivering building materials for several new military posts and even transporting huge "railroad rifles" on the Coast Line to the upper Santa Barbara Channel for target practice.[2]

Government traffic increased in 1941. During the several months preceding this country's entrance into the war, the SP handled thirty to fifty special passenger trains per week for the Civilian Conservation Corps, army, and navy. Its "number one job," said the company in April, 1941, was "the speedy and efficient movement of freight and passenger traffic involved in Uncle Sam's gigantic defense program of construction and training." A steady flow of freight passed daily over what the company called the "'Burma Road' of National Defense" to a bewildering array of military installations as diverse as Mather Field near Sacramento and sprawling Fort Bliss near El Paso. Major shipbuilding centers at Richmond, San Francisco, Oakland, Wilmington, and Vallejo in California, Houston and Orange in Texas, and Portland, Oregon, provided additional tonnage of monumental dimensions.[3]

Even before December 7, 1941, the SP was experiencing both labor and equipment shortages. Many from SP's family had been drafted and others had volunteered, especially for the army's new Military Railroad Units. At the same time, Joseph H. Dyer, SP's vice-president for operations, urged employees and shippers alike to do whatever was required to relieve the national car shortage; and the mechanical department reported the temporary lease of motive power from several other railroads, including the Texas & Pacific, the Rock Island, the Burlington, and the Great Northern. Privately, SP officers worried that the property was already taxed to the limit. It was not.[4]

The day that President Franklin Roosevelt said would live in infamy brought immediate and dramatic change to the very fiber of the country. The victories of Japanese forces in the Pacific were made more ominous by the ignorance of where they might strike next. Rumors on the West Coast were rampant. One SP officer, Donald J. Russell, was awakened two nights after the Pearl Harbor attack by a caller who urgently reported that the Japanese were at that moment bombing Taylor Yard in Los Angeles; on the next day another caller excitedly announced to him that Japanese infantry had landed near the Golden Gate. The army received similar bizarre reports in greater number and detail; in partial response, it hastily equipped flatcars with anti-aircraft weapons that for several days dutifully patrolled the coastline aboard special SP trains. Somewhat later a Japanese submarine did harass the Santa Barbara area but fortunately failed to shell SP's high viaducts nearby.[5]

Response around the country to the Japanese bombardment of Pearl Harbor resulted in a seemingly contradictory blend of stern determination and hysteria that was reflected on the SP. The naval threat on both coasts, as well as the Gulf of Mexico, meant the immediate diversion of coastwise and Panama Canal traffic to the nation's rails and thus a growing glut of freight business, which the carriers pledged themselves to handle without government intervention of the type experienced in World War I. It was much the same in terms of passenger carriage. Six days following Pearl Harbor Day, A. T. Mercier told the passenger department to stop "soliciting extra trains for the movement of special parties to any point." The meaning was clear: "Temporarily our en-

tire facilities will have to be used to handle military business." Part of that business, sad to say, was to move Americans of Japanese ancestry by the thousands to internment camps in the interior.[6]

SP's response to new conditions took varying forms. President Mercier urged close, calm teamwork among all hands and further urged each person to "be alert and refrain from gossip." Hoods were applied to locomotive headlights, train markers, and trackside signals, and blinds were drawn at night or windows blacked on all passenger, mail, and express cars. It was much the same at the general office building in San Francisco. A twenty-four-hour air raid and fire watch was established on the building's roof, and all windows were darkened. On the Cotton Belt employees were ordered to refrain from commenting publicly on "plans of the armed forces for movement of personnel, material or equipment" and were reminded that, to guard against espionage, visitors were barred from the train shed at Saint Louis Union Station. At Klamath Falls and elsewhere "railroad defense" organizations were established. Company shops turned their talents to unusual tasks: Sacramento fashioned steel plates and shafts for shipyards and hot metal cars for the steel industry, while at West Oakland, navy mechanics studied diesel maintenance procedures aboard units from the *City of San Francisco* as well as SP's new fleet of switchers. For its part, the Northwestern Pacific aided in the construction of ocean-going dry docks to assist vessels damaged in battle. Even SP's remaining ferry operations were affected. The U.S. Coast Guard requested that SP deploy the vessels variously in the Bay Area instead of concentrating them at Oakland Pier, where they were susceptible to air attack and fire.[7]

Across the entire system scrap drives took on a patriotic fervor. Such feelings ironically surrounded the abandonment and dismantling of 120.8 miles of Central Pacific's historic main line above Utah's Great Salt Lake between Lucin and Corrine. Much emotion at-

Hoods were applied to locomotive headlights and trackside signals.

tached to the line. It included not only the stretch where ten miles of track had been laid in one day (on April 28, 1869) to win a wager with the Union Pacific but also historic Promontory, where the Central Pacific and the UP joined on May 10, 1869, to set off national jubilation. The Lucin Cut-off had rendered the old line redundant in 1904, but the SP had been unsuccessful in abandonment efforts until the navy requisitioned all track metal and serviceable ties. Appropriate "unspiking" ceremonies were held at Promontory on September 8, 1942. Two diminutive locomotives owned by the dismantler, Hyman-Michaels Company, faced each other; a crowd between them watched as the first spike was removed by representatives of the SP and UP.[8]

The spirit of patriotism reached a fever pitch in 1942. Railroaders by the thousands joined the armed forces. By the end of the year, 6,192 from the Pacific Lines alone had "joined up." Those who stayed behind found other ways to serve. The SP Club at Los An-

geles provided transportation for servicemen to USO clubs in Hollywood and elsewhere; several persons in the general office building performed as air raid wardens, and others volunteered as members of the building rescue squad; women from the San Francisco office force served as hostesses for army and marine dances; and virtually all purchased war bonds and stamps.[9]

The rush of business placed a great demand on SP's rolling stock. Cars were patched, painted, and in some cases modernized. More were acquired—87 passenger cars and 8,798 freight cars from the end of 1938 through 1942. Shortages persisted, nevertheless. On the T&NO cabooses were in such short supply that boxcars were fashioned into side-door, or what crews called "Bull Moose," cabooses.[10]

The need for motive power presented special problems. Every locomotive SP owned, regardless of age, was reconditioned and restored to service. Additional power was leased from other roads, and on Tehachapi Pass helpers belonging to the SP and Santa Fe were pooled. Rehabilitation programs and cooperative ventures were laudible, but inadequate. Still more power was necessary. Immediate needs could be eased somewhat by the purchase of diesel-electric switch engines to relieve steam road power then assigned to yards. Diesels had other advantages. Mechanical officers admitted that one diesel switcher was the equivalent of one and one-half steam switchers. This same understanding, strange to say, did not extend to the relative value of General Motors' FT freighters, which neighbor Santa Fe embraced with such gusto. In the end, SP purchased 120 diesel switchers during the war years but for road service stayed with steam: 130 new GS 4-8-4s and AC 4-8-8-2s, plus used locomotives including ten 2-8-4s from the Boston & Maine. Because of the large increase in GS and AC locomotives, and because the Sacramento shops could not be economically expanded, a new erecting shop with twelve pits was placed in service at Sparks,

Unspiking at Promontory on September 8, 1942. What would Bret Harte have said?

Nevada, during 1944. Interestingly, the SP utilized structural steel and overhead cranes from the T&NO's abandoned complex in El Paso for the Sparks facility.[11]

Neither was the physical plant ignored. SP crews accomplished herculean tasks as they installed additional CTC equipment and upgraded track under the press of time-sensitive traffic in great volume. Military authorities were concerned that Beaumont Hill east of Colton, California, on the Sunset Route would become a bottleneck; for SP management the question was whether to add a second main track or install CTC. Ultimately, it was included on the list of lines for which CTC was authorized. By the end of the war such capability was extended by 375.2 miles systemwide, including: Redding–Black Butte in Northern California; Colton to Indio in Southern California; a stretch east of Sparks, Nevada, and another west of Ogden on the Overland Route; and parts of the San Joaquin and Coast lines. The volume of track work was even more impressive. In 1929 SP had only 1,532 track miles boasting rail of 110 pounds-per-yard or heavier, and that figure was not appreciably increased until shortly

before the outbreak of war. However, during the years 1940–45 an amazing total of 2,619 track miles were fitted with the heavier rail. And that did not tell the whole story; older rail thus released was cascaded to secondary mains, branches, sidings, and elsewhere to generally upgrade the entire track plant.[12]

Bridges received similar attention. Several were strengthened and new ones installed at various locations. None, however, were as spectacular as the 1,390-foot continuous cantilever, single-track steel bridge over the Pecos River gorge on the Sunset Route in West Texas. The bridge it replaced, a spindly 1892 structure, was, as board member Harvey S. Mudd said, "a weak link in a most strategic route." Consulting engineers in 1941 recommended a new structure, but the extent of war traffic was not yet apparent and SP's own engineers thought replacement unnecessary. By October, 1942, however, 408 freight and 209 passenger trains passed over the bridge per month. "I think the minds of all of us would rest easier if we had two strings in our bow," said Mudd. Consequently, on January 12, 1943, SP directors authorized construction of the new structure in addition to a requisite

A new erecting shop was placed in service at Sparks, Nevada, in 1944 because the Sacramento facility was overtaxed.

line change of nearly two miles. The million-dollar project was placed in service on December 21, 1944, but the old bridge remained intact as Mudd's "second string" and would not be dismantled until 1949. Meanwhile, as had been the case during World War I and earlier border disturbances, army personnel guarded the bridge area against "saboteurs or others who might recognize its importance to the transportation phase of the nation's war effort."[13]

The fortunes of SP's subsidiaries were mixed during these years. The Northwestern Pacific continued to pile up net deficits, but because of generally better business conditions the SPdeMex had net earnings in 1942 and 1943. Results for Pacific Electric during 1941 were

disappointing, and its management continued a policy of contracting rail operations and purchasing additional buses as a substitute for specified rail passenger operations. Sixty-nine rail cars were modernized in that season, however, and the decision proved wise, as PE in 1942 was deluged with war business plus a flood of domestic traffic, reflecting the rationing of both tires and gasoline. Because of the resulting increase in revenues, and because of a refinancing plan that reduced bond interest, Pacific Electric earned net income from 1942 through 1945.[14]

On SP's Pacific Lines, the Texas & New Orleans and the Cotton Belt, there was continuous consternation as each struggled to handle the flood of business. Some traditions

As director Harvey S. Mudd said, the spindly bridge over the Pecos was a "weak link."

The magnificent structure replacing the 1892 bridge was placed in service on December 21, 1944.

were retained, others dropped. Special merchandise service such as that provided by the *Overnighters* was canceled for the duration in order to conserve power and crews. Freight traffic was diverted to the most direct connections instead of maintaining the longest possible haul for the SP, and late in 1942 transcontinental freight schedules were lengthened by twenty-four hours. Nevertheless, when requested by the military to do so, SP went "the limit" to provide essential service. On one occasion the SP transferred a load of fighter plane landing wheels from a boxcar to an express car and then rushed it westward on the *Argonaut* to a desperate California assembly plant. Elsewhere, crews such as that of Extra 978 west from Valentine to El Paso late in 1942 took expedited trains over the railroad at speeds well in excess of those authorized. Operating officials, who were "encouraged to get trains over the road," discreetly looked the other way. Municipal officials similarly looked the other way when, on demand, the SP moved naval munitions along Alameda Street—right through downtown Los Angeles—to ordnance installations at Seal Beach and elsewhere in the area. On the busy Overland Route "barge trains" carrying steel hulls for landing craft were a periodic phenomenon, and, because of potential submarine attack on coastal shipping, there was a constant stream of symbol oil trains moving crude and refined petroleum products from the T&NO to the Cotton Belt and other connections. Indeed, during the thirty-six months following September 15, 1941, the T&NO billed 533,540 carloads of petroleum products from its stations. Similarly, entire trainloads of munitions moved to and from several locations such as the Sierra Army Ordnance Depot at Herlong, California (on the Modoc), the Naval Ammunition Depot at Hawthorne, Nevada (on the Mina Branch), and the Benicia Arsenal, across the straits from Martinez, California.[15]

Problems in moving the growing throng of passengers were, if anything, even more complex. Revenue passenger miles rose by 109.5

A constant stream of symbol oil trains moved from the T&NO to the Cotton Belt and other carriers. This elderly switcher assembles such a train at Beaumont.

percent in 1942. Early that year the SP dropped thirty-five passenger trains, including the profitable *Noon Daylight* and the *Sunset Limited* (between San Francisco and Los Angeles), in order to gain equipment. Later that year numerous long-distance passenger schedules were lengthened and the sale of liquor on most trains was discontinued, as was the sale of beer by news agents. It was not a matter of morality but of expediency; most of SP's lounge, club, and tavern cars had already disappeared, to become coaches and diners.[16]

The war even had impact on SP's commuter operations. Significant problems arose on the historic San Francisco–San Jose route as more and more patrons flocked to it because of gasoline rationing and shortages of rubber tires. The situation was worsened when the usual sturdy 4-6-2s were removed for freight and troop train service, to be replaced by lighter and older power. Equipment shortages also resulted periodically when commuter coaches were pressed into temporary military duty. In Texas the expanding shipbuilding industry demanded reliable and inexpensive commuter operations, which the T&NO was called upon to establish. For a brief period such service extended from Houston's Grand Central Station to that city's Brown Ship Yard, but at Beaumont it lasted throughout the conflict. An A-1 4-4-2 performed yeoman duty hauling several cars on twice daily trips to the Livingston Yard near Orange.[17]

As the military's Pacific campaigns gained momentum, space available for civilian travel became even more restricted. Holidays brought special problems. The SP, along with all of the nation's carriers, pledged that such space would go "to Uncle Sam's boys first" and frankly discouraged travel by others during those periods. Pullman space could easily be proctored but that was not the case for "first come, first served" coach accommodations. Consequently, on June 16, 1943, the SP instituted a "train assignment plan" under which boarding passes were issued on a priority basis; troops "traveling on orders" were at the head of the list, and "civilian traffic to the capacity of our trains" was last. Throughout the war SP's Reservation and Information Bureau was swamped; in 1943 the San Francisco office received an average of 16,000 calls daily and that at Los Angeles another 15,000.[18]

Before the dawn of 1944, 65 percent of SP's passenger revenues derived from military business. The numbers were awesome. During the first seven weeks of the war SP operated 573 military trains; during the thirty-four months following December 1, 1941, it handled 20,511 of these in addition to dozens of cars of military personnel that moved on regular trains. In 1943 alone it transported approximately five million personnel aboard 136,234 "military cars." This, of course, said nothing of the thousands more who traveled "on orders" aboard SP's regular trains.[19]

Representatives of SP's passenger traffic de-

Throughout the war, SP's Reservation and Information Bureau was swamped.

In 1943 alone, the SP transported five million personnel in "military cars."

partment were assigned to important on-line installations, and others rode MAIN (military) trains and dealt with any number of problems. These often took the form of emergency requests for food and refreshments, which passenger representatives passed to the harried commissary department or to local bakers, soft drink bottlers, and dairies. As an example, a midnight request by a military train commander was satisfied less than three hours later at Tucson when a bakery truck met the train with one hundred loaves of fresh, hot bread. And, in the dead of a cold winter night during 1942, SP personnel even delivered stove pipe, elbows, and bailing wire to an ailing kitchen car on a MAIN train at Dunsmuir.[20]

The greatest attention of all was given to hospital trains, many of which originated at the Presidio of San Francisco. After the establishment of Hospital Train Units by the Army Medical Corps in July, 1944, the SP moved 486 of them plus 408 single cars, or a total of 164,267 patients. Equipment included standard Pullmans in addition to the army's own ambulance and kitchen cars. "Convoy personnel" was composed of military doctors, nurses, and medical technicians. Some, but not all, of these "mercy trains" were destined for the thirty-two military hospitals located in SP's service area.[21]

Among a host of unsung heroes during the war years was SP's hard-pressed dining car and commissary staff. Although itself subject to shortages and rationing restrictions, the SP by the fall of 1943 had become, as the *Wall Street Journal* observed, the "biggest food buyer in the West." Indeed, during the last quarter of 1942, the Pacific Lines alone served more meals than any other carrier—including the Pennsylvania Railroad, the traditional leader. It was an incredible accomplishment. New diners could not be obtained because of War Production Board restrictions and, for a while, even the longest of SP's trains had to make do with a single dining car. Personnel turnover was great because of the draft, but the department grew, nevertheless, to a 2,400-man force in 1943. Civilians were restricted to two meals daily on almost all trains and in every instance were urged to have eaten a meal before boarding. By the end of 1942, menu entrees were restricted to three, and box lunches were sold on every long-distance train.[22]

All of this reduced, but hardly eliminated, pressure on the dining cars and their overworked crews. Niceties were curtailed. Table flowers disappeared, waiters wore plainer uniforms, the cars—now making two trips whereas before the war they made one—went without new paint, and fresh fish, poultry, pasta, and eggs often replaced red meat on the menu. Indeed, menus themselves were often in short supply, as was linen. Dirty windows frequently greeted patrons when they finally found a seat; tight turn-around times simply prohibited doing anything more than watering, icing, and cleaning car interiors.[23]

The dining car situation mirrored the glut of military and domestic travel needs. These could not always be anticipated. In one case, on very short notice, the SP was obligated to move a large contingent of troops—requiring thirteen diners and a crew of 150 cooks, waiters, stewards. Incidents such as this placed an inordinate stress on the entire operation. As

Any day saw hundreds of military personnel arriving at or departing from the Oakland Mole.

one company officer recalled, "on one Friday we had 19 tons of meat in the [West Oakland] commissary refrigerators, but because of heavy military and domestic requirements the inventory was down to only ten pounds of ham hocks Monday morning." The skill and dedication of the dining car and commissary personnel was reflected in an amazing set of records: 1,029 luncheons served one noon on the *Daylight* in 1943, and a staggering total of 14,080,000 "military meals" prepared during the years of war.[24]

Others likewise toiled with special diligence and practically without recognition. Mail handlers, express messengers, and Railway Post Office clerks shuddered, but did not falter, under a load that grew with each day of the war. The Christmas season required special energy; that of 1944 was memorable. With the Pacific campaign in full swing, the SP found itself moving solid trains of mail on the Overland Route from late September

to early November. In all, 2,931 carloads of overseas mail were moved into the Oakland and San Francisco terminals during that brief period.[25]

Accidents are an inevitable, if highly unpleasant, part of the railroad business. The sheer volume of trains and the nature of their lading during World War II increased the potential for disaster. Nevertheless, SP's safety record during those hectic years was noteworthy. A hair-raising derailment of seventeen cars of munitions early in 1944 near Wabuska, Nevada, fortunately resulted in no injuries, and all cars were rerailed without explosion or fire. A few months later, however, several SP employees were injured and damage to property was extensive when a mighty explosion tore through the navy's Port Chicago facility northeast of Oakland. Windows in nine coaches of the *San Francisco Challenger* were knocked out by the blast just as the train was moving off the Martinez-Benicia bridge (over

Nothing on the SP had greater priority than the Hospital Trains.

Soldiers prepared to roll at San Luis Obispo.

five miles away), but only one patron was injured. Not so fortunate were passengers on the *Pacific Limited* when the second section collided with the rear of the first near Bagley, Utah, on New Year's Eve, 1944. Fifty persons died and 168 were injured, many of them military personnel.[26]

Because of its essentially fine safety record, because it did perform with obvious dedication in trying times, and because the public tended to understand the exigencies of wartime, SP's reputation generally was improved between 1940 and the end of 1945. The Lord & Thomas Agency surveyed freight shippers in May, 1942, and found the SP well regarded among nearly all. "We have had cars held up but feel that SP is doing as well as can be expected under present conditions," said a representative of the Rath Packing Company. "Even if our shipments are a few days late," echoed the traffic manager of Fairbanks Morse Company, "it is only part of our contribution for defense."[27]

Throughout those years of war the SP held

massive "War Service Day" rallies each June at principal locations around the entire system. In all cases, said President A. T. Mercier, the 95,000 men and women of the Southern Pacific at home saluted those from the family serving with "Uncle Sam's fighting forces." These events obviously served to demonstrate the solid bond between those at home and those abroad, but they also were useful vehicles for promoting donations of blood, for increasing participation in payroll savings plans, and for memorializing those who had fallen in battle. The war bond and blood donor programs were the obvious means by which all could contribute to the war effort, but there were others. Cotton Belt employees took pride in their Victory Gardens, and several from the T&NO offices in Houston volunteered their time for Traveler's Aid, USO, and Red Cross projects. And in Arizona members of a bridge and building gang even apprehended two German POWs who had escaped from a nearby camp.[28]

The number of SP employees in the armed forces grew to 15,196 in June, 1944, and to 19,000 by V-E Day, 1945. They served as officers and enlisted personnel in all branches and in both theaters of war. Several from the T&NO were assigned to the 719th and 734th Railway Operating Battalions, while others from the Pacific Lines joined the 705th Head-

SP's rhetoric was matched by reality: the military had first lien on the company's transportation assets.

The draft and competition for labor resulted in a constant shortfall. Recruiting was intense.

quarters Company and 754th Railway Shops Battalion.[29]

Of all the problems faced by the Southern Pacific during World War II, none was greater than meeting its employment needs. During 1940–41 more than 18,000 employees were added to forces on the Pacific Lines and more than 2,100 on the T&NO. War traffic grew and so did SP's need for personnel, but the draft and competition for labor resulted in a constant shortfall. To give concerted atten-

tion to this problem, the SP in September, 1942, established a Labor Employment Department with offices in San Francisco, Los Angeles, and far-off Chicago. Recruiting was intense. Meanwhile, most shops worked ten-hour shifts, and the accounting offices went on two-shift days. In the operating area, the employee shortage was accentuated by so-called full-crew laws, which unreasonably demanded several brakemen on freights, and by maximum-car laws that required extra trains. California and Arizona requirements were especially difficult.[30]

The problem grew. Older personnel postponed their pensions and retirees returned to work. In 1942 and 1943 nonunion personnel from the San Francisco headquarters spent weekends as track laborers. So, too, did local businessmen, professors, bankers, students, and others who answered SP's patriotic appeal to "help win the war." More permanent help came from the reservations of the Navajo, Hopi, Pima, and Apache Indians; they were concentrated on section gangs across Arizona.[31]

Women represented a vast labor pool, one that had not been tapped much in the past because of social traditions. Those customs passed quickly during World War II. By March, 1943, over 1,300 women were employed by the Pacific Lines in its accounting department. Dozens more signed on as clerks, telegraphers, and traffic representatives. Others donned overalls to become blacksmith help-

Uncle Sam asks S.P to do its biggest job

WE NEED LOTS OF MEN AND WOMEN TO HELP
ASK YOUR **Southern Pacific** AGENT TODAY

ers, engine wipers, yard clerks, fire lighters, painters, coach cleaners, rodmen, and even section laborers. On the railroad, as elsewhere, they were often referred to as "Rosie the Riveter" but at Watsonville, women track workers were called "George Burdusis' Angels" (after the local section foreman of that name), and at Mojave the female roundhouse crew was affectionately labeled "Piston Packing Mammas." Eventually more than 4,000 women were assigned to nonclerical positions formerly held exclusively by men.[32]

Labor shortages persisted, nevertheless. As early as the summer of 1941 the SP had asked the U.S. Immigration and Naturalization Service for permission to import 5,000 Mexican laborers under the Alien Contract Labor Act. The request was vigorously opposed by labor organizations in this country, and the application was denied. At the insistence of the Railroad Retirement Board and organized labor, the SP then agreed to solicit track laborers from east of the Mississippi River and pay for transporting them to job locations. The plan failed miserably. Of the 2,896 men thus recruited, only 1,501 actually went on the payroll, and most of these worked only a few days. They had simply used the SP for free transportation and sustenance and then "deserted" for even better paying jobs among the ballooning war industries on the West Coast.[33]

A second attempt to contract Mexican labor was successful, however. The first trainload of 509 workers was delivered to the SP at Nogales, Arizona, on May 16, 1943; the last was received at El Paso on August 13, 1945.

None of these Mexican nationals were assigned to the T&NO but were sent instead to the Pacific Lines, the San Diego & Arizona Eastern (SD&AE), NWP, and PFE. A few of the 36,711 who eventually arrived served in the mechanical and stores departments, but most were assigned to track gangs. Indeed, by D-day in 1944 a full 78 percent of track jobs on the Pacific Lines were held by Mexican nationals under contract. They proved to be excellent workers and did much to serve the war effort. Total wages for them amounted to $48,097,714.[34]

The need for a constant and reliable labor force was one of several themes promoted through SP's impressive World War II advertising campaigns. These were designed to explain the company's wartime difficulties and responsibilities, to supply necessary current information, and to create a feeling of understanding and goodwill. It worked. "Our advertising," said the passenger department's F. S. McGinnis in 1942, "has been based on the principle that an informed and understanding public will be considerate in view of the current crisis."[35]

The SP chose the specific messages to impart through local and national newspapers and magazines, window displays, posters, billboards, and radio. As its labor requirements increased, the SP moved from classified to more sophisticated display and institutional advertising and finally to radio spots. It was the same with other messages that management considered worthy—the need to purchase war bonds, the need to give military re-

Eventually more than four thousand women were assigned to nonclerical positions formerly held by men, as shown by this "Sunbonnet Gang," Elko, Nevada, in 1943. *Harry Williamson Collection.*

Women were tapped in great numbers, even for the most difficult tasks.

quirements priority over civilian, the need for safety in all cases, and an appreciation for all hard-working railroaders, who were contributing mightily in the war effort. Other advertisements announced that SP would happily supply on request free copies of *Priority Special*, the story of a hospital train on the Los Angeles Division written by Harry Bedwell, a company telegrapher whose work frequently graced the pages of the *Saturday Evening Post* and other national magazines. Finally, SP advertised its own radio program.[36]

Begun in November, 1943, "Main Line" was a weekly thirty-minute evening program aired throughout the service area of the Pacific Lines by stations of the Mutual–Don Lee Broadcasting network. Because the program was spliced between "The Lone Ranger" and "Bulldog Drummond," its success was assured. The SP hoped to accomplish two objectives with the broadcast: to tell the story of the railroad and what its employees were doing to win the war, and to attract men and women to its service. The show's popularity

gained regularly in the Hooper ratings because, as the trade press said, "it dramatized real life incidents to show that a railroad is not just trains and tracks—it is also the people whose daily work keep things moving along this vital artery." In a sense, "Main Line" was a fitting exclamation mark for SP's entire wartime advertising program—likely the best public relations project in the company's history.[37]

As Douglas MacArthur prosecuted his famous island-hopping campaign in the Pacific, Dwight Eisenhower pushed into the German homeland along a broad front. Throughout the war Europe had been the primary theater, and when the conflict there ended on May 8, 1945, the SP warned "This War Isn't Over Yet!" in bold newspaper ads that appeared on V-E Day. Indeed, with the Third Reich vanquished, the West Coast would become, as the SP said, "the great marshalling yard" for the "big push" against Japan. The railroad, already straining under its load, was certain to be assigned an even greater tide of troops and material now released in Europe. That would mean more restrictions and hardships for non-military patrons—freight and passenger alike. In sum, said the SP, "first things come first until this war is over—and it isn't over yet."[38]

The redeployment necessary to prosecute

SP's advertising was based on the principle that an informed public would be understanding.

the "big push" did, indeed, focus on the Pacific coast as springboard for the remaining theater of war. President Harry Truman told the country that U.S. forces in Europe would be transferred to the Pacific over a ten-month period, promised that "various transportation restrictions" would not only "be retained but increased," and urged citizens to avoid needless travel. The swell of traffic to the West was both immediate and dramatic; the movement of troops subsequent to V-E Day represented the heaviest passenger load of the entire war for the SP. Transportation shortages were severe. On July 6 the Office of Defense Transportation issued an order requiring the discontinuance of all sleeping-car runs between cities less than 450 miles apart. A. T. Mercier announced that the SP would carry out the order "to the letter" and added that it would, for the time being, accept no reservations for train space made more than five days in advance. The public grumbled, but the government's decision freed 892 sleepers around the

country for military use, which meant that 68 percent of all sleeping cars could be assigned for troop movement. Additional capacity had been promised somewhat earlier when the War Production Board authorized construction of 1,200 troop sleepers (1,200 others had been built in 1943) to be leased to and paid for by the railroads on a mileage basis, and to be operated by the Pullman Company exclusively for the services. These troop sleepers accommodated thirty persons each; standard sleepers were ordered by the military on the basis of three persons per section; three were also assigned to two double seats in coaches.[39]

Then, suddenly, it was over. Atomic bombs dropped on Hiroshima and Nagasaki brought Japan to its knees. Surrender occurred on August 15, 1945; America understandably indulged itself in long-awaited victory celebration.

For the country's railroads, especially those in the West, however, there was hardly a moment to celebrate. The military placed an im-

Then, suddenly, it was over: V-J Day in San Francisco along Market Street in front of SP's general office building.

mediate embargo on material destined for ports of embarkation; freight cars backed up across the country, clogging yards. It was much the same with troops headed for the Pacific. Where should they go? The military services eventually unscrambled the mess, but not before the carriers received undue criticism for a situation not of their making.

As the West Coast's premier railroad, the SP had been instrumental in staging for the Pacific offensives; now it would play a similar role in reverse. The heavy eastbound growth of traffic resulting from V-J Day began in September, grew in October, and exploded in November, to exceed SP's peak wartime load. "Get the boys home for Christmas" was the rallying cry. Thousands were so delivered. On December 1 alone there were forty-nine special military trains spread across the system. For the 1945 Christmas season, only 18 percent of space on eastbound Overland trains was available for civilian use. Nevertheless,

the demobilization process proved lengthy. The last of the troop sleepers was not taken out of service until early 1947.[40]

As the wartime frenzy passed, SP's officers could reflect on the company's record for those years. Foremost in their minds was that over 20,000 from the SP family had been in the military at war's end and, sadly, 268 died in the service of their country. The effort at home produced its own war stories. The SP claimed, probably correctly, that it had served more military installations (290) than any other railroad. In any event, the traffic handled for them and for all others was, simply stated, prodigious. On the Sierra, an average of seventy-three trains and helper engines passed Colfax, California, daily over a three-month test period in 1943, but on September 1, 1945 —before the real crush of eastbound traffic began—"the mountain" witnessed sixty-two train and fifty-three helper movements. Farther south, on Beaumont Hill, east of Colton, California, on the Sunset Route, it was much the same. Traffic there was so fierce during the war that local freights, stuck in sidings for superior trains, lost their crews—and even relief crews—to the "16-hour law." Helpers congregated at the top of the hill but frequently could not return because of the velocity of traffic. This, of course, compounded problems because upbound trains could not proceed without assistance. Consequently, dispatchers periodically ordered several helpers, coupled, down the hill as fast-moving second sections of passenger trains. Ton miles told the story: an increase from 545.5 million in 1940 to 1.6 billion in 1944 over the Sierra, and 582.1 million in 1940 to 1.1 billion in 1944 over Beaumont. The traffic situation on the Cotton Belt can be stated rather more cryptically. This was the order given to northward trains during the evening of May 23, 1943, at Fordyce, Arkansas, and may be considered representative:

No. 17 Engine 807 meet Extra 544 North and Fourth and Fifth 24 Engines 574 and 575 and Engine 809 at Faith and meet Sixth and Seventh 24

Wartime traffic on the Cotton Belt was as dramatic as on the lines of its parent. Here, the first #119 leaves Texarkana in 1943.

Engines 810 and 802 at Cabool and has right over Eighth and Ninth 24 and No. 26 Pine Bluff to Rison.[41]

Traffic records fell, especially in 1944 and 1945, as these statements show:

1944—The highest number of revenue passengers since 1919 (only World War I years were ever higher)
—The highest average number of persons per intercity train (326.7)
—The greatest revenue ever from passenger service (not including mail, express, etc.)
—The highest total revenue from freight
—The highest average number of revenue freight tons per train
1945—The highest average distance traveled per person (330.2 miles—more than four times the World War I high)
—The greatest passenger contribution to total operating revenues since 1921
—The greatest average distance hauled per freight ton (423.9 miles)

These records were established with 227 fewer locomotives, 929 fewer passenger cars, and 22,208 fewer units of freight equipment than the SP had owned in the late 1920s. This, of course, reflected the constrictions of the 1930s, greater unit capacity for newer cars, and better equipment utilization. Fortunately, during the war years, the SP was actually able to establish a net gain of 197 locomotives, 378 passenger cars, and 1,547 freight cars. Newer motive power advanced the average tractive effort per locomotive by approximately 25 percent. Furthermore, system shops had kept the number of "bad order" locomotives and cars at very low levels—4.5 percent and 2.4 percent, respectively, in 1943.[42]

The SP received several commendations for its war efforts and issued its own messages of congratulations. The Twelfth Naval District, the Los Angeles Port of Embarkation (Army), and the Bureau of Naval Personnel were among several government agencies expressing thanks and best wishes to the SP and its employees, and Standard Oil of California's *Summer Bulletin* for 1945 celebrated "the War Job of a Great Railroad." For his part, SP president A. T. Mercier congratulated the entire company family for "a truly splendid job in helping win the war." Mercier had other if similarly upbeat news for SP's owners. The company's debt, he told them, had been substantially reduced during the war years (from $721 million at the end of 1940 to $534 million at the end of 1945) and, as they already knew, the SP had renewed divided payments—$1.00 per share in 1942, rising to $2.25 in 1945.[43]

The Southern Pacific, like the country itself, had been on a roller-coaster ride for a decade and a half. It had experienced the darkest days of its existence during the Great Depression and its finest hour during World War II. Its leaders could but wonder what the future held.

CHAPTER 14

Into a Bright Future

"The success or failure of Southern Pacific will depend almost entirely on our ability to meet competition."—S. K. Burke to J. T. Saunders

No management ever lacks problems; the challenges vary in time and circumstance. For A. D. McDonald they had involved keeping the company out of bankruptcy courts during the depression of the 1930s. For Armand Theodore Mercier they centered first on complexities resulting from World War II and then on positioning the Southern Pacific for successful conversion to a profitable peacetime economy.

Born in New Orleans, Mercier graduated from Tulane University with a degree in civil engineering before joining the SP as a transit-man and roadmaster's clerk in 1904. He rose quickly through the engineering and operating departments, served briefly in the executive departments of the San Diego & Arizona Eastern and Pacific Electric and, on his sixtieth birthday, December 11, 1941, assumed the presidency of the Southern Pacific. During the war years Mercier spent much of his time "out on the line," determining where and how to make the property more efficient and leaving the executive suite in charge of Vice-President Donald J. Russell. He was friendly and jovial, an expert in human relations, and one who inspired hard work and devotion on the part of subordinates as well as the rank and file of employees. His devotion to SP's slogan—"The Friendly Railroad"—was legendary. Mercier's message to the SP family at the end of World War II was typical of the man:

"Let us go forward harmoniously as a unit with high morale within the organization to establish the company outstandingly a a progressive and friendly public servic institution."[1]

Mercier did not order a broadly based and systematic approach to postwar planning until mid-1944. Individuals within various departments, however, took it upon themselves to speculate in this regard and to offer suggestions. Those of S. K. Burke, assistant vice-president—freight traffic, were especially noteworthy. Appropriately styled "In Time of War Prepare for Peace!" Burke's dry-eyed views were submitted to his superiors only a month after the Pearl Harbor invasion. Burke underscored the erosion of traffic to competitive modes during the decade preceding but argued that it had been nothing more than a "prelude" to that sure to follow in peacetime since air, water, and vehicular competitors all stood to gain from the technological advances that result from war. Burke's assessment was not pessimistic; he simply counseled expedient countermeasures. First of all, he urged the company to jettison any financial or emotional attachment to unprofitable affiliate companies or even traditional operations. "The success or failure of Southern Pacific will depend," said Burke, "almost entirely on our ability to meet competition." That, he argued, meant not only "a very high standard of per-

Leadership of the SP during the trying days of World War II and the optimistic times following fell to Armand Theodore Mercier (*center*).

formance" and "an intensive planned campaign of selling our product in the competitive market," but also reduction of "the volume of transportation produced," the "rejection of traffic that cannot be handled profitably," and reductions "in the cost of providing said transportation."[2]

Others were neither as direct as Burke nor as macrocosmic. Rather, they anticipated the future in circumscribed ways. The advertising department, for instance, as early as March, 1943, speculated on its postwar responsibilities, and the passenger department actively solicited ideas as to what its future posture should be.

President Mercier took a cautious approach. In planning for postwar service he would be guided by the past: "We intend to extend the new service that public approval and patronage made profitable during the years immediately before the war," he told stockholders early in 1945. That notion was clear in his mind, but other issues seemed more vexing. Mercier worried, for example, about maintaining equity between those who had labored hard and long to keep the trains rolling during the war and those who were re-

turning to claim jobs that they perceived were rightfully theirs as a reward for saving the country from fascism. It would require a delicate juggling act, he understood.[3]

At the same time, Mercier and his staff were mindful of changes occurring in SP's service area, particularly in California and Texas. Both states had experienced regular if not spectacular growth during the first four decades of the century, but the growth in California during the 1940s was phenomenal. The great explosion in Texas, particularly in the Gulf Coast region, would not be far behind. Already, firms such as Anderson, Clayton & Company, the Houston-based diversified foods concern, were urging "returning war veterans" and "released war workers" to find their fortunes in the Lone Star State. It augured well for the future of the Texas & New Orleans as well as its parent. Hundreds of new industries had developed along spurs of both during the war, and more were sure to follow.[4]

These considerations colored the recommendations of L. B. McDonald, vice-president of operations, who in 1947 told Mercier that important traffic, much of it susceptible to competitive attack, was being delayed, particularly during peak movements, because of "insufficient locomotives." The SP, he recalled, had placed every available locomotive in service as a consequence of heavy war traffic; many of these had been worn out even before and were certainly so now. Relief in the form of new power was essential. Furthermore, McDonald urged construction of longer sidings, second tracks, expansion of CTC, and improvements to terminal facilities. He was especially concerned with expanding capacity on the Sunset Route and between Los Angeles and Bakersfield on the San Joaquin line. Most of all, however, he worried about SP's ability to protect its potential in the Los Angeles Basin. The population of Los Angeles County alone had grown yearly by an average of 90,000 since World War I. This growth was reflected in freight business. The number of

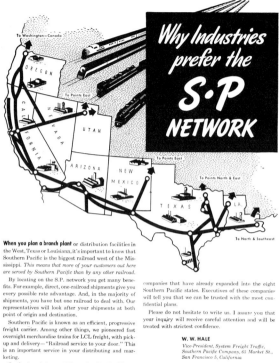

Why Industries prefer the S·P NETWORK

When you plan a branch plant or distribution facilities in the West, Texas or Louisiana, it's important to know that Southern Pacific is the biggest railroad west of the Mississippi. *This means that more of your customers out here are served by Southern Pacific than by any other railroad.*

By locating on the S.P. network you get many benefits. For example, direct, one-railroad shipments give you every possible rate advantage. And, in the majority of shipments, you have but one railroad to deal with. Our representatives will look after your shipments at both point of origin and destination.

Southern Pacific is known as an efficient, progressive freight carrier. Among other things, we pioneered fast overnight merchandise trains for LCL freight, with pick-up and delivery—"Railroad service to your door." This is an important service in your distributing and marketing.

Our business is *transportation*, not real estate. We are more interested in the success of your operation than in its specific location. You may be sure, therefore, that any advice we give you about a site in this region will be honest and unbiased.

Our Industrial Department has been helpful to many companies that have already expanded into the eight Southern Pacific states. Executives of these companies will tell you that we can be trusted with the most confidential plans.

Please do not hesitate to write us. I assure you that your inquiry will receive careful attention and will be treated with strictest confidence.

W. W. HALE
Vice-President, System Freight Traffic, Southern Pacific Company, 65 Market St., San Francisco 5, California

S·P

The friendly Southern Pacific

Hundreds of industries had located along the SP during the war, and more were sure to follow. Yet the SP left nothing to chance; its recruitment was aggressive.

cars loaded or unloaded in the city of Los Angeles by all carriers in 1945 was more than three times greater than the depression low of 1933, and SP researchers forecast a continued growth of business even after war's end.[5]

The SP had enjoyed a generally favorable public image during the war and, in the main, possessed a favorable image of itself. Mercier cherished these as important assets and worked hard to enhance them after the conflict. He was adept in the field of public relations and encouraged policies that would yield a "good press." In Houston, for example, the T&NO worked regularly with several universities to give their students a firsthand view of railroading, with public schoolteachers in business education, with agricultural specialists from Texas A&M College, as well

as with countless elementary schoolteachers who took their pupils on tours and trips sponsored by the railroad. These activities, Mercier understood, demonstrated the company's public spirit, offered the company important opportunities to "show itself off," and increased morale. SP's president saw the company's new sixty-minute color motion picture "This Is My Railroad" in the same vein. Emphasizing the role of employees at all levels in the company and filmed at various locations from New Orleans to Portland, it drew rave reviews from thousands of SP personnel, families, and friends who attended the premier showing in Houston on October 1, 1947, and thereafter at special showings around the system. The film was designed to instill pride in the company but, more than that, to instill pride in all who worked for the SP and in the specific jobs for which they were responsible. It was a smashing success.[6]

Mercier further understood that increased morale was the corollary of capital spending. During the six years from 1946 through 1951, an average of 439 track miles per year was outfitted with new and heavier rail; nearly 90 miles of additional CTC were installed; sidings on all main lines were extended to facilitate longer freight trains; a large grade-separation project (depressed trainway) project at El Paso was initiated; a bridge-strengthening program was executed on the Sunset Route east of El Paso; work was begun on a hump yard at Roseville, California; and many significant line changes were completed in Oregon and Texas. Following L. B. McDonald's urging, special attention was also given to the Los Angeles area, where nearly six miles of track was built in 1946 for a new automobile assembly plant near Van Nuys at Raymer. Equally important, another 8.6 miles of construction and a 6.6-mile trackage rights agreement with the Union Pacific in 1951 served to expedite the flow of freight traffic to and from the harbor and industrial areas at San Pedro and Long Beach.[7]

More pedestrian, but nevertheless essential,

A dramatic growth occurred in the Gulf Coast region. Metropolitan Houston posted incredible gains.

were a variety of improvements made to SP's communications system. These included radio telephones on Bay Area switchers and, when perfected, caboose-to-engine radios for road trains. Additional teletypes linking offices across the system were also acquired. The need for adequate communication was obvious; in 1951 SP's telegraph department handled 80,000 written telegrams and over 30,000 telephone calls daily.[8]

Some of the most impressive changes during the brief interim between World War II and the Korean conflict involved SP's motive power fleet. Steam still ruled; a modern "standing test laboratory" for the scientific testing of such locomotives was installed at Sacramento after the war, and company shops continued

to perform heavy repair on steam power. Yet the era was nearly ended; no new steam power would be ordered. Indeed, in 1946 SP acquired its first diesel freighters, four-unit (6,000-hp) F3s from General Motors' Electro-Motive Division to be assigned on the Sunset Route between Los Angeles and Lordsburg, New Mexico. Diesels for passenger service were ordered, too, with more following each year. By the end of 1951 SP owned 993 diesel freight, passenger, road-switcher, and switching units. Service and repair facilities for the new power were established at Los Angeles, Roseville, Houston, San Antonio, and Ogden in 1949, and at Eugene, Klamath Falls, Dunsmuir, and Lafayette in 1950.[9]

Some of these new locomotives were pur-

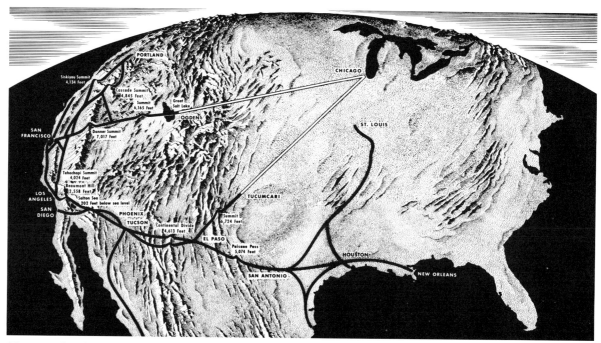

Topographical map of Southern Pacific

chased as power for SP's fleet of postwar streamlined trains. The program for upgrading SP's passenger fleet had begun during the depression but, except for the delivery of various new passenger cars, had been shelved during World War II. Shortly before that conflict began, however, the SP had placed in service a handsome overnight streamlined train between San Francisco and Los Angeles. Styled the *Lark*, these eighteen-car trains represented the finest in overnight rail travel. Experience gained with the streamlined *Lark*, its *Daylight* counterparts, and the *City of San Francisco* proved to be valuable as study for postwar passenger improvements began on a formal basis early in 1943.[10]

The planning program was broadly gauged. Each member of the passenger and advertising departments was asked for recommendations. Suggestions were noteworthy for their vigor and vision; they unmistakably anticipated competition from aviation and automobiles. For example, H. K. Reynolds believed that the patron of the future should find on "the trains the same comforts and conveniences he has at home." Moreover, said Reynolds, all cars

should be equipped with public address systems, car windows should have tinted glass, motion pictures should be shown in diners and lounges, stewardesses should be assigned to each major train, and train-board "cigar stores" where passengers could purchase "cigarettes, magazines, and candy bars" should replace "the news butcher." One of Reynolds's colleagues further proposed acquisition of "a fleet of small streamliners that could be operated for less than $1.00 per mile, to be run on fast schedules between San Francisco and Sacramento, Monterey, and other points." He also suggested "all room" Pullmans for the long-distance trains. Additionally, there was general agreement among members from both departments that each of SP's "Four Great Routes" should have a "leading daily train" identifying that route and that each should also be served by a "popular economy train."[11]

As it developed, the Shasta Route received first consideration because, said the passenger department's Claude E. Peterson, it was one of "the natural areas" where SP could "retain traffic previously enjoyed" as well as generate new business "by means of attractive and

The *Lark*, shown here coming up the Peninsula toward San Francisco, provided luxurious overnight service between Los Angeles and the Bay area.

expeditious service." Specifically, Peterson suggested two fourteen-hour trains—a new *Shasta Daylight* and a reequipped overnight *Cascade*, the latter to run through to Seattle in cooperation with the Northern Pacific. Vice-President D. J. Russell had reservations. On the one hand, he was convinced that "from a passenger revenue standpoint," SP's greatest opportunity was "in providing luxurious coach type trains with the most comfortable accommodations, low fares, reasonable dining car prices, and with lounge and bar facilities available." On the other, Russell believed that "after a reasonable time, the greater part of the sleeping car traffic will be lost to air lines. . . . From a long range viewpoint, some day we will be scrapping Pullman cars." Additional internal discussions followed, but the SP announced expansive plans for both trains early in 1946. Meanwhile, *Cascade*'s schedule was tightened and its older equipment was replaced on a piecemeal basis. Peterson's hope to extend the *Cascade* to Seattle over the North-

ern Pacific, however, was never realized, although the SP and NP did agree to a modest through-car arrangement. After protracted delays, the *Shasta Daylight* began service on July 10, 1949, and, finally, on August 13, 1950, a fully streamlined *Cascade* made its initial trip. Both trains were diesel powered.[12]

For several years preceding the war the Rock Island had pressed the SP for improvements that would make passenger service on the Golden State Route more competitive with that provided in the Chicago–Los Angeles corridor by the Santa Fe. Rock Island representatives observed that freight shippers often made invidious comparisons between the joint SP-CRI&P operation and Santa Fe's single-line route based on passenger train schedules. This, they added pointedly, hurt both companies. The SP, with several routes to maintain and protect, hedged and, in any event, the war made the issue moot for the duration. The SP dragged its feet even after V-J Day; it anticipated a continuing volume of

The *Shasta Daylight* entered service on July 10, 1949. Its dining car offerings could be summarized in a word: excellent.

eastbound military traffic on the Golden State Route for several months, and this, said Peterson, would not allow SP to "promptly set up postwar plans." Nevertheless, Peterson and others from the SP met with their counterparts from the Rock Island earlier in 1946 to make long-range plans.[13]

That meeting promised much for the Golden State Route. The two companies agreed to sponsor four trains in each direction with a new flagship—the thrice-weekly *Golden Rocket* on a 39-hour and 45-minute schedule. Additionally, the *Golden State* was to become "Pullman only" while the *Californian* and a through local were to handle most of the headend business. Complications, however, developed quickly. After the war ended, shippers and others in the Imperial Valley, long sensitive to SP's exclusive dominion there, pressured for "better passenger service." Consequently the SP, with the reluctant concurrence of the Rock Island, established a new Chicago–Los Angeles train—the *Imperial*—which detoured through Baja California west of Yuma and then turned back into the Imperial Valley to serve Calexico, El Centro, and Brawley with a "through train."[14]

Establishing a new train with old equipment was one thing, but fashioning a new train with new equipment—on an expedited

schedule—was quite another. The Rock Island dutifully ordered cars for the fancy *Golden Rocket*, and the SP told patrons and shareholders alike that the new train was "on the way." Nevertheless, the SP had cold feet; it stalled until the early fall of 1947, when, much to the Rock Island's consternation, the *Golden Rocket* project was scrapped. Rock Island's president, John D. Farrington, complained bitterly, but the best he could get from Mercier was a promise to speed up the schedule of the *Golden State Limited* to forty-five hours and divert equipment to it that would have been assigned to the now stillborn *Rocket*. Even this caused confusion. The Rock Island already had ordered its portion of observation lounges for the *Golden Rocket*, but the SP argued that such "cars were not popular, did not have enough room, and receipts were about 50% under those of full lounges placed next to the diner." The SP simply would not order its complement but substituted instead "two rounded 10-6 sleepers" to maintain symmetry for all train sets. In any event, "an improved *Golden State*" employing a strange mixture of rebuilt and new equipment was inaugurated on January 4, 1948. The SP promised that its full share of the train's new cars would be on hand before the end of the next year. The entire episode was ironic. SP management frequently found reasons to complain about real or imagined problems with connecting carriers on through routes—the CRI&P, UP, C&NW—but in this case the Rock Island was the aggrieved party.[15]

Plans for the premier train on the Sunset Route were similarly complex. As early as 1938 SP's advertising department had suggested "the inauguration of coast-to-coast streamlined service via New Orleans" as the best way to "focus national attention on the company's long haul Sunset Route." The "Union Pacific and the Santa Fe," complained F. Q. Tredway, "have whole fleets of streamlined trains." What the SP needed, he continued, was "a progressive, sensational move." That could be accomplished, he enthused, by

The *Golden Rocket* failed to birth, but a refurbished and speedier *Golden State* took to the rails on January 4, 1948. This one is at El Paso, in 1952.

establishment of "the first truly transcontinental run"—the *Robert E. Lee*, on a fifty-nine-hour schedule. This one train, said Tredway, "would steal the show" from the competition and be "front page news" everywhere. A. D. McDonald was intrigued with the idea and noted that cooperation could be expected from both the Louisville & Nashville and the Southern Railway as connecting carriers on the Washington–Los Angeles run, but he advised that the project "would have to be tabled until some future time." Mercier took the same position in 1943 and again in 1947, and the project died.[16]

Neither McDonald nor Mercier argued with Tredway's contention that "no halfway measure will ever revive passenger travel on the Sunset Route." Yet there were problems. When the *Robert E. Lee* failed to win approval, Claude Peterson suggested a thirty-nine-hour all-Pullman streamliner between Los Angeles and New Orleans, but the route was characterized by significant "intermediate

business" on both ends—Los Angeles, Phoenix, Tucson on the west and San Antonio, Houston, New Orleans on the east—with a long stretch between Tucson and San Antonio that yielded little passenger business of any kind. Furthermore, noted one of Peterson's associates, there was "the always-present negro problem in Texas and Louisiana," which required "separate but equal" or duplicate facilities. These problems militated against Peterson's dream.[17]

Nevertheless, something had to be done. The motive power and equipment assigned to the *Sunset Limited* had been severely taxed by wartime travel and was clearly shabby compared with the *Daylight*, the *Lark*, and the new trains planned for the Golden State and Shasta routes. All that could be done in the short term, though, was to speed *Sunset*'s schedule to just under forty-eight hours in 1946, and to reestablish a through New York–Los Angeles sleeper for it a year later. Finally, in 1948 SP's board authorized expenditures for five new train sets and power to pull them. The fifteen-car trains that resulted were gorgeous in every detail. Designers from the Budd Company, which built the cars, created interior decor representative of the regions traversed by the train. Especially impressive were the Audubon Dining Room, the Pride of Texas Coffee Shop, and the French Quarter Lounge—painted in a shade of pink called Sunset that even inspired a woman's fashion trend. The new trains took to the rails on forty-three-hour schedules effective August 20, 1950. "Now," enthused a beaming Claude Peterson, "we have streamliners to sell on all four routes."[18]

The earliest of these, the famous *City of San Francisco* increased its "sailing dates" to three times weekly late in 1946 and was made daily on September 1, 1947. New equipment ordered for it in 1948 would be delivered over the next two years. Changes also affected other trains on the Overland Route. Through sleepers to New York and Washington via Chicago and both the New York Central and

The newly equipped *Sunset Limited* was properly christened at New Orleans before its departure on August 20, 1950.

Pennsylvania railroads were assigned to the historic *Overland Limited* in 1946. The *Gold Coast* and a mail train protected the remaining business in 1950.[19]

Elsewhere, on April 14, 1946, the SP reinstated the *Noon Daylight* to aid its hard-pressed sisters, the original *Daylight* (now renamed *Morning Daylight*) and the *San Joaquin Daylight* between the Bay Area and Los Angeles. Also in 1946 the SP initiated expedited service between Sacramento and Los Angeles by way of the *Sacramento Daylight* and a connection with the *San Joaquin Daylight*. This pattern of service was modified in the fall of 1949 when the *Noon Daylight* was

replaced by the *Starlight*, a streamlined evening coach train running about an hour ahead of the all-Pullman *Lark* over the Coast Line. Most mail and express moved via the San Joaquin line on the *Owl* and the *West Coast*.[20]

One innovative idea that was "on the drawing boards" for nearly thirty years involved the broadly based operation of interline passenger trains from one coast to the other. The eastern roads—the Baltimore & Ohio, the New York Central (NYC), and the Pennsylvania (PRR)—and their western counterparts—the Santa Fe, the Southern Pacific, and the Union Pacific—had no difficulty embracing the concept but bickered endlessly over details. Simply stated,

"Now we have streamliners to sell on all four routes," SP's Claude Peterson exulted. The *Sunset* nears Morgan City, Louisiana, in 1953.

each protected itself as well as its presumed advantages against cooperative welfare. Shortly after the war the idea was resurrected by M. W. Clement, president of the Pennsylvania, who suggested that his road join with the New York Central in dispatching six trains per week (three each) from New York City to Chicago (or Englewood) for: Los Angeles via AT&SF (3) or CRI&P-SP (3); San Francisco via C&NW-UP-SP (6); Seattle via CB&Q-GN (3) or Milwaukee Road (3). In this way, both of the eastern roads would have one train per week to Los Angeles, San Francisco, and Seattle and, conversely, each of the western roads would have trains to New York City.[21]

Virtually all of the potential participants found fault with Clement's proposal. The Great Northern and Milwaukee doubted there was adequate through business between New York and Puget Sound; the Baltimore & Ohio had not been included and objected on that count; the Santa Fe felt it should monopolize the Los Angeles trade; the SP took exception to Santa Fe's position; and the Pennsy and NYC quarreled as a matter of policy. Privately, the SP simply wanted to stall; it was straining yet with the load of government business re-

sulting from the unexpectedly swift conclusion of World War II, and it wished to go to the bargaining table with a strengthened hand resulting from an upgraded service on the Golden State Route (the *Golden Rocket* or a much-improved *Golden State Limited*). However, the SP could not accomplish the latter goal, it reasoned, until military traffic subsided. Clement persisted with a mix of charm and vigor. His company completed arrangements with the Missouri Pacific and Texas & Pacific for through sleepers to the Southwest and hinted at plans for entire trains. Not surprisingly, the management of the T&P then approached Mercier with a proposal for "the first transcontinental route with coast-to-coast passenger trains" via SP-T&P-MoPac-PRR. Mercier would have none of it. The disappointed Clement pestered in support of his general plan through 1946 and 1947 but in the end accomplished only the assignment of New York–Oakland and Washington-Oakland sleepers on the Overland Route and New York–Los Angeles sleepers on the Golden State Route.[22]

Sleeping car service was central to long-haul passenger business, but the entire nature of that trade was clouded by a government antitrust suit against the Pullman Company. The matter was solved only when participating railroads, including the SP, purchased Pullman Incorporated's subsidiary, the Pullman Company, which actually operated the cars. The plan was approved on May 6, 1947, and took effect the following July 1; SP's interest totaled 8.5 percent.[23]

All of this represented substantial change for the SP in the postwar environment. The flood of military traffic eventually passed, and as gasoline and tire rationing ended, the public rediscovered its fascination with the automobile. Bus and air competition also increased, as did that from competing railroads that raised speeds, added classier equipment, and promoted themselves broadly in the lucrative long-haul business.

The SP responded with its own classy equip-

The beauty of SP's Santa Barbara station is properly matched by that of the *Daylight*.

ment, new trains, and advertising. It also brought back popular trains such as the *Suntan Special*, which took eager excursionists from San Francisco to Santa Cruz each Sunday of the summer. As equipment became available again, SP representatives similarly solicited a variety of excursions as expansive as the fifty-day *Hadacol Caravan* promoting that popular over-the-counter elixir, annual specials from the Bay Area to Sacramento for the California state fair, and a flamboyant tour from San Francisco to New York for the annual convention of the American Legion. Football specials took fans from California's St. Mary's College to see their favorite team play Fordham in New York's Polo Grounds, to annual gridiron collisions between the University of Texas and archrival Texas A&M, and in 1950 six fifteen-car trains were used for the Cotton Bowl contest between Rice and Southern Methodist. More dignified were special trains for the 1945 United Nations conference in San Francisco, and more publicized were President Harry Truman's campaign specials in 1948. The most unusual was likely the Lordsburg Mercy Train, which in January,

1949, rescued nearly four hundred motorists who had been stranded by a blizzard near that New Mexico community. Finally, numerous excursions on the San Diego & Arizona Eastern, the Northwestern Pacific, and over lines of the parent company were handled on behalf of camera fans and railroad buffs.[24]

After SP's board of directors authorized new streamliners and physical improvements necessary to advance their schedules, it fell to the passenger department to promote the company's modernized service. It did so with relish. The advertising budget exceeded $1 million in 1946 and hovered at that level for the half-dozen years following the war. "Next Time Try the Train" was the theme stressed on billboards that were placed to attract the attention of motorists likely to be fatigued and otherwise concerned with safety. The SP also took on the airlines with an award-winning ad that admitted air's primary advantage, speed, but argued that "trains have a lot of advantages, too, including economy and plenty of room to move around." The SP additionally promoted "installment plan" travel through credit and missed no opportunity to cooper-

The *Daylight*'s schedule afforded a splendid ride through gorgeous Southern California.

ate with radio personalities such as Jana Lee, who conducted her "Women's Magazine of the Air" in 1947 from the West Oakland commissary. Neither did it miss opportunities to ballyhoo travel on SP trains by celebrities such as entertainers Jack Benny, Tony Martin, George Burns, Donald O'Connor, and Ronald Reagan, who arrived together from Hollywood at SP's San Francisco station shortly before Christmas, 1948. Internally, Claude Peterson reminded SP personnel that "We've got plenty to sell" and added, "Let's all be salesmen." Beyond that, Peterson urged every employee to embrace a simple philosophy that acknowledged the passenger as "our friend" and asked all hands to do whatever was neces-

sary to keep the fine new equipment clean and neat. Team effort paid off. The SP in 1950 won the prestigious annual Railway Passenger Service Award of the Federation for Railway Progress.[25]

The number of revenue passengers handled by the SP in 1950 was only half the number of 1945 but was nearly the same as that of 1929; revenues from passengers followed a similar trend. The passenger picture, then, was mixed. For A. T. Mercier it posed a dilemma. He had committed millions of dollars to SP's postwar passenger program but the return on this investment appeared uncertain. He hedged. "Any money we may have in the immediate future must be spent for something other than

After the war the SP could again ballyhoo its popular *Suntan Special*.

It also celebrated, at least briefly, *Snowball Specials* to Norden and Truckee.

additional passenger equipment," Mercier told D. J. Russell in June, 1948. A few days later he expanded on this theme in a letter to Rock Island's J. D. Farrington: "I do not feel we should obligate ourselves [for new passenger equipment] until we have a somewhat better estimate . . . as to the revenues that follow these large expenditures." Mercier mirrored his contemporaries on other railroads when he complained about government subsidies for vehicular and air modes and urged the formulation of "fair competitive conditions." Meanwhile, circumstances demanded contraction of at least certain segments of the system's passenger offerings. Several trains on the Texas & New Orleans were discontinued, as was service in Arizona between Tucson and Nogales and on the San Diego & Arizona Eastern. Even the venerable tourist sleeping cars disappeared; the last one on the Golden State Route was removed in December, 1950, and the final car, on the San Francisco–Los Angeles run, was removed on February 14, 1951. Discontinuances in the six years follow-

ing V-J Day, Mercier noted, saved 4.7 million train miles.[26]

The decline in passenger volume following the end of the war was only one of several changes affecting employee numbers, working arrangements, and morale. By the end of 1947 most of the women who had entered the employ of the SP because of the war as well as men who had come back from or who had postponed retirements were no longer on the payroll; total numbers dropped to 83,346 and overtime was rare. These reductions and more promised by technological advances such as diesel-electric locomotives for road assignments caused nervousness among employees covered by labor agreements. Furthermore, they argued that their diligent service and hard work during the war ought to be recognized through better wages, shorter work weeks, and longer vacations. Enginemen considered further that each diesel road unit should have both an engineer and a fireman. Several work-rule concessions and wage increases followed. Overall, SP's rates of pay increased by 119 percent during the 1940s, and by 1951 forty-nine cents of every operating dollar expended by the company was for wages. Nevertheless, the high morale and good feelings between management and labor—increased during the common struggle of the depression and war—were shaken by confrontation and even strikes following V-J Day.[27]

Just as there were changes in the work place so, too, were there changes in SP's corporate structure. The Southern Pacific Company had been incorporated by an act of the Kentucky legislature in 1884, and subsequently had paid taxes there as a franchise company. The State of Kentucky, however, changed its interpretation in 1944 to insist that the SP pay an ad valorem tax on nonoperating intangibles (stocks and bonds owned by the company). Litigation followed, and in the end SP settled with Kentucky but was reincorporated in Delaware on September 30, 1947. In other corporate matters, the Dawson Railway & Coal Company was dissolved on October 18, 1948, and the Union Belt Railway of Oakland was acquired on November 15, 1948.[28]

The investment assets of the "new" company were noteworthy. In 1950 they included the 12,441-mile Southern Pacific Transportation System plus 2,546 additional miles of affiliated railroads (the Northwestern Pacific, the San Diego & Arizona Eastern, SPdeMex, etc.). They also included:

Pacific Motor Trucking (100 percent ownership),
Land companies (4,135,797 acres plus 4,236 town lots),
Rio Bravo Oil (100 percent ownership),
Los Angeles Union Terminal (100 percent ownership),
Southern Pacific Building Company (100 percent ownership),
West Coast Hotel Company (100 percent ownership),
Pacific Fruit Express (50 percent ownership),
Railroad terminals (12.5 percent to 50 percent ownership),
Miscellaneous physical properties (100 percent ownership), and U.S. Treasury

obligations and securities of other companies.

In addition, the SP owned 88.34 percent of the 1,569-mile St. Louis Southwestern Railway.[29]

On July 24, 1947, the St. Louis Southwestern emerged from nearly twelve years of bankruptcy. That historic event was all the more notable since the road had been able to do it without reorganization through a voluntary readjustment of its financial structure. In fact, on the day Berryman Henwood was discharged as trustee, the company paid $18.5 million to satisfy all of its creditors and at the same time retired three groups of mortgage bonds. Moreover, the Cotton Belt was in good physical condition. During its years of travail, it had laid heavier rail on 665 miles of track, installed 191 miles of CTC, and purchased heavy steam locomotives, twenty-three diesel switchers, and five multiple-unit road diesels plus air-conditioned coaches and hundreds of freight cars. Business had boomed for the road during the war—it was four times greater in 1943 than 1929, the previous peak—but war traffic records alone did not explain the company's fine accomplishment. Management earned much of the credit. The SSW, for instance, turned in a highly enviable operating ratio of 46.4 in 1943 and averaged 51.8 for the war years.[30]

Ironically, the SP near the end of the war undertook a searching study of its options regarding the SSW. Cotton Belt's inability to stand alone because of light on-line loadings, its recent financial instability, and its "long mileage" Los Angeles–Saint Louis route were noted as liabilities. However, its value as an integral part of an "all system route" between the Pacific Ocean and the Mississippi River, as an essential outlet to and from the Texas & New Orleans, and its well-maintained and tightly operated property were listed as assets. There were other considerations. Should the larger road sell its interest in the SSW, the proceeds could be used to redeem SP's 5 percent bonds. Early in 1947, however, A. T. Mercier concurred with the findings of the research team: "The Southern Pacific should retain an interest in the line and continue to coordinate, wherever possible, service and facilities of the T&NO and Cotton Belt, and that the Pacific Lines and the SSW should continue to work for the development of traffic to be interchanged between the two for their mutual advantage." It was a fortuitous decision. The SSW renewed dividend payments in 1948, $5.00 a share on preferred, and in 1950 authorized that amount for preferred and common stock alike. Moreover, it thereafter paid and even prepaid various obligations due on the SP.[31]

Interestingly, SP's investment in the Cotton Belt was threatened somewhat by the strategic goals of the Santa Fe, which long had cast a covetous eye toward Saint Louis. As early as 1887 the Santa Fe had purchased the St. Louis, Kansas City & Colorado Railroad with the hope of extending it to a connection with Santa Fe's main line at Kansas City. Construction was made to Union, about sixty miles west of Saint Louis, but the Santa Fe lost control and the line passed eventually to the Chicago, Rock Island & Pacific Railroad for completion. That did not end the Santa Fe's interest, however. Its system map for 1930 showed a projected line to Saint Louis in conjunction with the Chicago, Burlington & Quincy Railroad; Hale Holden recalled that "these negotiations were now more than fifteen years old." The depression and World War II again postponed Santa Fe's plans, but before V-J Day it renewed them. This predictably energized most of the railroads entering Saint Louis from the west in a campaign of opposition. Specifically, the Santa Fe and the Burlington wished to acquire a 156-mile line between Kansas City and Mexico, Missouri, from the Gulf, Mobile & Ohio Railroad; the Burlington would then grant the Santa Fe rights from Mexico to Saint Louis. Ultimately, however, in the summer of 1948, the Interstate Commerce Commission denied the applica-

tion, much to the relief of the Cotton Belt and its fellow protestants.[32]

Just as it had scrutinized the Cotton Belt, SP's management studied prospects offered by the Southern Pacific of Mexico. That company had consistently turned in net losses, although the parent and the Texas & New Orleans each derived substantial revenues from traffic moving to or from the SPdeMex. Yet it was insufficient. As D. J. Russell said, the road had "no future, no possibilities." Thus, late in 1950 SP's management determined to dispose of the "West Coast Route," as it was known. A year later, on December 21, 1951, the SP sold the Mexican government 1,227 miles of railroad, rolling stock, materials, supplies, and concessions for $12 million. SP's historic investment in the SPdeMex was $51.7 million; against this it had received net revenues from overhead (interchange) in the amount of $41 million, another $12 million from its sale, and a tax benefit of $11.9 million for a total of $64.9 million. This represented a very disappointing profit of only $13.2 million over forty-six years of operation. The SPdeMex would be dissolved on August 23, 1955, and its remaining assets distributed to the Southern Pacific Company.[33]

The course of the West Coast Hotel Company was similar. To stimulate tourist travel the SPdeMex had organized this enterprise to foster the Plaza del Cortes Hotel at Miramar Beach near Guaymas in 1935. Its facilities were handsome but profits were spare. Its stock was transferred to the Tijuana & Tecate Railway in 1940; on September 1, 1945, the property was leased to Mexico Hotels, Ltd., and sold to that firm nine years later.[34]

Meanwhile, SP's managers increasingly turned their attention to matters of freight transportation. Much of the accumulated need for postwar goods had been satisfied by the end of 1948. Wholesalers reduced their inventories in 1949 as a result, but a sudden upsurge in civilian and government buying followed the outbreak of the Korean conflict

SP's managers increasingly turned their attention to matters of freight transportation. A long drag comes off the former EP&SW line into El Paso in the late 1940s.

The postwar building splurge resulted in a heavy forest products business from SP's lines in Oregon. Here one of SP's famous Cab-Forward locomotives wrestles tonnage over the Cascade Line near Mt. Shasta.

in 1950. A "freight car shortage" followed, in spite of SP's constant campaign to expand its fleet; the company owned approximately 10,000 more freight cars in 1950 than it had at the end of World War II. Revenues from cargoes hauled in those cars hit a peacetime high in 1947. Indeed, the importance of freight to SP's corporate health increased impressively after the war. Total receipts from freight, revenue tons per train, average cars per train, average distance hauled, and percentage of contribution to operating revenue all rose. Except for LCL business, which in 1950 was only half of what it had been at war's end, tonnage in all commodity classes remained stable.[35]

On his retirement at the end of 1951, Armand (Ted) Mercier could look back on the accomplishments of the SP during the postwar years with justifiable pride. The property was in good shape, new streamliners were in service, the road's equipment inventory was laudable, and several unproductive activities had been trimmed. Furthermore, the SP had been able to reduce some of its funded debt while paying regular dividends—$4.00 annually from 1946 through 1948, $5.00 each year thereafter. And the future looked good. Operating revenues for the company in 1951 were the highest in its history, and 550 new industries had been located on SP lines in that year. Finally, Mercier had the pleasure of turning over the helm to a trusted subordinate, Donald J. Russell.[36]

CHAPTER 15

The Russell Years

> "Iron will, coupled with engineering savvy, has kept Southern Pacific operational from below sea level to 8000 feet above, against the worst that the Colorado River and the Great Salt Lake and the Richter Scale can hurl at its fixed plant."—David P. Morgan

CLOUDS on the Southern Pacific's horizon in 1952 were scarce. Its service area was growing in population and in relative national prominence; commodities historically important to SP's traffic mix continued to promise prodigious tonnage; and the property was well maintained. The company, it seemed, could not fail to prosper. Yet to reach its full potential, the SP required the strong hand of a truly outstanding chief executive. Donald Joseph Russell was precisely that man. His leadership would prove to be the strongest since the respected Julius Kruttschnitt.

Born in Denver, Colorado, on January 3, 1900, Russell grew up in Oregon and California. He served in the Imperial Royal Flying Corps (Canada) during World War I, attended Stanford University, and entered the employ of the SP as timekeeper for a maintenance gang in 1920. Russell held numerous positions in the engineering and operating departments before his appointment as assistant to the president in 1941; there was little doubt that he was headed for the corner suite in the executive department.

Russell's views on managing the property were clear and uncomplex. An axiom advanced many years before by James J. Hill—and one that Russell may not have been aware of—was nevertheless embraced by him: "A railroad's success is in direct proportion to the closeness with which its affairs are looked after." Russell's view was similar, but he stated it more colorfully: "Railroading is like athletics—you eat and sleep it 24 hours a

Clouds were scarce on SP's horizon when Donald J. Russell took the helm.

day or go to work elsewhere." He held that standard for himself and expected it of others. "The company—he lived and breathed it," recalled an associate. Others remembered that his was an imperial presidency, that he rarely delegated authority, and that he appeared to be an awesome figure. They also recalled, however, that his "bark was worse than his bite," that he was firm but fair, and that he was an aggressive, capable, and inventive manager. Richard D. Spence, who served as vice-president–operations before leaving to head Conrail, especially admired Russell's "hands-on feel" for the railroad. Indeed, nobody doubted either his knowledge of the property or his ability to spend the company's money to the greatest advantage.[1]

An SP trainmaster once told the editor of *Trains Magazine* how upset the general office became over a snow blockade in the mountains. The rationality of this reaction was lost on the journalist, who protested that a heavy snowfall represented "an Act of God." Replied the trainmaster, "Mr. Russell doesn't believe in Acts of God." This may explain, in part, the chagrin at 65 Market Street when the westbound *City of San Francisco* was marooned at Yuba Gap just days after Russell became president. A fierce storm, which one mountain officer called "a wild nightmare," began on January 10, 1952, and lasted until the sixteenth. Before it was over, 84 inches of new snow whipped by raging winds created mammoth drifts and fearsome slides. The *City* hit one of these slides on the thirteenth and could not be extricated before snow inundated it. For three days the elements defeated all of SP's valiant efforts to free the 196 passengers and 30 crewmen. Sadly, the engineer on a relief plow train was killed in another slide, but fortunately no serious health problems arose among the passengers, and on the sixteenth a rescue train finally delivered them to Oakland. Another three days were required to free the *City* itself. President Russell praised the unceasing efforts of company personnel, but nobody doubted he was sorely displeased

An act of God; Russell frowned on such.

that the honor and reputation of the SP had been besmirched.[2]

Mother Nature struck the SP again six months later when "an earthquake of notable severity" hit south-central California on July 21, 1952. The municipality of Tehachapi was nearly demolished, and SP's important San Joaquin line was closed by collapsed tunnels and numerous slides. Over a thousand men and approximately 175 heavy machines toiled twenty-five days, and more than $2 million was expended before the line could be reopened. Russell himself spent considerable time on the scene and served to "expedite matters." Nobody was more appreciative than Fred Gurley, whose Santa Fe Railway shared the important artery. Russell was clearly proud of the way the company had responded to this emergency, but he also expected that kind of response to be routine: "The things that people look on as great catastrophes," he said, "are commonplace with us. We get out and fix them."[3]

It was that kind of mentality—"no problem is too big to overcome"—that Russell wished to see in his subordinates. Yet he was not naive. The first requisite of a successful manager, he told students at Stanford University's Graduate School of Business in the summer of 1956, was "the ability to grasp specific situations quickly and relate them to broad, long-range considerations." Russell perceived that these skills, inadequately developed in otherwise talented officers, might be made to flourish by sending them to college for what he called "broadening." The SP paid full salaries as well as all expenses for those managers selected. During one phase of the program in 1958, seventy-nine persons were enrolled in advanced management, engineering, and liberal arts courses at colleges and universities across the country. "We are happy of course, to be able to give more education to some of our people," Russell noted, "but the primary purpose also represents a hardheaded business effort."[4]

Russell also expected the SP's subsidiaries to perform at the same high levels as the parent, and he sent their executives back to school as well. Indeed, the first candidate for the program was Harold J. McKenzie, Texas & New Orleans's chief engineer, who was sent to the Advanced Management Program at Harvard in 1950. McKenzie then went to the Cotton Belt as executive vice-president, becoming its president on July 1, 1951. He replaced F. W. Green, who had replaced Daniel Upthegrove in 1947. Russell had grown impatient with the elderly Green, however, because he seemed unable or unwilling to vigorously prosecute programs using SSW earnings otherwise subject to excess-profits tax. McKenzie had no such difficulties. A graduate of Texas A&M college, he had begun his career with the engineering department at Houston in 1926, served as project engineer for the Pecos River Bridge undertaking during World War II, and became T&NO's chief engineer in 1945. McKenzie was an excellent choice for the Cotton Belt presidency. He had a fine sense of humor as well as a flair for working with people and getting them to "pull in harness." One subordinate explained his success in turning the Cotton Belt into a most admirable

property: "McKenzie knew that he did not know everything. He was not ashamed to learn from anybody, anywhere. He consulted all persons involved, asked for their advice, pondered it, and then made his own decision."[5]

McKenzie's line of command and marching orders were clearly stated; he was to answer only to the chairman of the Cotton Belt board of directors (A. T. Mercier, and after January 1, 1952, D. J. Russell), and he was to do his utmost to streamline the Cotton Belt and maximize its profits. That process included, among other things, combining, as quickly as possible, the St. Louis Southwestern Railway and the redundant St. Louis Southwestern Railway of Texas. On December 18, 1953, the ICC authorized the SSW to lease and operate all railroad properties of the Texas company, which itself ceased to exist as an operating property on March 1, 1954. Such might otherwise have violated the sensibilities of the proud Texans, but McKenzie smoothed the issue by moving SSW's corporate headquarters from Saint Louis to Tyler. A new $1.5 million general office building opened there in 1955.[6]

Since the Cotton Belt had only a small bonded indebtedness and a handsome surplus for dividends, McKenzie was in the enviable position of paying cash for improvements such as CTC, new rail, and a fleet of rolling stock. The CTC program, begun in 1943, was completed in 1956, when the entire main line from Illmo, Missouri, to Corsicana, Texas, was so equipped. Yard improvements at Valley Junction in East Saint Louis, Jonesboro, and Tyler; welded rail for major portions of the main line; hot journal detectors; and mobile inspection units at East Saint Louis and Pine Bluff all represented impressive plant improvements. New cars in traditional form—box, flat, and gondola—were joined by special equipment—bulkhead flats, insulated boxcars, flats for trailers, and eventually tri-level flats for automobiles.[7]

McKenzie also vigorously prosecuted Cot-

"I'm turning in my broom.
Next year, I'm going by **BLUE STREAK.**"

For *speedy delivery,* you can't beat the COTTON BELT.

H. J. McKenzie happily authorized innovative advertising to maximize profits.

Cotton Belt's smaller locomotives and about half of its handsome fleet of 4-8-4s were sold to parent SP where they rolled out their final miles. In gestures of goodwill, the Cotton Belt distributed bells from dismantled locomotives to area churches and happily donated 4-8-4 number 819, built by the Pine Bluff Shops in 1943, to the city of Pine Bluff for display.[8]

With an excellent physical plant and new power and equipment for his railroad, McKenzie turned to the matter of industrial development. Attractive sites were purchased at North Little Rock, Texarkana, Waco, Tyler, and Bossier City (across the Red River from Shreveport); special attention was given Fort Worth and Dallas, where several valuable tracts were acquired. "We definitely need more industries to strengthen our company and we are going to do what is necessary to locate them on our line," McKenzie told the Cotton Belt's far-flung sales organization in 1955.[9]

McKenzie had reason to be concerned about on-line business. More than 60 percent of Cotton Belt's traffic was overhead, and there was a clear and steady erosion of certain traditional local traffic—tomatoes, roses, livestock, and even cotton. The road was pleased, however, to record significant movements of

ton Belt's program of dieselization. Road switchers from Alco and road and switching units from GM's Electro Motive Division (EMD) were present in sufficient numbers by the end of 1953 to write finis to the era of steam. Ironically, the final run was made by an elderly 2-8-0, number 502, which without fanfare delivered a work train from Corsicana to Tyler on October 28, 1953. A few of

The end of steam on the Cotton Belt came in 1953.

soybeans and a growing volume of rice, especially to and from Stuttgart, Arkansas.

Even the Cotton Belt's involvement with trailer-on-flat car (TOFC) reflected efforts to retain or recapture business local to the railroad. Begun on September 1, 1954, SSW's piggyback operations served ramps at thirteen on-line locations. Service was extended through interline agreements with twenty-one other carriers in 1956, and during the following season the Cotton Belt and SP joined with others to forge transcontinental TOFC service. The SSW handled approximately 64,000 tons of piggyback traffic in 1956.[10]

By the mid-1950s shippers acknowledged the Cotton Belt's growing reputation for dependable service, speed, and concentration on the needs of freight traffic. The rewards were sweet: increased market share in its own territory and, in close cooperation with parent SP, in the highly competitive transcontinental business, too. By 1967 Cotton Belt speedsters aggregated nearly as many miles of "50 mph or over" running as did much larger roads such as the Chicago, Burlington & Quincy and the Union Pacific. Its premier trains included the eastbound *Colton Block*, westbound *Motor Special*, and, of course, the most venerable of them all, the westbound *Blue Streak Merchandise.*[11]

The *BSM* celebrated its twenty-fifth birthday in October, 1956. South Texas and California LCL cars had long since been added to the train and, indeed, it had evolved to serve both transcontinental and regional patrons. During the 1960s the *BSM* frequently held the title as the world's fastest freight train; this was ballyhooed far and wide through Cotton Belt's eye-catching advertisements and through its aggressive sales department. Small wonder the *BSM* became one of the country's best-known freight trains.[12]

If the Cotton Belt was willing to go head to head with all comers in competition for freight traffic, it took quite another approach to its marginal passenger operations. Conductors and engineers still took pride in bringing the company's few passenger trains "in on time," and in 1957 the SSW assisted Warner Brothers Studio and motion picture personalities Andy Griffith and Patricia Neal in filming "A Face in the Crowd" aboard a Cotton Belt train and at the depot in Piggot, Arkansas. Nevertheless, the end of the passenger train era on the Cotton Belt rapidly approached. Service to Memphis ended in 1952, and by early 1956 Cotton Belt's sole operation was one daily train between Saint Louis and Texarkana with an SSW bus connection to Tyler. Even that was tenuous. The Cotton Belt vacated the huge Saint Louis Union Depot on January 1, 1958; buses shuttled the few passengers between East Saint Louis and Saint Louis. Pullman service ended on February 8, 1959, with the remaining mixed trains having been discontinued, on the first day of the year. The end came with little remark and no ceremony when trains 7 and 8 completed their respective runs between East Saint Louis and Pine Bluff on November 29, 1959.[13]

During the years that Cotton Belt was terminating passenger operations, one of its important subsidiaries, the Southwestern Transportation Company, expanded its trucking services. Begun in October, 1928, with a route structure of under one hundred miles, Southwestern Transportation thirty years later owned 550 pieces of equipment, employed nearly 600 persons, had operating authority in all six states served by the Cotton Belt, and sported new terminals at Memphis, Dallas, Texarkana, and Tyler. It also teamed with its parent in providing TOFC service. Indeed, it had toyed with the piggyback concept as early as 1930 but did not mature its interest until the mid-1950s, when coordinated St. Louis Southwestern–Southwestern Transportation

SWT joined with its parent, the Cotton Belt, to provide TOFC service as early as 1930.

TOFC service was established to on-line points in addition to Houston and San Antonio on the SP. Although the trucking line always stood in the shadow of its larger railroad parent, its employees took pride in the company motto—"perfect delivery"—and in the several National Safety Council awards that the company earned.[14]

McKenzie and his subordinates implicitly understood that work habits, levels of productivity, morale, and attitudes regarding safety are inextricably linked. Consequently, they were understandably elated when SSW earned three gold and two lesser Harriman safety awards during the 1950s and 1960s. They were likewise pleased with news from the auditor's office. In the fifteen years following 1953, the SSW doubled the tonnage it carried and more than doubled its net income. Furthermore, it did so with only half the number of employees in 1968 as the company had required in 1954. SSW's operating ratio reflected this: it averaged only 63.74 for the fifteen-year period. There was additional pleasant news. Cotton Belt provided a 6.63 percent rate of return on investment for 1954, but the rate stood at an impressive 12.11 percent in 1967. Some SP vice-presidents and department heads thought McKenzie "got away with murder" in his annual requests for SSW capital and maintenance projects, but D. J.

Russell found little to cheer about in the performance of Pacific Electric.

Russell, in approving them, understood that money spent on the Cotton Belt would return a handsome profit. Indeed, Yale University's Kent T. Healy argued that the St. Louis Southwestern was the most efficiently run railroad in the country.[15]

Russell found little to cheer about in the performance of another subsidiary, however. Pacific Electric had enjoyed a renaissance of business during World War II when every piece of its equipment had been pressed into service. In fact, a new rail branch—from Terminal Island to the Los Angeles–San Pedro line—alone required 116 cars daily to carry shipyard workers to and from their jobs during those hectic years. In 1945, as another example, PE carried more than 109 million passengers. Yet after V-J Day patronage plunged to prewar levels. Faced with declining demand, worn plant and equipment, and a parent that was openly skeptical of rewards from further heavy investment, Pacific Electric's president, O. A. Smith, was confronted with only difficult alternatives.[16]

The company's problems were deeply rooted in the changing landscape of Los Angeles and in the changing patterns of American transport. Pacific Electric's management had early recognized the threat that motor vehicles posed to company fortunes, but rather than submitting to corporate handwringing, it had purchased buses as early as 1917 to serve as a low-cost feeder system to the main rail routes. Twenty years later studies by PE and by the California Railroad Commission even urged substitution of buses for certain rail lines; several of these recommendations were implemented between 1938 and 1943. Subsequently an SP study pointed out that impaired clearances on several routes and high maintenance costs of the "electrical overhead system" argued in favor of a ten-year program for dieselization of freight service and an accelerated time table for elimination of all electric service in favor of motor coaches. The process began in 1950; buses replaced rail cars on several lines, "one-man" passenger cars were employed for most of the remaining electric service, and diesels replaced electrics on specified freight routes. Pacific Electric put

Pacific Electric conveyed all of its passenger transit operations to Metropolitan Coach Lines as of October 1, 1953.

on a happy face for its golden jubilee in 1952, but prospects were bleak.[17]

Dramatic changes followed. On October 1, 1953, after intensive negotiations, Pacific Electric conveyed all of its passenger transit operations to the newly formed Metropolitan Coach Lines for $7.2 million. Metropolitan intended to convert all remaining PE rail passenger operations to bus and in 1954–55 did so on the Los Angeles–Hollywood–Beverly Hills and Los Angeles–Glendale–Burbank lines, but failed to win regulatory agency approval for the remaining four routes. Profits eluded the Metropolitan Lines, however, and on April 1, 1958, the tax-supported Los Angeles Metropolitan Transport Authority took over. The axe fell quickly. The "Big Red Cars" made their last trips to San Pedro and to Bellflower in 1958, to Watts in 1959, and the final operation—to Long Beach—ended on April 9, 1961. In the process Pacific Electric became "freight only" and diesel powered. As late as 1953, fully 50 percent of its revenue had come from passenger operations, although PE at that time generated freight revenues from 900 industries at 117 stations; in 1956 it handled 170,900 carloads and employed over 2,000 persons. Nevertheless, Pacific Electric's life as an independent entity soon ended; on August 12, 1965, the Pacific Electric was merged into the Southern Pacific.[18]

Many mourned the passage of the "World's Greatest Electric Railway System," and some charged SP with "years of . . . neglect" in its administration of Pacific Electric's affairs. Others believed that PE's decision to convert electric rail passenger operations to motor coach could be explained solely by sinister collusions between parent SP and bus-builder General Motors—although Pacific Electric purchased GM vehicles only after World War II and then only because it offered a better product coupled with attractive financing arrangements. In fact, rail passenger car miles had peaked in the mid-1920s; PE's passenger bus miles surpassed rail in 1940, and in 1950 its buses carried more passengers than did the electric cars. This said nothing of total passenger traffic that moved increasingly by private automobile—a fact that was central to PE's grim financial picture. After 1923 Pacific Electric had posted annual deficits until World War II. Interline freight divisions favoring PE resulted, however, in generally offsetting advantages for SP's system at large; this consideration was overriding until PE faced the need to renew plant and equipment following the war. Meanwhile, the ability of Pacific Electric's rail operation to compete was impaired by the construction of highways on either side of its private rights-of-way and by a plethora of right-angle grade crossings as the public roadway system exploded. Accidents followed as a matter of course; there was a public outcry; the company was forced to lengthen schedules, which put its rail service at a disadvantage. Indeed, the California Highway Department had the last word when its planners rejected Pacific Electric's suggestion that rights-of-way for high-speed, grade-separated electric passenger service be included in the Los Angeles freeway network.[19]

President Russell found more pleasurable notice in events more than two thousand miles to the east. Indeed, the mood was measurably upbeat in 1954 when New Orleans celebrated the official opening of its long-awaited and impressive new Union Passenger Terminal to serve seven railroads and their forty-eight daily trains. The new station produced a monumental relocation project, replaced five older stations, eliminated 144 grade crossings, and cost a staggering $57 million. The station building alone cost over $16 million. SP's Russell and the other railroad presidents who were there for the dedication on May 1 may have had a bittersweet reaction, however, knowing that the railroads would pay for this new facility while taxpayers would foot the bill for the New Orleans airport and terminal only a few miles away. SP's share of the cost amounted to 16.5 percent of the total.[20]

The opening of the New Orleans Union Passenger Terminal generally reflected SP's positive feelings regarding passenger service in 1954. Film and television celebrities such as Jack Benny, Don McNeill, Kim Novak, and Forrest Tucker continued to ride SP's finest trains; additional new equipment—including dome lounges—was on order or had been delivered; the Chicago Cubs baseball team still arrived in Mesa, Arizona, each year aboard the *Golden State Limited* for spring training; and Claude E. Peterson, in charge of SP's passenger business, was featured in both *Business Week* and *Modern Railroads* for his im-

The passenger railroads paid for the new station opened in New Orleans on May 1, 1954.

Rita Hayworth arrived in San Francisco aboard an SP train for the filming of "Pal Joey" in 1957.

pressive efforts in promotion of the company's trains. There was other visible evidence of SP's enthusiasm for passenger business: modern city ticket offices were opened in Los Angeles and San Francisco; the company had streamlined its ticketing system; and SP embraced a "family fare plan" to promote vacation travel. Its fleet of premier long-distance trains—the *Shasta Daylight, City of San Francisco,*

In 1954, a lot of new passenger equipment—including dome lounges—was on order or had been delivered.

Golden State Limited, and *Sunset Limited*— maintained the popularity of SP's "Four Great Routes West" by catering to patrons who were interested in comfort, convenience, and service. Lucius Beebe, the writer, bon vivant, and rail enthusiast extraordinaire, lavished praise on several SP trains, especially the *Golden State* and *Sunset*. Furthermore, the dining car service, however costly, maintained its reputation for high quality. In 1954 SP also began to operate "hamburger grill" or cafeteria cars on certain trains in an attempt to reduce expenses and gain revenues from those who considered dining car meals too expensive. And, for those who wanted their own automobiles when they arrived at their destination, the SP experimented briefly with what it called "Private Auto Piggyback" between Portland and Oakland and Los Angeles.[21]

Passenger specials in varying forms remained popular throughout the 1950s and into the next decade. On the Texas & New Orleans they included Cub Scout Specials to Houston, annual Christmas Orphans Specials from San Antonio to outlying points, as well as the annual Fun Tours to New Orleans

Mardi Gras festivities. On the SP itself they included forty-five trainloads of Boy Scouts in 1953 to an annual jamboree in California, several special trains for the 1960 Winter Olympics at Squaw Valley, California, popular Reno Fun Trains, as well as campaign trains for Harry S Truman, Dwight D. Eisenhower, Adlai E. Stevenson, John F. Kennedy, and Richard M. Nixon. Less spectacular but of great importance locally were specials on the T&NO that carried workers to their jobs near Lake Charles, Louisiana, when floods blocked highways in 1958 and in Oregon during 1956 when the SP transported school children from Scholfield Road to Reedsport after mud slides closed roads. The most remarkable special of all, however, was that which carried Soviet Premier Nikita S. Krushchev and his entourage plus accompanying newsmen (over four hundred persons) aboard an eighteen-car train along the Coast Route from Los Angeles to San Francisco on September 20, 1959. Krushchev obviously enjoyed the experience. "This is a fine train and a nice route," he told Ambassador Henry Cabot Lodge, and praised the dining car service, commenting especially

Russell insisted on Hamburger Grill cars after he watched passengers leave the train during a mail stop at Eugene to purchase sandwiches at a nearby cafe.

on SP's famous salad and the tasty cornbread. The Soviet contingent fooled the commissary department, though, by ordering gin instead of vodka.[22]

Sparkling equipment, innovative marketing, and newsworthy special trains notwithstanding, all was not well with SP's passenger operations. Except for the Korean war years of 1951–52, the SP suffered annual declines in the number of passengers handled from 1946 to 1960. The average distance each passenger traveled fell as did the ratio of ticket revenues to total operations revenues. SP sought fiscal relief by discontinuing little-used trains, but the issue proved volatile. For instance, when the company sought to remove a pair of trains between Grants Pass, Oregon, and Dunsmuir, California, the overall question of SP's interest in passenger service was raised by protestants. Russell was characteristically direct: "We feel that the logical measure of the need for a passenger train is whether it is sufficiently patronized to pay at least its out-of-pocket cost of operation." To be sure, as more and more former patrons chose alternate means of transport, passenger trains became a greater financial burden for the SP and increasingly an emotional issue for the public.[23]

SP's passenger philosophy during the last half of the 1950s was to protect the reputation of its premier trains, to cover out-of-pocket costs on the secondary trains, and to eliminate all others. There were times, though, when Russell felt his subordinates were not pressing the issue with adequate vigor. Early in 1955 he told Claude Peterson to make "a realistic short and long range forecast of the passenger service" that SP might expect to maintain. In this regard, Russell reminded Peterson it was not likely "that the mail will continue on our trains indefinitely." He was especially concerned that money not be wasted on new diesel locomotives if SP intended to significantly reduce its passenger train miles. Peterson counseled against "drastic action," proposing instead a systematic reduction through 1957. Russell's response was blunt: "I am disappointed in your long range thinking on this subject, and had hoped you would take a more realistic and aggressive approach thereto." A further indication of Russell's feeling came a few months later when the passenger department was downgraded and merged with public relations.[24]

Russell's pessimism regarding the future of railroad passenger business was based on his perceptions of the relative advantages enjoyed by the train's principal competitors—the automobile and the airliner. "There will never be a thing as valuable as rubber tires going where the people are," Russell said in noting the flexibility of the automobile for the short haul. It did not end there. Congress had established the first federal highway program in 1916 and forty years later passed the Federal-Aid Highway Act, which inaugurated the interstate highway network that gave the automobile an advantage for long-distance travel as well. Similarly, commercial aviation, which profited greatly from technological advances as a result of World War II, grew astonishingly during the late 1940s and throughout the following decade. Russell's views, molded in part by his experiences in the Imperial Royal Flying Corps during World War I, were in ad-

Ike liked trains, and he used them extensively in his campaigns. In 1956, the SP assigned the car *Sunset* for his use.

vance of conventional wisdom—a fact that frequently put him at odds with his fellow railroad leaders and with the public at large. As early as 1942 he had warned that passenger revenues provided only a small portion of SP's income but consumed a disproportionate percentage of management's time and the company's resources. In 1956 Russell observed that losses in passenger patronage came despite the millions of dollars expended after the war to provide the finest trains in the country. In 1955 alone, he continued, the SP had lost $4 million in the dining car service because, as Russell noted, the company "tried to give the best we could for what people could afford to pay." Yet the slippage in pas-

senger numbers continued. "It's just a change in the American way of life," said the SP president. "You can't make people do what they don't want to." The "jet plane will spell the end of the transcontinental [passenger] train"; the "Pullman car will be extinct within 20 years," Russell predicted in 1957.[25]

Even the irrepressible Claude Peterson had to admit that "the long-term outlook for passenger travel" was not good, although like Russell he expected continued need for short-distance trains in urban areas. Both men agreed that the SP would provide "trains which the public needs . . . and will support by actual use" and both pledged in 1956 to operate those same trains as "the finest in the

Khrushchev's entourage confounded SP's commissary personnel by ordering gin instead of vodka.

Lightly patronized trains such as the *Gila Tomahawk*, running in Arizona between Bowie and Globe, did not pay out-of-pocket costs.

SP's 1948 study spelled doom for the unconventional Cab-Forwards used to hurry perishables over the Sierra Nevada from Roseville.

country." Results were mixed. During the 1958 vacation season business was up significantly on the *Sunset Limited* and the *Golden State* but down disappointingly on the *Shasta Daylight* and *Coast Daylight*. Russell insisted that unremunerative trains and service be curtailed. At the same time SP initiated a program of selling airline tickets at locations along the SP where the air carriers had no offices. "This," said the SP, "is in line with our policy of giving customers a complete travel service" and keeping "them coming back to SP ticket offices." Russell's determination to cut costs and the company's campaign to sell international airline tickets appeared to some, however, as duplicitous efforts to get out of the passenger train business. In California, Arizona, and Oregon, state regulatory bodies frequently denied SP's discontinuance applications and insisted that the company continue to operate money-losing and lightly patronized trains. Ironically, public sentiment hardened against train discontinuances even as travelers abandoned the rails. The SP pro-

claimed "We Want to Run Passenger Trains" but warned it was "only sensible to discontinue those trains which so few people use that the trains obviously are no longer needed." The public, however, was not persuaded. It perceived that the SP embraced a policy of wholesale abandonment of the trains. SP's general advertising, some observed, now featured the advantages of its freight service *as well as* its passenger offerings—a distinct break with the past. The issue was volatile and acrimonious debate would persist through the decade following.[26]

Meanwhile, after a slow start, SP moved to effect the complete dieselization of its operation. SP's lethargy in this matter is explained by the presence of strong-minded steam-oriented men in the mechanical department and by the fleet of modern GS and AC locomotives that it had purchased during the 1930s and 1940s. The die was cast, however, in 1948 when the company completed an exhaustive motor power survey that projected a gross savings of $66.7 million following

The AC-9 monsters that lugged dead freight from El Paso to Tucumcari were victims, too.

dieselization accomplished in an orderly fashion over a ten-year period. The plan would be executed, in part, on the basis of internal research dealing with steam locomotive maintenance procedures. For instance, SP found that although higher standards of maintenance were applied to passenger locomotives, the cost of maintaining freight locomotives was more than 60 percent greater per ton mile; and that, in terms of locomotive ton miles, those engines running on level terrain and those pulling light loads cost less to repair than those working mountain grades or pulling heavy loads. In other words, the intensity of use and not locomotive miles or locomotive ton miles

was the criterion used to determine maintenance procedures and costs. The same criterion would be employed to determine retirement patterns for SP's steam locomotive fleet.[27]

SP's steam locomotive retirement program thus considered the age and size of the machines, but these factors were not controlling. The company had found that the age of a locomotive did not contribute to high repair costs if it was properly maintained; and it also determined that heavy locomotives, because of more intense use during their overall life periods, could not be expected to last as long as smaller types less intensively utilized. Conse-

The old and the new; the new would win out.

quently, elderly and lighter locomotives could be expected to remain on the roster after heavier and in some cases newer engines were gone. Maximum annual savings per locomotive, predicted SP planners, could be realized by dieselizing freight districts having heavy grades; conversely, minimum savings could be expected from replacing steam on the San Francisco–San Jose commute line. Planners similarly recommended the gradual replacement of steam for switching, local freight, and secondary passenger assignments. Finally, they also urged the full dieselization of the San Diego & Arizona Eastern by 1956, and the Northwestern Pacific and T&NO in 1957.[28]

Actually, the need for new power on the T&NO was relatively greater than on the Pacific Lines. In 1948, when the first diesel road units arrived, the average age of T&NO's 450 locomotives was 43.1 years. By the end of 1952 the road had 212 diesels; three years later only 34 steamers remained, including

nine 0-6-0s and seven 2-10-2s (T&NO's GS engines already had gone to the Pacific Lines). The last steam locomotive in road service on the T&NO took a train from Avondale to Lafayette on December 23, 1956, and a few weeks into the new year the last of T&NO steam locomotives was retired.[29]

Dieselization on the Pacific Lines followed a similar pattern. Over 90 percent of through freights on the Sunset Route between Los Angeles and El Paso were diesel powered by early 1952, and at the end of the next year SP's Pacific Lines owned more diesel units than steam locomotives. Following the 1948 plan, SP retained steam for much of its passenger service—handling 64.2 percent of passenger miles as late as 1952. Savings in passenger service were not as dramatic as in freight, and, moreover, President Russell frowned on spending money for passenger units if SP was going to trim its offerings in that area. Steam, nevertheless, was on its last legs. The era of external combustion ended on the north end of the

A frequent scene along SP lines during the mid-1950s. Here an Alco switcher lugs a "train" of locomotives from scrapper.

Portland Division on October 5, 1955, when 4-10-2 number 5021 handled a freight train from Brooklyn Yard to Eugene. The ACs were still found wrestling tonnage on the Modoc while GS and 4-8-2 locomotives handled the commuter fleet, but orders for new diesels in 1955 and 1956 plus an unexpected downturn in the economy promised to end it all. AC number 4211 was the last cab-forward to handle revenue freight, from Oakland to Roseville, on November 30, 1956; GS number 4430 drew the last steam-powered commute on January 22, 1957. The operating department early in 1957 anticipated that sixteen heavy and forty-three light steam locomotives "which had remaining mileage" would be required to see the SP through "the peak season" of 1958, although the SP actually declared itself "fully dieselized" at the end of 1957. It did agree, however, to operate a series of railfan excursions in 1958, the last being an emotional weekend trip to Reno on October 18–19 using GS 4460. Then it was over. The SP and its subsidiaries fittingly donated sixty locomotives for display in honor of an era now passed. Yet not even the most hardened industrial engineer would argue that there was any substitute for the sight, sound, and wonder of those awesome steel giants under steam.[30]

The capital requirements necessary for dieselization were stupendous, but Russell correctly observed that "the investment was worth every cent." The diesel proved to be

Before the era of steam in commute service ended in 1957, magnificent GS locomotives replaced older and lighter power.

more efficient than steam. More importantly, steam required massive service facilities and a huge attending labor force that the diesel did not. Steam power, in fact, served to point up one of the industry's trying liabilities—it was at once capital intensive *and* labor intensive. Russell saw no immediate way to avoid the constant need for massive infusions of capital, but he did set out to "get rid of bodies." Dieselization certainly reduced the number of employees necessary for the company to do its work; Russell was pleased by this and looked elsewhere for opportunities to reduce the work force. He was, for instance, enraged when an internal study showed that an average of thirty-three persons handled or, in Russell's word "touched," a company requisition. A streamlined system, instituted shortly thereafter, reduced the number who "touched" the requisition to five—with a correspondingly smaller number of persons on the payroll. "A large number of employees," said Russell, was "fine in a time when wages were low" and when there was little modal

competition. It was not "fine," however, in an era of escalating wages and intense modal competition.[31]

Russell constantly looked for better ways to do business. He complained bitterly that "the railroad industry was far behind others" in the area of research, and under his direction SP's own Bureau of Transportation Research and the Department of Research and Mechanical Standards were nurtured. Additionally, he engaged Stanford Research Institute in 1953 to search for a cure to the constant problem of freight claims. "I wanted PhDs who knew nothing about railroads to study the problem," Russell explained. Two years later the institute and SP's own Sacramento shops unveiled the prototype of what soon would be called the "Hydra-Cushion" freight car, which featured hydraulic dampening devices to reduce coupling and train slack impact. The results were marvelous. During a six-month test in which the car hauled only automobile windshields, no claim was filed by shippers. Early in 1958 SP sold the Hydra-

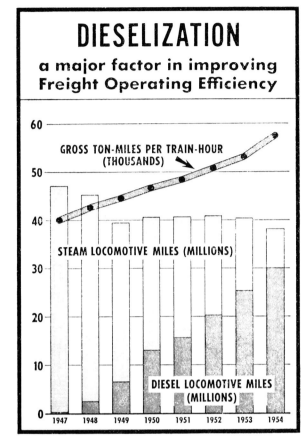

DIESELIZATION
a major factor in improving
Freight Operating Efficiency

GROSS TON-MILES PER TRAIN-HOUR
(THOUSANDS)

STEAM LOCOMOTIVE MILES (MILLIONS)

DIESEL LOCOMOTIVE MILES
(MILLIONS)

1947 1948 1949 1950 1951 1952 1953 1954

Cushion rights and patents to private manufacturers; consequently, the entire national car fleet benefited from the new technology. SP also looked to SRI for advice on the application of magnetic drum data storage devices for various accounting and car-reporting functions.[32]

Russell was equally interested in capitalizing on the dramatic growth that had occurred in SP's service area during the fifteen-year period following 1940. SP's industrial department focused on California, where the increase in economic expansion was most dramatic, but did not ignore the rest of the company's sprawling route structure that served what SP called the "Golden Empire." The fruits of these efforts were sweet. Russell gleefully reported that "new industries, each requiring a spur track, are being located along the Southern Pacific's rail lines—at the rate of 1-½ a day in 1955." Four years later the SP

led all rail carriers in the number of new industries located along its lines.[33]

This phenomenal growth plus the burgeoning development of previously established industries placed great stress on SP's freight car fleet. The company responded dramatically—spending $267 million to acquire 46,604 cars in the ten years following World War II. This, in addition to the company's stringent policy of maintenance (the percentage of unserviceable cars in 1955 was a mere 1.9), increased SP's carrying capacity by nearly one-half.[34]

Traditional as well as specialized cars were employed to handle SP's growing volume of revenue freight during the 1950s; the total for 1956 even exceeded that of 1943, the peak year of World War II traffic. The portion of operating revenue attributed to freight rose similarly, to 91.4 in 1959. Exotic shipments such as fractionating towers, massive generators, and even miniature submarines gained headlines, but SP's bread-and-butter freight revenues continued to come from manufacturers and products of mines, forests, and agriculture: automobile parts; set-up autos; copper concentrates and anodes; iron ore; petroleum and chemical products; logs, lumber, and paper; and, food products ranging from bananas and raisins to lemons and oranges.[35]

Traffic in bulk commodities generally increased or remained stable during this period, but time-sensitive merchandise traffic and LCL business were increasingly subject to truck competition. SP's response was to somewhat tardily, but then with gusto, embrace TOFC service—a technology that was not new but one that came into its own gradually after the war. On May 4, 1953, the Texas & New Orleans initiated TOFC service between Houston and on-line cities in Louisiana for LCL shipments, and two months later the SP initiated the concept on the West Coast for hauling trailers of the subsidiary Pacific Motor Trucking between San Francisco and Los Angeles aboard the *Overnighter* merchandise trains. This service was expanded during 1954 and 1955 to principal locations on the

The portion of operating revenue attributed to freight rose to 91.4 percent in 1959. Trains like this one at Crescent Lake, Oregon, told the story.

During the late 1950s, the SP embraced the TOFC concept with gusto. In this view a piggyback train is leaving San Francisco.

Here another piggyback train traverses the famous loop near San Luis Obispo.

SP and further through connections with the Union Pacific at Ogden, the Northern Pacific and the Great Northern at Portland, and the Cotton Belt at Corsicana. The SP hauled its 100,000th trailer in 1956. SP's efforts in this regard were remarkable. Indeed, one writer called the SP "the Piggyback Champion of U.S. railroading."[36]

SP's TOFC efforts retained, regained, or expanded traffic in high-rated commodities and, as operations were broadened, also attracted business from freight forwarders and even common carrier truckers. Postal business was retained and not lost to trucks by diversion to TOFC from passenger head-end cars; automobile shipments increased astonishingly as SP instituted TOFC options for that highly competitive business. Initially, SP modified existing flatcars with special tie-down devices but later purchased specially built 79-foot and then 85-foot cars for the operation. At first SP's trucking subsidiaries provided all trailers, and by 1960 SP claimed to have the nation's largest fleet of piggyback equipment. That approach changed, however, as first the Cotton Belt and then the SP purchased shares in Trailer Train Company, a piggyback car leasing agency that owned and leased equipment to its owners. Was there profit in any of this? Internal studies showed mixed results. In 1959 TOFC business moving between the Bay Area and Los Angeles showed a net loss, primarily because of inadequate or inefficient use of equipment and facilities and because of a high percentage of northbound empties. One year later TOFC service in that corridor showed an overall profit; automobile traffic was especially lucrative, but "rail-billed"

TOFC business resulted in "a substantial loss." Technological advances, it seemed, had proved greater than those of marketing and pricing.[37]

Some TOFC business moved at "passenger train speed" on dedicated trains such as the *Pacific Coast Expediter* between Portland and Oakland or the *Coast Merchandiser* between San Francisco and Los Angeles, but other piggyback shipments were assigned to expedited trains such as Cotton Belt's famous *Blue Streak Merchandise*. That train, in fact, was rapidly becoming the premier train of SSW's parent, too. The *Blue Streak* typically handled high-rated merchandise forwarder business and auto parts to Southern California. This and similar lading was subject to competitive forces that conspired to demand speedier schedules for time-sensitive business throughout the 1950s. To emphasize its determination to meet these forces, SP instituted several additional name trains as diverse as the *West Coaster* on the Overland Route and the *Arizona Zipper* on the Sunset Route between Los Angeles and Tucson via Phoenix. By early 1956 SP's Pacific Lines boasted thirty-nine symbol or name freight trains.[38]

Increased train speeds required substantial expenditures for track and signaling improvements. In this regard, the SP continued its program of installing new and heavier rail, expanded its radio-telephone system, and added capacity by the installation of more CTC. Throughout the 1950s Russell pushed CTC programs on SP's major routes: "It does the business for less money than double tracking," he said. Capacity on the Sunset Route, for example, was increased in 1955 between Colton and Yuma with a combination of CTC, lengthened sidings, and construction of second main for 9 miles on the west approach to Beaumont Hill. By the end of the 1950s CTC extended from Los Angeles as far east as Sierra Blanca, Texas, on the T&NO. Special attention was given the entire Sunset Route at mid-decade because traffic via the El Paso

Several line changes in West Texas reduced mileage and increased maximum track speed.

gateway to and from the T&NO had nearly doubled since 1940. Studies were made for a modern yard west of El Paso, and that city's Alfalfa Yard was expanded. Additional line changes in West Texas, including one that eliminated the famous "horseshoe curve" at Torcer, 79 miles east of El Paso, and another resulting from the damming of the Devil's River west of Del Rio, reduced mileage and increased maximum track speed.[39]

Of the many betterment projects approved during the Russell years, none was more dramatic in scope and undertaking than the Salt Lake fill. The impressive cross-lake trestle, in use since 1904, incurred increased maintenance problems with age, and if SP chose to renew it, the work would have to be done "under traffic." SP engineers and outside consultants considered various alternatives, among them: renewing the old trestle; building a concrete trestle; a solid fill; and a combination of these. Eventually they concluded

The new track at the Mofeta-Feodora cut-off in West Texas has been tied into the main line before the old track is taken up.

One improvement eliminated the famous "horse-shoe curve" at Torcer, seventy-nine miles east of El Paso.

that a fill would be the best choice. Work began on 1955 and was conducted by SP forces in addition to those from the Morrison-Knudsen Construction Company.[40]

The fill required a prodigious effort. To provide maximum stability, a 25-foot trench was dug in the lake bottom, 30 feet beneath the surface. This trench varied in width from 175 feet to 600 feet; when filled with rock and gravel, it provided a stronger foundation for the fill than if materials had been poured directly onto the lake bottom. Above the surface, the top of the fill would be 38 feet wide. Originally, it was designated to an elevation of 4,217 feet above sea level, the same as the 1904 trestle, but after engineers' tests determined that the fill would not be stable at the elevation, the level was reduced to 4,212 feet—still 12 feet above the level of the lake at that time. The fill's length was 12.68 miles; its maximum height was 97 feet. Material handled totaled an enormous 60,832,000 cubic yards. Ironically, fire consumed 645 feet of the elderly trestle on May 4, 1956; for the first time in its history the trestle was out of service (for six days), and traffic normally moving

over it was rerouted or annulled. For Russell the fire emphatically proved the wisdom of constructing the fill. Work on the project went well, and on July 27, 1959, the first revenue train passed over it. Russell was delighted. The enterprise had been completed almost a full year ahead of schedule.[41]

Completion of the fill allowed the SP to increase train speeds on the Overland Route and thereby improve the efficiency of the Ogden Gateway. This pleased the Union Pacific, SP's historic partner at Ogden, but it also pleased the much smaller Denver & Rio Grande Western with which it also connected at that point. Even before the SP completed work on the fill, the Rio Grande had pledged itself as a competitor of Union Pacific for SP's favor. Yet for the smaller road it was a grim battle. During the early twentieth century the road had been part of George Gould's empire, the intermediate carrier for his Missouri Pacific and his new Western Pacific. In the process Gould had looted Rio Grande's treasury, and when his empire crumbled, the road passed into receivership during 1918. Some years earlier the Harriman-controlled SP and

Of the many betterment projects from the Russell years, none was more impressive than the Salt Lake fill.

UP had added to the woes of the smaller road when they determined to close the Ogden Gateway to the Rio Grande and, after the SP and UP were separated, the latter determined to keep the gateway closed, a position affirmed by an ICC decision of 1915. Rio Grande's circumstances were further eroded in 1923 by the so-called Central Pacific Conditions, which pledged the Southern Pacific to preferentially solicit traffic to and from prescribed areas in the West via Ogden for the benefit of the Union Pacific.[42]

On the surface all this made little difference anyway, as the Rio Grande's route from Denver to Ogden was long and indirect compared with Union Pacific's. However, completion of its Dotsero Cut-off in 1934—shortening the route by 175 miles—placed the Rio Grande in a position to at least claim competitive ability. Another important variable was introduced at about the same time when SP gained control of the St. Louis Southwestern. The SP, of course, was obligated under the Central Pacific Conditions but the Cotton Belt was not. Consequently SSW's sales force could and did

solicit traffic to the advantage of the SP and to the Rio Grande via Ogden. Conversely, the Rio Grande was not bound by any restrictions and campaigned vigorously for interchange business with the Southern Pacific. These marketing changes posed a delicate problem for the SP. On the one hand, it wished to keep its options open and maximize opportunities; on the other, it needed to maintain proper if not necessarily cordial relations with the UP. For its part, the D&RGW in 1949 filed papers with the ICC to force the UP to establish joint rates to and from the Northwest—a case that it eventually won. The aggressive Rio Grande also sought, in 1957, and gained, in 1966, modifications of the Central Pacific conditions that gave it an improved competitive environment. As a result of these events, SP became D&RGW's principal source of interchange business, a fact that was not lost on Rio Grande's president, Wilson J. McCarthy, who constantly reminded his successor, Gus B. Aydelott, to "remember the SP."[43]

Meanwhile, the Southern Pacific Company sought to simplify its complex corporate struc-

The first revenue train passed over the Salt Lake fill on July 27, 1959. Note the earlier fill and trestle at left.

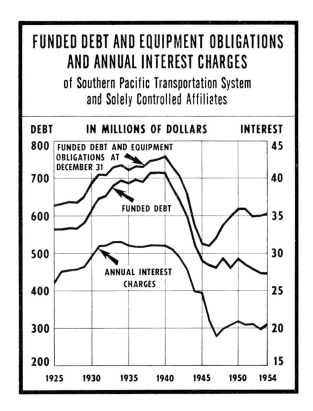

ture through a series of internal mergers. Five corporate names—the Southern Pacific Railroad, Arizona Eastern, Dawson Railway, El Paso & Rock Island, and the El Paso & Southwestern—disappeared in 1955. The venerable Central Pacific followed four years later. In 1961 the ICC approved the merger of three more subsidiaries into the parent company. These were the El Paso & Southwestern of Texas, El Paso Southern, as well as the much larger Texas & New Orleans Railroad. Russell noted that these mergers would not result in any substantial change in the total assets and liabilities of the SP but would yield further centralized control and simplify financial, accounting, legal, and administrative procedures.[44]

Another matter of internal importance concerned SP's ownership of stock, amounting to 34 percent, in Pacific Greyhound. This ownership gave the SP four members on the bus company's eleven-member board, an agreement in effect since 1929. Shortly after the

war, however, the federal government brought suit under the Sherman Antitrust Act to force SP's divestiture of its Pacific Greyhound stock. The issue dragged on until SP sold its common stock in 1954 and its preferred two years later. SSW's trucking company, Southwestern Transportation Company, would similarly sell its holdings in what had become the Greyhound Corporation during 1969. The venture had proven profitable over the long run; in addition to receiving dividends over the years, SP made a three-to-one profit on its investment in Pacific Greyhound. Southwestern Transportation's net, if anything, was larger.[45]

These profits and those from routine business, plus reductions in SP's funded debt and equipment obligations, allowed Russell to present the company's growing number of shareholders with an increasingly rosy picture. SP paid annual dividends of $3.00 per share from 1952 through 1958 and split two-for-one in 1952 and three-for-one in 1959. Funded debt and equipment obligations had stood at just under $800 million in 1940 but, even after massive acquisitions of freight cars, stream-lined passenger equipment, and diesels, stood at only slightly over $600 million by the mid-1950s. Interest charges declined similarly.[46]

Russell was concerned, nevertheless, with the need to raise the company's stature in the financial community. This resulted in a redirection of SP's advertising strategies— "to impress on the money-lenders, investment counselors, trust administrators and the like that Southern Pacific is a railroad with a great future." Whether it was because of this cam-paign or because of SP's noteworthy perfor-mance during the 1950s, the SP did gain con-siderable popular attention. In 1954 the SP ranked third among all domestic railroads in terms of operating revenues and in the same year it ranked ninth among all companies (ex-cluding banks and insurance firms) as mea-sured by total assets. Moreover, SP's manage-ment received plaudits from *Forbes* and the American Institute of Management, and the company received "buy notices" from stock brokers who, as one noted, admired the SP because the "price risk is small and longer term prospects are substantial." There was one discordant note. SP's return on investment was only 3.5 percent in the ten-year period following World War II.[47]

Russell's mark on the Southern Pacific dur-ing the 1950s was distinct and emphatic. No-body doubted that his vigorous leadership would have the same positive impact on the company during the decade upcoming. In-deed, his tenure would be distinguished by the admiring label "The Russell Years."

CHAPTER 16

The New Standard Railroad of the World?

"The machines that have been invented for
saving the labor of men's hands have come
to stay, and every intelligent business man
recognizes it."—C. P. Huntington, 1900

THE tumultuous 1960s proved to be a period of extraordinary stress for the United States. The country was confronted by a variety of controversial social and political issues; four men of widely differing persuasions occupied the White House; and, the war in Viet Nam threatened to dissolve the national spirit. Those who managed or worked for the Southern Pacific were not removed from these movements and events, but the company itself forged ahead under the steady guidance of Donald Joseph Russell. Yet, just as there was constancy at 65 Market Street so, too, was there change. Russell recognized that dramatic alterations had occurred, were occurring, or certainly were necessary in the fabric of the nation's transportation plant—especially within the railroad industry. With this in mind, Russell determined to position the SP in a fashion that would maximize its potential for profitability and assure its future.

Russell's efforts went forward against the backdrop of strained relationships between the company and those who worked for it. The SP had long been known as a company where one familial generation followed another in employment and where there was a "true sense of family"; insiders felt it, and outsiders recognized it. This sense of closeness had been reinforced during the hard times of the depression and in the urgency of war years that followed. Much of the "glue" that had held the family together, however, sub-

sequently eroded. Ordinary employees no longer had an opportunity to directly solicit business for the company since the haulage of LCL freight had nearly disappeared and, indeed, the small rail shipper himself faced extinction. A similar situation obtained as passenger trains disappeared. Furthermore, management authority itself was increasingly centralized in San Francisco. All of this served to create greater distances between labor and management.

Such was reflected in many of the company's traditions and customs. SP glee clubs, athletic groups, and service organizations continued to function, but without the previous vigor and level of participation. Annual Christmas parties for office personnel in San Francisco, Houston, and elsewhere ended. Of more tangible importance were changes in health care. On January 31, 1968, the Hospital Association of the Southern Pacific Lines in Texas and Louisiana was dissolved and its Houston hospital closed. At about the same time the Cotton Belt deeded its facility at Texarkana to employees, but the hospital would finally close in 1972. Even earlier, in 1963, SP's Pacific Lines hospital department had been reorganized. Although a few company physicians remained, employees no longer had direct contact with company-sponsored health providers. Henceforth these benefits were provided through company-paid contracts with various health insurance companies.[1]

Tangible changes occurred in many of SP's traditions and customs, including in the important area of health care. SP's hospitals were closed during the 1960s.

Labor-management relations were especially subject to friction over the industry's and SP's diligent efforts to reduce the work force. Management complained bitterly of "make work" policies that it labeled "featherbedding." Some rules were, to be sure, ridiculously wasteful of company resources. Yet the term *featherbedding* was perceived by labor as an indictment of all contract workers. The result was an acrimonious and, certainly in terms of morale, counterproductive conflict. In the end, arbitration awards and compromise agreements allowed the carriers to reduce numbers in specified crafts. The number of firemen, whose necessity on diesel locomotives was certainly questionable, was reduced beginning in 1964, and "third brakeman rules" (on freight trains) mandated by law in New Mexico, Arizona, and California were gradually rescinded. However, "full crew laws" in Oregon and Arkansas would not be repealed until 1972.[2]

As important as it was to trim the number of employees, Russell understood that it was even more urgent to provide educational opportunities for the remaining work force—opportunities that would benefit individual employees and the company, too. During 1963 the SP initiated a program of reimburs-ing employees who worked toward degrees offered by accredited colleges and universities, and shortly thereafter instituted a series of free home study courses available through its Training Bureau. There was a special program for locomotive engineers; in 1968 the SP announced that it had ordered the industry's first "locomotive simulator." This sophisticated $1 million computer-aided teaching device would be used, the company noted, to provide standardized training for enginemen.[3]

At the same time Russell decided to beef up SP's officer recruitment and improvement programs. "We need to take advantage of all the thinking we can get," Russell said: the company needed "an adequate pool of people capable of taking on high level responsibility." To this end, SP sent more and more of its managers to advanced programs at universities such as Harvard, MIT, and Stanford and simultaneously recruited young talent from campuses across the country. The newcomers were then sent through SP's intensive two-year management training program.[4]

In a related manner, the Southern Pacific on June 22, 1962, became the first railroad in the country to voluntarily pledge its support for President John F. Kennedy's "Plan for Progress"—a joint effort between the nation's major corporations and the President's Committee on Equal Employment Opportunity to advance the principle of equal consideration and treatment for all applicants and all employees. The plan predated the Civil Rights acts. As Russell told SP's officers and supervisors, "equal employment opportunity without regard to race, creed, color or national origin is a vital part of our American heritage." Whether Russell knew it or not, he was affirming a principle advanced sixty-two years earlier by Collis P. Huntington. "If we deny to the individual, no matter what his creed, his color, or his nationality, the right to justice which every man possesses," Huntington had said in 1900, "there will be no enduring prosperity and decline will surely follow. If, on the contrary, we establish and maintain as a prin-

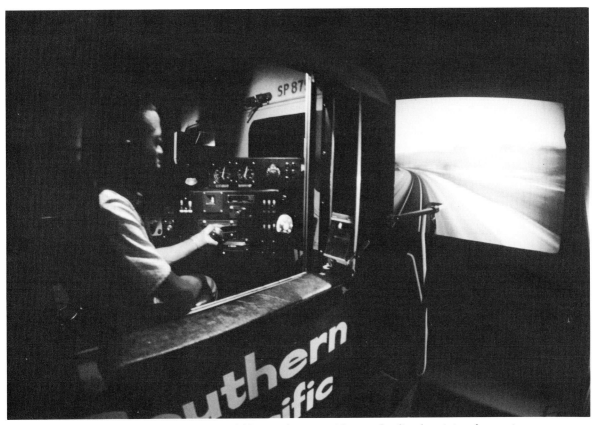

SP's innovative locomotive simulator would be used to provide standardized training for enginemen.

ciple of our national life the right of every man and of all property to be treated fairly and equally before the law, there is hardly a limit to the splendid success that the people of our republic can gain and hold. . . ." Huntington would have been proud of SP's advanced position on the matter.[5]

During this same time the Southern Pacific found other avenues to demonstrate its corporate responsibility. The SP delivered carloads of water without charge to a New Mexico village after its water system was disabled; donated an impressive collection of fossils and rocks to the University of Texas; sponsored an award-winning float that appeared in Pasadena's 1969 Tournament of Roses Parade; handled a two-car "Main Street U.S.A." exhibition belonging to the Henry Ford Museum and Greenfield Village to several on-line locations; provided vigorous support for the Junior Achievement program; and, with spe-

cial trains dispatched for the purpose, picked up motorists marooned by a devastating blizzard at Vaughn, New Mexico. SP's mountain forces likewise rescued a hapless skier who had become lost near Norden, in the Sierra Nevada.[6]

Much of this was newsworthy, and the media provided free advertising as a consequence. It fell to SP's advertising department, however, to place the company's overall self-image before the public. Russell was especially eager to improve the stature of the SP in the financial community; image ads thus stressed the company's constant efforts to reinvest in plant. On another front, outdoor billboards extolled SP's ability to handle fast freight, big loads, and provide excellent plant locations. These handsome specimens won first prize in the Outdoor Advertising Association's 1964 competition.[7]

On the other hand, one advertising campaign proved to be immediately controversial. Early in 1954 the SP had placed a huge two-directional lighted display sign atop its general office building in San Francisco. The message that it blinked each evening toward the Bay and toward downtown was the uncomplicated company slogan—"SP, Your Friendly Railroad." The public's response was anything but friendly. Letters to the editors of the city's newspapers charged the SP with callous disregard for the integrity of San Francisco's skyline. Photographer Ansel Adams was one of many prominent persons who complained of SP's "arrogance." Russell assured the famous environmentalist that "railroad people are not a breed apart" and that "we of the Southern Pacific are just as proud of San Francisco . . . and its beauties as you and other citizens." In spite of protests, the sign remained until 1961, when it was quietly dismantled. Russell later admitted "it [the sign] was a lousy thing."[8]

Nothing loomed so large on the Southern Pacific during the 1960s as Donald J. Russell himself. "With the railroadman's traditional gold watch chain slung across his vest" he "looks every inch the old-time railroad boss," wrote one observer in 1965. Russell was, indeed, a railroader's railroader—"the most dedicated railroadman I ever knew," said Cotton Belt's Harold J. McKenzie. Russell possessed a commanding presence: no subordinate even thought of calling him "Don"; it was always "Mr. Russell."[9]

Russell's success as a manager sprang from his very persona. The *San Francisco Examiner* called him "an unpretentious realist"; an associate referred to him as an "uncomplicated purist." Subordinates clearly respected his character, integrity, honesty, and his unfailing ability to make decisions. Nobody had to guess where Russell stood on issues. As his wife once said, he "is seldom wrong and never in doubt." Sternly self-disciplined, fearsome, and blunt nearly to rudeness, Russell was nevertheless an aggressive, capable, and inventive manager whose mind was restlessly independent. His style was at once traditional

and unorthodox. He was, fortunately for the SP, the right man at the right time.[10]

Russell was not without humor, but often it was sardonic. One example serves to illustrate this trait. On an inspection trip over the well-manicured Cotton Belt, Russell turned to Harold McKenzie and said, "Mac, if the property looks this bad after two weeks notice, I wonder how bad it is usually?"[11]

Russell showed no humor on one issue. He was emphatic in his belief that one of top management's major responsibilities was that of locating and cultivating talent for executive leadership. His views regarding desirable characteristics were typically straightforward. He looked for the person who could "gear his imaginative process to cold facts," who could "grasp specific situations quickly and relate them to broad, long-range considerations," who was an "innovatist," not what he called a "repeater." Additionally, he placed high value on a person's ability to make decisions and on his "courage to think out recommendations and then stand up for them." Equally important were emotional stamina, ambition, "a real love for the activity in which the company is engaged," and an "interest in affairs outside the company." Finally, the future executive must be "interested in people." He had to be "consistently fair," to "be able to see the other person's point of view," to "understand the emotional reasons behind it," and to "find a common ground for understanding." After all, said Russell, "his most important task will be to build a team which will do the job for him, and he will be able to do this only by motivating and inspiring the people around him."[12]

Awards and recognition for President Russell came as a matter of course. In 1957 he received the National Defense Transportation Association's annual award and in the same season was honored by *Forbes Magazine* as one of the fifty "foremost business leaders of America." More followed. Russell's countenance graced the cover of *Time* on August 11, 1961, and *Forbes* for November 1, 1965.[13]

Russell's efforts and accomplishments were properly recognized, as were those of the company he headed. In an industry that many saw as disintegrating and demoralized and others saw as dying, SP's star seemed to shine brightly. Russell had provided the company with personal and determined leadership, had demanded innovation and imagination from subordinates, and had, as one writer phrased it, forced the SP to "discard its conservatism." The same observer praised Russell and the SP for realizing "sooner than most that the rails were caught up in a fight for survival." Others noted—without taking anything away from Russell or the SP—that the company benefited from changes in demography that favored it. They pointed with admiration to SP's crescent-shaped route structure—stretching from Portland, in the Northwest, through California and Texas to Saint Louis, in the Midwest—and serving, in SP's idiom, the "Golden Empire." Many focused on the railroad itself. *Time* called it "aggressively modern," and *Forbes* said it was "one of the best-

run railroads in the U.S." Dean Witter & Company, the investment firm, argued that the SP was "in the forefront of railroad renaissance" because, in part, it boasted a management that had "demonstrated that it could keep the company competitively competent." Statistics told the tale. In 1963 SP led all railroads in ton-miles handled, and in 1967 it ranked third among all transportation companies (behind Penn Central and United Air Lines) in terms of operating revenues and second in terms of assets, net income, and invested capital. All of this moved David P. Morgan to speculate in *Trains Magazine* that the Southern Pacific might have become the new standard railroad of the world. Toward the end of the 1960s several analysts pointed to SP's broad income base that resulted from its diversification—and recommended its "common stock as one of the soundest values for good income and growth available today," as one brokerage firm put it.[14]

The general enthusiasm that surrounded the company was certainly based in part on SP's continuing dedication to research and development coupled with its willingness to experiment. SP's close association with the Stanford Research Institute continued throughout the 1960s, although it delegated a variety of other research projects to the company laboratory at Sacramento and to various teams from the engineering and mechanical departments.[15]

SP's interest in experimentation assumed concrete form in 1961, when it took delivery of new 4,000-hp diesel-hydraulic locomotives manufactured in West Germany by Kraus-Maffei AG. SP's interest in the diesel-hydraulic reflected not only a search for alternatives to diesel-electric power but also a disenchantment with domestic manufacturers, which, thought the company's management, were too complacent and backward in developing larger and more powerful locomotives. With a significant portion of its diesel fleet needing replacement, SP wished to have a look at what the Kraus-Maffeis could do under harsh

The Kraus-Maffeis are shown here with a dynamometer car at Monolith, California.

operating conditions before deciding whether to rebuild older units in its own shops, return them to the builders for upgrading, trade them on new power, or simply scrap and purchase new power. Ultimately, SP acquired twenty-four diesel-hydraulic units, including three manufactured by American Locomotive Company, and was impressed with their higher horsepower per unit, improved rail adhesion, and reliable propulsion through hydraulic transmissions, cardan shafting, and geared axle drives. However, problems with the high-speed engines were serious. Additionally, the German-made locomotives experienced air intake difficulties in mountain operations where long tunnels and heavy ascending grades were encountered. Consequently, beginning in 1967, as they came due for major repairs, the Kraus-Maffeis were retired; mechanical personnel continued to evaluate the Alcos, but eventually they, too, were scrapped. Meanwhile, domestic builders brought out the types of diesel-electric power that SP officers

had been seeking. At mid-decade the company received, for instance, 2,500-hp GP-35s and 3,600-hp SD-45s from General Motors as well as 3,000-hp Century 630s from Alco and 2,800-hp U28Cs from General Electric.[16]

Southern Pacific's freight car acquisitions during these years represented a blend of the new as well as the old and reflected traffic forecasts based on the period 1960 through 1964, when tonnage grew at a 6.5 percent annual rate. Special equipment orders included "damage free" and "compartmentized" boxes, stainless steel hoppers, trilevel flats, wood chip cars, and cabooses. Other orders brought a flood of conventional boxcars. At the same time, company shops modified older cars to increase capacity and in all cases kept the fleet in functional order. In 1969 a mere 2 percent of the company's inventory of rolling stock was "bad ordered."[17]

Other physical improvements were not as eye-catching as powerful locomotives and huge new freight cars but were just as important in advancing the company's efficient rail operations. CTC was expanded to cover nearly 2,500 miles by the end of 1962, and many of the earlier installations were upgraded to make them even more effective. Along its main routes the SP also installed wayside scanners to detect overheated journals on moving trains and thereby enhance safe passage. At the same time, the company's communications department—already one of the largest privately owned systems—prosecuted the expansion of a "storm-proof" microwave network. This was begun in 1956, with a modest 18-mile link between Dunsmuir and Black Butte in mountainous northern California. By the end of 1963 SP had 316 miles of microwave in service, and by 1969 the system had grown dramatically to 3,450 miles with more promised.[18]

An important corollary was SP's deepening interest in computers—an interest that came to full flower with the implementation of its Total Operations Processing System (TOPS), perhaps the most advanced and comprehensive management information and control system in the industry when "cut over" in 1968. Indeed, the system was so impressive that it would earn *Modern Railroads'* prestigious "Railroad Man of the Year" award in 1972, for James W. Germany, who headed the operation at the time.[19]

Interest in computers at SP developed early, and management learned much from the use of IBM's 650 and then IBM's 7070 and 1401 data processing systems during the late 1950s and early 1960s. Impressive progress was made, especially in accounting procedures, but problems resulted, too. Germany noted that inadequate attention had been paid "to the quality of input data"; an associate also pointed to "human resistance to change" that manifested itself in some quarters. This was understandable, as computers clearly implied change in historic procedures and implied a reduction of jobs. Furthermore, the matter coincided with a fierce jurisdictional dispute between members of the Order of Railroad Tele-

graphers and the Brotherhood of Railroad and Airline Clerks over the handling of "intercity messages of record." These and other problems notwithstanding, a feasibility study team composed of SP and IBM personnel was established in 1960 and labored into 1963. At that point senior management made decisions to "move on the jurisdictional dispute" and to simultaneously "develop and implement TOPS." Russell boldly authorized the design of a complete system—but one that would only gradually be implemented, forgoing immediate returns in favor of a greater yield later. Eventually, TOPS orientation sessions were held systemwide, clerks were retrained, programmers and systems analysts were hired, and on May 7, 1968, TOPS began to function when Portland's Brooklyn Yard was "cut over." By the end of 1969, TOPS was operational across the SP, Cotton Belt, and other rail subsidiaries.[20]

TOPS was designed to be a "living" computer system, one that could be adapted to new circumstances and expanded in its functional capacity. Among operating personnel, Richard D. Spence was especially enthusiastic about its potential. Spence saw TOPS as a management tool of many dimensions. For instance, it could be used to improve car and locomotive utilization; as a system for collecting, processing, and delivering cost and inventory information to various levels of management; as a master file of SP's equipment inventory; as a means by which to better account for per diem and car miles; as a device to provide passing records and revenue data for the sales department; as a funnel for waybill accounting; and as a way to speed up or otherwise improve accounting of all types. TOPS, of course, was not a decision-making system, but rather offered management a reliable means for monitoring and control. The heart of supervision, Germany noted, is communication; TOPS, utilizing SP's own microwave system, could and did provide the necessary vehicle. Collaterally, TOPS served the twin purposes of centralization and standard-

TOPS proved to be a model for the industry.

ization and at the same time put "cracks in departmental empires." Small wonder that several companies studied or replicated SP's $22 million model called TOPS.[21]

Russell did not shrink from such large price tags. "Capital expenditures are the prerequisite of profits," Russell was fond of saying. Yet that hardly meant he was a spendthrift. For those who advanced proposals for important improvements or capital expenditures, Russell posed his classic question: "What will your project do to improve earnings per share?" Well conceived and economically justifiable plans were approved. These were as diverse as a "cat whisker" clearance car to measure tunnel bores, strengthening approaches to the huge Dumbarton Bridge south of San Francisco, planting tamarisk trees to provide windbreaks along the busy main route in the desert east of Los Angeles, and "daylighting" or enlarging tunnels, renewing the remaining timber-lined tunnels with grout and steel sets, and replacing elderly timber snowsheds with new ones made of prestressed concrete. In other cases massive expenditures were authorized to create more "push button" or electronic hump yards. Earlier efforts had focused on Antelope at Roseville and Taylor at Los Angeles; later plans included Englewood at Houston (1956), Cotton Belt's facility at Pine Bluff (1959), and Eugene (1967). Collectively

these new yards cost over $16 million to implement.[22]

Even more capital was required to complete the impressive 78.3-mile Palmdale Cut-off, which provided a time-saving shortcut between the Sunset–Golden State Route at Colton and the San Joaquin line at Palmdale. SP's interest in such a route was not new. In 1928, for example, William Sproule had raised the question "as to what might be saved in cost of handling freight between the San Joaquin Valley and points east of Colton by using the Santa Fe from Mojave to Kramer, building a new SP line from Kramer to Oro Grande, and using the Santa Fe again from Oro Grande to Colton." SP's locating engineers could not find a feasible route between Kramer and Oro Grande, however, and suggested instead a new 57-mile line from Lancaster along the foothills of the San Gabriel Mountains to Cajon Pass, with trackage rights over the Santa Fe from Cajon's summit to San Bernardino, 27 miles. Internal studies showed that this project, if implemented, would result in an appreciable savings in operational expenses and in per diem charges, and would advance time-sensitive traffic by nearly half a day. Nevertheless, the proposed cut-off was shelved at that time because SP's extensive betterment activities elsewhere created a cash shortage and the depression and war followed soon thereafter.[23]

Russell revived the issue during the mid-1950s when he secured a "handshake agreement" from Santa Fe's Fred S. Gurley "to use the AT&SF from San Bernardino up Cajon Pass." Gurley retired in 1957, however, and his successor, Ernest S. Marsh, "reneged" on the deal. For Russell, who saw matters in terms of distinct ethics and morals, Marsh's conduct was shameful; Russell also felt that Marsh's strategy was shortsighted. Had the agreement been forged, the SP would have paid for another main track to Cajon Summit—with appropriate and sophisticated signaling and crossover—to be used commonly by the SP and the Santa Fe. In any event, Marsh's decision "left the SP with nothing to

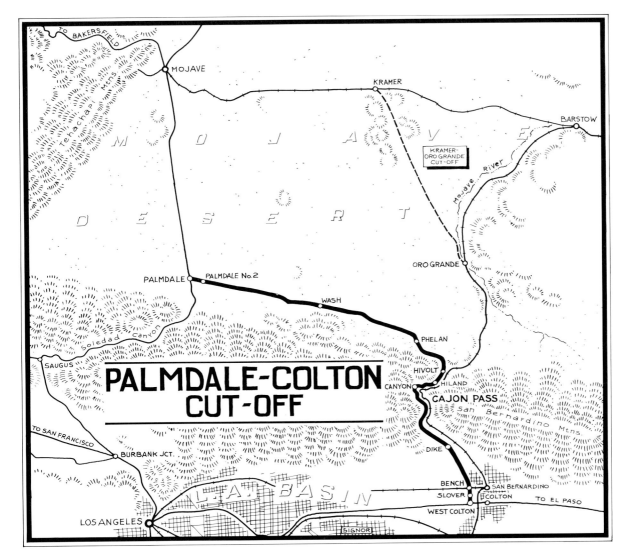

do but build its own line"—one that Russell determined would be better engineered and more efficient than that of rival Santa Fe. Work began early in 1966; on July 11, 1967, the Palmdale Cut-off was placed in service. It was the longest domestic railroad construction project in many years and cost $22 million. The price was justified, Russell thought, for the new route gave the SP a means by which to save both time and ton miles while avoiding the congestion of Los Angeles. Furthermore, noted a smiling Russell, "we built a line of such quality that our freight trains pass their [Santa Fe's] passenger trains."[24]

Russell's credentials as a railroader were, of course, unquestioned. Yet he was too nimble of mind to be wedded only to the concept of transportation provided by flanged wheels on steel rails. He was an early and energetic advocate of diversification in transportation service under one management. In his view "such a company would offer movement by rail, by air, by highways, by water, or by pipeline, in any combination best trailored to individual need." This led Russell to contemplate acquisition of the Railway Express Agency, which, he thought, if merged with SP's Pacific Motor Trucking, "would provide a very attractive operation" since Railway Express "had rights to go to so many places." The railroad or another subsidiary could provide TOFC equipment for the far-flung operation that Russell envisioned. It came to naught, however, after Russell concluded that the Interstate Commerce Commission would not approve the idea.[25]

This did not end Russell's interest in a fully integrated transportation network under one management. He chafed under laws and government regulations that stood in the way of his eminently logical aspirations but determined to do what he could under the circumstances. There was one opportunity immediately at hand. The SP, like other rail carriers, had watched in dismay as unregulated truckers captured a large portion of the petroleum products business that heretofore had gone by rail. "Why not lose the business to ourselves?" Russell asked rhetorically. Thus was born the Southern Pacific Pipe Lines, Incorporated (SPPL).[26]

SP's interest in pipelines was at once historic and contemporary. In 1906 the company had constructed its own 32-mile line in California for the purpose of transporting locomotive fuel oil and, through its partial ownership of Associated Oil, SP had an indirect interest in the pipeline operations of that firm. Events bearing directly on the formation of SPPL, though, dated from 1951, when SP's traffic department warned President A. T. Mercier that the Texas Company contemplated construction of a pipeline from "El Paso to Arizona," threatening loss of rail traffic. The SP and other western railroads thereupon agreed to reduce their rates and the ICC concurred, but in September, 1953, a federal court overturned the regulatory agency's order. Texaco's plans failed to materialize, but, with rail rates locked at an arbitrarily high level by the court's ruling, additional traffic was lost to trucks. Moreover, SP's sales personnel knew that several oil companies were studying the possibility of constructing a "joint venture" pipeline between Los Angeles and Phoenix. Late in 1954 Russell asked William G. Peoples, head of SP's traffic department, for his views on the possibility of pipelines built by and for

the SP. Peoples expressed interest, and an interdepartmental committee soon recommended the project. Russell's approval was enthusiastic.[27]

The Southern Pacific Pipe Lines was born on February 18, 1955, and matured rapidly. Construction, generally following SP's Sunset–Golden State Route between the Los Angeles Basin and El Paso, began early in 1955; a year later operations began. Funding came through a $5 million advance from the railroad and from borrowing $29 million. Business response was both immediate and profitable, and expansion followed. Lateral lines were built in the Imperial Valley during the late 1950s, as were one primary and several laterals to link the Richmond-Concord refining area with Reno and Fallon, Nevada. Routes serving Portland-Albany-Eugene, Norwalk–San Diego (jointly with the Santa Fe), and Bakersfield-Fresno were completed by the mid-1960s. Eventually additional laterals were added, several in the Bay area, and the capacity of the original route between El Paso and Tucson was expanded. As a product line common carrier, SPPL service was available to a variety of customers, including producers and distributors as well as several military installations. The subsidiary's statistical profile was impressive. Although clearly capital intensive, SPPL proved hardly labor intensive; total employment in 1969 stood at only 310. In 1963 SPPL operated 1,760 miles of line, handled 53 million barrels of product, and generated $6.6 million in net profit; by 1969 it operated 2,438 miles of line, transported 134 million barrels of product, and turned a profit of $10.7 million. Moreover, after 1969 SPPL was debt free.[28]

Another and very different pipeline opportunity presented itself during the mid-1960s when Southern California Edison Company announced its intention to build a large coal-fired generating plant at Davis Dam near Bullhead City, Arizona. The utility considered the procurement of coal from Arizona, Utah, and New Mexico with delivery by rail or coal slurry pipeline. The Santa Fe understandably

SP's interest in pipelines was at once contemporary and historic.

urged rail delivery over an existing line from New Mexico or from Black Mesa, Arizona, by way of new construction; Shell Pipeline Company proposed a slurry operation from Emery County, Utah, or from Black Mesa. Southern California Edison eventually selected fuel from Peabody Coal Company's preserve at Black Mesa, northeast of Flagstaff above the Grand Canyon. By that time the Southern Pacific Pipe Line also involved itself in formal negotiations with the utility and with Peabody. To further promote its opportunities, SPPL formed the Black Mesa Pipeline Company, a wholly owned subsidiary, on April 29, 1966.[29]

Fortune eventually smiled on the new subsidiary, although Black Mesa initially faced a serious obstacle—the Atchison, Topeka & Santa Fe Railway. Black Mesa's projected slurry line would cross arteries of the Santa Fe at four locations, but SP's historic adversary stoutly refused to grant easements. Complicated maneuverings followed. In the end Peabody agreed to pay the Santa Fe a premium on each ton of coal crossing the railroad in exchange for easement rights favoring Black Mesa. Consequently, on January 6, 1967, formal agreements were signed between Peabody Coal and Southern California Edison for the purchase of fuel and between

Black Mesa and Peabody Coal for its transportation. With a thirty-five-year contract safely under its belt, Black Mesa began construction of its 273-mile, eighteen-inch, $39 million slurry line. Operations began late in 1970; soon the company was handling over 10,000 tons per day. By 1980 Black Mesa Pipeline would be free of debt.[30]

Russell was justifiably elated with the results of SP's involvement in the pipeline business, which, he noted wryly, "made good money and didn't block any grade crossings." He would not rest, however. Noting that there had been a tremendous growth in the volume of business handled by barge lines as well as a concomitantly heavy growth of industry along inland waterways, Russell in 1959 approved SP's joint application with Illinois Central Railroad to acquire the John I. Hay Company barge line. This, of course, was consistent with Russell's ambition to develop the SP into a broadly based and diversified transportation complex. Hay's common carrier barge operations extended over 2,500 miles, principally on the Mississippi and Illinois rivers and the Gulf's Intracoastal Waterway, connecting Chicago, Milwaukee, and Gary on the north with New Orleans, Houston, and Brownsville on the south. Its route structure was essentially that of the IC, but it also touched the SP or Cotton Belt at Saint Louis, Memphis, New Orleans, and variously along the Gulf Coast.

The SP and IC jointly pledged to establish through rail-water and truck-water rates and to use their respective sales departments to solicit business for Hay. Not surprisingly, however, powerful and active opposition developed. Barge operators, barge associations, truckers, and other railroads protested loudly that control of Hay by the two railroads would lead to destructive competition and higher charges for shippers. Santa Fe's E. S. Marsh worried about "Southern Pacific extending itself into Chicago by water with the prospect of diverting rail tonnage by barge. . . ." Marsh need not have worried. Early in 1962 the ICC ruled against the applicants and, observed a disgusted D. J. Russell, "transport diversification, so necessary to the financial stability of the railroads . . . suffered a setback. . . ."[31]

Rebuffed in his latest attempt to diversify Southern Pacific's transportation business, Russell turned to the task of strengthening the competitive capacity of the railroad itself. He looked close at hand. Through a subsidiary, the Southern Pacific Land Company, SP purchased a 10 percent interest in the stock of the 1,900-mile Western Pacific Railroad Company and then asked the ICC for permission to issue additional shares of authorized common to exchange on a share-for-share basis with holders of WP common. SP argued that its control of the Western Pacific would result in "an improved transportation service" made possible through important economies and efficiencies in the operation of the two properties. The Western Pacific and the Southern Pacific, after all, served a common territory in northern California, and WP's main line essentially paralleled SP's Overland Route into Utah.[32]

Exceptions were instant and vigorous. The Santa Fe, SP's old nemesis, through one of its own subsidiaries, the Chanslor-Western Oil & Development Company, quickly purchased 20 percent of WP's outstanding stock; the parent thereupon proposed control through a one-and-one-quarter-for-one share offer. The

Great Northern also entered the fray. To protect its "Inside Gateway," it purchased 10 percent of WP's common. With that, a full 40 percent of Western Pacific's stock was held by the three contestants. The WP itself took a dim view of SP's proposal and sided with the Santa Fe. On the other hand, SP found powerful support elsewhere. The Denver & Rio Grande Western hoped that the WP would remain independent but, as its president G. B. Aydelott explained, if confronted with a "controlled WP," the Denver & Rio Grande Western would "definitely prefer that it rest with the Southern Pacific rather than the Santa Fe." The Union Pacific, the Chicago, Rock Island & Pacific, and the Missouri Pacific similarly took SP's side. The debate heated. WP's F. B. Whitman charged that the SP contemplated monopoly, and Santa Fe's Marsh argued that SP would "suppress competition." Marsh also reasserted SP's image in California as "the Octopus." Russell and the SP denied such charges but were put on the defensive.[33]

Both the SP and Santa Fe mounted massive public relations campaigns, but a consensus did not develop. Finally, after protracted proceedings, the ICC on January 27, 1965, denied both the SP and Santa Fe petitions, claiming that the public interest required "the continued existence of Western Pacific as an independent carrier." Russell privately grumbled about the shortsightedness of government bureaucrats and the counterproductive nature of regulation, but publicly hoped "that further coordinations . . . can be put into effect promptly."[34]

Strangely, however, the SP was lethargic and ineffective in advancing opportunities on its eastern flank. The case of the Chicago & Eastern Illinois Railroad is illustrative. That company owned a major route south from Chicago that split at Woodland Junction, Illinois, with one leg continuing southward to Evansville, Indiana, and the other driving southwestward to Saint Louis, with a secondary route branching from Finlay, Illinois, to

Thebes, across the Mississippi River from Cotton Belt's terminal at Illmo, Missouri. The short (slightly over 900 miles in 1950) C&EI had reorganized itself in 1941, after eight years of trusteeship, and had enjoyed a brief period of relative prosperity during World War II, but its long-term prospects were clouded by negative alterations in its traffic base and by severe competition from all modes of transportation. The market value of its stock reflected this; it was a clear candidate for acquisition or merger. Discussions in this regard already had been held by the C&EI with the Chicago Great Western Railway, the Missouri-Kansas-Texas Railroad, and early in the 1950s the Cotton Belt's management recommended to the parent company that it be allowed to acquire the line. The "fit" was logical in that the C&EI offered the Cotton Belt a direct extension to Chicago from Thebes (one that avoided the congested Saint Louis area) as well as a competitive route between the important cities of Saint Louis and Chicago. The Woodland Junction–Danville–Evansville segment admittedly did not fit into SSW's route structure and, noted Cotton Belt's H. J. McKenzie, could be sold to the Louisville & Nashville Railroad as a logical enlargement of that road. In San Francisco, SP officials—especially in the traffic department—took a dim view of the idea. Friendly connections, they argued, would be offended by an "invasion" of the type Cotton Belt proposed and, since much of SP–St. Louis Southwestern's transcontinental traffic moved via East Saint Louis instead of Chicago, acquisition of the C&EI "could not be justified on the return that was forecast."[35]

Other suitors were understandably quick to call on the Chicago & Eastern Illinois. The Chicago, Indianapolis & Louisville Railway (Monon) was followed by the Missouri Pacific, the Chicago & North Western, and the Louisville & Nashville (L&N). Cotton Belt's archrival, the Missouri Pacific, in 1961 finally made a bold move after an earlier false start; the Illinois Central Railroad and the Louisville

& Nashville then made counterproposals. For the MoPac and the L&N, ownership or control of the C&EI represented logical extensions; for the Illinois Central, acquisition implied an opportunity to reduce excess rail capacity and eliminate competition. A lengthy regulatory examination and legal proceeding followed. Eventually, however, the Missouri Pacific prevailed, although it was obliged to sell the Woodland Junction–Danville–Evansville line to the Louisville & Nashville and also to grant it joint ownership from Woodland Junction into Chicago. The Cotton Belt was inexplicably restrained in these proceedings until the last hour; in the end its protestations went for naught. For the SSW—and for the SP as well—it was a double blow. The Cotton Belt not only failed to expand its own dominion by acquisition of the C&EI but, and equally important, archrival Missouri Pacific gained an incalculable advantage over the St. Louis Southwestern and its parent by securing for itself the Thebes–Saint Louis–Chicago route. Conventional wisdom in San Francisco had carried the day but, in retrospect, the decision was a monumental blunder.[36]

The Missouri Pacific proved to be a stern and uncompromising adversary on another matter of strategic importance for the Southern Pacific and Cotton Belt—the proposed acquisition of the Alton & Southern (A&S) Railroad. It had been organized on July 8, 1910, and developed as an important switching and terminal company connecting with all major railroads on the Illinois side of the Mississippi River opposite Saint Louis and with most carriers on the Missouri side via trackage rights over the city-owned McArthur Bridge. By the mid-1960s the Alton & Southern owned 138.4 miles of line and yard track and operated under trackage agreements over an additional 20.1 miles. It served approximately forty on-line shippers and enjoyed the prospect of luring more since extensive industrial property abutted Alton & Southern lines. Revenues derived principally from switching charges and divisions on line hauls; until recent times it had been profitable, and it had no funded debt. The Alton & Southern was owned by the Aluminum Company of America.[37]

Acquiring the A&S offered several advantages for the Cotton Belt. Alton & Southern handled about 35 percent of all traffic passing through the Saint Louis gateway, and its share seemed destined to increase with full operation of its new electronic Saint Louis Gateway Yard lying adjacent to Cotton Belt's own tiny Valley Junction facility. Ownership of the A&S would not only give the Cotton Belt more switching capacity but also would give it direct connection with fourteen other trunk roads in addition to the Terminal Railroad Association of Saint Louis, the Illinois Terminal, and Manufacturers Railway (Anheuser-Busch). More importantly for the SSW, it would create the possibility of moving solid trains including locomotives and cabooses through to primary eastern connections—the Pennsylvania Railroad, New York Central, Nickel Plate, Wabash, and Baltimore & Ohio—"in a matter of one or two hours." With all of this in mind, H. J. McKenzie signed an agreement with ALCOA on November 30, 1965, for the purchase of the Alton & Southern—subject to ICC approval. The price: $16 million.[38]

The prospect of the Southern Pacific's and the Cotton Belt's gaining this important advantage annoyed several other carriers, including the Terminal Railroad Association (TRRA) of Saint Louis—itself owned by the trunk railroads (including the SSW) serving metropolitan Saint Louis and the Alton & Southern's chief competitor. On June 14, 1965, just two days after SSW's own internal study team had urged purchase of the Alton & Southern, TRRA's president proposed to his board that a feasibility study be made to determine whether acquisition of the ALCOA property "would be advantageous." When completed, the TRRA study "was positive" and the president had planned to urge his board to "make an offer for the A&S" at the December meeting. By that time, however,

news of Cotton Belt's agreement with ALCOA confused the issue; nevertheless, he asked the board for authority "to acquire the A&S at the same price agreed to by the Cotton Belt." The resolution failed, but the board did direct management to oppose the SSW's application. The issue was awkward for H. J. McKenzie, who headed the SSW and was at the same time a member of the Terminal Railroad Association board, yet his opposition was forthright. TRRA handled essentially the same number of cars for the Cotton Belt as did the Alton & Southern—of westbound business, A&S got 55 percent and of eastbound, Terminal Railroad Association received 56 percent including all perishables—but frankly, said McKenzie, the latter's service suffered by comparison.[39]

A new variable was interjected on March 22, 1966, when the Missouri Pacific announced that it had gone before the ICC with an application to match Cotton Belt's offer. The Illinois Central and the Chicago & North Western (C&NW) also expressed interest. ALCOA favored the SSW, but the regulatory agency in March, 1968, denied Cotton Belt's application for independent ownership. The ICC instead favored the MoPac, but only after adding a provision that the other aspirants— SSW, C&NW, and IC—be allowed to unite in acquisition if they desired. Cotton Belt officials urged joining the MoPac in ownership; that, however, was "overruled" by D. J. Russell, who did not like joint ownership arrangements. "When you get into bed with a dog, you are bound to get his fleas," he complained. The IC also decided to back out, but the C&NW purchased a half-interest. The C&NW nevertheless soon found itself financially embarrassed and offered its holding to others. TRRA's management again urged its board to seek purchase of the entire Alton & Southern; late in 1969 the board instead approved acquisition of Chicago & North Western's half-interest—but only if Missouri Pacific would also sell its half to TRRA. MoPac was not interested. Meanwhile, several officers of both the SP and SSW recommended purchase of C&NW's interest to protect the vital Saint Louis gateway and to reduce delays on through business. Furthermore, warned SP's R. D. Spence, the MoPac was certain to seek full ownership if Cotton Belt failed to act. Senior SP executives finally changed their position, and on September 9, 1970, the Cotton Belt offered the Chicago & North Western $8 million for its interest in Alton & Southern. Approval would come from the ICC late in 1972 and on August 1, 1973, the purchase would be consummated.[40]

All of this was merely a preview to the main attraction. During the course of SP's 1962 annual meeting, Russell received a telephone call from Louis B. Neumiller, a member of the executive committee of the Chicago, Rock Island & Pacific Railroad. Neumiller asked bluntly: "Would the SP be interested in acquiring the Rock Island?" Russell responded that the SP would be interested in portions of the Rock Island and suggested that the Union Pacific might purchase other parts. Earlier, Robert A. Lovett, chairman of Union Pacific's executive committee, had asked Russell if the SP was interested in the CRI&P. Russell had given Lovett the same response. Frankly, he had no desire to "get into the Chicago and northern areas where there was too much duplication of rail service," and he did not wish to "go head-to-head with the Union Pacific." Nevertheless, both the SP and UP undertook individual studies analyzing the potential value of the entire Rock Island to their respective systems—apparently without advising each other of the fact. When UP's A. E. Stoddard heard of SP's study, he called G. B. Aydelott of the Rio Grande and exploded: "Those SOBS [the SP] are going all over the Rock Island with the idea of buying it. By God that's our baby," asserted the UP president.[41]

The Rock Island, older than either the SP or the Union Pacific companies, owned a rich and colorful history. Chartered on February 7, 1851, as the Chicago & Rock Island Railroad, it reached the Mississippi River from

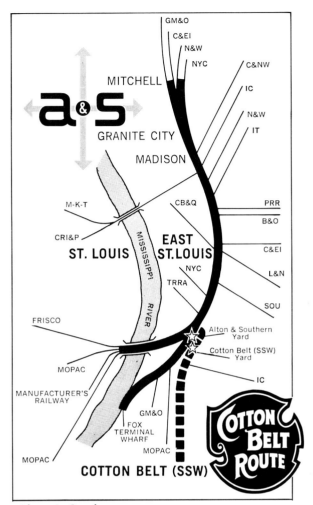

Alton & Southern

Chicago three years later, was the first railroad to bridge that formidable waterway (1856), and was the third railroad to connect with the Union Pacific at Council Bluffs (1869). Its route structure eventually included the original Chicago–Council Bluffs main extended to Colorado Springs and Denver; a strong second artery branching from near Davenport, Iowa, and angling southwestwardly to Tucumcari and Santa Rosa, New Mexico (the Golden State Route); the Choctaw Route, running along the thirty-fifth parallel from Memphis and Little Rock to Oklahoma City and Tucumcari; and a vital vertical-axis route from Minneapolis to Fort Worth, Dallas, Houston, and Galveston that crossed the original main at Des Moines, joined the Golden

State Route as far as Herington, Kansas, and bisected the Choctaw at El Reno, Oklahoma. The Rock Island also owned secondary mains from Kansas City to Saint Louis and Little Rock to Eunice, Louisiana. Approximately one-fifth of its 7,843 miles in 1962 consisted of branches.[42]

During the twentieth century the Rock Island found itself victimized by opportunists, and it otherwise suffered from the cyclical economic vagaries that historically plagued the Granger roads. It emerged from its latest round of bankruptcy proceedings on January 1, 1948, under the capable leadership of John D. Farrington, and for a few years all looked well for the CRI&P. Freight density remained fairly constant, and the road experienced improvements in gross revenues after 1956. At the same time, though, it was unable to absorb "upward adjustments" in wage rates through force reductions, and, as a consequence, the Rock Island experienced a sharp curtailment in net income. Problems mounted. "Interline received and bridge traffic," especially in the "manufacturing and miscellaneous commodity group," was of crucial importance to the CRI&P but such traffic was especially vulnerable to attack by other carriers as well as other modes of transportation. For the Rock Island's directors, these matters came to a head when Farrington died late in 1961. They then sought suitable marriage partners.[43]

Southern Pacific's exploratory study was delivered to Russell on August 1, 1962; its burden was mixed. The study team found the Rock Island's physical plant "in generally good order," but its locomotive and car fleet was in poor condition. Although the team evaluated the entire system, it focused on the Golden State Route, which Farrington had favored in the late 1930s and early 1940s with expensive line changes—among them the Arkalon Cut-off with a huge new bridge over the Cimarron River west of Kismet, Kansas—as well as automatic block signaling between Herington and Tucumcari. "The pri-

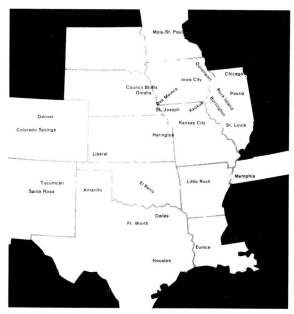

Route structure of the Chicago, Rock Island & Pacific

mary objective in acquiring the Rock Island," argued the study team, "would be to place the Southern Pacific in a more fully competitive position with the Santa Fe which presently has a one-line control of service and rate adjustments between Chicago—long terminus for transcontinental business—and Arizona-California." The advantage of being in a position to offer competitive and dependable service over a road built to SP's standards, particularly as regards the Tucumcari-Chicago route, "is of paramount importance," concluded the team.[44]

As senior officers analyzed this document, Russell agreed with the Union Pacific to jointly study the prospect of acquiring and dividing the Rock Island—generally speaking, into two segments, north and south. The notion implied gains for each company but also presented them with potential liabilities. If the idea was implemented, the SP would extend its line and influence into Oklahoma and into the important Kansas City gateway and thus establish controlled service between Kansas City and Arizona and California. For its part, the Union Pacific would gain crucial

Beaumont Hill, east of Colton, California, always presented challenges. Here a brawny U50 from General Electric heads tonnage toward an eventual connection with the Rock Island at Tucumcari.

gateways at Chicago, Saint Louis, and the Twin Cities and thereby add impressive line-haul privileges to its traditional service areas in the Pacific Northwest and Southern California. On the other hand, the UP would have new competition with the SP at Kansas City, and the Cotton Belt would be faced with the UP at Saint Louis; the SP could expect the loss of preferential solicitation at Chicago, Peoria, the Tri-Cities, Des Moines, and the Twin Cities, and would be dependent on the UP's benevolence for service between Chicago and Kansas City; and the UP would be confronted with high costs of gathering and distribution in the Midwest as well as the liability of offering commuter service in Chicago. Coverdale & Colpitts was commissioned by the two companies to offer an independent analysis.[45]

Events moved smoothly at first. On February 28, 1963, the SP and UP agreed that the latter would seek to acquire the entire CRI&P, subject to ICC approval, and that after the merger the southern portion of the Rock Island, i.e., those lines south of Kansas City—excluding the Kansas City–Saint Louis line but including the CRI&P's historic trackage rights over the UP between Kansas City and Topeka, would be sold to the SP. The SP would also retain rights between Armourdale Yard in Kansas City, Kansas, across the river to Kansas City Union Station and would further retain rights necessary for freight interchange in the metropolitan Kansas City area. Mileage accruing to the UP would aggregate 4,265; to the SP, 3,585. Subsequent arrangements would cover apportionment and acquisition cost of Rock Island's motive power, rolling stock, materials, and supplies. Rock Island's management concurred in this arrangement and so did its shareholders; by the summer of 1965, 92 percent of CRI&P stock was "deposited by owners in acceptance of UP's exchange offer." The merger agreement was filed with the ICC in September, 1964.[46]

If the acquisition and partitioning of the Rock Island by the Southern Pacific and Union Pacific offered important gains for each, it appeared to be quite the reverse for other carriers—many of which mounted active campaigns of their own. The Chicago & North Western, the historic eastern partner on the Overland Route and, like the Rock Island, a struggling Granger, saw its death warrant in the SP-UP concordance, for the UP would surely shift lucrative Council Bluffs–Chicago traffic away from the C&NW to its own line if the ICC approved the proposal. (In 1965 the C&NW was UP's primary connection at Council Bluffs, with 29.3 percent of the total interchange; Rock Island was fifth, with only 8.4 percent.) The North Western predictably responded with its own plan to purchase the CRI&P, and the Santa Fe, hardly bereft, nevertheless sought advantage by asking the commission for the southern portion of the Rock Island if the C&NW won over SP-UP. This alarmed the SP, which hardly wanted to see Santa Fe with any more competitive advantages; it especially did not wish to see it in possession of Rock Island's Memphis–Little Rock–Amarillo–Tucumcari route. The waters were further muddied when the Missouri Pacific and Santa Fe considered merger and when destitute Missouri-Kansas-Texas presented itself to the SP (and others, most likely) as a marriage partner. Eventually, a dozen railroads intervened in the case to one extent or another. UP's Arthur E. Stoddard early dismissed such opposition as "routine," but his assessment could not have been further from reality. Indeed, the Rock Island case became the vortex of a titanic struggle to sort out sur-

vivors in the Midwest and thus restructure the very face of railroading west of Chicago.[47]

The hearings held by the Interstate Commerce Commission seemed endless. They were not concluded until August 22, 1968, and a decision from the agency could not be expected until during the next decade. Meanwhile, the plight of the Rock Island worsened. SP officers had noted in 1962 that its facilities were "being taxed to the detriment of continued useful and economic lives." Rock Island's chairman echoed this assessment early in 1965. "Rock Island's problems cannot be postponed," said Jervis Langdon. "They are here now and must be dealt with." That was not to be the case. The condition of the CRI&P continued to deteriorate as the railroads warred among themselves, attorneys quarreled, and bureaucrats fumbled. Precious time was wasting.[48]

Even as the SP attempted to expand its domain through the Western Pacific and Rock Island cases, it was paring elsewhere. In addition to the numerous short branches it abandoned, SP also reduced its size by terminating service over longer segments of line. Included were the former El Paso & Southwestern route from Benson Junction to Mescal in Arizona, and from Douglas, Arizona, to near El Paso, Texas, and in western Nevada between Fernley and Flanigan. In the latter instance, the SP arranged for trackage rights between Flanigan and Weso, Nevada, over the Western Pacific to maintain through service on the Modoc Route. Elsewhere, the Inter-California Railway, a wholly owned subsidiary, sold its remaining 9.5-mile route to the Mexican government in 1964; a year later another subsidiary, the Nacozari Railroad, surrendered its line of 76 miles. In the case of the Nacozari, title had been held under terms of a ninety-nine-year concession from the Mexican government that had been signed in 1899. Meanwhile, on the Cotton Belt, the Commerce-Sherman Branch in Texas had been abandoned in 1953.[49]

Most of SP's narrow-gauge lines had long

since been abandoned or standard gauged. For instance, the Oakland–Santa Cruz "Picnic Line" had been fully converted to standard gauge in 1907. Yet one isolated fragment survived until 1960. This was the 71.5-mile remnant of the Carson & Colorado between Keeler and Laws in the Owens Valley of California. At one time, business over the dusty route had been brisk, but it diminished over the years. By 1954 triweekly service was adequate to handle tonnage of talc, pumice, dolomite, and other bulk commodities that were transloaded at Owenyo, where the "Slim Princess" connected with SP's standard gauge Owenyo-Mojave or "Jawbone" Branch. The SP went to the expense of dieselizing the line during the mid-1950s, but denouement was not far off. The end came on April 30, 1960, when SP closed the book on its final narrow-gauge route.[50]

On the passage of SP's narrow gauge, one devotee wrote: "the amazing thing was not that a part of the Old West had vanished, but that it had lasted so long." Those similarly attracted by SP's passenger operations were rarely as circumspect. Indeed, the company's policies of reducing staggering passenger deficits ($50 million in 1954, $16 million in 1966) brought a continuing and vocal outcry that reflected the public's perception of real or imagined loss of traditional transportation service. The problem was a result both of SP's handling of this sensitive issue and public reactionism and nostalgia.[51]

The matter demoralized Russell. In 1947 SP executives had predicted a handsome return on investment for new streamlined trains— 14.4 percent for the *Shasta Daylight*, 27.2 percent for the *Cascade*, and 35.7 for the *City of San Francisco*—and for a short time those rosy predictions held true. One train, the *Shasta*, earned a 21.4 percent return during the first three and one-half years of its life. And SP's executives had carefully monitored the quality of these trains. Early in 1956, for example, Russell severely chastised passenger

The end came for SP's romantic if unproductive narrow gauge in 1960.

and operating officers for mixing *Lark* cars in the consist of the *Sunset Limited*. There was "no excuse" for this, he roared. "It must be stopped." Nevertheless, several months later when Russell's office car was attached to the *Sunset Limited*, he made a personal inspection of the train and was appalled to learn that there were only nineteen Pullman and fifty-seven coach passengers on the nine-car train. "We have the finest equipment in the country and the best schedules on the *Sunset Limited*, but apparently to no avail," he ruefully concluded in a letter to top officers.[52]

Not surprisingly, SP's passenger policy took a new turn. Russell ordered the prosecution of a vigorous discontinuance policy. Ridership on most premier trains held up, but there had been a steady erosion on most locals and secondary runs, and the end had come already for some trains. No longer did the *Sunbeam* and the competition's *Sam Houston Zephyr* sprint side by side out of Dallas Union Terminal following their common late afternoon departure. Indeed, all SP passenger service between Houston and Dallas ended with final runs of T&NO's *Owl* on June 7, 1958. On the

The *Sunbeam* no longer raced the competition's *Sam Houston Zephyr* out of Dallas Union Terminal. Indeed, all SP passenger service between Dallas and Houston ended in 1958.

Pacific lines, the *Starlight* was combined with the *Lark* on the Coast Line, the *West Coast* was discontinued on the San Joaquin Route, and the *San Francisco Overland* was reduced to seasonal service and then discontinued altogether in 1964. A similar fate befell the much-touted *Shasta Daylight*. As early as 1956 Russell approved a plan to make that train triweekly except for the summer months and Christmas holidays; the plan was approved by the ICC in 1959, but costs accelerated nevertheless and the train rolled its last miles in 1966. It was the first of SP's premier trains to perish.[53]

A corollary to these trends and events unfolded predictably in the Bay Area when, on October 30, 1957, the SP filed for discontinuation of its historic ferry service between San Francisco's Ferry Building and the Oakland Mole. Commutation had ended a generation earlier; SP's ferries thereafter had functioned solely as accessory to the company's intercity passenger operation. The fleet had dwindled accordingly to just three vessels after World War II: the *Sacramento*, *Berkeley*, and *Eureka*. The *Sacramento* was retired in

1955; the *Eureka* was donated to the San Francisco Maritime Museum in 1956; and a "new" vessel, the *San Leandro*, built by the Key System in 1923 and later sold, was acquired from the army in 1954 and subsequently served in regular assignment. The *Berkeley* provided backup protection. Both active vessels required expensive maintenance, however, and would have to be replaced in the near future. Bus service provided under contract by Western Greyhound would, asserted the SP, provide more efficient and desirable service in lieu of the twelve daily round trips offered by the ferries. Removal of the old vessels, however, represented a monumental public relations problem. As one officer said, "taking them away from San Francisco would be like taking sidewalk cafes from Paris." Nevertheless, the SP ultimately received permission to substitute buses for ferries; the *San Leandro* made its last revenue tours on July 29, 1958. The final curtain came down the next day when SP hosted an invitation-only trip across the Bay. Guest conductor Arthur Fiedler led the San Francisco Municipal Band in an appropriate dirge, thus ending more

The end came for SP's famous ferry service on July 30, 1958.

TR SAN FRAN & LA 52

than a century of ferry operation on the Bay. The Oakland Mole predictably fell to the wrecker's ball late in 1965 to make way for a new deep-water shipping terminal.[54]

Before the East Bay said good-bye to the familiar Oakland Mole, it said hello to new mail-handling and express facilities. Head-end business, mail and express, had always been important to SP's passenger ledgers, but never more so than in the 1950s and 1960s as fewer and fewer revenue passengers boarded the trains. Sealed as well as "way" express cars filled with a multitude of parcels were found on locals and secondary runs; during the early summer, solid trains of express cars wheeled strawberries from the central coast counties of California to eastern markets. Yet the volume of express traffic gradually deteriorated, in part the result of low-priced parcel post service, and eventually REA Express, successor to the Railway Express Agency, would face liquidation. While the volume of express shipments declined, that of mail—especially letter mail—increased. Much of this was sorted en route by Railway Post Office (RPO) clerks, who performed yeoman duty aboard the swaying, lurching cars. During the 1950s and into the 1960s, the SP

owned nearly one hundred RPO cars, which were a normal complement on its locals and secondary trains and in some cases on its flagship trains, too. Alas, this class of business was susceptible to competition from trucks, air, and even the rails' own TOFC service. In 1967 the Post Office Department began a nationwide diversion of mail away from passenger trains, and the SP was caught in this net. Mobile postal service ended on the El Paso & Los Angeles RPO line at the end of March; on the San Francisco & Los Angeles and on the San Francisco, San Jose & Los Angeles lines late in September; and on the Ogden & San Francisco effective October 12. En route sorting of mail thus joined the Oakland Mole and the Bay ferries as part of the company's past.[55]

For Russell, loss of the mail contracts represented the "last straw." The "long-haul passenger train has outlived its usefulness," he told shareholders in 1967. SP's passenger operation was losing alarming amounts of money and at the same time the company's equipment was rapidly approaching obsolescence; should the SP be required to stay in that business, replacement costs would be staggering. "The company, therefore, has no alternative but to continue to press for discontinuation of passenger operations which are not used by the public," Russell concluded.[56]

This fully aroused SP's critics, who charged the company with an array of nefarious practices. Many accused the SP of actively discouraging patronage in its attempt to eliminate "intercity passenger service at all costs."

Others unfavorably compared SP's service standards and general philosophy regarding passengers to its principal rival, the Santa Fe. Some complained that SP advertised its service only in a negative fashion ("The Train Traveler—A Rare Breed These Days" in *Sunset Magazine* for October, 1965). One pro-passenger organization even argued that "railroads still enjoy a monopoly as compared to other forms of transportation for the bigger part of their most profitable freight business," that in SP's case, "shareholders have no valid complaint against absorbing passenger losses," and that it "should not be permitted to get out of the passenger business simply to increase the already-large profits of the company." The same group likewise implied that the SP should make massive expenditures in new technology to reattract passengers.[57]

The complaints in retrospect seem peevish and naive. There was no conscious effort at SP to drive passenger business away. Rather, management decisions were made to gain control of costs; in some cases these had the effect of downgrading overall service. In that sense SP's policies affected business negatively. All of this *followed*, Russell vigorously reminded, SP's massive expenditures for new equipment, a constant and effective advertising campaign, and aggressive marketing. "The handwriting was on the wall," he said. "It was so obvious that the kind of people who had justified the passenger train were gone. All you had to do was look at the airport." Always alert to innovative ways to deliver service and improve net profits, Russell saw no such opportunities in the passenger trade. As a result, the SP during the 1960s did not consider expenditures for new technology because there was no apparent potential return on such investment. Furthermore, speculation of that nature seemed especially foolish when the same monies could be expended to improve freight carriage with assured return.[58]

Any fair-minded assessment urges that SP's decision to seek relief from devastating passenger deficits was justified. There was little

use in quarreling over the origins of the situation. Indeed, the American railroad industry was no longer entertaining the prospect of a high-quality passenger market, but instead was confronted with the "leftovers." In the 1960s it was, in fact, confronted with a market that was exceedingly price-sensitive, exhibited great seasonal fluctuations in demand, and tended to be rooted in small towns. "You are not performing an essential service when the cost is exorbitant," Russell complained. Even the ICC eventually concluded that passenger deficits endangered "the present and future welfare of the railroad industry." Nor, believed the regulatory agency, would matters improve. "If the statistical trends of 25-odd years prove any one thing, it is the folly of awaiting more fortuitous events." Thus both history and logic favored SP's decisions. The business world applauded. SP's passenger policies represented "fiscal common sense," said *Forbes*.[59]

On the other hand, SP's cavalier style and abrupt tactics left much to be desired. Stanford Research Institute, which SP hired to evaluate the future of rail passenger service in the West, suggested that "a slow rate of decline in traffic volume purchased at the price of a large deficit is not preferable, in economic terms, to a faster rate of decline with smaller losses." After all, said SRI, "businesses in every field continually make decisions to discontinue products and activities that are declining and profitless. . . . The railroads also have an obligation to their stockholders to invest capital wisely and profitably." Yet SRI was not convinced that the railroads had followed a uniformly enlightened policy in the passenger train matter. In an oblique criticism of the SP, SRI stated that "the 'hard' pursuit of a deficit reduction policy practiced by some railroads has aroused considerable opposition in the segment of the public that is partial to railroads. . . ." Consequently, "a hard-line policy has been partially self-defeating." SRI felt that the industry had inadequately educated the public "in the economics of rail passenger service" and suffered as a consequence from the "large amount of misinformation current on the subject." The Southern Pacific stood condemned on this count. It had failed to heed the advice of one of its own publicists: "If you anticipate trouble with the community you serve, meet it more than half way. Give your neighbors the facts; make peace before they make war." A casualty of SP's "hard" approach to its passenger problem, sad to say, was the intangible goodwill necessary for the ultimate success of any corporation, especially one whose only product is service.[60]

The issue of SP's style and tactics aside, the era of privately operated intercity passenger trains in this country was nearly over. In addition to the remaining secondary trains, several of SP's "name" trains perished during the 1960s. These included the *San Francisco Overland* (1964), *Shasta Daylight* (1966), and even the *Golden State* (1968) and *Lark* (1968). Ridership was awful. During a test period early in 1968, a mere 624 persons per day boarded SP's long-distance trains. By the time the National Railroad Passenger Corporation (Amtrak) was formed late in 1970, SP's passenger listings were down to the daily *Coast Daylight*, *San Joaquin Daylight*, and connecting *Sacramento Daylight*; the *Del Monte* (to Monterey); triweekly *Cascade*, *Sunset Limited*, *City of San Francisco*; and, on the Northwestern Pacific, twice-weekly service between Willits and Eureka. Amtrak took over national intercity operations effective May 1, 1971, retaining service on the Cascade, Overland, Coast, and Sunset routes; it purchased some of SP's rolling stock, required a one-time entry fee of $9.3 million, and contracted with SP to provide train service. Thereafter SP's only direct financial involvement with passengers was its San Francisco–San Jose commute operation. A remarkable chapter in SP's history had closed.[61]

The company did not dispose of all passenger rolling stock. Some was retained for internal purposes, particularly for the use of the sales and industrial development forces, who

enthusiastically promoted the advantages of SP's "Golden Empire." In this regard, SP continued to offer land for sale or lease and to sponsor industrial parks and other development. During the five-year period 1958–62, an average of 397 industries were located along the Southern Pacific–St. Louis Southwestern annually, generating an estimated $10 million per year in additional revenues. The pattern continued throughout the decade, and in 1966 alone 598 new industries were attracted to SP's service. The company's efforts were systemwide, but were especially effective in the Los Angeles Basin, where in 1966 it won the Chamber of Commerce's "Gold Shovel Award" for "significant recent contribution to the economy" of that region.[62]

Given what the automobile did to SP's passenger fortunes, it is ironic that the company, in perhaps its most impressive industrial development coup, located every one of General Motors' West Coast assembly plants along its lines. Automobile business, however, was not new to the SP. Entire trainloads of Overlands, Dodges, Packards, and Durants had been delivered to California during the early 1920s. The location of assembly plants, such as GM's sprawling Southgate facility near Los Angeles a decade later, provided the railroad with revenues from inbound parts as well as outbound set-up or assembled autos. Other GM plants followed at Melrose (near Oakland), Van Nuys, and Fremont. In the latter case, General Motors initially favored a location served by competitor Western Pacific, but the SP scrambled to offer an alternative. "The Western Pacific cannot afford you," William G. Peoples told GM officials. Peoples, who headed the sales department, stressed SP's strong financial base, its overall expertise, and—in conjunction with PMT—its ability to provide full-service transportation. In sum, argued Peoples, the Western Pacific was weak by comparison; only the SP could give GM the long-term service it required. Peoples carried the day; the Fremont plant went "online" during May, 1963.[63]

Automobiles—long a staple in SP's traffic base. Oakland, 1959. *Photograph by Richard Steinheimer for SP.*

General Motors provided the SP with a handsome account, but it also proved to be a demanding customer. Traditional boxcars and old-fashioned auto boxes were simply inadequate for modern purposes, GM told the SP. New equipment was necessary for set-up autos as well as parts delivery. SP responded by experimenting with TOFC in hauling autos and by 1960 was using PMT trailers loaded on 85-foot Clejan piggyback cars. At the same time it joined other carriers and suppliers in testing 85-foot trilevel flatcars laden with set-up models. Later in the decade the SP introduced the 89-foot Vert-A-Pak car, which carried thirty subcompact Vegas, vertically packed in ten compartments. Special equipment was also necessary for parts manufactured in the Midwest and shipped to California. SP's answer was Hy-Cube Hydra-Cushion cars that could carry massive payloads and be quickly and efficiently loaded and unloaded through four sets of doors.[64]

General Motors' plants were among thousands located adjacent to SP's tracks or otherwise served by spurs. Many thousands of other manufacturing works or distribution centers, however, were located away from all rail facilities during the 1960s. These were served by SP's rapidly growing TOFC service. Fast, overnight TOFC trains whisked trailers between San Francisco/Oakland and Reno, San Francisco/Oakland and Los Angeles, Houston and Dallas, and Houston and New Orleans. Piggyback accounted for 5 percent of SP's tonnage in 1963; six years later the company handled 262,500 trailers, more than double the figure of 1960. Additional growth was assured.[65]

Whether auto parts or TOFC, a rising volume of long-haul business was expedited by run-through trains. The first of these resulted from agreement between the Cotton Belt and the New York Central to run connecting trains, with power and cabooses, through East Saint Louis from Pine Bluff to Indianapolis. Service began on September 7, 1966. Four months later, on January 11, 1967, the Pennsylvania Railroad—which had been told in advance of the SSW-NYC arrangement but had blithely shrugged "so what?"—joined in a similar operation between Pine Bluff and Enola, Pennsylvania. Run-through contracts were also forged with the Northern Pacific between Portland and Seattle, with the Union Pacific via Ogden, and, of course, with the Rock Island via Tucumcari. Other agreements followed, as the carriers cooperated to develop speedier and more efficient means of interchange.[66]

Piggyback, trilevel flats, and diesel-powered run-through freight trains were but a few of the improvements that characterized the first one hundred years of Southern Pacific's existence. The company had good reason to be proud of its accomplishments and of the positive impact that it had made on its vast service area. Celebrations were in order. The first of these commemorated the centennial of the New Orleans, Opelousas & Great Western Railroad; together, the state of Louisiana and the SP celebrated "A Century of Progress" in 1952. Eleven years later ceremonies were held in Sacramento to mark the one-hundredth birthday of groundbreaking for the Central Pacific. All of this was merely prologue to May 10, 1969, when over 25,000 persons watched a reenactment of the Golden Spike ceremony at Promontory, Utah. Singled out for special recognition at the event were more than one hundred descendants of the founders and builders of both the Central Pacific and Union Pacific who were present for the occa-

sion. Elsewhere, the Cotton Belt would honor its own centenary in 1977.[67]

SP shareholders, who numbered 84,455 by 1969, had reason to celebrate the present and the future as well as the past. After adjustments for the stock split in 1959, annual dividends per share rose from $1.12 in 1960 to $1.80 in 1969. Furthermore, after lengthy reflection, D. J. Russell recommended and the board of directors approved a plan to restructure the SP as a holding company that could engage in transportation as well as other diverse activities. On November 26, 1969, all railroad assets, rights, and obligations of the "old" Southern Pacific Company passed to the recently organized Southern Pacific Transportation Company. However, all stock of SPTCo was held by a "new" Southern Pacific Company, the holding corporation. In effect, SPTCo would direct the affairs of those companies related to transportation while, in general, nontransportation subsidiaries would be managed by the parent. Russell promised early efforts to develop nonrailroad real estate through "a broad range of urban, industrial, and recreational projects over the coming year." The future, he implied, was as bright as the company's past.[68]

The vigorous schedule that Russell had set for the Southern Pacific during the 1960s made it a property that was admired both inside and outside the industry. The railroads it owned were well managed and in generally fine physical condition; the new corporate structure and the opportunity to diversify outside regulated transportation made the company even more attractive. Furthermore, Russell, who would face retirement soon, had hand-picked an energetic successor to prosecute his aggressive management: Benjamin Franklin Biaggini. As a result, there was a strong sense of optimism at 65 Market Street as the 1960s ended.

CHAPTER 17

New Directions

"No business can stand still. It will either move ahead to keep out in front of the competitive parade, or it will quickly fall hopelessly behind."—Benjamin F. Biaggini

THE decision by Southern Pacific's management, with the concurrence of the shareholders, to further diversify the company's operations represented relative disappointment with the financial performance of its rail units. Their operating ratio during the 1960s had averaged 78.3, and in 1969 the return on equity for the company reached 9.1 percent. Nevertheless, there seemed little prospect that these figures could be improved or even maintained. Railroads, after all, remained both capital and labor intensive—a problem exacerbated by government regulations, counterproductive laws, and labor contracts restricting managerial opportunities. Categorical disinvestment of rail properties was not an alternative; the reallocation of investment through diversification was. The upshot was a Southern Pacific that, during the next several years, sought to redefine its raison d'etre. Successes followed; so did disappointments.[1]

Diversification, in a very real sense, was not new to the SP although its historic focus had been on transportation service and to a lesser extent on land development. President D. J. Russell enthusiastically embraced that philosophy. He had long dreamed of forging "a fully diversified transportation company" and chafed under unwarranted restrictions that prevented the SP from creating "a transportation supermarket," which would be sure, he said, to benefit the public interest. Frustrated in his greater goals, Russell nevertheless pressed for a policy of diversification within those constraints. "Basically," he said, "we have a policy of trying to get into businesses that are related to transportation—that is what we know something about—rather than spread out into areas where we are not familiar."[2]

In some cases the association with transportation was not readily apparent. For instance, in 1964 the Southern Pacific Land Company acquired the capital stock of the Bankers Leasing Company, which owned a variety of equipment including machine tools, fleets of motor vehicles, data processing equipment, and railroad freight cars that were leased to other firms. Russell, though, saw in Bankers Leasing an opportunity to acquire railroad "equipment without having to do so in the name of the Southern Pacific." Collaterally, ownership of the Evergreen Freight Car Corporation, established in 1966 specifically for the purpose of furnishing freight cars for the forest products industry of northern California and Oregon "under contracts of supply," was transferred the next year from the Southern Pacific Land Company to Bankers Leasing. Eight years later Evergreen's inventory totaled 3,128 cars. Bankers Leasing in 1975 listed 30 percent of its portfolio as railroad related; it included, incidentally, the fully automated 15-mile Muskingum Electric Railroad, constructed for the purpose of hauling coal from a mine to a generating plant in southeastern Ohio. In 1978 bankers enjoyed pretax net of $5 million on lease income of $19.9 million. Acquisition of Bankers Leasing, noted Russell with undue modesty, "worked out very satisfactorily over the years."[3]

To provide the full-service transportation package that Russell envisioned would, of course, require that SP reenter the steamship business, something he was loathe to do. "A desirable alternative," Russell believed, was the Southern Pacific Marine Transport, a non-vessel-operating common carrier chartered late in 1967, for the purpose of handling intermodal container traffic moving to or from foreign ports. In essence, SPMT would offer international shippers a single-billing transportation arrangement by consolidating lading into containers and utilizing SP's truck and rail components to provide overland delivery to and from dockside. Ocean movements would be accomplished by various steamship companies under contract. The SP was one of the first, if not in fact the first carrier, to provide such coordinated rail-truck-ship transport. In 1979, to expand such opportunities at several locations, another subsidiary—Southern Pacific International—acquired the stock of SPMT from the Southern Pacific Land Company.[4]

Given Russell's long and deep interest in aviation, it was not surprising that the SP involved itself in that enterprise as a part of its transportation diversification program. Years earlier, Russell had talked to the president of American Airlines about the prospect of building a canopy over SP's San Francisco passenger station to be used by futuristic vertical-takeoff aircraft and, of course, the company had cooperated with several air carriers by selling their tickets at railroad agencies. Nothing came of the vertical-takeoff project, but in July, 1967, Southern Pacific Air Freight was incorporated and began operations on January 14, 1971, following approval by the Civil Aeronautics Board. A wholly owned subsidiary of Southern Pacific Transportation Company, SPAF coordinated truck service (PMT) with that of established air freight car-

riers to forward shipments on one bill with single-carrier responsibility.[5]

Other diversification energies focused on developing the SP's general service area and thus enhancing the potential for the company's broadening transportation net. Much of this was the responsibility of the Southern Pacific Industrial Development Company and its cousin, the Southern Pacific Development Company. Both were established and owned by SPCo, the holding company parent, for the purpose of engaging in real estate investment, development, and management. By 1978 SPID had developed over seventy industrial parks which it owned and managed. Additionally, it actively recruited businesses for another 30,000 acres of undeveloped or lightly developed lands under its control. Southern Pacific Development Company's efforts centered on office-building expansion in cities from San Francisco to New Orleans.[6]

The grandfather of SP's diversified subsidiaries was the Southern Pacific Land Company. Formed on March 6, 1912, for the purpose of managing outlying lands of the Southern Pacific Railroad Company, its activities were expanded later by acquisition of properties formerly held by the Central Pacific Land Company. The powers of this subsidiary were broadened several times over the years, and on March 1, 1970, it was reorganized to embrace industrial development and natural resources as well as real estate operations. By December 31, 1980, it owned 3.62 million acres and held mineral rights for another 1.27 million acres of deeded lands. Particularly noteworthy were SPLC's timber lands in northern California and its agricultural holdings in the San Joaquin Valley. Until the SP accelerated its diversification program in the 1960s and 1970s, the company had almost singlemindedly viewed its real estate resources as a means to maximize rail traffic. Thereafter, however, the holding company embraced a philosophy of enhancing the earning power of those properties. The land company, managing SP's long-term investment properties—

The grandfather of SP's diversified subsidiaries was the Southern Pacific Land Company, which, among other things, was responsible for the timberlands.

including natural resource holdings—was central to the new policy. Its own subsidiaries, acting independently or in joint ventures, moved actively on projects as diverse as shopping centers, warehouses, family resorts, hotels, and even the development of geothermal energy in the Imperial Valley. If there had been any reason to doubt the wisdom of the new approach, it was dispelled by the result: net income from operations of the land company rose dramatically from $3.9 million in 1972 to $55.9 million in 1979.[7]

If the roots of the land company were deep in SP's history, those of TOPS On-Line Services were not. Using the principles and techniques developed through SP's much-heralded Total Operations Processing System (TOPS), the parent company and an outside management consulting firm formed On-Line Services late in 1969, to offer data processing and related communications services to commercial and governmental organizations. This subsidiary helped to install TOPS or similar systems at home and abroad; clients included the Burlington Northern, Missouri Pacific,

Union Pacific, and British Rail, among several others.[8]

Another new subsidiary, and one that would greatly affect the direction of parent itself over the next years, took the form of the Southern Pacific Communications Company. SPCC was created on January 23, 1970, to provide communication transmission services for business, government, and other customers over SP's extensive microwave system and leased connections in an eleven-state area (essentially the service territory of SP's railroads). Permission to sell time on its circuits came from the Federal Communications Commission late in 1972. This allowed SPCC to compete with American Telephone & Telegraph and Western Union, companies that traditionally enjoyed a monopoly on interstate telephone and message services. Other aspirants, such as Microwave Communications Incorporated (MCI), had similar interests, but the SP, with the largest private microwave network in the country, already had what one official called "a real telephone network in place." Revenue service began on December 26, 1973, when SPCC sent signals for its first customer. Acquisitions and expansion followed, first into the Midwest and then into the East. During July, 1974, SPCC became the first of the specialized common carrier communications companies to offer coast-to-coast voice transmissions by microwave.[9]

This impressive growth continued, and by the end of 1976 SPCC had virtually completed its own coast-to-coast microwave system (capacity had been leased briefly from competitors east of Saint Louis) and a major investment had been made in expensive switching equipment required for SPRINT, a new private-line service to be inaugurated shortly. None of this was without difficulty. Start-up costs were staggering and losses from operations were constant. Furthermore, AT&T retaliated with reduced rates and other roadblocks that were only gradually removed by legal action. Eventually, federal courts confirmed the right of specialized common carriers like SPCC to provide long-distance telephone services similar to those provided by the Bell system. The courts during the mid-1970s likewise decided that AT&T was obliged to provide local interconnections between switch connections owned by the specialized carriers and patrons' telephones. SPCC's customer base then leaped from 944 to 16,000; revenues reflected that happy development, with a rise of 90 percent. SPCC reported its first profit from operations in 1979.[10]

The most visible symbol of the increasingly diversified Southern Pacific Company was the transformation of its general office property in San Francisco from 65 Market Street to One Market Plaza. Plans were unveiled in 1971 by O. Greg Linde, president of the Southern Pacific Land Company, for two office towers that would be joined by a street-level galleria and pedestrian mall adjacent to the historic headquarters. Construction began two years later and occupancy followed in mid-1976. The $82 million project was a joint venture of the land company and the Equitable Life Assurance Society.[11]

Of equal symbolic as well as material importance was the retirement of Donald J. Russell on May 17, 1972. His mark on the Southern Pacific was, in a word, indelible. He could point to any number of accomplishments—diversification being just one—but for Russell the railroad always had been closest to his heart. He took justifiable pride in the performance of system railways, especially during the 1960s, when revenue ton miles increased by 51 percent, gross ton miles per train hour grew by 49 percent, and revenue tons per car rose by 35 percent. Russell thought the key to his success was "a lot of hard work and God-given faculty to think a little bit." His prized accomplishment, he thought, was "raising the overall quality of the property" and "reducing the debt of the company." As his successor, Benjamin F. Biaggini, put it, "the vision of his leadership will have a continuing effect on the Company for years to come." Indeed, the sterling characteristic of Russell's stewardship

Plans were unveiled in 1971 for two office towers joined by a street-level galleria-pedestrian mall adjacent to SP's historic headquarters building in San Francisco.

was his ability to make progressive decisions on major issues or projects.[12]

Biaggini's position was at once enviable and frightening. The company he now would lead was in good condition and well respected as a successful business enterprise, but clearly in a period of unpredictable evolution. SP's "Golden Empire" service area and the generous traffic mix it offered had enriched the company's railroads following the Great Depression, but the future was uncertain. For that matter, the very fabric of American railroading was in flux. But there were other variables. SP's success in becoming a leader of the rail industry reflected its unwillingness to tolerate the status quo; that attitude had bred a useful pride and internal confidence which

Benjamin Franklin Biaggini's position was at once enviable and frightening.

permeated the corporate culture. That same confidence and pride, however, sometimes bordered on an aloofness and arrogance that rejected ideas and viewpoints not originating in or finding favor with the San Francisco offices. It also irritated fellow railroaders and in some cases—particularly in California—the public at large. Finally, Russell's performance would be hard to follow; Biaggini would not be able to avoid invidious comparison.

Born on April 15, 1916, in New Orleans, where his father was an inspector for the Pullman Company, Biaggini earned a bachelor's degree at St. Mary's University in San Antonio, and later participated in Harvard's Advanced Management Program. His first railroad assignment was as a rodman in the engineering department of the Texas & New Orleans; in 1953 he was appointed to the executive de-

partment at Houston. Biaggini was named president of the SP in 1964, and four years later assumed additional duties as chief executive officer. Few doubted his ability. The president of a connecting railroad said: "He is smart, knows the business, and has a good overview." Another railroad president, who once had worked for him, especially admired Biaggini's speaking ability.[13]

Because of his geniality and his capacity for oratory, Biaggini frequently found himself on the speakers' circuit. His themes varied little: the importance of railroads in opening and prospering the West, the pressing need to deregulate the railroads, the value of free enterprise "as a bulwark of the American system," the obsolescence of the intercity passenger train, and optimism regarding the future of railroading.[14]

Biaggini perhaps felt most strongly about deregulation. "The industry's greatest problem has been its inability to earn an adequate rate of return on its investment," he said in a 1970 address before the National Press Club in Washington. This, he maintained, "has been the result of strict economic regulation and of a national policy that has actively promoted and financed the growth of other forms of transportation. . . ." Additionally, he fumed, railroads were subject to difficulties in changing "rates, service and plant" because they were treated as "pure public utilities enjoying protected monopoly status while in fact they fight to stave off government-subsidized transportation at every turn." This combination of counterproductive measures by the 1970s had resulted in the Penn Central debacle, left several major roads with severe liquidity problems because of decreased working capital, and spawned a potential crisis in the Middle West. SP's railroads were doing well by comparison, but their fate depended in part on that of others. "Even though we are many different companies, we are also an integrated rail system. The failures or disabilities of any parts of this system affect the health of the whole," warned Biaggini.[15]

Small wonder that Biaggini and most other rail executives were pleased as public sentiment gradually changed in favor of unshackling the carriers. This took substantive form with passage of the Regional Rail Reorganization Act (1973) to restructure the bankrupt railroads of the Northeast and the Railroad Revitalization and Regulatory Reform Act (1976). The latter included provisions for flexibility in rate making and encouraged Biaggini and others to plead for equal treatment for all modes of transport. To press the issue in 1978, the SPTCo challenged the "agricultural exemption" that allowed truckers to engage in interstate carriage of fresh fruits and vegetables without any rate regulation. SPTCo asked the Interstate Commerce Commission for the same exemption, which, thought Biaggini, was compatible with the intent of the 1976 legislation. The timing was propitious; both Congress and the Carter administration were receptive to the general notion of deregulation. In that mood the ICC agreed to SPTCo's request; it augured well for the future. And it was none too soon. "We have reached the absolute point of choice between either letting the railroads earn a fair return or else putting the whole country on notice to be prepared to pay the staggering bill for nationalization," said Biaggini.[16]

Meanwhile, the Southern Pacific Transportation Company labored hard to better its competitive position. An important reflection of this was the 560-acre, 5.7-mile long, $39 million West Colton Classification Yard located some 50 miles east of Los Angeles. The West Colton facility, which SP touted as "the most technologically advanced rail terminal in the world," had capacity for 7,100 freight cars and was located at the confluence of the Sunset–Golden State line and the new Palmdale Cut-off. Sophisticated computer and electronic equipment typified the operation, which was placed in service on July 19, 1973.[17]

The West Colton Yard, noted Biaggini, would assume even greater importance once the SP acquired the southern portion of the Rock Is-

land. That case, before the ICC since the mid-1960s, was yet to be resolved, but Biaggini remained confident. "If the regulators and the Supreme Court can approve Penn Central and then the Northern Lines [Burlington Northern], they pretty much have to approve any merger that comes along." The ICC's administrative law judge did eventually recommend granting the SP–Union Pacific applications, but only subject to major conditions including a "grand design" for substantially restructuring the nation's rail system west of the Mississippi River. Biaggini objected to this and, along with several others, the SP sought to dismiss the proceedings. Biaggini also considered that the physical and fiscal condition of the Rock Island no longer warranted the original purchase price. Thus, when the regulatory body finally on December 4, 1974, approved the merger of the Rock Island into the Union Pacific and concurrent purchase by SP of Rock Island lines south of Kansas City, the applicants hedged. Officers of the two companies made another hurried inspection of Rock Island's road and equipment property to determine the cost of rehabilitation, but the results were depressing: the cost in 1974 dollars for a five-year program would amount to $1.7 to $1.9 billion. This said nothing of acquisition costs, interest, and the like. It was the last straw. Both the SP and UP threw in the towel and, predictably if sadly, the Rock Island on March 17, 1975, filed a reorganization petition under section 77 of the Bankruptcy Act.[18]

That did not end SP's interest in the Rock Island or at least certain of its parts. When the Rock Island threatened an embargo of traffic and cessation of all operations, SPTCo volunteered to maintain service from Tucumcari to Kansas City (the Golden State Route) under temporary ICC authority. The SPTCo, of course, had a vested interest. Through connections had existed since 1902, when the Rock Island and two subsidiary companies finished the route to Tucumcari and Santa Rosa. Joint solicitation of traffic had persisted

The new West Colton Yard reflected confidence in SPTCo.

even after the SP brought the Cotton Belt into its fold, and the Golden State Route remained the premier funnel for perishable traffic from Southern California and Arizona. True, volume had fallen as trucks took more of the perishable business and as the Rock Island's plant deteriorated, but loss of the Golden State Route would clearly disadvantage SPTCo against the Santa Fe and, to a lesser extent, the Union Pacific—especially in competing for time-sensitive business. To be sure, the SPTCo–Cotton Belt route between Los Angeles and Saint Louis was important, but it was significantly longer (over 400 miles) than those of competitors—a comparative liability for shippers in terms of delivery times and for the company in terms of maintenance, fuel, and labor costs.[19]

With those thoughts in mind, management and the trustee of the bankrupt Rock Island came to an agreement in April, 1978, for the purchase of nearly 1,000 miles of line, plus trackage rights, from Santa Rosa, New Mexico, to Kansas City and Saint Louis along with the Bucklin–Dodge City Branch in Kansas. On December 29, 1978, the SP filed appropriate papers with the ICC. If approved, title would be held by SPTCo's St. Louis Southwestern Railway. The price: $57 million.[20]

Biaggini was characteristically frank regarding SPTCo's position. He had rejected the idea of seeking the northern segment of the Golden State Route from Kansas City to Chicago for several reasons, not the least of which was the poor condition of Rock Island's property and because it would have resulted in formidable opposition from many of the same carriers that earlier had plagued the joint SP-UP application. In this one, however, Biaggini thought the SPTCo was favored by "the logic of the former case," in which the regulatory body had finally agreed that SPTCo could acquire Rock Island lines south of Kansas City concurrently with a merger of the Rock Island into the Union Pacific. Additionally, thought Biaggini, there could be no opposition to Cotton Belt's acquisition of the Rock Island's Saint Louis–Kansas City line since SSW already served Saint Louis and thus was not asking for a "new" gateway.[21]

There was important support. On-line shippers and local governmental agencies rejoiced at the prospect of a healthy carrier's taking over the lines; the Rock Island's management and the court-appointed trustee heartily applauded; and the railroad brotherhoods approved. Sale to the SSW would, after all, preserve local service, restore competition on the historic transcontinental route, provide jobs, and generate tax revenues. For the Rock Island, money from the proposed sale could be used to enhance "an income-based reorganization" and thereby preserve "essential transportation for the benefit of the shipping public." Collaterally, the Chicago, Rock Island & Pacific promised to upgrade Armourdale Yard (which it would share with the SSW) in Kansas City, Kansas, as well as the line from Kansas City to Chicago so that it could "compete for the added Southern Pacific traffic north of Kansas City." The Rock Island likewise planned to rehabilitate trackage in Kansas between Topeka and Herington, where trains from its surviving Corn Belt–to–Gulf "spine line" and Kansas City–Denver line (from Topeka to McFarland) would operate with those of the Cotton Belt on property to be owned jointly.[22]

Reactions among other railroads were mixed. Only the Burlington Northern supported the SPTCo/SSW. The Chicago & North Western, Missouri-Kansas-Texas, Norfolk & Western, and St. Louis–San Francisco all opposed it in one fashion or another, while the Illinois Central Gulf, Milwaukee Road, Kansas City Terminal, and Western Pacific requested "conditions"; the Denver & Rio Grande Western sought to preserve the "Central Corridor" via Ogden. Major complaints came from the Atchison, Topeka & Santa Fe, which groused that it would lose $56.7 in gross revenues, and from the Missouri Pacific, which not only opposed the purchase plan but itself asked to acquire the Rock Island's Kansas City–Saint Louis line—one that duplicated MoPac's own route in that corridor. The Union Pacific, SPTCo's historic partner at Ogden, was thoroughly alarmed by the proposal. It feared that SPTCo would divert traffic away from Ogden to Tucumcari, insisted on strict adherence to the Central Pacific Conditions and, apparently in retaliation, asked for rights over SPTCo lines to serve new customers in far-off Southern California. On the surface, the Tucumcari case seemed minor compared with the earlier and abortive Rock Island merger application, but in reality it contained a germ adequate to spark massive transformation of the industry in the trans-Chicago West. Hearings by the ICC were concluded on February 6, 1980; a decision was promised later that year.[23]

All of this was a matter of great curiosity for the Cotton Belt. Retirement had claimed Harold J. McKenzie on October 31, 1969, and his successor as president, R. Maurice Nall, followed suit after only a brief tenure. Numerous personnel already had been shifted from SSW's headquarters at Tyler to locations on the parent road, and that process continued after the departure of McKenzie

and Nall; management decisions thereafter came from San Francisco and Houston, since the SSW no longer enjoyed a resident chief executive. SP's policy of gradually reducing Cotton Belt's autonomy reminded retired vice-president W. H. Hudson of "cutting the dog's tail off an inch at a time." This, however, did not diminish SP's interest in maintaining at least the facade of SSW independence—even as it increased its actual ownership (to 99.8 percent of its common and 99.6 percent of its preferred stock by 1977). Its chief value as a de facto independent entity sprung from the fact that although the SPTCo was bound by the Central Pacific Conditions to solicit preferentially for the Union Pacific via Ogden, the Cotton Belt was not and thus could solicit for itself—and indirectly its parent—for the longest haul (via Corsicana and East Saint Louis). This fact had long troubled the Union Pacific and later also bothered the Denver & Rio Grande Western because it allowed the SPTCo the luxury of internal debate over the net benefit of, say, handling loads from Oregon via Ogden or East Saint Louis. The response to that question usually hinged on SPTCo's cash-flow situation at the moment and whether it had surplus capacity on the home route to East Saint Louis. Admittedly, though, the system earned more net dollars per mile via Ogden. These same considerations would obtain and, in fact, become even more important should the ICC allow the Cotton Belt to acquire the Tucumcari–Kansas City–Saint Louis line from the Rock Island.[24]

Among other things, the internal debates over soliciting and routing traffic via Ogden versus Tucumcari also reflected SP's need for more sophisticated marketing procedures. Indeed, the entire concept of marketing was foreign to the railroad industry until the late 1950s, and even then it caught on very slowly. The SP was no exception. Its operating department traditionally calculated what trains it could conveniently and economically schedule, and then the traffic or sales department

Retirement claimed Cotton Belt's popular and respected Harold J. McKenzie late in 1969.

attempted to sell the service. In no case was the sales force responsible for profitability. An officer of an eastern carrier that was particularly progressive in this regard and who deeply admired SP's remarkable car fleet and its well-known operating skills complained, nevertheless, that SP's management had "little or no comprehension of the economics involved." At best, he said, "SP was the Pennsylvania Railroad of the West in terms of pricing and marketing." When the SP finally moved, however, it did so vigorously, hiring an outsider who previously had headed Crocker National Bank's marketing program. His task, simply stated, was to increase market share as well as profitability. Yet it was not a simple task, for marketing was not simply a matter of organization but rather more an internal perception of the very nature of doing business. In sum, marketing, properly approached,

required substantial alterations in the time-honored practices of several organizational areas—changes that ran counter to the culture of the company and threatened established fiefdoms. In the end, tradition won, the outsider and many of those he brought onto the marketing team left and, as one officer observed, "we lost a half-decade in marketing." He may have mildly overstated the matter since the marketing department was not actually dismantled and later recovered some of its momentum, but the issue demonstrated, as one outsider noted, that "logic, reason, and economics go out the window when there are problems of personality and turf." [25]

In the case of some commodities, modern marketing techniques might increase market share and profitability, but in others the railroad frankly was no match for competition. For instance, livestock and LCL shipments together made up less than one-tenth of one percent of all SPTCo tonnage by 1970. The truck was simply superior for the movement of live animals, and LCL similarly moved more expeditiously by motor carrier or by freight forwarders. On the other hand, gains were made in traditional categories such as ores, minerals, and fuels, manufactured goods, timber products, food and farm products, chemicals, and others. Commodities such as crude oil, sugar beets, cement, iron ore, steel coils, and grain were especially subject to efficient bulk movement by unit train. Lumber, wood chips, and paper products similarly continued to supply handsome revenues from mills in Oregon and northern California, and Arizona maintained its reputation for heavy tonnage in copper concentrates and anodes. A particularly bright spot in SPTCo's traffic mix derived from the Gulf Coast region, where volume in chemicals jumped from 8.9 percent of SPTCo's tonnage in 1970 to 14.7 percent in 1981. [26]

Throughout this period SPTCo paid strict attention to the needs of the automobile industry. In 1970 General Motors began unit train shipments of auto parts and assembled units that had been gathered at the Illinois

The motor truck was frankly superior to rail service in the carriage of livestock. Indeed, SPTCo's tariff for live animals was canceled before 1970.

Central's Markham Yard south of Chicago from twenty-three of its midwestern plants. These trains, headed for assembly plants and unloading points in the Los Angeles Basin, were handed to the Cotton Belt at East Saint Louis and then to SPTCo at Corsicana. This arrangement reduced transit time and saved money in inventory needs for GM, and it saved car miles and reduced equipment needs for the carriers. It was mutually advantageous and gave the auto maker an excuse to cancel other routings and gateways favoring competing railroads. The Southern Pacific–General Motors alliance was further cemented by mutual development of Stac-Pac container cars for shipments of Cadillacs (a dozen autos in four containers loaded on a standard 89-foot

flatcar) and in continued use of SP Vert-A-Pac cars for Chevrolet Vegas.[27]

Substantial growth likewise occurred in trailer (TOFC) and container (COFC) volume. Piggyback or intermodal traffic grew from 178,000 units (trailers or containers) handled in 1965 to 245,000 units in 1972, when SPTCo created a new intermodal traffic department to coordinate operating and sales functions. Overhead or straddle cranes and motorized Piggy Packers replaced "circus ramps" for loading and unloading at new or improved intermodal yards in Los Angeles, Oakland, Dallas, Phoenix, Houston, Portland, Memphis, East Saint Louis, and Avondale (New Orleans). Dedicated long-distance TOFC trains, such as that contracted for by

The Southern Pacific paid strict attention to the needs of the automobile industry. "Stac-Pac" reflected this.

the U.S. Postal Service between the Bay Area and Chicago, made their appearance early in the 1970s and grew in number throughout the decade. Similarly, two important innovations, "landbridge" and "mini-bridge"—port-to-port and point-to-point rail networks—utilized containers. Landbridge linked ocean routes by way of overland rail service between ports, e.g., Oakland and Houston; mini-bridge handled international shipments to and from domestic points in similar fashion.[28]

Mini-bridge and landbridge both shortened transit time by avoiding lengthy voyages through the Panama Canal and offered a competitive edge because break-bulk expenses were avoided. The entire process implied drastic changes for the ocean carriers and the ports they plied. The case of San Francisco and Oakland is illustrative. San Francisco historically was the more important of the two ports, but labor and work-rule problems, the demise of American flag lines, and the desire of that city for only "clean industries" combined to diminish its maritime importance. On the other hand, Oakland recognized the move away from break-bulk shipping to con-

tainerization and planned accordingly. Other ports served by the SPTCo—Portland, Los Angeles (San Pedro–Long Beach), and Houston—made the transition to containerization rather easily.[29]

Change also typified an old subsidiary—Pacific Fruit Express—and the transportation of perishable products associated with it. PFE gradually phased out its ice bunker cars (the use of ice as a refrigerant ended in 1971), replacing them with mechanical refrigerators. A total of 13,252 of these cars were leased or purchased between 1953 and 1971. During the 1960s PFE also acquired 3,314 refrigerated trailers and over a thousand flatcars for TOFC service. Piggyback proved especially attractive for the movement of lettuce and grapes, and the "reefers" wheeled heavy volumes of lettuce, potatoes, melons, citrus, and, increasingly, frozen foods. The shipment of the millionth carload of lettuce from the Salinas Valley on August 20, 1963, attested to the long relationship between PFE and the perishables producers. Yet change was in the offing. The volume of fresh fruits and vegetables handled nationwide by railroads and the trucking industry was about equal in 1960, but by 1978 trucks held a seven-to-one advantage. This was mirrored by PFE's performance; shipments dropped from 232,071 in 1960 to 62,083 in 1977. PFE consequently suffered net deficits beginning in 1971 and, except for 1975, each year through 1978. Unregulated trucks clearly had advantages, including plasticity in operations and rates as well as faster transit time (third-morning delivery to Chicago versus fifth-morning by rail). Ironically, PFE's efforts in TOFC proved unremunerative, and even its attempt to advance efficiency by providing higher capacity (130,000-pound) rail cars backfired when buyers favored the flexibility of smaller shipments.[30]

Joint ownership of PFE by the Southern Pacific and the Union Pacific always had been somewhat difficult, and that problem stood in bold relief as its market share deteriorated. Both owners simply wished to have closer identification with the shippers and producers on their respective lines; not surprisingly then, they agreed to a split-off and equal division of PFE's assets effective April 1, 1978. Under the agreement, Union Pacific established its own refrigerator car line while the SP retained the familiar name of Pacific Fruit Express for its "new" subsidiary.[31]

Another alteration in the company's conventional landscape involved the commute operation between San Francisco and San Jose. Although its out-of-pocket costs had risen regularly after World War II, the SP had continued to lavish close attention on the program. Even in the 1960s when the company struggled to get out of the intercity passenger business, it pledged to "continue operating the best commute service in the country, just as long as there is need for it or until it is eventually supplanted by some other form of rapid transit." To this end, SP had received ten new double-decker "gallery" cars in 1955, twenty-one more two years later, and would receive fifteen more in 1968. Not surprisingly, Peninsula patrons gave SP's service high marks and so did the national media, which compared it favorably with other operations in the East and Midwest. Festivities properly marked the centennial of SP's commute operations on January 16, 1964.[32]

The same year, however, marked growing distress among SP's managers regarding rising commute deficits. The California Public Utilities Commission inexcusably put off decisions on rate increase requests, and eventually the SP put the matter before the Interstate Commerce Commission. Even after increases were finally granted, SP's rail commute rates were among the lowest in the nation (round trip fare from San Francisco to San Jose was $1.75 in 1948, only $3.10 in 1967) and deficits continued to climb, from $670,000 in 1964 to over $1 million by 1968, while ridership held steady at about 12,000 daily. Matters came to a head in 1975, after SPTCo asked Price Waterhouse & Company, a nationally recognized accounting firm, to con-

duct an independent review of commute costs. The Price Waterhouse report concluded that the railroad received a mere $4.6 million annually in revenues but lost a staggering $5.3 million. Biaggini rightly concluded that this was an intolerable burden for the equity holders, but the California PUC was obdurate. When SPTCo asked for a fare increase of 111 percent "to offset losses from operations," the California regulators announced that they would "not be ready to proceed with hearings for approximately 14 months." Ridership fell to about 8,000 daily and losses mounted to $9 million in 1976. In utter despair Biaggini first offered to sell the commute line and then offered to purchase 1,000 eight-passenger motor vehicles and donate them for vanpools if relieved of the commute operation. Finally, he authorized company attorneys to seek "discontinuance of passenger service on the San Francisco Peninsula." In all of this, the PUC had not yet acted on SP's request for rate increases, fumed Biaggini. An accommodation was finally reached, however. On July 1, 1980, the California Department of Transportation assumed financial responsibility for the commute service; SPTCo agreed to maintain operations under a cost-reimbursable contract. Consequently the trains continued to roll—ironically, to and from a relatively new station in San Francisco. The old Mission style facility at Third & Townsend was the victim of freeway planners; the new one, a block away on Fourth Street, had opened on June 23, 1975.[33]

Just as it sought relief from commute deficits, SPTCo also found other areas to trim. It filed applications with the ICC to retire over 700 miles of track during the mid-1970s. Most of these were bits and pieces of branches around the system, but one was not. On September 10, 1976, Hurricane Kathleen inflicted $1.3 million in damages, destroyed three trestles, otherwise cut the line at more than fifty locations, and threatened the very life of the San Diego & Arizona Eastern (SD&AE). The road had other problems, how-

Price Waterhouse estimated that SPTCo received $4.6 million annually in revenues from commute operations, but lost a staggering $5.3 million each year in that service. Small wonder the company wanted out.

ever, which had not developed overnight. Carloads handled had dropped from 33,000 in 1958 to 20,000 in 1974, while difficulties of maintenance and operation on the "impossible railroad" were historic. Operations themselves had not been affected in 1970, when ownership of the Tijuana & Tecate Railway—a subsidiary that held title to the 44 miles of route in Mexico—was transferred from the SD&AE to the Sonora–Baja California Railway, part of the Mexican government's national system. It merely confused matters.[34]

Hurricane Kathleen's devastation, however, required that SPTCo's management face the issue of SD&AE's future earlier than might otherwise have been the case. In any event, it determined early in 1977 to abandon or sell all of the SD&AE except the eighteen easternmost miles from El Centro to an important United States Gypsum Company plant at Plaster City. Events then took a surprising course when on November 1, 1978, SPTCo concluded the sale of 108 miles of the roadway and all of the company's capital stock to San Diego's Metropolitan Transit Development Board for $18.1 million, less the cost of SPTCo's repairing those segments of line damaged by the hurricane in 1976. For SPTCo it represented a "sale-donation" that would yield a charitable deduction; for San Diego it represented an inexpensive opportunity to employ the western portion of the SD&AE for a new trolley system while leasing the entire line from San Diego to a connection with SPTCo at Plaster City to a short-line operator.

For the SD&AE, Hurricane Kathleen proved to be one storm too many.

In that way the San Diego & Arizona Eastern survived. San Diego's trolley system would get rave reviews, but short-line operators would find the rugged route through Carrizo Gorge as "impossible" as had the Southern Pacific.[35]

Fires and floods were a normal part of business on the SD&AE; challenges to operations elsewhere were just as normal for its parent. Continued sinking of the tracks in the Suisun Marshes between Benicia and Sacramento had plagued the SP early on; the collapse of a tunnel closed traffic on the Coast Line for sixty days in 1914; the Christmas week storm of 1964 knocked out the Northwestern Pacific, SP's Cascade Line, and others; and Hurricane Beulah in 1967 heavily damaged several lines in Texas. However unpleasant, SP forces handled these crises and others like them with aplomb. More difficult were disasters involving lading. An explosion of liquid petroleum gas in the Alton & Southern yard at East Saint Louis during 1972 produced heavy damage to rail facilities and the nearby area; a similar explosion occurred two years later in Houston's Englewood Yard; and the derailment of a Cotton Belt train followed by a fire among cars containing hazardous materials required the evacuation of 1,700 persons living in and around Lewisville, Arkansas, early in 1978. Worst of all was the devastation brought by multiple explosions in SPTCo's yard at Roseville, California, on April 28, 1973. In this case, several cars of bombs destined for Viet Nam blew up. Nearly two hundred persons were injured, but miraculously none died in the two-day ordeal. Hundreds of claims and dozens of lawsuits resulted; the monetary loss to the SPTCo was enormous, although neither the company nor its personnel were guilty of improper procedures or sloppy handling.[36]

These unanticipated liabilities were all the more debilitating given the general economic instability of the 1970s and the cash requirements necessary for the Southern Pacific to prosecute its diversification program. SP's dividends rose from $1.80 per share in 1970 on an uninterrupted curve to $2.45 in 1979. This index, however, did not represent the whole cloth. Neither did the fact that the company's revenues in 1977 exceeded $2 billion for the first time. As late as that same year railroad operations accounted for 86 percent of the Southern Pacific Company's revenues and 71 percent of its income from operations. SP's railroads were obviously central to the holding company's fortunes—they were generous "cash cows" necessary in providing funds to "lever up" the communications and land companies. Yet the railroads remained both capital and labor intensive—the latter element increasingly a matter of concern. Labor costs for the company's railroads rose 50 percent in the first half of the 1970s, and agreements pledged them to at least another 40 percent increase over the next three years. Unproductive work rules militated against advances in productivity and, as a consequence of energy shortages, fuel costs were up 117 percent in 1974 alone. The result was as unpleasant as it was predictable; SPTCo's operating ratio skyrocketed to 97.49 by the end of the decade. Moreover, the country's railroads were especially vulnerable to the vagaries of the business cycle; this was especially true of SPTCo since many of its principal customers were themselves susceptible to cyclical impact. Unfortunately, there were two severe slumps during the 1970s which, in contravention to the norm, were accompanied by inflation of severe proportions. During the recession year of 1975 SP's working capital dropped frighteningly; long-term debt rose to $1.5 billion by 1979, up from $844.2 million in 1972. Obviously, SP's diversification program had not yet reached full flower, at least in terms of contributing to net. Rather, it needed even more infusions of cash just when the company's railroads were having a very hard time with expenses.[37]

Indeed, the devastating recession of 1974–75 thoroughly traumatized SP's railroads (the holding company at one point had to advance $53 million to SPTCo for it to meet obligations) and that trauma had onerous short- and long-term implications. To slow the hemorrhage of cash, management postponed certain capital expenditures and embraced a

The nation's railroads in the 1970s remained both capital and labor intensive. On the Southern Pacific, operating costs were always an important issue because of the rugged nature of much of its service area.

program of "stringent cost control." No new locomotives were delivered in 1976 and 1977, and the number of track miles receiving new or relay rail dropped to 388 in 1976. Biaggini told shareholders that the company's rail properties were "well maintained," but cuts made during the recession hit the mechanical and maintenance-of-way departments hardest. The locomotive rebuilding program at the Sacramento Locomotive Works was curtailed, and ties installed on SPTCo's trackage averaged only 812,000 annually during the years 1973–76. (Maintenance engineers argued that these properties required 1.2 million renewal ties annually.)[38]

One officer labeled management's policy as "selective negligence"; another said flatly that not enough money was authorized for "system management and maintenance." Problems in track structure showed up earliest and were the most severe on the Texas & Louisiana Lines, where properties had been under-maintained longer. Ironically, the traffic base on the Texas & Louisiana Lines, especially in lucrative business from the petrochemical industry, had been increasing, but SPTCo managers failed to apprehend the volume of that growth and the importance of it to the entire system. When the national economy turned up, the Texas and Louisiana Gulf Coast economy boomed. SPTCo simply was not in condition to adequately handle the business offered. Track conditions demanded voluminous slow orders; crews "died" on line without getting their trains into terminals; traffic backed up from Los Angeles to East Saint Louis; congestion was so intense that loads were "stored" on remote unused track simply to achieve fluidity; and customers were driven to distraction. A shortage of motive power compounded the problem. Newer locomotives had been used during the recession while older power, as it became disabled, was stored as unserviceable rather than repaired. Now the new power needed attention as did the old; locomotives from other carriers that otherwise might have been leased were not available because of the national demand for transportation. A total of 1,197 miles of rail were laid and 2.5 million ties inserted during the last two years of the decade, the locomotive rebuilding program was renewed and accelerated, and nearly three hundred new locomotives were received, but in many ways it was too little too late. The competition, especially the Missouri Pacific, profited greatly from SPTCo's misfortunes. As one senior officer would observe, customers and potential customers as late as 1982 remained skittish, recalling SPTCo's poor performance of the late 1970s.[39]

These problems notwithstanding, Biaggini remained confident in the rail industry and the place of SP's railroads in it. Merger, he concluded, was the proper medicine. Consequently, he vigorously pursued creation of the nation's first truly transcontinental system. During the early 1970s Biaggini had held informal discussions in this regard with

W. Thomas Rice and Prime F. Osborn of the Seaboard Coast Line (SCL) Railroad and Hayes T. Watkins of the Chesapeake & Ohio Railway to see if a three-way partnership might be arranged—replicating, in a sense, the nineteenth-century dream of Collis P. Huntington. The Chesapeake & Ohio eventually dropped out, but in the summer of 1977 the SP and the SCL each authorized initial studies, followed by a more formal agreement of a few months later. Biaggini met with Osborn in March, 1978, and gave the SCL president a list of propositions, including the ratio of stock exchange and names for senior management positions and the board of directors. The burden of Biaggini's list implied that SP "would be the dominating or surviving" company. SCL officers thought well of SP's management and, according to Osborn, regarded SP's diversification as "the most attractive feature" that the San Francisco company brought to the potential marriage. Osborn promised to study Biaggini's list. Meanwhile, the SP purchased 700,000 shares or 4.8 percent of Seaboard Coast Line's outstanding stock.[40]

If merged, the SP-SCL would link the Pacific coast with that of the Atlantic by way of a 30,000-mile railway serving more than half of the nation's states. Yet there were problems. Definite long-haul advantages would accrue for transcontinental traffic, but, because of the end-to-end nature of this merger, operating savings by way of closing redundant facilities would be few. Many at SCL felt that SP's proposal offered little financial incentive and that forces at One Market Plaza interpreted the word *merger* as "takeover." Others at Seaboard were put off by Biaggini's "domineering style." In any event, Seaboard's board of directors rejected SP's offer on May 18, 1978. Biaggini attempted to change opinions at SCL and SP increased its holdings in Seaboard to 9.5 percent, but that brought complaints from Seaboard and an order from the ICC to terminate stock acquisitions. Seaboard and Chesapeake & Ohio soon thereafter announced their own plans for merger. SP voted its shares in favor of the plan and then sold its holdings in 1980 at an appreciable profit. Biaggini was philosophical. Had the merger been consummated, he noted, it not only would have created the first transcontinental but it also "would have initiated the ultimate wave of them." For better or for worse, it was not to be.[41]

Biaggini's ardor for some kind of expansion was not dampened. Early in 1978 he announced that SP would acquire the outstanding stock of Ticor, a financial service company headquartered in Los Angeles. Ticor, the oldest and largest title insurance company in California, had expanded in recent years into mortgage insurance, reinsurance, and financial and corporate printing. Critics, both inside and outside of the company, wondered why SP sought an operation such as this, for Ticor's fortunes—like those of SP's railroads—were subject to the vagaries of the business cycle. Nevertheless, Ticor became a member of the Southern Pacific family on July 27, 1979. The cost: $258 million in cash and debentures.[42]

Biaggini considered that "the 1970s, and particularly the last few years of the decade, marked a major turning point in Southern Pacific's" long history. Ten years ago, he noted, it had been "basically a railroad company with outside interests." Now, as it approached the 1980s the SP was, in Biaggini's words, "a strongly diversified corporation." True. But its raison d'etre still was not clearly defined and, as a consequence, its course was not predictable. Would further diversification cause disinvestment in its rail properties? Would SP acquire additional concerns such as Ticor, which seemed to have so little similarity to its other holdings? Would it sell some of its subsidiaries? The past seemed inadequate as a predictor as the new decade began.[43]

CHAPTER 18

Eye of the Storm

"Unfortunately, there is no certainty. There is
only reason and experience to guide us."—
Frederick S. Burbridge

CONDITIONS faced by the Southern Pacific
Company during the early 1980s remained in
a state of flux, partly because its own corporate direction was inadequately defined and
partly because of external circumstances over
which it had little or no control. Interest rates,
as an example, soared before finally moder-
ating as the country suffered its worst economic downturn since the Great Depression.
For that matter, the very core of the American
economy was under stress as its base gradually shifted from traditional heavy industries
to high technology and service-oriented concerns. All of this had a predictably forceful
impact on the SP and colored the decisions
of its managers, who faced yet another particularly vexing matter: The "mega-merger"
movement that had settled upon the railroad
industry.

Mergers were hardly new to the country's
railroads; SP's own development included a
bewildering plethora of such consolidations.
In the twentieth century the federal government had encouraged mergers of carriers into
strong systems through the Transportation
Act of 1920 as well as the Prince Plan of the
1930s, but little was accomplished until the
carriers themselves clamored for combinations as a cure for their collective ailments
during the late 1950s. Industry leaders such as
John W. Barriger, president of the Pittsburg &
Lake Erie, called for "super railroads," and in
1957 Northern Pacific's Robert S. MacFarlane
predicted the nation's railroads would be

merged into "perhaps 25 great systems" within
fifteen or twenty years. MacFarlane's predictions pointed to fruition during the 1960s.
In the Midwest the Chicago & North Western swallowed the smaller Minneapolis &
St. Louis and the Chicago Great Western, but
more important manifestations occurred east
of the Mississippi River, where the Chesapeake & Ohio and the Baltimore & Ohio
formed the Chessie System; the Atlantic Coast
Line and the Seaboard Air Line emerged as
the Seaboard Coast Line; the Erie and the
Delaware, Lackawanna & Western created the
Erie Lackawanna; and the Norfolk & Western
brought the Virginian and then the New York,
Chicago & St. Louis and the Wabash under
its flag. As impressive as these combinations
were, nothing in the East compared to the
new Penn Central, an amalgamation of the
Pennsylvania Railroad, New York Central,
and the New York, New Haven & Hartford.
Neither was the West left out. The Hill Lines—
the Chicago, Burlington & Quincy, Great
Northern, Northern Pacific, and the Spokane,
Portland & Seattle—finally pledged their four-
way troth early in 1970 under a new corporate
canopy, Burlington Northern (BN).[1]

Merger activity subsided dramatically during the 1970s, however, following the spectacular failure of Penn Central and the bankruptcy of several other railroads in the
Northeast. (These finally emerged as Conrail,
a child of the federal government, on April 1,
1976.) If the merger movement temporarily

decelerated, the problems of the industry did not. Focus shifted to the Midwest, where a long-anticipated crisis was at hand. The Illinois Central had merged with the Gulf, Mobile & Ohio in 1972, but anticipated benefits proved disappointing and the "new" Illinois Central Gulf quickly became an unwanted entity of the holding company that it had birthed. Many other midwestern roads suffered similarly from financial malnutrition. The Rock Island, of course, struggled with bankruptcy and faced dismemberment, and the Chicago, Milwaukee, St. Paul & Pacific similarly found refuge in the courts and eventually lopped off nearly two-thirds of its route miles in a desperate attempt to stay alive. It was against this backdrop that another round of mergers began; many executives agreed with SP's Ben Biaggini, who saw the issue quite simply: mergers were "a matter of survival."[2]

On the other hand, Biaggini soon learned that the merger knife was double-edged. The term *mega-merger* became popular during the late 1970s, but it might justifiably have been used to define both the earlier Penn Central and Burlington Northern combinations. The SP had taken no official position on the Penn Central merger but had labored to protect historic traffic patterns via Portland under the Burlington Northern plan. Its concerns deepened when the mid-sized St. Louis–San Francisco was folded into the much larger BN (1980), when the Chessie System and Seaboard Coast Line combined to form the huge CSX Corporation (1980), and again when Norfolk & Western joined with Southern Railway to form the equally formidable Norfolk Southern (1982). The most decisive blow of all, however, came on January 8, 1980, when the Union Pacific—SP's historic partner on the Overland Route—and the Missouri Pacific—its chief rival in the Texas and Louisiana Gulf Coast region—announced that they had agreed in principle to a merger. This trauma was compounded shortly thereafter when the UP announced that it would also

seek authority to control the Western Pacific, which paralleled SPTCo's portion of the Overland Route in California, Nevada, and Utah. If approved, "Mop Up," as it came to be called, would spread UP's influence over a vast domain from Portland, Oakland, and Los Angeles to Chicago, Saint Louis, Houston, and New Orleans. It would clearly, as one writer observed, represent the "first fundamental rearrangement of Western railroading since Edward H. Harriman strode the land."[3]

There was much irony in all of this. Harriman, after all, had joined the SP with the Union Pacific early in the century, but nettlesome government intervention eventually undid his handiwork. The matter was further confused by the activities of George Gould, whose Western Pacific finally constructed its line over a route that the Union Pacific itself would have used had the Central Pacific not made such rapid progress building eastward during the late 1860s. Robert S. Lovett, who headed the Union Pacific after the SP had been separated from it, could have acquired the Western Pacific interloper for the UP but chose not to "because of the inconsistency of such purchase with the obligation under the Pacific Railroad Acts for the continued use of the Union Pacific and Central Pacific as one continuous line of railroad." This notion was reinforced in 1923 by the ICC's so-called Central Pacific Conditions, which bound the SP to solicit preferentially for the UP via Ogden, and a year later by an agreement between the two historic partners in which the UP promised to view the Central Pacific Conditions as reciprocally obligatory—i.e., it would treat the SP preferentially at Ogden.[4]

Union Pacific's merger proposal, if approved, would disavow the relationship begun more than a century earlier with the driving of the Golden Spike at Promontory. More than that, it would negate the possibility of reuniting the former Harriman properties in an eminently logical modern-day end-to-end merger. W. Averell Harriman, who himself had once headed the Union Pacific, thought it "too bad" that a merged SP-UP "couldn't be," and SP's D. J. Russell and Ben Biaggini both agreed that such a marriage was both reasonable and desirable. Russell recalled that the Southern Pacific had made "very serious studies" and had held "casual discussions" with the UP to that end "over the last 20 years"; the benefits, he maintained, had not been "justified for the SP." UP's action now, though, struck Russell as a "double cross" since it sought direct access to the Bay Area by way of the Western Pacific—in contravention to the Central Pacific Conditions and other collateral agreements. Ben Biaggini took a similar position. He was long on record as favoring mergers to achieve a "nicely balanced, competitive" rail system for the nation, but he saw Union Pacific's effort to merge with the Missouri Pacific and then acquire the Western Pacific as "corporate treachery of the highest order." From SP's point of view there was very good reason to be concerned. Company accountants glumly calculated that the huge merger would essentially dry up SPTCo's part of the Overland Route. Furthermore, said Biaggini, there would be "no public benefit associated with transferring revenues from other railroads to the already embarrassingly rich Union Pacific." Correspondingly, the Southern Pacific threw itself into an earnest campaign against the UP-MoPac-WP combination, which it branded as "anticompetitive and otherwise contrary to the public interest."[5]

Biaggini worried openly that the merger might bankrupt the Southern Pacific Transportation Company. On the other hand, UP's actions were a predictable response to its historic needs. In 1901 E. H. Harriman had explained to UP shareholders that gaining control of the SP was necessary "to maintain and protect the position of the system and to safeguard its future against combinations of other lines which might divert much business by changes in existing channels of transportation." These same words might have been used in the present case by UP's John C. Kene-

fick, for in reality the government-mandated split of Southern Pacific and Union Pacific after Harriman's death had left the UP dependent on eastern connections at Council Bluffs and Kansas City and at Ogden on the west. The "Mop Up" proposal, coming eight decades after Harriman's pronouncement, would improve competition by opening new routes for more efficient and economical service, promised Kenefick. The argument was compelling from a historical as well as contemporary perspective. "Solicitation to secure the long through haul is always an effective argument before the ICC," Hale Holden had told Paul Shoup in 1930. The UP had this and other ammunition in its arsenal. It argued for parity with those western railroads that already enjoyed two-carrier transcontinental opportunities via Chicago or Mississippi River connections. These included, Kenefick noted pointedly, the Burlington Northern, Santa Fe, and Southern Pacific Transportation Co.[6]

Meanwhile, the railroad that Huddie "Leadbelly" Ledbetter had immortalized as "a mighty fine line" met an unfittingly bitter end. On August 28, 1979, the Brotherhood of Railway and Airline Clerks and the United Transportation Union struck the Chicago, Rock Island & Pacific Railroad over the issue of retroactive pay. Shortly thereafter, the ICC, in a highly controversial decision, ruled that the Rock Island was "cashless" and ordered service temporarily restored under the direction of the Kansas City Terminal Railway, itself owned by the trunk carriers serving that city. This peculiar arrangement lasted until March 31, 1980, when systemwide revenue operations across the Rock Island ended. The ICC thereupon authorized several carriers to serve specific Rock Island segments under temporary service orders. The Cotton Belt, for instance, performed such service in Arkansas on the Choctaw Route and over the Santa Rosa–Tucumcari–Kansas City–Saint Louis line while waiting for the ICC to render a decision on its request to purchase that important trackage. It was, for all parties, an

For the cities and towns along the Rock Island's Golden State route west of Kansas City, the Cotton Belt was clearly a white knight. Operation began under an ICC service order late in March, 1980. The first train at Hooker, Oklahoma.

The first train at Liberal, Kansas.

awkward situation; the Rock Island would eventually emerge as the Chicago Pacific Corporation after liquidating the assets of the former railroad company.[7]

As events surrounding the ill-fated Rock Island wound their way to conclusion, and as the Interstate Commerce Commission wrestled with the merits of the Union Pacific case, a new variable in the western railroad picture burst upon the scene. On May 15, 1980, the boards of directors of the Southern Pacific Company and Santa Fe Industries announced that they had jointly embraced a memorandum of intent to merge the SP into the Santa Fe. Casual discussions between Biaggini and Santa Fe's John S. Reed had gone on before, but the campaign by Union Pacific to expand its dominion through the Missouri Pacific and Western Pacific now forced these ancient rivals into an embrace. Santa Fe Industries and its railroad were more profitable than SP and its railroads, although SP's combined properties boasted larger gross revenues and net assets; Santa Fe would be the survivor if the merger was approved by shareholders and governmental bodies. The initial reaction to the merger proposal on Wall Street, however, was not flattering. Nevertheless, Biaggini thought the creation of Burlington Northern followed by its acquisition of the Frisco and then the massive Union Pacific proposal made the matter academic. "There would be no use in leaving the Southern Pacific alone and the Santa Fe alone to compete with railroads the size" of the Burlington Northern and the "Mop Up," he explained.[8]

The obvious need to unite in the face of major railroad restructuring west of the Mississippi River notwithstanding, major obstacles to a Santa Fe–SP merger remained. One centered on SPTCo's persistent interest in acquiring much of Rock Island's Golden State Route and, even as Santa Fe's and SP's managers studied the overall merger proposition, the ICC gave its permission for that $57 million line acquisition on June 10, 1980. SPTCo's Cotton Belt, which had been providing di-

On June 10, 1980, the ICC gave approval for SSW's acquisition of the Rock Island's Golden State line west of Kansas City. The task of renewing it would be awesome. *Photograph by Jim Johnson for SSW.*

The moment of transition. The Rock Island designation is replaced by the Cotton Belt on the division offices at Kansas City, Kansas. *Photograph by Jim Johnson for SSW.*

SSW's first train from Kansas City left from the Rock Island's formerly impressive Armourdale Yard—now in very great need of attention. *Photograph by J. David Ingles for SSW.*

rected service over the route since March 24, found business, both local and overhead, was initially slack; the sole train dispatched from Kansas City on April 1, for instance, handled only thirty-five cars, of which more than half were empty. There was no disputing the potential of the line, however, and that autumn the Cotton Belt committed itself to a massive rehabilitation program, using some funds generated internally and obtaining the remainder from a federal loan. This all presented the Southern Pacific and its potential merger partner, the Santa Fe, with a conundrum. SP's officers saw the revitalized Golden State Route as essential to survival if the merger with the Santa Fe failed, but Santa Fe's John Reed was "horrified" at the prospect of sinking money into what he considered a redundant line should the merger be completed. To make

it the high-speed route that SPTCo envisioned would require the expenditure of millions that, said Reed, was "not economically justified."[9]

SP's determination to follow through with not only acquisition but also with rehabilitation of the Golden State Route was hardly the sole problem plaguing merger negotiations. In fact, both companies issued terse statements on September 12, announcing that they had mutually determined to end such discussions. Biaggini cited several reasons: the management of nonrail properties, benefit programs for company officers, and accounting problems. Outsiders pointed to another element: the clash of corporate as well as individual egos.[10]

They might not be able to agree to merge; nevertheless, the SP and Santa Fe commonly

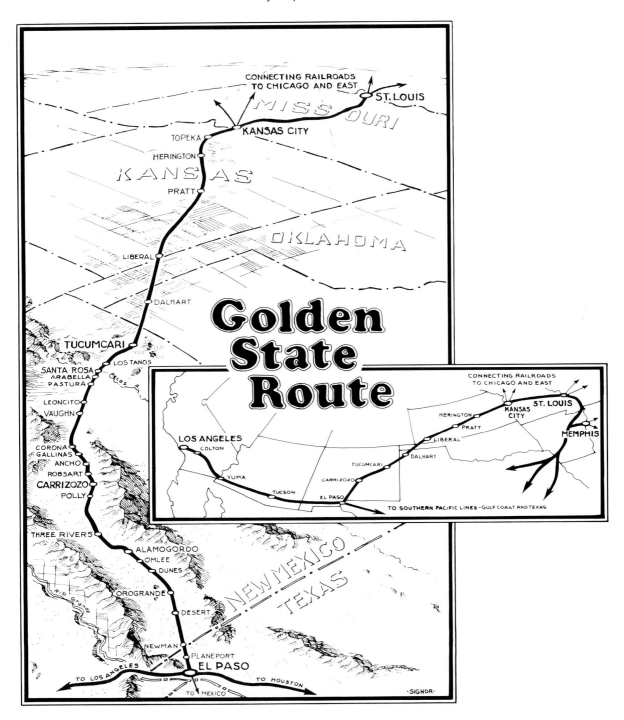

viewed the prospect of a strengthened Union Pacific as abhorrent to their individual interests. Both asked that the UP-MoPac-WP combination be rejected by the ICC; SPTCo estimated its annual loss, if the merger was approved, to be $100 million, and the Santa Fe expected annual losses of $92 million. Nevertheless, the ICC granted UP's wishes on September 13, 1982. The SPTCo immediately filed suit to stop the merger because, in its view, the combination would "destroy railroad competition in the West" and because, again in its view, the UP-WP affiliation would be "illegal under the Pacific Railroad Acts." This legal action and that brought by other carriers was of no avail. "Mop Up" became a very impressive element on the American transportation landscape when the Union Pacific more than doubled its size as a railroad on December 22, 1982. "DONE!" boasted the UP in full-page newspaper advertisements. "DONE," of course, was in mock reference to the message sent from Promontory on May 10, 1869, when the Central Pacific had met the Union Pacific to forge the nation's first transcontinental rail link. For those at One Market Plaza on December 22, 1982, however, "DONE" could only be translated as "UNDONE." [11]

The SPTCo was not the only rail carrier subject to altered conditions as a result of Union Pacific's expansion. Years earlier, the Rio Grande had suffered greatly when George Gould drained its treasury in construction of the Western Pacific, and it had suffered also as the result of restrictive policies imposed by Harriman and then by the ICC in the Central Pacific Conditions. The Denver & Rio Grande Western gamely survived, though, and even prospered by handling overhead business to and from the Missouri Pacific at Pueblo, the Chicago, Burlington & Quincy and the Rock Island at Denver, the Western Pacific at Salt Lake City, and the SP at Ogden. These opportunities shrank, however, when the CB&Q became an integral part of the Burlington Northern, when the Rock Island disappeared, and when the Western Pacific and the Missouri Pacific became extensions of the Union Pacific—Rio Grande's historic competitor. Meanwhile, SPTCo had long since become the Rio Grande's premier connection, and that important association predictably matured as SPTCo lost its own traditional partner at Ogden and as the Union Pacific diverted business to itself from the former Western Pacific at Salt Lake City and away from the Missouri Pacific's Pueblo gateway. Fortunately for both the D&RGW and SPTCo, the Rio Grande gained trackage rights concessions as

a result of the Missouri Pacific–Union Pacific merger over the Missouri Pacific from Pueblo to Kansas City, Missouri; these implied longhaul advantages for the Denver company and routing alternatives for SPTCo. For that matter, many considered that the well-managed Rio Grande was a logical and proper marriage partner for the Southern Pacific Transportation Company. [12]

Another important trackage rights concession from the Union Pacific proceedings had been gained by SPTCo's Cotton Belt. This one gave the SSW the right to close the strategic gap between Kansas City and Saint Louis by using rails of the Missouri Pacific. The Cotton Belt, of course, already had its own line between those points through acquisition of the former Rock Island trackage. That route was poorly engineered, however, and in wretched physical condition. Indeed, Biaggini estimated that such rehabilitation would cost at least $100 million and add capacity in a corridor that already had a sufficiency. The Cotton Belt willingly agreed to service the industrial zones on either end of the former Rock Island line near Kansas City and Saint Louis, but after the UP-MoPac-WP merger occurred, the Cotton Belt initiated service across Missouri on January 7, 1983. Appropriately, the first train to take advantage of the shorter East Saint Louis–to–Los Angeles route (via the Missouri Pacific to Kansas City and Golden State Route to El Paso) was the famous *Blue Streak Merchandise*. [13]

None of this was satisfactory as far as the Santa Fe was concerned. Among other problems, the AT&SF took exception to Cotton Belt's use of the Missouri Pacific between Kansas City and Saint Louis because MoPac itself used Santa Fe trackage for five miles near Kansas City and it considered intrusion by Cotton Belt trains as "unlawful appropriation of Santa Fe properties." Through operations prevailed, nevertheless. The Cotton Belt and the Santa Fe had also skirmished earlier over the fate of Rock Island's Choctaw line along the thirty-fifth parallel linking Memphis with

Little Rock, Oklahoma City, Amarillo, and Tucumcari. That route offered advantages to both rivals and, of course, the SSW already used the easternmost 65 miles under trackage rights to reach Memphis from Brinkley, Arkansas. Purchase of the Choctaw from Amarillo to Memphis would give the Santa Fe access to important eastern connections, and acquisition of it by SP and SSW would give them an air-line route from Tucumcari. SP managers had urged acquisition of this line several years earlier, and it would have fallen to the SP had the abortive UP-CRI&P merger occurred; however, little serious consideration was given the Memphis-Tucumcari line by SP officers after the Rock Island went bankrupt. That hardly meant that SPTCo looked with favor on Santa Fe's interest. Indeed, there was great relief at One Market Plaza when AT&SF's John S. Reed announced that his company had decided to withdraw from consideration and when late in 1982 the SSW took possession following purchase of the segment from Brinkley east to Memphis.[14]

Other events surrounding Santa Fe Industries were of note to the rail industry at large and to the SP in particular. The first of these involved a change in management. John Reed, whose devotion to the railroad was well documented, retired in April, 1983, and was replaced by John J. Schmidt, whom many considered more interested in the holding company's other subsidiaries. Under Reed, the holding company had functioned more or less as an offshoot of the railroad, but Schmidt soon changed the management structure to make Santa Fe Industries "a true holding company." Nevertheless, Schmidt—whether he wished it or not—remained actively involved in railroad matters. On March 1, 1983, the Norfolk Southern (NS) announced that it had acquired 4.2 million shares, or 5 percent, of Santa Fe Industries' common stock. NS, itself a new creation springing from the merger of the Norfolk & Western and the Southern, stated that the purchase was for "investment purposes," but the implication was that NS

was projecting a truly transcontinental structure; it connected with the Santa Fe at Chicago, Peoria, and Kansas City. On the other hand, Santa Fe shortly made headlines of its own when on July 27, 1983, Schmidt reported that Santa Fe might seek to acquire government-owned Conrail, with which it connected in Illinois at Chicago, Peoria, and Streator and in Indiana at Logansport. A Santa Fe–Conrail combination would create an impressive transcontinental route and seemed logical on its face; Conrail was Santa Fe's most important connection with over one-third of its interchange volume. Whatever the result of this maneuvering, Santa Fe seemed destined to play a major role in the mega-merger movement.[15]

That process was predictably accelerated by passage of the Staggers Act, signed into law by President Carter on October 14, 1980, and by the antiregulatory mood of the ICC and the federal government at large. For many years, SP managers had argued for such even-handed federal regulation of transportation and in recent times Ben Biaggini had been among the industry's most outspoken advocates of deregulation. When the ICC removed regulations governing the carriage of fresh produce by rail—after a major push by SPTCo—the industry properly hailed it as a harbinger of even better times to come. True enough. The Staggers Act, although it stopped short of wholesale deregulation, nevertheless substantially eased the regulatory burden on the railroads, and it provided significant changes in rate-making procedures, legalized contract rates, established new cost-accounting principles, and streamlined abandonment and merger standards, among other things.[16]

None of this, however, was without difficulty. Like many of the nation's carriers, SPTCo was not adequately prepared for the new environment. As the chief executive of another carrier said, "it was strong for the principle of deregulation, but weak on the practice." Competition, especially for contract business, proved unexpectedly keen, and although SPTCo locked up several important agreements and although ton miles were increased, net profits deteriorated. Traffic managers for major shippers were bemused by the way SPTCo and others sorted through the new circumstance. One said, "If a railroad moves freight at a loss today, it is usually because it is deliberately implementing a short range strategy to capture traffic or because it is not yet used to competing in the market place." There were other problems. Single-line service, always desirable from the carriers' point of view, became even more so as a result of Staggers. Previously, the railroads had been protected from antitrust action in the process of making joint rates, but under deregulation they had reason to worry about prosecution by the Justice Department when they sought to negotiate rates on point-to-point shipments. The easiest way to avoid such legal difficulty was, of course, to own the track from origin to destination. Short of this, and in an attempt to force shippers to accept, as much as possible, single-carrier service, SPTCo and other large railroads closed traditional gateways and raised rates via others. Customers were justifiably nervous, and eventually the carriers modified their positions. Still, competition remained intense.[17]

Competition was not restricted to rail companies; most, in fact, was with other modes. The volume of intercity freight traffic transported by rail carriers had dropped from 74.9 percent in 1929 to a disappointing 35.8 percent in 1982, although the number of tons handled nearly doubled over the same years. Trucks, waterway operators, and pipelines had exacted devastating tolls on the railroads. The Staggers Act, of course, significantly reduced artificial restrictions on the inherent efficiency of steel-wheel-on-steel-rail transport, but modal competition was clearly not going to disappear simply because of progressive legislation. The American railroads had dieselized, purchased thousands of high-capacity cars, dumped their money-losing passenger service, and trimmed branches. Yet they remained an asset-rich, cash-poor, high labor–cost industry with clearly inadequate returns on investment. Other than gaining productivity-enhancement contracts from the railroad brotherhoods or reducing investment in property, the only immediate opportunity for improvement seemed to be further effort in the merger field.[18]

Speculation was rife. Rumors circulated that the Southern Pacific would acquire all or a part of the Illinois Central Gulf, that it would purchase the Denver & Rio Grande Western, that SP would merge with Burlington Northern, or that the CSX Corporation would purchase SP. Many observers freely predicted that the next major merger would create the country's first truly transcontinental road, but others agreed with Hayes T. Watkins of CSX, who saw no financial advantage to such an arrangement—"although that may eventually come." On the other hand, none doubted that combination of Union Pacific with the Missouri Pacific and Western Pacific had so improved Union Pacific's economy of scale that another round of mergers was inevitable. Security analysts uniformly agreed that SP's railroads especially had been hurt by "Mop Up"; indeed, many referred to the expanded Union Pacific as "an unstoppable monster." The Santa Fe, too, had been hurt by "Mop Up," and John Schmidt admitted late in 1982 that Santa Fe Industries was "taking a hard look" at merging the AT&SF with another railroad. He predicted early action on the matter. At SPTCo a comprehensive merger study undertaken for the company by an outside firm was completed in the same year. Biaggini, in a reflective mood, thought SPTCo was the victim of cruel irony since it had been a leader in the campaign for deregulation and had laid the groundwork for the mega-merger movement but, to date at least, had not benefited thereby. Its options, sadly, were now severely restricted. "We would not want to be the one left out in the West," said Robert D. Krebs. Biaggini was more direct. "We do have to find a permanent home for our railroad," he told those attending the annual stockholders meeting in 1983.[19]

While storms of merger rumors surrounded the industry during the first years of the 1980s, nature's storms and operating problems plagued SP's railroads. The winters of 1981–82 and 1982–83 brought awesome snowfalls to the Sierra; for the first time since record keeping began in 1878, Norden experienced over 600 inches of snow two years in succession. Moreover, the snowfall in 1982–83 was the second highest, with a total of 796 inches. Dealing with this required the service of spreaders, flangers, and even the rotaries; it also resulted in heavy expense. To the southwest, rainstorms early in 1983 knocked out both the Coast and San Joaquin lines for two weeks and forced massive and expensive rerouting of trains over competing lines. Unseasonable downpours that autumn also inflicted heavy damage on the main line and various branches in Arizona. The SPTCo's historic annual storm damage cost was approximately $5 million; in 1983 it was over $30 million.[20]

A perennial problem, but one that grew in scope and expense, was the Salt Lake fill. Company engineers had properly calculated a rate of consolidation (the rate at which the fill would compact over time under passing tonnage) that required constant applications of ballast and grooming by maintenance forces. These calculations were confused, however, as the wet cycle returned and as the lake rose. In 1983 and 1984 heavy snows followed by record rains resulted in run-offs that raised the lake to an alarming level. Since the lake lies in a natural basin devoid of usual outlets, only evaporation can reduce its level, but the summers proved relatively cool and less than normal evaporation occurred. The difficulties were then compounded by periodic high-velocity winds that whipped fearsome waves against the fill, causing serious erosion. Railroad forces responded by raising the track,

unloading riprap, and "sinking" hundreds of redundant boxcars to form a seawall along the fill. The cost was enormous, and even then the Overland Route was out of service with disappointing frequency.[21]

More devastating by far was the vicious economic storm that swept the country early in the decade. Indeed, the "Reagan Recession" of 1981–82 was by almost all standards the worst economic downturn since the Great Depression. As always, the country's railroads—which must provide transportation on demand and cannot warehouse their products—mirrored the fate of the general industrial economy. The management of SPTCo—perhaps recalling its counterproductive program of storing unserviceable locomotives and trimming expenditures during the recessions of the 1970s—bravely continued an active program of maintenance, repair, and rehabilitation, and Biaggini put on a happy face for the 1982 stockholders meeting. But all was not well. Just a few days later, SPTCo announced substantial force reductions and subsequently confirmed an early retirement plan for eligible personnel. Furthermore, senior officers were even obliged to deal with unfounded rumors that the company was "about to declare Chapter 11." Such rumors were predictable, however, given the depressingly long lines of idle locomotives and cars; eventually over 20 percent of SPTCo's locomotive fleet—including several recently rebuilt and other brand-new units—was stored along with more than 20,000 freight cars. Elsewhere within the holding company, Ticor's title insurance business suffered greatly as a consequence of the recession in the housing industry. There was, however, at least a small silver lining since SP's communication company, pipelines, land, and natural resource units maintained profitability. The holding company's profit for 1982 was $120.1 million, but SPTCo suffered staggering operating losses of $51.9 million.[22]

Southern Pacific's officers underestimated the length and depth of the recession, but as it began to ebb, Biaggini maintained that the company, "leaner and stronger" as a consequence, was on the threshold of a bright future. Not everybody agreed. Critics noted that SP in 1982 dropped to twelfth place among the nation's transportation companies (measured by operating revenues). For that matter, some securities analysts spoke darkly of SP as "the Penn Central of the West," and *Forbes*, which had given the company an unflattering assessment in 1979, wondered rhetorically three years later if SP was "doomed." When Standard & Poors Corporation lowered debt ratings on certain obligations of both SP and SPTCo, the worst seemed confirmed.[23]

The reasons for SP's unpleasant predicament were complex. Its pretax net stagnated during the 1970s because the company had failed to generate adequate cash flow from earnings and depreciation to finance the heavy capital spending programs for its diversification. Consequently, the SP had borrowed heavily; outstanding debt nearly doubled and interest charges nearly quadrupled. This, in part, reflected the plight of SP's railroads, which during the same decade had seen their market share drop disappointingly from 20 percent to only 13 percent. The problem for SPTCo was made all the more obvious by the recession of 1981–82 when its historic traffic base eroded badly because of reduced copper mining activity in Arizona, the severely depressed housing and real estate market, and the unanticipated shutdown in 1982 of General Motors plants at South Gate and Fremont (Melrose had closed earlier, leaving only Van Nuys in production). Unable to adequately reduce costs, SPTCo saw its train-hour expenses accelerate and its rate of return plummet.[24]

The chief executive obviously has impact on the company he heads by way of his relative capacity, values, and style; it was no less so with SP's Benjamin Biaggini. As a consequence, much of the criticism that SP received centered—rightly or wrongly—on Biaggini himself. Nobody doubted his leadership abil-

ity. He was characterized by one writer as "an imperial presence, a towering monolith of a man." Yet others called him "unyielding," "aloof," "rigid," and "uncompromising." Specifically at issue were Biaggini's unpredictable and explosive personality, his age (he was sixty-six in 1982), his salary ($699,200 in 1981), his unwillingness to decentralize authority, his active political involvement with wealthy conservative Republicans, and ultimately the very course he had set for SP.[25]

These issues or difficulties notwithstanding, those who thought Biaggini or the company he headed would roll over and play dead were naive in the extreme. For instance, Biaggini shrewdly announced a shift in management personnel that was of both material and symbolic importance. In mid-1982 Denman K. McNear, who had served as president of SPTCo since 1976, was promoted to chairman and chief executive officer of SP's railroads and replaced as president by Robert D. Krebs, who formerly served as vice-president of operations. McNear, fifty-six, had joined the SP in 1948 after earning a degree from the Massachusetts Institute of Technology and serving in the navy; Krebs, forty, graduated from Stanford and then took a master's degree from the Harvard Business School before accepting employment with the SP in 1966. No personnel changes were made at the holding company, where Alan C. Furth remained president. With the SP since his graduation from the University of California at Berkeley, Furth had headed the law department when he was named president of SPCo in 1979.[26]

Krebs set out to improve SPTCo's service, efficiency, safety record, and internal communications and to make SP's railroads more "commercially driven" enterprises. Indeed, said Krebs, "the commercial side of the house is where the game will be won or lost." In a sense, he was reflecting on the relative advantages of SP's competition, which he characterized this way: the Burlington Northern, "market oriented"; the Santa Fe, "able to

Denman K. McNear.

compete on price because it produces ton miles at lower costs"; the Union Pacific–Missouri Pacific, "less a bridge carrier and more an originating carrier"; and trucks, "the greatest enemy of all because they have streamlined to lower costs." For a variety of reasons, he noted, SPTCo found it harder to "control traffic." Moreover its customers and potential customers were increasingly sophisticated and now bathed in the luxury of a "buyer's market." The only product SP's railroads had to offer, Krebs insisted, was service—"rail freight transportation." Krebs understood that to survive in the era of deregulation SPTCo would need to emphasize a combination of service and pricing that would be aggressively marketed by its sales force. "We are going to put emphasis on our salesmen to help drive the company," Krebs promised. This included domestic opportunities as well as foreign, the latter promoted in conjunction with Southern Pacific International. Particular attention was accorded to SPTCo's international connections at Eagle Pass, El Paso, Nogales, and elsewhere in an attempt to accelerate business opportunities with neighboring Mexico.[27]

An obvious requirement for the successful implementation of SPTCo's "service and pricing" policy was power, equipment, and a physical property adequate to facilitate the free flow of traffic. New and nearly new locomotives had been stored during the recent recession and were gradually returned to service as the economy improved. Meanwhile, the Sacramento Locomotive Works continued to rehabilitate and improve heavy road units under a program that vastly extended the service life of locomotives at two-thirds the cost of new power. This allowed SPTCo to forgo acquisition of additional locomotives until 1984, when fifty units were authorized in an order split between General Motors and General Electric. It was much the same with SPTCo's car fleet. Except for "doublestack" container flats and an experimental fiberglass hopper car, little was done to expand the roster of rolling stock. Instead, the company gradually drew on its inventory of stored equipment and, in some cases, made important modifications. Much of this work was done at Roseville, California, where heavy car maintenance and rehabilitation were concentrated after the move from Sacramento in 1980. Interestingly, the Roseville facility, under contract from a leasing company, converted 1,400 outmoded multilevel automobile cars to intermodal flatcars; these were then leased back to SPTCo as intermodal business increased.[28]

Krebs pressed hard for increased systemwide track maintenance while rebuilding the Golden State Route. Work crews carried out a massive program that soon made SP-SSW a worthy competitor in the important Kansas City–Los Angeles corridor. Welded rail, ballast, ties, and upgraded signaling—including CTC between Herington and Topeka (83 miles)—allowed the St. Louis Southwestern to raise authorized speeds to 60 and 70 miles per hour. Moreover, after Armourdale Yard in

No new power was required until 1984, when an order was split between General Motors and General Electric. *Photograph by GM.*

Kansas City was renewed, track gangs turned to the business of bringing SPTCo's El Paso–Tucumcari line, which had been neglected as traffic there evaporated because of Rock Island's hardship, up to standards. The rewards were heartening. Early in 1985 the Cotton Belt routinely handled a half-dozen through manifest and TOFC trains plus grain drags and locals in and out of Kansas City each day. Veteran railroaders, many of them former Rock Island employees, understandably rejoiced as the Golden State Route rose phoenix-like to reclaim its former status as one of SP's "Great Routes West."[29]

Additional improvement programs had begun earlier and still others were under consideration. For example, extensive track and yard rehabilitation in the Gulf Coast area had commenced in 1979 and was accelerated in the years following. Small wonder. Despite the fact that 38 percent of system carloading came

from the Texas & Louisiana Lines, much of SPTCo's track in Texas and Louisiana had been in need of work. Happily, as general manager L. G. Simpson observed, all primary routes and Houston's massive Englewood Yard eventually received attention. It was of more than symbolic importance. As the recession of 1981–82 ended, Krebs announced that SPTCo would make "a real commitment to the future" by launching a three-year "new rail" program aggregating 900 miles. Krebs's view was echoed by D. M. Mohan, vice-president for maintenance: "We have made a firm commitment to the railroad business, and we are going to invest more in plant to be competitive for service-sensitive traffic." Numbers told the story. In 1976 SP had 2,650 miles of slow orders; by the end of 1983 the number was reduced to 1,100. At the end of the same year, 6,314 miles of SPTCo's main track had been laid with continuous welded

General Electric's contribution to the 1984 split order for new locomotive power is shown here by engine no. 7769. *Photograph by GE.*

rail, and Krebs proudly forecast that "all of the core routes" would be "in shape"—with good ties and rail—by the end of 1985. The railroads' communication net would also be "in shape." Their microwave communications system grew from 7,839 miles in 1976 to 8,672 in 1985.[30]

Krebs understood that all of this was necessary if SP's railroads were to compete for time-sensitive traffic such as auto parts, assembled automobiles, and TOFC/COFC. Although auto production in California had been curtailed by plant closures during the first part of the decade, the Golden State remained the country's premier auto market, and distribution patterns mirrored this fact. SP's railroads still hauled parts to the GM plant at Van Nuys and, with the temporary absence of other assembly capacity in California, a growing volume of set-up autos to that state from domestic manufacturers. Ironically, many rail

cars handling parts and autos from the east were reloaded at Benicia and Long Beach with foreign parts and foreign-built autos destined for interior assembly plants and distribution points. These included the products of Nissan, Honda, and Toyota, among others. Additional alterations in previous patterns further reflected this international flavor. General Motors automobiles assembled in Mexico began arriving by the trainload at Eagle Pass, Texas, for nationwide delivery during the autumn of 1984, and GM joined with Toyota in a promise to reopen the Fremont assembly plant.[31]

It was much the same with piggyback business, which not only moved in greater volume each year but also with increasing directional balance. The impressive national growth in TOFC/COFC quickened following deregulation, although TOFC profitability was further diminished by cutthroat competition. The

SP's articulated "doublestack" carried two forty-foot containers on each car.

Santa Fe—historically disadvantaged in California by comparison to SPTCo, which served the majority of the state's shippers by way of direct spots—effectively embraced piggyback to "raid" SPTCo territories far from its own rail lines. With an extensive inventory of conventional equipment and direct spot trackage, however, SPTCo became the disadvantaged carrier when customers chose flexibility and smaller shipments during the harsh recession of 1981–82. The SPTCo fought back, though, with new equipment, more facilities, and lower rates. As a result, its intermodal business rose by nearly 55 percent in 1982–83. In 1983 alone, piggyback contributed 18 percent of rail freight revenues; on the Tucson Division fully 50 percent of all crew starts were for such intermodal runs.[32]

Much of this traffic—and less exotic cargoes, too—moved via a growing number of "dedicated trains." Some were laden exclu-sively with American President Lines containers, others with paper products from the Crown Zellerbach Corporation, and others were unit trains of coal, aggregates, or grain. Some were named: *Salad Bowl Express* (Fresno/Salinas–Chicago), *Golden State Piggyback Express* (Oakland-Chicago), and *West Coast Super Pig* (Portland–Los Angeles). One, the *Texas Overnight Piggyback Express* (Houston–Dallas), featured a single locomotive trailing fifteen trailer flats and was operated by a two-man crew. Most were solely on SP's railroads, but some were run-through operations like that between Seattle and Los Angeles (with Burlington Northern) and Oakland and Saint Louis (with Denver & Rio Grande Western via Kansas City). Indeed, as relations with the Union Pacific soured, the Rio Grande became SPTCo's favored connection at Ogden—providing an integral link with Chicago (via Denver and the BN) and Kansas

The rehabilitation of the Golden State Route was impressive in the extreme. *Photograph by Jim Johnson for SSW.*

City–Saint Louis (via Herington, Kansas, or Kansas City and the SSW).[33]

Not to be forgotten in all of this was the operation of Amtrak passenger trains on certain of SPTCo's major routes. Its performance on behalf of Amtrak during the 1970s was lackluster at best and likely reflected the views of Biaggini, who said in 1970: "The long distance passenger business is dead, and we ought to give it a decent burial." Biaggini expected the federal government to come around to the same view in time. "It is just as wrong for the taxpayers of the United States to support a service that isn't needed as it is for the Southern Pacific," he maintained. Biaggini's views and those of other like-minded rail executives notwithstanding, Amtrak survived and even showed signs of vitality. SPTCo-Amtrak relations reached their nadir in 1979 when congestion on the Sunset Route frazzled the nerves of all concerned. Amtrak sued the SP

The results of the rehabilitation were impressive, too. *Photograph by Jim Johnson for SSW.*

In 1985, SPTCo's microwave system linked the general office with outlying points over an 8,672-mile network.

over delays to its *Sunset Limited*, and Krebs admitted that there was an unfavorable attitude toward the operation of passenger trains at One Market Plaza. Yet Krebs was not an ideologue. He was quick to point out that Amtrak provided SPTCo with regular and reliable income—a fact that was especially appealing during the "Reagan Recession." Moreover, Amtrak sweetened the pot by adding an incentive payment codicil to promote on-time performance. Because of these factors and because of SPTCo's improved maintenance, the on-time statistics improved from 75.4 percent in 1979 to 96 percent by mid-1982. For its part, Amtrak purchased new locomotives and new passenger cars of all types, and when the first run of the re-equipped *Sunset* passed through the tiny village of Liberty, Texas, one woman who enthusiastically greeted the trains each day released several balloons in ceremonial salute. Those aboard rejoiced at the spectacle. Perhaps they understood implicitly what the editor of *Ameri-*

can West wrote shortly thereafter: "There's just no substitute for seeing the country by train," for "rolling across the country on the train a sense of time, history, and heartland reveals itself in the constantly changing scene."[34]

Just as it sought to improve some properties, SPTCo's management simultaneously sought to rid itself of others. During the 1970s SP's railroads abandoned nearly 800 miles of line, but the process accelerated in the following decade when another 1,400 miles were dropped by mid-1984. This included about 140 miles abandoned on January 1, 1980, in South Texas, but service to the lower Rio Grande Valley was maintained by way of trackage rights over the Missouri Pacific from near Victoria to Harlingen. Another 200 miles was cut in East Texas, while in California the SP was able to drop the historic Altamont Pass line between Niles and Tracy when operating rights were secured over the nearby Western Pacific. At the same time, SPTCo management analyzed every one of the company's branches to determine current and potential profitability and then classified each as to retention and improvement, sale, or abandonment. Among those that SP hoped to sell were the Austin, Mina, and Lakeview branches in Texas, Nevada, Oregon, and California.[35]

The Northwestern Pacific presented another opportunity for sale or abandonment. It had a long record of providing more by way of scenery than net profit, a problem that stood in bold relief following a devastating fire that closed a long tunnel at Island Mountain, between Willits and Eureka, on September 6, 1978. SPTCo officers thereupon considered the prospect of abandoning nearly 65 miles of line from near Willits through the difficult Eel River Canyon while instituting rail-barge operations to serve the Eureka area. Business on the NWP and on the parent road was brisk at that time, however, and SPTCo decided to spend several million dollars to repair the tunnel. Meanwhile, ten locomotives and nearly 500 cars (including 386 loads) were stranded north of Island Mountain. Because of an acute

SP piggyback (TOFC) ad.

equipment shortage, SPTCo arranged a spectacular "over hill and dale" evacuation of several locomotives and a seaborne removal of rail cars while repair crews restored the tunnel. Trains again rumbled over the entire length of the NWP after several months, but the decision to reopen the line was questionable at best. Business dropped precipitously during the recession of 1981–82, but nature maintained its constant assault on the property with slides and washouts. Krebs announced the inevitable in April, 1983: The Northwestern Pacific would seek abandonment of the northern portion of its railroad. An emotional and often acrimonious debate followed, but in the end rail service to California's north coast was preserved late in 1984 when 162 miles of line above Willits was sold and turned over to operation by a new short line, the Eureka Southern Railroad.[36]

Krebs was confronted with numerous additional problems and opportunities. Many of these centered on SP's traditional patterns of management and style of doing business. The company's senior management had long embraced the "heroic boss" syndrome, and the company's internal procedures were clearly militaristic. Moreover, SPTCo's corporate culture still pledged allegiance to the past and continued to define the company as a "rail-

road" rather than a "customer-oriented transportation firm." Because he was youthful and not as yet entrapped by the "this-is-the-way-we-have-always-done-it" mentality, and because of his educational background, Krebs could promote substantive changes in the way SP's railroads conducted their business. In particular, he was in a position to modify the traditional product-orientation in favor of a marketing and sales approach, to ease the confrontational style of labor-management relations, and to improve SPTCo's image within its service area. None of this could be easily accomplished, however, since traditions and values transmitted from generation to generation can not be rewritten by decree. Krebs faced a tricky task.

The new president of SPTCo often complained that company officers tended to get so wrapped up in the railroad business that they forgot the customer. This problem was confirmed by a study commissioned by SPTCo that showed that shippers compared rail service unfavorably with trucks and that they similarly compared SPTCo's service unfavorably with that of its principal rail competitors. Changes clearly were required. Personnel shifts in marketing and sales included the appointment of an outsider to head the area, and Krebs himself increasingly made it a point to

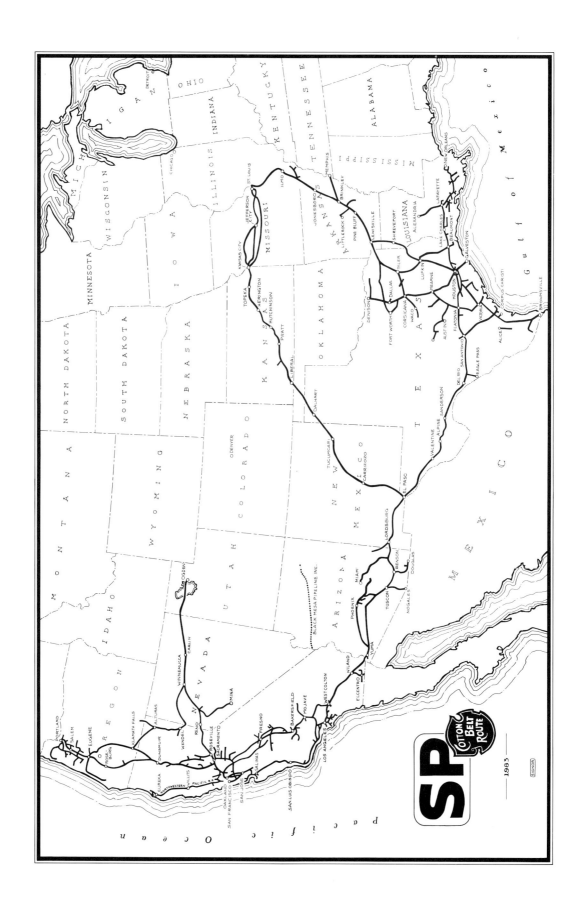

In 1984, 162 miles of NWP line above Willits was sold to the Eureka Southern, a new short-line railroad.

call on customers. SP's railroads also promised improved reliability on a dock-to-dock basis, reflecting Krebs's insistence that campaign verbiage—"the customer is king"—translate into reality.[37]

Problems in the relationship between management and labor were not unique to SP's railroads, but were as great there as on any American rail property. Ironically, the gulf between the two had widened even as the carriers agreed to higher wages, greater benefits, and better working conditions. Indeed, by 1983 average total earnings and fringe levels exceeded those paid to workers in all other transportation modes. During the year preceding, wage increases for the railroads aggregated 9.7 percent, but for the trucking industry only 2.6 percent. These mirrored earlier agreements such as that of 1975 which increased wages and benefits by 41 percent over three years. Figures for selected crafts

suggest the pattern. Clerks in 1923 were earning $4.83 a day; by 1950 their daily rate had risen to $14.97 and by 1980 it had skyrocketed to $64.05. Daily rates of pay showed a similar pattern for locomotive engineers, who in 1919 earned $7.28, in 1954, $14.08, and in 1980, $76.06. Track laborers in 1920 were paid $0.50 an hour; their daily wages in 1953 were $13.20 and in 1980 had risen to $64.16. During the era of regulation these increases could generally be passed on to customers, but that was not the case after passage of the Staggers Act. Furthermore, the striking growth in wages and benefits was not accompanied by simultaneous gains in productivity. In other words, the railroads generated more ton miles per train mile by way of more powerful locomotives, larger cars, and longer trains, but higher wages, improved benefits, and frequently counterproductive work rules negated any gain in net production. To be sure, technological advances and shifts in traffic routing left SPTCo in 1983 with approximately 2,500 redundant employees, costing the company more than $100 million annually.[38]

As the 1980s unfolded, most rail managers saw the situation clearly: Without a more productive labor force, the rails were doomed to play a reduced role in serving the country's transportation needs. This was especially true for SPTCo—surrounded as it was with larger and stronger rail carriers that could deliver freight at lower cost, menaced by an aggressive trucking industry, and faced with a drastically altered traffic base. Urged on by W. J. Lacy, vice-president–transportation, R. D. Bredenberg, general manager, and others, Krebs set out to improve employee communications and morale, to further stress safety, and to otherwise gain the trust of workers by acknowledging the importance of every employee in a team effort necessary to survive and prosper. To this end, Krebs and other senior officers held a series of productive "no holds barred" discussions with employees around the system, funded a variety of internal communications projects including division newsletters and magazines, and pushed forward with employee physical rehabilitation and drug-dependency assistance programs. Most impressive in terms of departing from previous wisdom was SPTCo's "Transportation Problem Solving" program, which centered on employees' interacting with management to find ways of making SP's railroads more competitive. The idea was not without its detractors among management and labor officers alike, but the energetic conviction of both Lacy and Bredenberg that SPTCo was "committed to finding a way by which employees can help run the railroad" eventually carried the day. "TPS" thus became a provocative, but productive, means of changing hidebound traditions by involving more and more of the railroad family in decisions of common importance.[39]

The one problem that seemed to defy re-

habilitation was SP's public image. Even before Frank Norris visited "the Octopus" epithet at its doorstep early in this century, the company labored against adverse and incorrect impressions of its purposes and actions. These sadly became integral parts of western folklore, to be repeated by succeeding generations of writers and others who invented history to satisfy strangely perverse needs. This was especially the case in California, where many insistently recalled Norris's work as valid historical gospel instead of memorable, if muckraking, fiction. Not all, of course, succumbed to this mythology. The *Los Angeles Express* in 1915 had noted that the service of the SP made "all of its agents ministers to our welfare." A few months later another California newspaper similarly had noted the symbiotic relationship between the carrier and its service area: "More power to the Southern Pacific Company and may its earnings increase, for its prosperity spells prosperity for the workingman and its deficit spells poverty," intoned the *Yolo Independent*. Respected University of California professor Stuart Daggett early in the 1920s similarly viewed the SP as a powerful machine for the promotion of industry and commerce on the Pacific Coast and further observed that public opinion in the Golden State was generally well disposed toward the SP, in part because of "the efficiency of its technical staff" and in part because of "the excellence of its service compared to other roads." Yet such praise seemed to matter little. Even in the 1980s, those who found themselves in disagreement with the SP invoked *The Octopus* and employed terms and phrases like those Norris used in his novel: "the mighty Southern Pacific," or "corporate leviathan," the "arrogant, greedy and thoughtless railroad," managed by "modern-day 'robber barons' . . . [whose attitude] . . . is 'the public be damned.'"[40]

The task of rebuttal was clearly difficult, but SP's response was often impressive in scope as well as imagination. Its railroads gave considerable support to the California State Railroad Museum at Sacramento and, to help celebrate the nation's bicentennial, assisted in operation of the *Freedom Train*, headed by former SP steam locomotive 4449, a GS-type donated to the city of Portland during the late 1950s. This handsome locomotive also drew the resplendent *Louisiana World's Fair Daylight* from Portland to New Orleans and back in 1984. Several hundred persons rode the sparkling, steam-powered train that was seen by thousands more. It had a wondrously unifying effect on all races and ages; every face turned to and lit up with an expression of appreciation and awe. As a result, SP's managers were forcefully reminded that Americans have always had a love affair with trains, if not always with the railroad companies that operate them. On another front, the Southern Pacific Company served as one of the official sponsors for the 1984 Olympic Games held in Los Angeles. It was historically appropriate, since the SP had similarly supported the 1932 Olympics, also held in the City of Angels. Finally, early in the summer of 1983 SPCo launched an impressive advertising campaign on national television and in the print media to create a greater public awareness of its diversified nature.[41]

The first subsidiary thus showcased was Southern Pacific Pipe Line, a stellar performer in any season. SPPL had gradually expanded its capacity with larger diameter pipe, additional pumping equipment, and new gathering lines. A major new artery between the Bay Area and Fresno along a SPTCo right-of-way entered service in 1984, bringing SPPL's petroleum product mileage to 2,668. Barrel miles rose from 23.8 billion in 1974 to 33.4 billion in 1984, but the cost of delivering product remained amazingly low—only 2¢ per gallon between Los Angeles and Phoenix, and 2.2¢ per gallon between the Bay Area and Reno. It was much the same for Black Mesa Pipeline, SPPL's coal slurry operation, which in 1983 alone moved a record 4.8 million tons of coal with 99 percent reliability. All of this brought a smile to the face of W. Theo Eskew, president of SPPL, who pointed to an enviable operating ratio of 53 cents to the dollar and a dramatic increase in income from operations—$53.4 million in 1984 compared with $19.0 million a decade earlier.[42]

The Southern Pacific Land Company represented another glittering jewel in the corporate crown. Its activities ranged from ethanol production and geothermal power to the development of mineral-bearing properties, industrial parks, agricultural lands, and other physical assets. The land company's most spectacular venture, however, was its proposal for the redevelopment of former rail properties in the China Basin area of San Francisco. Plans for "Mission Bay" called for a dramatic "city within a city"—a balanced mix of shops, offices, residential complexes, light industries, parks, and open spaces across nearly two hundred acres. As such, the venture represented one of the nation's largest privately funded urban development packages. Aggressive management paid off as the land company's income from operations jumped from $62.4 million in 1980 to $79 million in 1982.[43]

Another steady performer was Bankers Leasing Corporation, which, noted the SP, had one of the industry's most consistent records of profitability. Income before taxes increased from $10 million in 1980 to $21.1 million in 1982 and nearly tripled between 1978 and 1982. This represented, Bankers Leasing managers liked to point out, a profit of nearly $600,000 per employee. Small wonder that Bankers Leasing proudly anticipated an even rosier future.[44]

The same mood did not prevail at Pacific Motor Trucking and SPTCo's other regional trucking affiliates. By 1971 they collectively served shippers along 27,000 miles of highway routes and represented the nation's second-largest common carrier truck line (measured by intercity tonnage handled) as well as the country's largest railroad-owned truck subsidiary. PMT and the others had been established years before as handmaidens of SP's railroads, but ownership of them by those

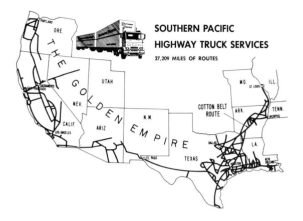

By 1971, PMT and SPTCo's regional affiliates formed a massive route structure in the West. But all was not well with the operation.

railroads resulted in severe government regulation that inhibited efficiency and reduced competitive capacity. Gross revenues in 1970 exceeded $100 million, although net was a mere $2.7 million. Future profits were even more elusive, as PMT and the others struggled under the burdens of regulation, inadequate rate increases, more costly fuel, expensive Teamster contracts, restrictive work rules, balkanized operations, the closing of GM auto-assembly plants in California and, finally if ironically, partial deregulation of the trucking industry. The ICC eventually eased restrictions so that PMT was finally able to interconnect its Oregon and Northern California routes with others serving Nevada, on the one hand, and Southern California and El Paso, on the other. Yet to come, strange to say, was permission to meld PMT operations with those of the Southern Pacific Transport Company of Texas and Louisiana and the Cotton Belt's Southwestern Transportation Company. That came on December 31, 1981, but by then PMT, the surviving entity, was awash in red ink.[45]

The task of restoring PMT to profitability fell to Alan D. DeMoss, who in 1981 left SPTCo to head the ailing subsidiary. DeMoss's chore was not enviable; PMT sustained losses of $39.8 million for the years 1981–82. During 1982, however, PMT was reorganized; its work force was eventually pared to under 2,000, excess equipment was sold off, and in 1984 its large and historic less-than-truckload

branch was eliminated. At the same time, Pacific Motor Transport—a dormant subsidiary of SPTCo—was reactivated as an essentially nonunion company. Problems remained, though, as DeMoss sought profitability for PMT in the era of deregulation. Especially troublesome was PMT's "long tail of employee liability"—workman's compensation, pensions, health protection, early retirement obligations—which had to be met from operating income. Nevertheless, DeMoss happily reported a net of $3.5 million for 1984 and predicted further progress in the year following.[46]

The case of the Pacific Fruit Express Company was similar. After the split-off in 1978, PFE's management quickly reduced system facilities and centralized repair at Tucson. Profitability, absent for much of the 1970s, returned in 1979 and aggregated $33.5 million over five years. Problems persisted, however, since cyclical loadings resulted in excess capacity for PFE during more than half of each

PMT's president, A. D. DeMoss, stands beside a shiny new addition to that operation.

year and finding return loads for its mechanical refrigerator cars was always difficult. Furthermore, despite deregulation, the company found it difficult to match the advantages of flexibility offered by over-the-road truckers. This was reflected ultimately in PFE's ledger books. It suffered a small net loss in 1984 and, in the year following, PFE's management determined to further reduce equipment and personnel. The policy, in fact, represented a desperate effort by this historic subsidiary to survive. The prospects were dim.[47]

The mood at Southern Pacific Communications Company, largest of SP's nontransportation subsidiaries, was predictably more upbeat. By the end of 1980 SPCC was handling 60,000 long-distance calls per day, was expanding its microwave operations, and was planning a network of communications satellites; SPRINT was coming of age. In 1981 its 200,000 customers enjoyed rates that were 20 to 50 percent lower than those offered by the American Telephone and Telegraph Company; the prospect of further growth was bright.

Moreover, SPCC and similarly oriented firms scored major gains against AT&T in 1982 as the consequence of antitrust litigation that resulted in the eventual breakup of that huge complex. SPCC's customer base in 1982 jumped to 900,000 in forty-five states. Profits reflected this, escalating from a pretax loss of $23.4 million in 1980 (due in part to unauthorized use of the system) to a pretax income of $19.3 million in 1981 and an impressive $73.1 million in 1982.[48]

Biaggini was understandably pleased. "In 10 years, the communications company will be bigger than the railroad in terms of investment, sales and profits," he told shareholders. To maintain this impressive growth, however, would require massive infusions of capital—a commodity required in similar volume by SP's railroads. This posed a dilemma, since SP's debt structure was already a matter of concern, and income from operations was not likely to provide requisite capital for the voracious appetites of the company's two largest entities. At the same time, changes resulting from court orders requiring AT&T to divest itself of local operating subsidiaries posed problems of another type for that company's major competitors, especially General Telephone & Electronic Corporation, AT&T's nearest rival. Given the respective needs of SP and GTE, few were surprised on October 1, 1982, when Biaggini announced that the board of directors had agreed to sell Southern Pacific Communications Company and some of its own subsidiaries to GTE. The price: approximately $740.5 million in cash plus SPCC's outstanding debt of $318 million. The arrangement, when completed on June 15, 1983, provided important fleshing-out for GTE and gave it immediate entry into the intercity telecommunications industry through acquisition of SPRINT's long-distance transmission facilities.[49]

There was similar news from Los Angeles-based Ticor, another wholly owned subsidiary of the Southern Pacific Company. One of the nation's leading sources of title insurance, mortgage insurance, and financial printing services, Ticor was hard hit by the recession of the early 1980s. It had pretax earnings of $39.1 million in 1979 but had only $53.0 million of pretax income during the three-year period from 1980 through 1982. Prospects for improvement hinged on recovery of the national economy, especially the real estate market, but that segment remained disappointingly sluggish. This was a disappointment for Biaggini and deprived the SP of much-needed profits. Relief came on February 1, 1984, however, when SP completed the sale of Ticor—less one subsidiary, Constellation Reinsurance Company—to the new TC Holding Corporation, which arranged a leveraged buyout. The price was $271.3 million, or $10.8 million above what SP paid for it.[50]

The sale of both the communications company and Ticor obviously changed the very fabric of the company. SP's railroads were again the corporate centerpiece, and proceeds from the sale of the two subsidiaries benefited the treasury by over $1 billion. Furthermore, the dramatic growth in capital expenditures for the communications company and the relative decrease in the amount available for the railroads was obviated by the sale of SPCC. It augured well for SPTCo and, in the view of most outside analysts, for the holding company as well. Biaggini considered that the SP now was "leaner and stronger" and ready for a "new future." Dividends held steady at $2.60 per share from 1980 through 1982, and SP's stock split two-for-one in 1983. This good news spurred many brokers to signal "buy orders" to clients while simultaneously speculating on the destiny of the Southern Pacific Company.[51]

What *was* its future? Speculation was rampant within the company and without. Meanwhile, Robert Krebs charted a course for SPTCo that took a dry-eyed view of its competitive circumstance and that promised an upgraded property as well as improved service and operating efficiency. Additionally, Krebs insisted that SPTCo concentrate its efforts on single-line and interline corridors where it could best compete. These included: (1) Los Angeles to Kansas City, Saint Louis, and Chicago; (2) Los Angeles to Houston, Memphis, and New Orleans; (3) Oakland to Kansas City, Saint Louis, and Chicago; (4) Portland to Oakland and Los Angeles; (5) Houston to Memphis and Saint Louis. He likewise targeted TOFC, grain, timber products, chemicals and petroleum, and coal for increased marketing and sales promotion. This implied that the Southern Pacific would attempt to go it alone. Some observers, however, thought that these plans were mere posturing and speculated that Biaggini would soon attempt to sell all of SP's rail assets and point the company in a new direction. Others argued that it would be impossible to find a buyer willing to pay book value for these rail properties. Most concluded that Biaggini would use some of the monies gained from the sale of SPCC and Ticor to improve the holding company's balance sheet and then seek logical acquisition in the rail field—perhaps the Rio Grande or the Illinois Central Gulf. A few mentioned SP as an integral element in some gigantic combination; active rumors linked SP with CSX, for example. There remained yet another option, one considered earlier: a combination of the Southern Pacific Company with Santa Fe Industries.[52]

CHAPTER 19

Denouement?

"The new company will combine basic transportation, natural resources, real estate and financial services, offering shareholders a broader-based enterprise and affording customers, employees and the communities we serve greater opportunities than either company might be expected to achieve alone."—Southern Pacific press release, 1983

THOSE who arrived for work early at the general office building in San Francisco on Monday, September 27, 1983, were greeted by astonishing news: trading of Southern Pacific Company stock on the New York Exchange had been temporarily halted. What did it mean? Soon another bit of information floated from floor to floor: trading of Santa Fe Industries stock similarly had been stopped. The implication was that the SP and Santa Fe would try another hand at the merger table; confirmation followed with joint announcements later in the day. Throughout the building and, indeed, across the breadth of the sprawling Southern Pacific property there were mixed feelings among all hands, who immediately desired knowledge of the details. Biaggini promised a face-to-face meeting with SP's San Francisco officers and a press conference on the morrow.[1]

The chairman's message for those who gathered in the galleria of the building was both upbeat and reassuring. A "business combination" of SPCo and Santa Fe Industries for the purpose of creating a new holding company—Santa Fe Southern Pacific Corporation—would bring together "complementary" properties and most importantly, he promised, "a merger of equals." The combined railroads,

for instance, would "utilize the most efficient routes between commercial centers" and "would be strong enough to compete with trucks." This would not require massive abandonment of lines and yards, Biaggini predicted. Much had changed since the earlier discussions with the Santa Fe in 1980, he noted, and now the two companies were motivated by a sense of urgency. The Southern Pacific and the Santa Fe were stronger in 1983 than they had been three years earlier, Biaggini thought, but competitive pressures flowing from Union Pacific's merger with the Missouri Pacific and additional acquisition of the Western Pacific were overpowering factors for both. Biaggini and Santa Fe's new chairman, John J. Schmidt, had held passing conversations earlier, but formal merger discussions did not begin until September 1; the two had come to an agreement on the twenty-fourth. It is necessary to "seize the opportunity when it comes along," Biaggini declared.[2]

The proposed combination represented a very impressive $5.2 billion plan that would create, among other things, a 25,000-mile railroad—third in size behind Burlington Northern and CSX Corporation. Each share of SP's common stock would be exchanged for 1.543 shares of common stock in the new

Officers of the Santa Fe Southern Pacific Company, announced December 23, 1983.

company; shares of Santa Fe Industries would be exchanged on a ratio of 1.203 for 1. Officers of the Santa Fe Southern Pacific Corporation would be John J. Schmidt (SFI), chairman and chief executive officer; Robert D. Krebs (SP), president and chief operating officer; W. John Schwartz (SFI), vice-chairman; and, Alan C. Furth (SP), vice-chairman. Biaggini would retire once the merger of the holding companies occurred; merger of the railroads would require permission from the Interstate Commerce Commission and thus would take longer to accomplish.[3]

As it developed, the combination of the Southern Pacific and the Santa Fe Industries took place "at the close of business" on December 23, 1983. The new Santa Fe Southern Pacific Corporation, shareholders were told, derived from "two strong compatible companies, rich in resources and rooted in the nation's history, with sound strategies for a dynamic future together." In a time of massive industrial mergers it proved to be what *Fortune* called "the biggest deal of all" for 1983.[4]

Meanwhile, the Southern Pacific Transportation Company found itself in a peculiarly awkward state. Its common stock was placed in an independent voting trust when the Southern Pacific Company, SPTCo's parent, became part of the Santa Fe Southern Pacific Corporation. At the same time, the parent gave SPTCo

$150 million to cover contingencies during the period prior to merger of the railroads—a pittance, some at SPTCo thought, since most of the parent's resources once had been those of its railroads. Simply stated, during the period of trusteeship SPTCo would "stand alone without the support of the parent," as SPTCo chairman Denman K. McNear put it, or, as controller Eric L. Johnson said, SPTCo on its own had to "generate funds adequate to provide service and maintain capital programs." A positive cash flow was essential; there would be no "sugar daddy" on which to lean. At the same time, SPTCo needed to prepare for merger with the AT&SF while, under penalty of law, it was obligated to compete earnestly with its potential partner.[5]

Documents weighing no less than forty-one pounds were filed with the Interstate Commerce Commission on March 22, 1984. What the Santa Fe Southern Pacific (SFSP) Corporation sought was authority to control the Southern Pacific Transportation Company and its subsidiaries through merger of SPTCo and AT&SF into a new, wholly owned subsidiary of SFSP—the Southern Pacific & Santa Fe Railway. Immediately prior to that merger, if approved, the St. Louis Southwestern Railway would be merged into SPTCo. In addition, SFSP sought authority to acquire control of Pacific Motor Trucking and SPTCo's other trucking arms. Under revised regulatory law, the ICC was obliged to render a decision by early autumn of 1986.[6]

After some initial hesitation, investors came to look generally with favor on SFSP. Many saw it as did Dean Witter Reynolds, which admired SFSP's enormous assets, low long-term debt, and amazing potential that could be exploited by "management drive and initiative." Dean Witter called Santa Fe Southern Pacific "a sleeping giant."[7]

Others viewed it similarly—but in a negative context. The Union Pacific Corporation, for instance, noted that the proposed Southern Pacific & Santa Fe would operate 90 percent of all Class One rail lines in New Mexico and 100 percent in Arizona, and that it would account for 90.1 percent of all rail tonnage originating in California and 78.7 percent terminating there. This, said the UP, would be "seriously anti-competitive unless the ICC imposes conditions to preserve competition." Several state and local governments favored the merger, but only with conditions of the type suggested by the UP. Not surprisingly, then, several railroads asked for concessions if the ICC agreed to merge SPTCo and AT&SF. These included the Union Pacific (nearly 2,000 miles of trackage rights from El Paso to Southern California and into the San Joaquin Valley); the Denver & Rio Grande Western (purchase of SPTCo's Overland Route from Ogden to Roseville, purchase of the Modoc Route to Klamath Falls, and various trackage rights in Oregon and California); the Kansas City Southern (trackage rights and acquisitions in Texas and Louisiana and single-line rate-making authority); and the Missouri-Kansas-Texas (extensive trackage rights over the SPTCo and Cotton Belt in Texas and Kansas).[8]

All of this brought an irate response from John J. Schmidt. Given the recent history of the ICC in approving mergers, e.g., the Northern Lines (1970), Burlington Northern–Frisco (1980), and Union Pacific–Missouri Pacific–Western Pacific (1982), there could be little doubt that the SPTCo-AT&SF application would be granted. On the other hand, the UP-MoPac-WP decision had carried with it important concessions granting right of entry to Kansas City by the D&RGW and use of MoPac's track between Kansas City and Saint Louis by the Cotton Belt. This suggested that corollary concessions in the Santa Fe Southern Pacific case might be anticipated, but Schmidt described the collective demands by Union Pacific, Denver & Rio Grande Western, Kansas City Southern, and Katy as "opportunistic and unwarranted." They were, in fact, "unacceptable" and threatened to undermine the entire application. Schmidt was emphatic that burdening the merger with the excessive conditions would result in the holding com-

As SPTCo's traditional sources of traffic eroded, gains were made in intermodal sales. But even these were soft at mid-decade, and margins were extremely thin.

pany's jettisoning either one or both of the rail lines. That was a serious matter, since few observers thought either SPTCo or AT&SF could survive alone in the harsh competitive environment of the late 1980s.[9]

Indeed, the initial experience of the Southern Pacific Transportation Company under the independent voting trust seemed to demonstrate that likelihood. In 1984 SPTCo handled more carloads than in either of the two years preceding, and its operating income reached $51.2 million but its operating ratio remained dangerously high—98.1. Adequate productivity, alas, was elusive. Moreover, SPTCo's traditional traffic base—forest products, auto parts and assembled autos, copper, and agricultural commodities—continued to erode and remained under competitive attack. Even TOFC loadings soon dropped off. Consequently, during the first quarter of 1985 SPTCo suffered a disappointing operating loss of $26.3 million. Cost-reduction programs were instituted but, in many cases, these hindered SPTCo's ability to maintain service levels adequate to hold or attract new business. It was, in a phrase of the time, a "Catch-22."[10]

When Lord Cornwallis found it necessary to surrender to George Washington at Yorktown on October 19, 1781, his regimental

These intermodal transports are loading at SP's Golden Pig TOFC facility.

band chose to play what it considered an appropriate tune: "The World Turned Upside Down." For Cornwallis and his troops—and, indeed, for the entire British empire—defeat by the colonial rebels reflected a world run amok. It was much the same for the Southern Pacific and those who directed its affairs or worked for that company in the 1980s. "How strange that a long-haul, Sunbelt, land-holding, Harriman-oriented colossus could be acting as caboose instead of locomotive in the final season of merger maneuverings!" opined David P. Morgan in *Trains* for December, 1984. "Nobody," he suggested, "buys Espee; Espee buys other railroads." Morgan was reflecting on SP's historically strong position in the industry as well as the reality of its situation 115 years after the celebration at Promontory. Biaggini had pledged and Schmidt

had affirmed that merger of the Southern Pacific Company and the Santa Fe Industries would be a "combination of equals," but as the merger took its course, few doubted a new reality: the Santa Fe was "more equal" than the SP and would be the dominant partner. The ghosts of Collis P. Huntington, Edward H. Harriman, and Julius Kruttschnitt must have recoiled at the idea; the world was truly upside down. Among those of SP persuasion there was a pervasive feeling of anxiety mirroring astonishment that the sun might, in truth, set on the Southern Pacific.[11]

Indeed, the Southern Pacific may very well pass from the scene. If it happens that way, the enormity of the void will be astonishing not just because of its size and the fact that it has been a part of the national landscape so long, but because it has had such a dramatically

If merger is approved, the Southern Pacific will live on—in bold new dress.

positive influence on American transportation history and on its far-flung service area. Over SP's long and colorful life, it has made money for its owners; has given direct employment to tens of thousands and indirect employment to many thousands more; paid millions of dollars in local, state, and federal taxes; and has served the manifold needs of countless patrons. Moreover, since the inception of the first predecessor more than a century and a quarter ago, SP's railroads have done as much as any carrier in furthering the American

westering process—a national goal of great dimension, it should be remembered. So the ghosts of Huntington, Harriman, and Kruttschnitt can be at rest—easily at rest, for the Southern Pacific enterprise has been a significant, exciting, and productive adventure. Moreover, should the merger of the SP and Santa Fe rail units be executed, as anticipated, SP's railroads will join the holding company they birthed and live on as a part of the Santa Fe Southern Pacific Corporation—in bold new dress.

Notes

CHAPTER ONE

1. Lucius Beebe, "Pandemonium at Promontory, *American Heritage* 9 (Feb., 1958): 20–23. On the first transcontinental rail line, see: Charles Edgar Ames, *Pioneering the Union Pacific: A Reappraisal of Building the Railroad*; William Francis Bailey, *The Story of the First Trans-Continental Railroads*; Barry B. Combs, *Westward to Promontory*; Everett L. Cooley, ed., "The Last Spike Is Driven," *Utah Historical Quarterly* 37 (Winter, 1969); Grenville M. Dodge, *How We Built the Union Pacific Railway and Other Railway Papers and Addresses by Grenville M. Dodge*; John Debo Galloway, *The First Transcontinental Railroad: The Central Pacific and Union Pacific, 1863–1869*; Wesley S. Griswold, *A Work of Giants: Building the First Transcontinental Railroad*; Garry Hogg, *Union Pacific: The Building of the First Transcontinental Railroad*; Robert West Howard, *The Great Iron Trail: The Story of the First Transcontinental Railroad*; Enid Johnson, *Rails across the Continent: The Story of the First Transcontinental Railroad*; George Kraus, *High Road to Promontory: Building the Central Pacific across the High Sierras*; Leonard O. Levi and Jack T. Johnson, *A Railroad to the Sea*; James McCague, *Moguls and Iron Men: The Story of the First Transcontinental Railroad*; David E. Miller, ed., *The Golden Spike*; Joseph Nichols, *History of the Construction of the Union Pacific Railway & Company*; E. L. Sabin, *Building the Pacific Railway*; and David F. Myrick, *Railroads of Nevada and Eastern California*, 2 vols.

2. R. S. Cotterill, "Early Agitations for a Pacific Railroad," *Missouri Valley Historical Review* 5 (March, 1919): 396–414; M. L. Brown, "Asa Whitney and His Pacific Railroad Publicity Campaign," *Mississippi Valley Historical Review* 20 (Sept., 1933): 209–24; William H. Goetzmann, *Army Exploration in the West, 1803–1863*.

3. On the Big Four and Theodore D. Judah, see: Helen Hinckley Jones, *Rails from the West: A Biography of Theodore D. Judah*; Oscar Lewis, *The Big Four: The Story of Huntington, Stanford, Hopkins, and Crocker, and the Building of the Central Pacific*; G. T. Clark, *Leland Stanford*; Cerinda W. Evans, *Collis Potter Huntington*, 2 vols.; Estelle Latta, *Controversial Mark Hopkins: The Great Swindle of American History*; David Lavender, *The Great Persuader*; Benjamin P. Redding, *A Sketch of the Life of Mark Hopkins of California*; Norman E. Totorow, *Leland Stanford: Man of Many Careers*; and Stuart Bruchey, ed., *Memoir of Three Railroad Pioneers*.

4. *Corporate History . . . as of December 31, 1962*, B-1, p. 1. On California railroads in general, see Ward McAfee, *California's Railroad Era, 1850–1911*.

5. *Corporate History*, C-2, pp. 3–4; Neill C. Wilson and Frank J. Taylor, *Southern Pacific: The Roaring Story of a Fighting Railroad*, pp. 47–48.

6. Southern Pacific (SP), Division Maps, Southern Pacific Company Lines as of June 30, 1916, San Francisco; David F. Myrick, *New Mexico's Railroads: An Historical Survey*, p. 59.

7. S. G. Reed, *A History of the Texas Railroads and of Transportation Conditions under Spain and Mexico and the Republic and the State*, p. 197.

8. Ibid., pp. 53–65.

9. SP, Division Maps, . . . as of June 30, 1916; Wilson and Taylor, p. 78.

10. H. M. Mayo, *History of the Southern Pacific Lines in Texas*, p. 3.

11. SP, Division Maps, . . . as of June 30, 1916.

12. SP, *Historical Memoranda*, I: "Formation of Southern Pacific System," p. 5, "Capital Stock," pp. 1–2, "SP Control of CP," pp. 1–5; Lavender, pp. 374–75; SP, Annual Reports, 1899, p. 13; 1900, p. 6, 1908, p. 28.

13. Evans, II, 509–12; *Louisville Courier-Journal*, March 9, 1882; *Railway World*, Dec. 23, 1893, p. 1201; SP, *Historical Memoranda*, I: "Formation of the SP System," pp. 5–6.

14. Richard J. Orsi, "The Octopus Reconsidered: The Southern Pacific and Agricultural Modernization in California, 1865–1915," *California Historical Quarterly* 54 (Fall, 1975): 196–220; W. H. Hutchinson, "Southern Pacific: Myth and Reality," *California Historical Society Quarterly* 48 (Dec., 1969): 325–34.

15. Kraus, pp. 294–97.

CHAPTER TWO

1. Burton J. Hendrick, "The Passing of a Great Railroad Dynasty," *McClure's* 38 (March, 1912): 656–59; George Kennan, *E. H. Harriman: A Biography*, 1:233–39; H. J. Eckenrode and Pocahontas Wright Edmunds, *E. H. Harriman: The Little Giant of Wall Street*, pp. 59–61; John F. Hippen, "A Wall Street Man and Western Railroad: A Chapter in Railroad Administration," *Bulletin of the Business Historical Society* 23 (Sept., 1949): 117–20.

2. Kennan, 238–39; Bernard M. Baruch, *Baruch: My Own Story*, p. 139; *Railway Age Gazette* 52 (Feb., 9, 1912): 237; Hippen, pp. 121–22; C. M. Keys, "Harriman II: The Building of His Empire," *World's Work* 13 (Feb., 1907): 8548–52; Interstate Commerce Commission, *Reports*, vol. 12, "Consolidations and Combinations of Carriers," pp. 281–82; Jacob Schiff, Feb. 4, 1901, to James J. Hill, James J. Hill Reference Library, Saint Paul.

3. Stuart Daggett, *Chapters on the Southern Pacific*, p. 456; Hendrick, p. 641; Albro Martin, *Enterprise Denied: Origins of the Decline of American Railroads, 1897–1917* (New York:

Columbia University Press, 1971), p. 90; Eckenrode and Edmunds, *Harriman*, p. 223; John Moody, *The Railroad Builders: A Chronicle of the Welding of the States*, p. 193.

4. Kennan, 1: 5, 12, 15, 60, 61.

5. Ibid., p. 71.

6. Frank H. Spearman, "Building Up a Great Railway System," *Outlook*, Feb. 27, 1909, p. 436; Grenville M. Dodge, *How We Built the Union Pacific and Other Railway Papers and Addresses*, pp. 78–79; Spearman, p. 435; C. M. Keys, "Harriman IV: Salvage of the Two Pacifics," *World's Work* 13 (April, 1907): 8791; Kennan, 1: 119, 124–25; Harriman, quoted in Martin, p. 370.

7. Kennan, 1: 119, 124–25; Dodge, p. 78; Charles E. Perkins, Aug. 8, 1893, to James J. Hill, James J. Hill Reference Library, Saint Paul.

8. Kennan, 1: 120–38, 151–64, Otto H. Kahn, "Edward Henry Harriman," *Memoirs of Three Railroad Pioneers*, ed. Stuart Bruchey (New York: Arno Press, 1981), pp. 10–11; Keys, "Harriman IV," 8795; Kennan, 1: 121.

9. Robert G. Athearn, *Rebel of the Rockies: A History of the Denver & Rio Grande Western Railroad* (New Haven: Yale University Press, 1962), pp. 122–24; Julius Grodinsky, *Jay Gould: His Business Career, 1867–1892*, p. 555; Memorandum of Agreement . . . Union Pacific Railway . . . and Southern Pacific Company (April 12, 1890), Executive Department box 35; ICC, "Consolidations and Combinations," pp. 281–82.

10. Robert G. Athearn, *Union Pacific Country*, pp. 268–72, 281, 315, 350; David F. Myrick, *Railroads of Nevada and Eastern California*, 1: 72.

11. O. Meredith Wilson, *The Denver and Rio Grande Project, 1870–1901: A History of the First Thirty Years of the Denver & Rio Grande Railroad*, pp. 63, 70, 71, 75, 76.

12. Ibid., p. 112.

13. Ibid., pp. 112–13; David F. Myrick, *Railroads of Arizona*, 1: 620–22, 632.

14. Richard C. Overton, *Burlington Route: A History of the Burlington Lines*, pp. 155, 197; Stuart Daggett, *Railroad Consolidation West of the Mississippi River*, p. 160; Morris Cafky, *Colorado Midland*, pp. 45, 175; *Railway Review*, March 31, 1888; Grodinsky, p. 564.

15. Hippen, p. 117; David Lavender, *The Great Persuader*, p. 375; Kennan, 1: 233; Hendrick, pp. 483–501; Moody, pp. 200–201.

16. Lavender, p. 376; SP, Annual Report, 1900, p. 20.

17. ICC, "Consolidations and Combinations of Carriers," p. 284; Kennan, 1: 236–39.

18. UP, Annual Report, 1901, p. 5; *Railway Gazette*, Jan. 3, 1902, p. 9; U.S., Industrial Commission, *Reports* 19: 309–10, 313; John S. Kennedy, Feb. 6, 1901, to James J. Hill, James J. Hill Reference Library, Saint Paul.

19. Moody, p. 201; Kennan, 1: 240–43; Dagget, pp. 349–51; Spearman, p. 436.

20. William Hood, June 21, 1922, to George Kennan, PR file 130.75; C. Vanderbilt, April 15, 1896, to C. P. Huntington, PR file 301; *Railway Gazette*, Feb. 8, 1901, p. 96; Hippen, pp. 137–38.

21. Moody, p. 20; Eckenrode and Edmund, p. 61; Kennan, 1: 233; Hendrick, p. 644; William Hood, June 21, 1922, to George Kennan, PR file 130.75.

22. Keys, "Harriman II," p. 8548; SP, Annual Reports, 1900–10; Hippen, p. 124.

23. Kennan, 1: 244–45; *Railway Gazette*, May 16, 1902, p. 359.

24. David F. Myrick, "Refinancing and Rebuilding the Central Pacific: 1899–1910," prepared for the Golden Spike Symposium, University of Utah (1969), p. 41; Kennan, 1: 245–46; SP, Annual Report, 1902, pp. 14–15.

25. William Hood, Memorandum—Biography of E. H. Harriman by George Kennan (June 21, 1922), PR file 130.75.

26. Myrick, "Refinancing and Rebuilding," pp. 39–40; Myrick, *Railroads of Nevada and Eastern California*, 1: 29–31.

27. Hood, Memorandum, and Memorandum—Great Salt Lake, PR file R10.1; A. W. Wright, June 30, 1929, to Erle Heath, PR file 130.75.

28. Memorandum—Great Salt Lake; William Hood, May 31, 1922, to George Kennan, PR file 130.75; *Ogden Standard Examiner*, Nov. 26, 1953.

29. SP, Annual Report, 1903, p. 16; Kennan, 1: 246–48; SP, *Bulletin*, Dec. 15, 1915, p. 4.

30. SP, Annual Report, 1907, p. 26, 1908, p. 15; Hood, Memorandum, and various data, PR file 130.8; *Santa Barbara Morning News*, March 27, 1900.

31. SP, Annual Report, 1904, p. 6; Kennan, 1: 251; Hood, Memorandum.

32. Hood, Memorandum; SP, Annual Report, 1909, p. 20.

33. Kennan, 1: 253–54; SP, Annual Report, 1906, p. 14, 1907, p. 18.

34. Kennan, 1: 249; SP, Annual Report, 1909, p. 20.

CHAPTER THREE

1. Otto H. Kahn, "Edward Henry Harriman," *Memoirs of Three Railroad Pioneers*, ed. Stuart Bruchey, p. 31; H. J. Eckenrode and Pocahontas Wright Edmunds, *E. H. Harriman: The Little Giant of Wall Street*, pp. 133, 137, 215, 127; George Kennan, *E. H. Harriman: A Biography*, 1: 27–30; W. Averell Harriman, interview, Dec. 14, 1982.

2. Robert A. Lovett, *Forty Years After: An Appreciation of the Genius of Edward Henry Harriman, 1848–1909*, pp. 14, 21; Kahn, p. 13; Grenville M. Dodge, *How We Built the Union Pacific and Other Railway Papers and Addresses*, pp. 77–78; Frank H. Spearman, *The Strategy of Great Railroads*, pp. 49, 67; Kennan, 1: 327; ICC, *Reports*, vol. 12, "Consolidations and Combinations of Carriers," p. 281.

3. Kennan, 1: 151–52; Eckenrode and Edmunds, p. 55; Kennan, 1: 364; Lovett, p. 24; Albro Martin, *Enterprise Denied: Origins of the Decline of American Railroads, 1897–1917*, p. 88.

4. C. M. Keys, "Harriman II: The Building of His Empire," *World's Work* 13 (Feb., 1907): 8550; Kennan, 1: 258, 281; ICC, "Consolidations and Combinations," pp. 278, 281.

5. Eckenrode and Edmunds, p. 213; Lovett, p. 21; Kennan, 1: 346–59; SP, Annual Reports, 1906, p. 8, 1907, p. 8, 1908, p. 8, 1909, p. 8.

6. Eckenrode and Edmunds, p. 214; Kennan, 2: 269.

7. Eckenrode and Edmunds, p. 230; Lovett, p. 15; Martin, p. 51; John Moody, *The Railroad Builders: A Chronicle of the Welding of the States*, p. 198.

8. Martin, pp. 361–62; Lovett, p. 13; John Muir, *Edward Henry Harriman*, pp. 35–36; *San Antonio Express*, Dec. 31, 1935.

9. Kahn, p. 30; Frank H. Spearman, "Building Up a Great

Railway System," *Outlook*, Feb. 27, 1909, p. 436; Kahn, pp. 25, 31; Dodge, p. 79.

10. Kennan, 1: 104, 108, and 2: 2, 347–50; C. M, Keys, "Harriman 1: The Man in the Making, His Early Life and Start," *World's Work* 13 (Jan., 1907): 8463; Muir, p. 50.

11. Dodge, p. 75; Kahn, pp. 2–7, Keys, "Harriman I," p. 8464.

12. Eckenrode and Edmunds, p. 210; Kahn, pp. 5, 34; Kennan, 1: 42 and 2: 356.

13. Eckenrode and Edmunds, p. 206; Lovett, pp. 22–23; Martin, pp. 19–20.

14. Eckenrode and Edmunds, p. 222; Martin, p. 116; Kahn, pp. 16–20; Kennan, 1: viii, ix.

15. Spearman, "Building Up a Great Railway System," pp. 444–47; John F. Hippen, "A Wall Street Man and a Western Railroad: A Chapter in Railroad Administration," *Bulletin of the Business Historical Society*, 23 (Sept., 1949): 146–47.

16. Hippen, pp. 128–29.

17. Kahn, p. 37; Eckenrode and Edmunds, pp. 33, 209; Kennan, 1: 187; C. M. Keys, "Harriman III: The Spinner of Golden Webs," *World's Work* 13 (March, 1907): 8659.

18. Harriman interview; Eckenrode and Edmunds, pp. 205, 225; Kahn, p. 30; Kennan, 2: 351; C. C. Goodwin, *As I Remember Them*, pp. 342–45; Kahn, p. 8; Keys, "Harriman II," p. 8550; Eckenrode and Edmunds, p. 222; ICC, "Consolidations and Combinations," p. 278; Keys, "Harriman I," p. 8464.

19. Lovett, p. 20; Stuart Daggett, *Chapters on the Southern Pacific*, p. 455; Spearman, "Building Up a Great Railway System," p. 436; Dodge, pp. 78–79; Eckenrode and Edmunds, p. 225; Hippen, p. 143.

20. ICC, "Consolidations and Combinations," p. 283; Spearman, "Building Up a Great Railway System," pp. 436–37; Goodwin, p. 344.

21. Hippen, p. 117.

22. Martin, p. 93; *The Biographical Directory of the Railway Officials of America*, 1922 ed., p. 356.

23. Hippen, p. 125.

24. *The Biographical Directory of the Railway Officials of America*, 1913 ed., p. 338.

25. Hippen, pp. 125–26.

26. *The Biographical Directory of the Railway Officials of America*, 1901 ed. (Chicago: Railway Age, 1901), p. 259.

27. *Railway Age*, April 22, 1904, pp. 38–39.

28. Hippen, pp. 131–32.

29. E. H. Harriman, June 28, 1904, to J. Kruttschnitt, Executive Department file 011.1-9, box 29.

30. *Railroad Gazette*, March 17, 1905, p. 248; *Railway Age*, Aug. 24, 1906, p. 224; Spearman, "Building Up a Great Railway System," p. 443; Kennan, 1: 277.

31. *Railway Gazette*, May 1, 1908, pp. 610–16; Spearman, "Building Up a Great Railway System," p. 444; J. Kruttschnitt, June 29, 1904, to B. H. Meyer, Executive Department file 011.1-9, box 29.

32. Kennan, 1: 274–76; Spearman, "Building Up a Great Railway System," p. 440.

33. *Railway Age Gazette*, Sept. 17, 1909, p. 484; R. B. Miller, Oct. 26, 1907, to A. A. Morse, Morse, Dec. 28, 1910, to Miller, and Oregon Railroad & Navigation Co., General Freight Department Circular No. 288 (Feb. 1, 1908), all three items from the Amos A. Morse Correspondence, 1908–1912, Oregon Collection, University of Oregon, Eugene.

34. J. Kruttschnitt, "Memorandum" (April 25, 1904), Executive Department file 011.1-9, box 29.

35. Ibid.; Spearman, "Building Up a Great Railway System," p. 441.

36. J. Kruttschnitt, June 29, 1904, to B. H. Meyer, Executive File 011.1-9, box 29; Hippen, p. 132.

37. Hippen, pp. 142–44; Martin, pp. 92–93; David F. Myrick, *Railroad of Arizona*, 2: 759, 948.

38. Spearman, "Building Up a Great Railway System," pp. 447–48; Eckenrode and Edmunds, p. 631; Hippen, pp. 129–30.

39. Hippen, pp. 129–30.

40. Kennan, 2: 354; Hippen, pp. 131, 144–45.

41. Lovett, p. 20; Spearman, "Building Up a Great Railway System," pp. 448–49.

CHAPTER FOUR

1. Frank Adams, "Imperial" (memorandum), p. 2, Executive Department file 048.

2. H. T. Cory, "Irrigation and River Control in the Colorado River Delta," *Transactions of the American Society of Civil Engineers* 76 (Dec., 1913): 1286–91.

3. Epes Randolph, Sept. 2, 1919, to Carl Hayden, Public Relations file 110.3; Otis B. Tout, *The First Thirty Years: Being an Account of the Principal Events in the History of Imperial Valley Southern California, U.S.A.*, pp. 100–101.

4. SP, Annual Report, 1907, p. 25; Tout, pp. 104–106; Margaret Romer, "From Boulder to the Gulf," *Southern California Historical Quarterly* (Sept., 1953): 279.

5. Epes Randolph, Sept. 2, 1919, to Carl Hayden, Public Relations file 110.3; Cory, p. 1362; Tout, p. 107; SP, Annual Report, 1907, p. 25.

6. Cory, pp. 1325–35; Tout, p. 107; Romer, pp. 282–86.

7. Tout, p. 107; Cory, pp. 1369–77; SP, Annual Report, 1907, p. 25.

8. SP, Annual Report, 1907, p. 25.

9. SP, Annual Report, 1905, p. 21; *San Francisco Call-Chronicle-Examiner*, April 19, 1906; SP, Annual Report, 1906, p. 23.

10. E. E. Calvin, June 18, 1906, to E. H. Harriman, PR File 190.5; SP, Annual Report, 1906, p. 25.

11. E. E. Calvin, June 18, 1906, to E. H. Harriman, PR File 190.5.

12. SP, Annual Report, 1906, p. 24.

13. E. E. Calvin, June 18, 1906, to E. H. Harriman, PR File 190.5.

14. Ibid.

15. SP, Annual Report, 1906, pp. 24–25.

16. Ibid.

17. Ibid.

18. Ibid.; E. H. Harriman, "San Francisco," *Sunset Magazine* 17 (May, 1906): 3.

19. *Railway World*, Sept. 3, 1909, p. 68; *New York Times*, Nov. 29, 1906; D. J. Russell, April 20, 1954, to E. Roland Harriman, PR File 190.5.

20. Parker Morell, *Diamond Jim*, p. 180; Superintendent of the Mason City & Fort Dodge Railroad, Oct. 3, 1898, to W. C. Toomey, James J. Hill Papers, Hill Reference Library, Saint Paul; Don L. Hofsommer, "A Chronology of Iowa Railroads," *Railroad History*, Spring, 1975: 78; Don L. Hofsommer, *Prairie*

Oasis: The Railroads, Steamboats and Resorts of Iowa's Spirit Lake Country, pp. 105, 107; Illinois Central Railroad, Annual Reports, 1899, p. 4, 1900, pp. 3–4, 1901, pp. 1–3.

21. Morell, p. 180. J. P. Morgan, Jan. 7, 1903, to James J. Hill (two telegrams), Hill, Jan. 7, 1903, to Morgan, and Hill, Jan. 10, 1903, to Morgan, all in the James J. Hill Papers, Hill Reference Library, Saint Paul.

22. James Blaine Hedges, *Henry Villard and the Railways of the Northwest*, pp. 59–61, 134–37, 143–63.

23. James J. Hill, April 4, 1898, to E. D. Adams: "In the matter of the Oregon Railroad & Navigation Company, Minutes of Conference, October 3, 1898," James J. Hill Papers, Hill Reference Library, Saint Paul.

24. James J. Hill, Sept. 12, 1899, to E. H. Harriman, W. T. Nichols, Jan. 29, 1900, to Hill, John S. Kennedy, Feb. 6, 1900, to Hill, D. Miller, July 24, 1902, to J. C. Stubbs, Stubbs, Sept. 3, 1902, to Miller, Miller, Sept. 14, 1902, to Hill, Hill, Sept. 16, 1902, to Miller, and Hill, July 22, 1904, to Lord Mount Stephen, all from James J. Hill Papers, Hill Reference Library, Saint Paul.

25. *Poor's Manual of Railroads 1914*, p. 1617; Albro Martin, *James J. Hill and the Opening of the Northwest*, pp. 563–65; James J. Hill, June 14, 1910, to George F. Baker, James J. Hill Papers, Hill Reference Library, Saint Paul.

26. Edwin D. Culp, *Stations West: The Story of the Oregon Railways*, pp. 123–24; Martin, p. 567; Robert S. Lovett, Feb. 7, 1910, to James J. Hill, and Hill, March 14, 1910, to Robert S. Lovett, both in James J. Hill Letterbook 2/20/06–1/31/14 (NY), pp. 370, 482, Hill Reference Library, Saint Paul; Northern Pacific Railway, Annual Report, 1912, p. 27.

27. Hugh Neill, Memorandum, Oct. 30, 1926, p. 2, Executive Department file 080.2, box 44; James J. Hill, July 10, 1890, to William H. Holcomb, James J. Hill Letterbook 8/11/90–10/21/90, p. 145, James J. Hill Papers, Hill Reference Library, Saint Paul; Julius Kruttschnitt, Dec. 16, 1908, to E. H. Harriman, Julius Kruttschnitt, Dec. 17, 1908, to Harriman, and Harriman, March 3, 1909, to R. S. Lovett, all in Executive Department file 080.2, box 44.

28. Julius Kruttschnitt, April 24, 1909, to E. H. Harriman, and "Memo of Agreement," May 21, 1909, both in Executive Department file 080.2, box 44; *Poor's Manual of Railroads 1914*, pp. 1505–1506; Louis Tuck Renz, *The History of the Northern Pacific Railroad*, p. 220; Northern Pacific Railway, Annual Report, 1911, p. 20; Union Pacific Railroad, Annual Reports, 1906, p. 19, 1911, p. 8.

29. Executive Committee Resolution, April 9, 1912, G. S. King, Dec. 23, 1913, to William Sproule, Sproule, Oct. 14, 1914, to Julius Kruttschnitt, Hugh Neill, March 4, 1931, to G. L. Buland, and Ben C. Dey, March 9, 1931, to Guy V. Shoup, all from Executive File 080.2, box 44.

30. SP, Annual Report, 1910, p. 26; SP *Corporate History of the Southern Pacific Company as of Date of Valuation, June 30, 1916* (compiled May 31, 1919), pp. SP Co. 10/40; James J. Hill, June 14, 1910, to George F. Baker, James H. Hill Papers, Hill Reference Library, Saint Paul.

31. SP, Annual Reports, 1907, pp. 26–27, 1906, p. 22; *Corporate History*, pp. CP 58, 59, 61; Neill, Memorandum, Oct. 30, 1926, Executive Department file 080.2, box 44.

32. David F. Myrick, *Railroads of Nevada and Eastern California*, 1: 181, 202–203, 208–210; SP, Annual Reports, 1905, p. 6; 1900, p. 6; "Construction or Acquisition of Railroad

Lines by Southern Pacific Company Since Approval of Anti-Trust Laws of July 2, 1890" (April 14, 1914), p. 19; Executive Department File 075-UP, box 13.

33. L. L. Waters, *Steel Trails to Santa Fe*, pp. 127–29; H. Craig Miner, *The St. Louis–San Francisco Transcontinental Railroad: The Thirty-Fifth Parallel Project, 1853–1890*, pp. 119–35.

34. Waters, pp. 129–30; SP, *Corporate History*, SPRR pp. 11–13/138; Julius Grodinsky, *Jay Gould: His Business Career, 1867–1892*, p. 380.

35. Keith L. Bryant, Jr., *History of the Atchison, Topeka & Santa Fe Railway*, pp. 99–104, 173–81; Waters, pp. 130–40; Burton J. Hendrick, "The Passing of a Great Railroad Dynasty," *McClure's* 38 (March, 1912): 648; Stuart Daggett, *Chapters on the Southern Pacific*, pp. 317–46.

36. James Marshall, *Santa Fe: The Railroad That Built an Empire*, p. 266; David F. Myrick, *Railroads of Arizona*, 2: 544–50, 1: 177–254.

37. Hendrick, p. 649; Marshall, pp. 424–30.

38. Myrick, *Railroads of Arizona*, 2:539; Epes Randolph, Jan. 3, 1906, to Julius Kruttschnitt, and Randolph, June 20, 1906, to Kruttschnitt, both in Executive Department file 110-1, box 37.

39. Epes Randolph, Feb. 18, 1904, to Julius Kruttschnitt, Randolph, March 19, 1904, to William F. Herrin; and Randolph, June 9, 1904, to Herrin, all in Executive Department file 87.02, box 71.

40. Bryant, p. 206; R. S. Lovett, Dec. 19, 1905, to Julius Kruttschnitt, and E. P. Ripley, Oct. 6, 1908, to Kruttschnitt, both in Executive Department file 110.1, box 37.

41. SP, Annual Report, 1907, pp. 26, 27; AT&SF, Annual Report, 1907, pp. 18–19; E. H. Harriman, Oct. 24, 1904, to Julius Kruttschnitt, Executive Department file 110-1, box 37.

42. Nelson Trottman, *History of the Union Pacific: A Financial and Economic Survey*, p. 330; ICC, *Reports*, vol. 12: "Consolidations and Combinations of Carriers," p. 280; Waters, p. 451.

43. SP, *Historical Memoranda*, 2: SPdeMex, pp. 1–7; SP, Annual Report, 1909, pp. 27, 29.

44. SP, *Historical Memoranda*, 2: SPdeMex, pp. 1–7; SP, Annual Report, 1909, pp. 27, 29.

45. SP, Annual Report, 1911, p. 27.

46. Stuart Daggett, *Railroad Consolidation West of the Mississippi River*, pp. 161–62; Trottman, pp. 316–25; *Moody's Analyses . . . Railroad Investments, 1922*, p. 199; ICC, "Consolidations and Combinations," p. 289.

47. Robert G. Athearn, *Rebel of the Rockies: A History of the Denver & Rio Grande Western Railroad*, pp. 191, 195; O. Meredith Wilson, *The Denver and Rio Grande Project, 1870–1901: A History of the First Thirty Years of the Denver and Rio Grande Railroad*, pp. 107–10; Ernest Howard, *Wall Street Fifty Years after Erie*, p. 13; Chicago, Burlington & Quincy, Annual Reports, 1901–1904, p. 2 each; SP, Annual Reports, 1901–1904, p. 2 each; Union Pacific, Annual Reports, 1898–1905, p. 2 each.

48. Athearn, pp. 125, 196–97; ICC, "Consolidations and Combinations," p. 304; Myrick, *Railroads of Arizona*, 1:316.

49. Burton J. Hendrick, "The Passing of a Great Railroad Dynasty," *McClure's* 38 (March, 1912): 497; *Railway Age*, Sept. 15, 1905; *Moody's 1922*, p. 1521; ICC, "Consolidations and Combinations," p. 304; Western Pacific, *The Feather River*

Route: A Brief History, p. 2; C. M. Keys, "Harriman II: The Building of His Empire," *World's Work* 13 (Feb., 1907): 8551; *Commercial and Financial Chronicle*, March 19, 1904, p. 1168; Athearn, p. 207.

50. Western Pacific, *Feather River Route*, p. 3; Wilson, pp. 112–13; Athearn, pp. 197, 204, 209; G. H. Kneiss, "Fifty Candles for the Western Pacific," *Western Pacific Mileposts*, March, 1983, p. 9; Myrick, *Railroads of Arizona*, 1:319.

51. Western Pacific, *Feather River Route*, p. 1; Kneiss, pp. 22–25; Athearn, pp. 214–15; Kendrick, p. 486; Athearn, pp. 192, 210, 214.

52. Henry Morgenthau, *All in a Lifetime*, p. 72; Albro Martin, *Enterprise Denied: Origins of the Decline of American Railroads, 1897–1917*, pp. 3–5.

53. On the general subject of Northern Securities, see Balthasar Meyer, "A History of the Northern Securities Case," *Bulletin of the University of Wisconsin* 1 (July, 1906): 215–350; George Kennan, *E. H. Harriman: A Biography*, 1: 286–339, 387–98; Richard C. Overton, *Burlington Route: A History of the Burlington Lines*, pp. 261–63; Martin, pp. 508–21, 592–93.

54. John Moody, *The Railroad Builders*, pp. 211–17.

55. Martin, pp. 79, 83; Kennan, 1:261.

56. Kennan, 2: 219, 228; Otto H. Kahn, "Edward Henry Harriman," *Memoirs of Three Railroad Pioneers*, ed. Stuart Bruchey, p. 38.

57. Martin, p. 84; Kahn, pp. 38–40; Union Pacific, Annual Report, 1909, p. 38; Moody, pp. 206–208.

58. Kahn, pp. 40–41.

59. Trottman, pp. 355–58; ICC, "Consolidations and Combinations," pp. 305–306; Martin, p. 117.

60. Martin, p. 117; *New York Times*, March 3, 1907; Frank H. Spearman, "Building Up a Great Railway System," *Outlook*, Feb. 27, 1909, p. 451; Myrick, *Railroads of Arizona*, 2: 615–34; Spearman, p. 452.

61. H. J. Eckenrode and Pocahontas Wright Edmunds, *E. H. Harriman: The Little Giant of Wall Street*, p. 237; *New York Times*, Sept. 10, 1909; Kennan, 2:350; Kahn, p. 46; *Illinois Central Employees Magazine* 1 (Oct., 1909): 317; Union Pacific, Annual Report, 1909, p. 23; SP, Annual Report, 1909, p. 27-A.

62. Kennan, 2: 272–273; tabular data from SP Annual Reports, 1901–1909; Spearman, p. 436.

CHAPTER FIVE

1. John Moody, *The Railroad Builders: A Chronicle of the Welding of the States*, pp. 199–210; Grenville M. Dodge, *How We Built the Union Pacific and Other Railway Papers and Addresses*, p. 77.

2. Burton J. Hendrick, "Mr. E. H. Harriman, the Most Powerful Man in America," *McClure's*, Oct., 1909, pp. 656–59; William Sproule, Feb. 11, 1913, to Julius Kruttschnitt, Executive Department file 075-USCP, box 13; Stuart Daggett, *Chapters on the Southern Pacific*, pp. 429, 433.

3. Daggett, pp. 430–31; United States v. Union Pacific Railroad, et al. 188 F. 102–27; Evan J. Foulds, "Historic Litigation: Southern Pacific Control of Central Pacific," S.P. Law Department (Dec. 7, 1953), pp. 7–9.

4. W. Averell Harriman, interview Dec. 14, 1982.

5. Daggett, pp. 425–36; Foulds, pp. 9–10; United States v. Union Pacific, et al. 226 U.S. 61–98.

6. W. G. Neimyer, Dec. 9, 1912, to William Sproule, Memoranda, "Withdrawal From Joint Agencies," Dec. 12, 1912, Sproule, Dec. 19, 1912, to E. E. Calvin, Calvin, Dec. 23, 1912, to Sproule, and Julius Kruttschnitt, March 3, 1913, to Sproule, all in Executive Department file 542-406, box 35.

7. SP, Annual Report, 1912, p. 31; Hugh Neill, March 4, 1931, to Hale Holden, Executive Department file 081 OWR&N, box 35.

8. United States v. Union Pacific Railroad, 226 U.S. 470–77; "Agreement of February 8, 1913, proposed between the Union Pacific RR, Southern Pacific Company, et al." Executive Department file 080.3-9, box 13; William Sproule, *Threatened Southern Pacific/Central Pacific Dismemberment* (pamphlet), Aug. 14, 1922, pp. 1–5; *San Francisco Chronicle*, Jan. 26, 1913.

9. 2 CRC 233; 2 CRC 248; 2 CRC 319; William F. Herrin, Feb. 25, 1913, to R. S. Lovett, and O. W. Durrow, March 1, 1913, to Herrin, both in Executive Department file 120.01, box 12; SP, *Historical Memoranda*, 1: Southern Pacific Control of Central Pacific, p. 11.

10. *San Francisco Chronicle*, Jan. 25, Feb. 11, March 17, May 17, May 28, June 3, 1913.

11. William Sproule, Feb. 25, 1913, to Julius Kruttschnitt, Executive Department file 120.01, box 12.

12. L. J. Spence, July 14, 1913, to William Sproule, Spence, Feb. 1, 1913, to C. M. Evans, and Spence, Feb. 20, 1913, to Sproule, all in Executive Department file 120.01, box 12; *San Francisco Call*, March 6, 1913.

13. Frederic V. S. Crosby, March 15, 1913, to Stockholders of the Union Pacific Railroad and Southern Pacific Company, Executive Department file 120.01, box 12; Nelson Trottman, *History of the Union Pacific: A Financial and Economic Survey*, pp. 366–67.

14. Union Pacific Railroad, Annual Reports, 1913, p. 25, 1914, pp. 23–25; *Poor's Manual of Railroads*, 1914, p. 1505; Frederic V. S. Crosby, July 11, 1913, to Stockholders of the Union Pacific Railroad, and SP, Executive Committee Vote, July 24, 1913, both in Executive Department file 110.1-UP, box 14.

15. William Sproule, May 9, 1913, to Julius Kruttschnitt, Kruttschnitt, May 21, 1913, to Sproule, Robert S. Lovett, May 24, 1913, to James C. McReynolds, William F. Herrin, June 19, 1913, to Maxwell Evarts, and Kruttschnitt, Sept. 15, 1913, to Sproule, all in Executive Department files 110.1, 120.01, 075-US(CP), boxes 12 and 13; *Morning Oregonian* (Portland), Sept. 14, 1913; *New York Times*, Sept. 14, 1913; *San Francisco Chronicle*, Oct. 20, 1913; Trottman, pp. 368–72.

16. *Morning Oregonian* (Portland), Sept. 14, 1913; William Sproule, March 19, 1913, to E. O. McCormick, and Julius Kruttschnitt, Sept. 5, 1913, to Sproule, both in Executive Department file 075-US, box 13.

17. SP, Annual Reports, 1909, p. 20, 1911, p. 12; E. E. Calvin, Dec. 14, 1912, to William Sproule, Executive Department file 120.01, box 12.

18. SP, Annual Reports, 1910, pp. 26–27, 1911, p. 29, Julius Kruttschnitt, Oct. 27, 1915, to J. P. Blair, Executive Department file 510–963, box 38; SP, Annual Report, 1899, p. 6, 1910, pp. 6, 27.

19. SP, *Corporate History of the Southern Pacific . . . as of June 30, 1916*: Inter-California Railway, p. 1/2.

20. SP, Annual Report, 1910, p. 26; SP, *Corporate History*: Southern Pacific Company, p. 10/40.

21. SP, Annual Reports, 1907, pp. 26–27, 1910, p. 20; C. J. Millis, Oct. 28, 1910, to E. E. Calvin, Executive Department file 081, box 62; *Coos Bay Times*, April 8, 1916; *Bulletin*, Sept. 15, 1916, pp. 2, 5; SP, *Corporate History*, p. 20/40.

22. *Poor's Manual of the Railroads, 1914*, p. 1484; Northern Pacific Railway, Annual Reports, 1911, p. 17, 1912, p. 17; Robert S. Lovett, Feb. 1910, to J. C. Stubbs, Julius Kruttschnitt, Sept. 20, 1911, to Lovett, both in Executive Department files, box 45; Edwin D. Culp, *Stations West: The Story of the Oregon Railways*, pp. 132, 198, 216.

23. SP, Annual Reports, 1912, p. 7, 1914, p. 22.

24. SP, Annual Reports, 1911, p. 29, 1916, p. 24, 1918, p. 29.

25. "History of the San Diego & Arizona Eastern Railway" (MJW-277), July 7, 1937, p. 1, Executive Department box 53.

26. Ibid., pp. 1–6.

27. Ibid., pp. 7–11; *Bulletin*, Sept. 15, 1924, p. 3.

28. Corporate History: Central Pacific Railway, pp. 40, 43, 57/73.

29. SP, Annual Report, 1911, pp. 27–28; *Official Guide of the Railways* (Aug., 1913), pp. 846–47, (Aug., 1916), p. 845.

30. SP, Annual Report, 1911, p. 28.

31. Ibid.; William D. Middleton, *When the Steam Railroads Electrified*, pp. 280, 283.

32. Thomas Ahearn, April 25, 1912, to E. O. McCormick, Executive Department file 083, box 65.

33. E. E. Calvin, Dec. 31, 1912, to William Sproule, Paul Shoup, Jan. 7, 1913, to Sproule, Sproule, Jan. 3, 1913, to Julius Kruttschnitt, and Sproule, Jan. 3, 1913, to Calvin, all in Executive Department file 083, box 65.

34. Robert S. Lovett, Sept. 6, 1912, to William Sproule, Sproule, Oct. 24, 1912, to W. F. Herrin, and Paul Shoup, Oct. 26, 1912, to Sproule, all in Executive Department file 083, box 29.

35. Culp, pp. 222–45; Robert E. Strahorn, Jan. 20, 1914, to E. E. Calvin, Executive Department file 083/000, box 62; *Bulletin*, Feb. 1, 1914, p. 7, and Feb. 15, 1914, p. 8.

36. *Sunday Oregonian* (Portland), Jan. 18, 1914; Robert E. Strahorn, May 15, 1914, to William Sproule, T. O. Edwards, Sept. 28, 1914, to Sproule, and Sproule, Oct. 5, 1914, to W. R. Scott, all in Executive Department file 083/000, box 62.

37. Allen H. Babcock, "Mountain Railway Electrification: A Study of the Tehachapi Pass," *Transactions of the American Institute of Electrical Engineers* (1913), pp. 1784–1815; E. P. Ripley, Nov. 14, 1912, to Julius Kruttschnitt, Executive Department file 081/360, box 28.

38. Julius Kruttschnitt, Nov. 15, 1912, to E. P. Ripley, G. C. Ward, May 8, 1913, to Paul Shoup, Shoup, May 10, 1913, to E. E. Calvin, William Sproule, May 19, 1913, to Ripley, Ripley, May 21, 1913, to Sproule, and C. J. Mills, July 1, 1913, to Ripley, all in Executive Department file 081-360, box 28; Babcock, p. 1784.

39. SP, Time Table, March, 1907, pp. 15, 35–36, 45–46; *Official Guide of the Railways* (March, 1906), p. 664, and (Aug., 1913), pp. 842–43.

40. *Official Guide of the Railways* (March, 1906), p. 664, and (Aug., 1913), p. 824; SP, Time Table, March, 1907, pp. 7–14; Lucius Beebe, *The Overland Limited*, p. 13.

41. *Official Guide of the Railways* (March, 1906), pp. 664–71, and (Aug., 1913), p. 830.

42. *Bulletin*, July 1, 1915, p. 2, Oct., 1956, p. 28; *San Francisco Chronicle*, Nov. 25, 1911; William Sproule, Jan. 6,

1912, to Julius Kruttschnitt, Executive Department file 9251/351, box 65; *San Francisco Chronicle*, June 12, Dec. 12, 1912; *San Francisco Examiner*, May 30, 1915.

43. SP, Annual Report, 1913, p. 26.

44. Ibid., 1914, p. 18, 1916, p. 19.

45. David P. Morgan, "Southern Pacific at the Panama-Pacific," *Trains* 37 (Sept., 1977): 48–51; *Bulletin*, March 15, 1915, pp. 1–2; *San Francisco Chronicle*, April 30, 1915; SP, Annual Report, 1916, p. 19.

46. SP, Advertising Proofs, 1916.

47. *Bulletin*, May, 1957, pp. 3–4; *Sunset Magazine*, 1898–1914; SP, Time Table, March, 1907, p. 1.

48. SP, "The Role of Central Pacific and Southern Pacific in Developing California and the West" (Public Relations Department, 1971), pp. 1–11.

49. Ibid., p. 11.

50. *Bulletin*, Oct., 1922, p. 3, Oct. 15, 1914, p. 8, Feb. 1, 1916, p. 7, March 15, 1916, p. 4, Feb. 1918, p. 2.

51. SP, "The Role . . . West," pp. 11–12; *Bulletin*, Jan. 15, 1914, p. 7.

52. *Bulletin*, Feb. 15, 1914, p. 1, Oct., 1922, p. 3.

53. Ibid., Jan. 15, 1914, p. 6, April 15, 1916, p. 3, and May 15, 1916, p. 2.

54. Ibid., July 1, 1914, p. 1.

55. Ibid., July 1, 1914, p. 2, Dec., 1922, p. 27; G. J. Blech, Nov. 17, 1939, to Lindsay Campbell, PR file 87; *Chicago Railway Review* July 20, 1878.

56. *Bulletin*, July 15, 1916, p. 1, Aug. 1, 1914, p. 1, May 15, 1917, p. 5, April, 1918, p. 2, May 15, 1913, p. 1, Feb. 1, 1915, p. 5.

57. Ibid., April 1, 1914, p. 2.

58. SP, Annual Report, 1907, p. 24; *Bulletin*, April 1, 1914, p. 1, Aug. 1, 1917, p. 1.

59. SP, Annual Report, 1915, p. 18; Julius Kruttschnitt, April 25, 1911, to W. A. Worthington, R. S. Lovett, May 5, 1911, to Kruttschnitt, and Kruttschnitt, May 13, 1911, to Lovett, all in Executive Department file 300.4-983, box 56.

60. SP, Annual Report, 1917, p. 19; E. O. McCormick, Nov. 25, 1913, to William Sproule, Executive Department file 354, box 65; *Bulletin*, Aug. 1, 1916, p. 3, May 1, 1917, pp. 1–2, Aug. 1, 1917, pp. 1–2; "Southern Pacific Building, San Francisco," Executive Department file 354.2, box 65.

61. SP, Annual Reports, 1913, p. 25, 1914, p. 20, 1915, p. 19, and 1916, p. 21.

62. *Bulletin*, Nov. 20, 1913, p. 2, and passim, 1913–16.

63. John Moody, *The Railroad Builders: A Chronicle of the Welding of the States*, pp. 234–38; SP, Annual Report, 1913, p. 26, 1914, p. 22; *Bulletin*, March 15, 1915, p. 2.

64. SP, Annual Report, 1912, p. 31; Moody, pp. 236–37.

65. Moody, p. 328; SP, Annual Report, 1918, pp. 8–9, 1926, p. 10; Albro Martin, *Enterprise Denied: Origins of the Decline of American Railroads, 1897–1917*, passim, esp. pp. 372–73; SP, Annual Report, 1917, pp. 7–8; Julius Kruttschnitt, July 28, 1913, to James W. Reagan, Executive Department file 110.1, box 14; *San Francisco Examiner*, March 12, 1915.

66. SP, Annual Report, 1915, p. 18.

67. Ibid., 1917, p. 8; John F. Stover, *American Railroads*, pp. 181–86; *Bulletin*, June 15, 1916, p. 1.

68. *Bulletin*, June 1, 1917, p. 1, Sept. 1, 1917, p. 1, Oct. 1, 1917, p. 1, and Nov. 15, 1917, p. 1.

69. Ibid., Jan. 15, 1918, pp. 3, 8, Sept. 1, 1917, p. 5, Aug. 1,

1917, p. 1, and April 1, 1918, p. 3.

70. Stover, pp. 185–97; Moody, pp. 238–41; K. Austin Kerr, "Decision for Federal Control: Wilson, McAdoo, and the Railroads, 1917," *Journal of American History* 3 (Dec., 1967): 550–60; SP, Annual Report, 1917, pp. 30–34; Julius Kruttschnitt, Dec. 28, 1917, to William Sproule, et al., Executive Department file 070.1, box 6; *Bulletin*, July 15, 1918, p. 1.

71. W. G. McAdoo, Dec. 28, 1917, to President and Directors, Southern Pacific Company; McAdoo, General Order No. 1, Dec. 29, 1917, McAdoo, Jan. 8, 1918, to All Railroad Officers and Employees, and McAdoo, "Policies in the Management of the Railroads: Summarized by Director General McAdoo," June 19, 1918, all in Executive Department file 070.1, box 6; *Bulletin*, July 15, 1918, p. 1.

72. William Sproule, Feb. 4, 1918, to Julius Kruttschnitt, Executive Department file 070.1, box 6; *Bulletin*, March 15, 1918, p. 1.

73. *Bulletin*, Aug. 15, 1918, p. 1; Julius Kruttschnitt, Aug. 5, 1918, to Director General of Railroads, Executive Department file 510.5, box 50; *Railway Age*, Nov. 8, 1918, p. 869.

74. *Bulletin*, June 1, 1918, p. 8, June 1, 1917, p. 1, Feb. 1, 1918, p. 1, Jan. 15, 1918, p. 1, Feb. 1, 1918, p. 2, April 1, 1918, p. 1, Sept. 15, 1917, pp. 1, 3, April 15, 1918, p. 5, Aug. 15, 1918, p. 1, April 1, 1918, p. 1.

75. Ibid., July 15, 1918, p. 1, Feb. 1, 1918, p. 3, Jan. 15, 1918, p. 3, Nov. 1, 1917, p. 5, Dec. 1, 1917, p. 3, July, 1919, p. 8, Feb. 15, 1918, p. 1, "Feb. 1, 1918, p. 3.

76. Ibid., April 15, 1918, p. 1, May, 1919, pp. 3–4; SP, Annual Report, 1918, p. 28; *Bulletin*, May 15, 1918, pp. 1–3, June, 1919, p. 6, Aug. 15, 1918, p. 1, April 1, 1918, p. 2.

77. *Bulletin*, April 1, 1918, p. 4, Sept. 1, 1917, p. 4, Dec., 1919, p. 1, June 1, 1918, p. 5, Oct. 1919, p. 7, Dec., 1919, p. 7.

78. Ibid., July 15, 1918, p. 1, April 1, 1918, p. 5; SP, Annual Report, 1918, p. 28.

79. *Bulletin*, Oct. 1, 1917, p. 1, Oct., 1919, pp. 1, 6.

80. Stover, pp. 194–97; Lewis J. Spence, Nov. 26, 1918, Address before the Traffic Club of New York, Epes Randolph, Dec. 18, 1918, to Paul Shoup, Frank Karr, Dec. 19, 1918, to Paul Shoup, Shoup, Dec. 26, 1918, to Randolph, Shoup, Jan. 16, 1919, to Julius Kruttschnitt, J. Ross Clark, Jan. 17, 1919, to Shoup; and Kruttschnitt, Nov. 29, 1919, to Shoup, all in Executive Department file 070.1, box 6.

81. Stover, pp. 195–97; Martin, pp. 363–64; SP, Annual Report, 1920, pp. 6–9.

82. Annual Report, 1920, pp. 6–9; *Bulletin*, June, 1922, p. 10; G. W. Mulks, Dec. 16, 1922, to William Sproule, Executive Department file 070.1, box 6.

CHAPTER SIX

1. Julius Kruttschnitt, Jan. 15, 1914, to William Sproule, Kruttschnitt, Feb. 5, 1914, to Stockholders, and Sproule, Jan. 20, 1914, to Kruttschnitt, all in Executive Department file 075-US, boxes 12 and 13; *Financial America*, Jan. 23, 1914.

2. SP, Annual Report, 1914, p. 21.

3. A. K. Van Deventer, Feb. 10, 1914, to Stockholders, W. H. Kaye, Feb. 20, 1914, to Van Deventer, and William Sproule, Jan. 9, 1914, to Julius Kruttschnitt, all in Executive Department file 075-US, box 13.

4. William Randolph Hearst, Feb. 10, 1914, to William Sproule, Executive Department file 075-US, box 12.

5. *New York American*, Feb. 14, 1914; *Chicago Examiner*, Feb. 21, 1914; *San Francisco Bulletin*, Jan. 22, 1914; *San Francisco Chronicle* Feb. 13, 1914, May 2, 1914; *New York American*, May 25, 1914; *Outlook*, Mar. 21, 1914, pp. 609–10, 642–46; *Leslie's Illustrated Weekly Newspaper*, Apr. 16, 1914, p. 365; *Railway and Marine News*, Mar. 1914, p. 27.

6. Paul Shoup, Mar. 1, 1914, to William Sproule, Executive Department file 075-US, box 12.

7. William H. Crocker, Feb. 28, 1914, to Lawrence F. Abbott, and William Sproule, Jan. 9, 1914, to Julius Kruttschnitt, both in Executive Department file 075-US, box 13.

8. *Bulletin*, May 1, 1914, pp. 1, 2, 5.

9. U.S. District Court Utah, *United States v. Southern Pacific Company, Central Pacific Railway Company, et al.*, I: 294–97.

10. Ibid., I: 182–84, 200–201.

11. Ibid., I: 728–31.

12. *San Francisco Chronicle*, Mar. 11, 1915.

13. Ibid., Sept. 14, 1914, Mar. 13, 1915; *New York American*, Aug. 7, 1916.

14. *San Francisco Examiner*, Mar. 11, 1917; 239 Federal Register 998–1009; SP, Press Release, Mar. 11, 1917, Executive Department file 075-USCP, box 13.

15. *San Francisco Bulletin*, May 2, 1917.

16. John F. Stover, *American Railroads*, pp. 195–96.

17. Julius Kruttschnitt, Jan. 3, 1921, to William Z. Ripley, R. S. Lovett, Jan. 14, 1921, to Ripley, Kruttschnitt, Feb. 18, 1921, to William Sproule, and William F. Herrin, memorandum, Mar. 5, 1921, all in Executive Department file 080-395, box 1. For full discussions of the government's efforts toward consolidation, see: Stuart Daggett, *Railroad Consolidation West of the Mississippi River*, and William Norris Leonard, *Railroad Consolidation under the Transportation Act of 1920*; 63 ICC 455–600; and 159 ICC 522–89.

18. Robert S. Lovett, Feb. 22, 1922, to Julius Kruttschnitt, and Kruttschnitt, Mar. 9, 1922, to Lovett, both in Executive Department file 080.3-9, box 1.

19. 259 U.S. 214–47; William Sproule, May 13, 1922, to Julius Kruttschnitt, Executive Department file 075-US, box 14.

20. Hugh Neill, Summary of Statements of H. W. de Forest at Executive Committee, June 1, 1922, R. E. Kelly, June 10, 1922, to Julius Kruttschnitt, both in Executive Department file 075-US, box 14; *What Californians Want* (pamphlet), published by the General Committee Against Dismemberment of the Southern Pacific–Central Pacific System, n.d. (1922), and *Central Pacific–Southern Pacific Dismemberment* (pamphlet), published by the San Francisco Chamber of Commerce, n.d. (1922), both in SP files.

21. William Sproule, June 10, 1922, to Julius Kruttschnitt, Executive Department file 075-US(CP), box 14.

22. *New York Times*, June 12, 1922; *Portland Oregonian*, June 29, 1922.

23. Evan J. Foulds, "Historic Litigation: Southern Pacific Control of the Central Pacific" (Dec. 7, 1953), p. 26; Fred G. Athearn, *The Separation of the Central Pacific and the Southern Pacific Railroads: A Plain Statement of the Facts* (pamphlet), published by the Union Pacific (July 7, 1922); Stuart Daggett, *The Unmerger of the Central Pacific and Southern Pacific Railways: A Broad Economic Advantage* (pamphlet), published by the Union Pacific, n.d. (1922), all in SP Law Department files.

24. William Sproule, Sept. 30, 1922, to Julius Kruttschnitt, and Sproule, Aug. 14, 1922, to Kruttschnitt, both in Executive

Department file 080.3-9, box 1; *Wall Street Journal*, June 14, July 17, 1922; Samuel Rea, June 14, 1922, to Kruttschnitt, Executive Department file 080.3-9, box 1.

25. Julius Kruttschnitt, July 13, 1922, to Paul Shoup, Executive Department file 075-US(CP), box 14.

26. *Bulletin*, Aug., 1922, p. 5; *San Francisco Chronicle*, Sept. 9, 1922; *Barron's*, Aug. 28, 1922.

27. *Morning Oregonian* (Portland), Oct. 10, 1922; *San Francisco Chronicle*, Oct. 12, 1922; *Salt Lake Telegram*, Oct. 22, 1922.

28. Hugh Neill, Summary of Statements of H. W. de Forest, June 1, 1922, and Julius Kruttschnitt, June 1, 1922, to William Sproule, both in Executive Department file 075-US(CP), box 14; Daggett, pp. 137–48.

29. Frank Karr, Address before the Meeting of World Traders, Oct. 5, 1922, Executive Department file 075-US(CP), box 14. The figures for the El Paso Gateway do not include traffic moving to or from El Paso & Southwestern–Chicago, Rock Island & Pacific on the Golden State Route.

30. Union Pacific, Annual Reports, 1922, pp. 16–17, 1923, p. 25; R. S. Lovett, "Opening Statement" before the ICC, Dec. 8, 1922, p. 16, in SP files.

31. Julius Kruttschnitt, Oct. 24, 1922, to Gen. Charles G. Dawes, Dawes, Oct. 26, 1922, to Kruttschnitt, F. E. Murphy, June 16, 1922, to Kruttschnitt, and A. G. Wells, Dec. 8, 1922, to Kruttschnitt, all in Executive Department file 080.3-9, box 1.

32. *Wall Street Journal*, Nov. 29, 1922; C. R. Gray, untitled pamphlet rebutting Kruttschnitt's testimony, published by the Union Pacific, Dec. 12, 1922, in SP files.

33. SP, *Historical Memoranda*, I: "Southern Pacific Control of Central Pacific," pp. 18–19.

34. Ibid., I: 20–21; 76 ICC 508–531.

35. *Historical Memoranda*, I: 20–21.

36. Ibid., I: 22–23.

37. Ibid., I: 17.

38. *Wall Street Journal*, Feb. 14, 1923; *San Francisco Chronicle*, Jan. 18, 1923.

39. 290 Federal Reporter 443–950; J. G. Scrugham, June 19, 1923, to Harry M. Daugherty, and Reed Smoot, June 14, 1923, to Daugherty, both in Executive Department file 075-US(CP), box 12.

40. William Z. Ripley, June 5, 1922, to Julius Kruttschnitt, Executive Department file 080.3-9, box 1; Daggett, *Railroad Consolidation*, pp. 143–48; R. S. Lovett, Feb. 22, 1922, to Kruttschnitt, Executive Department file 080.3-9, box 1.

41. L. J. Spence, "Attitude Toward Inclusion of Rock Island in Southern Pacific System," Oct. 10, 1922, Executive Department file 080.3-9, box 1.

42. Julius Kruttschnitt, Feb. 20, 1923, to J. P. Blair, Executive Department file 080.3-9, box 2.

CHAPTER SEVEN

1. *Bulletin*-T&L Lines, Feb., 1924, p. 3.

2. Donald J. Russell, interview, Feb. 25, 1982; *New York Evening Post*, Oct. 4, 1924.

3. Julius Kruttschnitt, "The Engineer as a Railroad Executive," address before the New York Section, American Society of Civil Engineers, March 18, 1925, p. 3.

4. Ibid., p. 18.

5. Ibid., pp. 3–5.

6. Julius Kruttschnitt, March 24, 1922, to William Sproule, Executive Department file 011.1-95, box 37; *New York Evening Post*, Oct. 4, 1924.

7. *New York Evening Post*, Oct. 4, 1924.

8. *Leslie's Weekly*, Aug. 7, 1913; *Bulletin*, Dec., 1920, pp. 8–9, 27, May, 1923, pp. 9–10; *Analyst*, April 20, 1924.

9. J. P. Blair, March 6, 1923, to W. F. Herrin, Julius Kruttschnitt, Aug. 20, 1924, to C. B. Seger, and Paul Shoup, April 2, 1927, to William Sproule, all in Executive Department, no file number, box 35.

10. SP, Annual Reports, 1923, p. 25, 1924, p. 24, 1929, p. 27; *Bulletin*, Oct., 1922, p. 10, Nov., 1927, p. 9.

11. Walter Douglas, July 23, 1926, to Henry W. de Forest, and A. D. McDonald, July 30, 1926, to William Sproule, both in Executive Department file 510.5/921, box 50.

12. SP, Executive Committee, June 15, 1922, Executive Department file 300-4, box 41; *Portland Oregonian*, March 25, 1923; *Portland Journal*, March 25, 1923.

13. William Sproule, Sept. 1, 1923, to Julius Kruttschnitt, Executive Department file 300.42, box 41; *Bulletin*, Nov., 1923, p. 25; Sproule, June 26, 1923, to E. L. King, and Sproule, April 25, 1924, to A. D. McDonald, both in Executive Department file 300.42, box 41.

14. William Sproule, March 18, 1924, to Julius Kruttschnitt, and Kruttschnitt, March 20, 1924, to Sproule, both in Executive Department file 300.42, box 35; *Railway Age*, Oct. 25, 1924, pp. 749–51.

15. *Portland Telegram*, Aug. 29, Sept. 12, 1924; Charles Donnelly, May 4, 1925, to William Sproule, Executive Department file 081 NP, box 44.

16. William Sproule, May 6, 1925, to Paul Shoup, W. A. Worthington, memorandum, July 20, 1925, and William Sproule, Sept. 30, 1925, to H. W. de Forest, all in Executive Department file 080.2, boxes 39 and 44.

17. *Railway Age*, May 15, 1926, pp. 1313–15.

18. Ibid.; *Portland Oregonian*, July 19, 1926.

19. William Sproule, Aug. 13, 1925, to Paul Shoup, Sproule, Aug. 29, 1926, to Shoup, and George W. Boschke, March 31, 1926, to Shoup, all in Executive Department file 300.42, box 41.

20. SP, Annual Report, 1926, p. 20; Paul Shoup, Aug. 31, 1926, to William Sproule, and Shoup, Sept. 20, 1926, to Sproule, both in Executive Department file 300.42, box 41; *Bulletin*, Sept., 1926, p. 11.

21. William Sproule and Ralph Budd, June 11, 1927, to Interstate Commerce Commission, and Sproule, May 29, 1928, to A. D. McDonald, both in Executive Department file 080.2, box 45; *Portland Oregonian*, June 30, 1927; SP, Annual Report, 1927, pp. 23–24; 138 ICC 95-105.

22. E. E. Calvin, June 26, 1911, to Julius Kruttschnitt, and Calvin, July 20, 1911, to Kruttschnitt, both in Executive Department file 081, box 63.

23. W. C. Dalton, Sept. 2, 1916, to William Sproule, Executive Department file 080.2, box 40; *Klamath Falls Herald*, Sept. 27, 1916; *San Francisco Chronicle*, Oct. 17, 1916, John M. Scott, July 5, 1922, to R. E. Kelly, Executive Department file 300.42, box 41.

24. Julius Kruttschnitt, June 6, 1923, to William Sproule, Executive Department file 080.2, box 40.

25. *Bulletin*, Sept., 1925, pp. 7–8, Nov., 1925, pp. 7–8; William Sproule, July 1, 1926, to A. D. McDonald, and

Sproule, Dec. 28, 1927, to C. R. Gray, both in Executive Department file 300.42, box 40.

26. Executive Department Resolution, May 17, 1928, Paul Shoup, Jan. 18, 1928, to William Sproule, and Shoup, May 18, 1928, to Frank Mulks, all in Executive Department file 081 NCO, box 63; *Bulletin*, Oct., 1928, pp. 9–11; George W. Boschke, Feb. 1, 1929, to Paul Shoup, and EMG, Oct. 14, 1929, to J. H. Dyer, both in Executive Department file 081 NCO, box 40; *Bulletin*, Oct., 1929, pp. 3–6; SP, Annual Report, 1929, p. 28; *Railway Age*, March 15, 1930, pp. 636–39.

27. *Bulletin*, April, 1929, pp. 17–24, May, 1929, pp. 5–6, May, 1929, pp. 5–6, June, 1929, pp. 7–9; 166 ICC 3; *Railway Age*, Feb. 20, 1932; 175 ICC 367; SP, Annual Report, 1929, p. 29; Paul Shoup, June 21, 1930, to Hale Holden, Executive Department file 110-1, box 50; *Railway Age*, Feb. 23, 1929, pp. 468–69, March 16, 1929, p. 628, Nov. 23, 1929, pp. 1205–1207, Dec. 7, 1929, pp. 1343–45, Nov. 30, 1929, pp. 1287–1302, and June 28, 1930, pp. 1595–98.

28. 162 ICC 37–70; William Sproule, March 11, 1927, to Paul Shoup, and Shoup, March 16, 1927, to Sproule, both in Executive Department file 120.01, box 45.

29. Paul Shoup, memorandum, July 4, 1925, Shoup, July 16, 1925, to A. D. McDonald, J. H. Dyer, March 25, 1926, to Shoup, J. T. Saunders, July 2, 1929, to Shoup, and D. C. Masson, office memo, July 19, 1929, all in Executive Department file 310-13, box 29.

30. Paul Shoup, July 21, 1925, to A. D. McDonald, Executive Department file 080.2, box 39; Shoup, memorandum, July 4, 1925, Executive Department file 310–13, box 29; Hale Holden, June 27, 1930, to Shoup, Executive Department file 110.1, box 50.

31. A. G. Wells, Dec. 26, 1912, to E. E. Calvin, William Sproule, March 8, 1912, to Calvin, William Hood, Sept. 5, 1913, to Calvin, Sproule, memorandum, Sept. 25, 1920, W. B. Storey, Dec. 27, 1921, to A. H. Payson, and General Manager, Traffic on Joint Line Kern Junction–Mojave, May 20, 1920, all in Executive Department file 300.421, box 59.

32. A. G. Wells, Dec. 20, 1927, to Paul Shoup, Executive Department file 300.421, box 59.

33. A. H. Babcock, March 31, 1927, to J. H. Dyer, Babcock, April 17, 1928, to Dyer, Dyer, Sept. 28, 1929, to Paul Shoup, Hale Holden, Sept. 10, 1930, to Shoup, Dyer, Dec. 20, 1929, to Shoup, Dyer, Sept. 19, 1930, to Shoup, Babcock, Nov. 6, 1930, to F. L. Burkhalter, H. L. Andrews, Dec. 27, 1934, to Shoup, and Shoup, Dec. 29, 1934, to H. L. Andrews, all in Executive Department file 360, box 28; John M. Scott, March 24, 1917, to William Sproule, Executive Department file 300.42, box 41.

34. For a more complete estimate of the El Paso & Southwestern, see David F. Myrick, *Railroads of Arizona*, 1: 177–254; "El Paso & Southwestern" (typescript, n.d.), Public Relations file 10.1; EP&SW, "Partial List of Construction Projects," n.d., Executive Department file 130-1, box 71; SP, *Historical Memoranda*, 1: "El Paso & Southwestern System," p. 1.

35. "EP&SW," typescript; EP&SW, "Construction Projects"; Myrick, 1: 196–99.

36. Myrick, 1:225; Paul Shoup, Oct. 20, 1930, to William Sproule, Executive Department file 081 SLSW, box 72.

37. Myrick, 1:201; EP&SW, "Construction Projects."

38. EP&SW, "Construction Projects."

39. EP&SW, Valuation Account 1923, Public Relations file 50.1.

40. SP, Annual Report, 1928, p. 11; EP&SW, Memo from Water Service Department, n.d., Public Relations file 50.1.

41. Julius Kruttschnitt, March 24, 1914, to Epes Randolph, Executive Department file 130-1, box 71.

42. T. M. Schumacher, March 24, 1914, to Epes Randolph, Executive Department file 103, box 71; Joy Christenberry with Bob Cunningham, "James S. Douglas and the Tucson, Phoenix & Tidewater Railroad," *Journal of Arizona History*, Spring, 1984.

43. H. B. Titcomb, April 10, 1923, to Julius Kruttschnitt, Executive Department file 130.1, box 71; E. P. Ripley, Oct. 6, 1908, to Kruttschnitt, Executive Department file AT-310-9, box 38; *Arizona Gazette* (Phoenix), April 18, 1924; Myrick, 1: 243–44.

44. *Arizona Gazette* (Phoenix), March 6, 1924, March 10, 1924.

45. William Sproule, March 18, 1924, to Julius Kruttschnitt, and William F. Herrin, June 11, 1924, to Sproule, both in Executive Department file 130.1, box 71; *Los Angeles Times*, June 11, 1924; *Arizona Republican*, June 12, 1924.

46. *El Paso Herald*, June 28, 1924; Julius Kruttschnitt, July 1, 1924, to William Sproule, Executive Department file 130.1, box 71; *Lordsburg* (N. Mex.) *Liberal*, Aug. 21, 1924; *Traffic World*, Sept. 13, 1924; *Bulletin*, Oct., 1924, p. 7, Nov., 1924, pp. 7–8.

47. *Wall Street Journal*, Oct. 1, 1924; *Bulletin*, Nov., 1924, pp. 3–6; *New York Herald-Tribune*, Oct. 1924; *Bulletin*, Dec., 1924, pp. 9–10; Myrick, 1:242.

48. SP, Annual Reports, 1925, p. 21, 1926, p. 20; *Bulletin*, July, 1926, p. 10, April, 1923, p. 11, Nov., 1926, pp. 9–10.

49. Extract from Memorandum, July 26, 1935, and Paul Shoup, May 14, 1928, to A. H. Payson, both in Executive Department file AT-310-9, box 38; Myrick, 2: 896–99; D. H. Thomas, *The Southwestern Indian Detours: The Story of Fred Harvey/Santa Fe Railway Experiments in Detourism*.

50. Paul Shoup, Sept. 26, 1925, to J. H. Dyer, and Dyer, Dec. 1, 1926, to Shoup, both in Executive Department file 620.4, box 50; SP, Annual Report, 1929, p. 29.

51. RRC, Feb. 1, 1929, to Paul Shoup, and Shoup, Jan. 29, 1927, to J. H. Dyer, both in Executive Department file 620.4, box 50; SP, Office Manual (6-1-70), Sunset Railway; SP, Annual Reports, 1927, p. 22, 1928, p. 24, 1929, p. 34. On the general matter of Los Angeles and transportation, see Richard W. Barsness, "Railroads and Los Angeles: The Quest for a Deep-Water Port," *Southern California Quarterly*, December, 1965, pp. 379–94.

52. SP, Office Manual (6-1-70), Holton Inter-Urban Railway; *Holton* (Calif.) *Tribune*, Jan. 29, 1976; SP, Annual Report, 1925, p. 23.

53. Paul Shoup, Feb. 7, 1927, to George W. Boschke, and Boschke, March 11, 1927, to Shoup, both in Executive Department, no file no., box 65.

54. SP, Annual Reports, 1920, p. 27, 1923, p. 27, 1927, p. 26, 1928, p. 25, 1929, p. 33; *Railway Age*, March 9, 1929, pp. 567–72.

CHAPTER EIGHT

1. Clifford R. Morrill, "History of the El Paso Division" (typescript, 1925), p. 69.

2. *Bulletin*, Feb. 15, 1918, p. 1, Oct., 1927, pp. 3–4, April, 1923, pp. 3–7.

3. Ibid., Jan., 1920, p. 11, Nov. 28, 1928, pp. 3–5.

4. Ibid., Dec., 1927, pp. 3–5; _Railway Age_, June 2, 1928, pp. 1293–94.

5. _Bulletin_, Sept., 1922, p. 23; Charles T. Fee, Jan. 20, 1923, to All Agents and Conductors, and Advertising Expenditures—Southern Pacific (Pacific Lines), 9/3/82, both in Advertising files; _Bulletin_, Feb., 1928, p. 5, May, 1929, p. 35; _Railway Age_, Aug. 24, 1929, pp. 450–52.

6. _Bulletin_, June, 1926, p. 5.

7. Keith L. Bryant, "The Atchison, Topeka & Santa Fe Railway and the Development of the Taos and Santa Fe Art Colonies," _Western Historical Quarterly_ 9 (Oct., 1978): 437–53; E. O. McCormick, Aug. 1, 1912, to William Sproule, Advertising Department file; Edith Hamlin, "Maynard Dixon: Painter of the West," _American West_ 19 (Nov./Dec., 1982): 50–59; David F. Myrick, _Railroads of Arizona_, 2:897.

8. _Bulletin_, April, 1928, pp. 6–7; _Railway Age_, May 5, 1928, p. 1059.

9. SP, Annual Report, 1920, pp. 27–28; _Produce Marketing_, June, 1958, pp. 1–15.

10. Julius Kruttschnitt, Nov. 15, 1921, to William Sproule, George McCormick, March 24, 1922, to J. H. Dyer, L. J. Spence, May 19, 1922, to Sproule, and G. W. Luce, May 20, 1922, to Sproule, all in Executive Department file 410-043-1, box 29.

11. L. J. Spence, May 23, 1922, to W. R. Scott, and Grafton Greenough, May 26, 1922, to Spence, both in Executive Department file 410-043-1, box 29.

12. W. R. Scott, May 27, 1922, to L. J. Spence, Executive Department file 410-043-1, box 29.

13. _Bulletin_, Aug., 1922, pp. 5–9; _Los Angeles Times_, July 1, 1922; _Los Angeles Record_, June 30, 1922; Samuel M. Vauclain, June 30, 1922, to William Sproule, L. J. Spence, July 7, 1922, to Sproule, and Statement . . . Purchase Order P-116, Dec. 6, 1922, all in Executive Department file 410-043-1, box 29.

14. _Bulletin_, Sept. 15, 1914, pp. 1, 3, April 1, 1917, pp. 1–2; SP, Annual Reports, 1928, p. 23, and 1929, p. 27.

15. _Bulletin_, May 15, 1914, pp. 1, 3, May, 1922, pp. 3–4, June, 1923, pp. 3–5.

16. _Bulletin_, March, 1922, pp. 10, 15, July 1, 1914, p. 3, Feb., 1922, pp. 9–10, 23, Feb. 1, 1916, p. 8, Jan., 1922, p. 29, July, 1927, pp. 24–27.

17. Ibid., April 15, 1914, p. 1, Nov., 1920, p. 28, March, 1920, pp. 11–12; _SP, Student Course in Railroading_ (SP, 1914), p. 3; SP, Annual Report, 1921, pp. 24–25.

18. _Bulletin_, Sept., 1922, p. 23, Jan., 1930, pp. 5–6, Jan., 1922, p. 25, June, 1922, p. 8; Julius Kruttschnitt, "The Engineer as Railroad Executive," address before the New York Section, American Society of Civil Engineers, March 18, 1925, pp. 11–12.

19. _Bulletin_, Feb., 1927, p. 6, March, 1928, pp. 6, 14, Sept., 1922, p. 28; SP, Annual Report, 1921, p. 10.

20. Ernest L. King and Robert E. Mahaffay, _Main Line: Fifty Years of Railroading with the Southern Pacific_, p. 135; _Bulletin_, April 15, 1917, p. 4.

21. "Southern Pacific Company–Hospital Department" (typescript, n.d.), pp. 1, 3–4; _Bulletin_, Oct., 1929, pp. 7–8, March 1, 1916, pp. 3–4; _Railway Age_, Sept. 5, 1878.

22. Hospital typescript, pp. 2, 5–7, 14; _Bulletin_, March, 1922, p. 19.

23. _Bulletin_, May 1, 1915, p. 5, July 15, 1916, p. 5, May, 1920, pp. 1, 4; King and Mahaffay, p. 155.

24. _Bulletin_, July, 1922, p. 8, Sept., 1922, p. 11; SP, Annual Reports, 1921, pp. 7–8, 1922, p. 8, 1926, p. 10, 1920, p. 9; William Sproule, Sept. 15, 1922, to Julius Kruttschnitt, Executive Department file 080-3.9, box 2; _Bulletin_, Feb., 1923, p. 17.

25. J. A. Taff, Dec. 2, 1926, to Guy V. Shoup, and Taff, Dec. 7, 1926, to Paul Shoup, both in Executive Department, no file number, box 29.

26. SP, _Historical Memoranda_, 1: "Separation of California Oil Properties from Railroad Properties," pp. 1–9.

27. Ibid., "Suits Involving Title to Oil Lands," pp. 1–10; Stuart Daggett, _Chapters on the Southern Pacific_, pp. 441–99; Pacific Oil Company, Annual Report (Final), 1927–1929, pp. 3–4; SP, Annual Reports, 1914, p. 21, 1919, p. 22, 1920, p. 26, 1921, p. 22.

28. SP, _Historical Memoranda_, 1: "Oregon Land Litigation," pp. 1–10; SP, Annual Reports, 1915, p. 20, 1925, p. 23, 1928, p. 23.

29. Paul Shoup, Nov. 10, 1926, to Calvin Coolidge, Executive Department file 089-4, box 28; Isidore B. Dockweiler, April 4, 1930, to Guy V. Shoup, and Hale Holden, April 1, 1930, to Paul Shoup, both in Executive Department file 345-1, box 28; SP, Annual Reports, 1928, p. 22, 1929, p. 30.

30. _Bulletin_, May, 1925, p. 2, July, 1925, pp. 3–4.

31. _Who's Who in Railroading, 1930_ (New York: Simmons-Boardman, 1930), p. 129.

32. Ibid., pp. 340–41.

33. _Biographical Directory of the Railway Officers of America, 1922_ (New York: Simmons-Boardman, 1922), p. 591.

34. _Who's Who in Railroading, 1930_, p. 472; _Railway Age_ 85 (Nov. 10, 1928): 942.

35. _Who's Who in Railroading, 1930_, pp. 242–43; SP, Annual Report, 1928, p. 26; _Railway Age_, Sept. 1, 1928, pp. 421–23.

36. _Railway Age_, April 23, 1927, p. 1261; _Barron's_, Aug. 15, 1927; _Southern Pacific Company: Pioneers of Western Progress_ (San Francisco: Strassburger, 1929), p. 63.

37. William Sproule, May 14, 1928, to Paul Shoup, and Shoup, May 15, 1928, to Sproule, both in Executive Department file 230.01, box 63; _Railway Age_, April 23, 1927, pp. 1261–64; SP, Annual Report, 1929, pp. 14–15; _Railway Age_, April 13, 1929, pp. 846–48, May 17, 1930, pp. 1189–91.

CHAPTER NINE

1. The term _dark decade_ was used by Jackson E. Reynolds, a director from 1929 to 1943.

2. Tabular data from SP Annual Reports, 1898–1941.

3. Ibid.

4. _Bulletin_, May–June, 1931, pp. 9–10; tabular data from SP Annual Reports, 1898–1941.

5. SP, Annual Reports, 1933, p. 19, 1934, p. 19; _Bulletin_, Oct., 1935, p. 6; V. S. Andrus, July 6, 1946, to K. C. Ingram, Executive Department file 216, box 29.

6. Executive Department memo, Rail Lines Abandoned and Trackage Rights Relinquished, Years 1921–1943, May 15, 1944.

7. SP, Annual Report, 1932, p. 13; _San Francisco Chronicle_, July 14, 1932; H. H. Hummell, Feb. 28, 1934, to Erle Heath, PR file R 10.1.

8. SP, Annual Reports, 1930, p. 34, 1931, p. 29, 1932, p. 29; *Bulletin*, May–June, 1931, p. 9, Jan., 1937, p. 14; *Railway Age*, Dec. 27, 1930, p. 1386.

9. *Bulletin*, May, 1922, pp. 14–15, Jan., 1922, p. 22; *Bulletin*–T&L Lines, June, 1939, pp. 2–3; SP, Annual Reports, 1926, p. 11, 1927, p. 12, 1933, p. 32, 1935, p. 35, 1937, p. 35.

10. *Bulletin*, Dec., 1919, p. 5; SP, Annual Report, 1933, p. 13; Memorandum, Nov. 30, 1928, Executive Department file 230, box 29; William D. Middleton, *When the Steam Railroads Electrified*, p. 283; SP, Annual Report, 1933, p. 29.

11. *Bulletin*, April, 1922, p. 21, July, 1922, pp. 18–19, April, 1923, pp. 22–23, April, 1929, p. 8, July, 1930, pp. 12–13, August, 1938, pp. 2–3, May, 1941, p. 7.

12. Ibid., March, 1923, p. 13, July, 1924, p. 11, Sept., 1924, p. 11, May, 1929, p. 35, July, 1940, p. 5, June, 1941, p. 7, June, 1939, p. 5.

13. Ibid., June, 1920, p. 8, Dec., 1922, pp. 17–18, Feb. 1923, p. 12. On the movie industry and the railroads, see Larry Jensen, *The Movie Railroads*.

14. SP, Annual Report, 1932, p. 12.

15. *Wall Street Journal*, Jan. 23, 1923; Julius Kruttschnitt, Jan. 24, 1923, to Marvin Hughitt, Executive Department file 080.3-9, box 2; L. J. Spence, May 1, 1924, to William Sproule, Sproule, May 10, 1924, to Spence, F. S. McGinnis, April 25, 1931, to Paul Shoup, and H. A. Scandrett, July 10, 1931, to Shoup, all in Executive Department file 110-1, box 17.

16. Paul Shoup, April 2, 1927, to William Sproule, Executive Department, no file number, box 35; Charles T. Fee, Aug. 2, 1913, to E. P. McCormick, Executive Department file 120.01, box 72; Passengers Interchanged Portland, Nov. 28, 1928, Executive Department file 081 GN, box 45; Shoup, Oct. 6, 1928, to Sproule, Executive Department file 120, box 72.

17. John F. Hippen, "A Wall Street Man and Western Railroad: A Chapter in Railroad Administration," *Bulletin of the Business Historical Society* 23 (Sept. 1949): 145–47; *Bulletin*, Dec. 15, 1913, p. 8, Jan., 1923, p. 18, Dec., 1929, p. 5; *Railway Age*, March 3, 1928, p. 508, Nov. 17, 1928, p. 971; *Bulletin*, Sept., 1927, p. 5; *Railway Age*, Feb. 1, 1930, pp. 343–44.

18. *Bulletin*, May, 1922, p. 5, Sept., 1922, p. 18, March, 1922, p. 31, Oct., 1922, p. 14, Nov., 1926, p. 13, Feb., 1914, p. 3.

19. Ibid., Oct., 1922, p. 3, June, 1920, pp. 5–6, Aug., 1920, pp. 9–10.

20. Various notations in ibid., 1907–41, also Aug., 1922, pp. 13–14, July, 1929, p. 608, Dec., 1929, pp. 6–7, Feb., 1940, pp. 2–3; Louis P. Hopkins, "A Lifetime of Railroading," p. 56, in Oregon Collection, University of Oregon.

21. "The First Presidential Train to the Pacific Coast—1901," Public Relations file 200.5; *Bulletin*, Oct., 1919, p. 1, Sept., 1923, pp. 7–8, Sept., 1928, pp. 3–5, Aug., 1938, pp. 8–9.

22. Tabular data from SP annual reports, 1920–41.

23. Executive Department, Statement 50 (annual), 1925–1941; memo, June 30, 1912, Executive Department file 075-USCP, box 13; *Morning Oregonian* (Portland), Sept. 14, 1913.

24. Executive Department, Statement 50 (annual), 1925–41; memo, June 30, 1912, Executive Department file 075-USCP, box 13; William Sproule, Oct. 13, 1928, to A. D. McDonald, Executive Department file 081, box 72.

25. *Bulletin*, Feb. 15, 1916, p. 5, April, 1920, p. 10, Sept., 1922, p. 28, June, 1928, p. 17.

26. Ibid., Dec. 10, 1913, p. 3, June, 1922, p. 26, June 1, 1914, p. 2, March, 1920, p. 20, March, 1939, p. 6; C. M. Keys, "Harriman IV: Salvage of the Two Pacifics," *World's Work* 13 (April, 1907): 8799.

27. *Packer* (Watsonville-Salinas, Calif), May 20, 1907; *Railway Age*, Nov. 30, 1929, pp. 1270–72; *Bulletin*, Oct., 1922, p. 27, July 24, 1924, p. 5.

28. *Bulletin*, Aug., 1927, p. 3; Ernest L. King and Robert E. Mahaffay, *Main Line: Fifty Years of Railroading with the Southern Pacific*, p. 28; *Bulletin*, Sept., 1929, pp. 7–10; W. B. Kirkland, Feb. 15, 1932, to R. E. Kelly, Public Relations file 70.2; William Sproule, Aug. 23, 1922, to Julius Kruttschnitt, Executive Department file 080.3-9, box 1; *Railway Age*, June 22, 1929, pp. 1404–10, Nov. 30, 1929, pp. 1270–72.

29. Superintendent of Transportation, "Transcontinental Freight Schedules," Aug. 1, 1932.

30. "Report on Schedules of Perishable and Manifest Trains," March 19, 1941; *Bulletin*, Dec., 1936, p. 6, July, 1937, p. 4.

31. Paul Shoup, March 29, 1929, to Hale Holden, Executive Department, no file number, box 59; *Railway Age*, Jan. 12, 1929, pp. 144–47, July 19, 1930, pp. 98–102; *Bulletin*, May, 1930, pp. 3–4, SP, Annual Reports, 1929, p. 27, 1941, p. 21.

32. "Report on Suisun Bay Bridge December, 1927," Office of the President; "The Suisun Bay Bridge," June 4, 1928, Executive Department, no file number, box 53; *Bulletin*, April, 1930, p. 14; *Railway Age*, June 21, 1930, pp. 1458–64; *Bulletin*, Nov., 1930, pp. 3–5; *Railway Age*, Dec. 13, 1930, p. 1297; SP, Annual Reports, 1928, p. 24, 1929, p. 26, 1930, p. 22.

33. SP, Annual Reports, 1930, p. 30, 1939, p. 28, 1940, p. 24, 1931, pp. 27–29; Richard M. Murdock, "Life on the Old Southern Pacific Train-Ferries," *Railroad Magazine*, Jan., 1967, pp. 46–47, and "Memories of the Old Benicia Depot," ibid., May, 1968, pp. 18–21; George W. Hilton, "Carquinez Train Ferries," *Trains*, Aug., 1946, 36–39.

34. *Railway Age*, Dec. 5, 1925, pp. 18–19, Dec. 12, 1925, pp. 30–31, July 28, 1928, pp. 190–94, July 28, 1928, pp. 179–80, Feb. 23, 1929, pp. 509–10, Sept. 28, 1929, p. 762; SP, Annual Report, 1929, p. 31.

35. Paul Shoup, March 25, 1931, to Ralph Budd, Executive Department file 081GN, box 45.

36. SP, Annual Report, 1930, pp. 13, 28, 29; *Railway Age*, June 22, 1929, pp. 1503–1506, Oct. 30, 1930, pp. 882–87; *Wall Street Journal*, May 9, 1931; *Railway Age*, April 26, 1930, pp. 1019–20.

37. Paul Shoup, March 15, 1929, to Hale Holden, Executive Department file PE089-2, box 21; SP, Annual Reports, 1930, p. 29, 1933, pp. 28–29; *Railway Age*, March 23, 1929, pp. 708–710, June 22, 1929, p. 1525.

38. L. B. Young, Memo, June 15, 1942, Executive Department file 280PMT, box 22; C. J. McDonald, Feb. 13, 1936, to John C. Emery, Executive Department file 120-1, box 22; *Bulletin*, Oct., 1935, pp. 8, 9, 12, March, 1936, pp. 4–5, 12–13, July, 1939, p. 8.

39. SP, Annual Report, p. 30.

40. *Bulletin*, Oct., 1935, p. 3.

CHAPTER TEN

1. SP, Annual Reports, 1930, p. 31, 1931, p. 32, 1935, pp. 28–29, 1936, p. 30, 1934, p. 34.

2. Ibid., 1939, p. 28; Executive Department, Statement 193 (April 14, 1941); SP, Annual Report, 1941, p. 26.

3. SP, Annual Report, 1936, p. 24; PFE, *History and Development of Pacific Fruit Express Company* (January 1, 1945), p. 2; PFE, *History and Functions of Pacific Fruit Express Company* (January 1, 1967), pp. 4–5; *Bulletin*, June, 1937, pp. 1–5.

4. SP, Annual Report, 1939, p. 27; Fred A. Stindt, *The Northwestern Pacific Railroad: Redwood Empire Route*, pp. 54–55; SP, Annual Reports, 1940, p. 26, 1941, p. 26.

5. H. K. Reynolds, April 5, 1933, to F. Q. Tredway, Advertising Department files.

6. Ibid.

7. *Bulletin*, Feb. 15, 1914, p. 6, June, 1929, p. 9, May–June, 1931, p. 8; Edmund Keilty, *Doodlebug Country: The Rail Motorcar on the Class I Railroads of the United States*, pp. 161–65.

8. Paul Shoup, Aug. 4, 1926, to F. S. McGinnis, VP&GM file 415-22; Richard K. Wright, *Southern Pacific Daylight: Train 98–99*, pp. 36–39. Wright presents an exhaustive study of the *Daylight*.

9. Hale Holden, Dec. 12, 1935, to A. D. McDonald and J. H. Dyer, Dec. 18, 1935, to McDonald, both in VP&GM file 415-22.

10. J. H. Dyer, Dec. 20, 1935, to A. D. McDonald, VP&GM file 415-22; John F. Stover, *The Life and Decline of the American Railroad*, pp. 206–209; Jim Scribbins, *The Hiawatha Story*, p. 26; Stan Repp, *The Super Chief—Train of the Stars*, p. 19.

11. A. D. McDonald, March 23, 1936, to F. H. McGinnis, A. T. Mercier, Memorandum, April 13, 1936, and J. H. Dyer, May 22, 1936, to George McCormick, all in VP&GM file 415-22.

12. *Bulletin*, April, 1937, pp. 2–7; SP, Annual Reports, 1939, pp. 12, 23, 1941, p. 25.

13. *Bulletin*, July, 1936, pp. 12–15, Jan., 1938, pp. 5–8; *Union Pacific Magazine*, April, 1924, pp. 8–9; SP, Western Division Time Table 231 (Sept. 29, 1940), pp. 2, 21; SP, Salt Lake Division Time Table 54 (June 17, 1940), pp. 2–3, 17.

14. "Chronology Air-Conditioning of Passenger Equipment on Southern Pacific," Executive Department, no file number, box 28; SP, Annual Reports, 1932, p. 21, 1939, p. 24; *Bulletin*, (Oct. 1935, pp. 10–11; Paul Shoup, April 6, 1930, to F. S. McGinnis, VP&GM file 541-401; *Bulletin*, Oct., 1935, p. 12, Sept., 1936, pp. 2–3.

15. *Bulletin*, Oct., 1936, p. 3, Aug., 1938, pp. 6–7, 9, May, 1941, pp. 9–10.

16. Ibid., Sept., 1940, p. 9; SP, Annual Report, 1938, p. 14.

17. Tabular data from SP Annual Reports, 1930–41.

18. *Bulletin*, Nov., 1925, pp. 3–5.

19. Ibid., Jan., 1924, pp. 23–24, Feb., 1924, pp. 8–9; Julius Kruttschnitt, "The Engineer as a Railroad Executive," address before the New York Section, American Society of Civil Engineers, March 18, 1925, p. 12.

20. William Sproule, June 30, 1922, to Samuel M. Vauclain, Executive Department file 410-043-1, box 29; *Bulletin*, Sept., 1924, pp. 3–6, Feb., 1925, pp. 3–4, July, 1925, p. 7. On the Southern Pacific–type locomotives, see James E. Boynton, *The 4-10-2: Three Barrels of Steam*.

21. On SP's famous articulated locomotives, see Robert J. Church, *Cab-Forward: The Story of Southern Pacific Articulateds*; *Bulletin*, Dec., 1928, pp. 3–5, 16–17, July, 1936, p. 3, Feb., 1937, pp. 2–5, Nov., 1939, pp. 12–13; Ralph D. Ranger, Jr., "Those Go-Ahead and Back-Up Locomotives," *Trains*, Aug., 1968, pp. 20–39; *Railway Age*, Dec. 15, 1928, pp. 1181–85.

22. On SP's GS engines, see R. J. Church, *Those Daylight 4-8-4s: The Story of Southern Pacific GS Class Locomotives*; David P. Morgan, "Famous Steam Locomotives 8: The Dressy but Durable Daylights," *Trains*, Oct., 1952, pp. 20–21; Memo, Office of General Superintendent Motive Power, Dec. 7, 1954; SP, Annual Reports, 1940, p. 21; 1941, p. 20. On SP's steam power generally, see Guy L. Dunscomb, *A Century of Southern Pacific Steam Locomotives, 1862–1962*; Donald Duke, *Southern Pacific Steam Locomotives: A Pictorial Anthology of Western Railroading*, and Gerald M. Best and David L. Joslyn, "Locomotives of the Southern Pacific Company," *R&LHS Bulletin No. 94* (March, 1956).

23. SP, Annual Reports, 1938, p. 32, 1941, p. 25.

24. Ibid., 1935, p. 34, 1938, pp. 26, 32.

25. *Bulletin*, June, 1925, pp. 5–7, July, 1925, pp. 5–6, March, 1938, pp. 6–9; *Railroad Magazine* 28 (June, 1940): 24–33; Fitzhugh Turner, "Railroad in a Barn," *American Heritage*, Dec., 1958, pp. 52–57, 107–109; George Kraus, *High Road to Promontory: Building the Central Pacific (Now the Southern Pacific) across the High Sierra*, pp. 121, 123, 144–49, 182–98. On rotaries, see Gerald M. Best, *Snowplow: Clearing Mountain Rails*.

26. SP, Annual Report, 1936, p. 21; H. C. Hallmark, April 8, 1942, to J. T. Saunders, Executive Department file 601-1, box 35; SP, Annual Reports, 1938, pp. 15, 21, 23, 1939, p. 22, 1940, p. 20, 1941, pp. 17–18; *Bulletin*, Jan., 1939, p. 3.

27. Charles T. Babers, interviews, Oct. 26, 1984, and Sept. 18, 1985.

28. David F. Myrick, *Railroads of Arizona*, 1: 99–105; Dan O'Connell, "Train Robberies on the Southern Pacific Lines" (typescript, PR file 071-2); *Phoenix Gazette*, May 25, 1977; *Bulletin*, Nov., 1923, pp. 11–12. On the Siskiyou robbery, see Art Chipman, *"Tunnel 13:" The Story of the De Autrement Brothers and the West's Last Great Train Hold Up*; Ernest L. King and Robert E. Mahaffay, *Main Line: Fifty Years of Railroading with the Southern Pacific*, p. 75; Clifford R. Morrill, "History of the El Paso Division" (typescript, 1925), p. 38; *San Francisco Chronicle*, Dec. 1, 1930; *Railway Age*, Nov. 23, 1929, p. 1210.

29. Memorandum on Major Passenger Train Accidents, March 31, 1958, Executive Department file 160.9, box 28.

30. J. H. Dyer, Aug. 13, 1939, to A. D. McDonald, and A. T. Mercier, Aug. 17, 1939, to McDonald, both in Executive Department file 581-1/922, box 1; *Wall Street Journal*, Dec. 30, 1939; SP, Annual Report, 1939, p. 14.

31. *Bulletin*, March, 1939, pp. 4–5, May, 1939, p. 4, June, 1940, p. 3.

32. Ibid., June, 1939, pp. 2–4, July, 1940, pp. 2–4.

33. Ibid., July 1, 1915, p. 2; Paul Shoup, March 20, 1929, to Hale Holden, Executive Department file 510-5/924, box 38; AT&SF, Annual Report, 1933, p. 16; SP, Annual Report, 1938, pp. 24–25; *Bulletin*, Aug., 1938, pp. 10–11, June, 1939, p. 9, July, 1939, pp. 2–5.

34. SP, Portland Division Time Table No. 116 (Feb. 17, 1929), pp. 11–14; SP, Annual Reports, 1939, p. 26, 1938,

p. 30, 1941, p. 26. On Northwestern Pacific's electric commuter lines, see Harre W. De Moro, *Electric Railway Pioneer: Commuting on the Northwestern Pacific, 1903–1941*; SP, Annual Report, 1928, p. 23, 1939, p. 26, 1941, p. 25.

35. Southern Pacific Company Report on the Interurban Electric Railway Company, January 16, 1940, Executive Department box 53; *Bulletin*, Feb., 1938, pp. 2–4, Jan., 1939, pp. 4–7, Feb., 1939, p. 7; SP, Annual Reports, 1938, pp. 13, 25, 31, 1939, p. 27; *Berkeley Gazette*, Jan. 14, 1939; *San Francisco Examiner*, Jan. 15, 1939.

36. SP, Annual Reports, 1940, pp. 12, 26, 1941, p. 26; *Bulletin*, March, 1940, p. 4, July, 1942, p. 14. See also Paul C. Trimble, *Interurban Railways of the Bay Area*.

37. Cerinda W. Evans, *Collis Porter Huntington*, 1: 270–72; James Horsburgh, Feb. 9, 1919, to G. E. Weeks, PR file 34; *Bulletin*, Jan., 1928, pp. 3–5; *Railway Age*, Jan. 18, 1930, pp. 187–89.

38. SP, Annual Report, 1929, p. 23; James Holden, "93 Years of Railway Ferries on San Francisco Bay," *Railroad Magazine*, Jan., 1965, pp. 13–17; *Bulletin*, Nov., 1936, pp. 2–5; J. H. Dyer, April 8, 1933, to A. D. McDonald, Executive Department file 510-5/924, box 38; *Bulletin*, Nov., 1938, pp. 2–8, Dec., 1938, pp. 10–13; *San Francisco Examiner*, Jan. 15, 1939; SP, Annual Reports, 1939, p. 28, 1940, p. 27, 1941, p. 27; *Bulletin*, June, 1940, p. 11. On San Francisco Bay, see John Haskell Kemble, *San Francisco Bay: A Pictorial Maritime History*; on ferryboats, see George H. Harlan, *San Francisco Ferryboats*.

39. C. P. Huntington, "California—Her Past, Present and Future," speech before the Chiefs of Department, Southern Pacific Company, May 16, 1900, p. 16; James J. Hill, "Their Advantages to the Community," *North American Review*, July 29, 1901, p. 654.

40. Evans, 1: 273–79; John Haskell Kemble, "The Big Four at Sea: The History of the Occidental and Oriental Steamship Company," *Huntington Library Quarterly* 3 (April, 1940): 339–57; SP, Annual Report, 1901, p. 6; SP, Time Table (March, 1907), pp. 53–54.

41. William Sproule, Sept. 21, 1912, to L. J. Spence, Executive Department file 082, box 21; *Bulletin*, Oct. 1, 1914, p. 8.

42. William Sproule, Sept. 30, 1912, to R. S. Lovett, Executive Department file 082, box 21; *Bulletin*, "Aug. 15, 1915, p. 3; SP, Annual Report, 1915, p. 21; *Bulletin*, Nov. 15, 1915, pp. 1–2; Julius Kruttschnitt, Feb. 2, 1916, to Stockholders of the Pacific Mail Steamship Company, Executive Department file 082, box 21.

43. SP, Time Table (March, 1907), pp. 53–54; SP, Passenger Department Circular No. 351 (Nov. 20, 1906); SP, Passenger Department Circular No. 699 (June 11, 1907).

44. SP, *A Financial History of the Southern Pacific* (n.d.), p. 31-1; "Southern Pacific Steamship Lines, 'Morgan Line'" (Oct. 1, 1961), pp. 1–2, Executive Department, box 53. On Charles Morgan, see James P. Baughman, *Charles Morgan and the Development of Southern Transportation*.

45. "Southern Pacific Steamship Lines, 'Morgan Line,'" p. 1.

46. SP, Time Table (March, 1907), pp. 53–54; *Official Guide of the Railways* (Aug., 1913), p. 844; *Bulletin*, Jan., 1922, p. 8; L. J. Spence, Oct. 3, 1914, to Julius Kruttschnitt, Executive Department file 075-USCP, box 13.

47. SP, Annual Reports, 1922, p. 24, 1918, p. 8.

48. *Bulletin*, Jan., 1924, pp. 7–9; A. M. Sullivan, "'Morgan Line: A Pioneer in Coastwise Trade," *Port of New York and Ship News* 5 (Feb., 1926): 3–9; *Bulletin*, Jan., 1927, pp. 3–4; various data, Public Relations file 290.2.

49. *Bulletin*, Sept., 1927, p. 7, Oct., 1935, pp. 4–5, Dec., 1935, p. 9, Jan., 1936, pp. 7, 12.

50. W. A. Worthington, May 10, 1937, to M. J. Wise, H. M. Lull, June 1, 1937, to A. D. McDonald, and "Report on the Conditions of Southern Pacific Steamship Lines" (June 8, 1937), all in Executive Department files.

51. SP, Annual Report, 1940, p. 25; SP, press release, Feb. 27, 1941; *Bulletin*, Feb., 1941, p. 10; SP, Annual Report, 1941, p. 25.

52. Evans, 1: 272–73; *Bulletin*, June 1, 1914, p. 3, Oct. 15, 1914, p. 4; SP, Annual Report, 1930, p. 31; Robert Hancock, Jr., "Riverboats," *Sacramento County Historical Golden Notes* 9 (July, 1963): 1–20.

53. F. Q. Treadway, Dec. 9, 1939, to F. S. McGinnis, Advertising Department files; *Bulletin*, June, 1940, back cover, Jan., 1940, pp. 10–12, Dec., 1941, pp. 8–9, Aug., 1939, p. 7, Dec., 1939, p. 2; F. Q. Treadway, *Selling Train Travel* (booklet, 1937); SP, Annual Reports, 1936, p. 13, 1937, pp. 14, 26, 1940, p. 9.

54. SP, Annual Reports, 1933, p. 28, 1937, pp. 34–35, 1934, p. 29.

55. Ibid., 1939, p. 32; *Bulletin*, Aug., 1939, pp. 2–6, Sept., 1939, p. 5; Donald J. Russell, June 15, 1984, to the author.

56. SP, Annual Report, 1936, p. 36, 1937, pp. 15–16, 37, 1938, pp. 14, 25, 1939, pp. 23–24, 1940, pp. 9, 24, 1941, p. 20.

57. *San Francisco News*, April 23, 1937; *Rails*, July, 1937, pp. 1–24; *Fortune* 16 (Nov., 1937): 91–104; *Magazine of Wall Street*, July 12, 1930, pp. 75–79.

58. *Fortune* 16 (Nov., 1937): 1868; *Bulletin*, Jan., 1941, p. 2; Dec., 1941, pp. 2–6; Louis P. Hopkins, "A Lifetime of Railroading," autobiographical typescript, pp. 81–82, Oregon Collection, University of Oregon, Eugene.

59. *Bulletin*, Dec., 1941, p. 3.

CHAPTER ELEVEN

1. Donovan L. Hofsommer, "Texas Railroads," *Texas: A Sesquicentennial Celebration*, ed. Donald W. Whisenhunt, p. 244.

2. SP, *A Financial History of the Southern Pacific Transportation Company* (n.d.), p. 34-1 (hereinafter cited as *Financial History*); *Poor's Manual of Railroads, 1887*, p. 89; James P. Baughman, *Charles Morgan and the Development of Southern Transportation*, pp. 154–77, 190–205, 208–11.

3. *Financial History*, pp. 34-1, 32-1. For an expansive history of SP operations in Louisiana, see *Bulletin*–T&L Lines, Oct., 1952, pp. 1–55.

4. *Financial History*, p. 55-1; *Poor's Manual of Railroads, 1896*, p. 891. On Texas railroads in general and the SP and its subsidiaries in particular, see S. G. Reed, *A History of the Texas Railroads and of Transportation Conditions under Spain and Mexico and the Republic and the State*. See also Charles P. Zlatkovich, *Texas Railroads: A Record of Construction and Abandonment*.

5. *Financial History*, p. 14-1; SP, *History of the Southern Pacific Organization & Development of the Lines in Texas & Louisiana* (1927), pp. 88–91, in Executive Department box 53; Baughman, pp. 193, 198, 200, 216.

6. *Financial History*, p. 23-1; *Poor's Manual of Railroads, 1888*, p. 933.

7. *Poor's Manual of Railroads, 1888,* p. 933.

8. George C. Werner, "Sunset Route Centennial," *National Railway Bulletin* 48, no. 6 (1983): 4–13, reprinted as *Sunset Route: The Centennial of Its Completion, 1883–1983;* Julius Grodinsky, *Jay Gould: His Business Career: 1867–1892,* pp. 346–51.

9. *Financial History,* p. 23-1.

10. *Poor's Manual of Railroads, 1900,* pp. 627, 634; *Financial History,* pp. 55-1, 34-1; George C. Werner, "Railroads of the Magnolia City," *National Railway Bulletin,* no. 1 (1982): 4–21, 42–43.

11. *Poor's Manual of Railroads, 1902,* pp. 610–11; *Financial History,* p. 28-1; Baughman, pp. 205–206; *Bulletin,* June, 1929, pp. 11–14.

12. Financial History, p. 24-1; SP, Annual Report, 1900, p. 6.

13. *Financial History,* p. 26-1; *Poor's Manual of Railroads, 1889,* pp. 763–64; *Bulletin*–T&L Lines, Oct., 1957, pp. 20–24. On the HE&WT, see Robert S. Maxwell, *Whistle in the Piney Woods: Paul Bremond and the Houston, East & West Texas Railway.*

14. *Poor's Manual of Railroads, 1924,* pp. 555–57, *Financial History,* p. 44-1; Reed, p. 247. On the San Antonio & Aransas Pass, see J. L. Allhands, *Gringo Builders,* pp. 253–54.

15. Reed, pp. 264–65; *Financial History,* p. 38-1; John C. Rayburn, "Count Telfener and the New York, Texas & Mexican Railway Company," *Southwestern Historical Quarterly* (July, 1964): 29–42. On the New York, Texas & Mexican, see Allhands, pp. 75–78.

16. *Financial History,* p. 25-1; Baughman, p. 188.

17. *Corporate History of the Galveston, Harrisburg & San Antonio Railway as of June 30, 1918,* pp. 5–6, Houston Public Relations office.

18. For a general history of the T&L Lines, its operations and antecedents, see *Bulletin,* July, 1929, pp. 15–17, and Aug., 1929, pp. 15–17.

19. *Bulletin*–T&L Lines, Dec., 1923, pp. 14–15.

20. SP, Annual Reports, 1926, p. 23, 1928, p. 25; Arthur H. Lewis, *The Day They Shook the Plum Tree,* pp. 177, 235; "Hetty Green's Railroad," *Railroad Magazine,* Oct., 1963, pp. 17–23.

21. *Laredo Times,* Dec. 5, 1981; Reed, pp. 472–76; W. R. Scott, May 18, 1920, to Julius Kruttschnitt, no file number, VP&GM files, Houston.

22. J. S. Pyeatt, May 26, 1922, to E. E. Bashford, W. R. Scott, March 4, 1925, to Julius Kruttschnitt, Executive Committee statement, Feb. 19, 1925, H. M. Lull, May 6, 1927, to G. R. Cottingham, and Memorandum of Meetings, June 25, 1930, all in Texas Mexican Railway file, VP&GM, Houston; H. Craig Miner, *The Rebirth of the Missouri Pacific, 1956–1983,* p. xiii.

23. SP, Annual Report, 1926, pp. 23–24.

24. *Bulletin*–T&L Lines, June, 1946, p. 13, Jan., 1923, p. 5, Sept., 1927, p. 15; Patrick J. Bruner, "'Can't Hurt, and May Do You Good': A Study of the Pamphlets the Southern Pacific Railroad Used to Induce Immigration to Texas, 1880–1930," *East Texas Historical Journal* 16 (1978): 35–45; T&NO, *East-Southeast Texas on the Texas & New Orleans Railroad* (1907); SP, *Agricultural Achievements and Possibilities along the Southern Pacific Lines in Texas* (1923); SP, *Southwest Louisiana: Its Agricultural and Industrial Developments and Its Potential Wealth* (1927).

25. SP, Annual Report, 1925, p. 23; W. R. Scott, Jan. 15, 1926, to A. D. McDonald, Executive Department file 120, box 72; L. W. Baldwin, Nov. 24, 1926, to H. W. deForest, Executive Department file 310-985, box 56; *Bulletin*–T&L Lines, Nov., 1926, pp. 2–5, Feb., 1927, pp. 4–7; SP, Annual Report, 1927, p. 25; 124 ICC 513-522; *Bulletin*–T&L Lines, April, 1927, p. 6, Dec., 1927, pp. 2–4; *San Antonio Express,* Nov. 6, 1927; *Brownsville Herald,* Nov. 14, 1927.

26. Paul Shoup, Nov. 14, 1932, to Walter Douglas, H. M. Lull, Oct. 14, 1943, to A. T. Mercier, both in Executive Department file 310-985, box 56; Julia Cameron Montgomery, *A Little Journey through the Lower Rio Grande Valley of Texas;* SP, *The Magic Valley of the Lower Rio Grande: The Land of Golden Fruit;* Hofsommer, p. 246; SP, Annual Report, 1928, p. 11.

27. *Bulletin*–T&L Lines, Aug., 1937, pp. 4–5, May, 1927, p. 6, May, 1937, pp. 4–5; SP, Annual Report, 1929, p. 21.

28. *Bulletin*–T&L Lines, June, 1936, p. 11, Aug., 1936, p. 17, April, 1940, p. 7; El Paso Division, Survey of Operations 1928, pp. 9–14, in Executive Department box 53.

29. *Bulletin*–T&L Lines, Jan., 1931, p. 13, Jan., 1945, pp. 12–13; SP-T&L Lines Circular 7-55 (July 1, 1926(, pp. 49–50, 52–53; W. Roland Earle, interview, April 7, 1982; SP/T&NO Circular No. 9, "Instructions Governing the Handling of Livestock" (April 1, 1949), p. 15.

30. *Bulletin*–T&L Lines, Dec., 1945, pp. 12–13, Feb., 1954, pp. 12–15.

31. SP, *Historical Memoranda,* 2: "Rio Bravo Oil Company," 1–3; "Spindletop (Texas) Oil Field Judgement," ibid., pp. 1–2; SP, Annual Report, 1933, p. 31.

32. The name of the train varied over the years but the word *Sunset* was always part of the title. In fact, in 1916 the SP operated both the *Sunset Limited* and the *Sunset Express* on the San Francisco–Los Angeles–New Orleans route (*Official Guide of the Railways,* June, 1916, pp. 632–33, Jan., 1930, p. 932).

33. *Official Guide of the Railways,* Jan., 1930, pp. 936–41; Edmund Keilty, *Doodlebug Country: The Rail Motorcar on the Class I Railroads of the United States,* pp. 167–68; *Bulletin*–T&L Lines, Aug., 1929, p. 5, Feb., 1930, p. 5; Paul M. Betts, interview, March 21, 1983; *Bulletin*–T&L Lines, June, 1936, p. 15, June, 1936, pp. 7–8; SP, Annual Report, 1934, p. 23; *Bulletin*–T&L Lines, Dec., 1939, pp. 2–3, May, 1939, back cover, Jan., 1936, p. 9, Oct., 1936, p. 20.

34. *Railway Age,* March 9, 1940, pp. 449–51; *Bulletin*–T&L Lines, July, 1938, p. 8, Oct., 1936, p. 4, Nov., 1937, p. 7, July, 1940, pp. 6–7.

35. *Bulletin*–T&L Lines, Feb., 1926, p. 9, Nov., 1927, p. 2, Sept., 1927, p. 5.

36. Ibid., Dec., 1945, pp. 2–5; *Railroad Magazine* 31 (March, 1942): 132–35; Clifford R. Morrill, "History of the El Paso Division" (typescript, 1925), pp. 14, 89; Gerald M. Best and David L. Joslyn, "Locomotives of the Southern Pacific Company," *R&LHS Bulletin No. 94,* March, 1956, pp. 27–62.

37. *Bulletin*–T&L Lines, Jan., 1931, pp. 1–2, June, 1937, pp. 10–11; Compiled Data, Superintendent MP&E Houston, March 22, 1932, in Houston files.

38. *Bulletin*–T&L Lines, Jan., 1931, pp. 10–11.

39. Ibid., Jan., 1936, p. 1, Oct., 1939, p. 9, Oct., 1939, p. 2, July, 1924, pp. 2–3, July, 1924, p. 1, Feb., 1926, p. 15.

40. *Bulletin*–T&L Lines, passim 1914–32, 1936–41, and April, 1930, p. 23, April, 1940, p. 6.

41. Ibid., April, 1924, pp. 1–5, Oct., 1940, pp. 8–14.

42. Ibid., March, 1937, pp. 10–12.

43. SP, Brief Summary—Industrial and Railroad Development—New Orleans, Louisiana (May 20, 1929), Executive Department box 53; Frank M. Masters, *Mississippi River Bridge at New Orleans, Louisiana: Final Report to the Belt Railroad Commission of the City of New Orleans*, pp. 7–13.

44. Masters, pp. 13, 18–19; SP, Annual Reports, 1932, p. 25, 1936, p. 27; *Bulletin*–T&L Lines, Jan., 1936, pp. 4–6, 12; Morrill, p. 92.

45. *Bulletin*–T&L Lines, Sept., 1937, pp. 4–9, June, 1938, pp. 6–7, Sept., 1940, p. 9.

CHAPTER TWELVE

1. C. D. Purdon, "History of the Cotton Belt," n.d., SSW Public Relations office, Kansas City, pp. 1–4; George W. Hilton, "The Grand Narrow Gauge Trunk," *Railroad History*, Spring, 1983, pp. 23–41.

2. Purdon, p. 5; *Cotton Belt News*, Third Quarter, 1969, pp. 17–20; "Corporate History St. Louis Southwestern Railway System and Subsidiary Companies," n.d., SSW Public Relations office, Kansas City (file 70-2-6), p. 6 (hereinafter cited as "History").

3. "History," pp. 7–8, 18–19, 24–29; Purdon, pp. 5–7, 11–15; Illinois Central Railroad, Annual Report, 1898, p. 5.

4. Purdon, pp. 7–10.

5. Ibid., pp. 13–15.

6. Ibid., pp. 10–11.

7. Ibid. (Addendum), p. 6; *St. Louis Southwestern Railway Company: An Examination of This System's Record with Reference to the Fundamental Position of Its Mortgage Obligations* (New York: Shields & Company, 1935), pp. 5–8 (hereinafter cited as *Examination*); SSW, Annual Reports, 1929, pp. 5–6, 1930, p. 3.

8. *Examination*, pp. 23–31.

9. Ibid., p. 13; *Tyler Courier Times*, March 20, 1955.

10. SSW, *Report on Certain Special Features of the St. Louis Southwestern Railway* (1915), pp. 153–65; Purdon, p. 19; *Railway Age*, Jan. 26, 1929, p. 298, July 27, 1929, p. 302.

11. F. W. Green, Oct. 17, 1947, to A. T. Mercier, Executive Department file SLSW 220, box 74; SSW, *Malaria Control: A Demonstration of Its Value to Railroads Based on Experience of the St. Louis Southwestern Railway Lines, 1917–1920* (1921), pp. 7–8, 12, 19–20, 27–28, 63.

12. Purdon (Addendum), pp. 2–3.

13. SSW, Northern Division Time Table 4 (Dec. 9, 1928); SSW, Texas Division Time Table 8 (May 16, 1926); *Examination*, pp. 31–33; *Official Guide of the Railways*, May, 1926, pp. 708–11, Jan., 1930, pp. 749–53; Edmund Keilty, *Doodlebug Country: The Rail Motorcar on the Class I Railroads of the United States*, pp. 154–55.

14. William Edward Hayes, *Iron Road to Empire: The History of 100 Years of the Progress and Achievements of the Rock Island Lines*, p. 210; Purdon (Addendum), p. 5; SSW, *Factual Report of Operating, Traffic and Financial Affairs* (1946), Exhibit 4, p. 1, Executive Department file 72 (hereinafter cited as *Report*); *Chicago Journal of Commerce*, Jan. 25, 1926; SSW, Annual Reports, 1924, p. 8, 1925, p. 8.

15. *Report*, Exhibit 4, p. 1; *Dallas Morning News*, Jan. 13, 1927; *Railway Age*, July 7, 1928, pp. 28–30, July 20, 1929, p. 213; SSW, Annual Reports, 1926, p. 8, 1927, p. 8, 1928, p. 8.

16. *Report*, pp. 170–73; Purdon (Addendum), p. 4; *Railway Age*, June 8, 1929, pp. 1337–38; *Examination*, pp. 15–19, 36–39. On Cotton Belt's motive power, see Joseph A. Strapac, *Cotton Belt Locomotives*.

17. *Railway Age*, Oct. 26, 1929, pp. 981–83, May 26, 1928, pp. 1256–58, Dec. 22, 1928, pp. 1269–70, April 27, 1929, pp. 1003–1006, Sept. 28, 1929, pp. 762, 781–82, April 26, 1930, pp. 1014–18, Nov. 22, 1930, pp. 1134–36; *Report*, Exhibit 5, pp. 1–3.

18. Daniel Upthegrove, Oct. 2, 1931, to William M. Greve, SSW Fn 428-185 (Tyler).

19. J. R. Turney, Sept. 30, 1931, to "All Shippers," E. L. Primm, Oct. 3, 1931, to Daniel Upthegrove, L. W. Baldwin, Sept. 30, 1931, to Upthegrove, J. M. Kurn, Sept. 30, 1931, to Upthegrove, all in SSW FN 428-185 (Tyler); *St. Louis Globe–Democrat*, Oct. 1, 2, 1931.

20. H. M. Lull, July 18, 1928, to A. D. McDonald, Executive Department file 081 SLSW, box 72; William Ripley, March 7, 1921, to Julius Kruttschnitt, Executive Department file 080.395, box 1; Stuart Daggett, *Railroad Consolidation West of the Mississippi River*, p. 255.

21. F. F. Green, May 6, 1935, to J. W. Barriger III, SSW VP files (Tyler); Survey of Operations, El Paso Division, 1928, pp. 12, 14, Executive Department box 53.

22. W. R. Scott, Jan. 15, 1926, to A. D. McDonald, and Scott, Jan. 24, 1926, to McDonald, both in Executive Department file 120, box 72.

23. T. M. Schumacher, April 9, 1926, to William Sproule, Paul Shoup, May 7, 1926, to Sproule, Shoup, May 31, 1926, to W. R. Scott, and Scott, May 22, 1926, to A. D. McDonald, all in Executive Department file 120, box 72.

24. F. H. Plaisted, June 2, 1926, to T. M. Schumacher, Plaisted, July 16, 1928, to A. D. McDonald, J. T. Saunders, July 19, 1928, to Paul Shoup, Saunders, July 20, 1928, to Shoup, and Shoup, July 28, 1928, to William Sproule, all in Executive Department file 081, box 72.

25. F. H. Plaisted, June 2, 1926, to T. H. Schumacher, and Paul Shoup, March 15, 1930, memorandum, both in Executive Department file 081SLSW, box 72.

26. Hale Holden, June 27, 1930, to Paul Shoup, Executive Department file 110.1, box 50.

27. Daggett, p. 155; Hale Holden, July 17, 1930, to Paul Shoup, Executive Department file 081SLSW, box 72; *Railway Age*, Aug. 9, 1930, pp. 283–84.

28. *Railway Age*, Nov. 1, 1930, pp. 924–25, Dec. 6, 1930, p. 1234; 180 ICC 175–217; 180 ICC 710–11.

29. Elizabeth M. Fowler, "The Turntable Fortunes of the Cotton Belt," *Railway Progress*, Nov., 1948, pp. 16–17; *Report*, Exhibit 50; SP, *Historical Memoranda*, 1: "Acquisition of St. Louis Southwestern Railway Company," 3–8.

30. *Examination*, pp. 49–50; *Official Guide of the Railways*, Oct., 1936, p. 861; Examination, p. 25; *Report*, pp. 11, 130–31, Exhibit 73—pp. 1, 5.

CHAPTER THIRTEEN

1. Statement by Director Jackson E. Reynolds at meeting of board of directors, Oct. 15, 1942, pp. 1–18, Executive Department, box 29.

2. *Bulletin*, Sept., 1939, p. 9, Sept., 1940, pp. 3–5, Oct., 1940, pp. 3–5, Nov., 1940, p. 5; various data, VP&GM file 611-1, San Francisco.

3. *Bulletin*, April, 1941, p. 3, Sept., 1941, pp. 2–21, Oct., 1941, p. 7.

4. Ibid., Nov., 1941, pp. 2–6.

5. Donald J. Russell, interview, May 21, 1982.

6. Ibid.; *Bulletin*, Dec., 1941, p. 7, F. S. McGinnis, Dec. 13, 1941, to C. E. Peterson, Advertising files; *Bulletin*, April, 1942, p. 10.

7. *Bulletin*, Jan., 1942, p. 2, Feb., 1942, pp. 3–5, March, 1942, pp. 3–4, April, 1942, pp. 3–6, 20, Sept., 1942, pp. 3–4, Dec., 1942, pp. 2–3, 11, Dec., 1943, pp. 6–7, March, 1944, p. 19; *Cotton Belter*, March 27, 1942, p. 2, July 10, 1942, p. 1; L. B. McDonald, April 23, 1942, to A. T. Mercier, Advertising files.

8. *Bulletin*, Oct., 1942, pp. 8–9; SP, Annual Report, 1942, p. 22; *Ogden Standard Examiner*, Sept. 13, 1942.

9. *Bulletin*, Feb., 1942, pp. 6–7, Dec., 1942, p. 15, April, 1942, pp. 13, 19, July, 1942, pp. 6–7, Sept., 1942, p. 13.

10. SP, Annual Reports, 1941, pp. 19–20, 1942, pp. 19–20, 1943, pp. 19–20, 1944, p. 19; J. T. McNamara, interview, Jan. 19, 1982.

11. SP, Annual Reports, 1941, pp. 19–20, 1942, pp. 19–20, 1943, pp. 19–20, 1944, p. 25, 1945, p. 23; SP, Executive Department Statement No. 457 (May 29, 1942), pp. 7–8; SP, Maximum Utilization of Transportation Facilities Under War Conditions, Statement No. 471 (Dec. 7, 1942), pp. 6, 15.

12. *Bulletin*, March, 1944, pp. 3–5; Randolph Karr, interview, Sept. 29, 1983; SP, Annual Report, 1945, p. 23; Statement 471, p. 3; tabular data from SP Statistical Reports 1940–45, inclusive.

13. SP, Annual Report, 1944, p. 24; R. W. Barnes, Nov. 12, 1941, to H. M. Lull, Harvey S. Mudd, Nov. 7, 1942, to A. T. Mercier, and Statement Showing Number of Trains, Locomotives, and Cars Across Pecos High Bridge—1936–1942 (Dec. 10, 1942), all in Executive Department file 331.-983PR, box 56; *Bulletin*–T&L Lines, July, 1945, pp. 14–15; *Railway Age*, May 26, 1945, pp. 930–32; *Texas Professional Engineer*, March–April, 1947, pp. 2–3, 22–23; *Bulletin*–T&L Lines, May–June, 1949, pp. 2–5.

14. Tabular data from SP Annual Reports, 1941–1945; Frank P. Donovan, Jr., "Pacific Electric," *Trains*, June, 1942, pp. 10–31; *Pacific Electric Magazine*, Feb., 1944, pp. 4–10.

15. Statement 471, pp. 13, 20; Frank J. Taylor, "Brother Can You Spare a Locomotive," *Saturday Evening Post*, June 26, 1943, pp. 71, 73, 75; Clifford R. Morrill, "History of the El Paso Division" (typescript, 1925—retyped and expanded 1970), p. 70; Randolph Karr, interview, Sept. 29, 1983; *Trainline*, Aug., 1983, p. 2; W. Roland Earle, interview, April 7, 1982; H. M. Lull, Oct. 30, 1944, to K. C. Ingram, PR file 1110.3; *Bulletin*, Nov., 1945, p. 11, Aug., 1944, pp. 5–6.

16. SP, Annual Report, 1942, p. 9; various data, PR file 120.7; Louis P. Hopkins, "A Lifetime of Railroading" (autobiographical typescript, Oregon Collection, University of Oregon, Eugene), p. 129.

17. Various data, PR file 120.7; W. Roland Earle, interview, Jan. 22, 1982; John F. Lindow, interview, Jan. 21, 1982; SP/

T&NO, Houston Division Time Table 26 (April 2, 1944), p. 2; Jo Rogers, interview, Jan. 22, 1982.

18. *Bulletin*, Dec., 1942, p. 4, Dec., 1944, p. 11.

19. Various data, PR file 120.8.

20. Ibid.

21. *Travel Items*, April 1, 1945, p. 4; various data, PR file 120.8; War Department Press Release 56806-2 (July 22, 1945); *Bulletin*, Feb., 1944, pp. 12–13, Dec., 1945, pp. 4–5.

22. *Wall Street Journal*, Sept. 27, 1943; H. A. Butler, Jan. 29, 1943, to D. J. Russell, Advertising files: F. Q. Tredway, speech before the Redding, California, Chamber of Commerce, Jan. 20, 1943, p. 11; *Bulletin*, Feb., 1944, pp. 3–5; various data, PR file 120.7; SP, Time Table, Sept. 9, 1945, back page.

23. *Bulletin*, Feb., 1944, pp. 3–5; *Cotton Belter*, July 10, 1942, p. 1; R. S. Gilmore, March 9, 1945, to F. S. McGinnis, Advertising files.

24. Tredway speech, pp. 12–13; *Wall Street Journal*, Sept. 27, 1943; various data, PR file 120.8.

25. *Bulletin*, Dec., 1944, p. 10.

26. Hopkins autobiography, p. 83; *Bulletin*, Aug., 1944, p. 6; "Memorandum of Major Passenger Train Accidents" PRE: Ref. 160.9 (March 31, 1958), p. 3, Executive Department, box 28; Robert B. Shaw, *A History of Railroad Accidents, Safety Precautions and Operating Practices* (privately published, 1978), p. 103.

27. "Opinion Survey as to Southern Pacific May 1942," Advertising file.

28. *Bulletin*, July, 1943, pp. 2–17, July, 1944, pp. 2–13, 16–17; *Bulletin*–T&L Lines, July, 1945, pp. 2–9; *Bulletin*, July, 1945, pp. 3–13; *Bulletin*–T&L Lines, June, 1945, pp. 4–5; *Bulletin*, May, 1945, p. 13.

29. *Bulletin*, June, 1944, p. 5, June, 1945, pp. 2, 8–9, Sept., 1945, pp. 17–18, May, 1943, pp. 3–4, March, 1944, pp. 8–10.

30. Tredway speech, p. 9; *Bulletin*, Aug., 1943, p. 2, July, 1945, p. 3.

31. Guerdon S. Sines, interview, June 29, 1984; *Bulletin*, March, 1943, pp. 3–4, Feb., 1942, p. 6; *Time*, Feb. 15, 1943, pp. 17–18; *Bulletin*, April, 1943, p. 3.

32. *Bulletin*, Nov., 1942, pp. 3–7; *Colliers*, Jan. 2, 1943, p. 54; *Bulletin*, April, 1943, pp. 4–6, Dec., 1944, p. 19.

33. Historical Data in Connection with Employment of Mexican National Laborers Imported from Mexico, Engineering Department (Aug., 1950), pp. 1–2.

34. Ibid., pp. 4, 11, 20, 21, 48, 68; *Bulletin*, June, 1943, pp. 6–7, Oct., 1943, pp. 4–7, Oct., 1944, p. 8, May, 1945, pp. 8–9, Oct., 1945, p. 23.

35. *Cotton Belter*, Dec. 14, 1942, p. 3; Tredway speech, p. 20; various data, PR file 120.7; F. S. McGinnis, Sept. 24, 1942, to Charles Laying, Advertising file.

36. "Southern Pacific's Campaign to Recruit Track Labor Through Advertising" (March 8, 1944), passim, in Advertising files; *Bulletin*, June, 1943, p. 12; Harry Bedwell, *Priority Special*; *Bulletin*, July, 1945, p. 20.

37. *Bulletin*, Nov., 1943, p. 5, Dec., 1943, p. 10, March, 1945, p. 10, May, 1945, p. 13; various data and scripts, Advertising file.

38. This advertisement, prepared in 1944, ran in several western newspapers on V-E Day.

39. J. J. Pelley, July 20, 1945, to Sen. Scott Lucas, PR file 120.7; *Bulletin*, Dec., 1943, p. 11, July, 1945, p. 2, back page.

40. *Bulletin*, Dec., 1945, pp. 6–8; various data, PR file 120.8; *Bulletin*–T&L Lines, May, 1947, p. 17.

41. *Bulletin*, Oct., 1945, p. 14, June, 1946, p. 6; various data, PR file 120.8; SP, Sacramento Division Dispatcher's Record of Movement of Trains (Sept. 1, 1945); Robert M. Gregory, interview, May 6, 1983; SP, Estimated Net Ton Miles (Jan. 8, 1946), and SSW, Train Order 231 (May 23, 1943), in author's files.

42. Tabular data from SP annual reports, 1940–46; Statement 471, p. 3.

43. *Bulletin*, April, 1946, p. 5; various data, PR file 120.8; *Standard Oil of California Summer Bulletin* 32 (Summer, 1945): 1–17; *Bulletin*, Sept., 1945, p. 2; SP, Annual Reports, 1944, pp. 21, 22, 27, 1945, p. 22.

CHAPTER FOURTEEN

1. *Bulletin*, Jan., 1942, p. 3; Donald J. Russell, interviews, Feb. 24, 1982, Dec. 10, 1982, Jan. 11, 1983; Ed P. Ahearn, interview, Jan. 10, 1983; SP, *Facts About the Southern Pacific: The Friendly Railroad* (1946), p. 1.

2. S. K. Burke, Memorandum for J. T. Saunders, Jan., 1942, Advertising files.

3. SP, Annual Statistical Reports, 1944, pp. 27–28.

4. SP, Annual Statistical Reports, 1940, p. 27, 1946, p. 28, 1947, p. 25.

5. L. B. McDonald, Nov. 3, 1947, to A. T. Mercier (with accompanying tabular data), Executive file 520.3.

6. *Bulletin*–T&L Lines, May, 1948, pp. 12–13, May, 1949, pp. 16–17, Nov., 1950, pp. 2–6, Aug., 1951, pp. 6–9, Sept., 1947, pp. 2–5; *Bulletin*, Nov.–Dec., 1947, pp. 11–13, March–April, 1948, p. 11.

7. Tabular data from SP's Annual Statistical Reports, 1945–51; SP, Statistical Reports, 1951, pp. 18–19, 1949, p. 19, 1946, p. 24, 1951, p. 18.

8. *Bulletin*, Feb., 1945, pp. 3–5, Sept.–Oct., 1949, p. 9, April, 1951, pp. 4–5.

9. SP, Statistical Reports, 1947, pp. 10, 22, 1949, p. 19, 1950, p. 17, 1951, p. 47.

10. *Bulletin*, May, 1941, p. 3.

11. H. K. Reynolds, March 22, 1943, to F. Q. Tredway, and A. L. Kohn, March 31, 1943, to Tredway, both in Advertising files.

12. C. E. Peterson, June 22, 1945, to A. T. Mercier, and D. J. Russell, June 27, 1945, to Mercier, both in Executive file 521-3; *Bulletin*, Feb., 1946, pp. 3–4; *Inside Track*, July, 1949, pp. 1–2, Aug., 1950, pp. 1–4.

13. C. E. Peterson, June 22, 1945, to A. T. Mercier, Executive file 521-3.

14. *Bulletin*, Nov.–Dec., 1946, p. 11; SP, Statistical Report, 1946, p. 27.

15. *Inside Track*, April, 1947, pp. 1–2; C. E. Peterson, July 5, 1949, to A. T. Mercier, Mercier, July 6, 1948, to J. D. Farrington, and C. E. Peterson, Nov. 17, 1949, to Mercier, all in Executive file 521-3; Donald J. Russell, interview, Feb. 24, 1982; SP, Statistical Reports, 1947, p. 11, 1948, p. 5.

16. A. L. Kohn, Dec. 5, 1938, to F. S. McGinnis, F. Q. Tredway, June 24, 1939, to McGinnis, and McGinnis, March 1, 1943, to A. T. Mercier, all in Advertising files.

17. F. Q. Tredway, June 24, 1939, to F. S. McGinnis, and H. K. Reynolds, March 22, 1943, to Tredway, both in Advertising files.

18. *Bulletin*–T&L Lines, Jan., 1946, pp. 2–3, April, 1946, pp. 2–4; *Inside Track*, May, 1947, pp. 1–2; *Bulletin*–T&L

Lines, May, 1948, p. 4, July, 1950, pp. 2–11; *Inside Track*, Aug., 1950, pp. 1–2; *Harper's Bazaar*, Jan., 1951, 110–15.

19. *Inside Track*, May, 1947, p. 2, Aug., 1947, p. 1, Feb., 1948, p. 4; SP, Statistical Report, 1947, p. 11; *Official Guide of the Railways*, Nov., 1950, p. 875.

20. *Bulletin*, May, 1946, p. 13; Willard V. Anderson, "$7.50 to L.A.,: *Trains* 10 (Aug., 1950): 36–42; *Inside Track*, Sept., 1949, pp. 1, 4.

21. F. S. McGinnis, Feb. 1, 1945, to D. J. Russell, and M. W. Clement, Sept. 27, 1945, to A. T. Mercier, both in Executive file 521.3.

22. C. E. Peterson, Feb. 12, 1946, to A. T. Mercier, Peterson, Jan. 4, 1946, to D. J. Russell, Peterson, March 19, 1946, to Mercier, W. G. Vollmer, April 30, 1947, to Mercier, Mercier, May 8, 1947, to Vollmer, and Peterson, March 19, 1946, to Mercier, all in Executive file 521-3.

23. SP, Statistical Supplements, 1946, p. 31, 1947, p. 29.

24. *Bulletin*, July, 1947, p. 3; *Bulletin*–T&L Lines, Dec., 1951, pp. 34–35, Jan., 1950, p. 17; *Bulletin*, May, 1945, p. 12, Aug., 1945, pp. 6–7, July–Aug., 1948, p. 8; *Bulletin*–T&L Lines, Sept., 1948, pp. 8–9; *Bulletin*, Jan.–Feb., 1949, p. 19, May–June, 1947, p. 15, Nov.–Dec., 1948, p. 9.

25. *Bulletin*, Sept.–Oct., 1946, back cover, March–April, 1950, p. 15; *Inside Track*, Aug., 1947, pp. 1, 4; *Bulletin*, July–Aug., 1946, p. 8, Nov.–Dec., 1948, p. 9, Nov.–Dec., 1950, pp. 6–7, Nov.–Dec., 1946, pp. 3–4, May–June, 1950, pp. 3–6; June, 1951, p. 8.

26. A. T. Mercier, June 30, 1948, to D. J. Russell, and Mercier, July 6, 1948, to J. D. Farrington, both in Executive file 521.3; SP, Statistical Reports, 1949, p. 21, 1950, p. 8, 1951, p. 8; W. A. Waisanen, comp., "Trains and Time Tables in the West, 1864–1976" (typescript, 1976), p. 367, SP Public Relations files.

27. SP, Statistical Reports, 1946, pp. 28–29, 1947, p. 11; SP, Annual Report, 1948, pp. 9–10; SP, Statistical Reports, 1948, pp. 25–26, 1949, pp. 21–22, 1950, pp. 9–10, 21, 1951, pp. 10–11.

28. SP, Statistical Reports, 1946, p. 30, 1947, p. 27, 1948, p. 27.

29. SP, Statistical Report, 1950, pp. 14–16.

30. SP, Statistical Reports, 1946, p. 31, 1947, pp. 28–29; *Railway Age*, Aug. 2, 1947, p. 203; *St. Louis Globe-Democrat*, Sept. 25, 1947; *St. Louis Star-Times*, Oct. 2, 1947; *Railway Progress*, Nov., 1948, pp. 16–19.

31. "Analysis of Value of St. Louis Southwestern Railway Company to Southern Pacific Transportation System" (n.d., 1945?), and SP, "Opinion Report on St. Louis Southwestern Lines" (March 25, 1947), pp. 44–45, both in Executive file, no number; SP, Statistical Reports, 1951, p. 22, 1948, pp. 16–17.

32. L. L. Waters, *Steel Trails to Santa Fe*, pp. 89–90, 371–73; William Edward Hayes, *Iron Road to Empire: The History of 100 Years of the Progress and Achievements of the Rock Island Lines*, pp. 162–64, 174; *St. Louis Post-Dispatch*, Jan. 15, 1931; Hale Holden, Jan. 19, 1931, to F. H. Plaisted, Executive file 310-9, box 38; *New York Journal of Commerce*, Jan. 29, 1931; *St. Louis Post-Dispatch*, Nov. 10, 1946; various data, SSW Law Department file 163-7-15365 (Houston); 271 ICC 63–167.

33. Rufus Kay Wyllys, "Sud-Pacifico: Postscript on Railroad," *Historical Society of Southern California Quarterly* 37 (March, 1955): 23–32; Robert A. Trennert, Jr., "Southern Pacific Railroad of Mexico," *Pacific Historical Review* 25 (Aug.,

1966): 265–84; Donald J. Russell, interview, Feb. 24, 1982; SP, Statistical Report, 1951, p. 13; Syllabus Southern Pacific Railroad Company of Mexico (as of June 30, 1948); D. J. Russell, Dec. 26, 1951, to James B. Black, and Southern Pacific Railroad Company of Mexico (n.d., 1955?), both in Executive file SPdeMex, box 53; various data, VP&GM file: Dissolution of SPdeMex (Houston).

34. Executive Committee Statement, Nov. 7, 1934, Executive Committee Statement, Jan. 11, 1940, and P. J. Kendall, July 28, 1955, to John B. Reid, all in Executive file 78-25, box 53; SP, "A Letter from Mexico's Hotel Playa de Cortes, Guaymas, Mexico" (1948); SP, "Hotel Playa de Cortes," Circular Letter No. 4526 (Nov. 1, 1941).

35. Various data from SP Statistical Reports, 1946–51.

36. SP, Statistical Reports, 1946, p. 28, 1951, p. 5.

CHAPTER FIFTEEN

1. Albro Martin, *James J. Hill and the Opening of the Northwest*, p. 564; Donald J. Russell, interview, Sept. 26, 1983; E. P. Ahearn, interview, Jan. 10, 1983; Richard D. Spence, interview, Dec. 1, 1982.

2. *Trains*, Aug., 1983, p. 3; unlabeled narrative account of events, Jan. 10–15, 1950, by Robert A. Miller, Superintendent's office, Sacramento, in Executive files, San Francisco; *Bulletin*, Feb., 1952, pp. 2–11; *San Francisco Examiner*, Jan. 18, 1982.

3. *Bulletin*, Aug., 1952, pp. 7–9, Sept., 1952, pp. 2–7; D. J. Russell, Sept. 22, 1952, to the stockholders; *San Francisco Call-Bulletin*, June 5, 1953; Russell, interview, May 20, 1982.

4. *Bulletin*, July, 1956, p. 7; D. J. Russell, interview, May 20, 1982; *Bulletin*, Jan., 1956, p. 9; SP, Annual Report, 1958, p. 12.

5. H. J. McKenzie, "History of the McKenzie Family and Autobiography of H. J. McKenzie" (unpublished MS, 1982, in author's files), pp. 1–32; Marshall Hamil, interview, Oct. 13, 1981.

6. H. J. McKenzie, interview, April 22, 1982; SSW, Annual Reports, 1954, pp. 5, 14, 1955, p. 12; *Cotton Belt News*, March, 1955, passim, April, 1955, pp. 2–8.

7. *Railway Age*, April 7, 1957, pp. 34–35, Sept. 16, 1957, pp. 37–40; *Cotton Belt News*, May, 1954, pp. 2–4, May–June, 1963, pp. 2–9, Fourth Quarter, 1965, pp. 12–17, Fourth Quarter, 1968, pp. 16–19.

8. SSW, Annual Report, 1953, p. 15; Lloyd Wilson, May 17, 1956, to A. F. Bartels, R. M. Nall files, SSW offices, Tyler; *Cotton Belt News*, Nov., 1953, pp. 2–6, Feb., 1954, p. 33, Sept., 1955, pp. 8–9.

9. *Cotton Belt News*, April, 1951, pp. 10–13, March, 1954, p. 6; "Remarks of H. J. McKenzie at Opening of Traffic Department Family Meeting, Tyler, 4-26-55," H. J. McKenzie files, SSW offices, Tyler.

10. SSW, Annual Report, 1957, p. 9; *Cotton Belt News*, Nov., 1956, pp. 7–8, May, 1957, pp. 5–6.

11. David P. Morgan, "Fast Freight," *Trains Magazine*, Nov., 1949, pp. 44–49; "Cotton Belt Speed and Performance Teamed for Better Service," *Railway Age*, June 2, 1952, pp. 77–81; *Cotton Belt News*, May, 1958, pp. 2–10; *Trains*, May, 1967, p. 42; Steve Patterson, "In a Race With MoP's Red Balls, Cotton Belt Goes Like a Blue Streak," *Trains*, Nov., 1962, pp. 18–27.

12. *Cotton Belt News*, Oct., 1956, pp. 8–9; *Railway Age*, June 2, 1952, p. 81.

13. *Cotton Belt News*, Jan., 1957, pp. 10–11, Nov., 1956, p. 27; various data, R. M. Nall files, SSW offices, Tyler.

14. *Cotton Belt News*, Oct., 1953, pp. 2–15, Oct., 1958, pp. 2–4, March–April, 1961, pp. 8–15, May–June, 1964, pp. 2–3, Third Quaerter, 1965, pp. 8–11, Fourth Quarter, 1967, pp. 14–17, Second Quarter, 1970, pp. 14–18, Aug., 1955, pp. 4–6.

15. *Cotton Belt News*, Second Quarter, 1974, pp. 2–4; SSW, Accounting Department statement of 1-25-69, File 11600 (Tyler); *Railway Age*, Feb. 4, 1963, p. 23.

16. On the Pacific Electric, see Spencer Crump, *Ride the Big Red Cars: How Trolleys Helped Build Southern California*; Eli Bail, *From Railway to Freeway: Pacific Electric and the Motor Coach*, pp. 117–25.

17. Bail, pp. 11, 70, 114; SP, *Ten Year Motive Power Survey* (Aug. 15, 1948), Exhibit 6, pp. 1–2; SP, Statistical Report, 1951, p. 13; *Pacific Electric Magazine*, July–Aug., 1949, pp. 3–4, Feb., 1952, passim, PE, "This Is Pacific Electric" (1952), passim.

18. PE, news release, March 4, 1953; *Pacific Electric Magazine*, April, 1953, pp. 3–6; William D. Middleton, "Twilight on the Pacific Electric," *Railroad Magazine*, Aug., 1954, pp. 48–63; O. J. Russell, Oct. 2, 1953, to Everett L. DeGolyer, Executive Department file PE 120-01, box 21; D. R. Lewis, Nov. 21, 1961, to J. C. Jaspar, Public Relations file, Los Angeles: Bail, p. 190; *Bulletin*, Nov., 1953, p. 9, Sept., 1956, pp. 14–19, Oct., 1965, pp. 2–3; 327 ICC 38-49.

19. Bail, pp. 113, 190; W. A. Worthington, April 30, 1937, to A. D. McDonald, Executive Department file 083, PE, box 21; Randolph Karr, "Rail Passenger Service History of Pacific Electric Railway Company" (1973), Public Relations file, Los Angeles; "The Truth about 'American Ground Transport'—A Reply by General Motors," submitted to the Subcommittee on Antitrust and Monopoly of the Committee of the Judiciary of the U.S. Senate (April, 1954), pp. 19–37, Law Department files, Los Angeles.

20. "New Orleans Union Passenger Terminal Dedication Program, Saturday, May 1, 1954," Public Relations files, Houston; *Bulletin–T&L Lines*, May, 1954, pp. 2–9, July, 1954, p. 6; "Union Passenger Terminal," *Trains*, Sept., 1954, pp. 14–19.

21. *Bulletin*, April, 1951, p. 13, April, 1961, p. 29; *Inside Track*, July, 1952, p. 4, Feb., 1953, p. 2, July, 1958, p. 2; *Bulletin*, March, 1953, p. 20; SP, Annual Report, 1954, p. 10; *Arizona Republic*, June 23, 1982; *Bulletin*, Dec., 1953, p. 8; *Inside Track*, March 1950, p. 4; *Bulletin*, Nov., 1952, pp. 4–5, Oct., 1954, pp. 10–11; *Inside Track*, Jan., 1952, pp. 1, 4, June, 1954, pp. 1, 4; Lucius Beebe, "My Favorite Train Rides," *Holiday*, July, 1961, pp. 1–6; Lucius Beebe, "Along the Boulevards," *Gourmet*, April, 1962, pp. 6–7; *Inside Track*, Nov., 1954, pp. 1–2, 4; *Bulletin*, Nov., 1954, p. 16; *Railway Purchases and Stores*, Dec., 1960, p. 15.

22. *Bulletin–T&L Lines*, May, 1953, pp. 18–19, Dec., 1953, pp. 6–7; SP, News Release (Houston), Feb., 27, 1957; *Bulletin*, Aug., 1953, pp. 3–5, April, 1960, pp. 12–13; *Reno Herald's Herald*, Oct., 1965, p. 3; *Inside Track*, Oct., 1952, pp. 1, 3–4; *Bulletin*, Sept., 1956, pp. 12–13, Oct., 1960, pp. 3–5; *Bulletin–T&L Lines*, Oct., 1958, p. 15; *Bulletin*, Feb., 1956, pp. 28–29; *San Francisco Chronicle*, Sept., 19–21, 1959; *Inside Track*, Oct., 1959, p. 2; *Bulletin*, Oct., 1959, pp. 3–5.

23. Tabular data from SP annual reports, 1946–60; *Bulletin*, May, 1952, p. 2.

24. Albert L. Kohn, May 28, 1953, to F. Q. Tredway, Advertising files; SP, Statistical Report, 1956, p. 5; D. J. Russell, May 6, 1955, to C. E. Peterson, J. W. Corbett, July 11, 1955, to D. J. Russell, Russell, July 18, 1955, to Peterson, VP&GM files, San Francisco; *Bulletin*, Sept., 1955, pp. 8–10.

25. D. J. Russell, interview, Feb. 24, 1982; John F. Stover, *The Life and Decline of the American Railroad*, pp. 127–57; Donald J. Russell, speech to the San Francisco Rotary, Jan. 21, 1942; *San Francisco Examiner*, July 12, 1956; *Railway Age*, June 17, 1957, p. 14; *San Francisco News*, Sept. 26, 1957.

26. *Inside Track*, Sept., 1956, p. 1; *San Francisco Examiner*, July 12, 1956; *Railway Age*, Dec. 1, 1958, p. 21, Sept. 24, 1956, p. 11, Feb. 18, 1957, p. 11, July 1, 1957, p. 40; *Inside Track*, June, 1957, p. 1; *Railway Age*, July 1, 1957, p. 40; *Inside Track*, April, 1959, p. 4; Railway Age, Dec. 21, 1959, p. 49.

27. E. C. Poole, "Fuel Used vs. Locomotive Miles as a Measure for Locomotive Repairs," June 20, 1952, BTR file M-287-1A; E. C. Poole, "Fuel Consumed vs. Locomotive Miles and Locomotive Ton Miles as a Measure of Locomotive Repairs," Oct. 20, 1953, BTR file M-359-1.

28. SP, *Ten Year Motive Power Survey*, Aug. 15, 1948, pp. 2, 7, 10–11, Exhibit 1, pp. 5–6, Exhibit 2, pp. 8–9, Exhibit 3, pp. 4–5, Exhibit 4, p. 5, Exhibit 6, pp. 11, 13.

29. Tabular data from annual reports of the Motive Power Department, Southern Pacific in Texas and Louisiana (1923–57); *Bulletin*–T&L Lines, March, 1957, pp. 2–7.

30. A. T. Mercier, "Diesel Power for Railroads," *Military Engineer*, Nov.–Dec., 1950, pp. 463–65; J. W. Corbett, "Moving Transcontinental Trains with Diesel Power," *Railway Age*, March 5, 1951, pp. 51–53; "Relative Use of Diesel and Steam Power in Through Freight Service for the First Four Months of 1952 and Year 1951," BTR file, I&S 6010; SP, Statistical Report, 1953, p. 47; SP, Annual Report, 1952, p. 6; *Bulletin*, Nov., 1955, pp. 14–15; *Trains*, April, 1956, pp. 14–15; David P. Morgan, "Diesels on the Desk Top," *Trains*, May, 1956, pp. 25–27; SP, news release, June 27, 1956; *Bulletin*, Dec., 1956, pp. 24–27; J. W. Corbett, Jan. 12, 1957, to D. J. Russell, VP&GM files, San Francisco; SP, Annual Report, 1957, p. 9; Fred A. Stindt, "The Last Days of Southern Pacific Steam," *Railroad History No. 149*, Autumn, 1983, pp. 100–13; *Bulletin*, Nov., 1958, pp. 3–5. Although officially dieselized, the SP used a 2-8-0 at Sacramento in 1958 during "high water," at an industry at Pittsburgh, Calif., during the same season, occasionally on the Owens Valley narrow gauge, and on subsidiary Nacozari Railroad until the last run there, on January 19, 1959.

31. SP, news release, June 27, 1956; D. J. Russel, interviews, Dec. 17, 1981, July 20, 1982.

32. D. J. Russell, interview, July 20, 1982; *Bulletin*, April, 1955, pp. 14–16, Dec., 1953, p. 4, Oct., 1955, p. 16; *SRI Journal*, 1958, pp. 44–45; SP, Statistical Report, 1956, pp. 15–16.

33. SP, Statistical Report, 1954, p. 5; *Bulletin*, Dec., 1957, pp. 10–15; SP, Statistical Report, 1955, p. 5; *Railway Age*, May 30, 1960, p. 58.

34. SP, news release, Oct. 3, 1955; *Railway Age*, April 15, 1957, p. 35, April 7, 1958, p. 52; *Bulletin*–T&L Lines, Aug., 1958, pp. 10–11.

35. Tabular data from SP, Statistical Reports, 1950–60; *Inside Track*, May, 1958, p. 1; *Bulletin*, Feb., 1955, p. 11, March 1959, back cover, Feb., 1957, pp. 6–10; *Railway Age*, Dec. 22, 1958, pp. 16–22; *Bulletin*, Sept., 1958, pp. 22–26, Dec., 1958, pp. 6–10, Aug., 1956, pp. 14–18.

36. *Railway Age*, May 11, 1953, p. 14, Aug. 10, 1953, p. 13; *Bulletin*, Aug., 1953, p. 6; *Bulletin*–T&L Lines, Feb. 1954, pp. 22–24; *Bulletin*, Feb., 1955, p. 9, Nov., 1954, p. 17; Gilbert A. Lathrop, "Mile-a-Minute Boxcars," *Railroad Magazine*, Aug., 1950, pp. 10–25; SP, Statistical Report, 1955, p. 7; William D. Middleton, "Piggyback Champ," *Trains*, Sept., 1956, pp. 16–20.

37. *Railway Age*, Aug. 11, 1958, pp. 9–10; SP, Annual Report, 1959, p. 4; *Bulletin*–T&L Lines, Jan., 1957, p. 6; *Bulletin*, Jan., 1957, p. 21; *Railway Age*, Aug. 24, 1959, pp. 8–9; *Bulletin*, July, 1954, p. 45; *Inside Track*, Sept., 1960, p. 1; *Railway Age*, June 26, 1961, pp. 40–41, April 6, 1959, p. 36; SP, Annual Report, 1960, p. 9; BTR files M-368-2, M-368-3.

38. *Bulletin*–T&L Lines, Sept., 1951, pp. 28–31; Chicago & North Western Railway, press release, July 8, 1953; *Bulletin*–T&L Lines, April, 1958, pp. 2–11; *Bulletin*, Nov., 1958, pp. 24–27, March, 1957, pp. 12–16.

39. SP, Statistical Report, 1955, p. 9; D. J. Russell, interview, Jan. 11, 1983; SP, Annual Report, 1952, p. 14; *Bulletin*, July, 1960, p. 17; SP, Statistical Report, 1955, p. 11; SP, Annual Report, 1959, p. 8; T&NO, "Long Range Planning Program," Item no. 1 (n.d., 1954–56?), pp. 3–6, VP&GM files, Houston; SP, Statistical Report, 1954, p. 12; SP, Annual Report, 1952, p. 14; *Bulletin*, April, 1959, pp. 20–21; *Railway Age*, June 8, 1959, p. 33; *Bulletin*, May, 1962, pp. 4–7, June, 1963, p. 23.

40. Donald J. Russell, interview, Feb. 24, 1982; *Bulletin*, Nov., 1955, pp. 2–6.

41. *Railway Age*, Feb. 4, 1957, pp. 30–33; *Bulletin*, Feb., 1957, pp. 24–27, Aug., 1957, pp. 18–19, SP, *Operation Fill* (1959).

42. Robert G. Athearn, *Rebel of the Rockies: A History of the Denver & Rio Grande Western Railroad*, pp. 197, 230, 237.

43. Ibid., pp. 231, 237, 337–42, 355–56; E. N. Brown, interview, March 1, 1982; *Modern Railroads*, July, 1957, p. 13; *Railway Age*, July 22, 1957, p. 42; G. B. Aydelott, interview, Feb. 17, 1982.

44. SP, press release, Oct. 4, 1955; *Railway Age*, May 25, 1959, p. 74; 312 ICC 598–606; SP, *Historical Memoranda*, 1: "Simplification of Corporate Structure," pp. 1–12; SP, *A Financial History of the Southern Pacific Transportation System*, sec. 45, pp. 71–73.

45. D. J. Russell, Oct. 25, 1945, to A. T. Mercier, SP, Board of Directors Resolution, Aug. 21, 1947, F. W. Ackerman, July 10, 1952, to Russell, Russell, Aug. 5, 1952, to D. W. Ackerman, and Department of Justice, press release, Oct. 24, 1945, all in Executive Department file 075, box 22; SP, Statistical Reports, 1947, p. 28, 1953, p. 14, 1954, p. 13, 1955, p. 13, 1956, p. 13; SP, Annual Report, 1969, p. 10; SP, *Historical Memoranda*, 2: "Motor Coach Operations," pp. 4–8.

46. Tabular data from annual statistical reports, 1952–60; *Bulletin* July, 1952, p. 2; *Railway Age*, Aug. 31, 1959, p. 60; SP, Annual Reports, 1952, p. 17, 1954, p. 16.

47. Albert L. Kohn, Dec. 30, 1954, to F. Q. Tredway, Advertising files; *San Francisco News*, June 11, 1952; *Forbes*, Jan. 1, 1957, pp. 93–98; Management Audit No. 133 (Oct., 1955), pp. 1–8, SP, Executive files, *Railway Age*, May 9, 1960, p. 34; J. R. Williston, Bruce & Company, "Southern Pacific Company" (May, 1953), pp. 1–12; SP, news release, Oct. 3, 1955.

CHAPTER SIXTEEN

1. *Bulletin*, Jan., 1967, p. 12, Aug., 1961, pp. 4–5, March, 1963, pp. 6–7, Jan., 1968, p. 10, Jan., 1955, pp. 32–33, Feb., 1968, p. 8; Ray Robertson, interview, June 17, 1982; *Bulletin*, Nov., 1963, pp. 6–8.

2. *Railway Age*, Oct. 27, 1958, pp. 9–10, Jan. 6–13, 1964, pp. 15–18; SP, Annual Report, 1972, p. 6.

3. *Bulletin*, July, 1963, pp. 2–3, March, 1965, pp. 14–15, Dec., 1967, p. 18; *Railway Age*, Dec. 8, 1969, pp. 14–17.

4. *Railway Age*, Feb. 11, 1963, p. 28; H. M. Williamson, "Wanted: Men to Meet Leadership Challenge," *Railway Age*, April 6, 1964, pp. 22–24; *Bulletin*, April, 1964, pp. 10–11, 26, June, 1964, pp. 8–11, Nov., 1967, pp. 6–7; SP, Annual Report, 1968, p. 10; *Trains*, April, 1970, p. 47.

5. SP, "Plan for Progress: A Statement of Southern Pacific Policy to Maintain Emphasis on Equal Employment Opportunity and Equal Treatment for All Qualified Persons," July 1, 1962, Public Relations files, San Francisco; *Bulletin*, July, 1964, p. 5; C. P. Huntington, *California—Her Past, Present and Future*, speech before the annual dinner of the Chiefs of Departments of the Southern Pacific Company, May 16, 1900, p. 27, Executive Department files, San Francisco; SP, Annual Report, 1900, p. 20; Lonnie M. Fox, interview, Feb. 25, 1982.

6. *Bulletin*, Aug., 1961, p. 21, May, 1963, pp. 6–7, Jan., 1969, p. 5, March, 1965, pp. 12–13, Dec., 1965, pp. 20–21, June, 1966, p. 11, Jan.–Feb., 1960, p. 23, Feb.–March, 1962, p. 9.

7. Albert L. Kohn, Dec. 30, 1954, to F. Q. Tredway, Advertising files; *Inside Track*, July, 1961, p. 4, July, 1963, p. 4; *Bulletin*, July, 1964, pp. 14–15.

8. *Inside Track*, May, 1954, p. 4; D. J. Russell, April 20, 1954, to Ansel Adams, Executive Deparment file 602; Donald J. Russell, interview, July 20, 1982.

9. *Forbes*, Nov. 1, 1965, p. 25; H. J. McKenzie, interview, June 16, 1982.

10. *San Francisco Examiner*, July 12, 1956; *Time*, Aug. 11, 1961, p. 58; Frank J. Longo, Dec. 30, 1981, to D. J. Russell, DJR Scrapbook 4, San Francisco; R. E. Hallawell, . . . *A Look at Today—A Glance Into Tomorrow*, remarks made at his retirement, Jan. 31, 1956, (pamphlet), p. 6; E. P. Ahearn, interview, Jan. 10, 1983; Richard D. Spence, interview, Dec. 1, 1982; Harold J. McKenzie, interview, June 16, 1982.

11. *Time*, Aug. 11, 1961, p. 58; H. J. McKenzie, interview, Nov. 8, 1982.

12. D. J. Russell, "The Need For Executive Training," address at the Transportation Management Program, Stanford University, June 25, 1956, and D. J. Russell, "People Are Individuals," address before the Tenth Annual Meeting of the American Society of Traffic and Transportation, San Francisco, Sept. 20, 1956, both in Public Relations files.

13. *Modern Railroads*, Oct., 1957, p. 12; *Bulletin*, Dec., 1957, pp. 5–7; *Time*, Aug. 11, 1961; *Forbes*, Nov. 1, 1965.

14. *Time*, Aug. 11, 1961, p. 58; *Forbes*, Nov. 1, 1965, p. 24; Witter & Company, "Special Study of the Southern Pacific Company" (Sept., 1964); *Railway Age*, Sept. 9, 1963, pp. 8–10; *Fortune*, June 15, 1968, pp. 214–15; David P. Morgan, "Is SP the New Standard Railroad of the World?" *Trains*, Nov., 1965, pp. 36–37; Hooker & Fay, "Southern Pacific Company," March, 1962; *Business Week*, Feb. 3, 1968, pp. 84–87; *Financial World*, Feb. 4, 1970, p. 5.

15. SP, Annual Report, 1970, p. 11; *Bulletin*, April, 1971, pp. 7–8, Aug.–Sept., 1972, pp. 6–7.

16. Donald J. Russell, interview, Feb. 24, 1982; *Railway Age*, Aug. 15, 1960, p. 20, July 24, 1961, pp. 20–24; *Modern Railroads*, Sept., 1961, pp. 98–100; *Railway Age*, Nov. 13, 1961, p. 39; American Locomotive Company, press release, Sept. 15, 1964; *Railway Age*, March 30, 1964, pp. 14–15; *Bulletin*, Sept., 1966, pp. 4–5.

17. SP, "Ten-Year Forecast of Freight Car and Locomotive Requirements" (Feb. 4, 1965), pp. 4–5; *Bulletin*, Nov., 1962, pp. 14–17; *Railway Age*, Nov. 12, 1962, p. 12; *Bulletin*, Nov., 1970, p. 10; *Inside Track*, Sept.–Oct., 1965, p. 3; SP, Annual Report, 1970, p. 6.

18. *Railway Age*, Dec. 18–25, 1961, pp. 35–37; *Bulletin*, Oct., 1962, pp. 3–6; Aug., 1963, pp. 6–9, July, 1962, pp. 3–7, Oct., 1955, pp. 2–3; *Railway Age*, June 20, 1960, p. 31; Aug., 1962, pp. 21–27, April, 1965, pp. 16–17, Nov. 11, 1963, pp. 19–21; *Bulletin*, July, 1968, pp. 6–7.

19. *Modern Railroads*, Jan., 1973, pp. 38–41.

20. *Bulletin*, Jan., 1957, p. 5; *Modern Railroads*, Jan., 1960, p. 154; *Bulletin*, Nov., 1962, pp. 19–21; James W. Germany, interview, Dec. 11, 1981; Guerdon S. Sines, interviews, June 29, Oct. 8, 1984; *Bulletin*, June, 1960, p. 10, March, 1967, pp. 6–7, May, 1967, p. 10, June, 1968, p. 6, Dec., 1968, pp. 3–5, July, 1969, p. 5; SP, Annual Report, 1968, p. 8.

21. James W. Germany, interview, Dec. 11, 1981; *Modern Railroads*, Jan., 1973, pp. 38–41, Dec., 1969, pp. 30–34; *Bulletin*, June, 1972, pp. 12–14.

22. *Forbes*, Jan. 1, 1957, p. 94; Donald J. Russell, interview, July 20, 1982; *Bulletin*, May, 1954, p. 11, April, 1960, p. 17, March, 1968, pp. 2–4, Sept., 1967, pp. 2–3; *Trains*, April, 1956, pp. 57–59; *Cotton Belt News*, July, 1957, p. 9; *Inside Track*, Jan.–Feb., 1967, pp. 1–2.

23. William Sproule, April 12, 1928, to Paul Shoup, Shoup, June 28, 1928, to Sproule, Sproule, July 19, 1928, to A. D. McDonald, and SP, "Financial Results of Operations Between Lancaster and Colton; Present Operated Line vs. Proposed New Line Lancaster to Cajon Summit, Thence Via Santa Fe to Colton," Report No. 24, Bureau of Commerce & Research (June 7, 1928), all in Executive Files 300-4/431, 510, 5/982, box 64.

24. Donald J. Russell, interviews, Feb. 24, May 20, May 21, 1982; *Bulletin*, July, 1967, pp. 3–6.

25. *Railway Age*, April 14, 1958, p. 27; Donald J. Russell, interview, July 20, 1982, and Jan. 11, 1983.

26. *Railway Age*, Nov. 23, 1959, p. 34; *Bulletin*, Aug., 1959, pp. 10–12, Dec., 1959, pp. 12–13; Donald J. Russell, interview, Feb. 24, 1982.

27. SP, Annual Report, 1906, p. 14; W. W. Hale, Oct. 4, 1951, to A. T. Mercier, H. W. Klein, Feb. 25, 1952, to E. B. Johnson, ICC, Investigation and Suspension Docket 6010, and W. G. Peoples, Oct. 29, 1954, all in BTR file 1428, box M-362; W. Theo Eskew, interview, Feb. 14, 1983.

28. SP, Statistical Report, 1955, p. 14; *Forbes*, Nov. 1, 1965, p. 25; *Southern Pacific Pipe Lines, Inc.*, pamphlet containing historical and tabular data prepared by the Office of President & General Manager, Los Angeles (Feb. 3, 1982).

29. E. T. S., Jan. 23, 1967, to B. F. Biaggini, SPPL Executive file, Los Angeles.

30. J. G. Montfoot, "Operations of the Black Mesa Pipeline System," and "General Description: Black Mesa Pipe Line, Engineering Management, Inc." (May 10, 1968), both in Black Mesa VP&GM files, Flagstaff; Dave Deason, "Black Mesa's 'River of Coal' Spans Arizona's Navajo Land," *Pipe Line In-*

dustry, Aug., 1969, pp. 49–52; Frank H. Love, "The Black Mesa Story," *Pipeline Engineer International*, Nov., 1969, pp. 38–44; Bill Quarles, "Black Mesa Is First Major Pipe Line in West," *Pipeline and Underground Utilities Construction*, Dec., 1969, pp. 14–18; *Bulletin*, Dec., 1970, pp. 3–6.

31. *Railway Age*, March 14, 1960, p. 60, Feb. 6, 1961, p. 9; E. S. Marsh, Feb. 23, 1960, to D. J. Russell, Executive Department box 37; SP, Annual Report, 1962, p. 3.

32. *Railway Age*, Oct. 17, 1960, p. 9, Oct. 31, 1960, p. 9.

33. *Railway Age*, Nov. 14, 1960, p. 9, Jan. 9, 1961, p. 32; *Modern Railroads*, July, 1961, p. 31; *Railway Age*, July 17, 1961, pp. 9, 34, Aug. 7, 1961, pp. 9–10, 39; 327 ICC 387–432; *Bulletin*, March, 1965, pp. 10–11.

34. David F. Myrick, *Railroads of Nevada and Eastern California*, 1: 332–39; Keith L. Bryant, Jr., *History of the Atchison, Topeka & Santa Fe Railway*, pp. 299–300.

35. *Moody's Manual 1950*, pp. 224–35; H. Roger Grant, *The Corn Belt Route: A History of the Chicago Great Western Railroad Company*, pp. 136, 161; Harold J. McKenzie, interview, June 16, 1982; Donald J. Russell, interview, May 21, 1982; H. J. McKenzie, March 21, 1984, to the author; Douglas C. Munski, "Modeling the Historical Geography of the Chicago & Eastern Illinois Railroad, 1849–1969" (Ph.D. diss., University of Illinois, 1978), pp. 126–31; E. N. Brown, interview, July 19, 1982.

36. *Moody's Manual 1958*, p. 480; Munski, pp. 182–96, 202–23; *Wall Street Journal*, Nov. 25, 1960; *Chicago News*, Dec. 29, 1961; *Traffic World*, March 13, 1965, pp. 38–40; *Wall Street Journal*, Jan. 10, 1967, May 15, 1967, Oct. 30, 1968; H. Craig Miner, *The Rebirth of the Missouri Pacific, 1956–1983*, pp. 57–81.

37. SSW, Exploratory Study of the Alton & Southern—The Purchase of Which Would Provide Direct Connection with Principal Trunk Line Railroads Through the St. Louis Gateway (June 11, 1965), pp. 1, 14, 20, 23, SSW Executive file 380-44, Tyler (hereafter cited as SSW Exploratory Study); Alton & Southern Railroad, Annual Report to the Interstate Commerce Commission, 1915, p. 109; 1967, p. 105.

38. SSW Exploratory Study, pp. 24–26; SSW-A&S Agreement (Nov. 30, 1965), SSW Executive file 380-44, Tyler.

39. George P. Mueller, Oct. 30, 1969, to E. T. Rucker, and TRRA, minutes of the Board (Jan. 10, 1966), both in SSW Executive file 380-44, Tyler; SSW Exploratory Study, p. 24.

40. *Wall Street Journal*, March 30, 1966; *St. Louis Post-Dispatch*, Aug. 8, 1966; *St. Louis Globe-Democrat*, Aug. 19, 1966; *Wall Street Journal*, April 5, 1967; SP, Annual Report, 1967, p. 10; *Traffic World*, March 9, 1968 pp. 47–48; C. H. Nelson, Nov. 11, 1969, to R. M. Nall (telephone transcript), SSW Executive file 380-44, Tyler; *Wall Street Journal*, April 1, 1968; *St. Louis Post-Dispatch*, April 5, 1968; *Wall Street Journal*, April 22, 1968; Larry S. Provo, Oct. 17, 1969, to H. J. McKenzie, George P. Mueller, Oct. 30, 1969, to E. T. Rucker, D. R. Kirk, Dec. 8, 1969, to R. M. Nall (telephone transcript), C. H. Nelson, Nov. 11, 1969, to Nall (telephone transcript), R. D. Spence, May 31, 1970, to B. F. Biaggini, and Nall, Sept. 9, 1970, to Larry S. Provo, all in SSW Executive file 380-44; *Traffic World* (March 6, 1972), pp. 9–10; *St. Louis Post-Dispatch*, Jan. 4, 1973; SP, Annual Report, 1973, p. 19; Miner, pp. 177–78.

41. Donald J. Russell, interviews, Dec. 17, 1981, Feb. 24, 1982; G. B. Aydelott, interview, Jan. 21, 1982; Exploratory Study of Possible Merger Southern Pacific Company and Rock Island Lines (Aug. 1, 1982), (hereafter cited as SP Exploratory Study).

42. On the Rock Island generally, see William Edward Hayes, *Iron Road to Empire: The History of 100 Years of the Progress and Achievements of the Rock Island Lines*; Donovan L. Hofsommer, "A Chronology of Iowa Railroads," *Railroad History No. 132*, Spring, 1975, pp. 70–83; CRI&P, Annual Report, 1962, p. 3; SP Exploratory Study, pp. 5, 16, 17.

43. SP Exploratory Study, pp. 29, 32, 36; CRI&P, Annual Report, 1961, p. 2.

44. SP Exploratory Study, pp. 7, 41.

45. *Railway Age*, Sept., 1962, p. 10.

46. B. F. Biaggini and R. M. Sulton, Sept. 24, 1962, to Coverdale & Colpitts, Executive files; SP, Annual Report, 1963, p. 10; Coverdale & Colpitts, Report on the Valuation of Chicago, Rock Island & Pacific Railroad Company as of Dec. 31, 1961 (1966), p. 2, VP&GM files, Houston; CRI&P, Annual Report, 1964, p. 5; UP and CRI&P, Merger Reference Manual for Proposed Merger of Union Pacific and Chicago, Rock Island & Pacific Railroad Company (Aug. 14, 1965), pp. 2–4, VP&GM files, Houston.

47. *Railway Age*, June 10, 1963, pp. 46–47, July 1, 1963, p. 9, Aug. 5, 1963, p. 30, Feb. 24, 1964, p. 9; H. J. Walker, June 30, 1965, to B. F. Biaggini, Executive files; *Forbes Magazine*, April 1, 1965, pp. 52–56; W. D. Lamprecht, July 20, 1965, to Biaggini, Executive files; *Wall Street Journal*, Dec. 18, 1964; Richard Saunders, *The Railroad Mergers and the Coming of Conrail*, pp. 223–45; Miner, pp. 112–36.

48. SP, Annual Report, 1968, p. 10; SP Exploratory Study, p. 21; CRI&P, Annual Report, 1965, p. 5.

49. *Railway Age*, Dec. 11, 1961, pp. 10–11; SP, Annual Report, 1963, p. 7, 1970, p. 8, 1964, p. 10, 1965, p. 10.

50. Dick Houton, "SP's Picnic Line," *Trains*, July, 1948, pp. 46–51; Lucius Beebe, "Southern Pacific Narrow Gauge," *Trains*, March, 1947, pp. 14–21; *Bulletin*, Nov., 1954, pp. 3–7, June, 1960, p. 10; Mallory Hope Ferrel, *Southern Pacific Narrow Gauge*; Lucius Beebe and Charles Clegg, *Steamcars to the Comstock: The Virginia & Truckee Railroad, the Carson & Colorado Railroad*.

51. Ferrell, p. 10.

52. A. T. Mercier, July 15, 1947, to John G. Walsh, Memo—Earnings of *Shasta Daylight*, Trains No. 9 and 10 (Feb. 6, 1953), D. J. Russell, Jan. 28, 1956, to C. E. Peterson, et al., and Russell, Nov. 5, 1956, to C. E. Peterson, et al., all in Executive file 521-3.

53. Daily Average Loadings of Passenger Trains (Based on Form 3646 figures), April 7, 1958, VP&GM files, San Francisco; *Dallas Morning News*, June 9, 1958; *Bulletin*, June, 1956, p. 25, May, 1957, pp. 28–31; *Railway Age*, Jan. 13, 1958, p. 12, March 30, 1959, p. 54, May 18, 1959, p. 33; C. E. Peterson, et al., July 8, 1947, to D. J. Russell, Executive file 521-3; SP, Annual Report, 1959, p. 5; Fred Matthews, "Queen of the Daylights," *Passenger Train Journal*, April, 1982, pp. 21–27.

54. *Bulletin*, Sept., 1958, pp. 12–18; *Inside Track*, Sept., 1958, p. 1; various materials PR file 280; *Oakland Tribune*, Sept. 14, 1965.

55. *Railway Age*, July 24, 1961, p. 33; *Bulletin*, Sept. 1961, p. 16, June–July, 1958, pp. 16–17, Oct. 1, 1914, p. 5; *Proceedings: The Journal of the Pacific Railway Club*, Jan., 1938, pp. 3–23; *Bulletin*—T&L Lines, Jan., 1957, p. 9; *Phoenix Arizona Republic*, March 28, 1967; *San Francisco Chronicle*,

Sept. 25, 1967; *Ogden Standard Examiner*, Sept. 21, 1967.

56. SP, Annual Report, 1966, p. 3.

57. J. B. McCall, "Corporate Attitudes toward a Declining Market: Santa Fe and Southern Pacific Rail Passenger Service, 1950–1965," Department of Economics, *Working Paper Series 82-7* (University of Texas at Arlington, n.d.), p. ii; 320 ICC 59–84; *Wall Street Journal*, June 1, 1966, Dec. 20, 1967; *Sunset Magazine*, Oct., 1965, p. 38; *The Southern Pacific and Railroad Passenger Service*, pp. 2, 10, 14, 19, 25.

58. R. E. Wyncoop, interview, May 21, 1982; D. J. Russell, interview, Dec. 11, 1981.

59. David P. Morgan, "Who Shot the Passenger Train?" *Trains*, April, 1959, pp. 14–51; D. J. Russell, interview, Dec. 11, 1981; 306 ICC 417–79; *Forbes*, Nov. 1, 1965, p. 25.

60. Ely M. Brandes and Alan E. Lazar, *The Future of Rail Passenger Traffic in the West*, pp. 3–5; *Inside Track*, Sept., 1958, p. 4.

61. SP, Annual Report, 1968, pp. 4–5; *San Francisco Examiner*, April 8, 1968; *Bulletin*, July, 1969, p. 6, April, 1970, p. 11; SP, Time Table, Oct. 20, 1970; SP, Annual Report, 1970, p. 14, 1971, pp. 4–5.

62. *Bulletin*, July, 1963, pp. 12–16; *Railway Age*, Sept. 23, 1963, pp. 23–25; SP, Annual Report, 1966, p. 4; *Bulletin*, July, 1966, p. 5; F. M. Guerin, interview, Feb. 15, 1983.

63. *Bulletin*, Jan., 1922, p. 10, July, 1936, pp. 8–9; William G. Peoples, interview, Feb. 17, 1983.

64. *Inside Track*, Jan., 1960, p. 3; *Railway Age*, May 16, 1960, p. 48; *Bulletin*, Nov., 1970, pp. 3–7; SP, Annual Report, 1970, p. 8; *Railway Age*, May 13, 1963, pp. 12–13, Feb. 24, 1964, pp. 36–37.

65. *Railway Age*, Feb. 25, 1963, p. 60; *Bulletin*, March, 1963, pp. 6–10, March, 1970, p. 2.

66. H. J. McKenzie, interview, Oct. 13, 1981; E. N. Brown, interview, June 24, 1982; *Inside Track*, Jan.–Feb., 1967, p. 2; Steve Patterson, "In a Race with MoP's Red Balls, Cotton Belt Goes Like a Blue Streak," *Trains*, Nov., 1962, p. 23; W. C. Hoenig, interview, Oct. 27, 1984.

67. *Bulletin*–T&L Lines, Oct., 1952, pp. 1–55; *Bulletin*, Jan.–Feb., 1963, pp. 11–13; May–June, 1969, pp. 1–24; SSW, *Centennial: 1877–1977*, pp. 1–8; *Bulletin*, Oct.–Nov., 1977, pp. 1–17.

68. SP, Annual Report, 1968, p. 7; 334 ICC 866–73; SP, Annual Reports, 1969, p. 3, 1970, p. 13.

CHAPTER SEVENTEEN

1. Tabular data from SP Annual Reports, 1960–69; D. E. Enright, Nov. 1, 1984, to the author; A. D. DeMoss, interview, Jan. 3, 1985.

2. *Railway Age*, April 14, 1958, p. 27; D. J. Russell, interview, Feb. 24, 1982.

3. SP, Annual Report, 1964, p. 10; D. J. Russell, Nov. 20, 1984, to the author; SP, Annual Reports, 1967, p. 8, 1975, p. 14, 1968, p. 10, 1975, p. 18, 1978, p. 22.

4. D. J. Russell, Nov. 30, 1984, to the author; SP, Annual Report, 1967, p. 10; *Inside Track*, Feb.–March, 1968, pp. 1, 4.

5. D. J. Russell, interview, Dec. 17, 1981; SP, Annual Reports, 1967, p. 10, 1970, pp. 8, 13; *Traffic World*, Sept. 28, 1970, pp. 13–14; *Bulletin*, May, 1950, p. 7.

6. *Bulletin*, June, 1978, pp. 3–5.

7. SP, Annual Report, 1970, pp. 12–13; *Bulletin*, March,

1970, p. 4; *Modern Railroads*, July, 1972, pp. 119–120; *Bulletin*, Jan., 1958, p. 25, Sept., 1978, pp. 4–6, May, 1978, p. 11.

8. SP, Annual Report, 1969, p. 3; 1 *Bulletin*, Jan., 1977, pp. 8–10.

9. SP, Annual Reports, 1968, p. 3, 1970, p. 3; *Business Week*, Oct. 28, 1972, pp. 32–33; SP, Annual Report, 1973, pp. 14–15; *Bulletin*, Aug., 1974, pp. 2–5, 13; SP, Annual Report, 1974, p. 1.

10. *Bulletin*, Spring, 1975, p. 12; SP, Annual Reports, 1976, pp. 14–15, 1978, p. 21, 1979, p. 10; *Bulletin*, Aug., 1979, pp. 11–15.

11. *Bulletin*, June, 1971, p. 2, May, 1973, p. 4; *Inside Track*, Aug.–Sept., 1973, pp. 6, 8; *Bulletin*, Mid-Year, 1976, p. 6.

12. *Bulletin*, May, 1972, pp. 2–4; SP, Annual Report, 1970, p. 6; D. J. Russell, interview, Feb. 24, 1982.

13. B. F. Biaggini, interview, March 1, 1982; G. B. Aydelott, interview, Sept. 22, 1982; R. D. Spence, interview, Dec. 1, 1982.

14. *Railway Age*, June 27, 1970, pp. 29–35; *U.S. News & World Report*, Jan. 3, 1972, pp. 44–48; various speeches, on file in the Public Relations office, San Francisco.

15. B. F. Biaggini, "Nationalization versus Rationalization: What Future for the Railroads?" speech before the National Press Club, Washington, D.C., Dec. 14, 1970, Public Relations files; *Railway Age*, June 29, 1970, p. 32.

16. SP, Annual Reports, 1973, p. 1, 1975, p. 1, 1977, p. 1; *Bulletin*, March, 1978, p. 2; SP, Annual Report, 1978, pp. 2–3; *Bulletin*, April, 1979, pp. 2–11.

17. *Bulletin*, April, 1971, pp. 2–4, Aug.–Sept., 1973, pp. 2–7; *Inside Track*, Aug.–Sept., 1973, pp. 1–3.

18. *Railway Age*, June 27, 1970, p. 32; SP, Annual Reports, 1973, p. 20, 1974, p. 1974; 347 ICC 556–861; SP/UP, *Five Year Plan for Rehabilitation of Chicago, Rock Island & Pacific Railroad Company Rail Properties* (Feb., 1975), p. 3, VP&GM files, Houston.

19. *Bulletin*, Summer, 1975, pp. 6–7; CRI&P, Annual Report, 1902, pp. 11–12; Oliver Philip Byers, "Early History of the El Paso Line of the Chicago, Rock Island & Pacific Railway," *Collections of the Kansas State Historical Society 1919–1922*, ed. William E. Connelly.

20. SP, Annual Report, 1978, p. 9.

21. B. F. Biaggini, interview, Nov. 8, 1983.

22. Verified statement of William M. Gibbons, Finance Docket No. 28799 (March 28, 1979), verified statement of John W. Ingram, Finance Docket No. 28799 (March 27, 1979), Law Department files.

23. 363 ICC 320–599; SP, Annual Report, 1979, pp. 21–22.

24. *Bulletin*, Oct.–Nov., 1969), p. 4; W. H. Hudson, interview, Oct. 12, 1981; SP, Annual Report, 1976, p. 12; E. N. Brown, interview, July 19, 1982; William G. Peoples, interview, Feb. 17, 1983.

25. *Railway Age*, July 29, 1963, pp. 19–25; James R. Sullivan, interview, Dec. 13, 1982; *Bulletin*, May, 1977, p. 4, March, 1978, pp. 6–7, 14.

26. Tabular data from SP statistical reports, 1965–81.

27. *Inside Track*, April–May, 1970, pp. 1, 3; E. N. Brown, interview, July 19, 1982; W. G. Peoples, interview, Feb. 17, 1983; *Inside Track*, March–April, 1972, pp. 1, 4; *Bulletin*, Oct., 1974, pp. 6–7.

28. *Bulletin*, May, 1972, pp. 5–6, Oct., 1971, pp. 2–4, Aug.–Sept., 1972, p. 9; tabular data from SP Statistical Reports, 1965–76; *Modern Railroads*, Nov., 1979, pp. 58–65.

29. *Fortune*, Dec., 1972, pp. 44–62.

30. *Railway Age*, Feb. 8, 1960, pp. 14–26, July 11, 1960, pp. 22–23; *Bulletin*, Jan., 1966, p. 4; tabular data from PFE form CS-988, 1965–69; *Inside Track*, Oct.–Nov., 1963, p. 2; F. E. Kriebel, "Transporting Perishables, *Blue Anchor*, Summer, 1971, pp. 30–33; statistical data from PFE files, Brisbane, Calif.

31. Arnold I. Weber, interview, Jan. 7, 1985; *Bulletin*, Sept., 1978, pp. 8–9, 14; *Western Grower and Shipper*, Nov., 1978, pp. 67–72, 125, 137; SP, Annual Report, 1978, p. 9.

32. *Inside Track*, July, 1955, pp. 1–4; *Bulletin*, Aug., 1957, p. 11, Oct.–Nov., 1967, p. 7; Fred A. Stindt, "Peninsula Service: A Story of Southern Pacific Commuter Trains," *Western Railroader No. 213*, 1957, pp. 1–40; SP Public Relations Statement, Sept., 1960; *Bulletin*, Oct., 1969, p. 7, Jan., 1964, pp. 16–21.

33. *Bulletin*, Dec., 1967, p. 17; SP, Annual Reports, 1974, pp. 7–8, 1975, p. 4; *Bulletin*, Jan., 1976, pp. 2–3, Autumn, 1976, p. 6; SP, Annual Reports, 1976, pp. 4–5, 1977, p. 13, 1980, p. 20; *Bulletin*, Summer, 1975, p. 11.

34. SP, Annual Reports, 1978, p. 9, 1976, p. 6; *Bulletin*, Spring, 1975, pp. 16–17; James R. Moriarty III and Elaine P. Lamb, "The Old San Diego & Arizona," *Railroad Magazine*, May, 1973, pp. 18–21; *San Diego Union*, Jan. 8, 1961; *San Diego Evening Tribune*, June 14, 1976; SP, Annual Report, 1970, p. 13.

35. SP, Annual Report, 1977, p. 12, 1978, p. 9, 1979, p. 21; ICC, Finance Docket 28917, unpublished decision, Aug. 22, 1979; *Bulletin*, Oct., 1978, p. 11; Arnold I. Weber, interview, Jan. 7, 1985; *San Diego Business Journal*, June 8, 1981. On the SD&AE generally see Robert M. Hanft, *San Diego & Arizona: The Impossible Railroad*.

36. SP, Annual Report, 1914, p. 18; *Bulletin*, Jan., 1965, pp. 2–11, 29, Oct.–Nov., 1967, pp. 3–4; SP, Annual Report, 1974, p. 20; *Bulletin*, April, 1978, p. 14; SP, Annual Report, 1973, p. 21.

37. Tabular data from SP annual reports, 1970–79; SP, Annual Reports, 1977, pp. 2, 9, 1974, p. 1, 1975, p. 1, 1977, p. 2, 1976, p. 1, 1972, p. 11, 1979, pp. 2, 31; A. D. DeMoss, interview, Jan. 3, 1985. The rise in SPTCo's operating ratio is partially explained by modifications in ICC accounting procedures that allowed substantial expenses not heretofore included.

38. *Railway Age*, June 27, 1977, p. 24; SP, Annual Reports, 1974, p. 1, 1975, p. 1, 1976, p. 1, 1978, p. 2; *Bulletin*, Jan., 1972, pp. 3–5.

39. W. G. Lacy, interview, Oct. 21, 1981; Harry Williamson, interview, April 10, 1984; R. M. Frame, interview, Dec. 1, 1982; A. D. DeMoss, interview, Jan. 3, 1985; *Bulletin*, July, 1978, pp. 3–5, Nov., 1979, pp. 3–6, Feb., 1982, p. 3.

40. B. F. Biaggini, interview, Nov. 8, 1983; Prime F. Osborn, interview, Nov. 30, 1982; SP, Annual Report, 1977, p. 13.

41. *Washington Star*, May 18, 1978; *Wall Street Journal*, May 19, 1978; *San Francisco Examiner*, Aug. 1, 1978; *New York Journal of Commerce*, Aug. 10, 1978; SP, Annual Report, 1978, p. 3; *Traffic World*, April 23, 1979, pp. 43–44; *Wall Street Journal*, Aug. 7, 1980; B. F. Biaggini, interview, Nov. 8, 1983.

42. SP, Annual Report, 1978, p. 3; *Bulletin*, Aug., 1979, pp. 5–8; SP, Annual Report, 1979, pp. 4–9.

43. SP, Annual Report, 1979, pp. 2–3.

CHAPTER EIGHTEEN

1. *Railway Age*, Oct. 30, 1961, p. 63, Feb. 4, 1963, pp. 21–24; John W. Barriger, *Super Railroads for a Dynamic American Economy*; *Forbes*, Jan. 1, 1957, p. 94. On the issues of mergers generally, see Richard Saunders, *The Railroad Mergers and the Coming of Conrail*.

2. Saunders, pp. 295–323; *San Francisco Examiner*, May 22, 1980.

3. *Trains*, Dec., 1982, p. 3.

4. G. H. Kneiss, "Fifty Candles for the Western Pacific," *Western Pacific Mileposts*, March, 1983, p. 9; *San Francisco Chronicle*, March 11, 1917; Robert S. Lovett, Statement before the Interstate Commerce Commission, Dec. 8, 1922, pp. 8, 16, Executive Department file 080.3-9; SP, *Historical Memoranda*, 1: "Southern Pacific Control of Central Pacific," pp. 23–24.

5. W. Averell Harriman, interview, Dec. 14, 1982; D. J. Russell, interview, Feb. 24, 1982; B. F. Biaggini, interview, Jan. 13, 1983: *San Francisco Examiner*, May 22, 1980, July 14, 1981.

6. *Railway Age*, Aug. 9, 1982, p. 9; UP, Annual Report, 1901, p. 5; *Portland Oregonian*, Oct. 18, 1981; Hale Holden, June 27, 1930, to Paul Shoup, Executive Department file 110.1, box 50; *Traffic Manager*, Oct., 1981, p. 9. The Union Pacific, it should be noted, did have a two-carrier transcontinental option via Kansas City and the Norfolk & Western.

7. *Wall Street Journal*, Sept. 27, 1979; *Railway Age*, Oct. 29, 1979, pp. 8–9; *Des Moines Register*, Jan. 26, 1980; *Traffic World*, March 24, 1980, pp. 9–10, 13–14; *Wall Street Journal*, April 17, 1980; *Chicago Tribune*, April 21, 1984.

8. *San Francisco Examiner*, May 15, 1980; B. F. Biaggini, interview, Nov. 8, 1983; *San Francisco Chronicle*, May 17, 1980; *Sacramento Union*, May 18, 1980; *San Francisco Examiner*, May 20, 1980, May 22, 1980.

9. *Bulletin*, July–Aug., 1980, p. 2, May, 1980, pp. 2–6; SP, Annual Report, 1980, pp. 18, 39; *Herington* (Kans.) *Times*, Oct. 9, 1980; John S. Reed, remarks before a press conference in Chicago, May 15, 1980, AT&SF, Public Relations files, Chicago.

10. *San Francisco Chronicle*, Sept. 13, 1980; *Wall Street Journal*, Sept. 15, 1980; *Bulletin*, Nov.–Dec., 1980, p. 2; B. F. Biaggini, interview, Nov. 8, 1983.

11. *Railway Age*, Aug. 9, 1982, p. 9; *Topeka Capital-Journal*, July 23, 1982; Santa Fe Industries, Annual Report, 1981, p. 3; *New York Times*, Sept. 14, 1982; *San Francisco Examiner*, Sept. 14, 1982; 366 ICC 458–819; *Wall Street Journal*, Dec. 23, 1982; UP, Annual Report, 1982, pp. 5–9; H. Craig Miner, *The Rebirth of the Missouri Pacific, 1956–1983*, pp. 215–29; *Wall Street Journal*, Jan. 4, 1983.

12. *Wall Street Journal*, Sept. 15, 1982; Rio Grande Industries, Annual Report, 1982, p. 11; *Wall Street Journal*, Jan. 4, 1983; *Traffic World*, Feb. 13, 1984, pp. 13–14; *San Francisco Chronicle*, Feb. 29, 1984.

13. *Kansas City Times*, July 16, 1981; *Southeast Missourian* (Cape Girardeau), Jan. 7, 1983.

14. *Trains*, Dec., 1982, p. 4; *Arkansas Gazette* (Little Rock), July 16, 1981; *Chicago Tribune*, March 3, 1982; *Traffic World*, Aug. 24, 1982; *Railway Age*, Sept. 27, 1982, pp. 21–23; SSW, press release, Oct. 20, 1982.

15. *Chicago Tribune*, Dec. 2, 1982; *Wall Street Journal*, Sept. 1, 1983, March 1, 1983; *Chicago Tribune*, June 28, 1983; *New York Journal of Commerce*, Feb. 17, 1983.

16. SP, Annual Report, 1980, p. 18; B. F. Biaggini, "Deregulatory Trends in Transportation and Communication," address before the Association for Corporate Growth, San Francisco, March 11, 1981, Public Relations files.

17. G. B. Aydelott, interview, Sept. 22, 1982; R. D. Krebs, remarks at SP's Management Meeting, April 26, 1983; *Railway Age*, Aug. 30, 1982, pp. 29–35; *Fortune*, Sept. 20, 1982, pp. 22, 24, 28, 32, 36, 38; *New York Journal of Commerce*, Jun3 17, 1982, March 22, 1983; *Wall Street Journal*, Feb. 22, 1983, July 13, 1983.

18. *Railroad Facts*, p. 32.

19. *Chicago Tribune*, Oct. 16, 1983; *Trains*, Dec., 1982, p. 4; *Modern Railroads*, Feb., 1983, pp. 26–29; *Wall Street Journal*, July 13, 1983; Donald E. Enright, interview, April 15, 1983; B. F. Biaggini, interview, Jan. 13, 1983; *San Francisco Chronicle*, March 10, 1983; *San Francisco Examiner*, May 20, 1983; *New York Journal of Commerce*, May 20, 1983.

20. *San Francisco Chronicle*, Feb. 22, 1982; *Sacramento Bee*, Feb. 12, 1983; *Bulletin*, May–June, 1983, pp. 14–15; SP, Daily Situation Reports, March 5–10, 1983; *Bulletin*, March–April, 1983, pp. 2–4, Dec., 1983, pp. 3–5; Robert Byrne, remarks at SP's Management Meeting, Nov. 16, 1983, notes in author's files.

21. Harry B. Berkshire, interview, Nov. 9, 1983; *Deseret News* (Salt Lake City), Dec. 4, 1983; Don L. Hofsommer, "Huntington's Problem Continues," *Trains*, March, 1984, p. 8; *Bulletin*, Jan., 1984, pp. 16–18.

22. Benjamin F. Biaggini, Remarks before the Annual Meeting of Stockholders, San Francisco, May 20, 1982, notes in author's files; *Los Angeles Times*, May 27, 1982; R. D. Krebs, May 28, 1982, to All Operating Employees, Operating Department files; R. E. Wyncoop, June 22, 1982, to J. T. Bertram, et al., Sales Department files; *San Francisco Daily Financial News*, Aug. 5, 1982; *New York Times*, Nov. 20, 1982; *Business Week*, Nov. 22, 1982, pp. 38–41; B. F. Biaggini, Dec. 17, 1982, to A. C. Furth and D. K. McNear, Executive files; SP, press release, Jan. 20, 1983, Public Relations files.

23. D. K. McNear, remarks at SP's Management Meeting, April 26, 1983, notes in author's files; SP, press release, May 19, 1983, Public Relations files; *Fortune*, June 13, 1983, pp. 68–69; *California Business*, May, 1983, pp. 81–82; *Forbes*, Oct. 15, 1979, pp. 86–87, Aug. 16, 1982, pp. 57–60; *Wall Street Journal*, Aug. 6, 1982.

24. *Modern Railroads*, Oct., 1982, p. 43; *Traffic World*, Sept. 21, 1981, p. 15.

25. *Forbes*, Aug. 16, 1982, p. 60; *San Francisco Chronicle*, June 23, 1982; *San Francisco* (magazine), Sept., 1982, p. 22; *San Francisco Examiner*, June 6, 1982; *Business Week*, May 3, 1982, pp. 120–21; *New York Times*, Nov. 20, 1982; *San Francisco Examiner*, Aug. 8, 1982; *Management Today-British*, June, 1982, pp. 8–15; *Los Angeles Herald-Examiner*, Oct. 18, 1981.

26. SP, press release, June 18, 1982, Public Relations files; *Bulletin*, Feb., 1972, pp. 2–5.

27. *Bulletin*, Jan., 1982; R. D. Krebs, remarks at SP's Management Meeting, April 26, 1983, notes in author's files; *Bulletin*, Sept., 1982, p. 2.

28. *Bulletin*, March, 1977, pp. 7–8, March, 1984, pp. 3–5; SP, press release, May 23, 1984, Public Relations files.

29. *Topeka Capital-Journal*, Aug. 23, 1981; *Railway Age*, July 27, 1981, pp. 82–84; *New York Journal of Commerce*, Dec. 29, 1982; SP, Annual Report, 1982, pp. 16, 19–21; David P. Morgan, "The Rock Reborn," *Trains*, March, 1983, pp. 48–51; Carl Graves, "Workin' On the Railroad," *Kansas*, no. 3 (1983: 36–38; *Railway Age*, Nov., 1984, pp. 71, 74; *Bulletin*, March–April, 1983, pp. 12–15.

30. SP, Annual Report, 1979, p. 21, 1980, p. 18, 1981, p. 16; R. D. Krebs, remarks at SP's Management Meeting, April 26, 1983, notes in author's files; *Railway Age*, June, 1983, pp. 37–38; Robert Byrne, remarks at SP's Management Meeting, Nov. 16, 1983, notes in author's files; *Bulletin*, Oct., 1984, pp. 3–5; R. D. Krebs, interview, Nov. 30, 1984; SP, Annual Report, 1976, p. 7; M. C. Blanton, Jan. 23, 1985, to the author.

31. *Los Angeles Times*, Aug. 24, 1982; *San Francisco Examiner*, Feb. 6, 1983; *Bulletin*, Nov.–Dec., 1984, pp. 7, 15–17.

32. R. E. Sharp, interview, Dec. 11, 1981; *New York Journal of Commerce*, Dec. 7, 1981; *San Francisco Daily Commercial News*, Jan. 18, 1982; *Traffic World*, March 22, 1982, pp. 26–29; *San Francisco Daily Commercial News*, Dec. 20, 1982; *Bulletin*, April–May, 1984, pp. 9–12; W. J. Lacy, remarks at SP's Management Meeting, Nov. 16, 1983, notes in author's files.

33. *Oakland Tribune*, Dec. 20, 1981; *Progressive Railroading*, Sept., 1981, p. 19; *Bulletin*, May–June, 1983, pp. 2–4; *Houston Business Journal*, July 4, 1983.

34. *Railway Age*, June 29, 1970, pp. 34–35; *U.S. News & World Report*, Jan. 3, 1972, pp. 44–48; *Bulletin*, Feb.–March, 1980, p. 2; *San Francisco Chronicle*, May 31, 1981, Oct. 5, 1982; *Modern Railroads*, Sept., 1982, p. 11; May, 1983, pp. 34, 37; *American West*, March–April, 1982, p. 4.

35. SP, Annual Report, 1979, p. 21; SP/WP, press release, Nov. 13, 1981, Public Relations files; *Burnet* (Tex.) *Bulletin*, Dec. 1, 1983; *Mineral County Independent-News* (Hawthorne, Nev.), May 2, 1984; *Klamath Falls* (Ore.) *Herald & News*, June 7, 1984.

36. W. M. Jones, memorandum, Sept. 6, 1978, Jones, Sept. 22, 1978, to J. D. Ramsey, E. J. Seil, Sept. 22, 1978, to Jones, all in Superintendent's file 520-3, X013-297 (Oakland); *Bulletin*, Nov., 1978, p. 11, Sept., 1979, p. 11; SP, press releases, Feb. 15, April 14, 1983; *Ukiah* (Calif.) *Daily Journal*, May 25, 1983; *Eureka* (Calif.) *Times-Standard*, May 28, 1983; *Bulletin*, Nov.–Dec., 1984, p. 7.

37. J. P. Edwards, remarks at SP's Management Meeting, Nov. 16, 1983, notes in author's files; Diane L. Young, "Marketing & Sales vs. Operating" (student paper, author's files).

38. *New York Journal of Commerce*, Sept. 20, 1984; J. A. Sage, remarks at SP's Management Meeting, Nov. 16, 1983, notes in author's files; SP, Annual Report, 1975, p. 10; C. E. Lamb, Aug. 24, 1984, to the author; R. D. Krebs, remarks at SP's Management Meeting, April 23, 1983, notes in author's files; "The Productivity Dilemma," *Progressive Railroading* (June, 1985): 37–38; *Trains*, July, 1985, pp. 3–4.

39. *Railway Age*, Nov., 1984, pp. 31–34; Frank N. Wilner, *Railroads and Productivity: A Matter of Survival*, pp. 1–25; R. D. Krebs, remarks at SP's Management Meeting, April 26, 1983, notes in author's files; *Bulletin*, Dec., 1977, pp. 6–7, 12, Nov., 1982, pp. 6–7; Don L. Hofsommer, "TPS: SP Tries Participatory Management," *Modern Railroads*, March, 1984, pp. 40–42.

40. *San Francisco Bay Guardian*, Oct. 19, 26, 1983; Bruce MacGregor, "The Ties That Bind," *New West*, March 12, 1979, pp. 24–42; *San Francisco Chronicle*, Nov. 12, 1981;

Signal (Newhall, Calif.), Nov. 8, 1981; *Fremont* (Calif.) *Argus*, Oct. 15, 1981; *Los Angeles Express*, Dec. 9, 1915; *Yolo* (Calif.) *Independent*, Dec. 11, 1915; Stuart Daggett, *Chapters on the Southern Pacific*, pp. 454–59; *San Francisco Chronicle*, Nov. 12, 1981; *Signal* (Newhall, Calif.), Nov. 8, 1981; *Fremont* (Calif.) *Argus*, Oct. 15, 1981; *Camarillo* (Calif.) *Daily News*, Jan. 19, 1983.

41. *Railfan & Railroad*, Jan., 1982, p. 60; *Pacific Rail News No. 230*, Dec. 1981, p. 9; SP, Annual Report, 1975, p. 4; *Arizona Daily Star* (Tucson), May 20, 1984; *Portland Oregonian*, June 25, 1984; SP/Los Angeles Olympic Organizing Committee, press release, March 15, 1983, Public Relations files, Los Angeles; Thomas C. Buckley, interviews, July 20, Oct. 24, 1984; *Los Angeles Times*, Aug. 10, 1984; SP, press release, May 27, 1983, Public Relations files, Los Angeles.

42. SP, Annual Reports, 1980, p. 11, 1982, p. 9; *San Francisco Daily Commercial News*, July 20, 1984; SP, Annual Report, 1975, p. 9; *Pace*, Aug., 1984, pp. 18–21; *Bulletin*, July–Aug., 1983, pp. 12–14; Edward J. Wasp, "Slurry Pipelines," Nov., 1983, pp. 24–32; SP, Annual Report, 1977, p. 20; W. Theo Eskew, remarks at the SP Management Meeting, April 23, 1983, notes in author's files; SP, Annual Reports, 1981, p. 15, 1971, p. 7; W. Theo Eskew, March 29, 1985, to the author.

43. *San Francisco Examiner*, Aug. 5, 1982; *San Francisco Chronicle*, Aug. 3, 1984; SP, Annual Reports, 1982, pp. 4–7, 1980, p. 11.

44. SP, Annual Reports, 1980, p. 7, 1982, pp. 7–8; Bernard Goldman, remarks at SP's Management Meeting, April 26, 1983, notes in author's files; *Times* (San Mateo, Calif.), Feb. 12, 1982; *Pace*, March, 1984, pp. 8–9.

45. *Bulletin*, Dec., 1971, pp. 3–5; SP, Annual Reports, 1971, p. 7, 1974, p. 10, 1976, p. 8, 1977, pp. 4–5, 1978, p. 13, 1980, p. 22.

46. SP, press release, July 7, 1981, Public Relations files; *San Francisco Chronicle*, Nov. 23, 1981; SP, Annual Report, 1982, p. 22; SP, press release, Jan. 6, 1984, Public Relations files; A. D. DeMoss, Nov. 9, 1984, to the author; A. D. DeMoss, interview, Jan. 3, Feb. 11, 1985.

47. PFE, Annual Report, 1980, p. 2; SP, Annual Report, 1982, pp. 18–19; *Bulletin*, April–May, 1984, pp. 29–30; Duane M. Autrey, interview, Feb. 27, 1985.

48. SP, Annual Report, 1980, p. 13; *San Francisco Examiner*, Jan. 14, 1982; SP, Annual Reports, 1981, p. 12, 1982, pp. 14–15.

49. *Washington Post*, Sept. 26, 1982; *San Francisco Examiner*, Oct. 1, 1982; *Wall Street Journal*, Oct. 4, 1982; *Business Week*, Oct. 11, 1982, pp. 63–70, Oct. 18, 1982, p. 71; *Wall Street Journal*, June 20, 1983; SP, Annual Report, 1982, p. 36;

A. C. Furth, remarks at SP's Management Meeting, April 25, 1983, notes in author's files.

50. *Bulletin*, July–Aug., 1980, pp. 20–21; Ticor, *Year in Review*, 1980, pp. 1–3; SP, Annual Reports, 1980, pp. 5–7, 1981, pp. 4–7, 1982, pp. 9–12; *Los Angeles Times*, Oct. 3, 1983; SP, press release, Feb. 1, 1984, Public Relations files.

51. L. T. Wood, remarks at SP's Management Meeting, April 25, 1983, notes in author's files; *Fremont* (Calif.) *Argus*, May 31, 1983; A. G. Becker Paribas, Inc., "Basic Analysis: Southern Pacific Company," (May 26, 1983, pp. 1–48; *New York Times*, Dec. 26, 1982.

52. *Wall Street Journal*, Oct. 4, 1982; *Modern Railroads*, Feb., 1983, p. 12; SPTCo, *Railroad in Transition* (June 28, 1983), pp. 1–61.

CHAPTER NINETEEN

1. *San Francisco Examiner*, Sept. 27, 1983.

2. Comments of B. F. Biaggini in management and press meetings, Sept. 28, 1983, notes in author's files; *Bulletin*, Oct.–Nov., 1983, 2–5.

3. *Chicago Tribune*, Sept. 28, 1983.

4. *Wall Street Journal*, Dec. 27, 1983; *Traffic World*, Jan. 2, 1984, pp. 8–10; SFSP, Annual Report, 1983, front cover; *Fortune*, Jan. 23, 1983, pp. 20–26.

5. D. K. McNear, E. L. Johnson, D. A. Miller, and Thor A. Miller, comments at Management Meeting, Nov. 16, 1983, notes in author's files.

6. *New York Journal of Commerce*, March 26, 1984; SFSP, Railroad Merger Application, vol. 1A—Summary, Finance Docket 30400 (March, 1984), pp. 1–2, Law Department files.

7. John F. Kawa, "An Interview with John J. Schmidt, Chairman of the Board and Chief Executive Officer, Santa Fe Southern Pacific Corp" (Dean Witter Reynolds, Inc., Nov. 21, 1984), p. 3.

8. UP, 1984 Second Quarter Report, p. 6, 1985 First Quarter Report, p. 10; *New York Journal of Commerce*, March 26, 1985; *Fresno* (Calif.) *Bee*, March 13, 1985; *New York Journal of Commerce*, June 1, 1984; *Daily Traffic World*, July 20, 23, 25, 26, 1984.

9. SFSP, press release, June 7, 1984, SP Public Relations files; *PACE*, Oct., 1984, p. 2; *New York Journal of Commerce*, Oct. 29, 1984; *Topeka Capital-Journal*, March 24, 1985.

10. SFSP, Annual Report, 1984, p. 11; SFSP, press release, April 17, 1985, SP Public Relations files.

11. Jack Rudolph, "Triumph at Yorktown," *American Heritage*, Oct., 1981, p. 78; David P. Morgan, "Perhaps a Christmas Fable," *Trains*, Dec., 1984, p. 40; *Santa Fe Magazine*, Oct., 1983, p. 8.

Bibliography

PRIMARY MATERIALS

THE essential material for this book derives from primary sources of the Southern Pacific. At the time I used them, these were reposited, for the most part, in San Francisco at the General Office Building, Oriental Warehouse, and Brannon Street Warehouse; at Houston in the Topek Building; at Tyler, Texas, in Cotton Belt's General Office Building; and, at Kansas City, Kansas, in Cotton Belt's Kansas City Division offices. Unless otherwise noted, citations to company records refer to those then housed at San Francisco. Since the merger with Santa Fe Industries, many files have been moved. It is not yet possible to tell where they will rest, but I hope the information on where I found materials will allow other researchers in the future to trace them.

PUBLICATIONS AND ARCHIVAL MATERIALS OF THE SOUTHERN PACIFIC AND SUBSIDIARIES

Bedwell, Harry. *Priority Special*. San Francisco: Southern Pacific, 1945. Biaggini, Benjamin F. "Remarks before the Annual Meeting of Stockholders." San Francisco, May 20, 1982. Notes in author's files.

Bulletin. First published on November, 1913 (suspended from August, 1931, to October, 1935), to the present. Public Relations office, San Francisco.

Corporate History of the Galveston, Harrisburg & San Antonio Railway as of June 30, 1918. Public Relations office, Houston.

"Corporate History St. Louis Southwestern Railway System and Subsidiary Companies." N.d. SSW Public Relations office, Kansas City (file 70-2-6).

Cotton Belt News. Begun in January, 1936, as *The Cotton Belter*, changed in March, 1945, to *The Cotton Belt News*. Ceased publication 1st Quarter, 1975. Public Relations office, Kansas City.

"General Description: Black Mesa Pipeline," Engineering Management, Inc., May 10, 1968. Black Mesa VP&GM files, Flagstaff.

Heath, Erle. *Seventy-five Years of Progress: Historical Sketch of the Southern Pacific*. San Francisco: Southern Pacific, 1945.

Huntington, C. P. *California—Her Past, Present and Future*. Speech before the Chiefs of Department, Southern Pacific Company. May 16, 1900. Copy in Executive files.

Inside Track, The. Publication of the Traffic Department, begun shortly after World War II and ceased in the mid-1970s.

Karr, Randolph. "Rail Passenger Service History of Pacific Electric Railway Company." 1973. Public Relations file, Los Angeles.

Kruttschnitt, Julius. "The Engineer as a Railroad Executive." Address before the New York Section, American Society of Civil Engineers, March 18, 1925. Copy in Executive files.

Mayo, H. M. *History of the Southern Pacific Lines in Texas*. N.d. Public Relations office, Houston.

Montfoot, J. G. "Operations of the Black Mesa Pipeline System." Black Mesa VP&GM files, Flagstaff.

Montgomery, Julia Cameron. *A Little Journey through the Lower Rio Grande Valley of Texas*. Houston: Southern Pacific, 1928.

Morrill, Clifford R. "History of the El Paso Division," typescript, 1925—retyped and expanded, 1970. Public Relations office, Houston.

Myrick, David F. *Refinancing and Building the*

Central Pacific: 1899–1910. Prepared for the Golden Spike Symposium, University of Utah, 1969. Published and distributed by Southern Pacific.

"New Orleans Union Passenger Terminal Dedication Program, Saturday, May 1, 1954." Public Relations files, Houston.

Pacific Electric. "This is Pacific Electric." 1952. Los Angeles Public Relations office.

Pacific Electric Magazine. Publication begun on June 10, 1916, suspended 1932–36, ceased October, 1953. Public Relations office, Los Angeles.

Pacific Fruit Express. *History and Development of Pacific Fruit Express Company.* January 1, 1945.

———. *History and Functions of Pacific Fruit Express Company.* January 1, 1967.

Poole, E. C. "Fuel Consumed vs. Locomotive Miles and Locomotive Ton Miles as a Measure of Locomotive Repairs." October 20, 1953. BTR file M-359-1.

———. "Fuel Used vs. Locomotive Miles as a Measure for Locomotive Repairs." June 20, 1952. Bureau of Transportation Research (BTR) file M-287-1-A.

Purdon, C. D. "History of the Cotton Belt." N.d. SSW Public Relations office, Kansas City.

St. Louis Southwestern Railway. *Centennial: 1877–1977.* 1977. Public Relations office, Kansas City.

———. *Factual Report of Operating, Traffic and Financial Affairs.* 1946. Public Relations office, Kansas City.

———. *Malaria Control: A Demonstration of Its Value to Railroads Based on Experience of the St. Louis Southwestern Railway Lines, 1917–1920.* 1921. Public Relations office, Kansas City.

———. *Report on Certain Special Features of the St. Louis Southwestern Railways.* 1915. Executive files, Tyler.

Southern Pacific. *Agricultural Achievements and Possibilities along the Southern Pacific Lines in Texas.* 1923.

———. Annual Reports, 1899–1983.

———. *Brief History of Relations Between Southern Pacific Company and St. Louis Southwestern Railway Company.* 1936.

———. Circular 4. 1940.

———. *Corporate History of the Southern Pacific Company as of Date of Valuation, June 30, 1916.* Compiled May 31, 1919.

———. *Dead Companies.* N.d.

———. Division maps, Southern Pacific Company Lines as of June 30, 1916.

———. *Financial History of the Southern Pacific Transportation Company, A.* N.d.

———. Historical and Factual Data Pertaining to Central Pacific Railway Company. Executive Department, Statement No. 507. July 28, 1943.

———. *Historical Memoranda.* Two volumes. N.d. [1960s].

———. *Historical Sketch of the Origin and Development of the Transportation Properties Operated as a Part of the Southern Pacific System.* March, 1933.

———. *History of the Southern Pacific Organization & Development of the Lines in Texas & Louisiana.* 1927.

———. *The: Magic Valley of the Lower Rio Grande: The Land of Golden Fruit.* Houston: Southern Pacific, 1930.

———. *Official Register.* N.d.

———. *Operation Fill.* 1959.

———. "Plan for Progress: A Statement of Southern Pacific Policy to Maintain Emphasis on Equal Employment Opportunity and Equal Treatment for All Qualified Persons." July 1, 1962.

———. Salt Lake Division Time Table #54. June 17, 1940.

———. *Southern Pacific and Affiliated Companies, Office Manual.* June 1, 1970.

———. *Southern Pacific Co. Proprietary and Affiliated Companies: Mileage and Termini Covered by the Securities Pledged Under Mortgages and Indentures.* 1916.

———. *Southwest Louisiana: Its Agricultural and Industrial Developments and Its Potential Wealth.* 1927.

———. *Student Course in Railroading.* 1914.

———. "Ten-Year Forecast of Freight Car and Locomotive Requirements." February 4, 1965.

———. *Ten Year Motive Power Survey.* August 15, 1948.

———. Time Table. March, 1907.

———. Western Division Time Table #231. September 29, 1940.

Southern Pacific Pipe Lines, Inc. Pamphlet containing historical and tabular data, prepared by and available from the Office of President & General Manager, Los Angeles. February 3, 1982.

Southern Pacific Transportation Company. *Railroad in Transition.* June 28, 1983.

Southern Pacific/Union Pacific. *Five Year Plan for Rehabilitation of Chicago, Rock Island & Pacific Railroad Company Rail Properties.* February, 1975.

Texas & New Orleans Railroad. *East-Southeast Texas on the Texas & New Orleans Railroad.* 1907.

Ticor, *Year-in-Review.* SP, 1980.

PUBLICATIONS AND REPORTS BY OTHER CORPORATIONS

A. G. Becker Paribas, Inc. "Basic Analysis: Southern Pacific Company." May 26, 1983.

Atchison, Topeka & Santa Fe Railway. Annual Reports, 1900–82. Title varies. AT&SF Offices, Chicago.

Chicago, Burlington & Quincy Railroad., Annual Reports, 1901–1904. Burlington Northern Offices, Saint Paul.

The Feather River Route: A Brief History. Western Pacific. 1973.

Hooker & Fay. "Southern Pacific Company." March, 1962.

Illinois Central Railroad. Annual Reports, 1897–1910. ICG offices, Chicago.

J. R. Williston, Bruce & Company. "Southern Pacific Company." May, 1953. Copy in Southern Pacific Offices, San Francisco.

Northern Pacific Railway. Annual Reports, 1901–15. Burlington Northern offices, Saint Paul.

St. Louis Southwestern Railway Company: An Examination of This System's Records with Reference to the Fundamental Position of Its Mortgage Obligations. New York: Shields & Company, 1935. Copy in SSW offices, Tyler.

Southern Pacific Company: Pioneers of Western Progress. San Francisco: Strassburgert Company, 1929. Copy in SP offices, San Francisco.

"The Truth About 'American Ground Transport'— A Reply by General Motors." Submitted to the Subcommittee on Antitrust and Monopoly of the Committee of the Judiciary of the United States Senate. April, 1954. Copy in SP Law Department files, Los Angeles.

Union Pacific. Annual Reports, 1897–1925. UP offices, Omaha.

Witter & Company. "Special Study of the Southern Pacific Company." September, 1964. Copy in SP offices, San Francisco.

MANUSCRIPTS AND COLLECTIONS

Hill, James H. Papers. James J. Hill Reference Library, St. Paul.

Hopkins, Louis P. "A Lifetime of Railroading." Oregon Collection, University of Oregon, Eugene.

King, Ernest L. Papers. Typescript. Oregon Collection, University of Oregon, Eugene.

McKenzie, H. J. "History of the McKenzie Family and Autobiography of H. J. McKenzie." Manuscript, 1982. Author's files.

Morse, Amos A. Correspondence, 1908–1912. Oregon Collection, University of Oregon, Eugene.

PERSONAL INTERVIEWS

Ahearn, Ed P. Vice President, Southern Pacific Transportation Co. January 10, 1983.

Autrey, Duane M. Administrative Assistant, Pacific Fruit Express Company. February 27, 1985.

Aydelott, G. B. Retired President and Chairman of the Board, Denver & Rio Grande Western Railroad. January 21, September 22, 1982.

Babers, Charles T. General Manager, Southern Pacific Transportation Co. October 26, 1984, September 18, 1985.

Berkshire, Harry B. Assistant Vice President-Maintenance of Way, Southern Pacific Transportation Co. November 9, 1983.

Biaggini, Benjamin F. Chairman, Southern Pacific Company. March 1, 1982, January 13, November 8, 1983.

Brown, Ed N. Vice President-Sales, St. Louis Southwestern Railway. July 19, 1982.

Buckley, Thomas C. Assistant Vice President-Public Relations, Southern Pacific Transportation Co. July 20, October 24, 1984.

DeMoss, Allan D. Chairman, Pacific Motor Trucking Company. January 3, February 11, 1985.

Enright, Donald E. Assistant Vice President-Finance, Southern Pacific Transportation Co. April 15, 1983.

Eskew, W. Theo. President, Southern Pacific Pipe Lines. February 14, 1983.

Fox, Lonnie M. Assistant Vice President-Labor Relations, Southern Pacific Transportation Co. February 25, 1982.

Frame, Russell M. Chief Engineering Officer, Seaboard Coast Line. December 1, 1982.

Germany, James W. Vice President-Information Services, Southern Pacific Transportation Co. December 11, 1981.

Gregory, Robert M. Chief Dispatcher-Los Angeles, Southern Pacific Transportation Co. May 6, 1983.

Guerin, Frank M. Assistant Vice President-Sales, Southern Pacific Transportation Co. February 15, 1983.

Harriman, W. Averell. Former Chairman of the Board, Union Pacific Railroad. December 14, 1982.

Hoenig, William C. Vice President-Purchasing, Southern Pacific Transportation Co. October 27, 1984.

Hudson, W. Harry. Retired Vice President of Operations, St. Louis Southwestern Railway. October 12, 1981.

Karr, Randolph. Retired Attorney, Southern Pacific Transportation Co. September 29, 1983.

Krebs, Robert D. President, Santa Fe Southern Pacific Corporation. November 30, 1984.

Lacy, William J. Vice President-Operations, Southern Pacific Transportation Co. October 21, 1981.

Lindow, John F. Clerk, Beaumont, Texas, Southern Pacific Transportation Co. January 21, 1982.

McKenzie, Harold J. Retired President, St. Louis Southwestern Railway. October 13, 1981, April 22, June 16, 1982.

McNamara, James T. Assistant Superintendent, Houston, Southern Pacific Transportation Co. January 19, 1982.

Osborn, Prime F. Retired Chairman of the Board, Seaboard Coast Line. November 30, 1982.

Peoples, William G. Retired Vice President-Sales, Southern Pacific Transportation Co. February 17, 1983.

Rodgers, Jo. Operator, Houston Division, Southern Pacific Transportation Co. January 22, 1982.

Roland, W. Earle. Chief Dispatcher, Houston, Southern Pacific Transportation Co. January 22, April 7, 1982.

Russell, Donald J. Retired Chairman, Southern Pacific Company. December 11, 17, 1981, February 24, 25, May 20, 21, July 20, December 10, 1982, January 11, September 26, 1983.

Sharp, Robert E. Vice President-Traffic Department, Southern Pacific Transportation Co. December 11, 1981.

Sines, Guerdon S. Vice President-Information & Communications Systems, Union Pacific System. June 29, October 8, 1984.

Spence, Richard D. Executive Vice President-Operations, Seaboard Coast Line. December 1, 1982.

Sullivan, James R. Retired Vice President-Marketing, Conrail. December 13, 1982.

Weber, Arnold I. Senior General Attorney, Southern Pacific Transportation Co. January 7, 1985.

Williamson, Harry E. Retired Chief Engineer, Southern Pacific Transportation Co. April 10, 1984.

Wyncoop, Robert E. Vice President-Sales, Southern Pacific Transportation Co. May 21, 1982.

GOVERNMENT DOCUMENTS

2 California Railroad Commission 233.

2 California Railroad Commission 248.

2 California Railroad Commission 319.

162 Interstate Commerce Commission 37-70.

166 Interstate Commerce Commission 3.

175 Interstate Commerce Commission 367.

ICC. *Reports*. Vol. 12: "Consolidations and Combinations of Carriers." Washington, D.C.: Government Printing Office, 1908.

ICC. *Valuation Docket 1008, Southern Pacific Company, et al.* Washington, D.C.: Government Printing Office, 1934.

U.S. District Court Utah. *United States v. Southern Pacific Company, Central Pacific Railway Company, et al.* 3 vols. Washington, D.C.: Government Printing Office, 1915.

U.S. Industrial Commission. *Reports*, Vol. 19. Washington, D.C.: Government Printing Office, 1908.

United States v. Union Pacific Railroad, et al. 188 F. 102-127.

United States v. Union Pacific Railroad, 226 U.S. 470-477.

NEWSPAPERS

Arizona Daily Star [Tucson], 1984.
Arizona Gazette, 1924.
Arizona Republican, 1924, 1982.
Arkansas Gazette [Little Rock], 1981.
Berkeley Gazette, 1939.
Brownsville [Texas] *Herald*, 1927.

Burnet [Texas] *Bulletin*, 1983.
Camarillo [California] *Daily News*, 1983.
Chicago Examiner, 1914.
Chicago Journal of Commerce, 1926.
Chicago News, 1961.
Chicago Tribune, 1982–84.
Coos Bay [Oregon] *Times*, 1916.
Dallas Morning News, 1927, 1958.
Deseret News [Salt Lake City], 1983.
Des Moines Register, 1980.
El Paso Herald, 1924.
Eureka [California] *Times-Standard*, 1983.
Fremont [California] *Argus*, 1981–83.
Fresno [California] *Bee*, 1985.
Herington [Kansas] *Times*, 1980.
Kansas City Times, 1981.
Klamath Falls [Oregon] *Herald*, 1916.
Klamath Falls [Oregon] *Herald & News*, 1984.
Laredo Times, 1981.
Lordsburg Liberal, 1924.
Los Angeles Express, 1915.
Los Angeles Herald-Examiner, 1981.
Los Angeles Record, 1922.
Los Angeles Times, 1922, 1924, 1982–84.
Louisville Courier-Journal, 1882.
Mineral County Independent-News [Hawthorne, Nevada], 1984.
Morning Oregonian, 1913, 1922.
New York American, 1914–16.
New York Herald-Tribune, 1924.
New York Journal of Commerce, 1978–85.
New York Post, 1924.
New York Times, 1906–1909, 1913, 1922, 1982.
Oakland Tribune, 1965, 1981.
Ogden Standard Examiner, 1942, 1953, 1967.
Phoenix [Arizona] *Republic*, 1967.
Portland Journal, 1923.
Portland Oregonian, 1923–27, 1981, 1984.
Reno Herald's Herald, 1965.
Sacramento Bee, 1983.
Sacramento Union, 1980.
St. Louis Globe-Democrat, 1931, 1966.
St. Louis Post-Dispatch, 1966, 1968, 1973.
Salt Lake Telegram, 1922.
San Antonio Express, 1927, 1935.
San Diego Business Journal, 1981.
San Diego Evening Tribune, 1976.
San Diego Union, 1961.
San Francisco Bay Guardian, 1983.
San Francisco Bulletin, 1912, 1914.
San Francisco Call, 1913.

San Francisco Call-Bulletin, 1953.
San Francisco Call-Chronicle-Examiner, 1906.
San Francisco Chronicle, 1911–17, 1922–23, 1930–32, 1959, 1967, 1980–85.
San Francisco Daily Commercial News, 1982.
San Francisco Daily Financial News, 1982–85.
San Francisco Examiner, 1915–17, 1939, 1956, 1968, 1978, 1980–85.
San Francisco News, 1937, 1952, 1957.
Santa Barbara Morning News, 1900.
Signal, The [Newhall, California], 1981.
Southeast Missourian [Cape Girardeau], 1983.
Sunday Oregonian, 1914.
Times, The [San Mateo, California], 1982.
Topeka Capital-Journal, 1981–85.
Tyler [Texas] *Courier Times*, 1955.
Ukiah [California] *Daily Journal*, 1983.
Wall Street Journal, 1922–24, 1931, 1939, 1943, 1960, 1964, 1966–68, 1978–85.
Washington Post, 1982.
Washington Star, 1978.
Yolo [California] *Interdependent*, 1915.

SECONDARY WORKS

BOOKS

Allhands, J. L. *Gringo Builders.* Joplin: Privately printed, 1931.
Allhands, James L. *Railroads to the Rio.* Salado, Tex.: Anson Jones Press, 1960.
Ames, Charles Edgar. *Pioneering the Union Pacific: A Reappraisal of Building the Railroad.* New York: Appleton-Century-Crofts, 1969.
Athearn, Robert G. *Rebel of the Rockies: A History of the Denver & Rio Grande Western Railroad.* New Haven: Yale University Press, 1962.
———. *Union Pacific Country.* Chicago: Rand McNally & Co., 1971.
Bail, Eli. *From Railway to Freeway: Pacific Electric and the Motor Coach.* Glendale, Calif.: Interurban Press, 1984.
Bailey, William Francis. *The Story of the First Trans-Continental Railroads.* Pittsburgh: Pittsburgh Printing Co., 1906.
Barriger, John W. *Super Railroads for a Dynamic American Economy.* New York: Privately published, 1956.
Baruch, Bernard M. *Baruch: My Own Story.* New York: Henry Holt, 1957.
Baughman, James P. *Charles Morgan and the De-*

velopment of Southern Transportation. Nashville: Vanderbilt University Press, 1968.

Beebe, Lucius. *Central Pacific & Southern Pacific Centennial History of a Great Transcontinental.* Berkeley: Howell-North, 1963.

———. *The Overland Limited.* Berkeley: Howell-North, 1963.

Beebe, Lucius, and Charles Clegg. *Steamcars to the Comstock: The Virginia & Truckee Railroad, the Carson & Colorado Railroad.* Berkeley: Howell-North, 1957.

Best, Gerald M. *Ships and Narrow Gauge Rails: The Story of the Pacific Coast Company.* Berkeley: Howell-North, 1964.

———. *Snowplow: Clearing Mountain Rails.* Berkeley: Howell-North, 1966.

Biographical Directory of the Railway Officials of America. New York: Simmons-Boardman, 1900–85. Title and publisher varies.

Blackford, Mansel G. *The Politics of Business in California, 1890–1920.* Columbus: Ohio State University Press, 1977.

Boynton, James E. *The 4-10-2: Three Barrels of Steam.* Felton: Glenwood Publishers, 1973.

Bradley, Bill. *The Last of the Great Stations: 40 Years of the Los Angeles Union Passenger Terminal.* Glendale, Calif.: Interurban Press, 1979.

Brandes, Ely M., and Alan E. Lazar. *The Future of Rail Passenger Traffic in the West.* Menlo Park, Calif.: Stanford Research Institute, 1966.

Bruchey, Stuart, ed. *Memoir of Three Railroad Pioneers.* New York: Arno Press, 1981.

Bryant, Keith L., Jr. *History of the Atchison, Topeka & Santa Fe Railway.* New York: Macmillan Publishing, 1974.

Cafky, Morris. *Colorado Midland.* Denver: Rocky Mountain Railroad Club, 1965.

Chandler, Alfred D., Jr., ed. *The Railroads: The Nation's First Big Business.* New York: Harcourt, Brace & World, 1965.

Chappell, Gordon. *Rails to Carry Copper: A History of the Magma Arizona Railroad.* Boulder: Pruett Publishing, 1973.

Chipman, Art. *"Tunnel 13": The Story of the De Autrement Brothers and the West's Last Great Train Hold Up.* Medford, Ore.: Pine Cone Publishers, 1979.

Church, Robert J. *Cab-Forward: The Story of*

Southern Pacific Articulateds. Wilton, Calif.: Central Valley Railroad Publications, 1982.

———. *Those Daylight 4-8-4s: The Story of Southern Pacific GS Class Locomotives.* Omaha: Kratville Publications, 1966.

Clark, G. T. *Leland Stanford.* Stanford: Stanford University, 1931.

Clark, Ira G. *Then Came the Railroads: The Century from Steam to Diesel in the Southwest.* Norman: University of Oklahoma Press, 1958.

Cleland, Robert Glass. *A History of California: The American Period.* New York: Macmillan Company, 1927.

Combs, Barry B. *Westward to Promontory.* Palo Alto, Calif.: American West Publishing Co., 1969.

Crump, Spender. *Ride the Big Red Cars: How Trolleys Helped Build Southern California.* Los Angeles: Trans-Anglo Books, 1962.

———. *Western Pacific: The Railroad That Was Built Too Late.* Los Angeles: Trans-Anglo Books, 1963.

Culp, Edwin D. *Stations West: The Story of the Oregon Railways.* Caldwell, Idaho: Caxton Printers, 1972.

Daggett, Stuart. *Chapters on the Southern Pacific.* New York: A. M. Kelly, 1966.

———. *Railroad Consolidation West of the Mississippi River.* 1933. Reprint, New York: Arno Press, 1981.

De Moro, Harre W. *Electric Railway Pioneer: Commuting on the Northwestern Pacific, 1903–1941.* Glendale, Calif.: Interurban Press, 1983.

Dickinson, A. Bray, and Roy Graves. *Narrow Gauge to the Redwoods: The Story of the North Pacific Coast Railroads and San Francisco Bay Ferries.* Los Angeles: Trans-Anglo Books, 1967.

Dodge, Grenville M. *How We Built the Union Pacific and Other Railway Papers and Addresses of Grenville M. Dodge.* Denver: Sage Books, 1965.

Dorin, Patrick C. *Commuter Railroads: A Pictorial Review of the Most Travelled Trains.* Seattle: Superior Publishing, 1970.

Dubin, Arthur D. *More Classic Trains.* Milwaukee: Kalmbach Publishing, 1974.

———. *Some Classic Trains.* Milwaukee: Kalmbach Publishing, 1964.

Duke, Donald. *Pacific Electric: Pictorial History of the World's Greatest Interurban System.* San Marino: Golden West Books, n.d.

Duke, Donald, comp., *Southern Pacific Steam Locomotives: A Pictorial Anthology of Western Railroading.* San Marino, Calif.: Golden West Books, 1962.

Dunscomb, Guy L. *A Century of Southern Pacific Steam Locomotives, 1862–1962.* Modesto, Calif.: Privately published, 1963.

Eargle, Dolan, Jr. *Tickets Please: All About California Railroads.* San Francisco: California Living Books, 1979.

Eckenrode, H. J., and Pocahontas Wright Edmunds. *E. H. Harriman: The Little Giant of Wall Street.* New York: Greenburg Publishing, 1933.

Evans, Cerinda W. *Collis Potter Huntington.* 2 vols. Newport News, Va.: Mariners' Museum, 1954.

Ferrel, Mallory Hope. *Southern Pacific Narrow Gauge.* Edmonds, Wash.: Pacific Fast Mail, 1982.

Fisher, Kay. *A Baggage Car with Lace Curtains.* Colfax, Calif.: Privately printed, 1979.

Ford, Robert S. *Red Trains in the East Bay.* Glendale, Calif.: Interurban Press, 1977.

Galloway, John Debo. *The First Transcontinental Railroad: The Central Pacific and Union Pacific, 1863–1869.* New York: Simmons-Boardman, 1950.

Godfrey, Aaron Austin. *Government Operation of the Railroads, 1918–1920: Its Necessity, Success, and Consequences.* Austin, Tex.: Jenkins Publishing Co., 1974.

Goetzmann, William H. *Army Explorations in the West, 1803–1863.* New Haven: Yale University Press, 1959.

Goodwin, C. C. *As I Remember Them.* Salt Lake City: Salt Lake Commercial Club, 1913.

Grant, H. Roger. *The Corn Belt Route: A History of the Chicago Great Western Railroad Company.* Dekalb: Northern Illinois University Press, 1984.

Griswold, Wesley S. *A Work of Giants: Building the First Transcontinental Railroad.* New York: McGraw-Hill, 1962.

Grodinsky, Julius. *Jay Gould: His Business Career: 1867–1892.* Philadelphia: University of Pennsylvania Press, 1957.

Hanft, Robert M. *San Diego & Arizona: The Impossible Railroad.* Glendale, Calif.: Trans-Anglo Books, 1984.

Harlan, George H. *San Francisco Ferryboats.* Berkeley: Howell-North Books, 1967.

———. *Those Amazing Cab Forwards.* Greenbrae, Calif.: Privately printed, 1983.

Harlan, George H., and Clement Fisher, Jr. *Of Walking Beams and Paddle Wheels: A Chronicle of San Francisco Ferry Boats.* San Francisco: Bay Books Limited, 1951.

Hayes, William Edward. *Iron Road to Empire: The History of 100 Years of the Progress and Achievements of the Rock Island Lines.* New York: Simmons-Boardman, 1953.

Hedges, James Blaine. *Henry Villard and the Railways of the Northwest.* New Haven: Yale University Press, 1930.

Hofsommer, Don L. *Prairie Oasis: The Railroads, Steamboats and Resorts of Iowa's Spirit Lake Country.* Des Moines: Waukon Mississippi Press, 1975.

Hogg, Garry. *Union Pacific: The Building of the First Transcontinental Railroad.* New York: Walker, 1969.

Howard, Ernest. *Wall Street Fifty Years after Erie.* Boston: Privately printed, 1923.

Howard, Robert West. *The Great Iron Trail: The Story of the First Transcontinental Railroad.* New York: G. P. Putnam's Sons, 1962.

Hungerford, John B. *Cab-in-Front: The Half-Century of an Unconventional Locomotive.* Reseda, Calif.: Hungerford Press, 1959.

Itzkoff, Donald M. *Off the Track: The Decline of the Intercity Passenger Train in the United States.* Westport, Conn.: Greenwood Press, 1985.

Jensen, Larry. *The Movie Railroads.* Burbank, Calif.: Darwin Publications, 1981.

Jewell, Donald V. *Southern Pacific Motive Power Annual, 1977–1980.* Burlingame, Calif.: Chatham Publishing Co., 1981.

Johnson, Arthur M., and Barry E. Supple. *Boston Capitalists and Western Railroads: A Study in the Nineteenth-Century Railroad Investment Process.* Cambridge: Harvard University Press, 1967.

Johnson, Enid. *Rails Across the Continent: The Story of the First Trancontinental Railroad.* New York: J. Messner, 1965.

Jones, Helen Hinckley. *Rails from the West: A Biography of Theodore D. Judah.* San Marino, Calif.: Golden West Books, 1969.

Keilty, Edmund. *Doodlebug Country: The Rail Motorcar on the Class I Railroads of the United States.* Glendale, Calif.: Interurban Press, 1982.

Kemble, John Haskell. *San Francisco Bay: A Pictorial Maritime History.* New York: Bonanza Books, 1972.

Kennan, George. *E. H. Harriman: A Biography.* 2 vols. Boston: Houghton-Mifflin, 1922.

King, Ernest L., and Robert E. Mahaffay. *Main Line: Fifty Years of Railroading with the Southern Pacific.* Garden City, N.Y.: Doubleday & Company, 1948.

Kneis, Gilbert H. *Bonanza Railroads.* Stanford: Stanford University Press, 1941.

Kraus, George. *High Road to Promontory: Building the Central Pacific (Now the Southern Pacific) across the High Sierras.* Palo Alto, Calif.: American West Publishing Co., 1969.

Latta, Estelle. *Controversial Mark Hopkins: The Great Swindle of American History.* New York: Greenburg, 1953.

Lavender, David. *The Great Persuader.* New York: Doubleday, 1970.

Leonard, Edward A. *Rails at the Pass of the North.* El Paso: Texas Western Press, 1981.

Leonard, William Norris. *Railroad Consolidation under the Transportation Act of 1920.* New York: Columbia University Press, 1946.

Levi, Leonard O., and Jack T. Johnson. *A Railroad to the Sea.* Iowa City: Midland House, 1939.

Lewis, Arthur H. *The Day They Shook the Plum Tree.* New York: Harcourt, Brace & World, 1963.

Lewis, Oscar. *The Big Four: The Story of Huntington, Stanford, Hopkins, and Crocker, and the Building of the Central Pacific.* New York: Alfred A. Knopf, 1938.

Lovett, Robert A. *Forty Years After: An Appreciation of the Genius of Edward Henry Harriman, 1848–1909.* New York: Newcomen Society, 1949.

McAfee, Ward. *California's Railroad Era, 1850–1911.* San Marino, Calif.: Golden West Books, 1973.

McCague, James. *Moguls and Iron Men: The Story of the First Transcontinental Railroad.* New York: Harper & Row, 1964.

McCall, J. B. "Corporate Attitudes toward a Declining Market: Santa Fe and Southern Pacific Rail Passenger Service, 1950–1965," Department of Economics *Working Paper Series 82-7.* Arlington, Tex.: University of Texas at Arlington, n.d.

MacGregor, Bruce A., and Richard Truesdale. *South Pacific Coast—A Centennial.* Boulder: Pruett Publishing, 1982.

Marshall, James. *Santa Fe: The Railroad That Built an Empire.* New York: Random House, 1945.

Martin, Albro. *Enterprise Denied: Origins of the Decline of American Railroads, 1897–1917.* New York: Columbia University Press, 1971.

———. *James J. Hill and the Opening of the Northwest.* New York: Oxford University Press, 1976.

Masters, Frank M. *Mississippi River Bridge at New Orleans, Louisiana: Final Report to the Belt Railroad Commission of the City of New Orleans.* Harrisburg, Pa.: Modjeski & Masters, Consulting Engineers, 1941.

Maxwell, Robert S. *Whistle in the Piney Woods: Paul Bremond and the Houston, East & West Texas Railway.* Houston: Texas Gulf Coast Historical Association, 1963.

Middleton, William D. *When the Steam Railroads Electrified.* Milwaukee: Kalmbach Publishing, 1974.

Miller, David E., ed. *The Golden Spike.* Salt Lake City: University of Utah Press, 1974.

Mills, Randall V. *Railroads Down the Valleys: Some Short Lines of the Oregon Country.* Palo Alto: Pacific Books, 1950.

Miner, H. Craig. *The Rebirth of the Missouri Pacific, 1956–1983.* College Station: Texas A&M University Press, 1983.

———. *The St. Louis–San Francisco Transcontinental Railroad: The Thirty-fifth Parallel Project, 1853–1890.* Lawrence: University Press of Kansas, 1972.

Moody, John. *The Railroad Builders: A Chronicle of the Welding of the States.* New Haven: Yale University Press, 1919.

Moody's Analyses . . . Railroad Investments, 1922–1984. Title varies.

Morell, Parker. *Diamond Jim.* Garden City, N.Y.: Garden City Publishing Co., 1934.

Morgenthau, Henry. *All in a Lifetime.* Garden City, N.Y.: 1922.

Muir, John. *Edward Henry Harriman*. New York: Doubleday, Page & Co., 1911.

Murdock, Dick. *Early Call for the Perishables: A Day at the Throttle*. Ross, Calif.: May Murdock Publications, 1983.

———. *Port Costa 1879–1941: A Saga of Sails, Sacks and Rails*. Port Costa, Calif.: Murdock-Endom Publications, 1977.

Myrick, David F. *New Mexico's Railroads: An Historical Survey*. Golden, Colo.: Colorado Railroad Museum, 1970.

———. *Railroads of Arizona*. 3 vols. San Diego: Howell-North, 1975–84.

———. *Railroads of Nevada and Eastern California*. 2 vols. Berkeley: Howell-North, 1962–63.

———. *Rails Around the Bohemian Grove*. San Francisco: Privately printed, 1973.

Neal, Dorothy J. *The Cloud-Climbing Railroad: A Story of Timber, Trestles and Trains*. Alamagordo, N. Mex.: Alamagordo Printing Co., 1966.

Nichols, Joseph. *History of the Construction of the Union Pacific Railway & Company*. Omaha: Klopp Bartlett, 1892.

Ostrander, G. M. *Nevada: The Great Rotten Borough*. New York: Knopf, 1966.

Overton, Richard C. *Burlington Route: A History of the Burlington Lines*. New York: Alfred A. Knopf, 1965.

Potts, C. S. *Railroad Transportation in Texas*. University of Texas Bulletin No. 119, Humanistic Studies. Austin: University of Texas, 1909.

Pyle, Joseph Gilpin. *The Life of James J. Hill*. Gloucester, Mass.: Peter Smith, 1968.

Railroad Facts. Washington: Association of American Railroads, 1984.

Redding, Benjamin P. *A Sketch of the Life of Mark Hopkins of California*. San Francisco: Bancroft, 1881.

Reed, S. G. *A History of the Texas Railroads and of Transportation Conditions under Spain and Mexico and the Republic and the State*. Houston: St. Clair Publishing Co., 1941.

Renz, Louis Tuck. *The History of the Northern Pacific Railroad*. Fairfield, Wash.: Ye Galleon Press, 1980.

Repp, Stan. *The Super Chief—Train of the Stars*. San Marino, Calif.: Golden West Books, 1980.

Riegel, Robert E. *The Story of the Western Railroads*. New York: Macmillan Company, 1926.

Sabin, E. L. *Building the Pacific Railway*. Philadelphia: Lippincott, 1919.

Salt Lake City and the State of Utah. San Francisco: Sunset Magazine Homeseekers' Bureau of Information, n.d. [1912?].

Sanjani, Sally Springmeyer. *The Unspiked Rail*. Reno: University of Nevada Press, 1981.

Saunders, Richard. *The Railroad Mergers and the Coming of Conrail*. Westport, Conn.: Greenwood Press, 1978.

Scribbins, Jim. *The Hiawatha Story*. Milwaukee: Kalmbach Publishing, 1970.

Shaw, Robert B. *A History of Railroad Accidents, Safety Precautions and Operating Practices*. Privately published, 1978.

Signor, John R. *Rails in the Shadow of Mt. Shasta: 100 Years of Railroading along Southern Pacific's Shasta Division*. San Diego: Howell-North, 1982.

———. *Southern Pacific–Santa Fe: Tehachapi*. San Marino, Calif.: Golden West Books, 1983.

Sonnichsen, C. L. *Tucson: The Life and Times of an American City*. Norman: University of Oklahoma Press, 1982.

Southern Pacific and Railroad Passenger Service. Chicago: National Association of Railroad Passengers, 1967.

Spearman, Frank H. *The Strategy of Great Railroads*. New York: Charles Scribner's Sons, 1904.

Staff, Virgil. *D-Day on the Western Pacific: A Railroad's Decision to Dieselize*. Glendale, Calif.: Interurban Press, 1982.

Stindt, Fred A. *The Northwestern Pacific Railroad: Redwood Empire Route*. Kelseyville, Calif.: Privately printed, 1964.

Stover, John F. *American Railroads*. Chicago: University of Chicago Press, 1961.

———. *The Life and Decline of the American Railroad*. New York: Oxford University Press, 1970.

Strapac, Joseph A. *Cotton Belt Locomotives*. Huntington Beach, Calif.: Shade Tree Books, 1977.

———. *Southern Pacific Review 1977*. Pacific Coast Chapter of the Railway & Locomotive Historical Society, 1978.

———. *Southern Pacific Review 1978–79*. Pacific Coast Chapter of the Railway & Locomotive Historical Society, 1979.

Strapac, Joseph A., and Tim Diebert. *Southern Pacific Steam Locomotive Roster*. Huntington

Beach, Calif.: Shade Tree Books, 1986.

Sturholm, Larry, and John Howard. *All for Nothing: The True Story of the Last Great American Train Robbery.* Portland: BLS Publishing Co., 1976.

Thomas, D. H. *The Southwestern Indian Detours: The Story of Fred Harvey/Santa Fe Railway Experiments in Detourism.* Phoenix: Hunter Publishing, 1978.

Totorow, Norman E. *Leland Stanford: Man of Many Careers.* Menlo Park, Calif.: Pacific Coast Publishers, 1971.

Tout, Otis B. *The First Thirty Years: Being an Account of the Principal Events in the History of the Imperial Valley Southern California U.S.A.* San Diego: Privately printed, 1932.

Trimble, Paul C. *Interurban Railways of the Bay Area.* Fresno: Valley Publishers, 1977.

Trottman, Nelson. *History of the Union Pacific: A Financial and Economic Survey.* New York: Ronald Press, 1923.

Turner, George. *Slim Rails through the Sand.* Los Angeles: Trans-Anglo Books, 1964.

Wagner, Jack R. *The Last Whistle: Oregon Shore Railroad.* Berkeley: Howell-North Books, 1974.

Waters, L. L. *Steel Trails to Santa Fe.* Lawrence: University of Kansas, 1950.

Wilner, Frank N. *Railroads and Productivity: A Matter of Survival.* Washington, D.C.: Association of American Railroads, 1985.

Wiebe, Robert H. *The Search for Order: 1877–1920.* New York: Hill and Wang, 1967.

Wilson, Neill C., and Frank J. Taylor. *Southern Pacific: The Roaring Story of a Fighting Railroad.* New York: McGraw-Hill, 1952.

Wilson, O. Meredith. *The Denver and Rio Grande Project, 1870–1901: A History of the First Thirty Years of the Denver & Rio Grande Railroad.* Salt Lake City: Howe Bros., 1982.

Wright, Richard K. *Southern Pacific Daylight: Train 98-99.* Thousand Oaks, Calif.: Wright Enterprises, 1970.

Zlatkovich, Charles P. *Texas Railroads: A Record of Construction and Abandonment.* Austin: Bureau of Business Research, University of Texas, 1981.

ARTICLES

Babcock, Allen H. "Mountain Railway Electrification: A Study of the Tehachapi Pass." *Transactions of the American Institute of Electrical Engineers* (1913): 1784–1815.

Baker, Robert A. "Hold-Up of the Golden State Limited." *Pacific Historian* 8 (February, 1964): 53–55.

Barsness, Richard W. "Railroads and Los Angeles: The Quest for a Deep-Water Port." *Southern California Quarterly* (December, 1965): 379–94.

Beebe, Lucius. "Along the Boulevards. *Gourmet,* April, 1962, pp. 6–7.

———. "My Favorite Train Rides." *Holiday Magazine,* July, 1961, pp. 1–6.

———. "Pandemonium at Promontory." *American Heritage,* 9 (February, 1958): 20–23.

———. "Southern Pacific Narrow Gauge." *Trains,* March, 1947, pp. 14–21.

Best, Gerald M., and David L. Joslyn. "Locomotives of the Southern Pacific Company." *R&LHS Bulletin No. 94* (March, 1956).

Brown, M. L. "Asa Whitney and His Pacific Railroad Publicity Campaign." *Mississippi Valley Historical Review* 20 (September, 1933): 209–24.

Bruner, Patrick J. "'Can't Hurt, and May Do You Good': A Study of the Pamphlets the Southern Pacific Railroad Used to Induce Immigration to Texas, 1880–1930." *East Texas Historical Journal* 16 (1978): 35–45.

Bryant, Keith L. "The Atchison, Topeka & Santa Fe Railway and the Development of the Taos and Santa Fe Art Colonies." *Western Historical Quarterly* 9 (October, 1978): 437–53.

Byers, Oliver Philip. "Early History of the El Paso Line of the Chicago, Rock Island & Pacific Railway." *Collections of the Kansas State Historical Society, 1919–1922,* ed. William E. Connelly. Topeka: Kansas State Printer, 1923.

Christenberry, Joy, with Bob Cunningham. "James S. Douglas and the Tucson, Phoenix & Tidewater Railroad." *Journal of Arizona History* (Spring, 1984).

Cooley, Everett L., ed. "The Last Spike Is Driven." *Utah Historical Quarterly* 37 (Winter, 1969).

Corbett, J. W. "Moving Transcontinental Trains with Diesel Power." *Railway Age,* March 5, 1951, pp. 51–53.

Cory, H. T. "Irrigation and River Control in the Colorado River Delta." *Transactions of the*

American Society of Civil Engineers 76 (December, 1913): 1286–91.

Cotterill, R. S. "Early Agitations for a Pacific Railroad." *Missouri Valley Historical Review* 5 (March, 1919): 396–414.

"Cotton Belt Speed and Performance Teamed for Better Service." *Railway Age*, June 2, 1952, pp. 77–81.

Deason, Dave. "Black Mesa's 'River of Coal' Spans Arizona's Navajo Land." *Pipe Line Industry*, August, 1969, pp. 49–52.

Donovan, Frank P., Jr. "Pacific Electric." *Trains*, June, 1942, pp. 10–31.

Fowler, Elizabeth M. "The Turntable Fortunes of the Cotton Belt." *Railway Progress*, November, 1948, pp. 16–17.

Graves, Carl. "Workin' On the Railroad." *Kansas*, no. 3 (1983): 36–38.

Greever, William S. "Railway Development in the Southwest." *New Mexico Historical Review* 32 (April, 1957): 151–203.

Gross, H. H. "The Pecos Legends." *Railroad Magazine*, July, 1949, pp. 42–57.

Hamlin, Edith. "Maynard Dixon: Painter of the West." *American West*, November-December, 1982, pp. 50–59.

Hancock, Robert, Jr. "Riverboats." *Sacramento County Historical Golden Notes* 9 (July, 1963): 1–20.

Harriman, E. H. "San Francisco." *Sunset Magazine*, May, 1906, pp. 1–5.

Hendrick, Burton J. "Mr. E. H. Harriman, the Most Powerful Man in America." *McClure's* 35 (October, 1909): 656–59.

———. "The Passing of a Great Railroad Dynasty." *McClure's* 38 (March, 1912): 483–501.

"Hetty Green's Railroad." *Railroad Magazine*, October, 1963, pp. 17–23.

Hill, James J. "Their Advantages to the Community." *North American Review*, July 29, 1901, pp. 654–56.

Hilton, George W. "Carquinez Train Ferries." *Trains*, August 6, 1946, pp. 36–39.

———. "The Grand Narrow Gauge Trunk." *Railroad History*, Spring, 1983, pp. 23–41.

Hippen, John F. "A Wall Street Man and Western Railroad: A Chapter in Railroad Administration." *Bulletin of the Business Historical Society* 23 (September, 1949): 117–20.

Hofsommer, Don L. "A Chronology of Iowa Railroads." *Railroad History*, Spring, 1975, pp. 70–83.

———. "Huntington's Problem Continues." *Trains*, March, 1984, p. 8.

———. "Texas Railroads." *Texas: A Sesquicentennial Celebration*. Edited by Donald W. Whisenhunt. Austin: Eakin Press, 1984, p. 244.

———. "TPS: SP Tries Participatory Management." *Modern Railroads*, March, 1984, pp. 40–42.

Holden, James. "93 Years of Railway Ferries on San Francisco Bay." *Railroad Magazine*, January, 1965, pp. 13–17.

Houton, Dick. "SP's Picnic Line." *Trains*, July, 1948, pp. 46–51.

Hutchinson, W. H. "Prologue to Reform: The California Anti-Railroad Republicans, 1899–1905." *Southern California Quarterly* 44 (September, 1962): 175–218.

———. "Southern Pacific: Myth and Reality." *California Historical Society Quarterly* 48 (December, 1969): 325–34.

Kahn, Otto H. "Edward Henry Harriman." *Memoirs of Three Railroad Pioneers*, ed. Stuart Bruchey. New York: Arno Press, 1981.

Kemble, John Haskell. "The Big Four at Sea: The History of the Occidental and Oriental Steamship Company." *Huntington Library Quarterly* 3 (April, 1940): 339–57.

Kerr, K. Austin. "Decision for Federal Control: Wilson, McAdoo, and the Railroads, 1917." *Journal of American History* 3 (December, 1967): 550–60.

Keys, C. M. "Harriman I: The Man in the Making, His Early Life and Start." *World's Work* 13 (January, 1907): 8455–64.

———. "Harriman II: The Building of His Empire." *World's Work* 13 (February, 1907): 8548–52.

———. "Harriman III: The Spinner of Golden Webs." *World's Work* 13 (March, 1907).

———. "Harriman IV: Salvage of the Two Pacifics." *World's Work* 13 (April, 1907): 8791–803.

Kirkland, Edward C. "The Robber Barons Revisited." *American Historical Review* 66 (October, 1960): 68–73.

Klein, Maury. "In Search of Jay Gould." *Business History Review* 52 (Summer, 1978): 164–99.

Kneiss, G. H. "Fifty Candles for the Western Pacific." *Western Pacific Mileposts*, March, 1983.

Kriebel, F. E. "Transporting Perishables." *Blue Anchor*, Summer, 1971, pp. 30–33.

Lathrop, Gilbert A. "Mile-a-Minute Boxcars." *Railroad Magazine* August, 1950, pp. 10–25.

Love, Frank H. "The Black Mesa Story." *Pipeline Engineer International* (November, 1969): 38–44.

MacGregor, Bruce. "The Ties That Bind." *New West*, March 12, 1979, pp. 24–42.

Matthews, Fred. "Queen of the Daylights." *Passenger Train Journal*, April, 1982, pp. 21–27.

Mercier, A. T. "Diesel Power for Railroads." *Military Engineer*, November–December, 1950, pp. 463–65.

Meyer, Balthasar. "A History of the Northern Securities Case." *Bulletin of the University of Wisconsin* 1 (July, 1906): 215–350.

Middleton, William D. "Piggyback Champ." *Trains*, September, 1956, pp. 16–20.

———. "Twilight on the Pacific Electric." *Railroad Magazine*, August, 1954, pp. 48–63.

Morgan, David P. "Diesels on the Desk Top." *Trains*, May, 1956, pp. 25–27.

———. "Famous Steam Locomotives 8: The Dressy but Durable Daylights." *Trains*, October, 1952, pp. 20–21.

———. "Fast Freight." *Trains*, November, 1949, pp. 44–49.

———. "Is SP the New Standard Railroad of the World?" *Trains*, November, 1965, pp. 36–37.

———. "Perhaps a Christmas Fable." *Trains*, December, 1984, p. 40.

———. "The Rock Reborn." *Trains*, March, 1983, pp. 48–51.

———. "Southern Pacific at the Panama-Pacific." *Trains*, September, 1977, pp. 48–51.

———. "Who Shot the Passenger Train?" *Trains*, April, 1959, pp. 14–51.

Moriarty, James R., III, and Elaine P. Lamb. "The Old San Diego & Arizona." *Railroad Magazine*, May, 1973, pp. 18–21.

Murdock, Richard M. "Life on the Old Southern Pacific Train-Ferries." *Railroad Magazine*, January, 1967, pp. 46–47.

———. "Memories of the Old Benicia Depot." *Railroad Magazine*, May, 1968, pp. 18–21.

Orsi, Richard J. "The Octopus Reconsidered: The Southern Pacific and Agricultural Modernization in California, 1865–1915." *California Historical Quarterly* 54 (Fall, 1975): 196–220.

Patterson, Steve. "In a Race with MoP's Red Balls, Cotton Belt Goes Like a Blue Streak." *Trains*, November, 1962, pp. 18–27.

Pratt, Sereno S. "Our Financial Oligarchy." *World's Work* 10 (October, 1905): 6704–14.

Prichard, Walter. "A Forgotten Louisiana Engineer: G. W. R. Bayley and 'His History of the Railroads of Louisiana'." *Louisiana Historical Quarterly* 30 (October, 1947): 1065–1325.

Quarles, Bill. "Black Mesa Is First Major Pipe Line in West." *Pipeline and Underground Utilities Construction*, December, 1969, pp. 14–18.

Ranger, Ralph D., Jr. "Those Go-Ahead and Back-Up Locomotives." *Trains*, August, 1968, pp. 20–39.

Rayburn, John C. "Count Telfener and the New York, Texas & Mexican Railway Company." *Southwestern Historical Quarterly* (July, 1964): 29–42.

Romer, Margaret. "From Boulder to the Gulf." *Southern California Quarterly* (September, 1953): 278–81.

Rudolph, Jack. "Triumph at Yorktown." *American Heritage*, October, 1981, p. 78.

Sage, Russell, James H. Hill, et al. "Industrial and Railroad Consolidations." *North American Review* (May, 1901): 641–700.

Spearman, Frank H. "Building Up a Great Railway System." *Outlook*, February 27, 1909, pp. 435–52.

Stindt, Fred A. "The Last Days of Southern Pacific Steam." *Railroad History*, No. 149, Autumn, 1983, pp. 100–13.

———. "Peninsula Service: A Story of Southern Pacific Commuter Trains." *Western Railroader* (1957): 1–40.

Sullivan, A. M. "Morgan Line: A Pioneer in Coastwise Trade." *Port of New York and Ship News*, 5 (February, 1926): 3–9.

Taylor, Frank J. "Brother Can You Spare a Locomotive." *Saturday Evening Post*, June 26, 1943, pp. 71, 73, 75.

Turner, Fitzhugh. "Railroad in a Barn." *American Heritage*, December, 1958, pp. 52–57, 107–109.

"Union Passenger Terminal." *Trains*, September, 1954, pp. 14–19.

Werner, George C. "Railroads of the Magnolia

City." *National Railway Bulletin* (1982): 4–21, 42–43.

———. "Sunset Route Centennial." *National Railway Bulletin* (1983): 4–13. Reprinted as *Sunset Route: The Centennial of Its Completion, 1883–1983*. Houston: Gulf Coast Chapter, National Railway Historical Society, 1983.

Williamson, H. M. "Wanted: Men to Meet Leadership Challenge." *Railway Age*, April 6, 1964, pp. 22–24.

THESES, DISSERTATIONS, AND REPORTS

Anderson, Jacob E. "History of the St. Louis Southwestern Railroad." Master's thesis, East Texas State Teachers College, 1939.

Barriger, John W., IV. "The Development of the Santa Fe, 1935–1948." Senior thesis, Massachusetts Institute of Technology, 1949.

Batson, Kate Allen. "Railroad Development in Texas in Relation to Population Trends." Master's thesis, Baylor University, 1937.

Elliott, Claude. "The Building of the Southern Pacific Railroad through Texas." Master's thesis, University of Texas, 1928.

Jordan, Mildred L. "Railroads in the El Paso Area." Master's thesis, Texas Western College [University of Texas at El Paso], 1957.

Kawa, John F. "An Interview with John J. Schmidt, Chairman of the Board and Chief Executive Officer, Santa Fe Southern Pacific Corp." Dean Witter Reynolds, Inc. (November, 21, 1984), p. 3.

Muir, A. F. "The Buffalo Bayou, Brazos, and Colorado Railway Company, 1850–1861." Master's thesis, Rice Institute, 1942.

Munski, Douglas C. "Modeling the Historical Geography of the Chicago & Eastern Illinois Railroad, 1849–1969." Ph.D. dissertation, University of Illinois, 1978.

Odisho, William C. "Salt Lake to Oakland: The Western Pacific Link in the Continental Railroad System." Ph.D. dissertation, University of California-Berkeley, 1941.

Peterson, Robert Lewis. "State Regulation of Railroads in Texas, 1836–1920." Ph.D. dissertation, University of Texas, 1960.

Ramsey, Volney E. "History of Land Grants to Texas Railroads, 1852–1882." Master's thesis, North Texas State College, 1949.

Index